1001
ILLUSTRATIONS
THAT CONNECT

Also by Craig Brian Larson

750 Engaging Illustrations for Preachers, Teachers, and Writers (Baker, 2002), a compilation of Baker's three previous illustrations books

The Art and Craft of Biblical Preaching (Zondervan, 2004), coedited with Haddon Robinson

Choice Contemporary Stories and Illustrations for Preachers, Teachers, and Writers (Baker, 2000)

Contemporary Illustrations for Preachers, Teachers, and Writers (Baker, 1999)

Hang in There ... to the Better End (Spire, 1996), originally published under the title *Running the Midnight Marathon* (Revell, 1991)

Illustrations for Preaching and Teaching: From "Leadership Journal" (Baker, 1999)

More Perfect Illustrations for Every Topic and Occasion (Tyndale, 2003), coedited/compiled with Drew Zahn

Movie-Based Illustrations for Preaching and Teaching, volume 1 (Zondervan, 2003), coedited/compiled with Drew Zahn

Movie-Based Illustrations for Preaching and Teaching, volume 2 (Zondervan, 2004), coedited/compiled with Laurie Quicke

Perfect Illustrations for Every Topic and Occasion (Tyndale, 2002), coedited/compiled with Drew Zahn

Preaching That Connects (Zondervan, 1994), cowritten with Mark Galli

Staying Power (Baker, 2005), originally published under the title *Pastoral Grit* (Bethany House, 1998)

Also by Phyllis Ten Elshof

Church Leader's Answer Book (Tyndale, 2006), general editor with Lee Eclov

Couples' Devotional Bible (Zondervan, 2008), general editor

Leadership Handbook of Management and Administration (Baker, 2007), general editor of revision

Men of Integrity Devotional Bible (Tyndale, 2002), general editor

Quest Study Bible (Zondervan, 2003), general editor of revised edition

Questions Women Ask (Nelson, 2008), general editor

Real Questions, Real Answers about Sex (Zondervan, 2005), general editor

Sweet Talk of Success (Nelson, 2007), general editor

What Cancer Cannot Do (Zondervan, 2006), writer and compiler

1001 ILLUSTRATIONS THAT CONNECT

Compelling Stories, Stats, and News Items for Preaching, Teaching, and Writing

CRAIG BRIAN LARSON
PHYLLIS TEN ELSHOF

GENERAL
EDITORS

 ZONDERVAN®    PreachingToday.com
Advancing the Art of Biblical Preaching

ZONDERVAN.com/
AUTHORTRACKER
follow your favorite authors

ZONDERVAN®

1001 Illustrations That Connect
Copyright © 2008 by Christianity Today International

Requests for information should be addressed to:

Zondervan, *Grand Rapids, Michigan 49530*

Library of Congress Cataloging-in-Publication Data

1001 illustrations that connect : stories, stats, and news items for preaching, teaching, or writing / Craig Brian Larson and Phyllis Ten Elshof, general editors.
    p. cm.
Includes bibliographical references and index.
ISBN 978-0-310-28037-8
1. Homiletical illustrations. I. Larson, Craig Brian. II. Ten Elshof, Phyllis, 1945– III. Title:
One thousand one illustrations that connect.
BV4225.3.A14 2008
251'.08—dc22
                                            2008013126

Interior design by Michelle Espinoza

Printed in the United States of America

09 10 11 12 13 14 • 23 22 21 20 19 18 17 16 15 14 13 12 11 10 9 8 7 6 5 4 3

CONTENTS

INTRODUCTION:

TELL ME A STORY

"Will you tell me a story?" My kids asked that; now the grandkids ask it too. They love to be read their favorite stories, of course, which include the adventures of the Berenstein Bears, Dr. Seuss's *Green Eggs and Ham*, and *If You Give a Moose a Muffin*, as well as the stories of Bible characters such as Daniel, Moses, and Samson.

But when the lights are off and we're snuggling after prayers or we're in the car minus books, it's begging time for custom stories—ones that tap into a fear, teach a lesson, warn about the consequences of messing up, or rejoice in the fun of getting something right. The stories can be wise, witty, scary, or sad, but the ones that go over best involve the kids themselves or grown-ups they know in real-life situations.

These are the kinds of illustrations that work best in preaching and teaching too. As John Ortberg, pastor of Menlo Park Presbyterian Church, in Menlo, California, says, the single largest source of his illustrations are stories about real people in real-life situations, "because story communicates deeply." Illustrations bring color, verve, personality, and emotion to sermons and Bible study, which themselves are rich with Bible story.

For example, a sermon on the Good Samaritan hits home with a story Gordon MacDonald tells about failing to help a homeless man who fell and split open his chin in front of MacDonald's taxi (#320). "If you're dumb enough to get that drunk, why should someone stop and help you?" MacDonald asks, sounding very much like the Pharisee and Levite in Jesus' parable—as well

as we who fail to help someone in self-inflicted trouble.

Likewise, the apostle Paul's teaching that "the whole world is a prisoner of sin" (Galatians 3:22) gets to us in Rich Doebler's tale of his out-of-control ride on a Tilt-O-Whirl at a carnival in northern Minnesota (#329). "After a few minutes the ride became miserable," Doebler writes. "I was caught, going around in circles, held down by a merciless carnival ride operator."

Stories help sermons hit home. They are natural teaching tools. But they are also just plain fun to read. Take a stroll through the 1001 illustrations covering everything from aging, evangelism, and faith to suffering, temptation, and work. Perhaps in the dark of night, these stories will come back to you, offering hope, inspiration, peace, and strength for your daily walk with Christ.

—Phyllis Ten Elshof, general editor

Editors' note: Many illustrations in this book have been adapted from the sources cited in the credit lines.

PART 1: AGING

ILLUSTRATION 1

FORGETTING TIMES THREE

Topics: Aging; Forgetfulness; Human Condition; Limitations; Perspective; Seasons; Time; Weakness

References: Deuteronomy 4:9; 6:10–12; Psalm 71:9; Proverbs 16:31; 20:29; Isaiah 46:4; Jeremiah 3:21

Three sisters, ages ninety-two, ninety-four, and ninety-six, lived together. One night the ninety-six-year-old drew a bath. She put one foot in and then paused. "Was I getting in the tub or out?" she yelled.

The ninety-four-year-old hollered back, "I don't know; I'll come and see." She started up the stairs but stopped on the first step, shouting, "Was I going up or coming down?"

The ninety-two-year-old was sitting at the kitchen table having tea, listening to her sisters. She shook her head and said, "I sure hope I never get that forgetful," and knocked on wood for good measure. Then she yelled, "I'll come up and help both of you as soon as I see who's at the door."

— Van Morris,
Mount Washington, Kentucky

ILLUSTRATION 2

MOURNING HIS SIXTIETH

Topics: Disappointment; Emptiness; Eternal Versus Temporary; Future; Limitations; Mortality; Old Age; Perspective; Reality; Seasons; Time; Transience

References: Job 8:9; Psalm 71:9; 90:12; Proverbs 16:31; 20:29; Isaiah 40:6–8; James 4:14

Bill Clinton was thirty years old when he was appointed attorney general of Arkansas. He was elected governor of Arkansas two years later, easily becoming the youngest person in the nation to hold that position. He was a youthful forty-four when elected president of the United States, and he still holds the distinction of being the youngest person ever to leave the office of president. In other words, the vast majority of Bill Clinton's life and accomplishments were characterized by youth.

In August 2006, during his sixtieth birthday celebration, a melancholy Clinton reluctantly admitted that life had changed. No longer the youthful saxophonist wailing away on MTV, the white-haired former president said, "For most of my working life, I was the youngest person doing what I was doing. Then one day I woke up and

I was the oldest person in every room. In just a few days, I will be sixty years old. I hate it, but it's true."

—"I'm 60 and I Hate It: Bill Clinton,"
Breitbart.com (August 15, 2006)

ILLUSTRATION 3

PICKING THE PERFECT AGE

Topics: Beauty; Change; Culture; Eternal Life; Immortality; Mortality; Perfection; Self-image; Time; Women

References: Proverbs 31:30; 1 Corinthians 3:16; 6:19–20; Galatians 2:6; 1 Peter 3:3–4

"What age would you want to stay eternally?" asked a Kelton survey of 1,019 adult women. Their response:

- under 18: 2 percent
- 18 to 20: 4 percent
- 21 to 30: 35 percent
- 31 to 40: 29 percent
- 41 to 50: 14 percent
- 51 to 60: 6 percent
- over 61: 3 percent
- don't know: 7 percent

—Mary Cadden and Dave Merrill,
USA Today "Snapshots" (November 14, 2006)

ILLUSTRATION 4

BILLY ON AGING

Topics: Death; Example; Great Commandment; Life; Mortality; Old Age; Perspective; Priorities; Seasons; Time; Waiting on God

References: Genesis 15:15; Deuteronomy 34:7; Psalm 71:9; Proverbs 16:31; Matthew 22:37–40; Luke 2:25–38; John 13:34; James 2:8

Anne Graham Lotz recounted a conversation with her father, Billy Graham, on the subject of aging. "All my life, I've been taught how to die," Billy told her, "but no one ever taught me how to grow old."

She replied, "Well, Daddy, you are now teaching all of us."

Lotz said she has already learned from her father: "When you get older, secondary things, like politics, begin to fall away, and the primary things become primary again. For Daddy, the primary thing is, as Jesus said, to try to love God totally and to love our neighbor as ourselves."

—Jon Meacham, "Pilgrim's Progress,"
Newsweek (August 14, 2006)

ILLUSTRATION 5

STAYING YOUNG WITH SUPPLEMENTS

Topics: Aging; Death; Human Condition; Human Nature;

Immortality; Limitations; Mortality; New Life; Old Age; Regeneration; Youth

References: Psalm 71:9; 90:12; Ecclesiastes 8:8; John 11:25–26; Romans 6:23; 1 Corinthians 15:54; 2 Corinthians 5:1

Retirement is close for about 77 million baby boomers. Meantime, the antiaging industry is trying to keep them young enough to enjoy it.

Doctors are prescribing large doses of supplements that they believe prevent the decay of the body's organs. Human growth hormones are reported to increase muscle mass and improve memory and heart function. Natural estrogen and progesterone are believed to guard against Alzheimer's and osteoporosis, as well as to relieve symptoms of menopause. Testosterone is believed to aid memory and bone mass, relieve menopause, and help sexual function.

The American Academy of Anti-Aging Medicine reports that the antiaging industry annually makes $56 billion. At least $79 billion of income is expected by 2009. More than 1,500 doctors have been certified as antiaging practitioners.

Most of these alternative treatments may be scientifically unproven but are supported by vast anecdotal evidence. One person who has become convinced of their effectiveness is retired dentist Dr. Howard Benedict, sixty-one. He spends $10,000 a year on testosterone gel, injections of human growth hormones, and thirty vitamins and supplements. He claims to feel like a twenty-year-old.

—Arlene Weintraub,
"Selling the Promise of Youth,"
Business Week (March 20, 2006)

ILLUSTRATION 6

WHEN YOU GROW UP

Topics: Busyness; Children; Responsibility; Rest; Stress; Weariness; Work

References: Genesis 2:1–3; Ecclesiastes 2:17; Matthew 11:28–30; Romans 12:2; Hebrews 4:9–11

A photographer was snapping pictures of first graders at an elementary school, making small talk to put his subjects at ease.

"What are you going to be when you grow up?" he asked one little girl.

"Tired," she said.

—J. R. Love, Rushton, Louisiana

ILLUSTRATION 7

END OF LIFE TESTIMONY

Topics: Assurance; Death; Eternal Life; Evangelism; Example; Faith; Heaven; Intimacy; Love; Marriage; Mortality

References: Genesis 2:20–24; Joshua 14:11; Psalm 23:4; Proverbs 16:31; Matthew 19:4–6; Romans 14:8; 1 Thessalonians 4:13–18

Ruth and Billy Graham offered a priceless testimony as they approached their final chapters on earth together. "We pray together and read the Bible together every night," Billy said in a recent interview. "It's a wonderful period of life for both of us. We've never had a love like we do now—we feel each other's hearts.

"I think about heaven a great deal," Billy continued. "I think about the failures in my life in the past but know they have been covered by the blood of Christ. And that gives me a great sense of confidence. I have a certainty about eternity that is a wonderful thing, and I thank God for giving me that certainty. I do not fear death. I may fear a little bit about the process, but not death itself, because I think the moment that my spirit leaves this body, I will be in the presence of the Lord."

—Jon Meacham, "Pilgrim's Progress,"
Newsweek (August 14, 2006)

ILLUSTRATION 8

GETTING OLD

Topics: Aging; Attitudes; Human Condition; Limitations; Mortality; Old Age; Seasons; Time; Transience

References: Psalm 71:9; Proverbs 16:31; Isaiah 46:4; Titus 2:2–3

You know you're getting old when:

- you look forward to a dull evening at home
- your mind makes commitments your body cannot keep
- everything hurts, and what doesn't hurt doesn't work
- you sink your teeth into a big, juicy steak—and they stay there

- you dim the lights for economic reasons, not romantic ones
- you've owned clothes for so long they've come back into style twice
- you sing along to elevator music
- you quit trying to hold your stomach in, no matter who walks into the room

—Greg Laurie, "God's Cure for Heart Trouble," Preaching Today Audio, no. 282

ILLUSTRATION 9

HAVING FUN IN RETIREMENT

Topics: Aging; Contentment; Leisure; Lifestyle; Retirement

Reference: Ecclesiastes 8:15

As Americans age, 60 percent say they expect to enjoy life more. According to a Belden Russonello & Stewart poll of 1,000 people in May 2001, here are the activities they are looking forward to in their golden years:

- spending more time with family and friends: 81 percent
- having more leisure time: 65 percent
- pursuing hobbies: 61 percent
- traveling: 51 percent

—Lori Joseph and Sam Ward,
USA Today "Snapshots" (August 7, 2001)

ILLUSTRATION 10

KNOWING WHEN TO QUIT

Topics: Ambition; Anxiety; Career; Contentment; Fatherhood; Fear; Greed; Idolatry; Money; Motives; Retirement; Stress; Success; Work

References: Ecclesiastes 4:8; 5:10; Matthew 6:19–34; Luke 12:22–34; Philippians 4:10–19

His health was in tatters and his life mired in financial wrangles, but Frank Sinatra refused to stop giving concerts. "I've got to earn more money," he said.

His performances, sad to say, were becoming more and more uneven. Uncertain of his memory, he became dependent on teleprompters. When his daughter, Tina, saw her father at Desert Inn in Las Vegas, he struggled through the show and felt so sick at the end that he needed oxygen from a tank that he kept on hand. At another show he forgot the lyrics to "Second Time Around," a ballad he had sung a thousand times. His adoring audience finished it for him.

"I couldn't bear to see Dad struggle," Tina said. "I remembered all the times he had repeated the old boxing maxim 'You gotta get out before you hit the mat.' He wanted to retire at the top of his game, and I always thought he would know when his time came, but in pushing eighty he lost track of when to quit. After seeing one too many of these fiascoes, I told him, 'Pop, you can stop now; you don't have to stay on the road.'"

With a stricken expression he said, "No, I've got to earn more money. I have to make sure everyone is taken care of."

Since Sinatra's death, there has been constant family wrangling over his fortune.

—Tina Sinatra with Jeff Coplon, *My Father's Daughter* (Simon & Schuster, 2000)

ILLUSTRATION 11

WORKING TO THE END

Topics: Diligence; Healing; Ministry; Miracles; Missions; Results; Retirement; Sacrifice; Work

References: Acts 20:35; 1 Corinthians 15:9–11, 58; 2 Corinthians 6:5; Hebrews 13:7

Before J. Oswald Sanders was fifty, he had arthritis so bad that he could hardly get out of bed. He could have taken a nice retirement. Instead, he entered the most productive years of his life.

At age fifty, he left a prosperous career as an attorney in New Zealand to lead the China Inland Mission (now Overseas Missionary Fellowship). After several years of leading the mission, he retired, only to take on the directorship of a Christian college. Then he retired again.

As a two-time widower, he certainly deserved a rest. But rather than taking it easy, he accelerated, spending his last twenty years speaking around the world more than three hundred times per year. His respect grew even though he never sought the limelight or tried to maintain his position. He was almost ninety and working on a book when he died.

—Jerry White, *Dangers Men Face* (NavPress, 1997)

ILLUSTRATION 12

MULTIPLYING CONFUSION

Topics: Aging; Confusion; Knowledge; Understanding

References: Psalm 90:10; Ecclesiastes 12:1–5; Isaiah 46:4

Three old men went to the doctor for a memory test. The doctor asked the first old man, "What is one plus one?"

"Two hundred seventy-four," he said.

The doctor asked the same question of the second man, "What is one plus one?"

"Tuesday," he said.

The doctor tried the third man, "What's one plus one?"

"Two," said the third man.

"That's great!" said the doctor. "How did you get that?"

"Simple," said the third man. "I subtracted 274 from Tuesday."

—John Fehlen, Stanwood, Washington

ILLUSTRATION 13

WISING UP WITH AGE

Topics: Aging; Fruitfulness; Perseverance; Service; Work

References: Job 12:12; Proverbs 3:13–16

Some of the greatest accomplishments in history were carried out by people late in life.

- Immanuel Kant wrote one of his best philosophical works at the age of seventy-four.
- Verdi wrote "Ave Maria" at eighty-five.
- Michelangelo was eighty-seven when he completed *The Pietá*, his greatest sculpture.
- Ronald Reagan was president of the United States at seventy-five.

This notion that life should be winding down at fifty or sixty years of age is just crazy.

—James Dobson,
Coming Home (Tyndale, 1998)

ILLUSTRATION 14

REMEMBERING YOU

Topics: Anxiety; Caring; Commitment; Disease; Faithfulness; Family; Fear; Husbands; Illness; Intimacy; Love; Loyalty; Marriage; Memories; Relationships; Wives

References: Genesis 2:24; Proverbs 12:4; 18:22; Song of Songs 8:6–7; Mark 10:9

Roger Zerbe, who suffered from early onset Alzheimer's disease, journaled this to his wife after a particularly troubling bout of forgetfulness.

Honey,

Today fear is taking over. The day is coming when all my memories of this life we share will be gone. You and the boys will be gone from me. I will lose you even as I am surrounded by you and your love.

I don't want to leave you. I want to grow old in the warmth of memories. Forgive me for leaving so slowly and painfully.

Blinking back tears, Becky wrote:

My sweet husband,

I will continue to go on loving you and caring for you—not because you know me or remember our life, but because I remember you. I will remember the man who proposed to me and told me he loved me, the look on his face when his children were born, the father he was, the way he loved our extended family. I'll recall his love for riding, hiking, and reading; his tears at sentimental movies; the unexpected witty remarks; and how he held my hand while he prayed. I cherish the pleasure, obligation, commitment, and opportunity to care for you because I remember you!

—Becky Zerbe, "Penning a Marriage,"
Marriage Partnership (Spring 2006)

PART 2: BIBLE

ILLUSTRATION 15

─────────────────────●

EQUIPPING US FOR BATTLE

Topics: Help from God; Protection; Security; Spiritual Armor; Spiritual Disciplines; Spiritual Formation; Spiritual Growth; Spiritual Warfare; Vulnerability; Weakness

References: Romans 13:11–12; 2 Corinthians 10:3–5; Ephesians 6:10–18; 1 Thessalonians 5:8

In December 2004, a single question from a young soldier touched off a media firestorm. U.S. Secretary of Defense Donald Rumsfeld had come to deliver a pep talk to the troops at Camp Buehring in Kuwait. But the usually unflappable secretary found himself blindsided by a bold query. As news cameras rolled, Army Specialist Thomas Wilson of the 278th Regimental Combat Team asked Rumsfeld, "Why do we soldiers have to dig through local landfills for pieces of scrap metal and compromised ballistic glass to up-armor our vehicles?"

Specialist Wilson clearly felt he was being sent into battle without proper protection. As Christians, however, we shouldn't have that fear. Our Supreme Commander generously equips us with the belt of truth, the breastplate of righteousness, the gospel of peace, the shield of faith, the helmet of salvation, and the sword of the Spirit.

But it's up to us to put them on and put them to use.

—Jim Bennett, "Troops Ask about Lack of Proper Equipment," Preaching.Today.com; source: "Troops Put Thorny Questions to Rumsfeld," CNN.com (December 9, 2004)

ILLUSTRATION 16

─────────────────────●

REJECTING AN AWARD-WINNING BOOK

Topics: Alertness; Books; Challenges; Complacency; Devotional Life; Diligence; Enthusiasm; Indifference; Obstacles; Persistence; Reputation; Word of God

References: Joshua 1:8; Matthew 24:35; Mark 13:31; Luke 21:33; Romans 10:17; 2 Timothy 3:16

Getting a novel published is extremely difficult, especially if you are an unknown author. Chuck Ross, a freelance writer, decided to test the system. He retyped the first twenty-one pages of a novel by Jerzy Kosinski, titled *Steps*, which had won the National Book Award six years before and sent them to four publishers, using the name Erik Demos as a fictitious byline.

All four publishers rejected the manuscript. Two years later, Ross retyped the entire novel *Steps* and submitted it under the pen name Erik Demos to several more publishers, including the original publisher, Random House. It was rejected by all with unhelpful comments, including Random House, which used a form letter. All told, fourteen publishers and thirteen literary agents failed to recognize a book that had already been published and had won an important award.

Sometimes our approach to the Bible is a similar "been there, done that."

—Noah Lukeman, *The First Five Pages*
(Simon & Schuster, 2000)

ILLUSTRATION 17

EASING ANGER WITH MEMORY VERSE

Topics: Anger; Change; Growth; Leading of the Holy Spirit; Overcoming; Scripture; Self-control; Temper

References: Psalm 37:8; Proverbs 14:7; 29:11; Ecclesiastes 7:9; Matthew 5:22; Ephesians 4:31; Colossians 3:8; James 1:19–20

As a new Christian, I was working through Colossians. The Holy Spirit caught my attention with Colossians 3:8 (NLT): "But now is the time to get rid of anger, rage, malicious behavior, slander, and dirty language." I tried to slide past the verse, but the Spirit kept bringing me back to the words "get rid of anger."

I had a violent temper. Whenever it flared, I'd haul up and bash my fist into the nearest door. Even though I often bloodied my knuckles and had once smashed a beautiful ring my wife had given me, I couldn't seem to stop. Yet here was God's Word saying, "Get rid of anger." This wasn't just advice given to the people of Colossae centuries ago. It was God speaking to me.

So I made a covenant with God. I promised him I would work on my anger. My first step was to memorize Colossians 3:8 and review it daily. I then asked the Lord to bring this verse to mind whenever I might be tempted to lose my temper. And I asked my wife to pray for me and remind me of this verse if she saw me failing in my promise to the Lord. In time, that text became a part of my life. Gradually the sin of anger lost its grip on me.

—Leroy Eims, *The Lost Art of Disciple Making*
(Zondervan, 1978)

ILLUSTRATION 18

FINDING OUR PRIME MERIDIAN

Topics: Authority; Bible; Creation; Doctrine; Guidance; Inerrancy; Inspiration of Scripture; Perspective; Promises; Purpose; Spiritual Direction; Theology; Truth

References: Deuteronomy 8:3; Psalm 12:6; 18:30; 119; Luke 11:28; John 16:13; Romans 1:16; 15:4; Colossians

2:8; 2 Timothy 3:16; Hebrews 4:12; James 1:22–25

My family and I recently saw the prime meridian at the Royal Observatory in Greenwich, England. I took a picture of my children straddling the meridian, each with one foot in the Eastern Hemisphere and the other foot in the Western Hemisphere.

The prime meridian itself is not impressive. You would not realize it was there if it were not for a bold line cut across the pavement. The demarcation is a human invention. Prior to the International Meridian Conference of 1884, each local region kept its own time, a system that, if continued, would have rendered impossible our current arrangements for trade and commerce. While the meridian is humanly derived, its relation to the stars is not, and that heavenly correspondence allows us to find our place on the map and in the world.

The prime meridian is the work of John Flamsteed, the first astronomer royal, who made it his life mission to produce a proper navigational chart of the heavens, mapping the location of thousands of stars. Based on Flamsteed's work, scientists were able to help people find their position on the planet, allowing them to answer that fundamental question of philosophy and physics: Where am I?

The prime meridian is a fixed position by which our knowledge of time and place can be understood. The Bible is like that with us. Scripture is our prime meridian. It is the fixed position, given by God himself, through which we can understand who we are, where we are, and where we must go from here.

—Kenton C. Anderson,
Choosing to Preach (Zondervan, 2006)

ILLUSTRATION 19
RANDOM GUIDANCE

Topics: Bible; Foolishness; Greed; Guidance; Interpretation; Money; Motives; Scripture; Success; Wishful Thinking

References: Matthew 22:29; Mark 12:24; 2 Corinthians 4:2; 2 Timothy 2:15; Hebrews 4:12

Two friends met after not seeing each other for a long time. One had gone to college and was now very successful. The other hadn't gone to college and never had much ambition, yet he still seemed to be doing well.

The college graduate asked his friend, "How has everything been going with you?"

The less-educated man replied, "Well, one day, I opened my Bible at random and dropped my finger on a page. The word under my finger was *oil*. So I invested in oil, and boy, did the oil wells gush. Then I tried the same method again, and my finger stopped on the word *gold*. So I invested in gold, and those mines really produced. Now I'm as rich as Rockefeller."

The college grad rushed to his hotel, grabbed a Gideon Bible, flipped it open, and dropped his finger on a page. When he opened his eyes, he saw that his finger rested on the words *Chapter Eleven*.

—Van Morris,
Mount Washington, Kentucky

ILLUSTRATION 20

BELIEVING THE BIBLE

Topics: Authority; Belief; Bible; Doubt; Inerrancy; Inspiration of Scripture; Interpretation; Postmodernism; Revelation; Skepticism; Unbelief; Word of God

References: Deuteronomy 8:3; Psalm 12:6; 119:105; Matthew 5:18; Luke 21:33; John 17:17; Acts 17:11; Romans 1:16; 2 Timothy 3:16

Americans who say the Bible is the actual word of God and should be taken word for word: 28 percent

Americans who said this thirty years ago: 38 percent

—Ted Olsen, "Go Figure," *Christianity Today* (August 2006)

ILLUSTRATION 21

WHEN READING ISN'T ENOUGH

Topics: Bible; Deliverance; Devotional Life; Faith; False Beliefs; Mistakes; Protection; Providence; Rescue; Safety; Spiritual Disciplines; Testing God; Trust; War

References: Psalm 91; Matthew 10:16–17; Mark 13:9; Acts 12:1–12; 2 Timothy 4:15

Although the first Pilgrims established a peaceful relationship with the natives in America, the following generation struggled with bloody warfare. The war between Pilgrims and Indians, known as King Philip's War, began in 1675 and lasted fourteen months.

In March 1676, a group of nearly fifteen hundred Indians attacked the village of Rehoboth. Nathaniel Philbrick writes, "As the inhabitants watched from their garrisons, 40 houses, 30 barns, and 2 mills went up in flames. Only one person was killed—a man who believed that as long as he continued reading the Bible, no harm would come to him. Refusing to abandon his home, he was found shot to death in his chair—the Bible still in his hands."

—Based on Nathaniel Philbrick, *Mayflower* (Viking, 2006)

ILLUSTRATION 22

STARRING IN THE BIBLE

Topics: Bible; Boasting; Depravity; Ego; Human Nature; Inspiration of Scripture; Pride; Self-centeredness; Self-image

References: Deuteronomy 18:20; Luke 15; John 3:16; Romans 3:23; James 4:6

Kanye West, a hip-hop producer and rapper, wants a new version of Scripture in which he's the lead.

"I bring up historical subjects in a way that makes kids want to learn about them," said West. "I'm an inspirational speaker. I changed the sound of music more than one time.... For all those reasons, I'd be a part of the Bible. I'm definitely in the history books already."

West may be one step shy of blasphemy. Or he is simply stating the obvious. He is already in the Bible — as are we all. Anytime Scripture speaks of sinners a holy God died to save, the Bible is talking about Kanye — and each one of us.

— "Cocky West: 'I Should Be in the Bible,'"
contactmusic.com (February 9, 2006)

ILLUSTRATION 23

TESTING THE KORAN AGAINST THE BIBLE

Topics: Authority of Scripture; Bible; Evangelism; Islam; Religion; Word of God

References: Isaiah 55:11; 2 Timothy 3:16; Hebrews 4:12

A Christian university student shared a room with a Muslim. As they became friends, their conversation turned to religion. The believer asked the Muslim if he'd ever read the Bible. He answered no, but then asked if the Christian had ever read the Koran.

The believer responded, "No, I haven't, but I'm sure it would be interesting. Why don't we read both together, once a week, alternating books?" The young man accepted the challenge, their friendship deepened, and during the second term he became a believer in Jesus.

One evening, late in the term, he burst into the room and shouted at the longtime believer, "You deceived me!"

"What are you talking about?" the believer asked.

The new believer opened his Bible and said, "I've been reading it through, like you told me, and just read that the Word is living and active!" He grinned. "You knew all along that the Bible contained God's power and that the Koran is a book like any other. I never had a chance!"

"Now you'll hate me for life?" asked the believer.

"No," he said, "but it was an unfair contest."

— Floyd Schneider, *Evangelism for the Fainthearted* (Kregel, 2000)

ILLUSTRATION 24

WHEN WORD TRUMPS THEOLOGY

Topics: Authority of Scripture; Preaching; Theology; Truth

References: 2 Timothy 3:16; 4:2

It has been my earnest endeavor ever since I have preached the Word, never to keep back a single doctrine that I believe to be taught of God. It is time that we had done with the old and rusty systems that have so long curbed the freeness of religious speech.

The Arminian trembles to go an inch beyond Arminius or Wesley, and many a Calvinist refers to John Gill or John Calvin as an ultimate authority. It is time that the systems were broken up, and that there was sufficient grace in all our hearts to believe everything taught in

God's Word, whether it was taught by either of these men or not.

If God teaches it, it is enough. If it is not in the Word, away with it! Away with it! But if it be in the Word, agreeable or disagreeable, systematic or disorderly, I believe it.

—Charles Haddon Spurgeon, in a sermon delivered at Exeter Hall, London (March 1860)

sis to the final chapter of Revelation. Weaving through all the diverse strands of the Bible is the overarching story of what God has been up to in the rescue and restoration of fallen human beings, from the first nanosecond of creation through the final cry of victory at the end of time.

—Timothy George, "Big-Picture Faith," *Christianity Today* (October 23, 2000)

ILLUSTRATION 25

GETTING THE BIG PICTURE

Topics: Bible; Grace; Inspiration of Scripture; Kingdom of God; Redemption; Salvation

References: Psalm 119:18–19; Luke 24:25–27

In *Mystery on the Desert*, Maria Reiche describes a series of strange lines made by the Nazea in the plains of Peru, some of them covering many square miles. For years, people assumed these lines were the remnants of ancient irrigation ditches.

Then in 1939, Dr. Paul Kosok of Long Island University discovered that their true meaning could only be seen from high in the air. When viewed from an airplane, these seemingly random lines are enormous drawings of birds, insects, and animals.

In a similar way, people often think of the Bible as a series of individual, unconnected stories. But if we survey the Scriptures as a whole, we discover that they form one great story of redemption—from the opening scenes of Gene-

ILLUSTRATION 26

USING OUR ENEMY'S PLANS

Topics: Bible; Satan; Spiritual Warfare; Temptation

References: 2 Corinthians 2:11; Ephesians 6:10–18; 1 Timothy 3:7; 1 Peter 5:8–9

The battle of Antietam in 1862 was the bloodiest day of the Civil War. In twelve hours, there were ten thousand Confederate casualties and even more on the Union side. "At last the sun went down and the battle ended, smoke heavy in the air, the twilight quivering with the anguished cries of thousands of wounded men," wrote one historian.

Though the battle appeared a draw, Union General George McClellan was able to end Robert E. Lee's thrust into Maryland, forcing him to retreat across the Potomac. This was possible because two Union soldiers found a copy of Lee's battle plans and delivered them to McClellan before the battle.

In some respects, we are no match for our adversary, Satan. But as with General McClellan, our enemy's plans have fallen into our hands. We know his strategies to entice us with lies, lust, greed, and the like. With such knowledge, given us by God's Word, and God's Spirit within, we too can resist the enemy's advances.

—Thomas Bailey and David Kennedy, eds., *The American Pageant*, 9th ed. (D. C. Heath, 1991)

Imagine looking at your own face in a mirror and not recognizing it. James 1:22–25 says that is what people do when they listen to God's Word but do not obey it.

—Lee Eclov, "Seeing or Just Looking," PreachingToday.com; source: Tom Hundley, *Chicago Tribune* (September 6, 2000)

ILLUSTRATION 27
NOT RECOGNIZING YOURSELF

Topics: Reflection; Self-deception; Self-examination

References: 1 Corinthians 11:28–29; James 1:22–25

Andras Tamas had been drafted into the army, but the authorities mistook his native Hungarian language for the gibberish of a lunatic and had him committed to a psychiatric hospital in Russia. Then they forgot about him for fifty-three years.

A few years ago, a doctor began to realize what had happened and helped Tamas recover the memories of who he was and where he came from. He recently returned home to Budapest as "the last prisoner of World War II."

This old man hadn't seen his own face in five decades. So for hours the old man studied his face in a mirror. The deep-set eyes. The gray stubble on the chin. The furrows of the brow. It was his face, but what a startling revelation to see it after fifty-three years.

ILLUSTRATION 28
TROUBLED BY GOSPEL TRUTH

Topics: Bible; Truth

References: Matthew 7:21–27; 1 Corinthians 6:9–11; Galatians 5:22–24; James 4:4; 1 John 2:15–17

Thomas Linacre was king's physician to Henry VII and Henry VIII of England, founder of the Royal College of Physicians, and friend of the great Renaissance thinkers Erasmus and Sir Thomas More.

Late in his life, Linacre studied to be a priest and was given a copy of the Gospels to read for the first time. Linacre lived through the darkest of the church's dark hours under the papacy of Alexander VI, the Borgia pope whose bribery, corruption, incest, and murder plumbed new depths in the annals of Christian shame.

Reading the Gospels for himself, Linacre was amazed and troubled. "Either these are not the Gospels," he said, "or we are not Christians."

—Os Guinness, *The Call* (Multnomah, 1998)

ILLUSTRATION 29

WEARYING OF SCRIPTURE

Topics: Devotional Life; Spiritual Disciplines; Word of God

References: Matthew 4:4; 1 Peter 2:2–3

Nothing is more perilous than to be weary of the Word of God. Thinking he knows enough, a person begins little by little to despise the Word until he has lost Christ and the gospel altogether.

—Martin Luther,
Galatians Commentary (on 2:14–16)

ILLUSTRATION 30

HOW BELIEF MULTIPLIES

Topics: Bible; Evangelism; Gospel; Missions; Outreach; Vision

References: Isaiah 55:10–11; Matthew 28:19; Acts 1:8; Romans 1:16; Hebrews 4:12

The people of the Hmar tribe of northeast India were once fierce headhunters known for their vicious slayings. But in 1910, Welsh missionary Watkin Roberts sent the gospel of John to a Hmar chief. The chief invited Roberts to come and explain the Scriptures, and within two generations the entire Hmar tribe was evangelized.

Soon after, the British government expelled Roberts from India, but his efforts continued to produce fruit. Today the Hmar tribe totals over a million people. Two members of that tribe—Rochunga and Mawii Pudaite—are continuing Roberts's work of evangelism. In 1971, they were convicted by God to give a free copy of the New Testament to all of the families of the world.

The Pudaites founded Bibles for the World ministries. To date, they have sent more than 16 million copies of the New Testament in various languages to homes all across the globe.

—"Quick Takes
—The Headhunter's Children,"
Today's Christian (January–February 2005)

ILLUSTRATION 31

TRANSFORMING A SKEPTIC

Topics: Agnosticism; Atheism; Belief; Bible; Conversion; Doubt; Jesus Christ; Truth; Unbelief

References: John 6:29; 1 Timothy 1:16; 1 John 5:6–12, 20

Lew Wallace, governor of New Mexico, was writing a book against Jesus Christ and in the process was converted to Christianity. He told a friend how it happened.

"I had always been an agnostic and denied Christianity," Wallace said. "Robert C. Ingersoll, a famous agnostic, was one of my most intimate friends. He once said, 'See here, Wallace, you are a learned man and a thinker. Why don't you gather material and write a book to prove the falsity concerning Jesus Christ, that no such man has ever lived, much less the author of the teachings found in the New Testament? Such a book would make you famous. It would be a masterpiece, and a way of putting an end to the foolishness about the so-called Christ.'"

Wallace went home and told his wife about the project. She was a member of the Methodist Church and did not like the idea. But Wallace began to collect material from libraries all over the world that covered the period in which Jesus Christ should have lived. He did that for several years and then began writing. He was four chapters into the book, he says, when it became clear to him that Jesus Christ was just as real a personality as Socrates, Plato, or Caesar. "The conviction became a certainty. I knew that Jesus Christ had lived because of the facts connected with the period in which he lived."

So he asked himself candidly, "If he was a real person, was he not then also the Son of God and the Savior of the world?" Gradually Wallace realized that since Jesus Christ was a real person, he probably was the one he claimed to be.

"I fell on my knees to pray for the first time in my life, and I asked God to reveal himself to me, forgive my sins, and help me to become a follower of Christ. Toward morning the light broke into my soul. I went into my bedroom, woke my wife, and told her that I had received Jesus Christ as my Lord and Savior.

"'O Lew,' she said, 'I have prayed for this ever since you told me of your purpose to write this book, that you would find him while you wrote it!'"

Wallace went on to write a famous book. Every time I watch the epic film *Ben Hur*, based on that book, I wonder at how it was written by a man who wanted to disprove that Jesus ever existed and instead became convinced that he was the greatest man who ever lived.

—David Holdaway, *The Life of Jesus* (Sovereign World, 1997)

ILLUSTRATION 32
SEEING SINS IN GOD'S LIGHT

Topics: Arrogance; Bible; Brokenness; Experiencing God; Hearing God; Humility; Prayer; Pride; Renewal; Seeking God; Spiritual Growth; Spiritual Perception

References: Isaiah 66:2; Jeremiah 33:3; Micah 6:8; 1 Corinthians 13:12

I wanted a deeper relationship with God, and I thought Isaiah 66:2 was speaking to me in the words "This is the one I esteem: he who is humble and contrite in spirit, and trembles at my word." But I didn't understand the connection between humility and trembling before God's Word. So I prayed, "Lord, please make this verse real to me."

Five days later, my wife and I were driving down the Oregon coast. I was meditating on 1 Corinthians 13:12, which says: "Now I know in part; then I shall know fully, even as I am fully known." I prayed, "God, please open my eyes to this evil in my heart."

As we followed Highway 101 south, I sensed a connection between Isaiah 66:2 and 1 Corinthians 13:12. So I prayed, "God, show me the connection between these verses."

A few minutes later, my wife began talking about a movie she liked. Irritated by the intrusion of such a trivial topic, I belittled her opinion. Instantly, three life-changing words knifed into my consciousness: *There it is!*

What was that? I wondered. Then I realized God had spoken. So I asked, "What is *it*?" An overwhelming sense of moral ugliness—my arrogance and pride—washed over me. For the first time I saw those sins in God's light.

My next sensation was the profound conviction that God had loved me for forty-five years despite these besetting sins. It was painful to see my pride as God saw it. Yet I was glad for that glimpse. I wept for my sin, and I wept because of God's indescribable love.

—William P. Farley,
"The Indispensable Virtue,"
Discipleship Journal (September/October 2001)

ILLUSTRATION 33

DOCUMENTING ISRAEL-EDOM RIVALRY

Topics: Apologetics; Belief; Bible; Doctrine; Doubt; Faith; Inerrancy; Insight; Inspiration of Scripture; Knowledge; Testing God; Truth; Unbelief; Uncertainties

References: Genesis 36; Numbers 20:14–21; 2 Samuel 8:11–14; 1 Kings 11:14–17; Isaiah 55:11; Galatians 1:11–12; 1 Thessalonians 2:13; 2 Timothy 3:16; 1 John 5:9

Scholars have long debated history in the Bible. For example, they have argued that the Edomites, who were a nomadic people, could not have become a cohesive society by the tenth century BC—thus negating the biblical accounts of a genuine rivalry between the Israelites in Judah and the Edomites. These scholars say that the biblical writers exaggerated the advancement of both states.

But Dr. Thomas Levy—an archaeologist from the University of California, San Diego, and a leader of an excavation in the lowlands of Jordan—has concluded that archaeology supports the biblical account. Radiocarbon dating of charred wood, grain, and fruit has yielded the first high-precision dates in the region, and the discovery of hammers, grinding stones, scarabs, and ceramics is telling evidence of Edom's stature at the time.

Levy and his fellow researcher, Dr. Mohammed Najjar, have received both enthusiastic support and heated criticism from their academic peers. Still, they maintain that the excavation of the copper works at Khirbat en-Nahas "demonstrates the weak reed on the basis of which a number of scholars have scoffed at the idea of a state or complex chiefdom in Edom at this early period."

They added, "The biblical references to the Edomites, especially their conflicts with David and subsequent Judahite kings, garner a new plausibility."

—John Noble Wilford,
"In a Ruined Copper Works:
Evidence That Bolsters a Doubted Biblical Tale,"
The New York Times (June 13, 2006)

ILLUSTRATION 34

PROVING THE RESURRECTION

Topics: Apologetics; Easter; Jesus Christ; Resurrection

References: Matthew 28:6; John 20:18; 1 Corinthians 15:20

In April 2002, the well-respected Oxford University philosophy professor Richard Swinburne used a broadly accepted probability theory to defend the truth of Christ's resurrection. He did this at a high-profile gathering of philosophy professors at Yale University.

"For someone dead for 36 hours to come to life again is, according to the laws of nature, extremely improbable," Swinburne said. "But if there is a God of the traditional kind, natural laws only operate because he makes them operate." Swinburne then used Bayes' Theorem to assign values to things like the probability of God's being real, Jesus' behavior during his lifetime, and the quality of witness testimony after Jesus' death. Then he plugged the numbers into a probability formula and added everything up.

The result: a 97 percent probability that the resurrection really happened.

—Emily Eakin,
"So God's Really in the Details?"
The New York Times (May 11, 2002)

ILLUSTRATION 35

TRIUMPHING OVER CONSPIRACY

Topics: Apologetics; Martyrdom; Resurrection; Testimony; Truth; Witnessing

References: Matthew 28:1–10; Luke 24:1–12; John 20:1–18

Whenever Charles Colson, onetime Watergate-criminal-turned-founder of Prison Fellowship, is challenged about the truth of Christ's resurrection, he responds, "My answer is always that the disciples and 500 others gave eyewitness accounts of seeing Jesus risen from the tomb. But then I'm asked, 'How do you know they were telling the truth? Maybe they were perpetuating a hoax.'" Colson says, "My answer to that comes from an unlikely source: Watergate." He writes:

Watergate involved a conspiracy perpetuated by the closest aides to the president of the United States—the most powerful men in America, who were intensely loyal to their president. But one of them, John Dean, turned state's evidence, that is, testified against Nixon, as he put it, "to save his own skin"—and he did so only two weeks after informing the president about what was really going on! The cover-up, the lie, could only be held together for two weeks, and then everybody else jumped ship to save themselves. Now, the fact is that all that those around the president were facing was embarrassment, maybe prison. Nobody's life was at stake.

But what about the disciples? Twelve powerless men, peasants really, were facing not just embarrassment or political disgrace, but beatings, stoning, execution. Every one of the disciples insisted, to their dying breaths, that they had physically seen Jesus bodily raised from the dead. Don't you think that one of those apostles would have cracked before being beheaded or stoned? That one of them would have made a deal with the authorities? None did. Men will give their lives for something they believe to be true; they will never give their lives for something they know to be false.

The Watergate cover-up reveals the true nature of humanity. Even political zealots at the pinnacle of power will, in the crunch, save their own necks, even at the expense of the ones they profess to serve so loyally. But the apostles could not deny Jesus, because they had seen him face to face, and they knew he had risen from the dead.

No, you can take it from an expert in cover-ups—I've lived through Watergate—that nothing less than a resurrected Christ could have caused those men to maintain to their dying whispers that Jesus is alive and is Lord. Two thousand years later, nothing less than the power of the risen Christ could inspire Christians around the world to remain faithful—despite prison, torture, and death. Jesus is Lord: That's the thrilling message of Easter. It's a historic fact, one convincingly established by the evidence—and one you can bet your life upon.

—Charles Colson, BreakPoint Online Commentaries (April 29, 2002)

ILLUSTRATION 36

FINDING THE BEATLES HOLLOW

Topics: Bible; Conversion; Emptiness; Repentance; Word of God

References: Matthew 11:28–30; John 6:27–35; 1 John 2:15–17

Ken Mansfield, the United States manager for Apple Records (the Beatles' label), tells about his wonderful times with the Beatles before they broke up. Things went downhill after that until, in the mid-1980s, he hit bottom.

Through a woman with whom he fell in love, Mansfield found Jesus. Before committing his life to Christ, he says *Billboard* magazine was his Bible; record charts, his God; and prestigious positions, his purpose. "The Holy Grail was a Grammy, and the best table at the Brown Derby, the Promised Land," Mansfield says.

After his conversion, he realized how hollow the way of the Beatles had been compared to the way of Christ. "They [the Father, Son, and Holy Spirit] are the authors of the map I needed for my journey," he wrote. "I needed a chart, a journal with clear directions, a log to refer to—a guidebook wherein their commands could speak to my wandering spirit. I needed a book so powerful that its very words could burn a living message into the absolute heart of my heart. I needed the irrefutable, holy Word of God, the Father Almighty, the Creator of the very seas I was lost upon!"

—Ken Mansfield,
The Beatles, the Bible, and Bodega Bay
(Broadman & Holman, 2000)

ILLUSTRATION 37

PROTECTING PEOPLE IN DEMOLITION

Topics: Evangelism; Judgment; Mercy; Preaching; Repentance; Warnings; Word of God

References: John 16:5 – 11; Romans 2:2 – 4

Seattle's famed Kingdome — home of the Seahawks, Mariners, and at times, the SuperSonics — was destroyed in March of 2000. Maryland-based Controlled Demolition Incorporated (CDI) was hired to do the job of imploding the 25,000-ton structure that had marked Seattle's skyline for two-dozen years.

Extreme measures were taken to ensure no one was hurt. CDI had experience with more than seven thousand demolitions and knew how to protect people. Engineers checked and rechecked the structure. The authorities evacuated several blocks around the Kingdome. Safety measures were in place to allow the countdown

to stop at any time if there were any concerns. All workers were individually accounted for by radio. A large public address system was used to announce the final countdown. In short, CDI took every reasonable measure and more to warn people of the impending danger.

The Bible teaches of a final judgment on this sinful world. Like the engineers who blew up the Kingdome, our heavenly Father has spared no expense to make sure everybody can "get out" safely. He warns us through our consciences, through the prophets, through the Word of God, through the Holy Spirit, through the church, and through his Son.

—Jon Mutchler,
"Preparing for Judgment,"
PreachingToday.com

PART 3: CHURCH

ILLUSTRATION 38

FINDING JOY IN GRATITUDE

Topics: Division; Gratitude; Joy; Love; Thanksgiving

References: Psalm 16:11; 100:4; Colossians 3:15; 1 Thessalonians 5:18; 1 Peter 1:8

I believe that the real difference in the American church is not between conservatives and liberals, fundamentalists and charismatics, or Republicans and Democrats. The real difference is between the aware and the unaware.

When somebody is aware of the love that the Father has for Jesus, that person is spontaneously grateful. Cries of thankfulness become the dominant characteristic of the interior life, and the byproduct of gratitude is joy. We're not joyful and then become grateful—we're grateful, and that makes us joyful.

—Brennan Manning, in "The Dick Staub Interview: Brennan Manning on Ruthless Trust," ChristianityToday.com (December 1, 2002)

ILLUSTRATION 39

SPELLING FINALIST SKIPS NATIONALS

Topics: Character; Choices; Church Attendance; Faithfulness; Obedience; Priorities; Respect; Responsibility; Sabbath; Sacrifice; Talents; Thankfulness; Worship

References: Genesis 2:1–3; 22; Exodus 20:8–11; Matthew 5:16; 11:28; Acts 20:7; Hebrews 10:25

Elliot Huck, a fourteen-year-old from Bloomington, Indiana, who had placed forty-fifth out of 250 spellers in semifinal competition, skipped the National Spelling Bee. The 2007 National Spelling Bee was held on a Sunday. In Elliot's eyes, the competition conflicted with the biblical command to rest on the Sabbath.

"I always try to glorify God with what I do in the spelling bee because he is the one who gave me the talent for spelling," said Elliot. "Now I'm not going to spell and try to give glory to God in that."

Dropping out wasn't an easy choice for Elliot. He loved his time in Washington, D.C., at the 2006 national competition and was looking forward to more of the same. Even so, the expert speller concluded, "I have accepted that

God knows what's best, and I'm just going to do what he says."

—Robert King, "Sunday Contest Spells the End for Student," *Indianapolis Star* (February 22, 2007)

ILLUSTRATION 40

SAYING FAREWELL TO CHURCH FREELOADERS

Topics: Apathy; Church Involvement; Complacency; Devotion; Faith and Works; Giving; Indifference; Sanctification; Service; Spiritual Formation; Spiritual Growth

References: Matthew 18:15 – 16; Romans 12:6 – 8, 11; Ephesians 4:11 – 16; 1 Timothy 3:10; Revelation 3:15 – 16

Julie and Bob Clark were stunned to receive a letter from their church in July asking them to "participate in the life of the church" or worship elsewhere. "They basically called us freeloaders," says Julie Clark. "We *were* freeloaders," says Bob Clark.

In a trend that may signal rough times for wallflower Christians, megachurch Faith Community of Winston-Salem has asked "non-participating members" to stop attending. "No more Mr. Nice Church," says the executive pastor, newly hired from Cingular Wireless. "Bigger is not always better. Providing free services indefinitely to complacent Christians is not our mission."

Freeloading Christians were straining the church's nursery and facility resources and harming the church's ability to reach the lost, says the pastor. "When your bottom line is saving souls, you get impatient with people who interfere with that goal."

Faith Community sent polite but firm letters to families who attended church services and freebie events but never volunteered, never tithed, and did not belong to a small group or other ministry. The church estimates that, of its 8,000 regular attendees, only half have volunteered in the past three years, and a third have never given to the church.

"Before now, we made people feel comfortable and welcome, and tried to coax them to give a little something in return," says a staff member. "That's changed. We're done being the community nanny."

Surprisingly, the move to disinvite people has drawn a positive response from men in the community who like the idea of an in-your-face church. "I thought, *A church that doesn't allow wussies—that rocks,*" says Bob Clark, who admires the church more since they told him to get lost.

P.S. This is not a true story, though we wish it were.

—Joel Kilpatrick, "Mega-Church Downsizes, Cuts Non-Essential Members," Larknews.com (September 2006)

ILLUSTRATION 41

TRAINING IN THE GYM OF THE SOUL

Topics: Accountability; Choices; Church Attendance; Community; Conversion; Self-reliance; Spiritual Disciplines; Spiritual Formation

References: Proverbs 22:6; 1 Corinthians 9:24–25; 1 Timothy 4:8; Hebrews 10:24–25; 12:1

Sylvester Stallone surprised the entertainment world by resurrecting his iconic movie hero, Rocky Balboa, for one last film in 2006. Then, while promoting the film, Stallone shocked Christian fans by saying that his faith in Jesus Christ had influenced the writing of the first *Rocky* screenplay. His renewed affiliation with Christianity had motivated him to write the last one.

In an interview with Citizenlink.com, Stallone said, "I was raised in a Christian home. I went to Catholic schools, and I was taught the faith. I went as far as I could with it until I got out into the so-called real world and was presented with temptation. I kinda lost my way and made a lot of bad choices."

Those bad choices, especially his decision to place fame and career ahead of his family, left Stallone unsatisfied. So he went back to church. "The more I go to church, the more I turn myself over to the process of believing in Jesus and listening to his Word and having him guide my hand," Stallone said.

Stallone also realized he had to trust Christ more than himself. "You need to have the expertise and the guidance of someone else," he said.

"You cannot train yourself. I feel the same way about Christianity and the church. The church is the gym of the soul."

—Stuart Shepard, "The Gym of the Soul," Citizenlink.com (November 15, 2006)

ILLUSTRATION 42

CHANGING THE OIL

Topics: Busyness; Health; Rest; Sabbath; Stress; Weariness; Work

References: Genesis 2:1–3; Exodus 20:8–11; Psalm 23:2–3; Matthew 11:28; Mark 6:31; Hebrews 4:9–11

A few years ago, I got a call from a girl in my department who said her car had broken down and left her stranded about two miles from the office. So I drove over there and found her leaning against her car, looking flustered.

I asked what happened.

"Well, I was just driving down the road, and the car quit running," she said.

"Could you be out of gas?" I asked.

"No, I just filled it up."

Well, that one question pretty well exhausted my automotive diagnostic abilities, but I persisted. "What happened? Did it make any noise?"

"Oh, yeah," she replied. "As I was driving down the hill, it went *brump, brump, brump, POW!*"

I asked, "When was the last time you changed the oil?"

She said, "Oil?" As it turned out, she had owned the car for a year and a half and had never changed the oil.

I get that same look when I ask frazzled friends, "When was the last time you took a Sabbath rest?"

—David Slagle, Atlanta, Georgia

ILLUSTRATION 43

FINDING JOY IN CHURCH DISCIPLINE

Topics: Adultery; Body of Christ; Church Discipline; Church Membership; Repentance; Restoration; Testimony

References: Matthew 18:15–20; Luke 17:1–4; 1 Corinthians 5:1–7; Galatians 6:1; Philippians 1:6; 2 Thessalonians 3:14–15; Titus 3:10

A few years ago, we had to discipline a man by removing him from membership for repeated and unrepentant adultery. We followed the guidelines of Matthew 18.

His response was, "I know what you have to do, so do what you must, because I don't care! I plan to never darken the doors of this church again anyway. So why should I care?" He proceeded to divorce his wife in civil court.

His wife continued to attend church. At cell group meetings, we prayed for God to do whatever was necessary to open this man's eyes and bring him back into a right relationship with God.

More than two years later, this man called me and asked if we could meet. In my office he broke down, saying the "Hound of Heaven" had been on his trail for nearly two years, and he couldn't take much more. He wanted to confess his sin, turn from his wicked ways, and renew his marriage. Even his wife, who had said she probably could never trust him again, was amazed at the change in his life.

After his divorce, this man, who was in the U.S. Army Reserves, had been sent overseas with his unit to process the bodies of soldiers who died in Iraq. Daily he was confronted with the brevity of life and permanence of eternity. After returning home, he met with the elders at our church, confessed his sin, and asked to be forgiven for his arrogance and the impact of his sin on the church. What a joy it was to later announce to the congregation that discipline against this man was lifted and he was restored to full fellowship in the church!

When we do things God's way, he does not always respond quickly with the results we desire, but his way is always right, best, and true. With praise, the whole church got to see God at work, restoring both the man and his marriage.

—Bob Ahlberg, Roscoe, Illinois

ILLUSTRATION 44

MULTIPLYING TALENTS

Topics: Blessings; Cooperation; Finances; Giving; Money; Sowing and Reaping; Stewardship; Talents; Testing God; Tithing; Vision

References: Malachi 3:10; Matthew 16:18; 25:14–30; Luke 19; Philippians 4:19; 1 Peter 4:10

St. Peter and St. Mary's Church in Stowmarket, England, needed repairs. So in December 2005, Reverend Michael Eden challenged his congregation to raise money with an application of the parable of the talents.

He gave each of the ninety parishioners 10 pounds (about $18) and instructed them to "go forth and multiply." That's what the people did. One person bought baking ingredients and made over $750 selling cakes and scones. Another bought wool and earned $138 selling scarves. In the end, the church raised more than $9,200.

Commenting on his unusual plan, Reverend Eden observed, "God gives us all sorts of things but does not expect us to waste them and do nothing."

—"It Wasn't All Bad,"
The Week (May 12, 2006)

ILLUSTRATION 45

CHRISTIAN CONTINENTAL SHIFT

Topics: Believers; Body of Christ; Christianity; Church; Evangelism; Family of God; Great Commission; Missions

References: Genesis 18:18; 22:18; Psalm 22:27; 96:3; Matthew 24:14; 28:18–20; Mark 16:15; Acts 1:8; 26:17–18

At the start of the twentieth century, only 10 percent of the world's Christians lived in the Southern continents and the East, while 90 percent lived in North America, Europe, Australia, and New Zealand.

Today at least 70 percent of the world's Christians live in the non-Western world. More Christians worship in Anglican churches in Nigeria each week than in all the Episcopal and Anglican churches of Britain, Europe, and North America combined. There are more Baptists in Congo than in Britain, more people in church every Sunday in communist China than in all of Western Europe, and ten times more Assemblies of God members in Latin America than in the United States.

—Christopher J. H. Wright, "An Upside-Down World," *Christianity Today* (January 2007)

ILLUSTRATION 46

SACRAMENTS OF LOVE

Topics: Assurance; Body of Christ; Communion; Doubt; Fellowship with God; Grace; Intimacy; Perseverance; Presence of God; Sacraments; Security; Self-worth; Trust

References: Matthew 26:26–29; Luke 22:19–20; John 3:16; 15:13; Romans 5:8; 1 John 3:16

My aunt died some time ago, having lived to be eighty or so. She had never married. While clearing out her possessions, we came across a battered photograph of a young man whom my aunt had loved. The relationship had ended tragically. She never loved anyone else and kept for the remainder of her life a photograph of the man she had loved.

Why? As she aged, she knew that she would have difficulty believing that, at one point in her life, someone had once cared for her and regarded her as his everything. It could all have seemed a dream, an illusion, something she had invented in her old age to console her in her declining years—except for the photo. The photo reminded her that she really had loved someone once and was loved in return. It was her sole link to a world in which she had been valued.

Communion bread and wine, like that photograph, reassure us that something that seems too good to be true—something that we might even be suspected of having invented—really did happen.

—Alister McGrath, *Doubting: Growing through the Uncertainties of Faith* (InterVarsity, 2006)

ILLUSTRATION 47

PREACHING BEYOND ASSAULT

Topics: Forgiveness; Preaching; Revenge; Violence

References: Matthew 5:38–44; Romans 12:17; 1 Thessalonians 5:15

A pastor in Tulsa, Oklahoma, recently had an opportunity to practice what he preaches about forgiveness.

The pastor was preaching when a man came up and punched him in the face. Victory Christian Center's pastor, Billy Joe Daugherty, continued his sermon, even though the blow had opened a cut above his eye that would later require two stitches.

Church members subdued the attacker, and police arrested Steven Rogers, age fifty. Daugherty prayed for his assailant during the church service and declined to press charges.

—"Pastor Punched in the Eye, Continues Sermon," firstcoastnews.com (November 23, 2005)

ILLUSTRATION 48

FINDING THEIR WINGS

Topics: Apathy; Dependence on God; Faith; Fear; Freedom; Power; Trust

References: Isaiah 40:31; Galatians 5:13

Every Sunday, the ducks in a certain town waddle out of their houses down Main Street to their church. They waddle into the sanctuary and squat in their proper pews.

The duck choir waddles in and takes its place, and then the duck minister comes forward and opens the duck Bible. He reads to them: "Ducks! God has given you wings! With wings you can fly! With wings you can mount up and soar like eagles. No walls can confine you! No fences can hold you! You have wings. God has given you wings, and you can fly like birds!"

All the ducks shout, "Amen!" And then they all waddle home.

—Tony Campolo, *Let Me Tell You a Story* (Word, 2000)

ILLUSTRATION 49

LOOKING BEYOND NUMBERS

Topics: Children; Church; Church Membership

References: Matthew 11:25 – 26; 18:1 – 3; 19:13 – 15

Forty years ago, a Philadelphia congregation watched as three nine-year-old boys were baptized and joined the church. Not long after, the church sold the building and disbanded.

One of those boys was Dr. Tony Campolo, Christian sociologist at Eastern University, Pennsylvania. Dr. Campolo remembers: "Years later when I was doing research in the archives of our denomination, I decided to look up the church report for the year of my baptism. There was my name and Dick White's—he is now a missionary—and Bert Newman is a professor of theology at an African seminary."

Then Campolo read the church report for the year he joined the church. It said, "It has not been a good year for our church. We have lost twenty-seven members. Three joined, and they were only children."

—Marlene LeFever,
Colorado Springs, Colorado

ILLUSTRATION 50

QUALIFYING FOR FIRST CLASS

Topics: Arrogance; Church; Community; Factions; Grace; Pride; Unity; Weakness

References: Romans 12:16; 15:5 – 7; 1 Corinthians 1:26 – 31; 4:6 – 13; Ephesians 2:8 – 9

After worrying for half an hour that we wouldn't get on an overbooked flight, my wife and I were summoned to the check-in desk. A smiling agent whispered that this was our lucky day. He was bumping us up to first class. This was the first and only time we have been pampered on an airplane with good food, hot coffee, and plenty of elbow room.

We played a little game, trying to guess who else didn't belong in first class. One man padded around the cabin in his socks, restlessly sampling magazines, playing with but never actually using the in-flight phones. Twice he sneezed so loudly we thought the oxygen masks would drop down. When the attendant brought linen tablecloths for our breakfast trays, he tucked his into his collar as a bib.

We see misfits at church too—people who obviously don't belong, people who embarrass us and cause us to feel superior. The truth is that we don't belong there any more than they do.

—Ken Langley, Zion, Illinois

ILLUSTRATION 51

CHRISTIANITY LEADS WORLD RELIGIONS

Topics: Belief Systems; Missions; Religions

References: Matthew 13:31–33; 28:19; Acts 1:8; Colossians 1:6

Christianity has become the most universal religion in history, with believers today a majority of the population in two-thirds of the world's 238 countries. So says the second edition of the *World Christian Encyclopedia* (Oxford University Press, 2001). Other statistics:

- Christianity began and ended the century as the world's biggest religion with 555 million believers or 32.2 percent of world population in 1900 and 1.9 billion or 31 percent as of last year.
- Those Christians are divided among 33,820 denominations or similar distinct organizations. Some 386 million believers are in independent churches. Apart from the historic Catholic, Orthodox, Anglican, and Protestant churches, Christians counted as belonging to "other" groups have quadrupled since 1970, with huge increases in Pentecostal and Charismatic movements.
- Islam ranks second worldwide. During the last century, it grew from 200 million, or 12.3 percent of the population, to 1.2 billion, or 19.6 percent.
- Other current totals: Hinduism, 811 million; Buddhism, 360 million; Sikhism, 23 million; Judaism, 14 million.
- In the United States there are 5.6 million Jews, 4.1 million Muslims (more than a fourfold increase in thirty years), 2.4 million Buddhists, and 1 million Hindus. There are 192 million people in U.S. Christian groups.

—Associated Press, "New Book Tallies Religions" (January 17, 2001)

ILLUSTRATION 52

WHY I STOPPED GOING

Topics: Church Attendance; Attitudes; Excuses

References: Romans 12:4–5, 10; Hebrews 10:25

I stopped going to ball games for the following reasons—which could apply just as easily to why I could stop going to church:

1. Whenever I go to a game, they ask for money.
2. The other fans don't care about me.
3. The seats are too hard.
4. Coach never visits me.
5. The referee makes calls I disagree with.
6. Some of the games go into overtime and make me late for dinner.
7. The band plays songs I don't know.
8. I have other things to do at game time.
9. My parents took me to too many games when I was growing up.

10. I know more than the coaches do anyway.

11. I can be just as good a fan at the lake.

12. I won't take my kids to a game either. They must choose for themselves what teams to follow.

—Mike and Amy Nappa,
A Heart Like His (Barbour, 1999)

ILLUSTRATION 53

STRADDLING THE MISSOURI

Topics: Beginnings; Church; Faith; Humility; Ministry; Small Things; Vision

References: Zechariah 4:10; Mark 4:30 – 32; 12:41 – 44

Almost two hundred years ago, Thomas Jefferson commissioned Meriwether Lewis and William Clark to find the source of the Missouri River, and from there to discover a relatively easy water route west to the Pacific. Such a waterway, they discovered, doesn't exist.

But they did succeed in mapping the Northwest. And fifteen months after pushing themselves upstream, they found the headwaters of the mighty Missouri River near the Montana-Idaho border: a tiny little rivulet, which a member of the expedition, Private Hugh McNeal, straddled, thanking God that he had lived to put one foot on either side of the mighty and heretofore deemed endless Missouri.

At its source, the Missouri looks a lot different from the powerful current that flows into the Mississippi River near St. Louis. Likewise,

in the kingdom of God, many great things start out small.

—Marshall Shelley, "Broader Pastures, More Breeds," *Leadership* (Fall 2000)

ILLUSTRATION 54

HOW WE ACT IN GOD'S FAMILY

Topics: Adoption; Belonging; Change; Children of God; Holiness; Sanctification; Spiritual Formation

References: Romans 7:24 – 25; 8:1 – 5; 2 Corinthians 7:1; Philippians 3:7 – 15

When I was a child, my father brought home a twelve-year-old boy named Roger, whose parents had died from a drug overdose. There was no one to care for Roger, so my folks decided they would raise him as their own.

At first it was difficult for Roger to adjust to his new home. Several times a day, I heard my parents saying to Roger, "No, no. That's not how we behave in this family." "No, no. You don't have to scream or fight or hurt other people to get what you want." "No, no, Roger, we expect you to show respect in this family."

In time, Roger began to change. Did he have to make those changes to become part of the family? No. He was part of the family by the grace of my father. But did he have to work hard because he was in the family? You bet he did. It was tough for Roger to change, and he had to work at it. But he was motivated by gratitude for the amazing love he had received.

Do you have a lot of hard work to do now that the Spirit has adopted you into God's family? Certainly. But not to become a son or a daughter of the heavenly Father. No, you make those changes *because* you are a son or daughter. And every time you start to revert back to the old addictions to sin, the Holy Spirit will say to you, "No, no. That's not how we act in this family."

—M. Craig Barnes, in the sermon "The Blessed Trinity," National Presbyterian Church, Washington, D.C. (May 30, 1999)

ILLUSTRATION 55

A FAMILY UNIT

Topics: Church; Conflict; Criticism; Cynicism; Family; Unity

Reference: Acts 2:42–47

While interviewing a young African-American soldier on the eve of Desert Storm, ABC correspondent Sam Donaldson asked, "How do you think the battle will go? Are you afraid?"

"We'll do OK. We're well trained," the soldier said, gesturing toward his fellow GIs. "And I'm not afraid, because I'm with my family."

The other soldiers shouted, "Tell him again. He didn't *hear* you."

The soldier repeated, "This is my family; we'll take care of each other."

We have to start thinking of America as a family. We have to stop screeching at each other, stop hurting each other, and instead start caring for, sacrificing for, and sharing with each other. We have to stop constantly criticizing, which is the way of the malcontent, and get back to the can-do attitude that made America. We have to keep trying and risk failing to solve this country's problems. We cannot move forward if cynics and critics swoop down and pick apart anything that goes wrong to a point where we lose sight of what is right, decent, and uniquely good about America.

That advice also applies to the body of Christ. We would do well to stop finding fault with each other and strive for unity.

—Colin Powell, *My American Journey* (Random House, 1995)

ILLUSTRATION 56

RADICAL INDIVIDUALISM

Topics: Body of Christ; Church; Community; Culture; Individualism; Revival

References: Romans 12:1–8; 1 Corinthians 12:12–31; Ephesians 1:22–23; 3:21

Many Christians have been infected with the most virulent virus of modern American life: radical individualism. They concentrate on personal obedience to Christ as if all that matters is "Jesus and me," but in doing so miss the point. For Christianity is not a solitary belief system. Any genuine resurgence of Christianity, as history demonstrates, depends on a reawakening and renewal of that which is the essence of the faith—the people of God, the new society, the body of Christ, which is made manifest in the world—the church.

—Chuck Colson, *The Body* (Word, 1992)

ILLUSTRATION 57

THE CURE FOR UNRULY BOYS

Topics: Discipline; Encouragement; Ministry; Pastors

References: 1 Timothy 5:17; Titus 2:6–8

I pastored a little congregation near Kaneohe Marine Corps Air Station in Hawaii. I always had a large supply of muscular recruits.

The young, mostly single marines had great hearts but not much tact. When out of uniform and away from their sergeant, they just stood around waiting for someone to tell them what to do.

At a Sunday school leaders' meeting, several women teachers described their discipline problems with young boys. They couldn't control the boys for the hour-long Bible lesson. They had tried everything and were ready to quit.

I grabbed a couple of marines and told them to go into the Sunday school rooms and put a couple of boys under each arm. "Rough them up and sit on them," I said.

The women were horrified, thinking the strategy bordered on child abuse, but the little boys loved it. Our discipline problems were solved by placing one marine per room to hold unruly boys while the teacher taught the lesson. In one Sunday I came to realize how every pastor needs a "few good men"!

—Robert Hicks,
in *Men of Integrity* (July/August 2000)

ILLUSTRATION 58

TURTLE RACING

Topics: Emotions; Enthusiasm; Joy; Praise; Worship

References: Psalm 150; Luke 19:40; Colossians 3:16

Nisswa, Minnesota, is known for its turtle races. Every Wednesday afternoon in the summer, the people of Nisswa and the surrounding communities gather at a designated parking lot for the races.

Vendors rent turtles; others sell "turtle products." And the fans gather early, placing their chairs and blankets in the best viewing sites. In a recent contest, 435 turtles raced in fifteen heats over a six-foot course.

The announcer calls the turtle holders to the mark and gives them the "Go!"—and the crowd goes wild as the handlers release the turtles and scream at them, jump up and down, wave furiously, and throw water, trying to urge the racers to the finish line. The winners of those heats then race their turtles in the championship race.

The winning handler receives $5—along with a turtle necklace. It's an uncharacteristic frenzy of emotion for the normally reserved folks of northern Minnesota. And to think that some people get upset when Christians are too expressive in church on a Sunday morning.

—Per Nilsen, Burnsville, Minnesota

ILLUSTRATION 59

YEARNING FOR HIS PRESENCE

Topics: Church; Joy; Longing; Passion; Prayer; Revival; Worship

References: Acts 1:14; Hebrews 11:6; James 4:8

If our churches don't pray, and if people don't have an appetite for God, what does it matter how many are attending the services? How would that impress God? Can you imagine the angels saying, "Oh, your pews! We can't believe how beautiful they are! Up here in heaven, we've been talking about them for years. Your sanctuary lighting—it's so clever. The way you have the steps coming up to the pulpit is wonderful"?

I don't think so.

If we don't want to experience God's closeness here on earth, why would we want to go to heaven, anyway? He is the center of everything there. If we don't enjoy being in his presence here and now, then heaven would not be heaven for us. Why would he send anyone there who doesn't long for him passionately here on earth?

—Jim Cymbala, *Fresh Wind, Fresh Fire* (Zondervan, 1997)

ILLUSTRATION 60

THREE-IN-ONE CHURCH

Topics: Attributes of God; Church; Theology; Trinity

Reference: John 4:23–24

The church is like the Trinity. It is a plant, with the Father as a deep root, the Son as the shoot that breaks forth into the world, and the Spirit as that which spreads beauty and fragrance.

—Tertullian (ca. 155–230), church leader and apologist

ILLUSTRATION 61

HARNESSING THE ORDINARY

Topics: Church; Community; Cooperation; Involvement; Ministry; Spiritual Gifts

Reference: Romans 12:3–8

The University of California at Berkley agreed to coordinate an international effort to locate extraterrestrial life.

To accomplish this impossible task, Berkley asked home computer users around the world to contact them over the Internet and download a program called SETI@home. The SETI software makes a connection over the Internet to a computer in California and downloads a "work unit"—that is, a set of measurements from a particular part of the sky. The work unit is not large, but it takes the computer a while to crunch the numbers.

When the work is done, the computer makes another Internet call to Berkeley, uploads its results, and downloads a new work unit. What today's largest supercomputer could never do alone, over a million ordinary home computers can easily do.

Sometimes the best way to accomplish the impossible is to harness the help of the ordinary. That is precisely how the church works best. No one can do it alone, but if we each do what we can, the unattainable becomes attainable, and the church can be all that God intended it to be.

—J. Kent Edwards, "Accomplishing the Impossible," PreachingToday.com

ILLUSTRATION 62

THE FIERY FORCE OF CHANGE

Topics: Change; Church; Leadership; Repentance; Spiritual Formation

Reference: 2 Peter 1:5 – 8

Growing up in the mountains of western New Mexico, I witnessed firsthand the hard work of containing forest fires.

One lesson hotshot crews and smoke jumpers learn early is that fire creates its own wind, and that wind can cause the fire to jump ahead much more quickly than anyone can anticipate. In the same way, change creates its own force. And the incendiary results may be more than anyone can bring under control.

—Ed Rowell, Monument, Colorado

ILLUSTRATION 63

DUMPING THE COTTON

Topics: Change; Habits; Traditions

Reference: Mark 7:1 – 13

Bayer Corporation has stopped putting cotton wads in its aspirin bottles. The company realized the aspirin would hold up fine without the maddening white clumps, which it had included since about 1914.

"We concluded there really wasn't any reason to keep the cotton except tradition," said Chris Allen, Bayer's vice president of technical operations. "Besides, it's hard to get out."

Likewise, long-standing traditions in the church can also be more annoying than helpful.

—Ed Rowell, "Parting from Tradition," PreachingToday.com

ILLUSTRATION 64

WRESTLING WITH BELIEF

Topics: Church; Community; Dependence on God; Help from God; Self-reliance; Weakness

References: Jeremiah 17:5 – 8; Ephesians 3:20 – 21; Hebrews 10:24 – 25

Organized religion is a sham and a crutch for weak-minded people.

—Jesse Ventura, former Minnesota governor and professional wrestler

ILLUSTRATION 65

CHURCH BEGINS WITH THANK YOU

Topics: Attitudes; Cross; Encouragement; Jesus Christ; Missions; Provision; Thankfulness

References: Psalm 100:4; Luke 17:18; Ephesians 5:20; Philippians 4:19; Colossians 1:12

When we started the PCA (Presbyterian Church in America) in 1973, we had no money — not a dime — and we were going to start a new denomination. One group gave us $90,000 for world missions. The only two missionaries we had — Dick Dye and a young woman named Ellen Barnett — were down in Acapulco.

Missionary Dick Dye had been in Acapulco for two months trying to start a church. Whenever he got discouraged, he looked up at a cross he could see on a nearby mountain. That encouraged him. Finally, he drove up the mountain to find out about that cross. And when he did, he found it attached to a big hotel. So Dye asked the secretary, "Can I speak to the man who runs this establishment?"

"Do you have an appointment?"

"No appointment, I just want to tell him something."

"What do you want to tell him?"

"I want to thank him."

The secretary got the owner. Dye said, "I'm a missionary from the United States here in Acapulco. I've been discouraged. But I see that cross and it encourages me. I want to thank you for having it up there."

The man looked at Dye, put his head down on his desk, and began to weep. He wept and wept. Finally he raised his head and said: "That cross has been up there for years. All I've heard is criticism. You're the first man who ever said thank you. Now, who are you and what do you need?"

"I'm just a missionary," Dick answered.

"Where do you meet?"

"We don't meet anywhere. I don't have any place to meet."

The owner said, "Come with me." He took Dick to a beautiful chapel and said, "We have church here at 9:00 a.m. and 11:00 a.m. From now on, it is yours at 10:00 a.m. You begin services next week."

That was the beginning of the first Presbyterian Church in America missionary plant. Within a few years, we turned four congregations over to the Presbyterian Church of Mexico. How did it start? With one guy who said thank you.

—James Baird, in the sermon "To Be Thankful," Independent Presbyterian Church, Savannah, Georgia

ILLUSTRATION 66

LOVING HIM TO CHURCH

Topics: Childlikeness; Church; Evangelism; Humility; Outreach; Questions

References: Matthew 18:1–4; Colossians 4:5–6; 1 Peter 3:15–16

British journalist Malcolm Muggeridge was captivated by Mother Teresa's deep compassion for the poorest of the poor in Calcutta's slums. But he, an unbeliever, could not accept her faith. He could not join the church, which was such a flawed institution.

Once, when Mother Teresa visited London, she and Muggeridge took a walk. "I took up my well-prepared defensive position about the church, whose deficiencies, crumbling barricades, and woeful future prospects, I expatiated upon, with little effect," the journalist said. Later Mother Teresa sent Muggeridge a small devotional book. Here are excerpts:

> I'm sure you will understand beautifully everything if you would only become a little child in God's hands. Your longing for God is so deep, and yet he keeps himself away from you. He must be forcing himself to do so, because he loves you so much, as to give Jesus to die for you and for me. Christ is longing to be your food. Surrounded with fullness of living food, you allow yourself to starve. The personal love Christ has for you is infinite. The small difficulty you have regarding his church is finite. Overcome the finite with the infinite. Christ has created you because he wanted you. I know what you feel, terrible longing with dark emptiness, and yet he is the one in love with you.

Eight years before he died in 1990, Muggeridge finally overcame his objections and joined the Christian church.

—Kevin Miller, Wheaton, Illinois

ILLUSTRATION 67

TEAMING FOR THE GOLD

Topics: Community; Competition; Individualism; Spiritual Gifts; Teamwork

References: 1 Corinthians 12:12–31; Ephesians 4:1–13

Jenny Thompson has won ten Olympic medals in swimming, eight of which are gold. However, she didn't win any of the golds in individual events; she won them in team events with three other swimmers.

As a result, some people have questioned whether Jenny's swimming accomplishments ought to rank her with the "great" Olympic champions. She asks that herself. "It's got to be very different to experience an individual gold versus a team gold," she says.

I find Jenny's accomplishments in the ego-driven United States culture refreshing. With ballplayers moving from team to team, demonstrating little team loyalty, Jenny is a marvelous example of someone whose genuine success came in the context of team play.

This is how the church should work. Our true "stardom" occurs when we participate as part of a winning team. On God's team, there is no room for superstars or mega-celebrities who do it on their own.

—Jon Mutchler, "Jenny Thompson's Gold-Medal Teamwork," PreachingToday.com

ILLUSTRATION 68

HELPING WITH HAND MOTIONS

Topics: Children; Church; Community; Compassion; Empathy; Family; Teens

References: Romans 12:3–8; 1 Corinthians 12:12–31; Ephesians 4:1–16

After an accident in which she lost her arm, Jamie refused to go to school or church. Finally, the young teen thought she could face her peers. In preparation her mother called her Sunday school teacher and asked that he not call attention to Jamie. The teacher promised, but then he got sick on Sunday and had to call a substitute.

At the conclusion of the lesson that day, which was about inviting friends to church, the substitute teacher led the class in doing the hand motions to the familiar children's poem:

Here is the church,
Here is the steeple.
Open the door
And see all the people.

Jamie's eyes filled with tears. A thirteen-year-old boy sensed Jamie's pain and knelt beside her. With one hand apiece, they supported each other, making the church, steeple, and people.

Together they illustrated what real church is.

—Billy Waters, *Teacher Touch* (Cook, 1999)

ILLUSTRATION 69

OFFERING A NEW VIEW OF THE WORLD

Topics: Awe; Beauty; Creation; Nature; Perception and Reality; Spiritual Perception

References: Psalm 119:18; John 9:25; 16:15; 2 Corinthians 5:17–18

Christo and Jeanne-Claude hung 142,000 square feet of orange nylon fabric between the mountains on either side of Rifle Gap in Colorado in the early 1970s. Ten years later they surrounded two islands off the Florida coast in bright pink fabric. Later they "wrapped" the German Reichstag and the Pont Neuf in France.

Since the early 1960s, Christo and Jeanne-Claude have been creating unique art installations for a public often skeptical, sometimes welcoming, and usually completely unprepared for what they are about to experience. The artists call their work "environmental art," because they use large pieces of fabric to highlight and set apart natural environments—urban or rural—for a short period of time. Each project typically requires years of logistical planning and negotiations with local governments. The artwork demands sophisticated feats of engineering and hundreds of crew members, not to mention lots of money.

What would possess anyone to create such massive (and temporary) works of art? What purpose could they possibly serve? According to Robert Storr, professor of modern art at the Institute of Fine Arts in New York, "They see it in terms of making what is already in the world more visible ... and visible to us in different ways." The installations are only a part of the artwork. The other part is the world that is already there, "which we often pass by without paying any attention to it," Storr says. The artists highlight one part of the environment. "In doing so, we see and perceive the whole environment with new eyes and a new consciousness," Christo and Jeanne-Claude say on their website.

Adam Cieselski and Jok Church, who were crew members on the artists' California coastline project titled *Running Fence*, said that the artwork served as "a landscape with an obstructive membrane in place to block and alter the view, which transforms the way people perceive it." Decades later Cieselski and Church can drive through Western Marin and Sonoma counties and still find *Running Fence*. The landscape is untouched, unaltered, and unchanged. "The thing that has been changed is us," they say.

Note: Images of the artworks can be viewed at www.christojeanneclaude.net.

—"Central Park's Bright New Clothes," npr.org (February 10, 2005)

ILLUSTRATION 70

FIGHTING FOR THE LAND

Topics: Beauty; Creation; Creator; Environmentalism; Nature; Unity; Vision

References: Genesis 1:28–30; Psalm 24:1–2; Revelation 11:18

Allen Johnson, a conservative evangelical Christian living in the mountains of West Virginia, is an environmental activist and cofounder of Christians for the Mountains, a group of people who have demonstrated against coal companies and participated in Rainbow Family gatherings.

Allen hopes that environmental stewardship will quickly become a unifying issue for Christians across the nation. "God has called all of us seriously," he says, "and we should agree on one thing: to take care of his earth."

Allen's passion for environmentalism began in 1993 while visiting Haiti with a Christian Peacemaker team. He saw desperate farmers cutting down grapefruit trees to make a cash crop of charcoal. "I just started sobbing," he says. "It really hit me that impoverishment is so closely tied to environmental destruction."

Since that day, Johnson has been a pioneer in a growing movement called "Eco-Christianity." His biggest challenge has been convincing other Christians to join him in the fight instead of labeling him a "New Age wing nut" or a liberal. "My identity is not as an environmentalist," says Johnson. "It's as a Christian. Because I am Christian, I should be involved with social justice—the poor,

the needy. Environmentalism is one thing in my circle, but it's not my center."

—Vanessa Juarez and David Gates,
"A Shepherd Protects His Own Backyard,"
Newsweek (September 5, 2005)

ILLUSTRATION 71

GOD'S WONDER BEES

Topics: Commitment; Community; Dedication; Determination; Diligence; Jobs; Nature; Sacrifice; Self-denial; Teamwork; Wonder; Work

References: Psalm 8:1–4; 19:1–3; Proverbs 6:6; 30:25; Romans 1:20; Colossians 1:16

That sixteen-ounce jar of honey in your pantry exists only because tens of thousands of bees flew some 112,000 miles in a relentless pursuit of nectar gathered from 4.5 million flowers. Every one of those foraging bees was female. By the time each died—living all of 6 weeks during honey-making season—she had flown about 500 miles in 20 days outside the hive.

As these bees were flying themselves to death, production inside the hive continued with stupendous efficiency, as follows: A bee brings nectar to the hive, carried tidily in her "honey stomach." The bee is greeted by a younger, homebody receiver bee, who relieves her of her load. A receiver bee deposits nectar into a cell, reducing its water content and raising its sugar level by fanning it with her wings and regurgitating it up to 200 times, killing microbes along the way. More bees surround this cell and others and fan them with their wings 25,000 times or so, turning nectar into honey. When the honey is ripe, wax specialists arrive to cap off the cells. That is how every single ounce of every single honey pot, bottle, or jar in the world—hundreds of thousands of them—is brought into being.

"Every gulp of raw honey is a distinct, unique, unadulterated medley of plant flavor; a sweet, condensed garden in your mouth," writes Holley Bishop, an awed amateur beekeeper trying her level best with ordinary English to capture a miracle.

—Eric Miller, "Shock and Awe,"
Books and Culture (September–October 2006)

ILLUSTRATION 72
UNFOLDING GRANDER VISTAS

Topics: Abundant Life; Calling; Conversion; Destiny; God; Growth; Illumination; Meaning of Life; Mysteries; New Life; Potential; Promises; Purpose; Revelation; Riches

References: Genesis 21:1–7; Acts 9:1–19; Ephesians 3

On my desk I like to display, on a bookstand, the kind of gift books you put on the coffee table—those filled with professional photos of nature or tourist destinations. My current book is *America's Spectacular National Parks* by Michael Duchemin. For several days I have had the book open to a photo of the Grand Teton Mountains, an extra-wide photo that fills the left page and crosses the fold to take up half of the right. It is a majestic display of deep blue sky; rugged, gray, snow-capped mountains; and a calm lake in the foreground.

This morning I decided to turn the page to the next photo, and as I did I discovered that I had missed something important. The right page of the Grand Tetons photo was an extra-long page folded over, covering part of the Grand Tetons. So when I opened it up, it added some sixteen inches to the width of the photo. Wow! The Grand Tetons became even grander.

The Christian life has unfolding moments like that, when we discover there is much more to God and his kingdom than we knew, much more to his purpose for us than we imagined. Abraham experienced that at age seventy-five, Moses at age eighty, the apostle Paul on the road to Damascus. Again and again in the Bible, when God met people, he opened a glorious page for them that had previously been folded.

—Craig Brian Larson,
Arlington Heights, Illinois

ILLUSTRATION 73
ANIMATING GOD'S WAY

Topics: Arts; Beauty; Creation; Creativity; God; Limitations; Movies; Nature; Perfection; Power

References: Genesis 1:1; Nehemiah 9:6; Psalm 19:1; 104:24; Romans 1:20; Colossians 1:16

John Lasseter, Pixar Animation Studios' genius and director of the hit film *Cars*, was talking to Michele Norris on National Public Radio. She commented on the amazing photo-realism of the film, which was entirely created by computers. "The cars glisten," she said. "It looks like we're seeing photography."

But she had a question for the moviemaker. "With everything you can do with computer-generated animation, are there still limitations?" Norris asked.

"Absolutely," Lasseter replied. "The more organic something is in the way it looks or the way it moves, the harder it is to create it with a computer." This was after he mentioned that every frame of the feature-length film required an average of seventeen hours to create. According to the *Los Angeles Times*, production costs for Pixar films average about $140 million.

However, no costs were mentioned in a *Wall Street Journal* review that appeared two weeks later describing a summer exhibit at Brooklyn Botanic Garden. The medium here was photography, not computer-generated anything, and the subject was totally organic. Here is a brief description from the review: "One canvas in magenta red has curling squares of what looked like skin or material; another has furry brown hairs sprouting on green and orange stripes; and on a third, lip-like shapes float on a gray-white background."

The subject of these abstract photos? Magnified close-ups of tree bark.

"The closer one gets to something man has made, the more its imperfections are obvious," said Dr. Lewis Foster many years ago. "The more we magnify something God has created, the more we see its perfection."

—Mark A. Taylor, "From the Editor,"
Christian Standard (August 6, 2006)

ILLUSTRATION 74

FINE-TUNING THE UNIVERSE

Topics: Creation; Evidence for God; Evolution; God's Omnipotence; God's Strength; Nature; Perfection

References: Genesis 1:1; Job 38:31–33; Psalm 19:1–3; 33:6; Romans 1:20

The fine-tuning of the universe is shown in the precise strengths of four basic forces. Gravity, the best known of these forces, is also the weakest, with a relative strength of 1. Next strongest is the weak nuclear force that holds neutrons together inside an atom. It is 1,034 times stronger than gravity but works only at subatomic distances. Electromagnetism is 1,000 times stronger than the weak nuclear force. And the strong nuclear force—which keeps protons together in the nucleus of an atom—is 100 times stronger yet.

If even one of these forces had a slightly different strength, the life-sustaining universe we know would be impossible. If gravity was slightly stronger, all stars would be large, like the ones that produce iron and other heavier elements, but they would burn out too rapidly for the development of life. If gravity was weaker, the stars would endure, but none would produce the heavier elements necessary to form planets.

The weak nuclear force controls the decay of neutrons. If it was stronger, neutrons would decay more rapidly, and there would be nothing in the universe but hydrogen. However, if this force was weaker, all the hydrogen would turn into helium and other elements.

The electromagnetic force binds atoms to one another to form molecules. If it was either weaker or stronger, no chemical bonds would form, so no life could exist.

Finally, the strong nuclear force overcomes the electromagnetic force and allows the atomic nucleus to exist. Like the weak nuclear force, changing its strength would produce a universe with only hydrogen or with no hydrogen.

In sum, without planets, hydrogen, and chemical bonds, there would be no life as we know it. Besides these four factors, there are at least twenty-five others that require pinpoint precision to produce a universe that contains life. Getting each of them exactly right suggests the presence of an Intelligent Designer.

—Charles Edward White, "God by the Numbers," *Christianity Today* (March 2006)

ILLUSTRATION 75

DUSTY VIEWS OF MAN'S CREATION

Topics: Creation; Creator; Dignity; Human Condition; Human Worth; Life; Perfection; Purpose

References: Genesis 1:26; 2:7; Job 32:8; Psalm 8:3–6; 139:13–16; John 3:16; Romans 5:8

Contrast the creation of the first man according to Genesis 2 with the creation of the first human beings according to Mesopotamian tradition. Both start with dust or clay, but then the accounts vary.

In the Mesopotamian creation account, *Enuma Elish*, humanity's dust is mixed with the blood of a demon god killed for his treachery against the second generation of gods. Humans are demons from the time they're born. According to *Atrahasis*, the second ingredient is the spit of the gods, a far cry from the glorious breath of the biblical Creator!

The creation process according to Mesopotamian tradition fits well with the overall low view of humanity professed by that culture. According to *Atrahasis*, humans were created with the express purpose of relieving the lesser gods from the arduous labor of digging irrigation ditches.

By contrast, the Genesis account teaches that human beings, male and female, were created in the image of God to rule over every living thing that has the breath of life in it (Genesis 1:30).

—Tremper Longman III, *Immanuel in Our Place* (P&R, 2001)

ILLUSTRATION 76

THE WONDROUS FLY

Topics: Animals; Beauty; Creation; Creator; Human Worth; Nature;

References: Psalm 8; 139:13–14; Matthew 10:29–31; Romans 1:20

The pesky housefly is the most talented aerodynamicist on the planet—superior to any bird, bat, or bee. According to a British scientist, "a housefly can make six turns a second, hover, fly straight up, fly straight down, fly backwards, do somersaults, land on the ceiling, and perform various other show-off maneuvers. And it has a brain smaller than a sesame seed."

Flies are also loaded with sensors. In addition to their compound eyes, which permit panoramic imagery and are excellent at detecting motion, flies have wind-sensitive hairs and antennae. They also have three light sensors, called *ocelli*, on the tops of their heads, which tell them which way is up. Roughly two-thirds of a fly's entire nervous system is devoted to processing visual images.

If God put so much wisdom into ordinary houseflies, imagine what it means to know that we are "fearfully and wonderfully made."

—Joel Achenbach, "Fly Like a Fly," *National Geographic* (June 2006)

The demotion was part of a shake-up in the Union's galactic guidelines. To qualify as a planet, a heavenly body must now "orbit the sun, be large enough to assume a round shape, and clear the neighborhood around its orbit." The third requirement disqualifies Pluto, which is surrounded by objects of similar size and characteristics.

"It's disappointing in a way, and confusing," said Patricia Tombaugh, ninety-three, widow of Clyde Tombaugh, who first discovered Pluto in 1930. "I don't know just how to handle it. It sounds like I just lost my job."

—William J. Kole, "Dinky Pluto Loses Its Status as a Planet," news.yahoo.com (August 25, 2006)

ILLUSTRATION 77
DEMOTING PLUTO

Topics: Authority; Change; Defeat; Ego; Failure; Fall of Humanity; Human Worth; Humility; Identity; Nature; Power; Powerlessness; Pride; Respect; Science; Self-image

References: Job 1:13–22; 2 Corinthians 13:5; Galatians 6:3; Philippians 2:3, 5–11; Revelation 12:9

Pluto has lost its place among the giants of our solar system. On August 24, 2006, the International Astronomical Union voted to strip Pluto of its planetary status, defining it instead as a "dwarf planet."

ILLUSTRATION 78
DESIGN PERSUADES ATHEIST

Topics: Arguments; Atheism; Beliefs; Change; Creation; Faith; Nature; Perfection; Results; Unbelief; Word of God

References: Psalm 19:1–6; 102:25; Isaiah 45:9–12

Legendary British philosopher Antony Flew gave up atheism at the age of eighty-one. A noted critic of God's existence for several decades, Flew wrote books such as *The Presumption of Atheism.*

When asked in 2004 what arguments for God's existence he found most persuasive, Flew answered: "The most impressive arguments for God's existence are those that are supported by recent scientific discoveries.... I think the argument to Intelligent Design is enormously stronger than when I first met it."

— "My Pilgrimage from Atheism to Theism: A Discussion between Antony Flew and Gary R. Habermas," in *Philosophia Christi* (Winter 2005)

ILLUSTRATION 79
CREATING OUR DIFFERENCES

Topics: Adam and Eve; Creator; Gender Differences; Men; Nature; Women

References: Genesis 2:18–25; 1 Corinthians 11:3–16

Men and women are different physically, psychologically, motivationally, and temperamentally. Anyone who has had exposure to babies and children can tell you that boys and girls respond differently to the world right from the start.

Give both a doll, and the girl will cuddle it, while the boy will more likely use it as a projectile or weapon. Give them two dolls, and the girl will have the dolls talking to each other, while the boy will have them engaged in combat.

— Laura Schlessinger, *The Proper Care and Feeding of Husbands* (HarperCollins, 2003)

ILLUSTRATION 80
OUR CARBON FOOTPRINTS

Topics: Consequences; Disobedience; Environmentalism; Example;

Godliness; Grace; Holiness; Integrity; Morality; Rebellion; Self-control; Sin; Temptation; Vices; Victorious Living; Weakness

References: Proverbs 20:9; 28:13; Romans 3:23; 6:23; 2 Corinthians 5:17; James 1:13–15; 1 John 1:8–9

Global warming seems to be on everyone's mind. Scientists are running tests in their laboratories. Political candidates are dreaming up "green" policies. The heavyweights of Hollywood are filming public service announcements and organizing benefit concerts.

Now even you can do your part in fighting global warming. Have you heard about the "carbon footprints" we all supposedly leave behind us? Stop at the site www.carbonfootprint.com and learn how these "footprints" are "a measure of the impact human activities have on the environment in terms of the amount of greenhouse gases produced." In other words, by the fuel we burn on the way to work and the hair products we use, we each leave a "footprint" in the wide, growing path of global destruction.

You can even figure out how big your personal carbon footprint is. Fill out the online form, which asks for estimates of natural gas usage, wattage settings, and the mileage of your car over the past year, and you're well on your way to figuring out just how much "damage" you are doing throughout your day. Take heart, though—the site goes on to offer a litany of suggestions for lifestyle change.

This really gets me thinking about a more inconvenient truth—*sin*. For every act of rebellion—every vicious word, every selfish act, every unhealthy state of mind—we press our footprint on the wide, growing path of spiritual destruction. By just one misstep, the world will never quite be the same again—and not for the better.

The good news, of course, is that we can leave another kind of print. With every act of redemption—every kind word, every selfless act, a healthy state of mind—we can deepen the personal footprint of the One who walked before us, ushering in his new kingdom with him. By just one sure step, the world will never quite be the same again.

—Brian Lowery, "The Inconvenient Truth of Sin," PreachingToday.com

ILLUSTRATION 81

UNCOVERING THE REAL MICHELANGELO

Topics: Cleansing; Grace; Redemption; Restoration; Sanctification

References: 2 Corinthians 5:17; Philippians 1:6

For five years in the early 1500s, the artist Michelangelo lay on his back and painted scenes depicting the fall and the flood on the ceiling of the Sistine Chapel in Rome.

But the magnificent art started to fade almost immediately. Within a century of completing his work, no one remembered what his original frescoes had looked like. Painter Biagio Biagetti said in 1936, "We see the colors of the Sistine ceiling as if through smoked glass."

In 1981, a scaffold was erected to clean the frescoes that adorn the chapel. With a special solution, Fabrizio Mancinelli and Gianluigi Colalucci gently washed a small corner of the painting. They then invited art experts to examine the work. The results were stunning. No one had imagined that beneath centuries of grime lay such vibrant colors.

This was not the Michelangelo known by art critics. That artist was the master of form, his paintings resembling sculpture more than painting. This "new" artist was also the master of color—azure, green, rose, and lavender.

Mancinelli and Colalucci's success prompted the restoration of the entire ceiling. The task was completed in December 1989. It took twice as much time to clean the ceiling as the artist utilized to paint it. But the result was breathtaking. For the first time in nearly five hundred years, people viewed this masterpiece the way it was intended, in all of its color and beauty.

—Al Janssen, *The Marriage Masterpiece* (Tyndale, 2001)

ILLUSTRATION 82

THE RIGHT ENVIRONMENT FOR LIFE

Topics: Creation; Creator; Life

References: Psalm 95:1–5; Isaiah 45:18

In the vast universe, few systems can support life. According to Dr. Seth Shostak, an astronomer with the SETI [Search for Extra-Terrestrial Intelligence] Institute, the following conditions must be present to support life:

- The system's star ("sun") must not be a giant star, because those burn out before life can fully develop.
- The system's star must not be a dwarf star, because such a star locks in the close planets, meaning "one side of the planet forever faces its sun, resulting in horrific weather and unlikely venues for life."
- The system's star cannot be a double star, because the unusual gravitational forces created by a double star sun might not allow stable planetary systems.
- The system's star must not be a young star, because stars less than one billion years old have not had enough time for life to develop.
- Ideally, the planet would have a large moon, which creates active tides.
- The planet should have tectonic activity, which causes metals to be pushed up to the surface, since metals are valuable to a technological civilization.
- The planet should have a large planet farther out in its solar system, which by its great gravitational pull cleans the inner solar system of deadly asteroids and comets.
- The planet should not have a highly elliptical orbit, which is unsuitable for incubating life.
- For life to live on the surface, the planet must have an atmosphere. "Very small planets lose their air, and very large planets tend to sport poisonous atmosphere. Earth-sized planets are ideal."

It just so happens that Earth meets all these conditions.

—"The Search for Intelligent Life in Space" course outline (The Teaching Company Limited Partnership, 1999)

ILLUSTRATION 83

GOING TO THE MAKER

Topics: Bible; Consequences; Disobedience; Guidance; Happiness; Obedience; Renewal

References: Psalm 119:105; John 10:10

My old laptop simply would not run the Mac-Bible software anymore. Though I had experimented with it for hours, nothing worked. My wife, wise woman that she is, suggested that I call the owners of the software for help, but no, I knew what I was doing.

That morning, after having exhausted every last idea, I gave in and called the MacBible Corporation. After speaking to a friendly voice, I was assured that the person to whom I was being referred would know exactly what to do. I wasn't convinced, but I called him anyway.

The name I had been given sounded familiar, and I soon learned why. The person on the other end of the line was none other than the man who had written the MacBible software. He gave me a brief set of instructions, which I wrote down. In minutes, my computer software program was up and running. I just had to go to the man who wrote the program.

How many times in life don't we try to work out our problems our own way? Finally, when all else has failed, we go to the one who designed us. Soon, if we obey, we find ourselves once again at peace with God and functioning as he planned.

—Tim Quinn, Holland, Michigan

Think of it: Biosphere 2 didn't work, yet the wonderfully integrated ecosystems of Earth supposedly just happened without intelligent design.

—"Lessons from Biosphere 2,"
Creation Ex Nihilo (June 1997)

ILLUSTRATION 84

ARTIFICIAL CREATION FLOPS

Topics: Creation; Creator; Evidence for God; God's Wisdom

Reference: Genesis 1:1

The experimental Biosphere 2 was an isolated living environment created to supply all the factors necessary for sustaining life. It was a self-contained microcosm of life on earth, containing soil, air, water, plants, and animals. It was an airtight enclosure covering 3.15 acres in Arizona.

Despite an investment of about $200 million from 1984 to 1991, a multimillion-dollar operating budget, almost unlimited technological support, and heroic effort, the Biosphere proved impossible to sustain eight human beings with adequate food, water, and air for two years.

Just fifteen months after the unit was enclosed in 1991, oxygen had to be added from the outside. Nineteen of twenty-five vertebrate species placed in the unit became extinct. All the species that could pollinate the plants became extinct, as did most insects. Water and air pollution became acute, and temperature control was a problem.

ILLUSTRATION 85

FINDING HOLINESS IN CREATION

Topics: Awe; Creation; Holiness; Spiritual Perception; Vision; Wonder; Worship

References: Exodus 3:5; Romans 1:20

Earth's crammed with heaven,
And every common bush afire with God;
But only he who sees takes off his shoes—
The rest sit round it and pluck blackberries.

—Elizabeth Barrett Browning,
from "Aurora Leigh"

ILLUSTRATION 86

ADMIRING SISTER NATURE

Topics: Beauty; Humanism; Naturalism; Nature; New Age; Worldview

Reference: Romans 1:18–23

The main point of Christianity is this: Nature is not our mother; Nature is our sister. We can be proud of her beauty, since we have the same Father; but she has no authority over us; we have to admire, but not to imitate. This gives to the typically Christian pleasure in this earth a strange touch of lightness that is almost frivolity.

Nature was a solemn mother to worshipers of Isis and Cybele. Nature was a solemn mother to Wordsworth or to Emerson. But Nature is not solemn to Francis of Assisi or to George Herbert. To St. Francis, Nature is sister, and even a younger sister: a little, dancing sister, to be laughed at as well as loved.

—G. K. Chesterton,
Orthodoxy (Ignatius, 1995)

ILLUSTRATION 87

VALIDATING CREATIVITY

Topics: Calling; Children; Creativity; Defeat; Direction; Encouragement; Fear; Goals; Influence; Mediocrity; Parenting; Peer Pressure; Purpose; Self-worth; Vision

References: Proverbs 3:27; Romans 15:2; Ephesians 4:29; 6:4; Colossians 3:21; 1 Thessalonians 5:11; 1 Timothy 4:12

For more than thirty years, Gordon MacKenzie worked at Hallmark. Along with challenging corporate normalcy at the card company, MacKenzie did a lot of creativity workshops for elementary schools. In those, MacKenzie would ask the kids up front: "How many artists are there in the room?"

The pattern of responses never varied. In the first grade, the entire class waved their arms like maniacs; every child was an artist. In the second grade, about half of the kids raised their hands. In the third grade, he'd get about ten out of thirty kids. And by the time he got to the sixth grade, only one or two kids would tentatively and self-consciously raise their hands.

All the schools he went to seemed to be involved in "the suppression of creative genius." They weren't doing it on purpose, but society's goal is to make us less foolish. As MacKenzie says, "From the cradle to the grave, the pressure is on: Be normal."

After his research, MacKenzie came to this conclusion: "There was a time—perhaps when you were very young—when you had at least a fleeting notion of your own genius and were just waiting for some authority figure to come along and validate it for you. But none ever came."

—Mark Batterson,
In a Pit with a Lion on a Snowy Day
(Multnomah, 2006)

PART 5: EVANGELISM

ILLUSTRATION 88

TAKING JESUS TO THE STREETS

Topics: Boldness; Evangelism; Gospel; Israel; Jesus Christ; Judaism; Messiah; Missions; Testimony; Witnessing

References: Matthew 28:18–20; Acts 1:8; 1 Corinthians 9:19–23; Galatians 3:28; Colossians 3:11; 1 Peter 3:15

In the summer of 2006, two hundred missionaries with Jews for Jesus worked the streets of New York City, which has the largest Jewish population in the world outside of Israel. They distributed a million tracts and collected contact information for more than five thousand people.

Members of Jews for Jesus, who are evangelicals with Jewish lineage, began the campaign by sending the *Jesus* film in Yiddish to eighty thousand Hasidic homes in the city. The organization also advertised in newspapers, on radio stations, and in the subway. These missionaries then worked the streets, trying to spark conversations by asking passersby who they thought Jesus was before explaining that they were both Jews and Christians.

"The bottom line is we're saying Jesus is the Messiah of Israel. What could be more Jewish?" David Brickner said. "My Jewish heritage is secondary to the fact that Jesus is the Messiah."

By mid-July, 157 Jews and 164 Gentiles became followers of Yeshua, mostly through street evangelism. Jews for Jesus is now working with a number of local evangelical churches, including Calvary Baptist Church, Brooklyn Tabernacle, and Christ Lutheran Church, to integrate the new believers into church fellowship.

—Sarah Pulliam, " 'Volcanic' Response," *Christianity Today* (September 2006)

ILLUSTRATION 89

CASTOR OIL LOVE

Topics: Beliefs; Evangelism; Judging Others; Legalism; Preaching; Religion; Teaching; Testimony; Witnessing

References: Matthew 6:5; 7:12; 28:19–20; 1 Corinthians 9:19–23; 1 Peter 3:15

Every day, at exactly the same time, Margaret would go to the bathroom cabinet, open it, and take out a huge bottle of castor oil. Then she would head to the kitchen to get a tablespoon.

At the sound of the drawer opening and the silverware rattling, Patches, her Yorkshire terrier, would run and hide—sometimes under the bed, at other times in the bathtub or behind Margaret's recliner.

Someone had convinced Margaret that Patches would have strong teeth, a beautiful coat, and a long life if she gave him a spoonful of castor oil every day. So, as an act of love every twenty-four hours, she cornered Patches, pinned him down, pried open his mouth, and poured a tablespoon of castor oil down his little doggie throat. Neither Patches nor Margaret enjoyed their daily wrestling match.

Then one day, in the middle of their battle royal, with one sideways kick, Patches sent the dreaded bottle of castor oil flying across the kitchen floor. It was a momentary victory for the canine, as Margaret let him go so she could run to the pantry and grab a towel to clean up the mess.

When Margaret got back, she was utterly shocked. There was Patches licking up the spilled castor oil with a look of satisfaction only a dog can make. Margaret began to laugh uncontrollably. In one moment, it all made sense. Patches liked castor oil. He just hated being pinned down and having it poured down his throat.

Welcome to the world of evangelism!

—Kevin G. Harney,
Seismic Shifts (Zondervan, 2005)

ILLUSTRATION 90

WISDOM SEEKER WINS CHINESE

Topics: Conduct; Culture; Evangelism; Humility; Judging Others; Lifestyle Evangelism; Ministry; Missions; Preaching; Seekers; Service; Teaching; Vision; Witnessing

References: Matthew 28:19–20; Acts 1:8; Romans 10:14; 1 Corinthians 9:19–23; 1 Peter 3:15

When Matteo Ricci, an Italian Jesuit scholar, finally gained permission to enter China in 1583 (the Chinese authorities generally didn't allow Europeans to enter at this time), he went dressed as a Buddhist monk speaking Chinese and presenting himself as a humble seeker after wisdom. He wasn't successful at first (the people of the area he arrived in, near Canton, didn't speak the Chinese dialect he had learned in Macao, and they didn't much like Buddhist monks either), but he persevered and won the trust of the people.

Ricci also made many contacts at the imperial court, where people were greatly impressed by his humble approach and his interest in Chinese learning. The emperor liked the gifts that Ricci brought him (especially a clock and a harpsichord), and Ricci sought to find new ways to express the Christian faith that made sense to the Chinese. He translated various Christian texts into Chinese, and in 1603 he wrote *The True Doctrine of the Lord of Heaven*, which presented Christianity in the form of a philosophical discussion in the Neo-Confucian tradition. The book, written in Chinese, was well received.

Ricci was the first great Jesuit missionary to China. Many more followed him and became closely involved in all kinds of scientific and cultural pursuits.

—Jonathan Hill, "Christianity's Cultural Contributions," ChristianityToday.com (May 3, 2006)

ILLUSTRATION 91

A PALESTINIAN PASTOR'S RADICAL LOVE

Topics: Courage; Decisions; Enemies; Evangelism; Love; Ministry; Persecution; Sanctification; Spiritual Formation; Witnessing

References: Matthew 5:43–44; Luke 6:27, 35; Acts 7:55–60; Romans 12:20

Bible college professor Yohanna Katanacho, who pastors a small church in Jerusalem, is subjected to much persecution. Israeli soldiers who patrol the city looking for potential terrorists impose spontaneous curfews on Palestinians and have the legal right to shoot at a Palestinian who does not respond quickly enough to their summons.

Yohanna tried and failed in his attempts to love his enemies. The Israeli soldiers' random daily checks for Palestinian identification cards—sometimes stopping them for hours—fed Yohanna's fear and anger. As he confessed his inability to God, Yohanna realized something significant. The radical love of Christ is not an emotion, but a decision. He decided to show love, however reluctantly, by sharing the gospel message with the soldiers on the street.

With new resolution, Yohanna began to carry copies of a flyer with him, written in Hebrew and English, with a quotation from Isaiah 53 and the words "Real Love" printed across the top. Every time a soldier stopped him, he handed him his ID card and the flyer. Because the quote came from the Hebrew Scriptures, the soldier usually asked him about it before letting him go.

After several months, Yohanna realized his feelings toward the soldiers had changed. "I was surprised, you know?" he says. "It was a process, but I didn't pay attention to that process. My older feelings were not there anymore. I would pass in the same street, see the same soldiers as before, but now find myself praying, 'Lord, let them stop me so that I can share with them the love of Christ.'"

—"When Love Is Impossible," *Trinity Magazine* (Fall 2005)

ILLUSTRATION 92

COFFEE SHOP WITNESS

Topics: Evangelism; Prayer; Testimony; Witnessing

References: Matthew 28:19; Mark 16:15; Acts 1:8; 3:1–8; 5:20; 1 Peter 3:15

The biggest hindrance for a lot of us in sharing Christ is that we don't see a natural and gracious opportunity to do that. I do a lot of evangelism at Einstein's Bagels, where I hang out for coffee.

I met a woman there, whom I'll call Barb, who told me that, though she was Jewish by birth, she was very interested in Christianity. "I guess you could say I'm a seeker," she said, to my surprise. I prayed for her regularly, and one day we started talking about the gospel. She was fascinated and curious. I discovered that the friend she was eating with was a strong Christian, and Barb had heard the gospel several times. She agreed with things that I said but was noncommittal. I said: "You know, Barb, someday you're going to have to make a choice. You can't be neutral about Christ forever." To my shock, she suddenly became very agitated and teary, even angry. She grabbed her things and ran out. After playing that tape back in my mind a few times to see if I had been out of line, I decided I had just seen the "offense of the gospel" at work.

Another morning I struck up a conversation with a young man who always wore black pants and a white shirt and carried a backpack full of self-help books, some in a foreign language. One day I said to him, "I see you like to read." I found he was eager to talk. His name, I eventually learned, was Dimitrij, and he was a waiter at a nearby restaurant. The second time we talked, he asked me if he could visit my church. The very next Sunday, he and his girlfriend were in church, and a guest speaker shared the gospel. Dimitrij raised his hand when I gave an invitation to accept Christ. We met several times over coffee until that interest in Jesus blossomed into faith.

Every now and then I'd see a fellow I'll call Jim — a dentist. I learned that he has a son who is an evangelical missionary. Jim is a sweet and generous guy, and I enjoyed talking with him. I invited him to church a few times, but nothing happened. Then one morning while we were getting coffee, he told me he had made a New Year's promise to his son to go to church. "I'm preaching this Sunday about the Good Shepherd and

lost sheep," I told him casually. He froze, coffee cup half filled, and just looked at me. "Are you kidding?" he asked. When I assured him I wasn't kidding, he said "I'll be there" — and he was.

— Lee Eclov, "Christ in a Coffee Shop,"
Trinity Magazine (Spring 2006)

ILLUSTRATION 93

EXHILARATING WITNESS

Topics: Anxiety; Courage; Evangelism; Fear; Guidance; Hearing God; Leading of the Holy Spirit; Seekers; Witnessing

References: Matthew 28:18 – 20; Mark 16:15; Luke 19:9 – 10; Acts 1:8; Romans 1:16; 1 Peter 3:15

On the flight from Chicago to Lincoln, Nebraska, I sat next to a Saudi Arabian guy, Ali, who was on his way to start college in Lincoln. As soon as I heard that he'd never been in the United States before and was from the Middle East, I felt Jesus tugging at my heart. After a little chitchat about his feelings about being so far from home and asking what he knew about American culture or life in Nebraska, I told him I was a follower of Jesus.

I asked Ali about his spiritual background. I told him that he'd probably meet a number of people in Nebraska who are Christians, and said it'd probably be helpful to understand a little of where they're coming from. I pulled out the *Four Spiritual Laws* and read through each point with him.

We talked a little bit more, and then I went back to reading my book. He opened the booklet and read it cover to cover. I was so excited. I prayed for him as he was reading it, thankful to have been reminded this morning that God is the one who works, convicting people of their need for him. After Ali finished reading, I asked him what he thought, and he said it was very interesting.

As the plane landed I told him I'd pray for him, then was convicted that I should do it right then. I asked if I could pray for him, and he immediately said yes. At the baggage claim I went over and met his cousin and invited them both to an American cultural event — Christmas Eve service at our church! We'll see!

This is why I love being a Christian — it's heart-pounding scary at times and exhilarating when I see someone I know Jesus wants to come to him, and I have the choice to step out in faith or stay in security.

— Email from Marilyn Adamson,
Orlando, Florida (December 2006)

ILLUSTRATION 94

SOUND CHECK FOR BILLY

Topics: Communication; Evangelism; Gospel; Opportunity; Purpose; Witnessing

References: Matthew 28:19 – 20; John 3:16; Ephesians 3:6 – 7; 5:15 – 16; Colossians 4:5; 2 Timothy 4:1 – 5

Billy Graham was so focused on bringing his message into every endeavor — even in something so simple as a sound check — that he would somehow always find a way to do it.

"One of the distinctives of Mr. Graham's ministry has been his ability to make positive points for the gospel in any situation," says Larry Ross, whose firm has handled media and public relations for Graham's organization for more than twenty-three years. "You can ask Billy Graham how he gets his suits dry-cleaned on the road, and he'll turn it into a gospel witness.

"I cut my teeth in the corporate world before I worked with Mr. Graham, and I set up numerous media interviews," Ross says. "Almost always before a TV interview, they do a microphone check, and they ask the interviewee to say something — anything — so they can adjust the audio settings. Often a corporate executive will count to ten, say their ABCs, or recite what he had for breakfast. Mr. Graham would always quote John 3:16 — 'For God so loved the world that he gave his only begotten Son, that whosoever believeth in him shall not perish but have everlasting life.'

"When I asked Mr. Graham why he does that, he replied, 'Because that way, if I am not able to communicate the gospel clearly during the interview, at least the cameraman will have heard it.'"

— Harold Myra and Marshall Shelley,
The Leadership Secrets of Billy Graham
(Zondervan, 2005)

ILLUSTRATION 95

SAVING A FAMILY

Topics: Deliverance; Depression; Despair; Emptiness; Guidance; Hearing God; Help from God; Hope; Overcoming; Perspective; Prayer; Suicide; Testimony; Trials; Witnessing; Worry

References: Psalm 23:4; Luke 19:9–10; John 8:32; Acts 16:25–34; Romans 8:28, 35–39

Kumar, a Christian in South India, was grieved because none of the thirteen people he had invited had come to watch a Billy Graham evangelistic broadcast at his home on December 23. He began to pray, and around 9:00 p.m. he felt compelled to invite his wife's sister's family to watch the next night's broadcast.

The family had no phone, so Kumar asked a neighbor to bring them to the phone for an urgent message. When his brother-in-law, Satish, reached the phone, Kumar asked him and his family to catch a bus to the city. Satish said he had no money. Kumar encouraged him to borrow the money and said that he would reimburse Satish for the tickets.

Satish consented, and at 4:00 a.m. he and his family boarded a bus for the long trip to Kumar's house. They arrived at 5:00 p.m., and an hour later they watched the *My Hope* telecast from the Billy Graham Evangelistic Association. Afterward, Kumar gave his testimony and asked if the others wanted to put their faith in Christ. They were all looking at each other, and Kumar wondered why. Then Satish, noticeably distressed, stood and explained that he had lost his job because the tea factory he worked for had closed. Further, the company was demanding that the family vacate their company-owned house. Seeing no hope, the family had decided that on December 25 they were all going to commit suicide.

Now they saw they had hope in Jesus, so they prayed with Kumar to accept Christ. Satish said he felt like a new man. After staying several more days with Kumar, the family returned home ready to face the future with Christ.

—Bob Paulson, "My Hope: India," *Decision* (March 2006)

ILLUSTRATION 96

EX-EVANGELIST MISSES JESUS

Topics: Atheism; Belief; Doubt; Faith; Gospel; Jesus Christ; Regret; Skepticism; Unbelief

References: Psalm 119:76; Matthew 14:31; Mark 4:1–20; John 9:35–41; 14:23–24; Romans 1:18–22; 1 Corinthians 10:12; 2 Peter 3:8–9; 1 John 5:10; Revelation 2:4

Charles Templeton was a close friend and preaching associate of Billy Graham in the 1940s. He effectively preached the gospel to large crowds in major arenas. However, intellectual doubts began to nag at him. He questioned the truth of Scripture and other core Christian beliefs. He finally abandoned his faith and made an unsuccessful attempt to persuade Billy to do the same. He felt sorry for Billy, saying, "He committed intellectual suicide by closing his mind." Templeton resigned from the ministry and became a novelist and news commentator. He also wrote a critique of the Christian faith titled *Farewell to God: My Reasons for Rejecting the Christian Faith.*

Interviewed when he was eighty-three and suffering from Alzheimer's disease, Templeton talked about some of the reasons he left the faith: "I started considering the plagues that sweep across parts of the planet and indiscriminately kill—more often than not, painfully—all kinds of people, the ordinary, the decent, and the rotten. And it just became crystal clear to me that it is not possible for an intelligent person to believe that there is a deity who loves."

When asked what he thought of Jesus Christ, Templeton would not acknowledge him as God. Rather, he responded: "He was the greatest human being who has ever lived. He was a moral genius. His ethical sense was unique. He was the intrinsically wisest person that I've ever encountered in my life or in my readings. He's the most important thing in my life. I know it may sound strange, but I have to say I adore him! Everything good I know, everything decent I know, everything pure I know, I learned from Jesus. He is the most important human being who has ever existed. And if I may put it this way, I miss him."

Templeton's eyes filled with tears and he wept freely. He refused to say more.

—Lee Strobel,
The Case for Faith (Zondervan, 2000)

ILLUSTRATION 97

GAS-STOP WITNESS

Topics: Boldness; Evangelism; Shame; Witnessing

References: Matthew 28:19; Mark 8:38; 1 Corinthians 9:19–23; 2 Corinthians 5:13–17; 2 Timothy 1:1–14

As a youth pastor, I'd just entered a convenience store with Jeff to pay for the gas I'd put in the church van. It was apparent that the woman behind the counter had been crying. I looked at her and said, "Has anybody told you that Jesus really loves you?" Jeff freaked out, took off, and dove into the van.

I talked to the woman for the next few minutes. After she asked Christ to come into her heart, her whole face changed.

When I got into the van, Jeff said, "Don't ever do that again!"

"Don't do what?" I asked.

"Witness to people like that," he replied. "Did you see how embarrassed that lady got?"

I responded, "Jeff, *you* got more embarrassed than she did. I prayed with her, and she received Christ."

I took Jeff back into the store to meet the woman, now radiant with the love of God—a complete contradiction of what she had been just a few minutes before.

—Eastman Curtis, *Raising Heaven-Bound Kids in a Hell-Bent World* (Nelson, 2000)

ILLUSTRATION 98

JOHNNY AND THE MISSIONARY

Topics: Discipleship; Evangelism; Ministry; Missions; Witnessing

References: Matthew 28:18–20; 2 Timothy 2:2

A veteran missionary met a new missionary, Johnny, who was a committed disciple of Jesus Christ but had a different approach to his work. He was spending most of his time meeting with a few young men in that country. The veteran missionary tried changing this tactic, but Johnny resisted. After several years, the veteran missionary found he had to leave the country because of visa restrictions.

"I've got little to show for my time there," he said, reviewing his work. "Oh, there is a group of people who meet in our assembly, but I wonder what will happen to them when I leave. They are not disciples. They have been faithful in listening to my sermons, but they do not witness. Few of them know how to lead another person to Christ. They know nothing about discipling others. And now that I'm leaving, I can see I've all but wasted my time here.

"Then I look at what has come out of Johnny's life. One of the men he worked with is now a professor at the university. This man is mightily used of God to reach and train scores of university students. Another is leading a witnessing and discipling team of about forty young men and women. Another is in a nearby city with a group of thirty-five growing disciples around him. Three have gone to other countries as missionaries and are now leading teams who are multiplying disciples.

"God is blessing their work. I see the contrast between my life and Johnny's. I was so sure I was right. What he was doing seemed so insignificant, but now I look at the results, and they are staggering."

—Billie Hanks and William Shell, eds., *Discipleship* (Zondervan, 1993)

ILLUSTRATION 99

WINNING A CHILD TO CHRIST

Topics: Children; Discipleship; Evangelism; Fruitfulness; Preaching

References: Matthew 19:13–15; Mark 4:3–20; Romans 10:14–15

Edward Kimball, a shoe store assistant and a Sunday school teacher in Chicago, spent hours of his free time visiting the young street urchins in Chicago's inner city, trying to win them for Christ. Through him, a young boy named D. L. Moody got saved in 1858. Moody grew up to be a preacher.

In 1879, Moody won F. B. Meyer to the Lord. Meyer became a preacher and won J. W. Chapman to Christ. Chapman became a preacher and brought the message of Christ to a baseball player named Billy Sunday.

Sunday held a revival in Charlotte, North Carolina, which was so successful that evangelist Mordecai Ham was invited to Charlotte to preach. Under Ham's preaching, a teenager named Billy Graham gave his life to Jesus.

It all started with winning one child to Jesus.

—Bill Wilson, *Streets of Pain* (Word, 1992)

ILLUSTRATION 100

"I GOTS COOKIES"

Topics: Boldness; Evangelism; Witnessing

Reference: Matthew 28:18–20

Our two older children, ages seven and nine, seemed to attract every child in our neighborhood for after-school games of hide-and-seek. Our youngest, Carrie, was not quite three and—in the minds of her older siblings—always in the way. Ten minutes into a game, our little one would get pushed aside or skin a knee.

One afternoon, Carrie came through the front door, again in tears. My wife, Elizabeth, tried to comfort her by giving her two freshly baked cookies. "Now don't tell the big kids yet," she cautioned. "I haven't got enough for everybody yet."

It took less than three seconds for Carrie to make it to the screen door, fling it wide, and announce to the big kids, "Cookies, I gots cookies!"

Great news should be shared with enthusiasm.

—Russell Brownworth,
Thomasville, North Carolina

ILLUSTRATION 101

SAVED BY A STORM

Topics: Boldness; Deliverance; Experiencing God; Help from God; Martyrdom; Persecution; Protection

References: Psalm 135:7; Jeremiah 10:13; 51:16; Mark 4:41; Acts 5:27–32; 16:22–34

While working with Christian youth in the southern part of Ethiopia under Communist rule (1974–91), Aberra Wata almost lost his life. He told the following story to fellow missionary John Cumbers:

Word came from the commandant that the Party leaders had studied my report about the work among the Christian young people. The authorities decided I had to be executed because of my "treasonous" words. "The only way you can overturn this sentence," said the commandant, "is for you to deny that you are one of the believers."

I told the commandant, "If they execute me, I will be immediately with the Lord."

The commandant replied, "That's what I expected you to say."

As I awaited execution in prison, my Savior gave me songs to sing I had never heard before. He turned me into a composer. [My fellow prisoners and I] reveled in the joys of praise to our God. The guards tried to silence us, but with the threat of execution hanging over us, why should we keep quiet? Seven men came to Christ in that prison, and we all sang together.

One guard took delight in mocking us. He would put filthy words to the tunes we sang. One night he patted his revolver and promised, "Tomorrow morning you won't be in the land of the living."

Just after midnight, a tremendous storm burst above us. Huge hailstones fell, wrecking several roofs, including the one where the insulting guard was sleeping. He was terrified, pulled out his revolver, and shot at random into the darkness, using up all his bullets. The storm took roofs off the commandant's house and the offices of the chief judge, the administrator, and his deputy. The prisoners in cells three, four, and five got a soaking from the rain too. We were in cell one and stayed dry.

At 9:00 the next morning, the nasty guard was pushed into our cell by the commandant, who was whipping him with his belt. Other people in the background were yelling, "We told this man to leave the believers alone, but he refused, and so God has sent this terrible punishment on the town and prison. He deserves to be given some of his own medicine."

After the guard was finally released, he told us, "I know that the Lord was with you. I know the way I should have treated you, but Satan persuaded me otherwise. Please forgive me." We did,

and several more men in the prison came to Christ.

—John Cumbers, SIM missionary in Ethiopia

ILLUSTRATION 102

BEYOND POOR RESULTS

Topics: Despair; Discouragement; Endurance; Evangelism; Fruitfulness; Ministry; Missions; Perseverance

References: 1 Chronicles 28:20; Psalm 31:9–24; 1 Corinthians 15:58; Galatians 6:9–10

"It seemed to me I should never have any success among the Indians. My soul was weary of my life; I longed for death, beyond measure."

That is what David Brainerd wrote in the early 1700s about his early weeks as a missionary to Native Americans. Things didn't improve much for the first two years. Brainerd felt his prospects of winning converts were "as dark as midnight."

Three years into the work, though, he finally witnessed a revival among the Indians of Crossweesung in New England, and eighteen months later, the number of converts numbered 150 — which was profoundly significant in his day. Brainerd died after only five years on the mission field, at age twenty-nine.

After Brainerd's death, Jonathan Edwards — whom some consider America's greatest theologian — published Brainerd's journals. These were read widely in America and Europe. William Carey, the man who ignited the modern Protestant missionary movement, which has resulted in millions of conversions worldwide, said Brainerd's journals were a key source of his inspiration to take up the missionary life.

Who, then, can judge whether our work is worthwhile? Certainly we cannot when we are in the midst of discouragement.

—Ruth Tucker, *From Jerusalem to Irian Jaya*
(Zondervan, 1983)

ILLUSTRATION 103

RECRUITMENT POSTER

Topics: Comfort; Convenience; Courage; Discipleship; Persecution; Risk; Suffering; Trials

References: Romans 5:3–4; Philippians 1:29; 2 Corinthians 6:3–10; James 1:2–4

Recruitment posters for our country's armed forces may emphasize seeing the world or getting financial help with college, but the harsh truth is that enlistment in the military carries serious risks. The crew and families of the USS *Cole* were reminded of that on October 12, 2000, when terrorists caused the deaths of seventeen and injured dozens more while the ship was refueling in Yemen.

Likewise, dare we present the Christian faith like a recruitment poster that talks about the "perks" of being a church member without letting people know that one's life is on the line for following Christ?

—Rubel Shelly, "Discipleship Is Serious Business," PreachingToday.com

ILLUSTRATION 104

CABBY WITNESS

Topics: Consideration; Evangelism; Gospel; Testimony

References: Matthew 10:7–8; Colossians 4:3–6

While in seminary I discovered that a Promise Keepers convention was coming to Soldier Field in Chicago. A group of us took a commuter train downtown and then caught a cab to the stadium.

We were running late but still hoped to get good seats. I'm sure our driver, a man who spoke little English, felt intimidated as the six of us piled into his taxi, jabbering loudly. Traffic was heavy and got worse near the stadium. We slowed to a crawl. We weren't going to get those good seats after all.

Some of us started talking about running the rest of the way to the stadium. Michael argued against that. He was concerned about the cabby; if we got out at that point, the driver would be stuck in traffic without being able to refill his taxi. He'd be losing money.

Michael then talked to the cabby about the conference we were going to, and he shared the Good News of Jesus Christ.

I don't know if the man was affected by the message, but I do know Michael's concern provided a base of credibility for sharing the gospel that the rest of us had overlooked.

—Greg Huffer, Lebanon, Indiana

ILLUSTRATION 105

CATCHING THE FIRE

Topics: Abundant Life; Evangelism; Fellowship with God; Joy; Knowing God; New Life

References: Matthew 5:13–16; John 10:10; Titus 2:9–10; 1 Peter 3:15

Evangelism is not what we tell people, unless what we tell is totally consistent with who we are. It is who we are that is going to make the difference.

If we do not truly enjoy our faith, nobody is going to catch the fire of enjoyment from us. If our lives are not totally centered on Christ, we will not be Christ-bearers for others, no matter how pious our words.

—Madeleine L'Engle,
A Swiftly Tilting Planet (Yearling, 1980)

ILLUSTRATION 106

YO-YO MA'S LOST CELLO

Topics: Evangelism; Great Commission; Lostness; Seekers

References: Matthew 28:18–20; Romans 10:1

Following an exhilarating performance at New York's Carnegie Hall, classical cellist Yo-Yo Ma went home, slept, and awoke the next day, still exhausted. He hailed a cab to take him to a hotel on the other side of Manhattan, then placed his cello, which was handcrafted in Vienna in 1733 and valued at $2.5 million, in the trunk of the taxi.

When he reached his destination, Ma paid the driver but forgot the cello.

He realized what he had done after the cab disappeared and began a desperate search for the missing instrument. Fortunately, he had the receipt with the cabby's ID number. Before the day ended, the taxi was located in a garage in Queens with the priceless cello still in the trunk. Ma's smile could not be contained as he spoke to reporters about the recovered cello. His evening performance in Brooklyn went on as planned.

Even more desperate than Yo-Yo Ma's search for his precious cello is the pursuit by God of the lost. We should imitate his passion for priceless people gone astray.

—Greg Asimakoupoulos, "Search for
Priceless Possession," PreachingToday.com

ILLUSTRATION 107

DIGITAL FROG DISSECTION

Topics: Compassion; Evangelism; Incarnation

References: Luke 10:30–37; Romans 10:14

Today high school students can get through biology class without smelling like formaldehyde. That's because they can now dissect frogs digitally.

Digital Frog International Inc. sells an interactive CD-ROM for $170 that allows students to probe a croaker's internal workings without lifting a scalpel. The impetus behind the digital frog program was company cofounder Simon Clark's squeamishness over cutting critters as a veterinarian student. Clark disliked dissection so much that he decided to find a less distasteful way to teach students anatomy and physiology.

Thanks to this program, students in more than nine hundred schools across North America are now making incisions into virtual frogs with a computer mouse. Throughout the virtual dissection, the computer program's speech component explains various organ functions while the program's three-dimensional animation allows the user to add cartilage and muscle to the frog's skeleton and get a beneath-the-skin view of how the amphibian moves.

The advantages of using this program are obvious: mistakes made on virtual frogs are easily corrected, no real frogs are hurt, and, perhaps best of all, students don't get their hands dirty. The whole procedure remains distant and antiseptic.

What is possible with biology is impossible with evangelism. We cannot do effective evangelism without touching the messy lives of sinners.

— J. Kent Edwards, "No Antiseptic Evangelism," PreachingToday.com

ILLUSTRATION 108

WRITING HIM OFF

Topics: Conversion; Evangelism; Great Commission

References: Matthew 9:12 – 13; 28:18 – 20; Mark 2:13 – 22; Luke 19:10

I was at a banquet in a secular setting. A group of us were sitting at a table when a guy sat down in the one empty seat. He was smooth. He said to the very attractive woman on one side, "Well, what have you been doing here except turning the heads of everybody in the room?"

I said, "Well, just eating lunch."

Later the discussion turned toward spiritual things, and at one point I talked about being at a church for people who don't like church. He told me about his background. He grew up Jewish and had no involvement in that faith beyond age twelve. He had been to a Unitarian church a couple of times and had been divorced three times.

If I had to assess someone on the basis of one conversation who was as far away from faith in Christ as could be, it would have been this guy, Steve. I invited him to come to our church, but I never thought I'd see him again.

The next Sunday, he came to our worship service and sat in the front row. He talked with me afterward and asked where we got our material. I told him about the Bible, and he got a New Testament. He had never read a New Testament before. He started getting up early to read twenty or thirty pages of the Bible every day. He came back to church the next week and the next. We kept talking, and he started thinking about making a decision to believe in Christ. It would be a costly thing for him because of his heritage — his family told him if he became a Christian, he would be dead to them. But he finally said yes to God.

The last time I saw him he was with a friend. He threw his arms around me and said to his friend, "I want you to meet the person who helped bring me to Jesus."

I almost missed doing that because I almost said no for him.

—John Ortberg, in the sermon "Three Habits of Highly Contagious Christians," Willow Creek Community Church, South Barrington, Illinois

ILLUSTRATION 109

BEFRIENDING MUSLIMS

Topics: Evangelism; Great Commission; Islam

Reference: Matthew 28:18–20

Hafsa, a Muslim, lives down my street. I have met her son, Mousa, who skateboards with my son and talks about religion. I told Mousa that I would like to meet his mother. He gave me her phone number, and I called her. She was not home. I called a week later. Mousa answered. He said that she wasn't home but that he would have his mother call me. She didn't.

A week later I tried again. Mousa answered and said he would "make it my mission" to have his mother call me. That was several weeks ago, and she still hasn't called. I'm told that many Muslim women possess as much reticence and misunderstanding toward Christian Americans as Christians do toward Muslims. They think our faith is corrupt and we hate them.

"When it comes to reaching Muslims, multitudes of people have stumbled for cultural, social, and linguistic reasons before they ever had the opportunity to stumble at the cross," says Robert Douglas, former director of the Zwemer Institute of Muslim Studies and now director of the Chicago Center for Urban Mission. He says Chris-

tians confront many obstacles that thwart them from understanding and relating to Muslims.

Nonetheless, we must try. "There is a desperate need for evangelical Christians to take the time to understand Islam and not to buy into the stereotypes that are floating out there," Douglas says. "We will have to work hard at building relationships with Muslims, which means a Christian presence where Muslims are concentrated."

—Wendy Murray Zoba, "Islam, U.S.A.," *Christianity Today* (April 3, 2000)

ILLUSTRATION 110

DRIVE-THROUGH WITNESS

Topics: Cross; Evangelism; Example; Great Commission; Jesus Christ; Simplicity; Testimony; Witnessing

References: Matthew 5:16; 28:18–20; Acts 1:8; Romans 1:16; Colossians 4:6; 1 Peter 2:12; 3:15

On a recent road trip, I stopped at a McDonald's. After placing my order, I came to the drive-up window to pay. I noticed an attractive, hand-carved cross hanging from the attendant's neck and said, "I like your cross."

Her reply showed how simple it is to share one's testimony. She said, "Thank you. I like the person who died on the cross for my sins. And I love the person who rose from the grave after having died on the cross."

She could have left it at "Thank you," but her faithful witness touched me and drew me closer to the Lord that day.

—Greg Huffer, Lebanon, Indiana

PART 6: FAITH AND CONDUCT

ILLUSTRATION 111

CHRISTIAN CONDUCT ON UPSWING

Topics: Behavior; Believers; Church Attendance; Devotional Life; Faith and Works; Good Deeds; Habits; Ministry; Prayer; Spiritual Disciplines; Spiritual Growth; Witnessing

References: Acts 2:42–47; 1 Timothy 4:7–16

A significant increase can be seen in five of the seven core religious behaviors that the Barna Group has studied over the past decade.

- In 1995, 31 percent of Americans read their Bibles at least once a week outside of a church setting; in 2006, that number jumped to 47 percent.
- In 1996, 37 percent of Americans attended church in a typical week; that number jumped to 47 percent in 2006.
- In 1996, 17 percent of Americans attended a small group outside of Sunday school or Christian education classes; in 2006, 23 percent attended.
- Church volunteerism hit a low of 20 percent in the mid-nineties; in 2006, 27 percent of Americans volunteered in a church setting.

- Sunday school attendance hit a low of 17 percent in 1995 and 1996; it climbed back to 24 percent in 2006.

Somewhat surprisingly, the only two religious behaviors that did not reflect significant change were prayer and evangelism. The number of Americans claiming to have prayed within the last week remained steady—around 84 percent in the period between 1993 and 2006. Similarly, the percentage of born-again Christians who claim to have shared their faith with a nonbeliever remained at about 60 percent in the decade between 1996 and 2006.

— "The Barna Update,"
barna.org (April 3, 2006)

ILLUSTRATION 112

THE ELECTRIC KINGDOM

Topics: Born Again; Christian Life; Kingdom of God; Power; Receiving Christ; Repentance; Salvation

References: Mark 1:15; John 3:3–5; Romans 1:16

As a child I lived in an area of southern Missouri where electricity was available only in the form of lightning. We had more of that than we could use. But in my senior year of high school, the REA (Rural Electrification Administration) extended its lines into the area where we lived, and electrical power became available to households and farms.

When those lines came by our farm, a very different way of living presented itself. Our relationships to fundamental aspects of life — daylight and dark, hot and cold, clean and dirty, work and leisure, preparing food and preserving it — could then be vastly changed for the better. But we still had to believe in the electricity — and take the practical steps involved in relying on it.

You may think the comparison rather crude, and in some respects it is. But it will help us to understand Jesus' basic message about the kingdom of heaven if we pause to reflect on those farmers who, in effect, heard the message "Repent, for electricity is at hand." Repent, or turn from their kerosene lamps and lanterns, their iceboxes and cellars, their scrub-boards and rug beaters, their woman-powered sewing machines and their radios with dry-cell batteries.

The power that could make their lives far better was right there near them where, by making relatively simple arrangements, they could utilize it. Strangely, a few did not accept it. They did not enter the kingdom of electricity. Some just didn't want to change. Others could not afford it, or so they thought.

To be sure, that kingdom has been here as long as we humans have been here, and longer. But it has been available to us through simple confidence in Jesus, the Anointed, only from the time he became a public figure.

— Dallas Willard,
The Divine Conspiracy
(Harper, 1997)

ILLUSTRATION 113

THE PROBLEM OF HAPPINESS

Topics: Anger; Complaining; Happiness; Joy; Piety; Witnessing

References: Nehemiah 8:10; Psalm 9:1 – 2; Proverbs 4:23; Matthew 5:13 – 16; John 10:10

I once asked a deeply religious man if he considered himself a truly pious person. He responded that while he aspired to be one, he felt that he fell short in two areas. One was his not being happy enough.

He said unhappy Christians reflect poorly on their religion and on their Creator. He was right — unhappy religious people do pose a real challenge to faith. If their faith is so impressive, why aren't they happy?

There are only two possible reasons: either they are not practicing their faith correctly, or they are practicing their faith correctly and the religion itself is not conducive to happiness. Most outsiders assume the latter reason.

Unhappy religious people should therefore think about how important being happy is — if not for themselves, then for the sake of their religion. Unhappy religious people provide more persuasive arguments for atheism and secularism than do all the arguments of atheists.

— Dennis Prager,
Happiness Is a Serious Problem
(HarperCollins, 1998)

ILLUSTRATION 114

A MARINE'S FINAL THANKS

Topics: Courage; Gratitude;
Testimony; Thanksgiving

References: Philippians 2:2–3;
1 John 2:6

Thirty-five years ago, I was a young second lieutenant who had just married after graduating from the Naval Academy. My wife and I went down to Quantico, Virginia, home of the school where officers learn about honor, courage, and commitment. I shared a room with another married officer, John Listerman, who was a Christian. That meant nothing to me other than that he was a really nice guy. Because of John, I guessed this Christian stuff must be pretty good.

After graduating from basic school, John and I went to Camp Pendleton, California, where we joined the same battalion preparing to go to Vietnam. I then saw John Listerman as a tremendous leader who was aggressive and technically proficient. People loved him. He was committed to his troops, and his troops were committed to him. He was a marine's marine.

In December 1965, John and I went to war. John Listerman's war lasted one day. While on patrol moving through the jungle, we came around a corner in the trail and ran into an ambush. John took a 50-caliber round in his kneecap. As his kneecap burst, he was thrown into the air. The second round hit him below the heart and exited out his side. I was wounded also, but not as badly. I crawled about thirty meters to John, but before I could ask, "Are you OK? Can

I do anything?" he said to me, "How are you doing, Chucker? Are you OK?"

When I said I was OK, he said, "Are my men safe?"

I said, "Your people are OK." He turned his head and looked to the sky and repeated over and over, "Thank you, Lord. Thank you for caring for my people. Thank you for caring for me."

(Note: John Listerman and Charles Krulak were evacuated. Krulak later became a Christian.)

—General Charles Krulak,
from a message given at the
Leadership Prayer Breakfast
in Wheaton, Illinois (October 2000)

ILLUSTRATION 115

ILLUMINATING THE WORLD

Topics: Evangelism; Light;
Missions; Witnessing

References: Matthew 5:14–16;
28:18–20; John 8:12

A missionary, home on leave, was shopping for a globe of the world to take back to her mission station. The clerk showed her a reasonably priced globe and another one with a light bulb inside. "This is nicer," the clerk said, pointing to the illuminated globe, "but of course, a lighted world costs more."

—Leonard Sweet,
Aqua Church (Group, 1999)

ILLUSTRATION 116

JOURNEY TO A GARBAGE DUMP

Topics: Christmas; Humility; Incarnation; Jesus Christ; Missions; Sacrifice

References: John 1:14; Philippians 2:5–8

Several years ago, I was visiting Manila and was taken, of all places, to the Manila garbage dump. Tens of thousands of people make their homes on that dump site. They have constructed shacks out of the things other people have thrown away. And they send their children out early every morning to scavenge for food in other people's garbage so they can have family meals.

People have been born and raised on the garbage dump. They have had their families and died there without ever going anywhere else, even in the city of Manila. It is an astonishing thing.

But Americans also live on that garbage dump. They are missionaries who have chosen to leave their own country to communicate the love of Jesus Christ to people who otherwise would never hear it. That is amazing, but not as amazing as the journey our Savior made from heaven to earth. The Son of God knew what he was doing. He knew where he was going. He knew what the sacrifice would be. He journeyed from heaven to earth on a mission to save the human race.

—Leith Anderson,
"A God's-Eye View of Christmas,"
Preaching Today Audio, no. 208

ILLUSTRATION 117

OUR LOUDSPEAKER

Topics: Boldness; Evangelism; Holy Spirit; Testimony

References: John 16:8–11; 1 Thessalonians 1:5

When doing sound tests, the audio engineer for the Republican Convention in July 2000 discovered that the noise the gavel actually made was not impressive enough to fill the huge hall in Philadelphia. So he recorded an "ideal gavel sound" that was played over the loudspeakers when the moderator struck the desk with the stand-in gavel, thereby signaling the start of the convention.

Likewise, we need to fill our own halls with the sound of Christ. Though our witness is weak, Jesus promises that the Holy Spirit will be our Loudspeaker if we will speak faithfully for him.

—Jeff Arthurs, "Holy Spirit Amplifies
Witness," PreachingToday.com

ILLUSTRATION 118

HIS SISTER'S FAITH

Topics: Apologetics; Conversion; Example; Salvation; Witnessing

Reference: Acts 1:8

Blaise Pascal, one of history's greatest scientists, was not converted through his scientific queries. Rather, when the scientist's carriage was once suspended on a bridge and the man was hanging between life and death, the only thing Pascal could think of was the Christian conviction of his sister and her witness of Christ.

Pascal was the inventor of the barometer. He was brilliant as a philosophical scientist. But the one thing that kept piercing his heart till he surrendered his all to Christ was the Christian witness of his sister.

—Ravi Zacharias, "Absolute Truth in Relative Terms," Just Thinking podcast

ILLUSTRATION 119

LIVING UP TO THE NAME

Topics: Christians; Church; Community; Example; Kindness; Lifestyle; Love; Testimony

References: John 8:47; 13:35

Dennis, from Katy, Texas, needed some same-day dry cleaning before he left on a trip. He remembered a store with a huge sign, "One-Hour Dry Cleaners," on the other side of town, so he drove there to drop off a suit. After filling out the tag, he told the clerk, "I need this in an hour."

She said, "I can't get this back to you until Thursday."

"I thought you did dry cleaning in an hour."

"No," she replied, "that's just the name of the store."

Likewise, we who say we are Christians but fail to act like the one whose name we bear create confusion and disillusionment for those who have yet to believe.

—Ed Rowell, senior pastor, Tri-Lakes Chapel, Monument, Colorado

ILLUSTRATION 120

STOCKPILING SALT

Topics: Evangelism; Influence; Salt

Reference: Matthew 5:13

A man walked into a little grocery store and asked, "Do you sell salt?"

"Ha!" said Pop, the proprietor. "Do we sell salt? Just look!" Pop showed the customer an entire wall of shelves stocked with nothing but salt: Morton salt, iodized salt, kosher salt, sea salt, rock salt, garlic salt—every kind of salt imaginable.

"Wow!" said the customer.

"You think that's something?" asked Pop. "That's nothing! Come look." And Pop led the customer to a back room filled with shelves and bins and cartons and barrels and boxes of salt. "Do we sell salt!" he said.

"Unbelievable!" said the customer.

"You think that's something?" said Pop. "I'll show you salt!" And Pop led the customer down steps into a huge basement, five times as large as the back room. It was filled, floor to ceiling, with every imaginable form of salt—even ten-pound salt licks for cows.

"Incredible!" said the customer. "You really do sell salt."

"That's just the problem!" Pop said. "We never sell salt. But that salt salesman—hoo-boy, does he sell salt!"

Salt that stays on the shelf doesn't do any good at all.

—D. James Kennedy, *Led by the Carpenter* (Nelson, 1999)

ILLUSTRATION 121

ARGUING BY EXAMPLE

Topics: Arguments; Example

References: 2 Timothy 1:13;
1 Peter 5:1–4

One example is worth a thousand arguments.

—Thomas Carlyle,
Scottish essayist (1795–1881)

ILLUSTRATION 122

SHAPING WITH WORDS

Topics: Betrayal; Lying; Preaching;
Tongue; Truth

References: Proverbs 18:21;
Ephesians 4:29; James 3:1–12

When a friend describes a beautiful sunset, a picture is created in your mind. The words enable you to make meaning. When a parent reacts to a child's artwork, meaning is created between child and parent, which can affect the child's self-concept for a lifetime.

Likewise, when a lie is spoken, a false reality is constructed that, once discovered, can rupture relationships. For example, when Bill Clinton's inner circle believed his lie that he hadn't had sex with Monica Lewinsky, their minds accepted an "unreal reality." Their eventual discovery of the truth and resulting feelings of betrayal were probably more dramatic than those who hadn't believed Clinton in the first place. This power to

affect one another is serious business. Our spoken words shape the reality of those with whom we interact.

—Lori Carrell, *The Great American Sermon
Survey* (Mainstay Church Resources, 1999)

ILLUSTRATION 123

BLOCKING RESCUE

Topics: Evangelism; Example;
Testimony

Reference: Matthew 28:19–20

I was touring China on a bus when the bus in front of us hit a patch of ice, skidded off the road, and tipped over on its side in a rice field.

I quickly jumped off my bus, ran to the overturned bus, and jumped on top. Windows were shattered, and people inside were obviously hurt. The emergency door was facing upward, so I grabbed the handle of the emergency door and pulled. The door would not open. I kept pulling hard, but it wouldn't budge.

By this time, others were pulling people out through the windows, so I gave up on the door and joined them. After I moved away from the door, another man went to the door. He turned the handle, and the door opened.

I suddenly realized why the door had not opened for me: I was standing on it as I tried to open it. With good intentions to save lives, I had become the biggest obstacle to rescue.

Likewise, those who want to lead others to Christ can become the biggest obstacle to their salvation.

—Charles Chu, "Bad Testimonies,"
PreachingToday.com

ILLUSTRATION 124

CHERISHING LIFE

Topics: Adversity; Crisis; Family; Hardship; Knowledge; Overcoming; Parents; Problems; Security; Significance; Suffering; Tragedy; Trials; Values; Worth

References: Genesis 1:26–27; Psalm 8:3–5; 23:4; 139:13–16; 2 Corinthians 1:3–4

Early in 2006, our daughter, Holly, eighteen, pulled in front of a Chevy Tahoe on a rainy, windswept night and got "T-boned" on the driver's side at about fifty miles per hour. Holly was pulled unconscious from her car. She had a broken pelvis, a chipped tailbone, a cracked collarbone, extensive facial lacerations, and most important, a "brain shearing" injury that left her with damage to her frontal lobe and other parts of her brain.

Everything changed for our family that night. When we first saw Holly, and for three long days following, she lay unconscious—bloodied and bruised and deeply silent. Every step after that was a step forward. She opened her eyes after three days. The next eleven days she drifted between wakefulness and sleep, a mute witness to the family and friends who rotated through her room, keeping watch. Then, on February 11, she rasped to her caretaker, "Could you rewind the movie, please?" By later that evening, she was talking happily with school friends. Doctors describe her progress as "miraculous."

As a professor of moral philosophy, my most recent book was about human nature. But I must say that I learned more about human nature in the month after Holly's accident than ever before. Many things I said in the book took on a whole new meaning. A wise friend called this the difference between knowledge and experience.

In that book, I emphasized how deep and mysterious the interconnections are between people, and how sacred human life is. I had no idea how true that was until I saw my Holly in the ER, sat by her bedside, and wondered whether she would ever wake up. The experience of getting her back as if from the dead awakened me to her immeasurable value, and by extension (because everyone is someone's child, and all are made in God's image) to the immeasurable value of every human being. I knew that before the accident. Now I *know* it.

—David P. Gushee, "Crash,"
Christianity Today (May 2006)

ILLUSTRATION 125

OUR POINT OF NO RETURN

Topics: Christians; Commitment; Dedication; Faith; Faithfulness; Loyalty; Self-denial; Submission; Surrender; Tenacity

References: Matthew 10:37–39; 16:24; Mark 8:34; Luke 9:23

If you were inside the cockpit of an airplane just before liftoff, you would hear the copilot or captain call out, "V1," which means the "point of no return."

As the airplane accelerates toward the end of the runway, the pilot must decide if the plane is moving fast enough for a safe takeoff. This speed must be determined preflight based on several factors, including the air pressure, temperature, speed of the wind, and weight of the aircraft.

The pilot holds the throttle as the plane approaches the V1 speed so that the takeoff can be aborted if something goes wrong. However, after V1 the plane *must* take off.

As Christians, we also have a V1 commitment. Once we have placed our faith in Christ alone, we have reached the point of no return. We need to adjust our sights, apply full throttle, and take off.

—Mike Silva, *Would You Like
Fries with That?* (Word, 2005)

ILLUSTRATION 126

THROWING HIM BACK

Topics: Crime; Gratitude; Ingratitude;
Rescue; Robbery; Thankfulness

References: Psalm 100:4; Luke 17:16;
Colossians 1:13; 3:15; 4:2; Hebrews
12:28

A South African man surprised nine men who were robbing his home. Eight of the robbers got away, but the homeowner managed to shove one into his backyard pool.

After realizing the robber couldn't swim, the homeowner jumped in to save him. Once out of the pool, the thief yelled to his friends to come back. Then he pulled a knife and threatened the man who had just rescued him.

The homeowner threw the thief back in the water.

—Kashiefa Ajam, "Homeowner Threatened by
the Robber He Saved," *Cape Times*,
Cape Town, South Africa (March 23, 2004)

ILLUSTRATION 127

UNHOLY AMERICANS

Topics: Believers; Holiness;
Purity; Redemption; Repentance;
Sanctification; Self-condemnation;
Self-image; Shame

References: Leviticus 11:45; Matthew
7:13–23; Romans 12:1; 2 Corinthians
6:14–18; 7:1; Colossians 3:12; Hebrews
3:12; 1 Peter 1:15–16; 1 John 3:3

Most Americans don't consider themselves to be holy, said a survey published by the Barna Group in 2006.

Three out of four Americans (73 percent) believe it is possible for someone to become holy regardless of their past. Only half of the adult population (50 percent), however, said that they knew someone they considered to be holy. That is more than twice as many as those who considered themselves to be holy (21 percent).

The views of born-again Christians were not much different from the national averages. Among believers, three-quarters (76 percent) said it is possible for a person to become holy regardless of his or her past. Slightly more than half of the group (55 percent) said they knew someone they would describe as holy. And roughly three out of ten Christians (29 percent) said they themselves were holy, which is marginally more than the national norm.

— "The Concept of Holiness Baffles Most Americans," barna.org (February 20, 2006)

ILLUSTRATION 128

THIS OLD HOUSE

Topics: Change; Christian Life; Conversion; New Life; Redemption; Regeneration; Repentance; Sanctification; Spiritual Formation

References: 2 Corinthians 5:1 – 17; Ephesians 4:20 – 32; 5:1 – 17; Philippians 3:7 – 16

In the late 1920s, my grandparents married and moved into Grandpa's old family home. It was a clapboard house with a hall down the middle. In the '30s they decided to tear down the old house and build another.

Much to my grandmother's dismay, many of the materials of the old house were recycled into the new house. They used old facings, doors, and other pieces of lumber. Everywhere my grandmother looked, she saw old doors that wouldn't shut properly, crown molding that was split and riddled with nail holes, and unfinished window trimming. It was a source of grief to her. All her life she had longed for a new house; now all she got was a recycled one.

When God brings us into the kingdom, the old way of living must be dismantled and discarded.

— Len Sullivan, Tupelo, Mississippi

ILLUSTRATION 129

PARKING SPACE THIEF

Topics: Heart; Temper; Tongue; Words

References: Matthew 15:17 – 20; James 3:1 – 12

I needed to do some last-minute Christmas shopping but was having difficulty finding a parking space. I finally spotted an old couple walking very slowly to their car. I thought, "If I can follow them down the aisle and wait for them to get into their car, that parking space will be mine!" So I waited patiently with my blinker on.

The couple put their gifts in the trunk, and he opened the door for his wife. I thought, "This is no time for chivalry. Get in the car and go!"

They pulled out slowly, and as I was ready to turn in, a beat-up old van pulled in front of me and stole my space. I got out of my car and had a chat with the driver. Had my mother been there, she would have washed my mouth out with soap. I chatted with such interesting words that he backed out of the parking space.

I felt good initially. I thought, "I'm good. I stood up for my rights. I'm pretty feisty." But then the verse came into my head that says, "The things that come out of the mouth come from the heart, and these make a man 'unclean'" (Matthew 15:18).

The painful truth is that the Bible says the condition of my heart is reflected by what comes out of my mouth and how I live my life. Many days later, I came to the conclusion I was wrong. I told God my actions and words did indeed reflect the condition of my heart, and I wasn't proud of it.

—Nancy Ortberg, in the sermon
"Matters of the Heart," Willow Creek Church
Seeds Tape Ministry, South Barrington, Illinois

ILLUSTRATION 130

BEHAVIOR CLUE

Topics: Belief; Disobedience; Love for Christ; Morality; Obedience; Sin

References: Galatians 5:6; James 2:14–26

Your behavior is a reflection of what you truly believe.

—Hyrum W. Smith,
*The 10 Natural Laws of Successful
Time and Life Management* (Warner, 1994)

ILLUSTRATION 131

BUCKLE UP WARNING

Topics: Behavior; Change; Consequences; Fear; Illumination; Knowledge; Perspective; Repentance; Spiritual Formation; Spiritual Growth; Warnings; Wisdom

References: Luke 19:1–10; John 13:35; 1 Corinthians 8:1–2; James 1:22

My brother-in-law would never wear a seat belt in the car. I berated him for it. Then one day he picked me up at the airport, and he had on his seat belt and shoulder harness. I asked, "What happened? What changed you?"

"I went to visit a friend of mine in the hospital who was in a car accident and went through the windshield," my brother-in-law said. "He had two or three hundred stitches in his face. I said to myself, 'I'd better wear my seat belt.'"

"Did you not know that if you didn't wear your seat belt you would go through the windshield if you had an accident?" I asked.

"Of course I knew it," he said. "When I went to the hospital to see my friend, I got no new information, but the information I had became new. The information got real to my heart and finally sank down and affected the way I live."

—Tim Keller, "Unintentional Preaching Models," *Preaching to the Heart*, Ockenga Institute of Gordon-Conwell Theological Seminary

ILLUSTRATION 132

JUST A LITTLE PORN

Topics: Addiction; Character; Double-mindedness; Faith and Works; Guilt; Hypocrisy; Lust; Pleasure; Pornography; Purity; Self-control; Self-indulgence; Vices

References: Job 31:1; Matthew 5:28; Romans 6:16; 1 Corinthians 6:18; Colossians 3:5; Hebrews 13:4; 1 Peter 2:11; 2 Peter 2:19

My friend looked like a good Christian. He was a faithful elder in the church and a devout husband and father. He had a reputation for honesty, courage, and integrity. But he also had an issue with pornography.

He said he wasn't addicted to porn, and there was no reason not to believe him. He could go weeks without it, he said. Porn didn't affect his relationship with his wife. It didn't interfere with his church work or prayer life. It was just a little recreational pleasure that he indulged in now and then, especially after working long hours for his company or the church.

"I've justified it in my mind a thousand times," he said, "and I could out-argue anyone who wants to give me all that bull about potential addiction and how it ruins your marriage. Well, it's only made my marriage easier, since I don't pester my wife as often, and yet I don't do porn so much that I don't have any ardor for her when she's ready. Still," he conceded, "I feel so unclean."

At first he thought the guilt was just a leftover from his fundamentalist upbringing. But he noticed he didn't feel bad about other post-fundamentalist behaviors, such as drinking wine or going to the movies. Just porn. I suggested that this feeling might be the prodding of the Spirit. "Why don't you just give up porn?"

"I've thought about that," he replied. "If God does want me to give it up, I know it's because that's ultimately good for me. Yet the thought of giving up porn cold turkey is one of the most frightening things I can imagine right now. And I don't know why."

— Mark Galli,
Jesus Mean and Wild (Baker, 2006)

ILLUSTRATION 133

LOVING BEYOND ABILITY

Topics: Compassion; Experiencing God; Giving; Grace; Love; Mercy; Strength

References: Luke 10:30–37; Philippians 4:13

Francis of Assisi was riding a horse down the road that went by a leper hospital situated far from Assisi, for then, as in biblical times, lepers were a rejected lot. Francis was not yet the saint of history; he was still caught between the lure of wealth and glory and the life of discipleship. As he rode along, he was absorbed in his thoughts.

Suddenly the horse jerked to the side of the road. With difficulty Francis pulled him back on course, but as Francis looked up, he recoiled at the sight of a leper in the middle of the road. He was a grey specter with stained face and shaved head, dressed in gray sackcloth. He did not speak and showed no sign of moving or of getting out of the way. He looked at the horseman fixedly, strangely, with an acute and penetrating gaze.

An instant that seemed an eternity passed. Slowly Francis dismounted, went to the man, and took his hand. It was a poor emaciated hand, bloodstained and cold like that of a corpse. Francis pressed the hand and brought it to his lips. As he kissed the lacerated flesh of the creature, who was the most abject, the most hated, the most scorned of all human beings, he was flooded with a wave of emotion that shut out everything around him.

That was an early step in Francis's conversion, which took many months. But it taught him that following Christ may require doing some things that repulse us. What Francis didn't know then was that something greater was prompting him, allowing him to do that which, humanly speaking, he was incapable of doing.

—Arnoldo Fortini,
Francis of Assisi (Crossroad, 1992)

ILLUSTRATION 134

FELLED BY NEGLIGENCE

Topics: Church Leaders; Consequences; Ministry; Negligence; Pastors; Responsibility

References: Ezekiel 3:16–21; Acts 18:5–6; 20:26–28

On a warm autumn afternoon, Anna Flores, thirty-six, was walking with her toddler in downtown Chicago. Without warning a window from the twenty-ninth floor of the CNA building fell to the ground, striking Flores in the head and killing her.

The tragedy was heightened a week later when CNA officials admitted they had known the window had been broken since June. They hadn't fixed it because other building projects were considered more of a priority.

In a public building, negligence has serious consequences. Spiritual negligence also has great consequences. In various ways, we are responsible spiritually for the welfare of others.

—Greg Asimakoupoulos, "Consequence of Negligence," PreachingToday.com

ILLUSTRATION 135

MOTHER TERESA'S FEET

Topics: Brotherly Love; Example; Godliness; Humility; Kindness; Love; Sacrifice; Service; Virtue

References: Matthew 16:25; Luke 10:25–37; John 15:13; Romans 12:1; 1 Corinthians 10:24; Philippians 2:4–11; 1 John 3:16

Shane Claiborne, who spent a summer in the slums of Calcutta with Mother Teresa, wrote the following about one of his experiences:

People often ask me what Mother Teresa was like. Did she glow in the dark or have a halo? She was short, wrinkled, and precious, maybe even a little ornery—like a beautiful, wise old granny. But there is one thing I will never forget—her feet were deformed. Each morning during Mass, I would stare at those feet. I wondered if Mother Teresa had leprosy. But I wasn't going to ask, of course.

One day a sister asked us, "Have you noticed Mother's feet?" We nodded, curious. She said, "Her feet are deformed because we get just enough donated shoes for everyone, and Mother does not want anyone to get stuck with the worst pair, so she digs through and finds those. Years of wearing bad shoes have deformed her feet."

That is the kind of love that places our neighbors' needs above our own.

—Shane Claiborne, *The Irresistible Revolution* (Zondervan, 2006)

ILLUSTRATION 136

JUDGING APARTHEID ATROCITIES

Topics: Forgiveness; Grace; Hatred; Love for Enemies; Racism; Violence

References: Matthew 5:38–48; Luke 23:34

A South African woman stood in an emotionally charged courtroom listening to white police officers acknowledge the atrocities they had perpetrated in the name of apartheid. Officer van de Broek acknowledged his responsibility in the death of her son. Along with others, he had shot her eighteen-year-old son at point-blank range. He and the others partied while they burned his body, turning it over on the fire until it was ashes.

Eight years later, van de Broek and others arrived to seize her husband. Hours later, van de Broek came to fetch the woman. He took her to a woodpile where her husband lay bound. She was forced to watch as they poured gasoline over his body and ignited the flames that consumed his body. The last words her husband said were "Forgive them."

Now van de Broek stood awaiting judgment. South Africa's Truth and Reconciliation Commission asked the woman what she wanted.

"Three things," she said. "I want Mr. van de Broek to take me to the place where they burned my husband's body. I would like to gather up the dust and give him a decent burial.

"Second, Mr. van de Broek took all my family away from me, and I still have a lot of love to give. Twice a month, I would like for him to come to the ghetto and spend a day with me so I can be a mother to him.

"Third, I would like Mr. van de Broek to know that he is forgiven by God and that I forgive him, too. I would like someone to lead me to where he is seated so I can embrace him and he can know my forgiveness is real."

As the elderly woman was led across the courtroom, van de Broek fainted. Someone began singing "Amazing Grace." Gradually everyone joined in.

—Stanley W. Green,
Canadian Mennonite (September 4, 2000)

ILLUSTRATION 137

THROWING DARTS AT THE ENEMY

Topics: Hatred; Love; Unity

References: Matthew 25:31–46; 1 John 4:20–21

Sally took a seminary class taught by Professor Smith, who was known for his object lessons. One day, Sally walked into class to find a large target placed on the wall and several darts on a nearby table. Professor Smith told the students to draw a picture of someone they disliked or who had made them angry—then they could throw darts at the person's picture.

Sally's friend drew a picture of a woman who had stolen her boyfriend. Another friend drew a picture of his younger brother. Sally drew a detailed picture of Professor Smith, including pimples on his face. She was quite pleased with her effort.

The class lined up and began throwing darts. Some students threw with such force that they ripped apart their targets. But before Sally had a turn, Professor Smith asked the students to return to their seats so he could begin his lecture. As Sally fumed, the professor began removing the target from the wall.

Underneath it was a picture of Jesus. A hush fell over the room as students saw the mangled image of their Savior with holes and jagged marks covering his face. His eyes were virtually pierced out.

Professor Smith said only these words: "Inasmuch as ye have done it unto the least of these my brethren, ye have done it unto me."

—Lee Rhodes, Wheeler, Michigan

ILLUSTRATION 138

FORGIVING HIS SHOOTER

Topics: Courage; Forgiveness; Freedom; Grace; Healing; Mercy

References: Matthew 6:14–15; 18:21–35; Colossians 3:12–15

For two decades, Wayne Messmer, forty-nine, was an announcer and singer for sports teams in the Windy City. After singing "The Star-Spangled Banner" at a Chicago Blackhawks game in 1994, Messmer was shot by two teenage boys. The bullet passed through the singer's throat, so doctors weren't sure if Messmer would sing again. Amazingly, six months later, Messmer returned to the microphone.

Physical healing was one thing; emotional release of the hatred and resentment he felt was another. For that, Messmer had to trust Christ, his Savior, to help him reach the point where he could forgive his shooters. When he did, he found freedom. As he says in *The Voice of Victory*, "Over a period of contemplative and reflective prayer and meditation, I was confident I had set myself free from the chains that had connected me to the incident."

Although one of the boys had been released on a plea bargain, the other, James Hampton, was still in jail. To prove that he truly had forgiven his would-be killers, Messmer drove 225 miles to Galesburg Correctional Center and asked to see Hampton.

Several years had passed, but Messmer found the grace to say, "James, I'm here to see how you are doing." After a two-hour emotional visit, Messmer turned to leave. Reaching out and touching Hampton's forearm, he offered a benediction: "James, I bid you peace."

—Pat Karlak, "Messmer Writes of Recovery, Forgiveness," *Daily Herald*, Arlington Heights, Illinois (January 16, 2000)

ILLUSTRATION 139

WANDA'S LEGACY

Topics: Depression; Evangelism; Excuses; Witnessing

References: Matthew 28:19–20; John 14:6–7; Colossians 4:3–6; 1 Peter 3:15

My job as a psychiatric nurse brought me in touch with many people who were searching for answers to problems in their lives. I knew that Jesus was the answer, but I couldn't bring myself to talk to them about him. I was the master of excuses. Then a patient changed my life.

Wanda, fifty-six, suffered with chronic depression. Many people in her family had died, some of them tragically. The loss and her grief became too great a burden for the widow. One day she quit her job, went home, pulled the curtains, and refused to leave her house. Eventually she stopped eating. Even the smallest task became too difficult for her.

A neighbor noticed the change in Wanda's behavior and made arrangements for her to be taken to a hospital, where she was admitted to the psychiatric ward. When Wanda went home, I was assigned to be her home health nurse. I visited her weekly to make sure she was taking care of herself.

Over the course of six months, Wanda continued to recover. Although I knew she needed to meet Jesus as her Savior, I reasoned that she would soon be attending church and would hear about him there.

One day I went to Wanda's house and was surprised to find the door ajar. I knocked, and when there was no response, I pushed the door open and stepped inside. I found her lifeless body in the bedroom. In her hand was a note to me, saying: "Dear Peggy, I'm so sorry. I tried it your way, but I got tired. Please forgive me."

I cried my heart out to my loving, forgiving Father, saying, "Lord Jesus, I gave her the best that I had. But it was my way. I didn't tell her about you. I didn't tell her about your way." I then promised God that I would never pass by another opportunity to tell someone about him.

— Peggy DesNoyers, "Silent No More,"
Decision (July–August 2000)

ILLUSTRATION 140

LAUNDERING EACH SIN

Topics: Apology; Confession; Forgiveness; Meditation; Pardon; Quiet Time; Reconciliation; Sin

References: Psalm 32:5; Proverbs 28:13; Acts 3:19; Hebrews 10:22; James 5:16; 1 John 1:9

When I left for college, my mother—who had always done my laundry—made a canvas duffel bag for me. "Put your dirty clothes in this every night," she said. "At the end of the week, wash them at the Laundromat."

Seven days later, I took my dirty clothes to the Laundromat. To save time, I threw the duffel bag in the washer, put in some laundry powder, inserted the proper change, and turned on the machine. Moments later, a loud *thump, thump, thump, thump* echoed through the Laundromat. A pretty coed approached me with a grin. "I watched you load your washer. I think the clothes would get cleaner if you took them out of the bag."

One day, when my relationship with God was hurting, I remembered my laundry episode. I realized the way I confessed sins — "Dear God, please forgive me for all the sins I've committed today" — was about as effective as my first attempt at washing clothes. Each sin needs individual attention.

—Roger Barrier, *Listening to the Voice of God* (Bethany, 1998)

ILLUSTRATION 141

ABSOLUTION FOR A WEEK

Topics: Character; Forgiveness; Guilt; Motives; Pardon; Redemption; Regret; Self-centeredness; Shame; Sin; Values

References: Psalm 39:6; Isaiah 45:13; 55:1 – 2; Colossians 3:12 – 13

Upon the death of Pope John Paul II, Rogers Cadenhead, a self-described "domain hoarder," registered www.BenedictXVI.com before the new pope's name was announced. Cadenhead had the name before Rome knew it was needed.

The right domain name can be lucrative. Another name, PopeBenedictXVI.com, secured $16,000 on eBay. Cadenhead, however, didn't want money. A Catholic himself, he was happy for the church to own the name. "I'm going to try and avoid angering 1.1 billion Catholics and my grandmother," he quipped.

He did want something in return, though:

1. one of those hats
2. a free stay at the Vatican hotel

3. complete absolution, no questions asked, for the third week of March 1987

Makes you wonder what happened that week, doesn't it? It may even remind you of a week of your own life.

—Max Lucado, *Facing Your Giants* (W Publishing Group, 2006)

ILLUSTRATION 142

VICTIM OF THROWN TURKEY

Topics: Compassion; Consequences; Foolishness; Forgiveness; Grace; Mercy; Pardon; Suffering; Values; Youth

References: Matthew 18:21 – 35; Romans 12:14 – 21; Galatians 6:1 – 10; Colossians 3:12 – 14

Victoria Ruvolo, forty-five, of Lake Ronkonkoma, New York, was driving to her niece's voice recital when she passed a car driven by Ryan Cushing, nineteen. Cushing was with five other teens and had just used a stolen credit card to go on a spending spree. One of their purchases was a frozen turkey, which Cushing decided to toss into oncoming traffic. The twenty-pound bird smashed through Ruvolo's windshield, crushing her face.

Ruvolo survived, though it took ten hours of surgery to repair her face and months of painful rehabilitation. On October 17, 2005, Ruvolo attended Cushing's sentencing and asked his judge for leniency. Part of her statement read, "Despite all the fear and the pain, I have learned from this horrific experience that I have much to be thankful for. Each day when I wake up, I thank God simply because I'm alive. I sincerely hope you have also learned from this awful experience, Ryan. There is no room for vengeance in my life, and I do not believe a long, hard prison term would do you, me, or society any good."

Cushing, who wept and expressed remorse for his action, was sentenced to six months in jail. He could have gotten a twenty-five-year prison sentence if Ruvolo had not intervened.

—Leah Ingram, "Compassionate Victim," beliefnet.com (December 2005)

ILLUSTRATION 143
WHOM WE FORGIVE

Topics: Anger; Forgiveness; Mistakes; Relationships; Stress

References: Psalm 25:11; 32:1–2; Matthew 6:12–15; 18:21–35; Mark 11:25; Luke 6:37; Acts 2:38–39; Colossians 3:13

According to a 2001 study of 1,423 adults by the University of Michigan Institute for Social Research:

- 52 percent of those surveyed have forgiven others for past transgressions
- 75 percent believe they have been forgiven by God for their mistakes
- 43 percent have asked others to forgive them of past offenses
- 63 percent have let themselves off the hook
- women are more forgiving than men

- middle-agers and older adults are more likely to forgive others than younger adults are
- forgiveness may be an antidote to anger, but asking for forgiveness can raise stress levels

—Van Morris, "Research about Forgiveness," PreachingToday.com

ILLUSTRATION 144
LOSING THE LEECHES

Topics: Bitterness; Forgiveness; God's Love; Resentment

Reference: Matthew 18:21–35

A traveler was making his way with a guide through the jungles of Burma. They came to a shallow, wide river and waded through it to the other side. When the traveler came out of the river, numerous leeches were on his torso and legs. His first instinct was to grab them and pull them off.

This guide stopped him, warning that doing so would leave tiny pieces of the leeches under the skin. Eventually, infection would set in. The best way to rid the body of the leeches, the guide advised, was to bathe in a warm balsam bath for several minutes. This would calm the leeches, and soon they would release their hold on the man's body.

Likewise, when I've been hurt by another person, I cannot simply yank the injury from myself and expect that all bitterness, malice, and emotion will be gone. Resentment still hides under the surface. The only way to become truly free of the offense and to forgive others is to bathe in the soothing bath of God's forgiveness.

When I finally fathom the extent of God's love in Jesus Christ, forgiveness of others will follow.

—Gary Preston, *Character Forged from Conflict* (Bethany, 1999)

be forgiven, I can certainly extend that same grace to you. I wanted you to know that."

Simon apologized and hugged the singer, and Mandisa discovered she had advanced to the next round.

—Based on *American Idol*, realitytvmagazine.com (February 15, 2006)

ILLUSTRATION 145
FORGIVING SIMON

Topics: Christlikeness; Grace; Imitation of Christ; Love; Mercy; Pardon; Reconciliation; Relationships

References: Matthew 5:43–48; 6:14–15; 18:21–35; Luke 6:27–36

Mandisa Hundley, a gospel singer, was one of the twelve finalists on *American Idol*. When she met with judges Simon Cowell, Paula Abdul, and Randy Jackson to find out if she had made it through to the next round of the competition, however, she got a stinging comment from Simon. Eyeing Mandisa, who was heavyset, Simon asked, "Do we have a bigger stage this year?"

When she entered the room to learn the judges' verdict, Mandisa looked right at Simon and said, "Simon, a lot of people want me to say a lot of things to you. But this is what I want to say: Yes, you hurt me, and I cried, and it was painful. But I want you to know that I've forgiven you, and that you don't need someone to apologize to forgive somebody. And I figure that if Jesus could die so that all of my wrongs could

ILLUSTRATION 146
RELIEVED OF STOLEN MONEY

Topics: Change; Confession; Conscience; Consequences; Emptiness; Forgiveness; Guilt; Honesty; Integrity; Pardon; Reconciliation; Shame

References: Psalm 32:5; Proverbs 28:13; Ezekiel 18:31; Acts 3:19; Romans 6:16; 2 Corinthians 7:10; Hebrews 10:22; 1 John 1:9

After John Jefferson robbed a Krispy Kreme Doughnut store in Kingsport, Tennessee, in 1999, he bought dope. But he couldn't enjoy it because he was plagued with guilt. Months later, even after moving to Kansas, the guilt remained. So Jefferson decided to confess.

Jefferson called Detective David Cole of the Kingsport Police Department and identified himself as the robber. "I couldn't take it anymore," Jefferson said in an interview. "I was sick and tired of the way I was living. I didn't want to die in a crack house, and I didn't want to smoke crack anymore."

After pleading guilty, Jefferson served a six-year sentence. Upon his release, he tried several times to return to the Krispy Kreme store and repay the money he had stolen, but he kept turning around before he could get there. Finally, Jefferson called David Cole again and asked him to accompany him to the store. Though he had stolen $300, Jefferson returned $400 to the robbery victim, who asked him to donate the money to St. Jude Children's Research Hospital.

"I felt like a million bucks when I walked out of that place," Jefferson said.

— "What Goes Around, Comes Around,"
FoxNews.com (December 21, 2005)

ILLUSTRATION 147

FORGIVING BIGOTRY

Topics: Bigotry; Conflict; Forgiveness; Hatred; Racism; Reconciliation

References: Matthew 5:43–48; 6:14–15; 18:21–35; 2 Corinthians 5:18–20; Hebrews 12:14–15

Vivian Malone, a young black woman, enrolled as a student at the University of Alabama in Tuscaloosa in 1963. Federal troops helped ensure her entrance into the school, but Governor George Wallace tried to block her way. When he failed, Malone became the first African-American student ever to graduate from the University of Alabama.

Years later, Governor Wallace was taken in his wheelchair to Dexter Avenue Baptist Church in Montgomery, where he asked black people to forgive him for his racism, bigotry, and specifically his ill-treatment of Vivian Malone. He asked Malone for forgiveness. Malone said she had forgiven the governor years before.

When asked why she had done that, Malone said, "I'm a Christian, and I grew up in the church. I was taught that we are all equal in the eyes of God. I was also taught that you forgive people, no matter what. And that was why I had to do it. I didn't feel as if I had a choice."

— "Transition—Vivian Malone Jones,"
Newsweek (October 24, 2005)

ILLUSTRATION 148

NO GRUDGE

Topics: Enemies; Forgiveness; Grace; Love; Tragedy

Reference: Matthew 5:43–48

In May 1987, thirty-nine American seamen were killed in the Persian Gulf when an Iraqi pilot hit their ship, the USS *Stark*, with a missile. The son of one of these seamen, John Kiser, age five, stood with his hand on his heart as his father's coffin was loaded onto a plane to go to the United States.

"I don't have to mourn or wear black, because I know my husband is in heaven," John's mother said to reporters. "I am happy, because I know he is better off."

Later she and John sent a letter and an Arabic New Testament to the pilot of the Iraqi plane, addressed to "the man who attacked the *Stark*, Dad's ship, in the hope that it will show that even the son and the wife do not hold any grudge and are at the same time praying for the one who took the life of our father."

—Roger Carswell,
How Small a Whisper (Kregel, 2000)

ILLUSTRATION 149

FORGIVING MURDERERS

Topics: Forgiveness; Grace; Mercy; Pardon

References: Matthew 6:14–15; Luke 7:36–50; Ephesians 4:32; Colossians 3:12–13

The parents of Matthew Shepard, the young gay man who was murdered in Wyoming in 1998, rejoiced over the guilty verdicts a Laramie jury handed down to Matthew's murderers in November 1999. The judge told a packed courtroom that the jury's verdicts "showed true courage" and sent a message that violence is not the solution to differing views on sexual orientation.

Courtroom observers were not prepared for what Dennis and Judy Shepard did next. After waiting thirteen months for guilty verdicts for their son's killers, Matthew Shepard's parents asked the judge to spare the lives of Aaron McKinney and Russell Henderson by giving them life sentences rather than the death penalty.

Cal Rerucha, who prosecuted the case, said, "The Shepards could look into the eyes of the men who killed their son and give them mercy."

—Greg Asimakoupoulos,
"Forgiveness Personified,"
PreachingToday.com

PART 8: GIVING

ILLUSTRATION 150

WESLEY'S GIVING

Topics: Benevolence; Generosity; Giving; Money; Possessions; Stewardship

References: Matthew 6:19–21; 2 Corinthians 9:6–10; 1 Peter 4:10

During John Wesley's life (1703–91), Britain experienced rapid urbanization and the beginnings of industrialization. This caused the collapse of rural economies and problems in city centers, such as overcrowding, disease, crime, unemployment, debt, substance abuse, and even insanity (London established its first asylum in 1781).

Meanwhile a small upper class spent large sums to distance itself, literally and figuratively, from the growing problems. This top 5 percent of the population controlled nearly one-third of the national income.

Wesley, part of the lower-middle class, interacted mostly with people who worked hard, owned little, and could never be certain of their financial future. But he eventually became so well known as a preacher that he earned 1,400 pounds per year—equivalent to more than $160,000 today. Still, he chose to live simply but comfortably on just 30 pounds while giving the rest away. He donated nearly all of the 30,000 pounds he earned in his lifetime. "If I leave behind me 10 pounds …, you and all mankind [can] bear witness against me that I have lived and died a thief and a robber," he said.

—Elesha Coffman, ed., *Christian History Newsletter* (November 30, 2001)

ILLUSTRATION 151

A TIMELY GIFT

Topics: Dependence on God; God's Faithfulness; Needs; Providence; Provision; Trust

References: Genesis 22:14; Isaiah 61:1–4; Matthew 8:23–27; 17:27; Mark 4:35–41; Luke 8:22–25

On a recent service trip to the Hurricane Katrina–ravaged coast of Mississippi, we worked at a home that was owned by a retired United Methodist pastor. Rev. Jones said he and his wife had left their home before Katrina struck and gone to a shelter. After the storm passed, they were allowed back into the city to grab a few belongings. When they entered their house, the water was still knee-high, but Jones was determined to see what he could salvage.

Jones saw several framed family photos floating in the water. He didn't see anything else to save, so he grabbed the pictures and left. Back at the shelter, he took the photos out of their frames so they could dry out. When he removed his father's picture, money fell out of the frame. He was astonished to count out $366. Even more astounding was that his father had died in 1942, when Jones himself was only twelve years old. He had no idea the money was in the frame.

The money was precisely what he and his wife needed to go to Atlanta after the storm to live with their daughter.

—Douglas Heiman, Evansville, Indiana

ILLUSTRATION 152

SMARTIES TO SHARE

Topics: Childlike Faith; Children; Contentment; Example; Friendship; Generosity; Giving; Kindness; Sharing; Stewardship; Tithing

References: Leviticus 27:30; Proverbs 11:24–25; Malachi 3:10; Luke 6:38; Acts 20:35; 2 Corinthians 9:6–8

You remember Smarties, a row of multicolored, chalklike, bite-size candies wrapped in clear plastic, about ten to twelve pieces in a pack? They are perfect for sharing.

I am not a huge fan of Smarties, but when I saw little Dustin come into church with a fresh roll, I just had to ask for one. Dustin peeled out a piece and handed it over with a smile. From that day on, for the next two years, every time Dustin got a pack of Smarties, he took out the first one

and set it aside for me. Every Sunday morning before the worship service, Dustin would track me down at church and offer me a Smarty.

Sometimes Dustin would open a pack of Smarties during the week, but he would still save me the first piece. By the time Sunday came, the Smarty was a little mangy and furry with lint, but he never forgot to bring it for me. I would thank him and put the candy in my pocket so I could "enjoy it later."

Sharing Smarties was a kind of Communion for Dustin and me. Jesus was present as we shared a conversation and candy.

Dustin's mother viewed this ritual as a kind of tithing; out of ten pieces in a pack, Dustin gave the first tenth to his pastor. What I saw was a little boy who loved to share and who understood the power of generosity. Since that time, I have asked myself many times, "How am I doing with my Smarties?"

—Kevin G. Harney,
Seismic Shifts (Zondervan, 2005)

ILLUSTRATION 153

THE CURE FOR WORLD POVERTY

Topics: Cost; Finances; Generosity; Giving; Materialism; Missions; Needs; Poverty; Social Action; Stewardship; Tithing

References: Deuteronomy 15:11; Proverbs 11:25; 22:9; Malachi 3:8–10; 2 Corinthians 9:5–11; 1 Timothy 6:8

If church members in the United States increased their giving to 10 percent of their income, there could be an additional $86 billion available for overseas missions. And according to researchers John and Sylvia Ronsvalle, founders of Empty Tomb, Inc., in Champaign, Illinois, that amount of money would meet the most essential human needs around the world.

"Projects for clean water and sanitation, prenatal and infant/maternal care, basic education, immunizations, and long-term development efforts are among the activities that could help overcome the poverty conditions that now kill and maim so many children and adults," the Ronsvalles say.

—Craig L. Blomberg, *Preaching the Parables* (Baker, 2004); statistics from www.emptytomb.com

ILLUSTRATION 154

A TITHE TOO MUCH

Topics: Contentment; Finances; Generosity; Giving; Greed; Luxury; Materialism; Perspective; Possessions; Prosperity; Riches; Stewardship; Stinginess; Tithing

References: Leviticus 27:30; Malachi 3:10; Matthew 25:14–30; Luke 12:48; 16:13; 2 Corinthians 9:6–8

A man once came to Peter Marshall, former chaplain of the Unites States Senate, with a concern about tithing. "I have a problem," he said. "I have been tithing for some time. It wasn't too bad when I was making $20,000 a year; I could afford to give up $2,000. But now that I am making $500,000, there is no way I can afford to give away $50,000 a year."

Peter Marshall reflected on this wealthy man's dilemma but gave no advice. He simply said, "Yes, sir. I see that you have a problem. I think we ought to pray about it. Is that all right?"

The man agreed, so Dr. Marshall bowed his head and prayed, "Dear Lord, this man has a problem, and I pray that you will help him. Please reduce his salary back to the place where he can afford to tithe."

—Kevin G. Harney, *Seismic Shifts* (Zondervan, 2005)

ILLUSTRATION 155

CONSERVATIVE CHRISTIANS GIVE MORE

Topics: Benevolence; Church Attendance; Community Impact; Compassion; Generosity; Giving; Godliness; Poverty; Sacrifice; Secularism; Self-denial; Self-discipline; Social Action; Stewardship; Tithing

References: Deuteronomy 15:7; Proverbs 19:17; Malachi 3; Matthew 19:21; Luke 6:38; 2 Corinthians 9:7

Conservative Christians put their money where their mouth is when it comes to giving. That's according to a study from Syracuse University published in 2006 by Arthur Brooks in *Who Really Cares: The Surprising Truth about Compassionate Conservatism*. "If you asked me, I would have expected to find that religious conservatives are stingy," said Brooks, a committed Catholic and political independent. "That's what we are told all the time." What he found instead was that conservative Christians give more in "every measurable way," from writing checks to volunteering time to donating blood.

Brooks attributes the difference to four factors: church attendance, two-parent families, a Protestant work ethic, and distaste for government social services. Of those, church attendance is the most telling. Ninety-one percent of regular church attendees give to charity each year, compared with 66 percent of those who said they do not have a religion. The gap adds up — the faithful give four times more money per year than their secular counterparts. While most of that money is given to churches, religious people also give more to a secular charity such as the Red Cross or to their alma mater.

Religious people also donate twice as much blood and are more likely to "behave in compassionate ways toward strangers," Brooks said. For example, they are much more likely to return extra change to a cashier when they are accidentally given too much.

Generous giving is part of the religious conservative identity, according to sociologist Tony Campolo. "The Religious Right, by conviction, is convinced that helping the poor is something that should be done individually or by the church," said Campolo. "[They say that] asking the state to do it is wrong."

— Sarah Eekhoff Zylstra,
"Compassionate Conservatives,"
Christianity Today (February 2007)

ILLUSTRATION 156

THIEVING MONEY

Topics: Character; Faithfulness; Finances; Generosity; Giving; Greed; Honesty; Prosperity; Riches; Stealing; Stewardship; Stinginess; Tithing

References: Deuteronomy 15:7; Malachi 3:6 – 12; Matthew 6:1 – 4; 19:21; Luke 6:38; Acts 5:1 – 11; 2 Corinthians 8:1 – 9:15

A twelve-year-old member of the church I pastor recently left a five-dollar bill on my desk with a note that read, "I have my thieving money," along with her signature.

I couldn't figure out what she meant. Had she stolen money she was now returning? When I saw the girl's father the next Sunday, I mentioned the money and note and asked if he could tell me what she meant. With no hesitation, he said that it was her tithe. She obviously had misspelled *tithing*.

As I thought about the misspelling, I realized that for those who do not tithe, they really do have a stash of "thieving" money, for as the Bible suggests, the one who refuses to tithe is stealing from God.

— Kirtes Calvery, Raymore, Missouri

ILLUSTRATION 157

TOOTH FAIRY FOR NEEDY KIDS

Topics: Childlike Faith; Compassion; Generosity; Giving; Kindness; Offerings; Sowing and Reaping; Spiritual Harvest; Stewardship; Tithing

References: Deuteronomy 15:7; Psalm 112:5; Proverbs 22:9; 2 Corinthians 8:12; 9:7; 1 John 3:17

Briton Nordemeyer, eight, of Brandon, South Dakota, wanted to help the children who had lost everything during Hurricane Katrina. So when Briton's tooth fell out in the fall of 2005, she decided to donate the money she'd get from the tooth fairy to the Red Cross.

Instead of waiting for the tooth fairy to arrive, however, Briton mailed her tooth to the Red Cross. She included a letter explaining that the tooth fairy would render payment upon arrival.

When news about Briton's generosity reached the public, the Red Cross received a $500 donation from an anonymous donor who heard about Briton's tooth and wanted to help provide a fairy-tale ending.

—Todd Hertz, "$500 Tooth Saves the Day," *Ignite Your Faith* (June 2006)

ILLUSTRATION 158

NO PAY PLATE

Topics: Children; Giving; Greed; Human Condition; Offerings; Self-centeredness; Sinful Nature; Stinginess; Tithing

References: Matthew 6:19–24; Luke 12:13–21; Ephesians 5:5; Colossians 3:1–6

A little boy wanted to help himself when the wine and wafers of Communion were passed out. His mother leaned over and told him that he was not old enough to take Communion.

Later, when the collection plate came by, his mother again leaned over and tried to coax a nickel out of the boy's clenched fist. He held on and shouted, "If I can't eat, I won't pay."

—J. R. Love, Rushton, Louisiana

ILLUSTRATION 159

GIVING MORE

Topics: Generosity; Giving; Missions; Money; Outreach; Poverty; Prosperity; Riches; Stewardship; Tithing

References: Proverbs 11:24; Acts 11:29; 20:35; 1 Corinthians 16:2; 2 Corinthians 9:7; Galatians 2:10; James 1:27; 5:1–6; 1 John 3:16–17

Most Americans are generous. According to a 2006 study, the vast majority of Americans make some contribution to the Red Cross, Salvation Army, American Cancer Society, local church, or other charitable organization every year. More Americans contribute to charities than bother to vote. U.S. donations rose from $1.7 billion in 1921 to more than $200 billion a year in 2006. There has been an 88 percent increase in the last decade alone.

Americans privately donated more than $4.2 billion to the Red Cross and other agencies to assist the survivors of hurricanes Katrina and Rita in 2005 and nearly $2 billion to relief efforts connected to the Indian Ocean tsunami.

"Philanthropy is no longer just for the very rich," says Robert Bremner, professor emeritus of history at Ohio State University. "Philanthropy is everybody's business now."

—Ted De Haas, "Philanthropy Is Everyone's Business," PreachingToday.com

ILLUSTRATION 160

GIVING TO GET

Topics: Eternal Life; Generosity; Heaven; Justification; Reconciliation; Salvation

References: Mark 10:25; John 3:16; 14:6; Acts 4:12; Romans 3:23; 6:23; Ephesians 2:8–9; Titus 3:5–7

Warren Buffet, the world's second-richest man, announced in June 2006 that he would donate 85 percent of his $44 billion fortune to five charitable foundations.

Commenting on this extreme level of generosity, Buffet said: "There is more than one way to get to heaven, but this is a great way."

—Associated Press, "How Do You Spend $1.5 Billion a Year?" CBSNews.com (June 27, 2006)

ILLUSTRATION 161

A GENEROUS HAND

Topics: Generosity; Giving; Money

References: Psalm 112:5; 2 Corinthians 9:11

Things themselves do not remain, but their effects do. Therefore we should not be mean and calculating with what we have but give with a generous hand. Look at how much people give to players and dancers—why not give just as much to Christ?

—John Chrysostom, early father of the church (347–404)

ILLUSTRATION 162

SLIGHTING GOD IN STINGINESS

Topics: Daily Bread; Giving; Gratitude; Provision; Thanksgiving; Tithing

References: Deuteronomy 26:1–11; Psalm 95:2; Luke 17:11–19; Acts 20:35; 2 Corinthians 8:1–15; 9:6–8; Ephesians 5:20

While hurrying through Chicago's commuter train station, I had an "Aha!" moment that stopped me in my tracks. I had just left the candy counter where I'd bought Valentine's treats for a party a few of us were planning for our church's single moms. Doing so took my thoughts back to a cookout the previous summer, for which I had covered the cost. The single moms, their children, and I enjoyed a glorious day at a local sunshine-drenched beach, conversing and stuffing ourselves with burgers, chips, and the trimmings.

As the afternoon ended, I sat among the moms at the picnic table as they enthusiastically divided up the leftover hot dogs, sodas, and desserts. No one thought to offer me a thing. My feelings were a little bruised. No, I didn't need the food. And most of the moms had given little thought to where the picnic spread had come from. But the slight was significant enough that I recalled it in the train station six months later.

Then it hit me! How much more slighted God must feel when, as recipients of his enormous generosity, we are reluctant to share a portion of our resources with him. Just as I didn't need the potato salad, he doesn't need our money. But he does crave our acknowledgment that all we have is from him.

—Judy Keene, Hoffman Estates, Illinois

ILLUSTRATION 163

TITHING BROOMS

Topics: Generosity; Giving; Money; Stinginess; Tithing

References: Matthew 6:21; Luke 21:1–4; 2 Corinthians 8:12

A church member stopped the pastor and angrily complained that the church had purchased five new brooms—an expenditure that he thought was completely unnecessary.

The pastor was surprised at the man's reaction and mentioned it to the church treasurer, who said, "It's understandable. How would you feel if you saw everything you gave in the past year tied up in five brooms?"

—Brad Estep, "Tithe Tied Up in Brooms," PreachingToday.com

ILLUSTRATION 164

PERSONALIZING GIVING

Topics: Benevolence; Generosity; Giving; Money; Stewardship; Tithing; Work

References: Proverbs 3:9–10; Malachi 3:10; Luke 6:38; 1 Corinthians 16:2; 2 Corinthians 9:6–8; Hebrews 7:5–6

Corporate giving is no longer about signing fat checks, public preening, and charity balls, says Jeff Skoll, vice president of strategic planning and analysis for eBay Inc. "Young, 'newly minted' givers anticipate seeing the effects of their gifts within their lifetimes and want a more hands-on role," he says.

For example, Ken Blanchard, coauthor of *How to Make Serious Money for Both You and Your Company*, says, "We tithe 10 percent of our profit.... We divide it among all our employees to give away. The lowest-paid employee gets to give $1,000 away, and the highest gets to give $3,500. We gave to 160 charities last year."

The results of this personalized giving are touching. "A guy in shipping came up to me with tears in his eyes," Blanchard said. "He got the chance to give $1,000 to his parish to buy robes for the choir. He's become a local hero."

—Lorenzo Della Foresta, "Twenty-first Century Giving," PreachingToday.com

ILLUSTRATION 165

GIFTS OF GIVING

Topics: Christian Culture; Giving; Money

References: Matthew 6:19–24; 16:24

When we give money, we are releasing a little more of our egocentric selves and a little more of our false security....

Giving frees us to care. It produces an air of expectancy as we anticipate what God will lead us to give. It makes life with God an adventure of discovery. We are being used to help make a difference in the world, and that is worth living for and giving for.

—Richard J. Foster, *Money, Sex and Power* (Harper, 1985)

ILLUSTRATION 166

GIVING FOR HOPE

Topics: Giving; Hope; Vision

Reference: Psalm 33:20–22

People give to achievement and promise and hope, not deficits.

—E. Burr Gibson, "Reflections," *Christianity Today* (June 12, 2000)

ILLUSTRATION 167

STEWARDS OF GIVING

Topics: Giving; Money; Stewardship

Reference: Matthew 25:14–30

John Wesley's famous formula "Get all you can; save all you can; give all you can" must be supplemented. It should read, "Get all you can; save all you can; freely use all you can within a properly disciplined spiritual life; and control all you can for the good of humankind and God's glory." Giving all you can would then naturally be a part of an overall wise stewardship.

—Dallas Willard, *The Spirit of the Disciplines* (Harper, 1988)

ILLUSTRATION 168

HOW GIVING SHAPES YOU

Topics: Giving; Greed; Money; Offerings

References: Psalm 50:8–15; Proverbs 11:24–25

I do not think I exaggerate when I say that some of us put our offering in the plate with a kind of triumphant bounce, as much as to say, "There—now God will feel better!"

I am obliged to tell you that God does not need anything you have. He does not need a dime of your money. It is your own spiritual welfare that is at stake in such matters as these.

You have the right to keep what you have all to yourself—but it will rust and decay, and ultimately ruin you.

—A. W. Tozer, *Christ, the Eternal Son* (Christian Publications, 1991)

ILLUSTRATION 169
PERFECTED IN GIVING

Topics: Attitudes; Giving; Holiness; Maturity; Sacrifice; Servanthood

References: Matthew 5:48; 19:21

Perfection, in a Christian sense, means becoming mature enough to give ourselves to others.

—Kathleen Norris, *Amazing Grace* (Riverhead Books, 1999)

ILLUSTRATION 170
GIVING EXAMPLE

Topics: Christian Life; Example; Giving

References: 2 Timothy 1:13; Titus 2:6–8

The first great gift we can bestow on others is a good example.

—Thomas Morell, classical scholar and librettist (1703–84)

ILLUSTRATION 171
MORE THAN WE CAN SPARE

Topics: Generosity; Giving; Money; Sacrifice

References: Matthew 19:23–24; 2 Corinthians 8:1–7; 9:6–15

I do not believe one can settle how much we ought to give. I am afraid the only safe rule is to give more than we can spare. In other words, if our expenditure on comforts, luxuries, amusements, etc., is up to the standard common among those with the same income as our own, we are probably giving away too little. If our charities do not at all pinch or hamper us, I should say they are too small. There ought to be things we should like to do and cannot do because our charitable expenditures excludes them.

—C. S. Lewis, *Mere Christianity* (Macmillan, 1952)

ILLUSTRATION 172
GIVING FOR LIFE

Topics: Generosity; Giving; Money; Sports

References: Amos 5:18 – 24;
1 Timothy 6:17 – 19

David Robinson, one of the best basketball players of all time, fed the homeless through his Feed My Sheep program. He also helped needy families get diapers and baby food through a charity called the Ruth Project.

He thought of this work as life-enhancers rather than sacrifices. "If I'm clutching my money with both hands, how can I be free to hug my wife and kids?" he asked.

—Rick Reilly, "Spur of the Moment,"
Sports Illustrated (June 23, 1999)

ILLUSTRATION 173

DOING WITHOUT

Topics: Contentment; Money

References: Acts 20:35;
Philippians 4:11 – 12

It is more blessed to give than to receive, but then it is also more blessed to be able to do without than to have to have.

—Søren Kierkegaard, Danish philosopher
(1813 – 55), submitted by Rubel Shelly,
Nashville, Tennessee

ILLUSTRATION 174

AN ENVELOPE FOR MIKE

Topics: Christian Life; Christmas;
Family; Gifts; Giving; Love; Ministry

Reference: Matthew 6:1 – 4

The small, white envelope stuck among the branches of our Christmas tree has peeked through the branches of our tree for the past ten years or so.

It all began because my husband, Mike, hated Christmas — oh, not the true meaning of Christmas, but the overspending, the frantic running around at the last minute, the gifts given in desperation. Knowing he felt that way, I decided to do something different.

Our son Kevin was wrestling at the junior high school. Shortly before Christmas his team played a team sponsored by an inner-city church. These youngsters, dressed in sneakers so ragged that shoestrings seemed to be the only thing holding them together, were a sharp contrast to our boys in their spiffy blue and gold uniforms and sparkling new wrestling shoes. As the match began, I was alarmed to see that the other team's boys were wrestling without headgear.

It was a luxury they obviously could not afford. We ended up walloping them. As each boy got up from the mat, he swaggered in his tatters with false bravado, a kind of street pride that couldn't acknowledge defeat. Mike shook his head sadly. "I wish just one of them could have won," he said. "They have a lot of potential, but losing like this could take the heart right out of them."

That afternoon I went to a local sporting goods store and bought an assortment of wrestling headgear and shoes and sent them anonymously to the inner-city church. On Christmas Eve, I placed an envelope on the tree with a note telling Mike what I had done as my gift to him. His smile was the brightest thing that Christmas.

Each Christmas after that, I sent Mike's gift money to a different group—one year sending a group of youngsters with mental disabilities to a hockey game, another year giving a check to elderly brothers whose home had burned down the week before Christmas.

We lost Mike to cancer. When Christmas rolled around, I was so wrapped up in grief that I barely got the tree up. But on Christmas Eve I placed an envelope on the tree, and in the morning it was joined by three more. Each of our children had placed an envelope on the tree for their dad.

—Anonymous

ILLUSTRATION 175

INSPIRATIONAL BLOOD GIFT

Topics: Giving; Sacrifice

References: Matthew 26:28; 1 Peter 1:18–19

The United States Red Cross has thirty-four blood-service regions across the country, and Jim Parker, a retired school superintendent, and his wife, Linda, a teacher, made a seventeen-month tour visiting each one of them to donate blood.

When asked about the pain of donating blood, the Parkers responded, "Pinch yourself hard; it doesn't hurt as bad as that."

The Parkers estimate their donations will save 130 lives. They also hope to inspire others to give, thereby saving even more lives.

—Keith Jordan, "Giving of Themselves," *Reader's Digest* (November 2005)

PART 9: GOD: THE FATHER, SON, AND HOLY SPIRIT

ILLUSTRATION 176

INSTINCT FOR GOD

Topics: Atheism; Childlike Faith; Creation; Creator; Evolution; God; Nature; Spiritual Perception

References: Genesis 1:1; Matthew 18:3; Mark 9:37; Luke 10:21; Romans 1:20

A little girl who grew up in an atheistic home where no one ever spoke of God once questioned her father about the origin of the world. "Where does the world come from?" asked the three-year-old.

Her father replied with a discourse that was materialistic in nature. Then he added, "However, there are those who say that all this comes from a very powerful being, and they call him God."

At this point the little girl began to run like a whirlwind around the room in a burst of joy and exclaimed, "I knew what you told me wasn't true; it is Him, it is Him!"

—Sofia Cavalletti, *The Religious Potential of the Child* (Paulist Press, 1983)

ILLUSTRATION 177

BEYOND UNDERSTANDING

Topics: God; Mysteries; Understanding

References: Psalm 139:6; Isaiah 55:8–9

Since it is God we are speaking of, you do not understand it. If you could understand it, it would not be God.

—Augustine, philosopher and theologian (354–430), in "Reflections," *Christianity Today* (July 20, 2000)

ILLUSTRATION 178

FINDING GOD IN SISTER'S ACCIDENT

Topics: Adversity; Attitudes; Crisis; Faith; Growth; Hardship; Knowing God; Perspective; Presence of God; Priorities; Salvation; Spiritual Growth; Suffering; Testimony; Tragedy; Trials

References: Luke 19:10; John 3:16; Romans 3:23–24; 8:28; 10:9–10; 2 Corinthians 7:10

Before I decided to live for Christ, I'd party with friends. As a guy who wanted to be a "cool and popular jock," I'd drink, act stupid, and end up making a fool of myself. But I didn't care, because I was popular and one of my school's top athletes. As for God, I thought he was for weak people. If Christians tried to tell me about Jesus, I'd make fun of them. Then something happened my sophomore year that changed everything.

My sister Ashley, who was a freshman at the time, was riding in a car driven by one of her friends. Worried about getting home late, Ashley's friend started speeding. The car hit a rough railroad track and flipped over. Ashley soon lay in a hospital on life support, very close to death.

At first I was angry with God for what happened to my sister. I shouted, "If you are who you say you are, how could you let this happen?" As angry as I was at God, I began to think about how much I loved my family. I had cared about them before, but all those trips to the hospital and all those times we cried together brought us much closer together. My family suddenly seemed more important than anything else in the whole world.

Even though my sister managed to survive, we were told her brain injury was so severe she'd probably never walk or talk again. But in the months that followed, I helped coach her as she struggled to stand, and then, eventually, take a few tiny steps. I listened in amazement as she began to put words together and form sentences. Very slowly, she was getting better. And very slowly, I was starting to change.

I thought a lot about God and his place in everything that had happened. Instead of blaming him for the accident, I began to thank him for my sister's life and for my family. I also began to see that all those things I'd lived for—like partying and acceptance by the popular crowd—weren't really important. Even sports no longer seemed important.

I started going to youth group and found I liked having conversations with my friends about God and Christianity. I wanted to know as much as I could about following God. During my junior year, I committed my life to Christ.

—Dustin Armstrong, "My Faith Is My Witness," *Ignite Your Faith* (June–July 2006)

ILLUSTRATION 179
THE SURVIVAL OF GOD

Topics: Atheism; Education; Faith; Modernism; Naturalism; Skepticism

Reference: Matthew 16:13–19

The most extraordinary thing about the twentieth century was the failure of God to die. The collapse of mass religious belief, especially among the educated and prosperous, had been widely and confidently predicted. It did not take place. Somehow, God survived—flourished even.

—Paul Johnson, *The Quest for God* (HarperCollins, 1997)

ILLUSTRATION 180

CALLING DAD FOR HELP

Topics: Communication; Crisis; Dependence on God; Desperation; Faith; Family; God as Father; Help from God; Needs; Prayer; Trust

References: Psalm 46:1; 1 Peter 5:7

While kayaking in southern England off the Isle of Wight, Mark Ashton-Smith, a lecturer at Cambridge University, capsized in treacherous waters. Clinging to his craft and reaching for his cell phone, Ashton-Smith, thirty-three, called his dad.

It didn't matter that his father, Alan Pimm-Smith, was training British troops in Dubai 3,500 miles away. Without delay, the father relayed his son's Mayday to the Coast Guard nearest to his son. Within twelve minutes, a helicopter retrieved the grateful Ashton-Smith.

Like this kayaker, when we are in peril, our first impulse should be to call our Father—the one we trust to help us.

— "Capsized Man Phones for Help 3,500 Miles Away," Reuters News Agency (September 11, 2001)

ILLUSTRATION 181

RUNNING FOR DADDY

Topics: Acceptance; God as Father; Grace; Love

References: Romans 8:15–16; 15:7; 1 Corinthians 1:26–31; 13:7–8; Colossians 1:21–22; Hebrews 4:14–16; 1 John 1:3–9

My twenty-one-month-old, who had just learned to say, "Daddy," had been struggling with asthma and an ear infection for two weeks. He coughed and sneezed continually, and his nose ran like a faucet. Each night when I came home, he ran to meet me at the door, smiling, coughing, nose running, yelling, "Daddy! Daddy!"

I was not repulsed by his runny nose or close-range sneezes in the least (he "slimed" every shirt I own!). I love him deeply and enjoy his love for me.

It does remind me, though, that when I am sick with sin, God loves me deeply and desires that I run to him as a son, crying, "Abba, Father."

— David Slagle, Lawrenceville, Georgia

ILLUSTRATION 182

HE WHO KNOWS MY NAME

Topics: God's Love; God's Omniscience; Intimacy; Lord's Prayer; Name

References: Exodus 33:17; Matthew 6:9; Luke 10:20; 12:6–7

Jonathan, four, was trying to learn the Lord's Prayer. He learned by listening at church each Sunday.

One Sunday as we were praying the Lord's Prayer, he could be heard above all the others, praying, "Our Father who art in heaven, I know you know my name."

— Jeff Newton, Lowell, Indiana

ILLUSTRATION 183

GREATNESS SNUFFED

Topics: Arrogance; Creator; Death; Fear; God; Irreverence; Judgment; Limitations; Power

References: Deuteronomy 3:24; Psalm 8:3–4; 19:1–6; 145:3; Isaiah 63:1; Revelation 1:12–16; 19:1–16

King Louis XIV of France, who preferred to be called "Louis the Great" and had declared, "I am the State!" died in 1717. His court was the most magnificent in Europe, and his funeral was the most spectacular.

In the church where the ceremony was performed, his body lay in a golden coffin. To dramatize his greatness, orders had been given that the cathedral would be very dimly lit with only one special candle that was to be set above the coffin.

The thousands of people in attendance waited in silence. Then Bishop Massillon began to speak. Slowly reaching down, he snuffed out the candle and said, "Only God is great."

—Jeff Arthurs, "Laying the Foundation for Peace," PreachingToday.com

ILLUSTRATION 184

HIS CRUCIAL DEATH

Topics: Cross; Death of Christ; Redeemer; Savior

References: Mark 10:45; Romans 6:3–9; 1 John 5:6–12

Of the biographies I have read—including biographies of men like Martin Luther King Jr. and Mahatma Gandhi, who died violent and politically significant deaths—few devote more than 10 percent of their pages to the subject's death. The Gospels, though, devote nearly a third of their length to the climactic last week of Jesus' life. Matthew, Mark, Luke, and John saw death as the central mystery of Jesus.

—Philip Yancey, *The Jesus I Never Knew* (Zondervan, 1995)

ILLUSTRATION 185

VOLUNTARY DEATH

Topics: Cross; Death of Christ; Deity of Christ; Dying to Self; Sacrifice

References: Ephesians 5:2; Philippians 2:5–11; 1 John 3:16

Christ died because he would die; other men admitted to the dignity of martyrdom are willing to die, but they die by the torments of the executioners; they cannot bid their souls go out and say, "Now I will die." And this was Christ's case: It was not only, "I lay down my life for my sheep" [John 10:15], but he says also, "No man can take away my soul; and I have power to lay it down" [10:18]. And, de facto, he did lay it down—he did die before the torments could have extorted his soul from him.

Many crucified men lived many days on a cross. The thieves were alive long after Christ was dead, and therefore Pilate wondered that he was already dead (Mark 15:44). His soul did not leave his body by force, but because he would, and when he would, and how he would.... Christ did not die naturally, nor violently, as all others do, but only voluntarily.

—John Donne, poet and preacher (1572–1631), in a sermon (March 28, 1619)

ILLUSTRATION 186

THE LANGUAGE OF RESURRECTION

Topics: Accepting Christ; Bible; Divine Power; Experiencing God; God's Love; Grace; Jesus Christ; Missions; Resurrection; Spiritual Perception; Surrender; Truth

References: Matthew 28:1–10; Mark 16:1–8; Luke 24:1–12; John 11:25; 14:6; 20:1–18; Romans 1:16; 1 Corinthians 15:17–20; Hebrews 4:12; 1 Peter 1:3

When I was about age six, a tall, pale white man stumbled into my home village of Dibagat in the northern jungles of the Philippine island of Luzon. The man didn't speak our language, so our elders asked him the best they knew how, "Why are you here?"

"I've come to learn your language," he said. "I'd like to write it down and then give you God's Word in your language."

We started teaching this man, Dick Roe, our language. Maybe his God could free us from the spirits.

When I was about thirteen, Dick had to return to the United States to raise support for his ministry. Before he left, he translated the gospel of Mark and gave me a copy. Sitting on top of a rock, I read the gospel of Mark in my heart language. It felt like I was actually there, seeing the characters.

The further I read, the more distressed I felt. A mob of people came to get Jesus out of the garden of Gethsemane. What did he do wrong? They accused him of all kinds of false things. They mocked him, spat on him, beat him, and took him before Pilate. Then came the scourge and the crown of thorns. It was excruciating to read that they forced him to carry a wooden cross and then nailed him to it.

Deep in my heart, a hatred of God swelled. I shook my fist and shouted, "I hate you, God, for being so powerless! Why should I believe in a powerless God like you?" I threw the gospel of Mark down to the rocks and started walking home. I couldn't understand why God wouldn't protect his own Son. Our headhunters defended us to the death. Because of them, no one could touch us. I wanted a god like that, someone who would protect me from the spirits that demanded we sacrifice our cows, chickens, pigs, and dogs. This God didn't even save his own Son.

Suddenly God reached down into my heart. "Nard, don't you understand?" I heard him say. "That's how much I love you. I gave my Son on your behalf." For the first time, I understood grace. I understood how much God loved me.

"God, if you love me that much," I prayed, "I want to give you my life, my heart. It's all yours." I went back and began to read further in Mark. I read that Jesus rose from the grave on the third day. Nobody in all of Dibagat, nobody from among the Isnag people, had ever risen from the grave. The resurrection story changed my life.

—Nard Pugyao, "Penetrating Power," *Decision* (July–August 2006)

ILLUSTRATION 187

SAVED BY THE FLEECE

Topics: Adoption; Atonement; Blood of Christ; Gift of Righteousness; Rescue; Salvation

References: John 1:29; Romans 8:15–17; Galatians 3:27; Ephesians 4:22–24; Colossians 3:9–10; 1 Peter 1:18–21

If you go to Scotland or anywhere there are a lot of sheep, sooner or later you will see a little lamb running around the field with what looks like an extra fleece tied onto its back. There are little holes in the fleece for its four legs and usually a hole for its head. If you see a little lamb running around like that, that usually means its mother has died.

Without the protection and nourishment of a mother, an orphaned lamb will die. If you try to introduce the orphaned lamb to another mother, the new mother will butt it away. She won't recognize the lamb's scent and will know the new baby is not one of her own lambs.

But thankfully, most flocks are large enough to have a ewe that recently lost a lamb. The shepherd skins the dead lamb and makes its fleece into a covering for the orphaned lamb. Then he takes the orphaned lamb to the mother whose baby just died. Now, when she sniffs the orphaned lamb, she smells her own lamb. Instead of butting the lamb away, she accepts it as one of her own.

In a similar way, we have become acceptable to God by being clothed with Christ.

—Peter Grant, in the sermon "In What Way Is Jesus Christ Different?"

ILLUSTRATION 188

BLOOD IN THE RIVER

Topics: Atonement; Changed Heart; Evangelism; Ministry; Missions; Obedience; Outreach; Rewards; Sacrifice; Vision

References: Matthew 6:19–20; 25:14–30; John 12:24; Romans 8:28; 2 Corinthians 5:10; Philippians 2:17; 2 Timothy 4:6

Assemblies of God missionary J. W. Tucker knew he was at risk when anarchy broke out in the Belgian Congo in 1964, but he stayed where God had placed him. One day a mob attacked and killed him with sticks, clubs, fists, and broken bottles. They took his body, threw it in the back of a truck, then tossed his corpse to the crocodiles in the Bomokande River, in what is now the Democratic Republic of the Congo.

J. W. Tucker had risked everything, yet he seemingly had nothing to show for it. But thirty years later, John Weidman, a close friend of Tucker, was in the country (by then known as Zaire) and learned how God had used that missionary's sacrifice.

The Bomokande River flows through the middle of the Mangbeto tribe, a people virtually without the gospel. During a civil war, the Mangbeto king appealed to the central government in Kinshasa for help. The government sent the brigadier, a policeman of strong stature and reputation who came from Isiro. Tucker had led the brigadier to the Lord two months before Tucker was killed.

As a new Christian, the brigadier had done his best to witness to others but had no response. Then one day he heard of a Mangbeto tradition that said, "If the blood of any man flows in the Bomokande River, you must listen to his message."

The brigadier called for the king and the village elders. They gathered in full assembly to hear the brigadier say, "Some time ago, a man was killed, and his body was thrown into your Bomokande River. The crocodiles in this river ate him up. His blood flowed in your river. But before he died, he left me a message. This message concerns God's Son, the Lord Jesus Christ, who came to this world to save people who were sinners. He died for the sins of the world; he died for my sins. I received this message, and it changed my life."

As the brigadier preached, the Spirit of God descended, and people began to fall on their knees and cry out to the Lord. Many were converted. Since that day, thousands of Mangbetos have come to Christ and dozens of Assemblies of God churches have opened.

—Marshall Shelley, "A Missionary's Sacrifice Was Worth the Cost," PreachingToday.com

ILLUSTRATION 189
THE DANGERS OF STRAYING

Topics: Atonement; Cross; Disobedience; Good Shepherd; Rebellion; Salvation; Sin

References: Isaiah 53:1–6; John 10:11; 1 Peter 2:24–25

It is the nature of sheep to stray and get in harm's way, whether from hungry wolves or steep canyons. For centuries, shepherds have used various methods — from staff to dog — to keep sheep from straying from the safety of their care.

In recent times shepherds have tried more sophisticated methods. One is a metal, hoof-proof grid that is built into the ground around the sheep's territory. The animals cannot walk over the grid, which is eight feet wide. This works well in keeping sheep in the protection of the pen.

But in 2006, shepherds in Yorkshire, England, found that their sheep were not only stubbornly prone to stray but also crafty. One of the sheep laid down and rolled over the grid. The other sheep in the herd followed the first, and soon the entire flock had spread over the countryside to neighborhood gardens, where they ate the food and flowers of local residents.

The shepherds eventually gathered up the troublesome sheep and returned them to their pen. But they escaped again and got into trouble. While the escape of this flock of "black" sheep may have seemed like an exciting adventure, it actually placed the animals in harm's way from cars and unfriendly dogs.

Thankfully, our Good Shepherd found another way to deal with stubborn, straying sheep. As Isaiah 53:6 says, "We all, like sheep, have gone astray, each of us has turned to his own way; and the LORD has laid on him [Jesus] the iniquity of us all."

—Craig Brian Larson, "Straying Sheep Endanger Themselves," PreachingToday.com; source: Jason Bellows, "The Great Sheep Escape," BBC online (January 30, 2006)

ILLUSTRATION 190

JESUS IN THE HOMELESS

Topics: Caring; Compassion; Generosity; Homelessness; Humility; Hunger; Ministry; Poverty; Presence of God; Sacrifice; Service; Sharing; Stewardship

References: Proverbs 29:7; Matthew 10:42; 25:31–46; Luke 6:20–21; 12:32–34; Acts 2:45; Galatians 2:10; 1 John 3:16–17

Shane Claiborne, who has taken the gospel beyond the streets of Philadelphia to the slums of Calcutta and the war zones of Iraq, describes how God revealed himself through the homeless:

I saw one woman in a crowd as she struggled to get a meal from one of the late-night food vans. When we asked her if the meals were really worth the fight, she said, "Oh yes, but I don't eat them myself. I get them for another homeless lady—an elderly woman around the corner who can't fight for a meal."

I saw a street kid get $20 panhandling outside of a store and then immediately run inside to share it with his friends. We saw a homeless man lay a pack of cigarettes in the offering plate because it was all he had. I met a blind street musician who was viciously abused by some young guys who would mock her, curse her, and one night even sprayed Lysol in her eyes as a practical joke. As we held her that night, one of us said, "There are a lot of bad folks in the world, aren't there?"

She said, "Oh, but there are a lot of good ones too. And the bad ones make you, the good ones, seem even sweeter."

We met a little girl who was homeless and asked her what she wanted to do when she grew up. "I want to own a grocery store," she said. We asked her why, and she said, "So I can give out food to all the hungry people."

Mother Teresa used to say, "In the poor we meet Jesus in his most distressing disguises." Now I knew what she meant.

—Shane Claiborne, *The Irresistible Revolution* (Zondervan, 2006)

ILLUSTRATION 191

INTERVIEWING CHRIST

Topics: Birth of Christ; Christmas; Incarnation; Jesus Christ

References: Isaiah 7:14; Matthew 1:18–25; Luke 2:1–7

When asked, "If you could select any one person across all of history to interview, who would it be?" talk-show host Larry King said he would like to interview Jesus Christ.

When asked, "What would you like to ask him?" King replied, "I would like to ask him if he was indeed virgin-born. The answer to that question would define history for me."

When Ravi Zacharias requested permission to quote Larry King, King responded, "Tell him I was not being facetious."

—Ravi Zacharias, "Questions I Would Like to Ask God," *Just Thinking* (Winter 1998)

ILLUSTRATION 192
LETTERS FROM THE KING

Topics: Bible; Christ's Love; Christ the King; Word of God

Reference: John 1:14

Bouch, a waiter at a tavern in Chicago, wrote to the king of his homeland, Morocco. King Mohammed VI, who often interacts with his subjects in public and has freed political prisoners as well as helped the poor and disabled, wrote back.

"Look at the letters," said Bouch. "These are letters from the king. If I meet him, I'll be so happy."

You think King Mohammed VI loves his subjects? You ought to meet Jesus, the King of Kings, and read his precious letters to you.

—Lee Eclov, "Letters from the King," PreachingToday.com; source: John Kass, "Waiter's Pen Pal Just a Cool Guy Who Runs a Country," *Chicago Tribune* (July 23, 2001)

ILLUSTRATION 193
RESURRECTION PROOF

Topics: Jesus Christ; Resurrection

Reference: Acts 1:3

Science says that if there is any such thing as infallible proof, it is the repetition of the same experiment.

> Experiment 1: Jesus rose from the dead, and Mary Magdalene encountered him.
> Experiment 2: The women encountered the risen Christ.
> Experiment 3: The disciples encountered Christ.
> Experiment 4: The apostles encountered him.
> Experiment 5: Christ was seen by five hundred people.

Each appearance of the risen Christ is the repetition of the same experiment. They all encountered the same phenomenon: Jesus, who died, was now alive! That's what changed the history of the world.

—Walter Martin and Jill Martin Rische, *Through the Windows of Heaven* (Broadman & Holman, 1999)

ILLUSTRATION 194
A SHEPHERD'S COMFORT

Topics: Circumstances and Faith; Comfort; Fear; Jesus Christ; Peace; Trust

References: John 14:27; 1 Peter 5:7

During a recent conflict in the Middle East, Ron and Joke Jones, who serve with the Christian and Missionary Alliance in Israel, wrote in their prayer letter:

> The result of the fighting and killing has left a profound sense of discouragement that hovers over the country. Several times we have come into closer contact with this conflict than our comfort zone allowed.
>
> Yesterday a friend said she was watching a shepherd caring for his flock near the area where guns are fired. Every time the shots rang out, the sheep scattered in fright. The shepherd touched each of them with his staff and spoke calmly to them, and the sheep settled down because they trusted the shepherd. Then another shot sounded, and the same routine happened. Each time, the sheep needed the shepherd to orient them again and to reassure them they were safe.

We are like those sheep. When we are frightened, our Shepherd reaches out and touches us with his staff, speaking words of calm and comfort.

—Greg Asimakoupoulos,
Mercer Island, Washington

ILLUSTRATION 195
FALLING DOWN BESIDE US

Topics: Caring; Comfort; Help; Holy Spirit

Reference: John 14:16–18

The Karre language of equatorial Africa was difficult for the translators of the New Testament, especially when it came to the word *Paraclete*. How could they describe the Holy Spirit?

One day the translators saw a group of porters going off into the bush carrying bundles on their heads. They noticed one didn't carry anything. They assumed he was the boss, who was present to make sure the others did their work. However, they discovered he was not the boss. Rather, he was present so that, should anyone fall over with exhaustion, this man would pick up the man's load and carry it for him. This porter was known in the Karre language as "the one who falls down beside us."

The translators had their word for *Paraclete*.

—Ian Coffey, "Deep Impact,"
Keswick '99 (OM Publishing)

ILLUSTRATION 196
HIS NATURAL BIRTH

Topics: Christmas; God; Humanity; Incarnation; Jesus Christ; Mysteries; Salvation

References: John 1:14; Philippians 2:1–11

God fills a bush with his glory, and it burns. God enters into the great mountain, and it rocks with an earthquake. When he comes to occupy a man, he must distort the humanity he occupies into some inhuman shape.

Instead of that, this new life into which God comes seems to be the quietest, most natural human life that was ever seen upon the earth.

It glides into its place like sunlight, seeming to make it evident that God and man are essentially so near together that the meeting of their natures in the life of a God-man is not strange.

So always does Christ deal with his own nature, accepting his divinity as you and I accept our humanity, and letting it shine out through the envelope with which it has most subtly and mysteriously mingled, as the soul is mingled with and shines out through the body.

—Phillips Brooks, Episcopalian preacher
(1835–93)

ILLUSTRATION 197

HUGS AND KISSES EVERY DAY

Topics: Children; Comfort; Cross; Drugs; Drunkenness; Family; Jesus Christ; Resurrection

References: Matthew 11:28–30; 19:13–15; 2 Corinthians 1:3–11

"The Little Girl," a ballad sung by John Michael Montgomery, tells the sad story of a little girl who hid behind the couch while her drug-addicted mother and alcoholic father continually fought. They never went to church or spoke of the Lord, except in vain. The parents eventually died in a murder-suicide.

The State placed the child in a foster home where she got kisses and hugs every day. The foster parents took the little girl to Sunday school where she saw a picture of Jesus hanging on a cross. With a smile, the girl pointed to the man in the picture. "I don't know his name," the little girl said. "But I know he got off the cross, because he was there in my old house. He held me close to his side as I hid behind our couch the night that my parents died."

—"The Little Girl," written by Harley Allen

ILLUSTRATION 198

STUDENTS SHOCKED BY PROFESSOR'S JUDGMENT

Topics: Consequences; Divine Power; Final Judgment; Goodness of God; Grace; Justice; Mercy; Patience; Punishment; Responsibility

References: Isaiah 66:15–16; Matthew 10:28; 12:36; Romans 2:4–5; 2 Corinthians 6:2; Colossians 3:25; 1 Peter 4:5; Revelation 20:11–15

On his first day of teaching his class of 250 college freshmen, R. C. Sproul carefully explained the assignment of three term papers—due on the last day of September, October, and November. Sproul clearly stated there would be no extensions (except for medical reasons). At the end of September, some 225 students dutifully turned in their papers, while 25 remorseful students quaked in fear. "We're so sorry," they said. "We didn't make the proper adjustments from high school to college, but we promise to do better next time." He bowed to their pleas for mercy and gave them an extension, but warned them not to be late next month.

The end of October rolled around, and about 200 students turned in their papers, while 50 students showed up empty-handed. "Oh, please," they begged, "it was homecoming weekend, and we ran out of time." Sproul relented once more but warned them, "This is it. No excuses next time. You will get an *F*."

The end of November came, and only 100 students turned in their papers. The rest told Sproul, "We'll get it in soon."

"Sorry," Sproul replied. "It's too late now. You get an *F*."

The students howled in protest, "That's not fair!"

"OK," Sproul replied, "you want justice, do you? Here's what's just: you'll get an *F* for all three papers that were late. That was the rule, right?"

"The students had quickly taken my mercy for granted," Sproul later reflected. "They assumed it. When justice suddenly fell, they were unprepared for it. It came as a shock, and they were outraged."

—Matt Woodley, "The Grieving Heart of God," PreachingToday.com

ILLUSTRATION 199

FINDING MESSIAH

Topics: Conversion; Family; Jesus Christ; Messiah; Prayer; Salvation; Seekers

References: Deuteronomy 18:18; Isaiah 43:18–25; Luke 2:11

Stan Telchin, a successful Jewish businessman, felt betrayed when his daughter, Judy, twenty-one, called home from college to say, "I believe Jesus is the Messiah."

To prove his daughter wrong, Telchin began an energetic quest for truth. So did Stan's wife, Ethel, and their other daughter, Ann. When the search created friction between Stan and Ethel, they agreed to pursue their studies independently.

Months later, Stan accepted an invitation to attend a National Convocation of Messianic Jews. He planned to "work the convention" just like any other business, meeting with anyone he thought could help him.

After a series of meetings, Stan lay awake in his dorm room, realizing he had arrived at a point of crisis. If the Bible was true—and he had concluded it was—then he really did believe in the God of Abraham, Isaac, and Jacob. He also admitted that he believed in the Bible as God's inspired Word. But he couldn't quite say, "Jesus is the Messiah."

He asked his roommate to pray for him. Art obliged, praying simply, "God, give Stan your peace, and resolve his inner conflict."

The next morning at breakfast, a man at Stan's table asked him to pray before the meal. Startled by the request, Stan bowed his head and said: "Praised be Thou, O Lord our God, King of the universe. I thank you for the fellowship and the friendship at this table. I thank you for what we have learned at this meeting. I ask you now to bless this food, and I do so ... in the name of Jesus, the Messiah."

For a moment, he sat there, amazed at what he had just prayed. The faces of others at the table were suddenly jubilant. "Stan," said one of them, "you're a believer!" One by one they got up from their seats and hugged Stan. Several cried with joy.

Stan began to weep too. He wasn't sure how his wife would take the news, but he called her, blurting out, "Ethel, honey, it's me. It's over. I've made my decision. Jesus is the Messiah!"

There was a pause on the other line as Stan held his breath. Then his wife said softly, "Thank God! That makes it unanimous. We've all been waiting for you."

Stan's entire family—his wife and both daughters—had decided to trust Christ as the Messiah. Each had been praying and waiting patiently for the Holy Spirit of Christ to draw Stan into a relationship with himself.

—Story told in Stan Telchin, *Betrayed* (Chosen, 1981)

ILLUSTRATION 200

READING CHRIST

Topics: Jesus Christ; Study; Truth; Understanding

References: Proverbs 2:1–11; 23:12; John 1:1

Reading ought to be an act of homage to the God of all truth. We open our hearts to words that reflect the reality he has created or the greater reality which he is. Christ, the incarnate Word, is the Book of Life in whom we read God.

—Thomas Merton, Thoughts in Solitude (Farrar, Straus and Giroux, 1958)

ILLUSTRATION 201

JESUS THE REFUGEE

Topics: Dependence on God; Hearing God; Holy Spirit; Inspiration; Jesus Christ; Preaching; Suffering

References: John 14:26; Acts 1:8; Hebrews 4:14–16

In Croatia I was asked to speak to a church gathering for about two hundred newly arrived refugees. Refugees from this area of the world are mostly women, because the men are dead or in camp or fighting.

This group of Muslims, Croats, and a few Serbs had fled to a seminary on the border of a battered Croatian town. The town was still in danger of sniper fire and bombing, but the church had escaped because there were apartment buildings between it and the guns. Attackers had tried to fire shells over the apartment buildings to the seminary, but they had failed, so the seminary became the refugee receiving and feeding place.

We worked all day visiting the refugees. At night we held a service in a huge, old church. I didn't know what to say. Everything I had prepared seemed totally inadequate, so I put my notes away and prayed, "God, give me something they can identify with."

I told the women about Jesus, who as a baby became a refugee. He was hunted by soldiers, and his parents had to flee to Egypt at night, leaving everything behind. I continued telling them about Jesus' life, and when I got to the cross, I said, "He hung there naked, not like pictures tell you." They knew what that meant. Some of them had been stripped naked and tortured.

At the end of the message, I said, "All these things have happened to you. You are homeless. You have had to flee. You have suffered unjustly. But you didn't have a choice. He had a choice. He knew all this would happen to him, but he still came." And then I told them why.

Many of the women knelt down, put their hands up, and wept. I said, "He's the only one who really understands. I cannot possibly understand, but he can. He's the suffering God. You can give your pain to him."

—Jill Briscoe, "Keeping the Adventure in Ministry," *Leadership* (Summer 1996)

ILLUSTRATION 202

A NOT-SO-CHEAP BUY

Topics: Christ's Sacrifice; Cross; Grace; Repentance; Sin

References: Luke 1:46–50; Romans 6:1–2; Hebrews 10:26–31; 1 Peter 1:17–19

I was in a store shopping for a sweater. The cost needed to be minimal, so I went to the clearance rack. As I flipped through the sweaters, one caught my eye. It was the right color and the right size, and, best of all, the price tag said $8. Without much more thought, I made my purchase.

At home I slipped on the sweater. Its texture was like silk. I had made my purchase so quickly that I hadn't noticed how smooth and elegant

the sweater was. Then I saw the original price tag: $124.

I gasped. I had never owned a sweater that expensive. I had come home with what I thought was a "cheap buy," but the original price was much higher. And I had been oblivious to its value.

At times I have treated the power of Jesus' blood like a cheap buy. God's grace, though free to me, carried the highest price tag of all: the life of his own Son.

—Karen R. Morerod, "Lesson Learned from a Sweater," *Decision* (November 1999)

ILLUSTRATION 203

SYNCING THE FATHER

Topics: Incarnation; Jesus, One with the Father

Reference: John 14:7–11

There were a few occasions in Brazil when I served as a translator for an English speaker. He stood before the audience, complete with the message; I stood at his side, equipped with the language. My job was to convey his story to the listeners.

I did my best to allow his words to come through me. I was not at liberty to embellish or subtract. When the speaker gestured, I gestured. As his volume increased, so did mine. When he got quiet, I did too.

When he walked this earth, Jesus was "translating" God all the time. When God got louder, Jesus got louder. When God gestured, Jesus gestured. He was so in sync with the Father that he could declare, "I am in the Father and the Father is in me" (John 14:11 NRSV).

—Max Lucado, *Just Like Jesus* (Nelson, 2003)

ILLUSTRATION 204

TALKING TO FISH

Topics: Fear; Goodness of God; Incarnation

Reference: John 1:14–18

I learned about incarnation when I kept a saltwater aquarium. Management of a marine aquarium, I discovered, is no easy task. I had to run a portable chemical laboratory to monitor the nitrate levels and the ammonia content. I pumped in vitamins and antibiotics and sulfa drugs and enough enzymes to make a rock grow. I filtered the water through glass fibers and charcoal and exposed it to ultraviolet light.

You would think, in view of all the energy expended on their behalf, that my fish would at least be grateful. Not so. Every time my shadow loomed above the tank, they dove for cover into the nearest shell. They showed me one emotion only: fear.

Although I opened the lid and dropped in food on a regular schedule, three times a day, they responded to each visit as a sure sign of my designs to torture them. I could not convince them of my true concern. To my fish I was deity. I was too large for them, my actions too incomprehensible. My acts of mercy they saw as cruelty; my attempts at healing they viewed as destruction.

To change their perceptions, I began to see, would require a form of incarnation. I would have to become a fish and speak to them in a language they could understand.

—Philip Yancey,
The Jesus I Never Knew (Zondervan, 1995)

ILLUSTRATION 205

JESUS UNTAMED

Topics: Convictions; Cross; Knowing God; Truth; Untamed Christ

References: Matthew 23; Mark 11:12–18

As I studied the life of Christ, one impression about Jesus struck me more forcefully than any other. We have tamed him.

The Jesus I learned about as a child was sweet and inoffensive, the kind of person whose lap you'd want to climb on. Mister Rogers with a beard. Indeed, Jesus did have qualities of gentleness and compassion that attracted little children. Mister Rogers, however, he assuredly was not. Not even the Romans would have crucified Mister Rogers.

—Philip Yancey, from the video
The Jesus I Never Knew
(Zondervan, 1998)

ILLUSTRATION 206

OUR UNIQUE GRACE

Topics: Buddhism; Grace; Hinduism; Islam; Judaism; Mercy; New Age; Religions; Unconditional Love; Worldview

References: John 3:16; Romans 5:1–11; Ephesians 2:8–9

During a British conference on comparative religions, experts from around the world debated what, if any, belief was unique to the Christian faith. They began eliminating possibilities. Incarnation? Other religions had different versions of gods appearing in human form. Resurrection? Again, other religions had accounts of return from death.

The debate went on for some time until C. S. Lewis wandered into the room. "What's the rumpus about?" he asked, and heard in reply that his colleagues were discussing Christianity's unique contribution among world religions. Lewis responded, "Oh, that's easy. It's grace." After some discussion, the conferees had to agree.

The notion of God's love coming to us free of charge, no strings attached, seems to go against every instinct of humanity. The Buddhist eightfold path, the Hindu doctrine of Karma, the Jewish covenant, and the Muslim code of law—each offers a way to earn approval. Only Christianity dares to make God's love unconditional.

—Philip Yancey,
What's So Amazing about Grace?
(Zondervan, 1997)

ILLUSTRATION 207

HUMAN-SIZED GOD

Topics: Incarnation; Jesus Christ; Jesus, One with the Father

References: John 1:18; Colossians 1:15–20

A village had a statue so immense that you couldn't see exactly what it represented. Someone finally miniaturized the statue so one could see the person it honored.

"That is what God did in his Son," said the early church father Origen. Paul tells us Christ is the visible icon or image of the invisible God (Colossians 1). In Christ we have God in a comprehensible way. In Christ we have God's own personal and definitive visit to the planet.

—Dale Bruner,
"Is Jesus Inclusive or Exclusive?"
Theology, News & Notes (October 1999)

ILLUSTRATION 208

FREEWAY TO GOD

Topics: Depravity; Gospel; Jesus Christ; Salvation; Savior

References: Isaiah 59:1–2; Romans 3:9–26; Ephesians 2:1–10; Titus 3:3–7

Whenever I drive to the east side of Portland over the Marquam Bridge, I'm reminded of what it took for God to save us. On the upper deck of that two-decker freeway spanning the wide Willamette River, you can catch a glimpse of an exit that drops off into empty space.

When the Marquam Bridge was built in the mid-1960s, it was designed to accommodate an east-running freeway still on the drawing boards, known as the Mount Hood Freeway. But the freeway was never built. Oregon voters opted for a light rail line instead, and plans for the highway were scrapped.

Even though there is no Mount Hood Freeway, you can certainly see Mount Hood from the top deck of the Marquam Bridge. On clear days it looms on the eastern horizon—a symmetrical, snow-capped beauty. And if you look carefully, you can see how the bridge was built to accommodate a freeway lane veering off to the southeast. It juts out just a bit from the bridge structure and then is cut off as though sliced by a giant knife.

The exit, permanently blocked, now goes nowhere—except into the waters of the Willamette far below. You can see Mount Hood in all its beauty, but you could never reach the high slopes of that mighty peak via the Mount Hood Freeway, because the freeway doesn't exist.

Likewise, we might understand there is a God. We might recognize his power and glory, his majesty and goodness, and desire with all our hearts to know him and be with him. But the distance is too great. The gulf is too wide.

Only through Jesus Christ can we cross that gulf to God the Father. And that freeway *does* exist.

—Ron Mehl,
Love Found a Way (WaterBrook, 1999)

ILLUSTRATION 209
A BENIGN JESUS

Topics: Buddhism; Cross; Hinduism; Islam; Jesus Christ; Judaism; Religions

References: John 14:6; 1 Corinthians 1:18–25

The cross is what separates the Christ of Christianity from every other Jesus. In Judaism there is no precedent for a Messiah who dies, much less as a criminal, as Jesus did. In Islam the story of Jesus' death is rejected as an affront to Allah himself. Hindus can accept only a Jesus who passes into peaceful *samadhi*, a yogi who escapes the degradation of death.

There is, in short, no room in other religions for a Christ who experiences the full burden of mortal existence—and hence there is no reason to believe in him as the divine Son whom the Father resurrects from the dead.

That the image of a benign Jesus has universal appeal should come as no surprise. That most of the world cannot accept the Jesus of the cross should not surprise us either. Thus the idea that Jesus can serve as a bridge uniting the world's religions is inviting but may be ultimately impossible.

—Kenneth L. Woodward,
"The Other Jesus,"
Newsweek (March 27, 2000)

ILLUSTRATION 210

SEEING GOD IN PEOPLE

Topics: God; Holy Spirit

Reference: 1 Corinthians 3:16–17

I stood at our window one Saturday afternoon and looked west. The sun was low, shining along the surface of the deep snow. A strong wind blew over the icy crust and carried snow particles along in its eddies. It made the wind visible in a curiously beautiful way, like a fast-moving river of light, with the snow dust catching and holding the glints from the sun. I think the Spirit of God is made visible in the individuals in our life stream. God shines on them and shows us in their lives the way the wind is blowing.

—Luci Shaw,
God in the Dark (Zondervan, 1989)

ILLUSTRATION 211

GREAT CAMERA

Topics: Praise; Thanksgiving; Worship

Reference: Romans 1:19–23

My wife and I recently went on vacation and took along a camera and several rolls of film. Upon our return, my wife began proudly showing off our latest set of vacation photos; she'd then tell me her coworkers' reactions. After a few days of this, I noticed a recurring theme. Invariably, people would say, "Wow, your husband must have a really nice camera!"

Even though people liked my photos, I was disappointed. I wanted them to acknowledge what a good photographer I am, not what a good camera I have.

I ranted to my wife: "Why do people do this? Nobody looks at a painting and says, 'Nice brushes!' Nobody looks at a skyscraper and says, 'Nice drafting table!' Nobody looks at a sculpture and says, 'Nice chisel!' What's wrong with these people?"

It felt good to get that off my chest. Until my wife reminded me, "So, how often do you look at creation and say, 'Nice work, God'?"

—Rich Tatum, Muskegon, Michigan

PART 10: GOOD AND EVIL

ILLUSTRATION 212

DYNAMITE AND THE PEACE PRIZE

Topics: Conviction of Sin; Death; Life; Mortality; Motivation; Perspective; Purpose; Repentance; Riches; Satisfaction; Shame; Spiritual Direction

References: Ecclesiastes 8:8; Matthew 16:26; Mark 8:36; Luke 9:25; Ephesians 5:15–16; 2 Peter 3:11–12

In 1867, Swedish chemist Alfred Nobel awoke one morning to read his own obituary in the local paper: "Alfred Nobel, the inventor of dynamite, who died yesterday, devised a way for more people to be killed in a war than ever before. He died a very rich man."

Actually, it was Alfred's older brother who had died. A newspaper reporter had made a mistake. But the account had a profound effect on Alfred. He decided he wanted to be known for something other than developing a means to kill people efficiently and amassing a fortune in the process.

So Nobel initiated the Nobel Prize—an award for scientists and writers who foster peace. "Every man ought to have the chance to correct his epitaph in midstream and write a new one," Nobel said.

—Doug Murren and Barb Sharin, *Is It Real When It Doesn't Work?* (Nelson, 1990)

ILLUSTRATION 213

GOOD AND EVIL AT THE WORLD'S FAIR

Topics: Depravity; Evil; Fall of Humanity; Free Will; Human Condition; Human Nature; Human Will; Power; Sinful Nature; Violence

References: Matthew 12:35; Luke 6:45; Romans 8:5–11

Set against Chicago World's Fair in 1893, Erik Larson's bestselling book *The Devil in the White City* tells the true story of two men, each serving as an extreme example of the good and evil in humans.

Daniel Burnham, one of the greatest architects of his day, was the driving force behind the Chicago World's Fair, transforming it into a phenomenon that forever changed his country. In less than two years, Burnham supervised the construction of more than two hundred buildings along the coast of Lake Michigan.

The largest exhibition, called the Manufactures and Liberal Arts Building, had enough interior volume to have housed the U.S. Capitol, the Great Pyramid, Winchester Cathedral, Madison Square Garden, and St. Paul's Cathedral, all at the same time.

The fair attracted more than 27.5 million visitors at a time when the nation's total population was 65 million.

Dr. H. H. Holmes also achieved notoriety during this era, but not for creating beauty. The year before the fair, Holmes constructed a block-long, three-story building that included a sound-proof vault, several gas chambers, and a specially crafted furnace designed to eliminate odors. Holmes called it "The World's Fair Hotel." In it he murdered at least twenty-seven men, women, and children. At least that's what he confessed to. Investigators believed the number was much higher, since fifty young women alone were traced to Holmes's hotel and were never seen or heard from again.

Burnham was quoted as saying, "Make no little plans; they have no magic to stir men's blood." Holmes, by contrast, stated, "I was born with the devil in me. I could not help the fact that I was a murderer, no more than the poet can help the inspiration to sing."

The Devil in the White City symbolizes the present condition of humanity. Even when we achieve our highest dreams and potential, there is evil afoot.

—Story told in Erik Larson,
The Devil in the White City
(Vintage, 2003)

ILLUSTRATION 214

WORDS TO TREASURE

Topics: Affirmation; Encouragement; Heart; Teachers

References: Romans 12:6–8; Colossians 4:8; 1 Thessalonians 5:11

"In an earlier grade, I'd taped Mark's mouth shut for talking too much in class. Now he was one of my students in junior high math," wrote Sister Helen Mrosia.

One Friday, in a break from work, the teacher asked her students to write the nicest thing they could about each other and hand it in. She compiled the results for each student and, on Monday, gave out the lists.

Several years later, Mark was killed in Vietnam. After the funeral, many classmates gathered with Mark's parents and Sister Mrosia for lunch. Mark's father took a wallet out of his pocket. "They found this on Mark when he was killed," he said. He carefully removed a folded, refolded, and taped paper—on which the teacher had listed the good things Mark's classmates had said about him.

Other students responded. Charlie smiled sheepishly and said, "I keep my list in my desk drawer."

Chuck's wife said, "Chuck put his in our wedding album."

"I have mine, too, in my diary," Marilyn said.

Vicky reached into her pocketbook and brought out her frazzled list.

—John Trent, *Choosing to Live the Blessing*
(WaterBrook, 1997)

ILLUSTRATION 215

ENCHANTING BUT DEADLY

Topics: Appearances; Beauty; Materialism; New Age; Occult; Spiritual Perception; Temptation; Worldliness

References: James 4:4; 2 Peter 1:3–4; 1 John 2:15–17

For years, workers and visitors flocked to the sight of silvery dust flakes that floated to the floor in a mill where steel strips rolled over pads in a tall cooling tower. In his book *The Heat: Steelworkers' Lives and Legends*, steelworker Joe Gutierrez tells how beautifully "the snow danced in August."

Then people discovered the dust was asbestos. "Everybody breathed it," wrote Gutierrez. He now suffers from the slow, choking grip of asbestosis, as do many plant workers.

"Who am I? I'm everybody. Can't walk too far now. I get tired real fast, and it hurts when I breathe sometimes. And to think we used to fight over that job," he says.

How many things in our culture resemble the silver flakes in that steel mill? They're enchanting but deadly.

—Lee Eclov, "Deceptive Appeal,"
PreachingToday.com

ILLUSTRATION 216

LEGALIZING MARIJUANA

Topics: Addiction; Bondage; Desires; Drugs

References: Romans 6:16; 8:5; 1 Peter 1:13–16; 2 Peter 2:19

Support for legalizing marijuana is at its highest level in more than thirty years, according to a *USA Today*/CNN/Gallup poll.

The poll found that 34 percent of American adults favor legalizing marijuana use while 62 percent oppose it. That's the most support for legalization since pollsters began asking the question in 1969.

Percentage of adults who say marijuana use should be legal:

1969 = 12	1980 = 25
1972 = 15	1985 = 23
1973 = 16	1995 = 25
1977 = 28	2000 = 31
1979 = 25	2001 = 34

—Dennis Cauchon, "Marijuana Attains Record Support," *USA Today* (August 24, 2001)

ILLUSTRATION 217

GUILT CHECK

Topics: Confession; Conscience; Guilt; Honesty; Integrity; Repentance; Restitution; Stealing

References: Exodus 20:15; Matthew 6:24; Ephesians 4:28

A shoplifter wrote to a department store, saying, "I've just become a Christian, and I can't sleep at night because I feel guilty. So here's $100 that I owe you."

He signed his name then added a little PS: "If I still can't sleep, I'll send you the rest."

—Bill White, Paramount, California

ILLUSTRATION 218

JAILED FOR A CAUSE

Topics: Christian Life; Compromise; Convictions; Courage; Evil; Sacrifice

References: 2 Timothy 1:8; 3:12

Martin Niemoeller, a World War I hero in Germany as a U-boat captain, was later imprisoned for eight years by Hitler on charges of treason. From 1937 to 1945, he spent time in prisons and concentration camps, including Dachau.

Still, Hitler realized much opposition would collapse if the influential Niemoeller, a leading figure in the German church, could be persuaded to join his cause, so he sent a former friend of Niemoeller.

Seeing Niemoeller in his cell, the onetime friend said, "Martin, Martin! Why are you here?"

The response? "My friend! Why are you *not* here?"

—Amos S. Cresswell,
I've Told You Twice (Vigo, 1995)

ILLUSTRATION 219

LIES FOR SALE

Topics: Adultery; Marriage; Sex; Sin; Temptation

References: Exodus 20:14; Romans 1:21–32; Hebrews 13:4

A publisher's review of a recent book describes it as "a thoughtful, detailed discussion of every aspect of considering, preparing for, beginning, and conducting a successful and emotionally fulfilling extramarital affair." The name of the book is *Affair! How to Manage Every Aspect of Your Extramarital Relationship with Passion, Discretion, and Dignity* by Cameron Barnes (UPublish.com, 1999).

For just $19.95, plus shipping and handling, you can get a practical summary of the lies the devil would have you believe concerning adultery.

—Bill White, Paramount, California

ILLUSTRATION 220

RECOGNIZING SATAN

Topics: Devil; Discernment; Evil; Satan; Truth

References: Genesis 3:1–7; John 8:44; 2 Corinthians 2:11; 11:14–15; Ephesians 6:10–18; 1 Peter 5:8

In a *Twilight Zone* episode from 1960, an American on a walking trip through Central Europe gets caught in a raging storm. Staggering through the blinding rain, he sees an imposing medieval castle, which is a hermitage for a brotherhood of monks. The reclusive monks reluctantly take him in.

Later that night, the American discovers a cell with a man locked inside. An ancient wooden staff bolts the door. The prisoner claims he is being held captive by the "insane" head monk, Brother Jerome. He pleads for the American to release him.

The prisoner's kind face and gentle voice win over the American. The American confronts Brother Jerome, who declares that the prisoner is Satan, "the father of lies," held captive by the Staff of Truth, the one barrier he cannot pass.

That convinces the American that Jerome is indeed mad. As soon as he gets the chance, he releases the prisoner — who immediately transforms into a hideous horned demon and vanishes in a puff of smoke.

The stunned American is horrified by what he has done. Jerome responds sympathetically. "I'm sorry for you, my son. All your life you will remember this night and whom you have turned loose upon the world."

"I didn't believe you," the American replies. "I saw him and didn't recognize him," to which Jerome responds: "That is man's weakness and Satan's strength."

— Kevin Stump, "Is the Devil Dead?"
The Plain Truth (March – April 2001)

ILLUSTRATION 221

SPREADING HONEY MUSHROOM

Topics: Human Condition; Human Nature; Original Sin; Sin

References: Romans 5:12 – 21; 1 Corinthians 15:19 – 26

In Oregon's Malheur National Forest, a fungus has spread through tree roots across twenty-two hundred acres, making it the largest living organism ever found. The Armillaria Ostoyae, also called "honey mushroom," started from a single microscopic spore. Yet it has been weaving its black shoestring filaments through the forest for an estimated twenty-four hundred years, killing trees as it grows.

"When you're on the ground, you don't notice the pattern. You just see dead trees in clusters," says Tina Dreisbach, a botanist and mycologist [botanist of fungi] with the United States Forest Service's Pacific Northwest Research Station in Corvallis, Oregon.

In the roots of an affected tree, researchers find something that looks like white latex paint. These are mats of mycelium, which draw water and carbohydrates from the tree to feed the fungus and interfere with the tree's absorption of nutrients. The shoestring filaments, called rhizomorphs, stretch as much as ten feet into the soil, invading tree roots through a combination of pressure and enzyme action.

Like the honey mushroom, sin began in a single act of disobedience but has spread across the entire human race.

— Gary Stewart, "How Sin Has Spread,"
PreachingToday.com

ILLUSTRATION 222

BLAMING GOD FOR EVIL

Topics: Blame; Free Will; Invitation; Salvation; Sin; Suffering

References: Isaiah 55:1–3; Matthew 23:37–39; Romans 2:4–5; 1 Timothy 2:1–6; James 1:13–15; 2 Peter 3:9; Revelation 22:17

A preacher and a barber were walking through city slums. "If God was as kind as you say, he wouldn't permit all this poverty, disease and squalor," the barber said. "He wouldn't allow these poor street people to get addicted. I cannot believe in a God who permits these things."

The minister was silent until they met a man whose hair was hanging down his neck and had a half inch of stubble on his face.

"You can't be a good barber, or you wouldn't permit a man like this to continue living here without a haircut and a shave," the preacher said.

Indignant, the barber answered, "Why blame me for that man's condition? He has never come to my shop. If he had, I could've fixed him up and made him look like a gentleman!"

"Then don't blame God for allowing people to continue in their evil ways," the preacher said. "He invites them to come and be saved."

—Brett Kays, Brownstown, Michigan

ILLUSTRATION 223

UNFORMED CONSCIENCES

Topics: Conscience; Crime; Parenting; Prisons; Youth

References: Romans 2:12–16; 3:9–26; 1 Timothy 4:1–3; Titus 1:15

More than ever before in American history—indeed in Western history—we are witnessing the near-death of conscience.

An incident in Indiana a few years ago brought this home to me. I had visited the prison several times before, but that day a young inmate responded to my proffered handshake by smacking my hand away. In many years of visiting prisons, I had never before encountered such direct and immediate hostility from a complete stranger. For obvious reasons, prisoners are rarely cheerful, but I saw in those eyes that day a chilling hardness I had never encountered before. Since then, however, I have seen a similar hardness reflected in the eyes of countless other inmates, particularly younger ones.

I asked the assistant warden, a Christian, what was happening. "This place has greatly changed," he said. "Ten years ago I could talk to these kids about right and wrong. Now they don't even know what I'm talking about." He said older prisoners were demanding protection from the newly arrived nineteen- or twenty-year-olds, an ominous reversal. Historically, younger guys needed protection from the older cons.

The horrifying truth is that we have bred a generation with unformed consciences.

—Charles Colson,
Wheaton College Magazine (Summer 2000)

ILLUSTRATION 224

WILDFIRE OF WORDS

Topics: Apology; Conflict; Negligence; Reconciliation; Relationships; Self-control; Tongue; Unity; Words

References: Proverbs 16:27; James 3:1 – 12

More than a thousand firefighters battled a wildfire for two weeks in the Black Hills of South Dakota. The fire started August 24, 2000, and was not contained until September 8. Meanwhile, more than eighty thousand acres of valuable timber burned.

Janice Stevenson, forty-six, was arrested on suspicion of starting the fire. She pled guilty to second-degree arson, was sentenced to twenty-five years in the South Dakota State Penitentiary, and ordered to pay restitution in the amount of $42,204,155.48.

Federal investigators who filed charges against Stevenson say she admits stopping by a road on August 24, lighting a cigarette, and tossing the still-burning match on the ground. "Rather than putting out the fire," an affidavit said, "she looked at it and decided to leave the area."

Like starting a forest fire, producing a "wildfire" with our tongues requires little effort. Rumors, half-truths, grumblings, sarcastic remarks, hurtful things said in the heat of anger—all of these smoldering matches have the potential for burning down acres of office morale, family peace, and church unity.

> — "Wyoming Woman Accused of Starting South Dakota Wildfire," CNN.com (September 30, 2000); 2001 Annual Report of the Attorney General to the Governor of South Dakota, www.state.sd.us

ILLUSTRATION 225

DUMBFOUNDED BY EVIL

Topics: Evil; Hatred; Human Condition; Human Nature; Inexplicability of Evil; Sin; Violence

References: Romans 1:18 – 32; 3:9 – 20

Former United Nations leader Kofi Annan traveled the world visiting areas of some of the worst violence and cruelty in human history. He often wonders about man's cruelty to man. "I'm still struggling with evil," he says. "I still don't understand how there can be so much evil.... You look at the impact; you see young people who have no hope."

Annan is most puzzled when he comes face-to-face with evil. Recounting his meetings with former Serbian leader and indicted war criminal Slobodan Milosevic, Annan says, "Milosevic will talk about the days when he was a banker here in New York City. He speaks English, sounds like a rational, reasonable person, and yet he is capable of all sorts of acts. How do they do it? How does someone behave like such a normal human being and suddenly turn so evil?"

> — Joshua Cooper Ramo, "The Five Virtues of Kofi Annan," *Time* (April 9, 2000)

ILLUSTRATION 226

JUST THE WAY IT IS

Topics: Children; Holiness; Human Condition; Lostness; Sin; Sinful Nature

References: Isaiah 53:6; Romans 3:10–23

I was sitting at my desk in my study after having scolded my daughter, four, for misbehaving. I heard a gentle knock on the door. "Come in," I said.

Bethany matter-of-factly said, "Daddy, sometimes I am good, and sometimes I am bad. And that is just the way it is." Then she left the room, acting as though she had completely explained her misbehavior for all time.

I later commented to her that she had described the problem we all face. We all do bad things, and the Bible says even the good things we do are not good enough to meet God's standard of holiness. That is why we need a Savior.

—Tony Smith, Gainesville, Georgia

ILLUSTRATION 227

POPULARIZING THE OCCULT

Topics: Entertainment; Influence; Occult; Satan; Television; Witchcraft

References: 1 Timothy 4:1; 2 Timothy 2:24–26

Great Britain's Pagan Federation, which represents druids and witches, says the TV shows *Buffy the Vampire Slayer* and *Sabrina the Teenage Witch* have fueled a rapidly growing interest in witchcraft among children. The organization averages one hundred inquiries a month from kids who want to become witches. In Septem-

ber, the federation appointed its first-ever youth officer to counsel young people.

A spokesman for the federation said his group is filling a spiritual need, picking up the baton dropped by the Christian church.

—Tracy Dawn, *Plugged In* (October 2000)

ILLUSTRATION 228

THE POISON IN EVERYDAY THINGS

Topics: Consumerism; Distractions; God's Love; Materialism; Passion

References: Mark 4:19; Luke 8:14; 14:18–20; 1 Timothy 4:4–5

The greatest enemy of hunger for God is not poison but apple pie. It is not the banquet of the wicked that dulls our appetite for heaven, but endless nibbling at the table of the world. It is not the X-rated video, but the prime-time dribble of triviality we drink in every night. For all the ill that Satan can do, when God describes what keeps us from the banquet table of his love, it is a piece of land, a yoke of oxen, and a wife (Luke 14:18–20). The greatest adversary of love to God is not his enemies but his gifts. And the deadliest appetites are not for the poison of evil, but for the simple pleasures of earth. For when these replace an appetite for God himself, the idolatry is scarcely recognizable and almost incurable.

Jesus said some people hear the word of God, and a desire for God is awakened in their hearts. But then "as they go on their way they are choked with worries and riches and pleasures of this life" (Luke 8:14 NASB). In another place he said, "The desires for other things enter in and choke the word, and it becomes unfruitful" (Mark 4:19 NASB). "The pleasures of this life" and "the desires for other things" are not evil in themselves. These are not vices. These are gifts of God. They are your basic meat and potatoes and coffee and gardening and reading and decorating and traveling and investing and TV-watching and Internet-surfing and shopping and exercising and collecting and talking.

And all of them can become deadly substitutes for God.

—John Piper,
A Hunger for God (Crossway, 1997)

ILLUSTRATION 229

DRIFTING FROM HOLINESS

Topics: Compromise; Holiness; Self-control; Spiritual Disciplines; Tolerance

Reference: 1 Thessalonians 5:1–10

People do not drift toward holiness. Apart from grace-driven effort, people do not gravitate toward godliness, prayer, obedience to Scripture, faith, and delight in the Lord. We drift toward compromise and call it tolerance; we drift toward disobedience and call it freedom; we drift toward superstition and call it faith. We cherish the indiscipline of lost self-control and call it relaxation; we slouch toward prayerlessness and delude ourselves into thinking we have escaped legalism; we

slide toward godlessness and convince ourselves we have been liberated.

—D. A. Carson,
For the Love of God (Crossway, 1999)

ILLUSTRATION 230

RENOUNCING CHRISTIANITY

Topics: Hardship; Oppression; Persecution; Suffering

Reference: 2 Corinthians 6:3–10

If you become an evangelical Christian in Laos, the communist neighbor of Vietnam and Cambodia, you likely will be "asked" to fill out and sign a form, which says, in part:

> I, [name], who live in [location], believe in a foreign religion, which the imperialists have used for their own benefit to divide the united front and to build power for themselves against the local authorities. Now I and my family clearly see the intentions of the enemy and regret the deeds which we have committed. We have clearly seen the goodness of the Party and the Government. Therefore, I and my family voluntarily and unequivocally resign from believing in this foreign religion.

If you sign the form, you promise not to participate in Christianity under punishment of law. If you don't sign, you can expect humiliation, harassment, and persecution, including probable imprisonment and torture.

The document's widespread use by Laotian officials has been authenticated by the World Evangelical Fellowship's Religious Liberty Commission and other sources. Hundreds of rural Christians reportedly have been forced to sign the form in public, then compelled to participate in animistic sacrifices.

— "Drive to Stamp Out Christianity in Laos Having Opposite Effect," *Baptist Press* (October 9, 2000)

ILLUSTRATION 231

LYING LAWYERS

Topics: Dishonesty; Lying; Truthfulness

References: Exodus 20:16; Ephesians 4:14–15

Lawyers are increasingly bending the truth, not telling the whole truth, or just plain lying. So said more than fifty state and federal judges, lawyers, and academics surveyed by the *ABA Journal*.

"On the basis of my academic and professional experience, I believe that no felony is committed more frequently in this country than crimes of perjury and false statements," says Alan Dershowitz, then professor at Harvard Law School.

— Joe M. Sprinkle, "A Call to Honesty," *Decision* (October 2000)

ILLUSTRATION 232

FEAR IN THE NIGHT

Topics: Fear; Prayer; Protection; Spiritual Perception; Trust

Reference: 2 Timothy 4:17–18

When Focus on the Family was in its early stages and our children were young, my husband, Jim, traveled often. I had grown accustomed to his absences and was never really frightened while he was away. Except once.

One night about 2:00 a.m., I awoke with a start. I was afraid and didn't know why. For a few minutes (it seemed like hours!), I lay in bed worrying. Finally, I forced myself out of bed and sank to my knees.

"Lord, I don't know why I'm so frightened," I prayed. "I ask you to watch over our home and to protect our family. Send your guardian angel to be with us." I climbed back into bed, and in about half an hour I was back asleep.

The next morning our babysitter, who lived across the street, came running over. "Mrs. Dobson, did you hear what happened? A burglar robbed your next-door neighbor's house last night!"

It was true. A thief had broken in, entered the couple's bedroom while they slept, and snatched the husband's wallet from a dresser. The burglar escaped with the family's vacation money, about $500. The police determined the time of the robbery: about 2:00 a.m. My mind reeled at the thought. "If a burglar wanted to break into our house," I said, "he would probably try to get in through the bathroom window near our children's bedrooms. There's a hedge, and he'd be shielded from view. Let's go look."

When we looked at the window on the other side of the house, we saw that the screen was bent and the sill splintered. Someone had indeed tried to break in!

I am convinced that God protected us that night. I was surprised, but I should not have been. For years, Jim and I had prayed and fasted, trusting God to protect our family. We knew God powerfully works through prayer. On that dark early morning, my trust was tested in a frantic moment, and God proved faithful.

I can't explain why God allows difficulties to come into our lives even though we are praying. But I know that in all circumstances, as the psalmist tells us, God is an ever-present help in trouble.

—Shirley Dobson, *Certain Peace in Uncertain Times* (Multnomah, 2002)

ILLUSTRATION 233

KILLER'S REMORSE

Topics: Despair; Fear; Worry

Reference: Matthew 11:28–30

"I have been dying since October. I wake up at night so afraid, so terrified, that I couldn't be that afraid while awake. It has taken its toll. I have come to hate this life and this system of things. I have come to have no hope."

So said Mark Orrin Barton, just before dawn on July 19, 1999, after killing his estranged wife and two children and gunning down nine workers at an investment firm in Atlanta.

—Adam Cohen, "A Portrait of the Killer," *Time* (August 9, 1999)

ILLUSTRATION 234

ORDERED TO KILL

Topics: Denial; Evil; Feelings; Guidance; Hearing God; Murder; Satan; Temptation

References: Exodus 20:13; John 8:42–47; 2 Corinthians 11:14–15

In 1992, Wayne Lo, a sophomore at Simon's Rock College in Massachusetts, killed two people and injured four others with a semiautomatic rifle. During the first years of his imprisonment, he said God had chosen him to commit carnage. Now he calls that a period of denial.

"At the time I thought I did the right thing," he said recently. "But as I look back, it doesn't make sense to me. I ask myself, why? Why did I do it?"

In December 1992, Lo said God told him to go to the gun store, order a weapon and ammunition with his mother's credit card, and then shoot people. He raged at his lawyers during his trial because they insisted that he was insane. He argued that his lawyers should have investigated his victims to uncover why a heavenly power had selected them to be shot.

After Lo realized God would not have chosen him to inflict so much pain, he struggled to understand what made him a killer. He remains convinced that it was something outside of himself. Perhaps it was a supernatural or satanic force. Either way, he appears not to be taking personal responsibility for the killing.

—William Glaberson, "Man and His Son's Slayer Unite to Ask Why," *The New York Times* (April 12, 2000)

ble. But I saw the interruption as a subtle demonic hindrance to distract this would-be believer from the gospel message. Not every negative event has a demonic source. But some do.

—Joseph Winger, "Our Call to Arms," *Discipleship Journal* (May–June 2006)

ILLUSTRATION 235

DEMONIC HORN

Topics: Bondage; Demons; Evil; Hindrances; Oppression; Satan; Spiritual Warfare; Supernatural Occurrences

References: Matthew 8:28–34; Mark 5:1–20; Luke 8:26–39; Ephesians 6:10–18; James 4:7; 1 Peter 5:8–9; 1 John 4:1–3

I was part of a church visitation team that had just spent twenty minutes explaining the gospel to a tenderhearted woman. When I asked her, "Are you ready to receive Christ as your Lord?" she responded, "Yes, I am!"

I said, "Then simply pray after me, 'Father, I thank you for sending your Son.'" She started repeating, "Father, I thank … "—but before she could finish, her car, parked nearby, started honking. The noise of the horn was so deafening that the woman couldn't hear my prayer.

We went to her car to investigate. We opened the hood, beat on the horn, and finally shut it off. Only then was I able to resume praying with this woman, but it was a struggle for her to focus again.

Many Christians would conclude that a mechanical failure had set off the horn. It's possi-

ILLUSTRATION 236

BELTWAY SNIPER'S NEXT TARGET

Topics: Children; Depravity; Evil; Parenting; Teens; Terrorism; Threats

References: Exodus 11:4–8; Matthew 18:6; Mark 9:42; Luke 17:2; 19:43–44

The "Beltway Sniper," John Allen Muhammad, was convicted in May 2006 in Maryland for murdering six people. He had already been sentenced to death in Virginia for murders committed there. However, during the trial, some frightening information was revealed about what Muhammad would have done if he had evaded capture.

According to Lee Boyd Malvo, Muhammad's accomplice in the sniper attacks, Muhammad planned to bomb schools and children's hospitals after the sniper phase of his plan was completed. When Malvo asked why, Muhammad said, "For the sheer terror of it, the worst thing you can do to people is aim at their children."

—"Quotables & 'Toons," *World* (June 10, 2006)

ILLUSTRATION 237

STEALING BACK TO JAIL

Topics: Addiction; Bondage; Depravity; Emptiness; Foolishness; Freedom; Powerlessness; Rebellion; Will

References: John 8:31–36; Romans 6:5–7, 16–18, 21–23; 2 Corinthians 3:17; Galatians 5:1, 13; James 1:25; 1 Peter 2:16

A man who robbed a bank ten years ago and was sentenced to seventy months in a federal penitentiary decided he liked prison life so much that he committed another crime so he could return. Danny Villegas walked inside a Federal Credit Union in Florida and told the teller he was robbing her, adding, "You might as well call the police right now."

Villegas then sat down on a couch in the lobby and waited for police to arrive. "He said he wanted to rob a federal bank because he wanted to go back to a federal penitentiary," said Lieutenant Ron Wright of the South Daytona Police Department. Villegas had worked in construction in Texas for five years but had grown tired of the work.

—Associated Press, "Police Say Man Staged Florida Robbery to Go Back to Prison," *Houston Chronicle* (January 9, 2007)

ILLUSTRATION 238

THE MONSTER INSIDE

Topics: Abuse; Anger; Cruelty; Depravity; Evil; Human Condition; Human Nature; Sin; Temper; Temptation; Violence

References: Ecclesiastes 9:3; Matthew 15:19; Mark 7:21; 14:38; Romans 7:14–21; Galatians 5:19–21

Journalist Hunter Thompson, longtime contributor to *Rolling Stone* magazine and author of *Fear and Loathing in Las Vegas*, committed suicide in 2005 at age sixty-seven. His addiction to drugs and alcohol and his abusive actions toward others were no secret. After his death, his first wife, Sandy Conklin-Thompson, wrote:

> He was, on the one hand, extremely loving and tender, brilliant and exciting, generous and kind. On the other end of the spectrum—he was full spectrum—he was extremely cruel....
>
> I will never forget something Hunter once said to me. In one of his tender moments, I asked him if he knew when he was about to become the Monster. He said, "Sandy, it's like this. I sense it first, and before I have completely turned around he is there. He is me."

—Sondi Wright, "He Was Full Spectrum," *Rolling Stone* (March 2005)

ILLUSTRATION 239

DREAM SENSE

Topics: Discernment; Fear; God as Father; God's Love; Hearing God; Spiritual Perception; Uncertainties; Visions and Dreams

References: Psalm 4:8; Matthew 7:7–11; Luke 11:11–13; James 1:16–18

One night in a dream, my wife saw the mangled body of one of our children. She tried to help, but nothing worked. She was helpless, desperate, and terrified. After waking, she agonized about her dream. She called me at the office and asked, "Roc, do you think this is God telling us to prepare for the death of our child?"

I listened and reasoned a bit. After all, the Bible gives examples of God telling people they are going to die. Then I thought about the nature of the dream (gruesome carnage and helpless despair) and the impact of the dream (fear and grief). I told Bev I was confident that this was not God speaking. It's not like him to frighten us for no reason. This sounded more like a message from her heart, which wrestled regularly with fears of losing a child, or a message from Satan, who is well known for lies and terror. Years have passed, and none of our children have died in a gruesome manner.

A similar "message," on the other hand, had a very different feel. While on vacation, my daughter Bethany was speeding down a California freeway with three teenage friends. One of them, Jody, said she had dreamed the night before that they were in a serious wreck and that she, the only one with a fastened seat belt on, had survived. Hearing that, everyone fastened their seat belts.

Later, their car swerved into the grass median and rolled. The investigating officer looked at the car and said, "If you hadn't had your seat belts on, the outcome would have been a lot different."

Where did Jody's dream come from? Consider the message: a warning of a danger that turned out to be very real. Consider the tone: an urging to do something that was right and reasonable, something that traveling teens often neglect. Consider the effect: saved lives. Who speaks in this way? A loving Father.

—Roc Bottomly, "May I Have a Word with You?" *Discipleship Journal* (November–December 2005)

ILLUSTRATION 240

ANGER ON A RAMPAGE

Topics: Anger; Enemies; Fighting; Grudges; Jealousy; Revenge; Self-control; Temper; Violence

References: Genesis 37:3–4; 1 Samuel 18; Proverbs 14:30; Romans 13:13; Galatians 5:26; 1 Peter 2:1

A guard dog ransacked a teddy bear museum in western England in the summer of 2006. Barney, a Doberman pinscher, went berserk, shredding about a hundred of the bears on display. Worst of all, Barney destroyed Mabel, Elvis Presley's teddy bear.

Mabel belonged to an English aristocrat, Benjamin Slade, who lived close to the museum. He had reportedly paid $75,000 for the bear at a Memphis auction, then loaned it to Wookey Hall Caves, the teddy bear museum. The museum's general manager, Daniel Medley, said, "I had a very embarrassing phone call with the owner. He's not very happy at all."

Barney's handler, Greg West, speculated that the dog went crazy because of a "rogue scent." Or it could have been pure jealousy. "I was stroking Mabel and saying what a nice little bear she was," West said.

West spent several minutes chasing Barney before he could wrestle him to the ground and end the carnage. Photos of the dog after he had been quieted show him sitting on his haunches and looking contrite. No dogs are allowed now at Wookey Hall Caves.

What are the triggers that send us into a rampage? What releases our anger and desire for revenge? Is it jealousy over the strokes that someone else got? More important, whom do we damage when we lose control? More than likely, it's something more valuable than a teddy bear.

—Lee Eclov, "Jealous Guard Dog Destroys Valuable Teddy Bears," PreachingToday.com; source: Alan Cowell, "Doberman on Guard Duty Whacks 100 Teddy Bears," *The New York Times* (August 3, 2006)

ILLUSTRATION 241
FUELING SEX ADDICTION

Topics: Addiction; Intimacy; Loneliness; Lust; Needs; Perversion; Self-control; Self-denial; Self-image; Sex; Sexual Immorality

References: Romans 13:13–14; 1 Corinthians 6:12–20; 1 Thessalonians 4:3–8

Sex is one of God's good gifts for a man and a woman to enjoy within the bounds of marriage. We have a tendency, however, to satisfy our deep longings for intimacy in unhealthy or even addictive ways, which usually results in brokenness and pain.

In February 2006 on her TV show, Oprah Winfrey interviewed people with sex addictions, such as Amy, who said:

It's not about sex with me. It's about the intimacy, or being close to someone, or feeling needed. Even though I'm totally out of control, I still feel that I am in control for that moment. I'm trying to think [of the] men that I've slept with, and I honestly can't remember—just 70 to 75, probably somewhere around there.

I'm tired of being alone. I don't want to be this way. I want to feel good enough within myself to not feel like I need to do this. I want to change. I want things to be better.

—"Oprah's Sex Talk," drudgereport.com (February 25, 2006)

ILLUSTRATION 242

CRIME IN THE UNITED STATES

Topics: Crime; Evil; Humanity; Lawlessness

References: Deuteronomy 8:19–20; Proverbs 1:10–19; Romans 1:21–32

According to the FBI Uniform Crime Report, these crimes occurred at the following rate in the United States in the year 2000:

- theft: every 4.5 seconds
- burglary: every 15.4 seconds
- motor vehicle theft: every 27.1 seconds
- aggravated assault: every 34.6 seconds
- robbery: every 1.3 minutes
- rape: every 5.8 minutes
- murder: every 33.9 minutes

— *USA Today* "Snapshots"
(December 11, 2001)

ILLUSTRATION 243

SEX AND GUILT

Topics: Behavior; Guilt; Sex; Shame; Uncleanness

References: Genesis 1:27–31; 2:24; Matthew 19:5; Ephesians 5:31

In *Music through the Eyes of Faith*, Harold Best tells the true story of a young man who became heavily involved in a satanic cult that developed an elaborate liturgy focusing on the compositions of Johann Sebastian Bach. The young man later became a Christian and started going to church. Everything went well until the church organist played a piece composed by Bach. The young believer was overcome by fear and fled the sanctuary.

Bach's work "represents some of the noblest music for Christian worship," Best writes. "To this young man, however, it ... epitomized all that was evil, horrible, and anti-Christian."

Sex is that way for some Christians. Past associations and guilty feelings about sexual behavior have created severe spiritual roadblocks. Christians try hard not to believe that sex is inherently evil, but because of previous experiences, it certainly feels evil.

— Gary Thomas,
"How Sex Points Us to God,"
Marriage Partnership (Winter 2005)

ILLUSTRATION 244

WHEN TYLER GOT HEALED

Topics: Faith; Healing; Miracles; Prayer; Supernatural Occurrences

References: Matthew 8:17; 1 Corinthians 12:6–10; James 5:13–16

Tyler Clarensau, fifteen, shuffled to the altar in Park Crest Assembly of God in Springfield, Missouri, to ask for healing. The surgery he'd had to correct his malformed knee joints had left him with swelling and terrible pain.

Forty Pentecostal teenagers formed a circle around Clarensau and began to pray. Gradually, the whole congregation joined in. Some forty-five minutes later, silence fell. Then one of the church volunteers announced that God had healed Clarensau. Clarensau shakily stood up, then did deep knee bends—something he hadn't accomplished in years.

Today Clarensau can walk—even run. "I'd heard about people getting healed," he says. "I thought it was pretty cool. But I didn't know for sure about such healing until it happened to me."

—Kenneth Woodward, "Should You Believe in Miracles?" *Newsweek* (May 1, 2000)

ILLUSTRATION 245

LOOK FOR JELLY BEANS

Topics: Discernment; Healing; Persistence; Spiritual Perception; Wisdom

Reference: Matthew 16:3

I was working as a nurse in a busy emergency room. We had a regular visitor, Billy, a cute two-year-old with freckles and tousled blond hair. For a year Billy had been in and out of the ER with what the doctors diagnosed as asthma.

The source of the illness was a mystery to the medical staff. Billy hadn't had asthma as an infant, there wasn't a family history of asthma, and there weren't obvious signs of allergies that would cause it. But the symptoms were asthmatic. Sometimes we treated Billy and sent him home; other times he would end up in the pediatrics ICU because his breathing was so labored.

This continued for about a year, and the staff grew fond of Billy. He came yet another day with breathing difficulties, and one of the medical interns decided, on a lark, to look up Billy's nose. He found a black jelly bean that Billy's brother had put there a year before. What came out with the jelly bean wasn't pretty.

We had treated Billy for the wrong condition for almost a year. In light of that circumstance, I put signs on the walls of the emergency room that said, "Look for jelly beans." When you're working in the ER, properly diagnosing a problem can be the difference between life and death.

—Nancy Ortberg, in the sermon
"Matters of the Heart," Willow Creek Church
Seeds Tape Ministry, South Barrington, Illinois

ILLUSTRATION 246

FINDING GOOD IN A TROUBLEMAKER

Topics: Affirmation; Children; Encouragement; Expectations; Parenting; Potential

Reference: Ephesians 6:4

He was always in trouble, so when the parents of the junior high boy received another call to meet with his teacher and the principal, they knew what was coming.

The teacher said, "Thanks for coming. I wanted you to hear what I have to say."

The father waited, thinking about what defense he could use this time. The teacher proceeded to go down a list of ten positive affirmations, or potential benefits, of the junior high "troublemaker." When she finished, the father said, "And what else? Let's hear the bad things."

"That's all I wanted to say," she said.

That night when the father got home, he repeated the conversation to his son. Almost overnight, the troublemaker's behavior changed.

All because a teacher looked past the negatives to see the potential in a young man.

—Peter Lord, former pastor, Park Avenue
Baptist Church, Titusville, Florida

ILLUSTRATION 247

NATHAN'S MIRACULOUS HEALING

Topics: Experiencing God; Healing; Miracles; Supernatural Occurrences

References: Matthew 8:17; James 5:13–16

In April 2000, my son Nathan was in a near-fatal car accident while trying to avoid a deer. When he arrived at the hospital, he had a broken leg, spinal cord damage, numerous lacerations, and a collapsed lung. To stabilize him, doctors put him into a drug-induced coma.

Nathan was in a coma for four days, but when the drugs were discontinued, he didn't come out of the coma. That night I prayed and read the Bible to Nathan, repeating the words Jesus said to Lazarus: "Come forth." I told him, "You've got to fight. You've got to wake up."

The next morning he came out of the coma. We were beside ourselves with joy.

But the spinal cord damage was a major concern. Nathan had a fracture in his neck, the same vertebra that actor Christopher Reeve had injured several years ago. The doctors gave Nathan a protective neck collar to prevent further separation of the vertebrae. He was in danger of full or partial paralysis.

For two weeks Nathan prayed earnestly for healing. One night as he was falling asleep, he heard and felt a popping in his neck. The next morning physicians performed three sets of X-rays to see if the vertebrae were continuing to separate. Instead, the tests showed that the vertebrae had fused back together. The doctors were stunned; there was no medical explanation for the healing.

Three months after the accident, doctors cleared Nathan to resume his participation in athletics, including football, wrestling, and track and field.

—Rev. James R. Christensen, Necedah, Wisconsin; adapted from *Pentecostal Evangel* (February 18, 2001)

ILLUSTRATION 248

HEALING FROM ANGER

Topics: Anger; Attitudes; Death; Healing; Illness; Miracles; Peace; Prayer;

References: James 1:20; 5:13–16

When Tony Campolo was in a church in Oregon, he prayed for a man who had cancer. In the middle of the week, he received a telephone call from the man's wife. She said, "You prayed for my husband. He had cancer." I said, "Had?" *Whoa,* he thought, *it's happened.*

She said, "He died." Campolo felt terrible.

"Don't feel bad," the woman said. "When he came into church that Sunday, he was filled with anger. He knew he was going to be dead in a short period of time, and he hated God. He was fifty-eight years old, and he wanted to see his children and grandchildren grow up.

"He was angry that this all-powerful God didn't take away his sickness and heal him. He would lie in bed and curse God. The more his anger grew toward God, the more miserable he was to everybody around him. It was an awful thing to be in his presence.

"After you prayed for him, a peace came over him and a joy came into him. The last three days have been the best days of our lives. We've sung. We've laughed. We've read Scripture. We've prayed. Oh, they've been wonderful days. And I called to thank you for laying your hands on him and praying for healing."

Then she said something incredibly profound: "He wasn't cured, but he was healed."

—Tony Campolo, "Year of Jubilee,"
Preaching Today Audio, no. 212

ILLUSTRATION 249

HEALING FETISH

Topics: Cross; Disease; Healing; Sickness; Suffering

References: 2 Kings 5:1–14; Isaiah 53:5; 1 Peter 2:24

In the lower Congo region of Africa, tribal artisans often craft *nkisi nkongi,* or "power objects." These wooden fetishes, usually in the shape of a human being, are thought to possess supernatural healing powers. When there is any kind of sickness in the village—physical, emotional, or spiritual—a priest will take something associated with the suffering person, such as a lock of hair or a piece of cloth, and nail it to the fetish. This tells the spirit what is wrong and calls on its power to heal the problem.

Christians don't need fetishes. When flesh just like ours was nailed to the cross, God healed us of our greatest problems: sin and death. By his wounds, we are healed.

—Elesha Coffman, Durham, North Carolina

ILLUSTRATION 250
BREAST CANCER HEALING

Topics: Healing; Help from God; Miracles; Power; Supernatural Occurrences

References: Psalm 103:3; Matthew 8:17; John 11:38–44; James 5:13–16

Innocentia, a highly regarded, devout woman Augustine knew in Carthage, discovered that she had breast cancer. A physician told her the disease was incurable. She could opt for amputation and possibly prolong her life a little, or she could follow the advice of Hippocrates and do nothing. Either way, death was not far away.

Dismayed, she turned for help to God in prayer, Augustine reports. In a dream, she was told to wait at the baptistry for the first woman who came out after being baptized and to ask this woman to make the sign of the cross over the cancerous breast.

Innocentia did as she was told and was completely cured. When she told her doctor what had happened, he responded with a contemptuous tone, "I thought you would reveal some great discovery to me!"

Seeing her horrified look, he backpedaled, saying, "What great thing was it for Christ to heal a cancer? He raised a man who had been dead for four days."

—Bruce Shelley, "Miracles Ended Long Ago—or Did They?" *Christian History* (Summer 2000)

ILLUSTRATION 251
SAVING THE BABY

Topics: Birth; Healing; Miracles; Prayer; Supernatural Occurrences

Reference: Isaiah 9:6–7

I was nearly sixteen weeks into pregnancy when my water broke. The doctor prescribed bed rest and instructed me to go to the emergency room when the miscarriage began. I stayed in bed for two weeks, praying for a miracle, but it was clear the pregnancy was slowly coming to an end.

The miscarriage was partially complete before we left for the hospital. The seasoned ER doctor who saw us mumbled to a nurse to get a fetal heart monitor on me and then dashed off to the next patient.

The nurse returned with the monitor and began searching my abdomen for signs of life. She tried from every angle until the monitor was as low as it would go. Nothing. Then, suddenly, there was the unmistakable steady thumping of a tiny heart. I stared at my husband in disbelief. How much longer could the baby survive if there was no fluid in the sac?

The nurse hastily examined what I had lost at home. "Massive blood clots," she told us as she quickly went in search of the doctor. My husband and I remained silent, not sure whether or not to be hopeful.

An obstetrician declared after his examination that we had a live baby who needed to be saved. He checked me into the hospital. The next day an ultrasound revealed perfect uterine conditions. I had plenty of fluid, a well-placed placenta, and an active eighteen-week-old baby. My doctor tried unsuccessfully to explain how several fist-sized blood clots could have escaped the sac along with large amounts of fluid and yet keep the pregnancy intact.

I went home from the hospital on Mother's Day, 1997. On October 21, 1997, my husband and I made another midnight run to the hospital, getting there just in time for our full-term son's marvelous birth. We named him Josiah, which means "Jehovah heals."

—Renee Duka, adapted from
Pentecostal Evangel (October 15, 2000)

ILLUSTRATION 252

SURGEON'S BLOOD SAVES PATIENT

Topics: Atonement; Blood of Christ; Christlikeness; Cross; Giving; Healing; Help from God; Imitation of Christ; Ministry; Receiving Christ;

Redemption; Righteousness; Sacrifice; Salvation; Savior

References: John 6:53; Ephesians 2:13; Hebrews 9:14; 13:12; 1 Peter 1:18–19; 1 John 1:7

Dr. Samuel Weinstein, chief of pediatric cardio-thoracic surgery for Children's Hospital at Montefiore Medical Center in New York City, went to El Salvador in 2006 with Heart Care International to provide life-saving operations for poor children.

It would take more than expertise and advanced equipment to save the life of Francisco Calderon Anthony Fernandez, eight, however. After twelve hours of surgery, the boy began to bleed out of control. The hospital lacked both the medicines to stop the bleeding and the blood to give the boy transfusions. Francisco's blood type was B-negative, which—according to the American Red Cross—is present in only 2 percent of the population.

Dr. Weinstein had the same blood type. So he set aside his scalpel, took off his gloves, and began washing his hands and forearm. Then he sat down and had his blood drawn.

When he had given his pint, Dr. Weinstein drank some bottled water and ate a Pop-Tart. Then—twenty minutes after stepping away from the table—he rejoined his colleagues, who watched as Weinstein's blood began flowing into the boy's small veins. Weinstein then completed the operation that saved Francisco's life.

—Jim Fitzgerald, "Doc Stops Surgery
to Give Own Blood to Patient,"
LiveScience.com (May 26, 2006)

ILLUSTRATION 253

APPENDIX ATTACKED

Topics: Faith; Healing; Illness; Miracles; Overcoming; Trust

References: Luke 4:38–39; 10:19; 13:10–13; Ephesians 1:18–23

When Heather, thirteen, complained of discomfort on her right side, I wasn't too concerned. But when, several days later, she was writhing and crying in pain, I knew something was terribly wrong. The doctor confirmed what I had suspected: appendicitis. "That appendix is going to have to come out," he said. "I'm sending you straight to the hospital."

We drove to the hospital, where I turned off the car and prepared to pray over Heather. Other cars were parking all around me. Even though I felt a little self-conscious, I prayed firmly and confidently. I remembered how Jesus had rebuked a fever and it had left. Some months earlier, my husband had tried that approach when one of our daughters had a fever, and it had worked. That increased my faith to pray now with Heather. I laid my hands on Heather and commanded the enemy to loose her in Jesus' name. I appropriated the authority I knew I had over the enemy. I prayed that God would comfort and heal Heather.

Then I practically had to carry her into the hospital. A nurse took one look at her and ordered a gurney. A blood test revealed a high white cell count. The nurse notified the waiting surgeon that Heather had arrived and sent her for an ultrasound.

As we waited, something began to happen. Until this point Heather had been unable to concentrate on anything except her pain. Now she entered into a lighthearted conversation with the woman next to her. Then she asked if she could get up and phone her best friend. I was incredulous.

"Look, Mom, I can jump," she said delightedly. "It doesn't hurt so much anymore."

The ultrasound technician tried for about ten minutes to see Heather's appendix but couldn't. He left the room and came back with the radiologist, who also failed. "There must be too much gas to see the appendix," the radiologist said. "But you should be screaming in pain the way I'm pressing on your stomach."

The radiologist told our doctors that he was unable to locate the appendix on the ultrasound and that Heather no longer seemed to be in pain. On that basis, he felt it would be unwise to do surgery. They agreed that Heather should be released but be brought back immediately at any recurrence of pain.

So, only a couple of hours after she arrived for surgery, Heather left the hospital with her appendix. She felt so good that she talked me into stopping on the way home to shop for a new pair of jeans. When we got home, the phone rang. It was our pastor, wanting to know how Heather was doing. "I'm fine," she said. "My mom prayed for me. And I was healed!"

—Arlyn Lawrence, *Pray!*
(January–February 2006)

ILLUSTRATION 254

LEUKEMIA CURE

Topics: Faith; Healing; Miracles; Receiving Christ; Supernatural Occurrences

References: Luke 4:38–39; John 14:12–14; James 5:13–16

Our friend Debbie was dying of leukemia at a cancer center in Seattle. She had slipped into a coma. Her two adult children had flown in to say their good-byes. Now her husband invited me to come and pray.

I asked a friend to drive with me to Seattle. As we drove, John 14:12–14 ran through my mind:

> "I tell you the truth, anyone who has faith in me will do what I have been doing. He will do even greater things than these, because I am going to the Father. And I will do whatever you ask in my name, so that the Son may bring glory to the Father. You may ask me for anything in my name, and I will do it."

Could we really do the things Jesus did? Would he really do the things we asked in his name?

At the hospital we approached Debbie's bed. I silently asked the Lord what to pray. Debbie was a sad sight. What I was about to pray seemed impossible.

Nevertheless, I prayed, "Lord, I come to you based on the authority and power you have given me because of Jesus. Jesus, you said we would do even greater things because of your power in us. You told me in John 15 that if I abide in you and your words abide in me, I can ask anything and it will be granted. So, right now, in the name and authority of Jesus in me, I rebuke the cancer and death. In Jesus' name I pronounce healing and abundant life." We left the hospital and drove home.

Debbie continued to be on my mind, but I also knew the Lord had heard my prayer. A week later my phone rang. It was Debbie. She had awakened from her coma and asked the medical team to unhook her life support. She was told that I had visited her several days before and had prayed for her. "Would you please come back?" she asked. So the next day I drove back to Seattle to see what the Lord had done.

Debbie—alert and smiling—told me the story. For three days after we prayed for her, while still in a coma, she sensed that an angel was standing by her bed. On the third day she woke up and knew that the Lord had completely healed her. The doctors' tests showed no sign of any cancer whatsoever.

We shared the gospel with her family. As a result of Debbie's healing, her son and his wife received Christ and are now joyfully serving him. Four years later, Debbie is still in remission.

—Cindy Riches, *Pray!*
(January–February 2006);
confirmed by Mike Riches, senior pastor, Clover
Creek Bible Fellowship, Tacoma, Washington

ILLUSTRATION 255

WATER OF HEALING

Topics: Confession; Healing; Help; Homelessness; Honesty; Needs; Thirst

References: John 4:1 – 15; 7:38;
Revelation 21:6

Mike, who works with homeless people, tells me that those who have hit bottom don't waste time building up an image or trying to conform. And they pray without pretense, a refreshing contrast to what is found in some churches.

I asked for an example. He said, "My friend and I were playing guitars and singing 'As the Deer Panteth for the Water' when David, a homeless man, started weeping. 'That's what I want, man,' he said. 'I want that water. I'm an alcoholic, and I want to be healed.'"

—Philip Yancey, "The Word on the Street,"
Christianity Today (January 2006)

PART 12: HEALTH AND BEAUTY

ILLUSTRATION 256

BRINGING BACK MODESTY

Topics: Beauty; Happiness; Lust; Modesty; Pleasure; Purity; Respect; Seduction; Stumbling Blocks

References: Matthew 5:27–28; 1 Timothy 2:9–10; 1 Peter 3:3–4

When asked in Paris about the conservative nature of his 2006 fall collection, world-famous designer Miuccia Prada replied, "The super-exposure of nudity seems not to have given much happiness to women."

> —Kate Betts, "Looks Like a Cover-up," *Time* (March 13, 2006)

ILLUSTRATION 257

DEADLY BEAUTY

Topics: Beauty; Character; Christian Life; Consequences; Death; Deception; Evil; Foolishness; Salvation; Satan; Sin; Temptation

References: Matthew 4:1–11; Romans 6:23; James 1:13–15; 1 John 2:15–17

The Huntington River Gorge, near Richmond, Vermont, is beautiful but deadly. In the last forty years, twenty persons (mostly young adults in their twenties and thirties) have lost their lives in the gorge. Hundreds of gorge swimmers have been injured.

On the surface the water of the gorge looks calm and placid, but beneath it are strong currents that run swiftly over treacherous waterfalls and whirlpools. Public safety officials have designated the gorge "the single most deadly place in the state." Warning signs have been posted on a side of the gorge, reading, "When the water is high due to rain or snowmelt, especially powerful currents can easily sweep you over the falls and trap you underneath the water."

People are debating about what to do about the gorge. Some argue for more public information about the gorge's risks. Others want to ban anyone from visiting the place. Meanwhile, swimmers continue to be attracted to the scene. One college student attending the University of Vermont—just fourteen miles from the gorge—said she had heard about the beauty of Huntington River Gorge and wanted to see it. She said people already know about the dangers and try their best to be careful.

"You can't change the water, and you can't stop people from going in," she said.

> —Katie Zezima, "An Enticing Gorge Poses a Deadly Problem," *The New York Times* (July 16, 2006)

ILLUSTRATION 258

DOC TAKES OWN ADVICE

Topics: Advice; Attitudes; Body; Change; Commitment; Food; Gluttony; Goals; Health; Lifestyle; Overcoming; Stewardship; Transformation

References: Proverbs 23:2; Romans 6:13; 1 Corinthians 6:12–20; 1 Thessalonians 5:23

Dr. Nick Yphantides used to tell his patients, "Do as I say, not as I do." That's because he weighed 470 pounds. But then God spoke to him about being a better steward of his body. In his own words, "God used testicular cancer to bring me to my knees. Here I had been healed of cancer and yet I was eating myself to death and committing suicide at the dining room table and going to fast-food places. I was overwhelmed with the conviction that my personal health was a God-given gift with which I had to honor him in the way that I cared for that gift."

Dr. Nick went on a spiritual, physical, and emotional journey to seek God's best for his body. He lost 270 pounds in eighteen months. In addition to founding a ministry focused on health, Dr. Nick has written the book *My Big Fat Greek Diet* and has done interviews with *Entertainment Weekly*, CNN, and *People* magazine, speaking to the issue of caring for our bodies.

— Bill White,
"Doctor Preaches Stewardship
of the Body," PreachingToday.com

ILLUSTRATION 259

FASHION ADVISERS

Topics: Advice; Appearance; Choices; Guidance; Marriage; Relationships; Spouses; Trust

References: Proverbs 12:15; Colossians 1:18; 3:16; 1 Thessalonians 5:12

When finding the right fit for clothing, women trust the advice of the following people:

self: 37 percent
husband/significant other: 26 percent
friend: 13 percent
daughter: 11 percent
mother: 5 percent
sister: 5 percent
other: 3 percent

— Mary Cadden and Marcy E. Mullins,
USA Today "Snapshots"
(November 15, 2006)

ILLUSTRATION 260

PRISONER OF APPETITE

Topics: Addiction; Appetites; Bondage; Food; Foolishness; Gluttony; Greed; Limitations; Self-control; Temptation

References: Proverbs 23:1–3, 21; John 8:34; Galatians 5:1; Philippians 3:19; 1 Timothy 6:9; 2 Peter 2:19

Raynald III, a fourteenth-century duke in what is now Belgium, was grossly overweight. His Latin nickname, Crassus, means "fat."

Raynald's younger brother Edward revolted against Raynald's rule. Edward captured Raynald but did not kill him. Instead, he built a room around Raynald in the Nieuwkerk castle and promised him he could regain his title and property when he left the room. This would not have been difficult for most people, since the room had several windows and a door of near-normal size, none of which were locked or barred. The problem was Raynald's size; to regain his freedom, he needed to lose weight.

Edward knew his older brother. Each day he sent a variety of delicious foods into the room. Instead of dieting his way out of prison, Raynald grew fatter. When Duke Edward was accused of cruelty, he had a ready answer: "My brother is not a prisoner. He may leave when he so wills." Raynald stayed in his room for ten years and wasn't released until after Edward died in battle. By then his health was so ruined that he died within a year—a prisoner of his own appetite.

—Thomas Costain,
The Three Edwards (Popular Library, 1964)

ILLUSTRATION 261

DILBERT CREATOR GETS VOICE BACK

Topics: Adversity; Body; Crisis; Disease; Healing; Health; Illness; Miracles; Overcoming; Power; Struggles; Testing

References: Nehemiah 9:17; Psalm 103:3; 145:8–9; Isaiah 64:3; Romans 10:8–13; James 1:2–4

Scott Adams, the creator and writer of the Dilbert cartoons, suffered from a vocal disorder—*spasmodic dysphonia*. With this rare disorder, a certain section of the brain simply shuts down, paralyzing the ability to speak with much command or volume. Think of it as a more permanent case of laryngitis.

Oddly enough, the condition is situational. For example, Adams could speak quite well when using his public speaking voice, but his more conversational, everyday voice eluded him.

Adams wrote on his personal website about how frustrating the condition was. He desperately wanted his normal voice back. One day he finally had a breakthrough. While helping his child with a simple homework assignment, Scott found that he could speak perfectly when using a rhyme scheme. He could say, "Jack be nimble, Jack be quick, Jack jump over the candlestick" with very little difficulty. As he noted on his website, it was "just different enough from normal speech that my brain handled it fine."

What is amazing is that Adams's regular voice returned as well. He likened the healing to starting up a car on a cold winter night—the words of the poem awakened a sleeping section of his brain, and his normal voice suddenly emerged.

In a similar way, the living Word can awaken and transform a heart that has been spiritually dysfunctional.

—Brian Lowery, "Dilbert Creator Healed of Mysterious Illness"; source: "Good News Day," dilbertblog.typepad.com (October 24, 2006)

ILLUSTRATION 262

SELF-HEALING ARROGANCE

Topics: Arrogance; Dependence; Depravity; Healing; Helplessness; Idealism; Limitations; Powerlessness; Self-reliance; Sinful Nature; Weakness

References: Exodus 15:26; Proverbs 14:12; Ecclesiastes 7:20; 8:8; Isaiah 5:21; Hosea 6:1; Romans 3:1–26; 1 Corinthians 1:18–31; 8:2

A global day of healing on December 8, the anniversary of John Lennon's death: that's what Yoko Ono asked for in a full-page ad in *The New York Times*.

"One day we will be able to say that we healed ourselves," Ono promised, "and by healing ourselves, we healed the world."

— "Good Week for … All Humanity," *The Week* (December 8, 2006)

ILLUSTRATION 263

SCARED OFF OF CHEWING TOBACCO

Topics: Appetites; Behavior; Change; Consequences; Desires; Fear; Growth; Habits; Motivation; New Life; Repentance; Spiritual Direction; Temptation

References: Genesis 4:7; 1 Corinthians 10:13; Hebrews 12:1

Several years ago, I chewed long-cut Wintergreen Skoal. I know, I know. It causes cancer of the mouth and is bad for your heart and your breath, and girls are never going to want to kiss you if you chew that stuff. I knew all that for years, yet I couldn't kick the habit—mainly because I didn't want to. The tobacco gave me a little buzz and helped me relax.

I tried to stop. I went to websites and looked up statistics about the health risks of chewing tobacco. I printed the statistics and placed them on my desk where I could read them when I was tempted. But it didn't help. I still bought a can of the stuff every other time I gassed up my car. This went on for at least a year, until …

I was listening to the radio one afternoon, when a voice came on, very distorted and troubled. The man sounded as though part of his face were missing—low and muffled and slobbery. Between songs, the radio station had inserted a commercial, a public service message about the danger of using chewing tobacco. The man in the commercial said half his jaw had been removed, he had no lower lip, and his face was deformed because for years he had used smokeless tobacco. He didn't list any facts; he didn't speak of any harmful ingredients; he didn't say he was going to die of cancer. Yet the image of a man without a chin speaking into the microphone was enough to convince me to stop. I never used the stuff again.

— Donald Miller, *Searching for God Knows What* (Nelson, 2004)

ILLUSTRATION 264

SCALE OF BEAUTY

Topics: Beauty; Body; Contentment; Coveting; Faultfinding; Intimacy; Judging Others; Lust; Perfection; Pornography; Satisfaction; Self-centeredness; Sex; Vanity

References: 1 Samuel 16:7; 2 Samuel 11:2–5; Proverbs 6:25; 31:30; John 7:24; Galatians 2:6; 1 Peter 3:3–5

A woman is beautiful—or not—depending on who she's with. That's according to psychologists Sara Gutierres and Douglas Kenrick of Arizona State University, who have studied the phenomenon of beauty for the past twenty years.

We judge both our own and other people's attractiveness based on the social situation we are in, research shows. If a woman of average beauty enters a room of extremely beautiful women, she will be perceived as less attractive than she actually is. If the same woman enters a room of unattractive women, she will be perceived as more attractive than she actually is. The same applies for men.

The researchers found that this contrast effect influences many women to devalue themselves: "Women who are surrounded by other attractive women—whether in the flesh, in films, or in photographs—rate themselves as less satisfied with their attractiveness and less desirable as a marriage partner." For the overwhelming majority of women who don't meet these impossible standards, multimillion-dollar industries are eager to help improve their appearance.

The effects on men are also damaging. The researchers note that "under a constant barrage of media images of beautiful women, these guys have an expectation of attractiveness that is unusually high—and that makes the people around them, in whom they might really be interested, seem lackluster, even if they are quite good-looking."

—Michael Levine (with Hara E. Morano), "Why I Hate Beauty," *Psychology Today* (July–August 2001)

ILLUSTRATION 265

FINED FOR DYING YOUNG

Topics: Death; Government; Health; Insensitivity; Law; Mortality

References: Psalm 49:5–15; Romans 5:12–19; 6:20–23; Hebrews 9:27–28

If someone in your family dies too young, your family could get fined or put in jail. That's the legislation Pereira da Silva, mayor of Biritiba-Mirim, in Brazil, is trying to pass to force the city's 28,000 residents to get adequate health care for themselves or family members—and the government to provide more burial space.

The state government promised the town a new vertical cemetery, but, to date, nothing has been done. Mayor da Silva offers his new proposal as an attempt to discourage death and resultant cemetery use.

Since announcement of the proposed law, both gym use and health care visits have increased.

— "Mayor Wants to Ban Death,"
ananova.com (December 13, 2005)

ILLUSTRATION 266

SHREDDED MAKEOVER

Topics: Appearance; Beauty; Body; Discouragement; Emptiness; Self-image; Shame; Tongue; Truth

References: Genesis 1:26–27; 1 Samuel 16:7; Proverbs 31:30; Ephesians 4:15; 1 Peter 3:3–5

Deleese Williams, a woman who was promised cosmetic surgeries on *Extreme Makeover* that would "transform her life and destiny," has sued the producers of the hit TV show. That dream was shattered when one of the dental surgeons reported that Williams' recovery time would be longer than expected. She was pulled from the show the night before her surgeries were scheduled to begin and sent home to Texas.

According to the lawsuit, Williams sobbed uncontrollably when she was given the news. "How can I go back as ugly as I left?" she said, "I was supposed to come home pretty." Wesley Cordova, an attorney for Williams, claims, "Deleese is so hurt and humiliated that she won't leave the house now. She grocery shops at midnight."

The lawsuit also claims that Williams' relationship with her family has been damaged. The producers coached family members not to accept Deleese's physical flaws and pushed them to verbally express their opinions on taped interviews — which Deleese later saw. The lawsuit claims, "Now that she returned in the same condition in which she left, there were no secrets, no hidden feelings, no rewards."

Finally, Cordova alleges that the emotional stress of the entire situation had a tragic impact on Deleese's sister, Kellie. "Kellie could not live with the fact that she had said horrible things that hurt her sister," said Cordova. "She fell to pieces. Four months later, she ended her life with an overdose of pills, alcohol, and cocaine." The lawsuit concludes, "The family is shredded. There is a human cost to this."

—Michelle Caruso, "Extreme Tragedy,"
nydailynews.com (September 18, 2005)

ILLUSTRATION 267

INNOVATIVE INOCULATION

Topics: Atonement; Blood of Christ; Body; Creativity; Determination; Diligence; Disease; Illness; Opportunity; Perseverance; Problems; Resourcefulness; Results; Salvation

References: Ecclesiastes 9:10; Matthew 26:28; John 6:56; Romans 5:9; 1 Corinthians 15:55

Dr. George Moore, a public health worker, was sent to Nepal in 1952. He found only one hospital in the country, which was for the royalty. Life expectancy of the people in Nepal was thirty-five years, and 98 percent of the population hadn't had any medical treatment in their short lives.

Moore and his colleague attacked malaria by spraying the inside of huts with insecticide. Their second major challenge, smallpox, was more difficult. Smallpox vaccine must be refrigerated, and in the early 1950s, there was no way to get refrigerators to primitive villages.

So Moore thought up a plan. He got a small batch of vaccine from the United States and stored it in the small kerosene refrigerator at his base camp. Then, using that vaccine, he inoculated some small boys and took those boys with him to the villages.

When someone is inoculated with smallpox vaccine, they get a mild case of the disease — too mild to make them sick, but strong enough to give them permanent immunity. They also develop a smallpox blister at the point of the injection.

Moore would break the smallpox blister in a vaccinated boy, dip the end of a string into the blister, then touch that infected string to a small opening in the skin of the person he wanted to protect. That was how the assault on the killer disease began.

—Marcus Rosenbaum,
"Dr. Moore's Mountaintop House Calls,"
NPR *Weekend Edition* (September 16, 2006)

ILLUSTRATION 268
HURTING YOURSELF

Topics: Consequences; Danger; Human Condition; Risk; Sowing and Reaping; Temptation; Vices

References: Proverbs 22:8; Amos 4:12; John 3:16 – 18; Romans 6:23; Galatians 6:7; Hebrews 9:27; Revelation 21:6 – 8

You could be injured brushing your teeth — or stapling a few pages together. Here are stats on the number of injuries sustained by people doing everyday activities during 2005:

brushing teeth and gargling: 3,925
reading: 11,243
barbecuing: 15,952
stapling paper: 15,974
bowling: 17,916
riding a stationary bike: 43,117
bicycling: 534,883
driving: 2,788,000

—Denis Boyle, "Five-Minute Guide to Risk,"
AARP (July – August 2006)

ILLUSTRATION 269
PAIN CAN BRING HEALING

Topics: Confession; Courage; Denial; Fear; Health; Pain; Repentance; Running from God; Self-deception; Self-reliance; Suffering; Truth

References: Jeremiah 6:13 – 14; 8:11; 2 Corinthians 7:8 – 11; Galatians 4:16; Colossians 3:16; James 1:2 – 4, 21 – 22; 1 John 1:7 – 9

All of us tend to avoid pain. Sometimes, though, avoiding pain can lead to much greater suffering.

Consider the story of William "the Refrigerator" Perry. Perry was a colorful defensive lineman for the Chicago Bears when they won the Super Bowl back in 1985. His nickname fit him well, because he was big and wide. Perry was also a friendly man with a wide grin.

Unfortunately for his grin, though he was a mammoth man playing in the tough world of the football trenches, he apparently was afraid of the dentist—so afraid that he didn't go to the dentist for twenty years. He didn't go to the dentist even though his teeth and gums hurt terribly, even though his teeth began falling out. Eventually he had lost half of his teeth—some he pulled out himself!—and his gums suffered chronic infection. He was suffering!

Finally, as he neared age forty-five, Perry went to a dentist, who had to pull out all of his remaining teeth, insert screws in his jaw, and implant new teeth—all of which would have cost him $60,000, except the dentist donated the procedure (apparently for the free publicity).

Now there's a story every mother will tell her son when she tells him he has to go to the dentist or brush his teeth. But this is also a story for all who avoid emotional and spiritual pain of any sort, for the body teaches you things about your soul. There are a lot of things that can cause pain to the soul but actually bring health—asking for help, hard work, repentance, looking honestly into our own souls, going to church, dealing with our problems, humbling ourselves, reading the Bible, listening to sermons, facing the truth. This list goes on. It takes courage to face pain. But as William Perry said of his new teeth, "It's unbelievable. And I love them.... I got tired of my mouth hurting all the time."

—Craig Brian Larson, " 'The Fridge' Gets New Teeth," Preachingtoday.com; source: "A Story with Some Teeth," *Chicago Tribune* (December 20, 2007)

ILLUSTRATION 270

BITING CANCER

Topics: Arguments; Conflict; Fighting; Gossip; Tongue

References: Psalm 5:9; 57:4; Proverbs 12:18; Jeremiah 9:8; Galatians 5:15; Hebrews 12:15; James 1:26; 3:5–10; 4:1–2, 11

In January 2006, Australian scientists discovered the cause of a mysterious disease that had killed thousands of Tasmanian devils on the island state of Tasmania, off the coast of Australia. The scientists initially believed the deaths were caused by a virus; however, their research ultimately uncovered a rare, fatal cancer. They named it Devil Facial Tumor Disease, or DFTD.

What is strange, according to cytogeneticist Anne-Marie Pearse, is that the abnormalities in the chromosomes of the cancer cells were the same in every tumor. That means the disease began in the mouth of a single sick devil. The ferocious little animal facilitated the spread of DFTD by biting its neighbors when squabbling for food, which, according to Pearse, is a natural behavior of Tasmanian devils. "Devils jaw-wrestle and bite each other a lot, usually in the face and around the mouth, and bits of tumor break off one devil and stick in the wounds of another," Pearse said.

Over the course of several years, infected devils continued to inflict deadly wounds with their mouths. Consequently, DFTD spread at an alarming rate, ultimately wiping out over 40 percent of the devil population.

A similar fate threatens the church if its members persist in the devilish behavior of wounding their neighbors with their mouths.

—Sam O'Neal, "Tasmanian Devils Spread Cancer with Their Mouths," PreachingToday.com

ILLUSTRATION 271
DEADLY TANS FOR TEENS

Topics: Addiction; Appearance; Beauty; Consequences; Coveting; Foolishness; Health; Human Nature; Popularity; Pride; Self-worth; Teens; Temptation; Vanity

References: 1 Samuel 16:7; Proverbs 11:22; 31:30; 1 Corinthians 6:19–20; Philippians 2:3; 1 Peter 3:3–4

An estimated 2.3 million teenagers go tanning at least once a year. That has helped indoor tanning become a $5 billion a year industry.

On their own, these numbers may not seem surprising or even noteworthy. But they become dangerous when you consider that since 1975, the occurrence of melanoma—the most lethal form of skin cancer—has doubled in the United States among women ages fifteen to twenty-nine.

"Skin cancer used to be something old people got," said Dr. James Spencer, a clinical professor of dermatology at New York City's Mount Sinai School of Medicine. "Now not a month goes by that I don't see somebody in their twenties. That was unheard of ten years ago."

The World Health Organization is also taking notice. It estimates that sixty thousand people die each year around the world because of excessive UV exposure and has urged youths under the age of eighteen to avoid indoor tanning.

But many experts fear that such warnings will not deter teens from tanning. Sabrina Hendershot, sixteen, says, "All the girls who are really tanned all through the year—they're the popular girls. And guys are always complimenting girls on their tans." Kylie-Ayn Kennedy, sixteen, who visits a tanning parlor several times each week, is also willing to take the risk. "Tanning may make my skin wrinkle a little bit earlier," she says, "but I'm going to look good while I can."

—Julie Rawe, "Why Teens Are Obsessed with Tanning," *Time* (August 7, 2006)

ILLUSTRATION 272
DOCTORS AND FAST FOOD

Topics: Character; Christian Life; Example; Hypocrisy; Imitation of Christ

References: Matthew 5:13–16; 1 Corinthians 11:1; 1 Timothy 4:16; James 1:22

At the 1993 annual meeting of the American Heart Association in Atlanta, three hundred thousand doctors, nurses, and researchers came together to discuss, among other things, the importance a low-fat diet plays in keeping our hearts healthy.

Yet during mealtimes, they consumed fat-filled fast food, such as bacon cheeseburgers and fries, at about the same rate as people from other conventions. When one cardiologist was asked whether or not his partaking in high-fat meals set a bad example, he replied, "Not me; I took my name tag off."

—Stephen Nordbye, "Always an Example,"
PreachingToday.com

ILLUSTRATION 273

QUANTUM WEIGHT LOSS

Topics: Adversity; Endurance; Perseverance; Trials

References: Romans 5:3–4; James 1:2–4; 1 Peter 1:6–7

I had put on weight and was out of shape, so a year ago I began working on my sagging waistline. Day after day, I worked hard on cardiovascular exercise and weight training, seeming to get nowhere. Straining. Sweating. Sucking wind. Questioning my sanity.

Finally, after several months, a quantum leap occurred. Weight began to drop off. Muscle began to get toned. And endurance increased. Medical friends tell me that during the constancy of working out, regardless of how I felt, a whole new freeway system of small blood vessels and capillaries was forming within my body. Then came the day when they decided it was time for a "grand opening." Suddenly, more blood came flooding into the muscle tissue, and the resulting benefits seemed to be exponential.

Likewise, when we're walking through the depths of trials, God is building up a secondary support system of endurance so that we might be even more prepared for the next time adversity comes our way.

—Bob Reccord, *Forged by Fire*
(Broadman & Holman, 2000)

ILLUSTRATION 274

WEIGHT-LIFTING TRIAL

Topics: Body; Commitment; Consequences; Dedication; Exercise; Laziness; Parenting; Promises; Responsibility; Teens

Reference: Galatians 6:9

Though skeptical of his teenage son's newfound determination to build muscles, one father followed his teenager to the store's weight-lifting department, where they admired a set of weights.

"Please, Dad," pleaded the teen, "I promise I'll use 'em every day."

"I don't know, Michael. It's really a commitment on your part," the father said.

"Please, Dad."

"They're not cheap," the father said.

"I'll use 'em, Dad, I promise. You'll see."

Finally won over, the father paid for the equipment and headed for the door. After a few steps, he heard his son behind him say, "What! You mean I have to carry them to the car?"

—Tim Davis,
Pastor Tim's CleanLaugh Collection
(Trafford, 2001)

ILLUSTRATION 275

HOW ATTRACTIVE ARE YOU?

Topics: Appearance; Beauty; Body; Self-image; Self-worth

Reference: 1 Samuel 16:7

Find out how attractive you are by sending your picture to AmIHotOrNot.com. The Internet audience will rate you on a scale of 1 to 10. If this is too intimidating, you can simply choose to rate other people.

—*Newsweek* (December 18, 2000)

ILLUSTRATION 276

WHY EVERYTHING HURTS

Topics: Consequences; Discernment; Disease; Pain; Self-examination; Sickness; Spiritual Perception

References: Matthew 7:1–5; Luke 12:57; John 7:24

A man went to his doctor in an acute state of anxiety. "Doctor, you have to help me; I'm dying," he said. "Everything I touch hurts. I touch my head and it hurts. I touch my leg and it hurts. I touch my stomach and it hurts. I touch my chest and it hurts. You have to help me, Doc; everything hurts."

The doctor gave him a complete examination. "I have good news and bad news for you," he said. "The good news is you are not dying. The bad news is you have a broken finger."

—David Holdaway, Kincardineshire, Scotland

ILLUSTRATION 277

NO GOLF REMEDY

Topics: Freedom; Free Will; God's Love; Goodness of God; Obedience; Physicians; Sin; Ten Commandments

References: Exodus 20:1–17; Psalm 19:7–11; Ephesians 6:1–3

Last summer a surgeon operated on my foot. While rehabilitating from that, I often did exercises that hurt because I knew that working through the soreness would allow my foot to regain its usefulness. On the other hand, the surgeon warned against bicycling, mountain climbing, running, and other activities that might endanger the healing process. Basically, anything that sounded fun, he vetoed.

On one visit I tried to talk him into letting me play golf. "Some friends get together once a year. It's important to me. I've been practicing my swing, and if I use only my upper body and keep my legs and hips very still, could I join them?"

Without a flicker of hesitation, my doctor replied, "It would make me very unhappy if you played golf within the next two months."

"I thought you were a golfer," I said, appealing to his sympathies.

"I am. That's how I know you can't swing without rolling that foot inward and putting weight on the parts that are trying to heal."

My doctor has nothing against my playing golf; as a fellow golfer, he sympathizes with me. But he has my best interests at heart. It will indeed make him unhappy if I do something that might damage my long-term recovery. He wants me to play golf next year, and the next, and the rest of my life, and for that reason he could not sanction a match too soon after my surgery.

As we talked, I began to appreciate my doctor's odd choice of words. If he had issued an edict—"No golf!"—I might have stubbornly rebelled. He left me the free choice and expressed the consequences in a most personal way: Disobedience would grieve him, for his job was to restore my health.

What a doctor does for me physically—guide me toward health—God does for me spiritually. I am learning to view sins not as an arbitrary list of rules drawn up by a cranky Judge, but rather as a list of dangers that must be avoided at all costs—for our own sakes.

—Philip Yancey, "Doctor's Orders,"
Christianity Today (December 6, 1999)

ILLUSTRATION 278

NO TIME FOR LIPSTICK

Topics: Appearance; Perspective; Pride; Priorities; Sickness; Values

References: Psalm 90:12; John 6:63

She's in a hospital smock, grimacing, unkempt, and sporting a hefty bandage on her hand. And she's on the cover of the July 2001 issue of her magazine, *Rosie*.

When asked why she was photographed in such a state, Rosie O'Donnell said she had nearly died from a staph infection following surgery on her hand. "I've just gotten out of the hospital and almost died," she said. "Who has time for lipstick?"

—"Quoteworthy,"
Chicago Tribune (June 6, 2001)

ILLUSTRATION 279

BEAUTY IN THE SCARS

Topics: Beauty; Grace; Scars; Trials; Worth

References: Mark 10:21; John 3:16; 2 Corinthians 11:16–33; Ephesians 2:8–9

A Nike commercial didn't say a word. It simply showed a series of people with one thing in common: a nasty injury or scar. There was a cowboy with a huge scar around his eye, a fellow with a bulbous cauliflower ear, and another man with horribly callused feet. There was no explanation—simply the Nike logo and "Just Do It."

The ad has been criticized as being incomprehensible and extreme. But the key to the commercial is the background music. Joe Cocker sings, "You are so beautiful . . . to me."

To the wrestler with the misshapen ear, the surfer with a shark bite, the bull rider blind in one eye, injuries are beauty marks. And to their fans, these athletes are beautiful because of their scars. "Beauty is in the eye of the beholder," says Mike Folino, the ad's creator.

God's grace is just as jarring. Our beauty is found not in us, but in the one who looks down at us—injured, blind, and scarred—and sings, "You are so beautiful . . . to me."

—Jim Congdon, Topeka, Kansas

ILLUSTRATION 280

THE MIRACULOUS HUMAN BODY

Topics: Body; Creation; God's Wisdom

Reference: Romans 1:20

The average human heart pumps more than a thousand gallons a day and more than fifty-five million gallons in a lifetime. That is enough to fill thirteen supertankers. The heart never sleeps, beating 2.5 billion times in a lifetime.

The lungs contain a thousand miles of capillaries. The process of exchanging oxygen for carbon dioxide is so complicated that it is more difficult to exchange O_2 for CO_2 than for a man shot out of a cannon to carve the Lord's Prayer on the head of a pin as he passes by.

Human DNA contains about two thousand genes per chromosome, and 1.8 meters of DNA are folded into each cell nucleus, which is six microns long. This is like putting thirty miles of fishing line into a cherry pit. And it isn't simply stuffed in. It is folded in. If folded one way, the cell becomes a skin cell; if another way, a liver cell; and so forth. To write out the information in one cell would take three hundred volumes, each five hundred pages thick. The human body

contains enough DNA that if it were stretched out, it would circle the sun 260 times.

The body uses energy efficiently. If an average adult rides a bike for one hour at ten miles per hour, the body uses the amount of energy contained in three ounces of carbohydrate. If a car were this efficient with gasoline, it would get nine hundred miles to the gallon.

—Dr. John Medina, genetic engineer, in a 1995 lecture at Multnomah Bible College, Portland, Oregon

ILLUSTRATION 281

KEEPING COD FRESH

Topics: Enemies; Spiritual Warfare; Temptation; Trials

References: John 15:18–27; 16:1–4; Ephesians 6:10–18

The only way to ship fresh North Atlantic cod from Boston to San Francisco during the nineteenth century was to sail around the South American continent. That trip took months, so, as you can imagine, the first attempts to dress the cod in Boston and pack it in ice failed miserably. The fish was inedible when it got to California.

In the next attempt, the cod were placed in holding tanks full of water, shipped to California alive, and dressed there. The results were also less than satisfactory. The fish didn't get much exercise during the trip, so they were pasty and relatively tasteless.

Finally, someone suggested, "Why don't we put some catfish in with the cod?" That wasn't such a wild idea, since catfish are the natural enemy of cod.

Sure enough, when a few catfish were placed in the tanks with them, the cod kept swimming to stay out of eating range. When they reached San Francisco, they were in perfect shape.

—Bill Myers and David Wimbish, *The Dark Side of the Supernatural* (Bethany, 1999)

ILLUSTRATION 282

CONNECTING FAITH AND HEALTH

Topics: Church Attendance; Health; Worship

References: Exodus 20:24; Hebrews 10:24–25

Recent studies indicate that men and women of faith live longer than people of no faith. They have fewer strokes, less heart disease, less clinical depression, better immune system function, lower blood pressure, and fewer anxiety attacks. They are also less likely to commit suicide.

These findings come from secular medical schools and schools of public health. What's more, Dr. Harold Koenig of Duke University Medical Center has calculated that the lack of religious involvement has an effect on mortality that is equivalent to forty years of smoking one pack of cigarettes per day.

And another study by researchers at the University of Texas found that those who regularly attended worship services lived an aver-

age of seven years longer than those who never attended.

—Gregg Easterbrook, *The New Republic* (July 1999)

ILLUSTRATION 283

MINISTERS OF BEAUTY

Topics: Beauty; Calling; Caring; Encouragement; Evangelism; Giving; Ministry; Respect; Self-image; Service; Stewardship; Talents; Witnessing

References: Matthew 25:14–30; Luke 19:11–27; Romans 12:4–8; 1 Corinthians 9:22; 1 Peter 4:10

Once a month, a group of professionals armed with blow dryers, scissors, nail polish—and love—venture forth to serve those less fortunate than themselves.

Hairdressers in the Marketplace (HIM), a ministry of Willow Creek Community Church in suburban Chicago, offers monthly Day of Beauty sessions in which needy women receive free haircuts and manicures. HIM volunteers also go to nursing homes for the poor, homeless shelters, and facilities for the mentally disabled to provide free services.

Hairstylist Teresa Russo-Cox founded HIM in 1998 after unsuccessfully trying numerous volunteer positions at Willow Creek. None felt like the right fit for her. She asked God, "Why did you give me a talent that's so much about vanity? How can I serve you?"

She says God answered those prayers with a vision for a group that not only communicates

God's love and care to women in need but also reaches out to stylists. "That's what sets us apart from other ministries that offer haircuts to the poor," says Teresa. "We focus on evangelism to the beauty industry, which is filled with so much darkness. Its underlying message is all about external things—glamour and glitz. I want to bring the light of God's Word into our industry."

Some "clients" surprise the HIM volunteers. At one Day of Beauty event in 2006, teen girls going through drug and alcohol rehab told Melissa they hadn't ever had "sober" fun before. "They had never experienced that," Melissa says.

"I had no self-esteem," says Doreen, who was invited to a Day of Beauty after she and her two preschool children left her alcoholic, abusive husband. "That day gave me a boost on the outside, but it helped me on the inside too. I felt beautiful, special, and deserving."

—Keri Wyatt Kent, "Pampered with a Purpose," *Today's Christian Woman* (November–December 2006)

PART 13: HEAVEN AND HELL

ILLUSTRATION 284

HOMESICK AT HOME

Topics: Afterlife; Children; Despair; Eternal Life; Family; God; Home; Longing; Parenting; Sadness

References: Ecclesiastes 3:11; Matthew 11:28–30; John 14:1–4; 2 Corinthians 4:18; 5:1–5; 2 Peter 3:13; Revelation 21; 22

My son, Brian, and his wife, Becky, were heading south to the Florida Keys for their fifteenth wedding anniversary. I had volunteered to housesit and watch my grandsons—Nathan, seven, and Joshua, five. The three of us were looking forward to our vacation, too: pool splashing, Happy Meals, park Olympics, and snuggle time.

The parents slipped into the boys' room around 5:00 a.m. to give last-minute hugs and kisses. When I woke up an hour or so later, I could hear the kids. "Up and at 'em," those sounds reported. "Your starting bell is ringing!" Sure enough, I found Nate and Josh wrapped in blankets and watching a cartoon on television.

The rainy day seemed to go on forever. The three of us played games, watched videos, and drew pictures. I got out my famous "Granny bag" filled with surprises and produced a puppy-and-mouse marionette show. After that, we all stood at the window looking wistfully at the pool as it filled with rainwater.

At last it was time for bed. Then the phone rang. It was Brian and Becky, and the boys jumped up to chat. As each one took a turn talking with their mom and dad, the tears began to flow. The boys were tired, their parents were far away, and as much as they loved Grandma, they wanted Mom and Dad.

I tried to quiet the boys. Josh eventually fell asleep with his mouth wide open, still crying. Nate couldn't stop thinking about his parents. He was like a record stuck in one spot. Through the wailing, he managed to eke out, "Grandma, I'm homesick, and I am *home*. How can that be?"

I took him into my bed. I rubbed his back and spoke soft words until he finally fell asleep.

We only had one night of tears. Mom and Dad learned to call during the day when the boys weren't so tired. Five days later, the parents returned. The boys' faces were filled with smiles, and they couldn't get close enough to their parents. At last, home was home.

—Pat Bailey, Batavia, Illinois

ILLUSTRATION 285

HEAVEN AND KINDERGARTEN

Topics: Afterlife; Children; Death; Eternal Life; Expectations; Heaven

References: Matthew 19:14; Mark 10:14; Luke 18:16; John 14:2

Kayse, five, was more and more excited about her first day of kindergarten. Jayme, three, watched her big sister with fascination. On the Sunday before the first day of school, Kayse fell and skinned her knee.

As Kayse cried, Jayme tried to comfort her by saying, "Don't worry, Kayse; if you die, you'll go to heaven."

But Kayse wailed even more. "I don't want to go to heaven," she said. "I want to go to kindergarten!"

—Hugh Poland, "Kids of the Kingdom," *Today's Christian* (July–August 2005)

ILLUSTRATION 286

LONGING FOR HEAVEN

Topics: Afterlife; Assurance; Beliefs; Desires; Eternal Life; Heaven; Hope; Human Nature; Immortality; Promises; Religion; Seeking God

References: Ecclesiastes 3:11; Luke 23:43; John 3:16, 36; 14:2; 1 Corinthians 2:9; 2 Corinthians 4:18; 5:1; 1 Thessalonians 4:13–18; 2 Peter 3:13; Revelation 21; 22

Australian aborigines pictured heaven as a distant island beyond the western horizon. The early Finns thought heaven was a distant island in the faraway East. Mexicans, Peruvians, and Polynesians believed they went to the sun or the moon after death. Native Americans believed that in the afterlife their spirits would hunt the spirits of buffalo.

The Gilgamesh Epic, an ancient Babylonian legend, refers to a resting place of heroes and hints at a tree of life. In the pyramids of Egypt, the embalmed bodies had maps placed beside them as guides to the future world. The Romans believed that the righteous would picnic in the Elysian fields while their horses grazed nearby. Seneca, the Roman philosopher, said, "The day thou fearest as the last is the birthday of eternity." Although these depictions of the afterlife differ, the unifying testimony of the human heart throughout history is belief in life after death. Anthropological evidence suggests that every culture has a God-given, innate sense of the eternal—that this world is not all there is.

—Randy Alcorn, *Heaven* (Tyndale, 2004)

ILLUSTRATION 287

WELCOME TO HEAVEN

Topics: Accepting Christ; Assurance; Belief; Eternal Death; Eternal Life; God as Father; Salvation; Spiritual Adoption; Tragedy; Unbelief

References: Psalm 68:5; Isaiah 64:8; John 3:16; 5:24–29; 14:6; Romans 8:15; Galatians 4:6–7; Hebrews 9:27

Anne Graham Lotz, daughter of evangelist Billy Graham and his wife, Ruth, was asked if those who died in the explosions of the World Trade Center on September 11, 2001, but had not confessed Christ as Savior would go to heaven. She replied:

In my little book *Heaven: My Father's House*, I tell about people who want to visit my father's home in western North Carolina. They drive up the long drive and come to the gate. They knock on the gate and say, "Billy Graham, let us in. We've read your books, we've watched you on TV, we've written to you, and we want to come to your house."

And my father says, "Depart from me, I don't know you. You're not a member of my family, and you've not made any arrangements to come."

But when I drive up that same driveway and knock on the gate, I say, "Daddy, this is Anne, and I've come home." The gate is thrown right open, and I go inside, because I'm the father's child.

Because heaven is God's house, he has the right to decide who comes in and who stays out. He says he will welcome anyone inside his home, but they have to be born again into his family through faith in Jesus Christ.

That gives us a wonderful hope that when the time comes—whether death comes as a thief in the night, as it did for those in the [World Trade Center] towers, or as an angel of mercy after a long illness—we can be assured that at the end of the journey, we'll step right into our Father's arms. We'll be welcomed there because we are our Father's children.

—Anne Graham Lotz, "Finding Meaning in September 11," CNN.com (December 11, 2006)

ILLUSTRATION 288
GETTING TO HEAVEN

Topics: Accepting Christ; Assurance; Born Again; Death; Eternal Life; Heaven; Salvation

References: 2 Samuel 14:14; Romans 5:12–14; 6:23; Hebrews 9:27; 11:5

A Sunday school teacher wanted to explain to the six-year-olds in his class what someone had to do to go to heaven. To find out what kids believed about the subject, he asked a few questions. "If I sold my house and my car, had a big garage sale, and gave all my money to the church, would that get me to heaven?" he asked.

"No!" the children answered. The teacher was encouraged.

"If I cleaned the church every day, mowed the yard, and kept everything neat and tidy, would that get me to heaven?"

Again the answer was, "No!"

"If I was kind to animals and gave candy to all the children and loved my wife, would that get me into heaven?"

Again they all shouted, "No!"

"Well then, how can I get to heaven?"

A boy in the back row stood up and shouted, "You gotta be dead!"

—Andy Stanley,
How Good Is Good Enough? (Multnomah, 2003)

ILLUSTRATION 289

PREACHING HEAVEN

Topics: Eternal Life; Heaven; Money; Riches; Wealth

References: 1 Corinthians 15:19; 2 Corinthians 4:16–18; 5:1–5; Revelation 21

For his first sermon in a preaching class, Lawrence, an African student, chose a text describing the joys we'll share when Christ returns and ushers us to our heavenly home.

"I've been in the United States for several months," he said. "I've seen the great wealth that is here—the fine homes and cars and clothes. I've listened to many sermons in churches here too. But I've yet to hear one sermon about heaven. Because everyone has so much in this country, no one preaches about heaven. People here don't seem to need it. In my country, most people have very little, so we preach on heaven all the time. We know how much we need it."

—Bryan Chapell,
The Wonder of It All (Crossway, 1999)

ILLUSTRATION 290

LIMITING GRACE

Topics: Day of the Lord; Grace; Judgment; Repentance; Urgency

References: Matthew 25:1–13; Romans 2:4–10; 2 Peter 3:9–12

Unlike other countries that have a pay-as-you-use toll system on major roads, Switzerland expects drivers using its autoroute system to pay an annual fee of 40 Swiss francs. When you pay, you get a windshield sticker you display for the rest of the year.

Traditionally, traffic police give motorists the whole month of January to purchase the sticker. There is no penalty for driving without it during that month—it is a month of grace. But when the first days of February come, expect to see the traffic police on the autoroute exit ramps checking for cars without the sticker. No more excuses are accepted; no more time is given.

The grace period has ended.

—Alan Wilson, Nyon, Switzerland

ILLUSTRATION 291

DRESSING FOR HEAVEN

Topics: Assurance; Christ, Our Righteousness; Heaven; Jesus Christ; Justification; Righteousness; Salvation

Reference: Galatians 3:26–29

I make no claim to being a good golfer, but I love to play golf and watch golf, and on good nights I even dream golf. So when I was invited to attend the Masters Golf Tournament, I was thrilled. A pass to the Masters is the golfer's holy grail. Mine came via pro golfer Scott Simpson.

Off we went to Augusta National Country Club in Georgia where golf heritage hangs like moss from the trees. I was a kid in a candy store. It wasn't enough to see the course and walk the grounds; I wanted to see the locker room, where the clubs of Ben Hogan and Paul Azinger are displayed.

But they wouldn't let me in. A guard stopped me at the entrance. I showed him my pass, but he shook his head. I told him I knew Scott, but that didn't matter. "Only caddies and players," he explained. Well, he knew I wasn't a player or a caddie. Caddies are required to wear white coveralls. So I left, knowing I had made it all the way to the door but was denied entrance.

God has one requirement for entrance into heaven: that we be clothed in Christ.

When someone prays, "Take away my [sinful] rags and clothe me in your grace," Jesus, in an act visible only to the eyes of heaven, removes the stained robe and replaces it with his robe of righteousness.

Jesus put on our coat of sin and wore it to the cross. As he died, his blood flowed over our sins and they were cleansed. Because of this, we have no fear of being turned away at the door of heaven.

—Max Lucado, "Back Door,"
Christian Reader (May–June 2000)

ILLUSTRATION 292

BULLYING REWARD

Topics: Conviction of Sin; Faith and Works; Final Judgment; Godliness; Hell; Repentance; Salvation; Truth

References: Matthew 7:13–27; 13:40–43; 2 Timothy 2:19

In *A Painted House*, John Grisham describes seven-year-old Luke Chandler's reaction to a Sunday school teacher's eulogy for a mean boy, Jerry Sisco, who had been killed the night before in a back alley fight after he picked on one person too many.

> "She made Jerry sound like a Christian, and an innocent victim," said a little boy who had seen the fight with his friend Dewayne. I [Luke] glanced at Dewayne, who had one eye on me. There was something odd about this. As Baptists, we'd been taught from the cradle that the only way you made it to heaven was by believing in Jesus and trying to follow his example in living a clean life and moral Christian life.
>
> Anyone who did not accept Jesus and live a Christian life simply went to hell. That's where Jerry Sisco was, and we all knew it.

—Based on John Grisham,
A Painted House (Doubleday, 2001)

ILLUSTRATION 293

MADE FOR ANOTHER WORLD

Topics: Desires; Eternity; Fulfillment; Heaven; Hunger; Satisfaction

References: Psalm 107:8–9; Isaiah 55:1–2; John 6:35; 7:37–39; Romans 8:8–25

Creatures are not born with desires unless satisfaction for those desires exists. A baby feels hunger; well, there is such a thing as food. A duckling wants to swim; well, there is such a thing as water. . . .

If I find in myself a desire that no experience in this world can satisfy, the most probable explanation is that I was made for another world. If none of my earthly pleasures satisfy it, that does not prove that the universe is a fraud. Probably, earthly pleasures were never meant to satisfy it, but only to arouse it, to suggest the real thing.

—C. S. Lewis, *Mere Christianity* (Macmillan, 1952)

ILLUSTRATION 294

FIRE IN THE BACKYARD

Topics: Assurance; Eternal Life; Hell

References: Mark 8:34–37; 9:43–48; Luke 12:5

Early on Friday morning, the phone rang. "David Noel?" I heard.

"Yes."

"This is your neighbor, Mrs. Waldron."

Not wanting to embarrass myself, I tried to place a Mrs. Waldron somewhere in my neighborhood. She continued, "There's a fire in back of your house by the fence, close to the gas tanks."

I don't have a fence, nor are there any gas tanks anywhere near my home. However, I immediately went outside to see if there was indeed a fire. Returning to the phone, I said, "Ma'am, I think you have the wrong David Noel."

"Aren't you the David Noel that lives on Avery?"

"No, ma'am."

"I'm very sorry," she said.

"That's quite all right," I said.

I hung up the phone with a smile—and one more glance at the backyard. Minutes later I found myself looking in the backyard again. The stakes were too high to let a little embarrassment keep me from making sure.

The scriptural teachings are clear on hell. No one ought to ignore those teachings without serious investigation into the claims of Jesus Christ.

—David Noel, pastor, First Alliance Church, Columbus, Ohio

ILLUSTRATION 295

KEEP YOUR FORK

Topics: Heaven; Hope; Resurrection

Reference: Philippians 1:21–24

A woman was diagnosed with a terminal illness. As she was getting her things in order, she contacted her pastor and asked him to come to her house to discuss some of her final wishes.

She told him the songs she wanted sung at her funeral service, the Scriptures she wanted read, and the outfit she wanted to be buried in. She also asked to be buried with her favorite Bible.

As the pastor prepared to leave, the woman remembered something else. "There's one more thing," she said excitedly.

"What's that?" said the pastor.

"I want to be buried with a fork in my right hand."

The pastor stood looking at the woman, not knowing what to say.

The woman explained. "In all my years of attending church socials and potluck dinners, when the dishes of the main course were being cleared, someone would inevitably say, 'Keep your fork.' It was my favorite part of the meal because I knew something better was coming—like velvety chocolate cake or deep-dish apple pie.

"So when people see me in that casket with a fork in my hand and they ask, 'What's with the fork?' I want you to tell them, 'Keep your fork. The best is yet to come!'"

—Brett Kays, Brownstown, Michigan

ILLUSTRATION 296

RAISING HOUSES

Topics: Caring; Childlike Faith; Children; Compassion; Example; Generosity; Giving; Good Deeds; Money; Sowing and Reaping; Stewardship; Talents

References: Proverbs 19:17; Matthew 11:25; 25:14–30; Luke 10:21; Acts 20:35; 2 Corinthians 9:7; Galatians 2:10; 1 Timothy 4:12

Jackson Rogers, ten, raised enough money to put up a house for the homeless. The young entrepreneur said he took on the fund-raising project for Habitat for Humanity in February when he accepted $100 and a challenge from his pastor at First Presbyterian Church.

"My pastor gave me a hundred dollars and told me to do something good to help someone," said Jackson, one of several congregants who accepted their pastor's challenge. They were told to use the money for good and then report on what they did.

At first Jackson's father was hesitant about letting his son take up such a daunting task, but Jackson was determined. "I was discouraging him from volunteering because I didn't know what the pastor intended. But he pulled away from me and ran down there," the father said.

Jackson knew he wanted to help a homeless family. But he wasn't sure how to do that, so he asked his dad. What they came up with was a letter-writing campaign asking for donations to raise $50,000 to build a house through Habitat for Humanity. Jackson then wrote a letter in his own handwriting on notebook paper. "I used the hundred dollars to buy stamps and paper," he said. He then sent out letters to friends and family.

One woman was so touched by his letter that she passed it on to several of her friends and colleagues. Soon, people from Tennessee, Virginia, and Idaho were sending in checks. The 170 people who responded contributed a total of $43,000. When the congregation at First Presbyterian learned the little miracle-worker was $7,000 short of his goal, people chipped in the rest.

"A little person can do something really good. You don't have to wait to be an adult," said Jackson's mother.

—Ron Wilson,
"Ten-Year-Old Raises $43,000
for Habitat for Humanity,"
San Antonio Express-News (August 5, 2006)

ILLUSTRATION 297

START WITH A HAMMER

Topics: Calling; Caring; Direction; Generosity; Giving; Good Deeds; Guidance; Help; Leadership; Ministry; Needs; Outreach; Service; Testimony; Witnessing

References: Matthew 5:13–16; Acts 20:35; Galatians 6:9–10; Ephesians 2:10; 2 Timothy 4:5; James 2:15–16

Clarence Jordan, a philosopher-farmer in Americus, Georgia, was convinced that poor people living in dilapidated shacks could improve themselves with a little support. "They don't need charity," he said to Millard Fuller, who visited Jordan's church community, Koinonia Farm. "They need a way to help themselves."

Millard Fuller, thirty, who was nearly a millionaire, was inspired by Jordan to begin what today is a worldwide organization to provide housing for the poor. Habitat for Humanity runs on what he calls "the theology of the hammer." The group raises money and recruits volunteers to renovate and build homes, which are sold at cost. Mortgages are interest free to qualified recipients. Habitat now builds or renovates twelve houses every day.

— Ward Williams,
"Jesus' Vacation," PreachingToday.com

ILLUSTRATION 298

BUBBLE WRAPPING AMPUTEES

Topics: Caring; Character; Community Impact; Compassion; Creativity; Goals; Healing; Ministry; Outreach; Poverty; Purpose; Talents; Teens; Values

References: Proverbs 29:7; Matthew 5:16; 10:42; Mark 10:43–44; John 13:14; Galatians 2:10; Ephesians 6:7; James 2:14–17

Grayson Rosenberger's mother lost both of her legs in a traffic accident. She and her husband founded Standing with Hope, a ministry that reaches out in music and prayer to amputees in Africa. Grayson, fifteen, wondered what he could do to help. So he entered the Sealed Air Corporation's Bubble Wrap Competition for young inventors.

Grayson used bubble wrap packing material to develop a cost-effective cosmetic skin covering for prosthetic limbs. He used a heat gun to mold sheets of bubble wrap to the steel rod of a prosthetic limb, giving it musclelike tone and shape.

He was one of eight hundred students who entered the contest. He won the grand prize, which included a $10,000 savings bond and a trip to New York City. He hopes to travel to Ghana later this year to fit amputees with the low-cost limb.

—Associated Press, "Teen Uses Bubble Wrap to Help Amputees," MSNBC.com (January 30, 2007)

ILLUSTRATION 299

WASHING THE FEET OF THE HOMELESS

Topics: Caring; Compassion; Godliness; Homelessness; Humility; Love; Missions; Outreach; Poor People; Social Justice; Submission; Witnessing

References: Proverbs 29:7; Matthew 5:16; 10:42; Mark 10:43–44; John 13:1–17; Galatians 2:10; Ephesians 6:7; James 2:14–17

On Friday nights, volunteers from Bridgetown Ministries help the homeless people gathered under the Burnside Bridge in Portland, Oregon. In addition to providing hot meals, shaves, and haircuts, some of the volunteers wash the homeless people's feet. Tom Krattenmaker, a writer for *USA Today*, was stunned when he saw that, calling it "one of the most audacious acts of compassion and humility I have ever witnessed."

This group of society's outcasts had their bare feet immersed in warm water, scrubbed, dried, powdered, and placed in clean socks. One man reported with a smile, "I can't find the words to describe how good that felt."

Krattenmaker later wrote, "Washing someone's feet is an act best performed while kneeling. Given the washer's position, and the unpleasant appearance and odor of a homeless person's feet, it's hard to imagine an act more humbling."

The leader of Bridgetown Ministries prepares volunteers for this ministry by saying, "When you go out there tonight, I want you to look for Jesus. You might see him in the eyes of a drunk person, a homeless person … we're just out there to love on people."

—Tom Krattenmaker, "A Witness to What Faith Can Be," *USA Today* (December 18, 2006)

ILLUSTRATION 300

RAISING THE MUSLIM VIEW OF THE UNITED STATES

Topics: Assumptions; Compassion; Enemies; Feelings; Grudges; Islam; Judging Others; Kindness; Love; Outreach; Prejudice; Respect; Servanthood

References: Proverbs 25:21; Matthew 5:43–44; Luke 6:27–36; Romans 12:17–21

Humanitarian aid is an effective way to improve how Muslim countries view the United States of America. That's what a poll conducted in January 2006 by the Terror Free Tomorrow organization showed.

In May 2003, research indicated that only 15 percent of people in Indonesia — the world's most populous Muslim nation — had a favorable view of the United States. However, after the country was devastated by a tsunami in December 2004, humanitarian aid poured into the affected areas from the United States and other Western nations. As a result, the favorable view of the United States nearly tripled, jumping to 44 percent. What's more, the well-respected Indonesian Survey Institute reported, "Support for bin Laden and terrorism has dropped to its lowest level since 9/11." And Indonesians with a "very unfavorable" view of the United States fell to 13 percent—down from 48 percent prior to the tsunami.

—Tom McCawley,
"U.S. Tsunami Aid Still Reaps Goodwill,"
Christian Science Monitor (February 28, 2006)

ILLUSTRATION 301

VOLUNTEERISM AND HEALTH

Topics: Caring; Community; Compassion; Empathy; Giving; Health; Illness; Kindness; Love; Relationships; Rewards; Sacrifice; Servanthood; Unselfishness

References: Luke 10:25 – 37; John 15:12 – 17; Philippians 2:1 – 4

People who help others are healthier and live longer. That was one of the conclusions of a team headed by Stephen G. Post, professor of bioethics at Case Western Reserve University School of Medicine, which evaluated fifty scientific studies of volunteers.

One of the studies, from Cornell University, spent thirty years following 427 women who were married and had children. Researchers found that only 36 percent of women who regularly volunteered had experienced a major illness, while 52 percent of those who never volunteered had a major illness. Other studies indicated that those who volunteered their time lived longer than those who didn't. Frequent volunteers had a 44 percent reduction in early death when compared to nonvolunteers.

Scientists also identified precise areas of the brain that are highly active during empathic and compassionate emotions. "These brain studies show this profound state of joy and delight that comes from giving to others," Post said. "It doesn't come from any dry action—where the act is out of duty in the narrowest sense, like writing a check for a good cause. It comes from working to cultivate a generous quality—from interacting with people. There is the smile, the tone in the voice, the touch on the shoulder. We're talking about altruistic love."

—Jeanie Lerche Davis, "The Science of Good Deeds," WebMD.com (November 28, 2005)

ILLUSTRATION 302

RESCUE REFUSED

Topics: Deliverance; Foolishness; Needs; Outreach; Powerlessness; Pride; Provision

References: Psalm 20:7; Matthew 23:37; Luke 13:34; Romans 5:6 – 8; Ephesians 2:1 – 10; Colossians 2:8 – 15

Some at-risk people would rather stay put than be led to safety. That's what helicopter pilot Iain McConnell and the rest of his air station crew discovered in the aftermath of Hurricane Katrina.

McConnell and his crew were told to keep five H-60 helicopters airborne on missions around the clock to airlift stranded people from their rooftops and deliver them to the Superdome in New Orleans. But they were only able to help relatively few survivors. "On our first three missions, we saved the lives of eighty-nine people, three dogs, and a cat," McConnell said. "On the fourth mission, to our great frustration, we saved no one—but not for lack of trying. The dozens we attempted to rescue refused pickup!

"Some people told us simply to bring them food and water. 'You are living in unhealthy conditions, and the water will stay high for a long time,' we warned them. Still they refused."

In truth, they did not know how desperate their situation was.

—Jocelyn C. Green, "A Rescuer's Journal,"
Today's Christian (January–February 2006)

ILLUSTRATION 303

RANDOM ACTS OF KINDNESS

Topics: Caring; Evangelism; Generosity; Kindness; Ministry; Outreach; Service; Witnessing

References: Matthew 6:1–4; Mark 9:41; John 13:34–35

Rena Garcia, twenty-four, is a wife, mother of two preschoolers, and a full-time nanny for two other children. She is busy, but her favorite part of the day is when she goes out to perform random acts of kindness.

She and her husband, Aaron, are part of RAOK (Random Acts of Kindness), through which Christians seek to anonymously bless other people in the name of Jesus. They have even started a website to help share ideas, www.raoked.com. Some of these ideas include:

- leaving a roll of quarters at the Laundromat
- paying for the person behind you at a drive-thru
- leaving grocery gift cards in mailboxes
- paying rent for a family in need
- handing out water or sports drinks on a biking trail.

Garcia hands out RAOK business cards that explain her motivation, information about her church, and the assurance that there are no strings attached. "People were drawn to Christ, not because he stood on a mountain and preached, but because he filled their needs," she says.

—John W. Kennedy,
"Winning Them with Kindness,"
Today's Christian (November–December 2005)

ILLUSTRATION 304

MISS MILDRED BLANKETS

Topics: Attitudes; Compassion; Good Deeds; Ministry; Needs; Outreach; Servanthood

References: Jeremiah 29:11; Romans 8:28; 2 Corinthians 1:3–7; 1 Timothy 4:12; 1 Peter 4:10

When she was thirteen, Lauren Blakemore was diagnosed with a rare form of neuroectodermal cancer, in which tumors invade bones and often lead to amputation. She had fourteen rounds of chemotherapy and twenty-five radiation treatments.

Throughout her battle, Lauren was comforted with a multicolored quilt that a neighbor, Mildred, had made for Lauren when she was a baby. Lauren snuggled with this "Miss Mildred" blanket through childhood and then through the nausea, fatigue, and sleepless nights that came with battling cancer.

After Lauren's dad visited a children's cancer ward in India, he returned home to tell her about the kids. Immediately, Lauren began to raise money by speaking at Rotary Club meetings and schools. She wanted every child to have a Miss Mildred blanket because "chemotherapy makes you cold all the time."

Thanks to women in Bosnia working at Peace Crafts, a cottage industry started by Southeast missionaries, whom Lauren asked to make the blankets, each child's bed in the cancer ward is now warmed by a Miss Mildred blanket.

"When I was first diagnosed with cancer, I knew God had a plan for my life," Lauren said. "This is part of that plan."

—Ruth Schenk, "Lauren's Mission," *Southeast Outlook* (November 24, 2005)

ILLUSTRATION 305

SOOTHING GRIEVING PARENTS

Topics: Grief; Loss; Ministry; Mothers; Purpose; Sacrifice; Service; Teens; Tragedy; Witnessing

References: John 19:25 – 27; Romans 8:28; 1 Corinthians 15:58; 2 Corinthians 1:3 – 7; 9:6 – 15; Galatians 5:6

In 1992, Rosemary and Luther Smith of Beattyville, Kentucky, lost two sons in a car wreck.

Darkness like nothing she had ever known settled over Rosemary. Yet she found solace in her faith. While following the hearses to the burial site, she heard church bells toll thirty-three times. "As I sat there and counted, it hit me that when Jesus died he was thirty-three, which was also the combined ages of my sons."

Not long after her loss, Rosemary began a ministry called Fellow Travelers, a ministry to other parents who have lost a child. "I now have a higher purpose than what I was doing, and the death of my sons took me there," she says.

Every day, Rosemary reads the newspaper and searches the Internet for child obituaries. She either calls the families or sends them special packets consisting of books on loss, a music CD, a notebook of inspirational messages, and more. She gets about fifty emails a day from people requesting one of her packets. More than five thousand packets—paid for by Rosemary and her husband—have been sent all over the world.

"We are here to help other people," said Rosemary. "It gives me great joy to think God is using me to help others."

—Kara Bussabarger, "A Fellow Traveler," *Southeast Outlook* (December 15, 2005)

ILLUSTRATION 306

FREED FROM GANG TATTOOS

Topics: Assurance; Atonement; Blood of Christ; Discipleship; Freedom;

Identity; Justification; Pardon; Purity; Rebirth; Repentance; Salvation; Sanctification; Sin

References: Proverbs 5:22; Romans 6:23; 8:2; 2 Corinthians 3:17; Galatians 5:1; Ephesians 2:13; 1 John 1:7

Father Greg Boyle, founder and director of Homeboy Industries in East Los Angeles, has put together a team of physicians trained to remove the tattoos of ex-gang members. The service is crucial for their success in making it outside the gang.

Gang-related tattoos prevent many former gang members from getting jobs or advancing in work. For others, the markings put them in serious danger on the streets. There is no fee or community service required to receive the service offered by Homeboy Industries; tattoo removal is strictly a gift. Currently, more than a thousand names are on the waiting list.

The seeming permanence of a gang tattoo fosters the attitude that the gang's claim is also permanent. It is a mark of ownership as much as identity. The emotional consequence is that the tie seems a part of a person that can never be shaken.

I suspect some of us have felt like this with past sins whose mark we cannot shake off though we know we have been cleansed by Christ. Perhaps the imagery of tattoo removal can evoke a renewed sense of our blessed assurance. Like former gang members who have had the marks of a former life removed, so our sins are blotted out by the blood of Christ. They are remembered no longer.

The process of tattoo removal is extremely painful. Patients describe the laser procedure as feeling like hot grease has been poured on their skin. Yet the list grows, each name representing a life that longs to be free and is willing to endure the pain to seize freedom.

—Jill Carattini, "A Slice of Infinity," rzim.org (June 23, 2006)

ILLUSTRATION 307

HERO OF HARLEM

Topics: Courage; Evangelism; Good Deeds; Great Commission; Heroes; Imitation of Christ; Love; Ministry; Redemption; Rescue; Rewards; Sacrifice; Salvation; Witnessing

References: Matthew 28:18–20; John 15:13; Romans 7:24–25; 10:14–15; Colossians 1:13–14; James 5:19–20; 1 Peter 3:15; 1 John 3:16–18

Cameron Hollopeter, nineteen, suffered a seizure while waiting for a train in a New York City subway station. As his body convulsed out of control, the young man stumbled down the platform and onto one of the tracks, directly into the path of an inbound train.

Wesley Autrey, fifty, a construction worker who was standing on the platform with his two daughters, saw Hollopeter fall. He jumped onto the tracks and grabbed hold of Hollopeter. With only seconds to spare, he rolled with the younger man into a drainage trough between two tracks. An instant later, the train cars thundered over both of them. Amazingly, neither man was injured.

In the ensuing days, Autrey was rewarded handsomely for his bravery. Mayor Michael Bloomberg presented him with the city's highest award for civic achievement, calling him "a man who makes us all proud to be New Yorkers." He was given $10,000 from Donald Trump, a trip to Disney World, and a year's supply of MetroCards from the Metropolitan Transportation Authority. His boss even bought him a "hero" sandwich.

Autrey is modest about his new status as the hero of Harlem. "I just did it because I saw someone in distress," he told reporters. "Someone needed help."

—Verena Dobnik, Associated Press, "NYC Subway Savior Showered with Gifts" (January 4, 2007)

ILLUSTRATION 308

DR. GOOD SAM

Topics: Brotherly Love; Caring; Christians; Compassion; Good Deeds; Great Commandment; Integrity; Involvement; Ministry; Outreach; Sacrifice; Service; Talents; Unselfishness

References: Matthew 9:36; 25:14–30; 28:19–20; Luke 10:29–37; 19:11–27; Romans 12:6–9; 1 Corinthians 4:2; James 4:17; 1 Peter 4:10

Dr. Scott Kurtzman, chief of surgery at Waterbury Hospital, was on his way to deliver an 8:00 a.m. lecture when he witnessed one of the worst crashes in Connecticut history. A dump truck,

whose driver had lost control, flipped on its side and skidded into oncoming traffic. The resulting accident involved twenty vehicles; four people died.

Kurtzman immediately shifted into trauma mode. He worked his way through the mangled mess of people and metal, calling out, "Who needs help?"

After about ninety minutes, when all sixteen victims had been triaged and taken to area hospitals, Kurtzman climbed back into his car, drove to the medical school, and gave his lecture—two hours late.

Over the years, Kurtzman has stopped at a half dozen crashes and assisted at three. "A person with my skills simply can't drive by someone who's injured," says Kurtzman. "I refuse to live my life that way."

—Hal Carp, "Roadside E.R.," *Reader's Digest* (August 2006)

ILLUSTRATION 309

JUST BEING THERE

Topics: Brotherly Love; Christlikeness; Comfort; Commitment; Companionship; Faithfulness; Friendship; Grief; Mourning; Needs; Relationships; Sacrifice; Service

References: Job 2:13; Proverbs 17:17; 27:10; Ecclesiastes 4:9–10; John 15:13–14

When during an already painful juncture in my life my wife died, I was so numb that I felt dead myself. In the hours after her death, as our children and I tried to figure out what to do next, how to get from hour to hour, the phone must have been ringing, but I have no recollection of it.

The next morning—one of those mornings when you awaken, blink to start the day, and then, a dispiriting second later, realize anew what has just happened and feel the boulder press you against the earth with such weight that you fear you will never be able to get up—the phone rang, and it was Jack.

I didn't want to hear any voice—even his voice. I just wanted to cover myself with darkness. I knew he would be asking if there was anything he could do. But I should have known that he'd already done it.

"I'm in Chicago," he said. "I took the first flight this morning.

"I know you probably don't want to see anyone," he went on. "That's all right. I've checked into a hotel, and I'll just sit here in case you need me to do anything. I can do whatever you want, or I can do nothing."

He meant it. He knew the best thing he could do was to be present in the same town—to tell me he was there. And he did just sit there—I assume he watched TV or did some work, but he waited until I gathered the strength to say I needed him. He helped me with things no man ever wants to need help with; mostly he sat with me and knew I did not require conversation, did not welcome chatter, did not need anything beyond the knowledge he was there. He brought food for my children, and by sharing my silence, he got me through those days.

—Bob Greene,
And You Know You Should Be Glad
(Morrow, 2006)

ILLUSTRATION 310

OFFERING A CUP OF COFFEE

Topics: Caring; Compassion; Discipleship; Generosity; Giving; Homelessness; Kindness; Needs; Poor People; Regret

References: Matthew 10:40–42; James 2:14–17

The Chicago-based newspaper *StreetWise* is sold by homeless people who collect a portion of the proceeds. One day as I walked to work, I passed a *StreetWise* vendor. It was a bitterly cold January morning, and I'd already stopped by Starbucks and paid more than a buck for a measly cup of coffee. Feeling noble, I struggled to find my wallet, reached in, and took out a dollar.

The homeless woman asked, "Do you really want the paper, or can I keep it to sell to someone else?"

"Keep the paper," I replied. Then I added, "How are you today?"

"I'm so cold," she said.

"I hope the sun comes out, it warms up, and you have a good day," I told her as I turned to go.

I continued on, with the cup of coffee warming my hand. About half a block later, the conversation finally registered. I wrestled for a moment with what I should do, but I was late, so I kept walking. Ever since, I've regretted not giving her a cup of hot coffee in Christ's name.

—Joseph Stowell,
A Heart for the City (Moody, 1999)

ILLUSTRATION 311

HELPING A MUSLIM MOM

Topics: Christian Life; Compassion; Poor People; Widows; Witnessing

References: Deuteronomy 10:18; James 1:27

Sheikha was born about sixty years ago to a Bedouin family that roamed across vast areas of the Middle East. Today her tribe is forced to live in one place because their nomadic ways are unwelcome by landowners and considered a security threat by governments.

Sheikha's life fell short of the noble designs her parents had for her. Where she lives is not part of any country. There is barely a government. Fierce fighting flares between Jews and Arabs only a few miles away. Also, the husband with whom she had six children abandoned her, leaving Sheikha to fend for herself and a severely disabled daughter.

Though uneducated, Sheikha is resourceful. She scraped together some cash, bought a couple of junkyard buses, and had them towed to her village of fifteen hundred people. Sheikha and her daughter live in one bus and planned to open a little convenience market in the shell of the other. With the help of HOPE, a Christian organization, she has done that.

HOPE loaned the money Sheikha needed to fill her shop with small items like soap, school supplies, and basic medicines. The store is a great service to the village, a great way for Sheikha to make a living, and a big witness to Muslims. "I prefer to be with Christians because they feel for the poor who need help," Sheikha says. "The others didn't look after me, not even my husband."

—Kevin Miller, "Christians Help Muslim Widow," PreachingToday.com

ILLUSTRATION 312

COSTLY RESCUE

Topics: Blood of Christ; Evangelism; God's Love; Great Commission; Redemption; Sacrifice; Salvation

Reference: 1 Peter 1:18–21

For four years Emperor Theodore III of Ethiopia had held a group of fifty-three European captives (thirty adults and twenty-three children), including some missionaries and a British consul. By letter Queen Victoria pleaded in vain with Theodore to release the captives, who were held in a remote nine-thousand-foot-high bastion deep in the interior.

Finally, the queen ordered a full-scale military expedition from India to march into Ethiopia, not to conquer the country and make it a British colony, but simply to rescue a tiny band of civilians.

The invasion force included thirty-two thousand men, heavy artillery, and forty-four elephants to carry the guns. Provisions included fifty thousand tons of beef and pork and thirty thousand gallons of rum. Engineers built landing piers, water treatment plants, a railroad, and a telegraph line to the interior, plus many bridges. All of this was necessary to fight one decisive battle, after which the prisoners were released. Then everyone packed up and went home. The

British expended millions of pounds to rescue a handful of captives.

—Jim Reapsome,
Current Thoughts and Trends (May 1999)

ILLUSTRATION 313
DYING FOR FRIENDS

Topics: Bible Study; Community; Courage; Love; Relationships; Sacrifice

References: John 13:34–35; 15:13

Prisoners of war in Japanese camps during World War II endured horrific conditions. A few Christians formed Bible study groups, which brought about amazing transformations within the camps. POWs who had stolen and cheated from one another became men who cared for and gave their lives for their friends.

Ernest Gordon, in *Miracle on the River Kwai*, writes:

> During one work detail, a shovel was missing, and the Japanese guard shouted, insisting someone had stolen it. Striding up and down before the men, he worked himself up into a paranoid fury. Screaming in broken English, he demanded that the guilty one step forward to take his punishment. When no one moved, the guard's rage reached new heights of violence. "All die! All die!" he shrieked. To show that he meant what he said, he cocked his rifle, put it to his shoulder, and looked down the gun sights, ready to fire at the first man at the end of the line.
>
> Another man stepped forward, stood at attention, and said calmly, "I did it."
>
> The guard kicked the helpless prisoner and beat him with his fists. He lifted his rifle high over his head and, with a final howl, brought it down on the soldier's skull, who sank limply to the ground and did not move. The men of the work detail picked up their comrade's body, shouldered their tools, and marched back to the camp. When the tools were counted again at the guardhouse, no shovel was missing.

—Ernest Gordon,
Miracle on the River Kwai (Collins, 1963)

ILLUSTRATION 314
DAMEON'S GIFT

Topics: Caring; Community; Compassion; Conversion; Disabilities; Giving; Help from God; Love; Mercy; Sacrifice; Sickness; Teens

References: Matthew 22:37–40; Mark 12:29–31; Luke 10:27; John 15:13; Acts 2:42–47; Romans 12:10; Ephesians 5:2

Jeff Leeland had just accepted a teaching position at Kamiakin Junior High in Seattle, Washington. The family had endured months of Dad's driving to and from work before the family could relocate from their previous home.

As winter struggled toward spring in 1992, Jeff and his wife, Kristi, heard the devastating news: "Your baby boy has cancer. Michael needs a bone marrow transplant." The good news was that Michael's six-year-old sister, Amy, was a perfect match for the transplant. But Jeff's insurance company wouldn't pay for it. A tiny clause in the contract stated that Jeff had to be on the job for at least a year before insurance would cover a transplant. He had only been teaching in the new job for six months.

By March, Michael's need for a transplant became urgent. If he couldn't receive the new marrow soon, he would die. The Leelands needed to raise $200,000 by May.

Fellow teacher Joe Kennedy told his class about Leeland's situation. Dameon, a seventh-grade boy who walked with a limp and struggled in special education classes, heard about Mr. Leeland's son, Michael, and made a visit to Jeff's house. "Mr. Leeland, if your baby is in trouble, I want to help," he said. The kid others teased then stuffed twelve five-dollar bills into the hand of a teacher who had made a difference in his life. It was the boy's life savings.

Word got out about Dameon's gift. Some kids organized a walk-a-thon. Others called a local newspaper with the story. Some held a car wash.

The Kamiakin kids' wave of compassion poured out across Seattle. On Friday, May 22, a man walked into the bank with a check for $10,000. One week after Dameon's gift, Michael's fund grew to $16,000. By late May, area TV stations picked up the story. By May 29, Michael's fund grew to $62,000. The Leelands were boosted with hope when the hospital moved Michael's transplant back by two weeks. By June 5, the fund had grown to $143,000; by June 8,

$160,000; by June 9, $185,000. Only four weeks after Dameon's gift of $60, the Michael Leeland Fund contained more than $220,000.

Michael got the marrow transplant and lived. Dameon accepted Jesus Christ as his Savior, partially due to his interaction with Michael's family. Soon after that, Dameon died from complications following an infection in one of his legs.

Dameon, the unlikely hero, gave his all to save the life of another. In the process he received life everlasting.

—Based on a phone interview and Jeff Leeland's account in *One Small Sparrow* (Multnomah, 2000)

ILLUSTRATION 315

FAILING TO HELP

Topics: Love; Mercy; Regret; Responsibility

Reference: Luke 10:30–37

I was driving to Chicago early one Sunday morning when I noticed a car in the ditch. I looked closer and saw an empty car with the driver's door wide open. Should I stop?

I remembered reading about an elderly woman whose car went off the highway in Florida. She was trapped in her car for three days and nearly died. Then I thought of Jesus' story of the Good Samaritan. Convicted, I slowed down and pulled off the road.

Forty yards ahead of me, another car stopped, and two young men got out. I walked toward them, yelling, "Do you have a cell phone?" Neither answered. I asked again, "Do you have a cell phone?" They just looked at me and walked toward me.

Suddenly I felt uneasy. "Did you see that car back in the ditch?" I asked. The two were now ten yards away. The man on the right was taller than me and thirty pounds heavier; the man on the left was at least sixty pounds heavier. "Uh-oh," I thought, "this was a mistake."

As I froze, the young men walked past me and continued down the road.

I jumped into my car and pulled back onto the expressway, feeling as if I had just dodged a bullet. How easy it would have been for those two to have jumped me, thrown me in the ditch, and stolen my car. My interest in the car in the ditch drained from me like milk from a broken bottle.

Still, my conscience bothered me. I should pull over and call 911. I drove past one exit, then another, then several more. Finally, fifteen minutes later I pulled into a McDonald's. *They'll have a phone,* I thought. They didn't.

When I arrived at church ten minutes later, I could have called, but I didn't. Later as I drove home, I looked to see what had happened to the car, but a concrete barrier blocked my view. I felt I had done wrong. If someone had been in that car in need, they got their help from someone other than me.

Later I asked God's forgiveness through Christ for failing to help the driver of the disabled car. I've thought about what I will do the next time I face that situation. I will be more careful, but I will try to help, for even though there are risks, I have a responsibility to my neighbor.

—Craig Brian Larson,
Arlington Heights, Illinois

ILLUSTRATION 316
THE RABBI'S DISCIPLE

Topics: Heaven; Humility; Love; Ministry; Servanthood

References: Matthew 25:31–40; John 13:1–17

In a small Jewish town in Russia, a rabbi disappeared each Friday morning for several hours. His devoted disciples boasted that during those hours their rabbi went to heaven and talked to God.

A stranger who moved into town was skeptical, so he decided to check things out. He hid and watched the rabbi. The rabbi got up in the morning, said his prayers, then dressed in peasant clothes. He grabbed an ax, went into the woods, and cut some firewood, which he then hauled to a shack on the outskirts of the village, where an old woman and her sick son lived. The rabbi left them the wood and went home.

The newcomer became the rabbi's disciple. Now, whenever he hears a villager say, "On Friday morning our rabbi ascends to heaven," the newcomer quietly adds, "if not higher."

—Jim McGuiggan,
Jesus, Hero of Thy Soul (Howard, 1998)

ILLUSTRATION 317
HELPED IN THE HELPING

Topics: Attitudes; Compassion; Empathy; Patience; Tolerance

References: Matthew 7:12; Galatians 6:7–10

How far you go in life depends on your being tender with the young, compassionate with the aged, sympathetic with the striving, and tolerant of the weak and strong. Because someday in life you will have been all of these.

—George Washington Carver,
in a 1923 New York City address

ILLUSTRATION 318

TAKING TIME FOR HOSPITALITY

Topics: Commitment; Hospitality; Kindness; Time

References: Isaiah 58:6–7; Matthew 25:34–46

In an era when many of us feel that time is our scarcest resource, hospitality falters.... "In a fast-food culture, you have to remind yourself that some things cannot be done quickly," said a wise Benedictine monk. "Hospitality takes time."

—Dorothy C. Bass,
Receiving the Day (Jossey-Bass, 2001)

ILLUSTRATION 319

REPAYING KINDNESS

Topics: Kindness; Power; Retribution; Revenge

Reference: Luke 11:30–37

Lewis and Clark's famous expedition to the Pacific Northwest in 1804 almost came to an untimely and deadly end. Half starved and almost frozen, the men staggered out of Idaho's snowy Bitterroot Mountains into the camp of the Nez Perce Indians.

A chief named Twisted Hair had to decide what to do with the weak but wealthy strangers suddenly in their midst. According to the tribe's oral tradition, some of the Nez Perce proposed killing the white men and confiscating their boxes of manufactured goods and weapons. The expedition's rifles and ammunition would have instantly made the Nez Perce the region's richest and most powerful tribe.

But an Indian woman came to the aid of the white men. As a young girl, she had been captured by an enemy tribe on the plains, who in turn sold her to another tribe. Eventually she was befriended and treated kindly by white people in Canada before escaping and making her way back to her own people. They called her Wat-kuweis, "Returned from a Faraway Country," and for years she told them stories about the fair-skinned people who lived toward the rising sun. She was aged and dying by the time the explorers arrived.

When she learned about plans to destroy the expedition, this woman intervened. "These are the people who helped me," she said. "Do them no hurt."

A little kindness can have amazing and unexpected results.

—Marshall Shelley, Wheaton, Illinois

ILLUSTRATION 320

HELPING MY DUMB NEIGHBOR

Topics: Compassion; Decisions; Generosity; Love; Mercy; Mistakes; Regret

Reference: Luke 10:25–37

Years ago I flew to Minneapolis to speak at a conference at the Minneapolis Convention Center. Near downtown Minneapolis my taxi stopped at a red light four cars back from the crosswalk. I noticed a homeless man lurching between the cars in the middle of the street. When he got to the front of my taxi, he fell and landed on his chin. His chin split open, and there was blood all over the place.

As I looked at this man six feet away, these thoughts went through my head:

1. I have a brand-new suit on that Gail just bought me. I can't afford to get messed up.
2. I have to get to the convention center to speak in fifteen minutes.
3. I'm in a strange city, and I don't know what to do.
4. I don't have any medical training. I wouldn't know how to help this guy.

I wonder if underneath there wasn't a fifth thought: *If you're dumb enough to get that drunk, why should someone stop and help you?*

For a few seconds those thoughts militated against any movement on my part. Before I could come to better senses, other people came rushing to this man's help, and I was able to get back into my taxi and go on to the convention center to

speak about sensitivity and caring for the needs of other human beings. Isn't that stupid?

—Gordon MacDonald, from the sermon "Pointing to Jesus: Generosity," Grace Chapel, Lexington, Massachusetts (February 22, 1998)

ILLUSTRATION 321

HELPING SLAVES TO FREEDOM

Topics: Courage; Freedom; Rescue; Risk

References: Joshua 1:9; Philippians 4:13

After Harriet Tubman escaped from slavery in 1849, she immediately became involved in the abolitionist movement, organizing meetings and speaking against slavery. But that wasn't enough; she returned to the South to help other slaves find freedom. If she had been caught, she would have been thrown back into slavery or killed as an example to other runaways.

Tubman returned to the South nineteen times to rescue some three hundred fellow slaves. Each trip became riskier as slave catchers became more aware of her. But each time with God's help, she said, she evaded the authorities.

—Matt Donnelly, "Black Moses: The Mystical Faith and No-Nonsense Tactics of the Underground Railroad," *Christian History and Biography* (April 1, 1999)

ILLUSTRATION 322

GETTING THE BALL TO SCOTTY

Topics: Body of Christ; Disabilities; Love; Teamwork

Reference: 1 Corinthians 12:21–27

Witts Springs, Arkansas, population one hundred, has a hard time producing athletes from a student body of forty-one in grades seven to twelve. But its athletes take team play to a new level.

In a basketball game with Leslie School, Witts Springs trailed by more than thirty points with just two minutes to go. The fans began to chant, "Put in Scotty." "Scot-TEE! Scot-TEE!" Coach Nash waved Scotty Harmon in.

Harmon, who has cerebral palsy, took a pass on the perimeter and flung the ball toward the hoop. He missed. His teammates scrambled for the rebound and gave Scotty a second chance. He missed again, which started another fight for the ball.

"The kids know when Scotty's in there, their game is over," Coach Nash said. "They're doing it for him. The atmosphere changes. If they're worn out, they'll break their necks to get that rebound. Our kids will go above everybody to get the ball to Scotty."

On his fourth try, Harmon sunk a three-pointer. Fans on both sides of the gym cheered wildly. The scoreboard showed Leslie, 89; Witts Springs, 58, but everybody left a winner.

—Larry Pillow, *Arkansas Democrat Gazette* (February 7, 1999)

ILLUSTRATION 323

STEP-IN NEIGHBOR

Topics: Mercy; Neighbors; Sacrifice

Reference: Luke 10:25–37

My wife, Gail, and I were flying to Boston. We were seated near the back of the airliner in the two aisle seats across from each other. As the plane loaded up, a woman with two small children took the row of seats in front of us. Another woman took a seat across the aisle next to one of the kids, and the mom held the other child on her lap. I hoped the kids wouldn't be noisy.

My prayer wasn't answered. The two children had a tough time. The air was turbulent, the children cried a lot—their ears hurt—and it was a miserable flight. The two women kept trying to help and comfort these children. The woman at the window played with the child in the middle seat, trying to make her feel good and paying her a lot of attention.

Things went downhill from there. As we got toward the last part of the flight, the child in the middle seat got sick. The next thing I knew she was losing everything from every part of her body. The diaper wasn't on tight, and before long a stench began to rise through the cabin. It was unbearable.

I watched as the woman next to the window patiently comforted the child and tried her best to clean up the mess and make something good out of a bad situation. The plane landed, and when we pulled up to the gate, all of us were ready to exit that plane as fast as we could. The flight attendant came up with paper towels and handed them to the woman in the window seat and said, "Here, ma'am, these are for your little girl."

The woman said, "This isn't my little girl."

"Aren't you traveling together?"

"No, I've never met this woman and these children before in my life."

Suddenly I realized this woman had found the opportunity to give mercy. She was, in the words of Christ, the person who was "a neighbor."

—Gordon MacDonald, in the sermon
"Pointing to Jesus: Generosity,"
Grace Chapel, Lexington, Massachusetts
(February 22, 1998)

ILLUSTRATION 324

PROVIDING A SAFETY MAT

Topics: Church; Cooperation; Ministry; Sacrifice; Spiritual Gifts; Teamwork

References: Acts 2:42–47; Galatians 6:1–2; James 5:19–20; 1 John 3:16–18

Soviet sport parachutist Yuri Belenko realized he was in trouble when he was three thousand feet above the ground. His main chute had malfunctioned, and his reserve chute was "barber poling" around the main, rendering them both useless.

Kicking his feet to slow the spiral caused by the whipping canopies above, Belenko yelled down to fellow jumpers on the ground. His jump buddies immediately sprang into action, grabbed a packing mat, and sprinted toward the impact point. All the way down Belenko yelled and

tugged at the static lines in an attempt to clear the tangled chutes. Below, his friends stretched the mat taut and waited.

Belenko plummeted into the canvas at bone-crushing speed, ripping the tarp from his rescuers' hands and knocking them to the ground. When the dust cleared, Belenko lay gasping for breath, complaining only of a sprained ankle and a few bruises.

His jump buddies were there for Belenko at the moment he needed them most. It's what God wants his people to do for others in need.

—Bud Sellick,
The Wild, Wonderful World of Parachutes and Parachutists
(Prentice-Hall, 1981)

PART 15: HOPE AND DESPAIR

ILLUSTRATION 325

TREES OF HOPE

Topics: Aging; Assurance; Commitment; Confidence; Example; Faith; Fathers; Fruitfulness; Hope; Optimism; Persistence; Promises; Waiting on God

References: Psalm 85:12; Isaiah 27:2–3; 44:4; Jeremiah 32:6–15; 48:47; Romans 5:3–5; 1 Corinthians 13:13; 1 Peter 1:3

In the darkest days of the Babylonian siege of Jerusalem, God asked Jeremiah to go out and buy a piece of real estate—complete with witnesses, a deed, and money (Jeremiah 32:6–15). This act seemed to make no sense, since Judah was about to be conquered and its people taken into exile. But in seventy years, as God reminded Jeremiah, the people would be set free and return to the land to rebuild homes and replant vineyards. Jeremiah's purchase of land was to provide a beacon of hope during the long years of captivity.

My father, at age seventy-five, planted a number of small fruit trees. "What an optimist," I said to him, somewhat mockingly. Dad passed away a few years ago. Now when I return to the old homestead, I have an option. I can go to the grassy cemetery on top of the hill and brood over his grave, or I can eat the fruit of his trees and reflect on a man who knew a great deal about hope.

—Bob Seiple, "The Gospel Blimp Revisited," *Princeton Seminary Bulletin*, vol. 27, no. 2 (2006)

ILLUSTRATION 326

"THIS WOULD BE ONE"

Topics: Cross; Death; Easter; Faith; Fall of Humanity; Hope; Jesus Christ; Life; Miracles; Peace; Resurrection; Trust

References: Genesis 3:1–24; John 3:16; Romans 3:1–26; 6; 8

The doctor said, "If you are a believer in miracles, this would be one."

The doctor was talking about Alcides Moreno. By every law of physics and medicine, Moreno should have died. Moreno was a window washer in Manhattan. He rode platforms with his brother Edgar high into the sky to wash skyscrapers. From there he could look down to see the pavement far below where the people looked like ants. On December 7, 2007, catastrophe struck the Moreno family. As the brothers worked on the forty-seventh story of a high-rise, their platform collapsed, and Alcides and Edgar fell from the sky.

If you are a believer in miracles, this would be one.

No, Alcides Moreno didn't land on a passing airplane or catch his shirt on a flagpole or have anything else amazing happen like you see in the movies; he fell the entire forty-seven stories to the pavement below. As would be expected, his brother Edgar died from the fall, but somehow Alcides did not. He lived. For two weeks he hung on to life by a thread. Then, on Christmas Day, he spoke and reached out to touch his nurse's face. One month later, the doctors were saying that he would probably walk again some day.

If you are a believer in miracles, this would be one.

In the beginning of the human race, Adam also fell from a great height. From sinless glory in the image of God, Adam rebelled against God and fell into sin, death, and judgment, and in this terrible fall he brought with him the whole human race. But "God so loved the world that he gave his one and only Son, that whoever believes in him shall not perish but have eternal life" (John 3:16). God the Son left the heights of heaven and descended to the earth to become a man. He lived a sinless life and then willingly went to the cross to die for the sins of Adam's fallen race. On the third day he rose again, and in his resurrection he made it possible for all to rise again and live forever.

If you are a believer in miracles, this would be one.

—Craig Brian Larson,
"Window Washer Falls 47 Stories, Survives,"
PreachingToday.com; source: "It Wasn't All Bad,"
The Week (January 18, 2008)

ILLUSTRATION 327

SEEING JESUS IN THE DARK

Topics: Challenges; Circumstances and Faith; Doubt; Experiencing God; Faith; Fear; Hope; Jesus Christ; Light; Lostness; Mysteries; Overcoming; Presence of God; Promises; Reality; Security in God; Seen and Unseen; Suffering; Trust

References: Job 23:10; Psalm 23:4; 27:1; John 16:33; Romans 5:1–5; 8:28; James 1:2–4; 1 Peter 5:10

When I was a student at Harvard Divinity School, I learned preaching from Dr. Gardner Taylor, a pastor in New York City. I'll never forget those lectures. I remember him telling a story from when he was preaching in Louisiana during the Depression. Electricity was just coming into that part of the country, and he was out in a rural, black church that had just one little light-bulb hanging down from the ceiling to light up the whole sanctuary. He was preaching away, and in the middle of his sermon, the electricity went out. The building went pitch-black, and Dr. Taylor didn't know what to say, being a young preacher. He stumbled around until one of the elderly deacons sitting in the back of the church cried out, "Preach on, preacher! We can still see Jesus in the dark."

Sometimes that's the only time we can see him—in the dark. And the good news of the gospel is that whether or not we can see him in the dark, he can see us in the dark.

—Timothy George, "Unseen Footprints,"
Preaching Today Audio, no. 290

ILLUSTRATION 328

YOU AND SUFFERING

Topics: Adversity; Despair; Hardship; Help from God; Jesus Christ; Overcoming; Pain; Presence of God; Problems; Questions; Security in God; Struggles; Suffering; Trials; Trust

References: Matthew 11:28–30; Romans 5:3–5; 2 Corinthians 4:11; Hebrews 4:15; James 1:2–4; 1 Peter 1:6–7; 2:24; 5:10

In an interview with Lee Strobel, Peter Kreeft concludes that the answer to suffering is not an answer at all. "It's the Answerer," says Kreeft. "It's Jesus himself. It's not a bunch of words, it's *the* Word. It's not a tightly woven philosophical argument; it's a person. *The* person. The answer to suffering cannot just be an abstract idea, because this isn't an abstract issue; it's a personal issue. It requires a personal response. The answer must be someone, not just something, because the issue involves someone— *God, where are you?*"

—Lee Strobel,
The Case for Faith (Zondervan, 2000)

ILLUSTRATION 329

SPINNING OUT OF CONTROL

Topics: Addiction; Control; Deliverance; Dependence; Despair; Emptiness; Helplessness; Limitations; Longing; Powerlessness; Salvation; Self-reliance; Sin; Waiting on God

References: John 14:6; Romans 3:23–24; 6:17–18; 7:14–25; 8:1–2; 2 Corinthians 5:17; Galatians 3:22; 5:1; 2 Peter 2:19

While vacationing in northern Minnesota, I took my kids to a small county fair near Babbitt. We were about the only ones visiting the carnival rides that morning. So when we climbed into the Tilt-O-Whirl, we hoped the operator would give us a decent ride, even though we were the only ones on it.

Little did we know. The first few minutes were rather fun. We laughed and enjoyed the funny feeling inside our stomachs. But after a while, the ride was not so much fun. And after more time—way past the length of an ordinary ride—I began to feel queasy.

I wanted to get out, but I couldn't. First, we were going too fast to escape. Second, the centrifugal force had me immobilized against the back of the car. Every time we spun past the operator, I looked pleadingly at him, trying to communicate "Please! I need to get off!" But the operator kept the ride going. I guess he thought he'd let it run until more customers showed up.

After another few minutes, the ride became miserable. The funny feeling inside my stomach turned into a churning concoction that included my morning breakfast. I had lost control. I was caught, going around in circles, held down by a merciless carnival ride operator.

After what seemed like three or four hours, the carnie finally stopped the ride. I'm sure I was green by that time. I staggered off the platform and lost my breakfast. Of course, my kids gathered around, cheering me on. They thought Dad's discomfort was the best part of the ride.

If you're caught spinning in a diabolical ride that started out fun but has turned into an addiction — if you're going around in circles, powerless to get off — you know the helpless feeling of losing control of your life. You know what it means to need God's supernatural help to stop the ride so you can escape.

—Rich Doebler, Cloquet, Minnesota

ILLUSTRATION 330

LOVE IN THE RUINS

Topics: Crisis; God's Love; Goodness of God; Loss; Mysteries; Tragedy

References: Ecclesiastes 3:11; John 13:7

Circumstances may appear to wreck our lives and God's plans, but God is not helpless among the ruins. Our broken lives are not lost or useless. God's love is still working. He comes in and takes the calamity and uses it victoriously, working out his wonderful plan of love.

—Eric Liddell, *The Disciplines of the Christian Life* (Ballantine, 1988)

ILLUSTRATION 331

YOUR WORTH

Topics: Depravity; Discouragement; Emptiness; Faithfulness; God; Grace; Guilt; Human Condition; Needs; Security; Self-image; Self-worth; Shame; Victorious Living

References: 1 Samuel 16:7; Matthew 10:29 – 31; Luke 12:6 – 7; John 3:16; Philippians 3:7 – 9

If someone offered you a twenty-dollar bill, would you take it? What if that person wadded up the bill and threw it on the ground — would you still want it? What if he stepped on it, kicked it, and even spit on it? Could you still go to the store and spend it?

The answer is yes. That bill has value because of what it is, not because of how it looks, where it's been, or what it has been used for. A crisp, clean twenty-dollar bill is worth the same amount as an ugly, old, abused one.

You may feel like you've been stepped on, beat up, or kicked around. You may feel dirty, unworthy, or useless. But be encouraged by the twenty-dollar bill — no matter what you've been through, you still have value to God!

—Mike Silva, *Would You Like Fries with That?* (Word, 2005)

ILLUSTRATION 332

TURNING ON THE SWITCH

Topics: Belief; Creator; Experiencing God; Fellowship with God; Gratitude; Happiness; Heaven; Joy; Life; Majesty of God; Nature; Optimism; Purpose; Reverence

References: Psalm 8:1 – 4; 19:1; Romans 1:20; 1 Corinthians 2:9; 2 Corinthians 12:1 – 4

After I had faith, living things became precious to me. I wanted to pet them, hug them—babies and dogs and lizards, whatever. For me the great fruit of belief is joy. There is a God, there is a purpose, there is a meaning to things, there are realities we cannot guess at, there is a big peace, and you are part of it.

"God is good." Near him is where you want to be. There is something called everlasting happiness, and Saint Paul—a fiercely imperfect man who was a great man—was granted visions of it, and that great user of words was floored by it and said that no one can imagine how wonderful it is. The human imagination cannot encompass it.

—Pope John Paul II, quoted in Peggy Noonan, *John Paul the Great* (Viking, 2005)

ILLUSTRATION 333

TRAPPED WORKER SEES JESUS

Topics: Despair; Discouragement; Encouragement; Experiencing God; Faith; Help from God; Hope; Jesus Christ; Miracles; Peace; Presence of God; Protection; Rescue; Supernatural Occurrences; Visions

References: Psalm 23:4; 46:1; Isaiah 40:31; Philippians 4:13; Hebrews 13:6; 1 Peter 1:3; 5:7

Port Authority Police Department officers Will Jimeno and John McLoughlin were the last two people rescued from the World Trade Center after the September 11 terrorist attack. For Will Jimeno, that tragic day represents a defining moment in his Christian faith.

Jimeno, McLoughlin, and three other officers entered Tower 1 to rescue civilians. But when they got inside, the building collapsed. McLoughlin and Jimeno were pinned under large blocks of concrete rubble and twisted steel. The other three officers were killed.

For the next ten hours, Jimeno and his partner fought pain and thirst inside a concrete tomb swirling with dust and smoke. At times, ruptured gas lines would hurl fireballs into the ruins, threatening to burn the two men to death. In another terrifying moment, heat from the fireballs "cooked off" the ammunition inside the firearm of a fallen officer, sending fifteen bullets ricocheting around the chamber.

Jimeno's hope began to falter. "I was exhausted. I had done everything as a police officer that I could do, and everything as a human being," he said. "I just knew I was going to die." Just then, Jimeno saw a figure coming toward him through the rubble. "He wore a glowing white robe and a rope belt," Jimeno said. "I couldn't see his face, but I knew it was Jesus."

The vision filled Jimeno with hope. "I had this resurgence of the will to fight," he said. Turning toward McLoughlin, he yelled, "We're going to get out of this hellhole!" Several hours later, U.S. Marines and NYPD rescue workers lifted the men out of their concrete prison.

The events of that day have given Jimeno a new perspective on the brevity of life. He noted that, even if a person lives to be ninety years old, that's only a little over thirty-two thousand days. "It's not that many," Jimeno said. "You have to do good and do right with the small period you have in between."

—Lynn Vincent, "Purpose-Driven Life," *World* (August 12, 2006)

ILLUSTRATION 334

HEEDLESS WORRIES

Topics: Appetites; Consequences; Danger; Decisions; Discernment; Eternal Death; Fear; Human Nature; Motivation; Priorities; Risk; Sinful Nature; Spiritual Direction; Temptation; Worry

References: Psalm 112:8; Matthew 6:25–27; 10:19

We all know the danger of risk. Yet we have a confounding habit of worrying about perceived dangers while ignoring real ones. Consider:

- We agonized over the avian flu, which [as of December 2006] had killed no one in the United States. Yet we had to be cajoled into getting vaccinated for the common flu, which contributes to the deaths of 36,000 Americans each year.
- White-knuckle fliers routinely choose to drive rather than fly when traveling long distances, heedless that a few hundred people die in U.S. commercial airline crashes in a year compared with 44,000 killed in motor vehicle wrecks.
- We wring our hands over the mad cow pathogen that might be (but almost certainly isn't) in our hamburger, yet we hardly worry about the cholesterol that contributes to the heart disease that annually kills 700,000 of us.
- Shoppers still look askance at a bag of spinach for fear of E. coli bacteria while filling their carts with fat-sodden French fries and salt-crusted nachos.
- We put filters on faucets, install air ionizers in our homes, and lather ourselves with antibacterial soap. At the same time, 20 percent of all adults smoke, nearly 20 percent of drivers and more than 30 percent of backseat passengers don't use seat belts, and two-thirds of us are overweight or obese.

In short, shadowed by peril, you would think we would get pretty good at distinguishing the risks likeliest to do us in from the ones that are statistical long shots. But you would be wrong.

—Jeffrey Kluger, "Why We Worry about the Things We Shouldn't," *Time* (December 4, 2006)

ILLUSTRATION 335

PREDICTING SURVIVAL

Topics: Circumstances and Faith; Comfort; Control; Death; Disease; Faith; Fear; Hope; Human Nature; Illness; Medicine; Mortality; Perspective; Powerlessness; Trials; Trust; Worry

References: Exodus 15:26; Job 14:5; Psalm 121:7–8; Isaiah 26:3; 2 Corinthians 5:1; James 5:13–16

"You're gonna be OK," the lady in pink had whispered as she wheeled me down the hall. "Eighty percent of breast lumps aren't cancer."

I stifled a sigh. So far, statistics had not been in my favor. My breast lump, which was big enough to be seen by the naked eye, hadn't shown up on a mammogram. Mammograms are effective only 80 percent of the time. The volunteer's prediction wasn't accurate, either; I discovered I *did* have breast cancer.

So why, years after surviving a mastectomy and treatment for breast cancer, was I still drawn to survival statistics like a mosquito to a lamp—especially after hearing that a fellow survivor had recurred?

The size of my lump plus five positive nodes had driven down my five-year survival rate to less than 25 percent. Yet I, like so many other cancer survivors, had learned how senseless statistics were in forecasting survival. As one doctor said, "Maybe only 10 percent of patients with your type and stage of cancer are cured, but within that 10 percent, your odds are 0 percent or 100 percent."

So what drove me to statistics? Perhaps it's the kind of fear that drove King Saul to consult a medium on the eve of a battle that would later claim his life (1 Samuel 28). God had stopped communicating with the king through ordinary means, so Saul tried to conjure up the spirit of Samuel to tell him what would happen to him. Saul got the message all right, but it knocked him to the ground.

Cancer knocks us to the ground, too. Still, rather than running to statistics (or doctors who quote them) to ease our fears, we should trust in our heavenly Father, who alone knows how long we will live.

—Phyllis Ten Elshof,
What Cancer Cannot Do (Zondervan, 2006)

ILLUSTRATION 336

HOPING IN A SENSELESS WORLD

Topics: Church; Culture; Despair; Discouragement; Emptiness; Hope; Human Condition; Limitations; Lostness; Ministry

References: Matthew 16:18; 1 Thessalonians 5:11; Hebrews 10:25

The nuclear bomb that was dropped on Hiroshima prompted Kurt Vonnegut to write *Cat's Cradle* to explore the technological ability of the human race combined with its stupidity. The main character, John, wants to write a book about the day the world ended. In the process of his research and travels, John comes across a chapter in a book related to his new religion. The title of the chapter is "What Can a Thoughtful Man Hope for Mankind on Earth, Given the Experience of the Past Million Years?" It doesn't take John long to read this chapter, because it consists of only one word followed by a period: "Nothing."

Vonnegut's book reveals what many in our world today think—there is no hope. Incidents like the tsunami in Southeast Asia, the genocidal activity found in many countries in the last couple of decades, and the daily death rates of HIV patients cause people to question where the hope is. Does Christianity have anything to say in this situation? Does the church have a message of hope in the apparent hopelessness?

—Terry G. Carter,
Preaching God's Word (Zondervan, 2005)

ILLUSTRATION 337

ART OF THE HOPELESS

Topics: Arrogance; Caring; Compassion; Hypocrisy; Indifference; Judging Others; Popular Culture; Postmodernism; Salvation

References: Matthew 9:36; Luke 15; 19:10

When we look at modern art or listen to modern music and are tempted to write it off (or find it amusing), we do well to remember the words of Francis Schaeffer:

> These paintings, these poems, and these demonstrations that we have been talking about are the expressions of men who are struggling with their appalling lostness. Dare we laugh at such things? Dare we feel superior when we view their tortured expressions in their art?
>
> Christians should stop laughing and take such men seriously. Then we shall have the right to speak again to our generation. These men are dying while they live, yet where is our compassion for them? There is nothing more ugly [sic] than an orthodoxy without understanding or without compassion.

> — Francis Schaeffer,
> *The God Who Is There* (InterVarsity, 1998)

ILLUSTRATION 338

OUR CHERNOBYL

Topics: Adam and Eve; Fall of Humanity; Human Condition; Salvation; Sin; Sinful Nature; Woundedness

References: Genesis 3; Romans 3:10; 5:12; 8:22

I have on my desktop a picture of Sasha, five, who was born in Chernobyl after the meltdown and explosions at the Russian nuclear facility in 1986. Sasha's tiny arm grips the side of a crib. His other hand flails upward toward his ear. His head and shoulders appear normal, but on Sasha's chest is a lump the size of a softball, and his belly is so big he looks pregnant.

His legs are oversized and blocky, and he has no knees, only rounded flesh flowing awkwardly to his oversized feet. From the bottom of his stomach protrudes a rounded flow of flesh as though it were a separate limb, stopped in half growth. Sasha lives in constant pain.

So do we.

I believe, without question, that none of us are happy in the way we were supposed to be happy. I believe that nobody on this planet is so secure, so confident, in their state that they feel the way Adam and Eve felt in the garden before they knew they were naked. I believe we are in the wreckage of a war, a kind of Hiroshima, a kind of Mount Saint Helens, with souls distorted like the children of Chernobyl. As terrible as it is to think about these things, as ugly as it is to face them, I have to see the world this way in order for it to make sense. I have to believe something happened, and we are walking around holding our wounds.

—Donald Miller,
Searching for God Knows What
(Nelson, 2004)

ILLUSTRATION 339

WISHING FOR FAITH

Topics: Christian Life; Comfort; Crisis; Faith; Mourning

References: Psalm 23:4; Romans 8:35 – 39; 2 Corinthians 1:3 – 7; 1 Thessalonians 4:13 – 18

Katie Couric lost her husband, forty-two, to colon cancer in 1998. Her sister died about four years later.

"I'm very interested in exploring a more spiritual side of me, and I'm in the process of doing that, both formally and informally," said the anchor of the *CBS Evening News* in a recent interview. "I really envy those who have a steadfast, unwavering faith, because I think it's probably so comforting and helpful during difficult times."

—Cable Neuhaus,
"Whatever Katie Wants,"
AARP (November – December 2005)

ILLUSTRATION 340

RESURRECTION TREE

Topics: Determination; Endurance; Healing; Hope; Overcoming; Patience; Perseverance; Persistence; Resilience; Strength; Testing; Trials; Victory

References: Genesis 9:12 – 17; Exodus 15:26; Hosea 6:1; Romans 5:3 – 5; James 1:2 – 4; 1 Peter 1:3; 5:10

A sprawling, shade-bearing, eighty-year-old American elm in Oklahoma City, Oklahoma, is a huge tourist attraction. People pose for pictures beneath her. Arborists carefully protect her. She adorns posters and letterhead. The city treasures the tree, not because of her appearance but her endurance.

She made it through the Oklahoma City bombing. Timothy McVeigh parked his death-laden truck only yards from her. His malice killed 168 people, wounded 850, destroyed the Alfred P. Murrah Federal Building, and buried the tree in rubble. No one expected it to survive. No one gave any thought to the dusty, branch-stripped tree.

But then she began to bud. Sprouts pressed through damaged bark; green leaves pushed away gray soot. Life rose from an acre of death. People noticed. The tree modeled the resilience the victims desired. So they named her the Survivor Tree.

—Max Lucado, *Facing Your Giants*
(W Publishing Group, 2006)

ILLUSTRATION 341

SINGING THROUGH INTERROGATION

Topics: Belief; Courage; Dedication; Faith; Fear; Integrity; Persecution; Persistence; Protection; Security in God

References: Psalm 9; Matthew 5:10–12; Luke 11:49; 21:12; John 15:20; 1 Corinthians 4:12; 2 Timothy 3:12

Chinese officials from the Public Security Bureau invaded a Sunday school room at a church in early 2005. They found thirty children inside and herded them into a van. Despite the scary situation, one child started to sing. In a few moments, all the children were singing.

Upon arrival at the police station, the children marched bravely into the interrogation room, still singing to the Lord. The Chinese officers attempted to force the children to write, "I do not believe in Jesus," telling them that they had to write it a hundred times before they would be released. Instead, the children wrote: "I believe in Jesus today. I will believe in Jesus tomorrow. I will believe in Jesus forever!"

Exasperated, the officials called the children's parents, some of whom renounced Christ. However, one widow refused to deny Jesus when she came to pick up her twin sons. The officers threatened her, saying, "If you do not deny Jesus, we will not release your sons."

She replied, "Well, I guess you will just have to keep them, because without Jesus, there would be no way for me to take care of them!"

The exasperated officials said, "Take your sons and go!"

—Lee Eclov,
"Chinese Children Stand for Christ,"
PreachingToday.com

ILLUSTRATION 342

FEELING ABANDONED

Topics: Calling; Devotion; Discouragement; Doubt; Experiencing God; Faith; God's Faithfulness; God's Sovereignty; Temptation; Trials

References: Psalm 27:13–14; Jeremiah 14:19–22; Hebrews 2:18

At times in her life, Mother Teresa felt abandoned by God. One day she had been walking the streets of Calcutta, searching for a house where she could start her work. At the end of the day, she wrote in her diary, "I wandered the streets the whole day. My feet are aching, and I have not been able to find a home. And I also get the Tempter telling me, 'Leave all this, go back to the convent from which you came.'"

Eventually Mother Teresa found her home—the Missionaries of Charity—which today feeds five hundred thousand families a year in Calcutta alone, treats ninety thousand leprosy patients, and educates twenty thousand children.

—Kevin Miller, Wheaton, Illinois

ILLUSTRATION 343

GETTING THE STORY RIGHT

Topics: Circumstances and Faith; Community; Discouragement; Experiencing God; Memories; Prayer; Providence; Relationships; Truth

Reference: Romans 8:28

Senator Max Cleland, who lost both of his legs and his right hand in Vietnam, came to the senators' Bible study withdrawn and tired. Another senator said, "Max, are you all right?"

"Not really," he said. "I've been having the same dream for thirty years. I accidentally drop that grenade, and I leap on it, and it explodes and blows my legs off." That night, the study group gathered around Max and prayed that the Lord would heal that memory.

Two days later, the History Channel broadcasted the story. A man from Annapolis saw it and phoned Max: "Senator, you have the story wrong. That wasn't your grenade. It was a young recruit behind you who had opened the pins on his grenades before jumping out of the helicopter. One of them popped out of the belt and rolled on the ground. You leaped on it to save us all. I wrapped you up myself and got you to the hospital. I was on the helicopter; I know how it happened."

Max came to the next Bible study saying a gigantic load had been lifted off his shoulders.

The study group had been studying Romans 8:28, which says, "God works all things together for good." So now, when Senator Cleland is hurrying around in his wheelchair, he'll call out to the Senate chaplain, "Remember, things don't work out; God works out things."

—Lloyd John Ogilvie, "Pastoring the Powerful," *Leadership* (Fall 2000)

ILLUSTRATION 344

BROKEN GLASS RESURFACES

Topics: Anger; Emotions; Feelings; Forgiveness; Healing; Memories; Pain; Suffering

Reference: Philippians 1:6

When my mother-in-law first married, she was in a serious car accident that threw her into the windshield (it was in the days before mandatory seat belts). Long after glass had been removed from her face and the scars healed, she would periodically find a small piece of glass rising to the surface of her skin.

Although the shard of glass didn't hurt her while it was lodged beneath her skin, it became very painful as it moved toward the surface.

In a similar way, we all have tragedies, accidents, and times when we "hit the windshield" in life. We go through the healing process and fight through the pain that accompanies it. We think all the "pieces of glass" are gone, only to have an event, a person, a holiday, or the like bring another piece to the surface, and we suffer pain all over again.

Complete healing often takes longer than we think.

—Gary Sinclair, Mahomet, Illinois

ILLUSTRATION 345

LEARNING FROM A BIRD

Topics: Attitudes; Circumstances and Faith; Joy; Pain; Perspective; Suffering; Thanksgiving; Worship

References: Psalm 30; Ephesians 5:20; Philippians 4:4–6; 1 Thessalonians 5:16–18; 1 Peter 1:3–9

I had a severe cervical spinal injury. The pain was so excruciating that the hospital staff couldn't do an MRI until I was significantly sedated. The MRI showed significant damage at three major points in the cervical area. Because of the swelling of injured nerve bundles, the only way I could relieve the pain was to use a strong, prescribed narcotic and to lie on bags of ice. Sleep, what little there was, came only by sitting in a reclining chair.

Approximately forty-eight hours from the onset of the injury, doctors estimated that I had lost about 80 percent of the strength in my left arm. Three fingers on my left hand totally lost feeling. The slightest movements would send pain waves hurtling down my left side and shoulder. I had to step away completely from my work (which I love) and wear a neck brace twenty-four hours a day for five weeks.

About halfway through that experience, I was sitting on the screened-in porch behind our home. The day was cold and blustery, but I needed a change of scenery. Suddenly a bird landed on the railing and began to sing. On that cold, rainy day, I couldn't believe any creature had a reason to sing. I wanted to shoot that bird!

But he continued to warble, and I had no choice but to listen.

The next day I was on the porch again, but this time it was bright, sunny, and warm. I was tempted to feel sorry for myself when suddenly the bird (at least it looked like the same one) returned. And he was singing again! Where was that shotgun?

Then it hit me: the bird sang in the cold rain as well as the sunny warmth. His song was not altered by outward circumstances, but it was held constant by an internal condition. It was as though God quietly said to me, "You've got the same choice, Bob. You will either let external circumstances mold your attitude, or your attitude will rise above the external circumstances. You choose!"

—Bob Reccord, *Forged by Fire* (Broadman & Holman, 2000)

ILLUSTRATION 346

GOD'S WAY IN TRAGEDY

Topics: Comfort; Death; Dependence on God; Faith; Guidance; Helplessness; Hope; Loss; Overcoming; Presence of God; Tragedy; Trust

References: Psalm 23:4; 2 Thessalonians 3:16

Don Moen's praise song "God Will Make a Way" affirms God's sovereign involvement in our lives. Here's how that song was written: Several years ago, Moen was awakened in the middle of the night. His mother-in-law called to tell him of a car accident involving his wife's sister, Susan.

Susan and her husband, Craig, and their four little boys were on a trip when the accident happened. Jeremy, age eight and the oldest of the four boys, was killed instantly. The others were seriously injured.

As Don and his wife grieved and poured out their hearts to the Lord, they felt helpless at communicating hope and grace to Susan and Craig. Don says God helped him through the tragedy by giving him these words:

God will make a way when there seems to be no way.
He works in ways we cannot see. He will make a way for me.
He will be my guide; hold me closely to his side.
With love and strength for each new day, he will make a way.

—Don Moen, "God Will Make a Way," © 1990 Integrity's Hosanna! Music/ASCAP

—Greg Asimakoupoulos, "Don Moen Faces Tragedy," PreachingToday.com

ILLUSTRATION 347
HOLDING MY HAND

Topics: Advocate; Comfort; Encouragement; Friendship of God; Presence of God; Security in God; Support

References: Psalm 16:8; John 14:27; 2 Corinthians 7:6; 2 Timothy 4:17; Hebrews 13:5–6

In Charles Dickens's *A Tale of Two Cities*, a story of the French revolution, a grim procession of prisoners was making its way on the streets of Paris to the guillotine. One prisoner, Sidney Carton, who had once lost his soul but now had it back, was giving his life for his friend. Beside him was a young girl. They had met before in the prison, and the girl had noticed the man's gentleness and courage. She said to him, "If I may ride with you, will you let me hold your hand? I am not afraid, but I am little and weak, and it will give me more courage."

So they rode together, her hand in his. When they reached the place of execution, there was no fear in her eyes. She looked up into the quiet composed face of her companion and said, "I think you were sent to me by heaven."

In all the dark valleys of life, God our Father, the God of all comfort, in the person of the Lord Jesus Christ, is at our side.

—Owen Bourgaize, "God at Our Side," PreachingToday.com

ILLUSTRATION 348
COMING TO BAT

Topics: Attitudes; Circumstances and Faith; Confidence; Encouragement; Overcoming; Perseverance; Persistence; Perspective; Problems; Trust; Victory

References: 2 Corinthians 5:7; Hebrews 10:36; 12:1–2

A man stopped to watch a Little League baseball game. He asked one of the youngsters what the score was. "We're losing 18 to nothing" was the answer.

"I must say, you don't look discouraged," the man said.

"Why should we be discouraged?" the boy asked, puzzled. "We haven't come to bat yet."

—Stan Toler, *God Has Never Failed Me,*
but He's Sure Scared Me to Death a Few Times
(Honor, 1995)

ILLUSTRATION 349
GOOD THINGS AHEAD

Topics: Birth of Christ; Christmas; Last Things; Second Coming

Reference: Revelation 22:20

When Pastor David Peterson was preparing a sermon, his little daughter came in and asked, "Daddy, can we play?"

"I'm awfully sorry, sweetheart, but I'm right in the middle of preparing this sermon. In about an hour I can play," her dad said.

"OK," she said. "When you're finished, I will give you a great big hug."

She went to the door, then did a U-turn and came back to give her dad a bone-breaking hug.

"You said you were going to give me a hug *after* I finished," her dad said, teasing.

"I just wanted you to know what you have to look forward to!" the little girl said.

God wants us to know, through this first coming at Christmas, how much we have to look forward to in his great second coming.

—Dale Bruner, "Is Jesus Inclusive or Exclusive?" *Theology, News & Notes* (October 1999)

ILLUSTRATION 350
DARRYL AND DRUGS

Topics: Addiction; Depression; Despair; Drugs; Pleasure; Purpose

References: John 4:13–14; 1 John 2:15–17

"Life has not been worth living for me. That's the honest truth." That's what former New York Yankees slugger Darryl Strawberry said in response to Circuit Judge Florence Foster's question about why he used drugs.

—Jack Curry, "Strawberry Still Missing and Faces Prison Time," *The New York Times* (April 2, 2001)

ILLUSTRATION 351
REMEMBERING KIM

Topics: Jesus Christ; Love; Regret; Sacrifice

References: Romans 5:8; 1 Peter 3:18

Ivan, a Vietnam veteran who lives in Denver, is tormented by something that happened more than three decades ago.

While in Vietnam, Ivan's squad befriended some Vietnamese village children who visited the men daily to peddle candy. Ivan became like a father to Kim, age seven, picking her up and whirling her around. He held her on his lap and told her he loved her.

Then one day Kim was used by the Vietcong as a *kamikaze*. She showed up alone at the soldiers' camp, wired with explosives. But before she got close, she unbuttoned her blouse to show the soldiers the bomb. It was her way of telling the Americans she would kill them if they allowed her to come any closer. Ivan was one of the men who shot her.

Kim gave her life so Ivan could live. And his life is a wreck because he could not save her.

— Bruce Weber, "Bill McCartney, Away from the Sideline, Brings His Inspirational Message to the Bowery," *The New York Times* (June 20, 1997)

ILLUSTRATION 352

STEALING DREAMS

Topics: Despair; Dreams; Hope; Potential; Vision

Reference: Proverbs 13:12

Our Little League coach had a picnic for the team at the beginning of the season. After we ate hot dogs and hamburgers, he gave us a pep talk. "How many of you have a dream to one day play in the major leagues?" he asked.

Almost every hand shot up. Every kid believed he could do it; you could see it in his eyes. "If that is to happen, that dream begins now," Coach said. We were so inspired that we practiced hard and played hard and went undefeated for the next few years. All-Star teams from other leagues played us and lost.

Years later, when I became a coach, I brought my kids together to give them the same pep talk. But when I asked, "How many of you have a dream to one day play in the major leagues?" not one hand went up. Not one kid believed he could do it. I was speechless.

The rest of my talk was meaningless, so I said, "Really? Nobody? Well, get your gloves and let's throw."

I thought about that day for a long time. What had happened in the twenty-five years since I was a kid? What had come into their lives to steal their dreams? What had convinced them they would never be more than what they were?

— Barry Merritt, Toledo, Ohio

ILLUSTRATION 353

LOVING THE LOSERS

Topics: Anxiety; Depression; Failure; Hope; Hopelessness; Insecurity; Insignificance

References: Proverbs 13:12; Ecclesiastes 1; Matthew 5:3–5; 1 Corinthians 1:26–31

Peanuts cartoonist Charles Schulz often reflected on the sadness of life through his characters. He seemed to love losers; even Charlie Brown's baseball idol, Joe Shlabotnik, was the worst player in the pros, and with that came the corollary of losing at love. Every major character has an unrequited love — Charlie Brown and the little red-haired girl, Lucy and Schroeder, Linus and Miss Othmar. Even Snoopy gets dumped at the altar.

Happiness may be a warm puppy, but as cartoonist Charles Schulz once said, "Happiness is not very funny." Schulz infused his Peanuts cartoons with his lifelong feelings of depression and insecurity — he had his heart broken by a real-life red-haired girl — and that showed how one could feel lonely even in a crowd.

Many of his cartoons have two characters outside, at night, staring at a field of stars. "Let's go inside and watch television," Charlie Brown says in one. "I'm beginning to feel insignificant."

— James Poniewozik,
"The Good and the Grief,"
Time (December 27, 1999)

ILLUSTRATION 354

MANSION FOR THE DEAD

Topics: Conscience; Guilt; Regret

Reference: Hebrews 10:1 – 4, 22

Sarah was very rich. Her income was $1,000 a day, but she had also inherited $20 million. That was in the late 1800s. By today's standards Sarah would have been a billionaire. But Sarah was also miserable. Her only child died at five weeks. Then her husband passed away. To get away from painful memories, Sarah moved from Connecticut to San Jose, California. She bought an eight-room farmhouse there, plus 160 adjoining acres.

Then she began a massive remodeling project. She hired sixteen carpenters to work on her house, twenty-four hours a day, every day, for the next thirty-eight years. The floor plan was bizarre. Corridors were put in at random. Some led nowhere. A set of stairs led to a ceiling that had no door, and one door opened to a blank wall. There were tunnels, trap doors, and secret passageways. The work on this mysterious mansion finally came to a halt after it covered six acres. It had six kitchens, thirteen bathrooms, forty stairways, forty-seven fireplaces, fifty-two skylights, 467 doors, ten thousand windows, 160 rooms, and one bell tower.

According to legend, Sarah Winchester had "visitors" every night. A servant would go to the bell tower at night via a secret passage and ring the bell. Sarah would then go into the "blue room," which was reserved for her and her guests, and stay there until 2:00 a.m. The bell would ring again, the visitors would depart, and Sarah Winchester would go to her room.

The visitors supposedly were U.S. soldiers and Indians killed on the frontier by that new invention, the repeating Winchester rifle. It brought millions of dollars to the Winchester family but death to thousands of people. That haunted Sarah Winchester the rest of her life. In an effort to appease the guilt, she built a mansion for the dead.

— H. Norman Wright,
Why Did This Happen to Me? (Servant, 1999)

ILLUSTRATION 355

BIBLE QUIZ

Topics: Bible; Questions

Reference: Proverbs 17:22

Q. What kind of man was Boaz before he married?

A. Ruthless.

Q. Who was the greatest financier in the Bible?

A. Noah. He was floating his stock while everyone else was in liquidation.

Q. Who was the greatest female financier in the Bible?

A. Pharaoh's daughter. She went down to the bank of the Nile and drew out a little prophet.

Q. What kinds of motor vehicles are in the Bible?

A. The Lord drove Adam and Eve out of the Garden in a Fury. David's Triumph was heard throughout the land. And a Honda, because the apostles were all in one Accord.

Q. Who was the greatest comedian in the Bible?

A. Samson. He brought the house down.

Q. What excuse did Adam give to his children about why they no longer lived in Eden?

A. "Your mother ate us out of house and home."

Q. Which servant of God was the most flagrant lawbreaker in the Bible?

A. Moses. He broke all Ten Commandments at once.

Q. Which area of Palestine was especially wealthy?

A. The area around Jordan. The banks were always overflowing.

Q. Who is the greatest babysitter mentioned in the Bible?

A. David. He rocked Goliath to a very deep sleep.

Q. Which Bible character had no parents?

A. Joshua, son of Nun.

—Anonymous

ILLUSTRATION 356

BRAIN TEASERS

Topics: Doubt; God; Limitations; Mysteries; Questions

References: Psalm 8:3–4; Isaiah 40:12–14; Romans 11:33–36

If you're pondering the imponderables, here are more to add to the list:

- You tell a man there are 400 billion stars, and he'll believe you. But tell him a bench has wet paint, and he has to touch it. Why?
- Why is the ground stuff called hamburger when it's made of beef?
- Why do you put suits in garment bags and put garments in suitcases?
- Why doesn't glue stick to the inside of the bottle?
- Why isn't there mouse-flavored cat food?
- Why do they lock gas station bathrooms—are they afraid someone will sneak in there and clean them?
- If man evolved from monkeys and apes, why do we still have monkeys and apes?
- Why are there five syllables in the word monosyllabic?
- When two airplanes almost collide, why do they call it a near miss instead of a near hit?
- Why do banks charge you a nonsufficient funds fee on money they know you don't have?
- Why do you drive in a parkway and park in a driveway?
- Why are they called apartments when they're stuck together?
- Why are they called buildings when they are already finished? Shouldn't we call them builts?
- If the black box flight recorder is never damaged during a plane crash, why isn't the whole airplane made out of that stuff?

At birth the human brain weighs, on average, fourteen ounces. It usually reaches its maximum size at age fifteen (proving the size of the brain has nothing to do with intelligence level). At its maximum size, the brain weighs an average of forty-six ounces, slightly less than three pounds. In liquid measurement, that's about a Big Gulp from the soda machine at the local gas station.

There is no way for medical professionals to prove this, but the old theory was that we use only about 10 percent of our brain capacity. If that were true and we start out with only a Big Gulp in the first place, we're down to about a quarter-pounder with cheese by the time we're done. And we think that with our quarter-pounder with cheese, we're going to comprehend the infinite, decipher the mysteries of the millennia, and answer all the questions? Right!

Isn't it logically impossible that we as finite creatures could ever fully understand the infinite?

—John Stumbo,
"God's Sovereignty: The Ultimate Question,"
Preaching Today Audio, no. 202

ILLUSTRATION 357

PIG ON A PLANE

Topics: Learning; Mistakes; Regret; Repentance; Teaching

References: 2 Corinthians 7:10; 2 Peter 2:22

Yes, a pig really flew—first class.

It flew US Airways, and the company, embarrassed, says it's never going to let it happen again.

On October 17, the six-hour flight from Philadelphia to Seattle carried 201 passengers — 200 people and one hog, which sat on the floor in the first row of first class. The pig was traveling with two women, who convinced the airline that the pig was a "therapeutic companion pet" — like a guide dog for the blind.

According to the airline's incident report, the animal became unruly as the plane taxied toward the Seattle terminal, running through the jet, squealing and trying to get into the cockpit. "Many people on board the aircraft were quite upset that there was a large uncontrollable pig on board, especially those in the first-class cabin," the report stated.

"We can confirm that the pig traveled, and we can confirm that it will never happen again," US Airways spokesman David Castelveter said. "Let me stress that. It will never happen again."

—Associated Press,
"When Pigs Fly, Airline Embarrassed,"
CNN.com (October 27, 2000)

ILLUSTRATION 358

ANY EXCUSE WILL DO

Topics: Excuses; Motives;
Self-centeredness

References: Zechariah 7:11 – 12;
Philippians 4:15 – 19

A fellow went next door to borrow his neighbor's lawn mower. The neighbor said he couldn't use the mower because all the flights had been canceled from New York to Los Angeles.

The borrower asked what canceled flights from New York to Los Angeles had to do with borrowing his lawn mower.

"It doesn't have anything to do with it, but if I don't want to let you use my lawn mower, one excuse is as good as another," the neighbor said.

—Zig Ziglar, *Something Else to Smile About* (Nelson, 1999)

ILLUSTRATION 359

LESSONS FROM NOAH

Topics: Attitudes; Christian Life;
Learning; Perspective; Teaching

Reference: 1 Peter 3:20

You may have learned everything you needed to know from kindergarten (as a popular book suggests). But here's everything I needed to know from Noah:

1. Don't miss the boat.
2. We're all in the same boat.
3. Plan ahead. It wasn't raining when Noah built the ark.
4. Stay fit. When you're six hundred years old, someone may ask you to do something big.
5. Don't listen to critics; just do the job that needs to be done.
6. Build your future on high ground.
7. For safety's sake, travel in pairs.
8. Speed isn't always an advantage. The snails were on board with the cheetahs.
9. When you're stressed, float awhile.

10. Remember, the ark was built by amateurs, the *Titanic* by professionals.
11. No matter the storm, when you are with God, there's always a rainbow waiting.

—Anonymous

ILLUSTRATION 360

PROOFING THE NOTE

Topics: Communication; Family; Relationships; Spouses

Reference: 2 Timothy 2:24

My farmer husband, Larry, isn't a cook. So when I accepted a lunch invitation with former coworkers, I put food for Larry in the oven and scribbled a note: "Dinner in oven." Returning at 4:00 p.m., I waved at Larry working outside, but he didn't wave back. *Guess he's had a bad day*, I thought.

In the kitchen, the plot thickened. There were no dirty dishes, and the casserole was still in the oven. Only a sandwich that I intended to throw away was missing from the refrigerator.

When Larry came in, I asked, "What did you have for dinner?"

Silence.

"Did you get my note?"

"Sure did," he replied gruffly. "It said, 'Dinner is over!'"

I now proofread all my notes.

—Evelyn Shetter, "Lite Fare,"
Christian Reader (May–June 2000)

ILLUSTRATION 361

PREACHING OUT OF ORDER

Topics: Christian Life; Giving; Ministry; Offerings; Preaching

References: Leviticus 27:32; Deuteronomy 25:4; 1 Timothy 5:18

Recently I tried something different in our worship service. Instead of preaching at the end, I did that first, followed by music, the offering, and Scripture reading.

As I began preaching, I could see people were preparing for the offering until they realized I was starting my message. Caitlyn, a first grader, was perplexed by this change of routine and whispered frantically to her mom, "Doesn't he know we haven't paid him to talk yet?"

—Gordon Wood, "Kids of the Kingdom,"
Christian Reader (July–August 2000)

ILLUSTRATION 362

TALKING TO FLOWERS

Topics: Confession; Counsel

References: Psalm 32:8; Matthew 13:24–43

I dragged my teenage son Matt outside to help me pull weeds one sunny morning, even though he snickers when he catches me talking to my plants.

"Be careful; the weeds are so thick here you could easily uproot a flower," I told him. "If you do, stick it back in the ground and tell it you're sorry."

My son sighed. "Mom," he said, "I just weed the plants. I don't counsel them."

—Marsha Gubser, "Lite Fare,"
Christian Reader (July–August 2000)

ILLUSTRATION 363

REMEMBERING GARBAGE DAY

Topics: Affection; Children; Family; Mothers; Values

Reference: 1 Corinthians 13:9–12

My three young children love to get up early and watch the garbage truck. They love watching the waste hauler empty the can and work the lever that causes the truck to compact the trash.

On the morning I turned thirty-five, my husband said to the children with a smile, "Kids, do you know what makes today so special?"

Our five-year-old rushed past my outstretched arms to the window and yelled, "It's garbage day!"

—Sheri B., Portage, Michigan,
"Life in Our House," *Christian Parenting Today*
(March–April 2000)

ILLUSTRATION 364

HE DID IT

Topics: Blame; Creation; Disorder

References: Genesis 2:2; 3:11–13; 1 Corinthians 14:33

My husband and I are always talking to our son about the wonderful things God has made. We ask questions like: "Who made the sun?" and "Who made the rain?"

One evening, I looked at the toys scattered on the floor and asked, "Who made this mess?"

"God did!" said my well-trained son.

—Shawne B., Warsaw, Indiana,
"Life in Our House," *Christian Parenting Today*
(March–April 2000)

ILLUSTRATION 365

DAD'S BAG

Topics: Character; Maturity; Spiritual Formation

Reference: 1 Corinthians 3:1–2

My husband usually sets his computer bag next to the front door before leaving home in the morning. One day he left the house but forgot to take his computer with him. Our two-year-old saw it and came running to find me. "Mama, Daddy forgot to take his diaper bag!"

—Sherilyn M., Lawrence, Kansas,
"Life in Our House," *Christian Parenting Today*
(May–June 2000)

ILLUSTRATION 366

SHORT ON MONEY

Topics: Dependence; Faith and Works; Grace; Salvation

References: Romans 3:20–28; Ephesians 2:8–9; Titus 3:5

I took Abby and Flannery out for something fun to drink. Abby got an apple juice, and Flannery got a Mango Surprise. Despite my insistence that I would pay, my daughters were prepared to be generous with the contents of their piggy banks.

As we were walking up to the counter, one of them said, "I want to pay for mine."

"Daddy's gonna get it," I said. She insisted, "I'm paying for mine."

The clerk, ringing up the drinks, said, "That'll be $2.06." One daughter put all the change, about 80 cents, on the counter. "Um, that's not enough," the clerk said.

I felt a little tug on my sweater. "I think I'd like to use your money," my other daughter said.

—Tom Allen, Seattle, Washington

ILLUSTRATION 367

DEATH NOTICE

Topics: Death; Life; Mortality

References: Job 8:9; 14:1–2; Psalm 39:4–6; 90:12; Isaiah 40:6–8; 1 Peter 1:24–25

A man had his annual checkup and then heard from his doctor a couple of days later. "I'm afraid I have some bad news for you," the doctor said. "You have only forty-eight hours to live."

"That *is* bad news!" said the shocked patient.

"I'm afraid I have even worse news," the doctor continued.

"What could be worse than what you've already told me?" the patient stammered.

"I've been trying to call you since yesterday."

—Rubel Shelly, Nashville, Tennessee

ILLUSTRATION 368

EXPLAINING BAPTISM

Topics: Baptism; Cleansing; Forgiveness; Grace; Punishment; Sin

References: Romans 6:1–14; Titus 3:3–7

Rena, age three, sat with us during the baptismal service last Sunday night, which was a new experience for her. "Why did Pastor Bob push that guy in the water?" she asked.

My wife quietly tried to explain, but Rena wasn't satisfied. Later that night we tried again. We talked about sin and how, when people decide to live for Jesus and "do good," they want everyone to know. We said water symbolizes Jesus' washing away people's sin; when they come out "clean," they will try to be "good."

A moment later, we realized we'd failed again when Rena asked, "Why didn't Pastor Bob just spank him?"

—Bob Beasley, pastor, Gregory Drive Alliance Church, West Chatham, Ontario

ILLUSTRATION 369

ASKING FOR IT

Topics: Comfort; Complaining; Convenience; Hardship; Laziness; Suffering

References: 2 Timothy 2:3; Hebrews 6:11–15

Comment cards given to the staff members at Bridger Wilderness Area in Wyoming in 1996 included the following:

- Trails need to be wider so people can walk while holding hands.
- Trails need to be reconstructed. Please avoid building trails that go uphill.
- Too many bugs and leeches and spiders and spiderwebs. Please spray the wilderness to rid the areas of these pests.
- Please pave the trails so they can be snow-plowed during the winter.
- Chairlifts need to be in some places so that we can get to wonderful views without having to hike to them.
- The coyotes made too much noise last night and kept me awake. Please eradicate these annoying animals.
- A small deer came into my camp and stole my jar of pickles. Is there a way I can get reimbursed?
- Reflectors need to be placed on trees every fifty feet so people can hike at night with flashlights.
- Escalators would help on steep uphill sections.
- A McDonald's would be nice at the trailhead.
- The places where trails do not exist are not well marked.
- Too many rocks in the mountains.

—Mike Neifert,
Light and Life (February 1997)

ILLUSTRATION 370

ON LIFE AND WORK

Topics: Attitudes; Experience; Failure; Foolishness; Money; Pessimism; Procrastination; Success; Wisdom; Work

Reference: Colossians 3:23

A few observations on life and work:

1. Nothing is foolproof to a talented fool.
2. The early bird may get the worm, but the second mouse gets the cheese.
3. Borrow money from a pessimist; they don't expect it back.
4. If at first you don't succeed, destroy all evidence that you tried.
5. Experience is something you don't get until just after you need it.
6. The sooner you fall behind, the more time you will have to catch up.
7. If at first you don't succeed, then sky-diving isn't for you.

—Anonymous

ILLUSTRATION 371

AUDACIOUS PREDICTIONS

Topics: Authority; Bible; Future; Prophecy

References: Deuteronomy 18:21–22; 1 Peter 1:23–25; 2 Peter 1:21

Some of the worst predictions of all time:

- "Inventions have long since reached their limit, and I see no hope for further developments." Said by Roman engineer Julius Sextus Frontinus in AD 100.
- "The abdomen, the chest, and the brain will forever be shut from the intrusion of the wise and humane surgeon." Said by John Eric Ericksen, surgeon to Queen Victoria in 1873.
- "Law will be simplified. Lawyers will have diminished, and their fees will have been vastly curtailed." Said by journalist Junius Henri Browne in 1893.
- "It doesn't matter what he does; he will never amount to anything." Said by Albert Einstein's teacher in 1895.
- "It would appear we have reached the limits of what it is possible to achieve with computer technology." Said by computer scientist John von Neumann in 1949.
- "The Japanese don't make anything the people in the U.S. would want." Said by Secretary of State John Foster Dulles in 1954.
- "Nuclear-powered vacuum cleaners will probably be a reality within ten years." Said by Alex Lewyt, president of the Lewyt Vacuum Cleaner Company in 1955.
- "Before man reaches the moon, your mail will be delivered within hours from New York to Australia by guided missiles. We stand on the threshold of rocket mail." Said by Arthur Summerfield, U.S. Postmaster General, in 1959.
- "By the turn of the century, we will live in a paperless society." Said by Roger Smith, chairman of General Motors in 1986.
- "I predict the Internet ... will go spectacularly supernova and in 1996 catastrophically collapse." Said by Bob Metcalfe, InfoWorld, in 1995.

—Laura Lee,
"Forecasts That Missed by a Mile,"
The Futurist (September–October 2000)

ILLUSTRATION 372

COMPETING IN HOLINESS

Topics: Arrogance; God's Holiness; Humility; Pride

References: Psalm 18:24–27; James 4:5–12

A pastor walked into his church and felt an overwhelming sense of God's holiness. He went to the front, knelt at the altar rail, and began to beat himself on the chest, crying out, "O Lord, I am nothing!"

Moments later, the minister of music entered the church. He too felt the overwhelming presence of God and knelt beside the pastor, striking his chest and saying, "O Lord, I am nothing. I am nothing."

One by one, other staff members entered: the minister of recreation, the minister of education, and more—who all knelt, bemoaning their "nothingness" before the Almighty.

The church custodian also got caught up in the revival, beating on his chest, and saying, "O Lord, I am nothing. I am nothing."

The pastor looked up, saw the janitor, and nudged the minister of music. "Well, well," he said. "Just look at who thinks he's nothing!"

—Don Aycock, Memphis, Tennessee

ILLUSTRATION 373

GERMS AND JESUS

Topics: Doubt; Faith; Unbelief

References: John 20:24–31; Hebrews 11:1–3; 1 Peter 1:6–9

A missionary family was visiting my aunt and uncle. When the missionary children were called in for dinner, their mother said, "Be sure to wash your hands. Get the germs off."

The little boy scowled and said, "Germs and Jesus. Germs and Jesus. That's all I hear, and I've never seen either one of them."

—Vesper Bauer, Audubon, Iowa, *Christian Reader* (September–October 1998)

ILLUSTRATION 374

KATIE'S CHECKUP

Topics: Christian Culture; Humor; Love for Christ; Youth

Reference: Matthew 18:1–4

Katie, three, had the flu and had to be taken to the pediatrician. As the doctor examined her ears, he asked, "Will I find Big Bird in here?"

"No," Katie said.

Before looking at her throat, the doctor asked, "Will I find Cookie Monster in here?"

"No."

Listening to her heart, he asked, "Will I find Barney in here?"

"No," Katie said firmly. "Jesus is in my heart. Barney is on my underwear."

—Judy Zmerold, *Minneapolis Star-Tribune* (January 17, 1998)

ILLUSTRATION 375

WHY MOM'S NOT HERE

Topics: Children; Communication; Reputation

References: Proverbs 21:23; James 3:1–12

My wife was busy one evening making porcelain dolls at a doll-making class, leaving me at home to watch our two children, Melinda, seven, and Craig, five. While I was chatting with a neighbor on the front porch, the phone rang.

Craig answered the phone promptly and politely. My pride in him vanished as I heard my son's response to the caller's request to speak to my wife: "No, my mom's not here. She's out making a baby. But my dad is here if you want to talk to him."

Of course, the phone call was from an elder in our church.

—Rick Eshbaugh, Birch Bay, Washington

ILLUSTRATION 376

COUNTING LAUGHS

Topics: Celebration; Gender Differences; Joy; Laughter

Reference: Luke 6:21

A man laughs, on average, 69 times a day. A woman laughs 55 times.

—Cindy Hall and Genevieve Lynn, *USA Today* "Snapshots" (March 4, 1999)

ILLUSTRATION 377

LAWS OF THE MOVIES

Topics: Morality; Movies; Reality

Reference: John 8:32

Watch enough movies, and you pick up a system of truisms. Some of them:

- All grocery shopping bags contain at least one stick of French bread.

- The ventilation system of any building is the perfect hiding place.
- The Eiffel Tower can be seen from any window in Paris.
- A man will show no pain while taking the most ferocious beating but will wince when a woman tries to clean his wounds.
- Cars that crash will almost always burst into flames.
- Persons knocked unconscious by a blow to the head will never suffer a concussion or brain damage.
- You can always park directly outside the building you are visiting.
- Any lock can be picked by a credit card or a paper clip in seconds—unless it's the door to a burning building with a child trapped inside; then the door must be knocked down.
- All bombs are fitted with electronic timing devices with large red readouts so you know exactly when they will go off.
- Medieval peasants had perfect teeth.
- It is not necessary to say hello or goodbye when beginning or ending phone conversations.
- Any person waking from a nightmare will sit bolt upright and pant.
- It doesn't matter if you are heavily outnumbered in a fight involving martial arts; your enemies will wait to attack you one by one by dancing around in a threatening manner until you have knocked out their predecessors.

—Anonymous

ILLUSTRATION 378

UGLY SHIRT

Topics: Family; Forgiveness; Marriage; Reconciliation

References: Matthew 6:14–15; 18:21–22; 2 Corinthians 2:7; Ephesians 4:32

During a children's sermon one Sunday morning, I held up a summer shirt that I wore around the house. I told the children that someone said the shirt was ugly and should be thrown away.

"I'm having trouble forgiving the person who said those mean things," I said. "Do you think I should forgive that person?"

My daughter, Alicia, six, raised her hand. "You should."

"But why? This person hurt my feelings," I said.

"Because you're married to her," Alicia replied.

—Glenn E. Schaeffer, "Kids of the Kingdom," *Christian Reader* (September–October 1997)

ILLUSTRATION 379

HOOKED ON A CAR

Topics: Envy; Greed; Materialism

References: Proverbs 14:30; Colossians 3:5–6

A hip young man bought one of the best cars around: a Ferrari GTO. He took it out for a spin and stopped at a red light. An old man on a moped pulled up next to him. The old man looked over at the sleek, shiny car and asked, "What kind of car ya got there, sonny?"

"A Ferrari GTO. It cost half a million dollars."

"That's a lot of money," said the old man. "Why does it cost so much?"

"Because this car can do up to 320 miles an hour!" said the young man proudly.

"Mind if I take a look inside?"

"No problem," replied the owner.

The old man poked his head in the window and looked around. "That's a pretty nice car, all right!"

Just then the light changed, and the driver decided to show the old man just what his car could do. He floored it, and within thirty seconds the speedometer read 160 miles per hour. Suddenly he noticed a dot in his rearview mirror. He slowed down to see what it could be, and—*whoosh*—something whipped by him going much faster.

"What on earth could be going faster than my Ferrari?" the young man said to himself. Then, ahead of him, he saw a dot coming toward him. *Whoosh!* It went by again, heading the opposite direction—and it looked like the old man on the moped.

Couldn't be, he thought. *How could a moped outrun a Ferrari?*

Once more, though, he saw the dot in his rearview mirror, followed by a bang as the speeding object crashed into the back of his car.

The young man jumped out and saw the old man lying on the pavement. He ran to him and asked, "How can I help?"

The old man whispered, "Unhook … my suspenders … from your side-view mirror."

The moral of the story: Be careful what you admire!

—Brett Kays, Brownstown, Michigan

ILLUSTRATION 380

PLAYING WITH GOD'S NUMBERS

Topics: Eternity; Money; Perspective; Time

Reference: 2 Peter 3:8

An economist who read 2 Peter 3:8 was amazed. "Lord, is it true that a thousand years for us is like one minute to you?"

"Yes," God said.

"Then a million dollars to us must be like one penny to you," the economist said.

"Well, yes," God said.

"Will you give me one of those pennies?" the economist asked.

"All right, I will," the Lord said. "Wait here a minute."

—John Ortberg, "Waiting on God," Preaching Today Audio, no. 199

ILLUSTRATION 381

ODE TO A FISH

Topics: Death; Fun; Happiness; Meaning of Life; Mortality; Youth

References: Job 14:1–2; Psalm 39:5; 90:12; James 4:14; 1 Peter 1:24

Nancy Walker of Newport Beach, California, was invited to attend the burial of a goldfish owned by her neighbor, Jimmy Yeargan, age five. Since Jimmy couldn't write, he asked Walker to do the honors for him, handing her a small, cardboard tombstone he had brought with him to the ceremony.

"What do you want to say?" she asked.

"His name was Mobert," Jimmy said.

Dutifully, Walker inscribed the name.

"Do you want anything else?" she asked.

Jimmy thought for a moment then nodded. "Put down, 'He was fun while he lasted.'"

—J. R. Love, Rushton, Louisiana

ILLUSTRATION 382

THE ROBBER AND THE PRIEST

Topics: Conscience; Fasting; Foolishness; Hypocrisy; Integrity; Lent; Resisting Temptation; Vices

References: Proverbs 20:11; Matthew 23:13–36; 1 Corinthians 8:8; Titus 1:16; 1 John 3:18

A priest was coming back to his rectory one evening in the dark when he was accosted by a robber who pulled a gun on him and demanded, "Your money or your life!"

As the priest reached into his coat pocket, the robber saw his Roman collar and said, "I see you're a priest. Never mind, you can go."

The priest tried to reciprocate by offering the robber a candy bar that he remembered was in his pocket.

The robber replied, "No thank you, Father. I don't eat candy during Lent."

—Harold A. Buetow,
Embrace Your Renewal
(Alba House, 2004)

ILLUSTRATION 383

THREE WEEKS TO LIVE

Topics: Death; Mortality

References: 2 Samuel 14:14; Psalm 49:10; Ecclesiastes 8:8; Hebrews 9:27

"I'm afraid you have only three weeks to live," the doctor told his patient.

"OK, then," the patient replied, "I'll take the last two weeks of July and the week between Christmas and New Year's."

—Van Morris, Mount Washington, Kentucky

ILLUSTRATION 384

TAKING ON THE FAMILY

Topics: Family; Marriage; Responsibility

Reference: Ephesians 5:22–33

When my youngest sister, Dorothy, and her boyfriend, Sonny, both nineteen, decided they wanted to get married, they approached my father with the news.

"You're mighty young to be taking on a family," Dad said to my future brother-in-law.

"But I don't want the whole family," protested Sonny. "I just want to marry Dorothy."

—Ruth A. Walton, "Lite Fare,"
Christian Reader (May–June 2000)

ILLUSTRATION 385

NO COOKIES FOR YOU

Topics: Indifference; Marriage; Mortality; Relationships

Reference: Titus 2:4

An old man was lying on his deathbed. He had only hours to live when he suddenly smelled chocolate chip cookies. He loved chocolate chip cookies more than anything in the world, so with his last bit of energy, he pulled himself out of bed, struggled across the floor to the stairs, and headed down the stairs into the kitchen. There his wife was baking cookies.

As he reached for one, his wife smacked him. "Leave those alone," she said. "They're for the funeral!"

—A Prairie Home Companion,
"Fifth Annual Joke Show"
(April 1, 2000)

ILLUSTRATION 386

CELEBRATING ANNIVERSARIES

Topics: Anniversaries; Commitment; Husbands; Love; Marriage; Spouses; Wives

References: Genesis 2:24; Proverbs 18:22; Song of Songs 8:6–7; Mark 10:9; 1 Corinthians 7:10; Ephesians 5:22–33; 1 Peter 3:7

Ralph and Janice were celebrating their fiftieth wedding anniversary, so Pastor Jones asked Ralph to come forward in church and talk about how he had managed to live with the same woman all those years.

Ralph turned to the congregation and said, "Well, I treated her with respect and spent money on her, but mostly I took her traveling on special occasions."

The pastor asked, "Trips to where?"

"For our twenty-fifth anniversary," Ralph answered, "I took her to Beijing, China."

The crowd nodded and murmured in appreciation. When things quieted down, the pastor winked and said, "What a terrific example you are to husbands, Ralph. So, tell us, where are you going now for your fiftieth anniversary?"

Ralph replied, "I'm going to go back and get her."

—Brett Kays, Brownstown, Michigan

ILLUSTRATION 387

INCREDIBLE METAPHORS

Topics: Communication; Creativity; Preaching; Teaching; Words

Reference: 1 Corinthians 13:11

Some attention-grabbing metaphors (for better or for worse) found in high school papers:

"He spoke with the wisdom that can only come from experience, like a guy who went blind because he looked at a solar eclipse without one of those boxes with a pinhole in it and now goes around the country speaking at high schools about the dangers of looking at a solar eclipse without one of those boxes with a pinhole in it."

"She caught your eye like one of those pointy hook latches that used to dangle from screen doors and would fly up whenever you banged the door open again."

"The little boat gently drifted across the pond exactly the way a bowling ball wouldn't."

"McBride fell twelve stories, hitting the pavement like a Hefty Bag filled with vegetable soup."

"From the attic came an unearthly howl. The whole scene had an eerie, surreal quality, like when you're on vacation in another city and *Jeopardy* comes on at 7:00 p.m. instead of 7:30."

"Her eyes were like two brown circles with big black dots in the center."

"Her vocabulary was as bad as, like, whatever."

"He was as tall as a six-foot-three-inch tree."

"The hailstones leaped from the pavement, just like maggots when you fry them in hot grease."

"Her date was pleasant enough, but she knew that if her life was a movie, this guy would be buried in the credits as something like 'Second Tall Man.'"

"Long separated by cruel fate, the star-crossed lovers raced across the grassy field toward each other like two freight trains, one having left Cleveland at 6:36 p.m. traveling at fifty-five miles per hour, the other from Topeka at 4:19 p.m. at a speed of thirty-five miles per hour."

"The politician was gone but unnoticed, like the period after the Dr on a Dr Pepper can."

"John and Mary had never met. They were like two hummingbirds who had also never met."

"The thunder was ominous sounding, much like the sound of a thin sheet of metal being shaken backstage during the storm scene in a play."

"The red brick wall was the color of a brick-red Crayola crayon."

—Anonymous

ILLUSTRATION 388

DYING IN THE SERVICE

Topics: Church; Joy; Worship

References: Psalm 103:15–17; Ecclesiastes 7:2–3

One Sunday morning, little Alex stared at the large plaque that hung in the foyer of the church. The seven-year-old had been staring at the plaque for some time, so Pastor McGhee walked up, stood beside the boy, and said quietly, "Good morning, Alex."

"Good morning," said the boy, still absorbed in the plaque. "Pastor McGhee, what is this?"

"Well, son, all of these people have died in the service," the pastor said.

Soberly they stood together, staring at the large plaque.

Then little Alex asked quietly, "Which one, the 9:00 or the 10:30 service?"

—Krista Carnet, Downers Grove, Illinois

ILLUSTRATION 389

TEARING DOWN THE WALLS

Topics: Biblical Literacy; Blame; Children; Communication; Confusion; Guilt; Sunday School

Reference: Joshua 6:1–20

A new pastor decided to visit the children's Sunday school. The teacher introduced him and said, "Pastor, this morning we're studying Joshua."

"That's wonderful," said the new pastor. "Let's see what you're learning. Who tore down the walls of Jericho?"

"I didn't do it," said Johnny shyly.

Taken aback, the pastor asked, "Come on, now, who tore down the walls of Jericho?"

The teacher said, "Pastor, little Johnny's a good boy. If he says he didn't do it, I believe he didn't do it."

Flustered, the pastor went to the Sunday school director to talk about the incident. The director, looking worried, said, "Well, sir, we've had some problems with Johnny before. Let me talk to him and see what we can do."

Really bothered now, the new pastor told the deacons the whole story, including the responses of the teacher and the director. A white-haired gentleman thoughtfully stroked his chin and said, "Well, Pastor, I move we just take the money from the general fund to pay for the walls and leave it at that."

—Cregg Puckett, Florence, Mississippi

ILLUSTRATION 390

YOUR BIGGEST SIN

Topics: Gossip; Humor; Pastors; Secrets; Sin

References: Proverbs 28:13; James 3:6; 5:16

Three preachers were on a fishing trip, They weren't catching many fish, so one preacher said he thought it would be nice if they confessed their biggest sins to each other and then prayed for each other. They all agreed.

The first preacher said that his biggest sin was that he liked to sit at the beach now and then and watch pretty women stroll by.

The second preacher confessed that his biggest sin was going to the racetrack every so often and putting a small bet on a horse.

Turning to the third preacher, they asked, "Brother, what is your biggest sin?"

With a grin, he said, "My biggest sin is gossiping."

—Van Morris, Mount Washington, Kentucky

ILLUSTRATION 391

BOOT TRIAL

Topics: Attitudes; Children; Humility; Patience; Perseverance; Persistence; Self-control; Testing; Tolerance; Trials

References: Psalm 27:14; Ecclesiastes 7:8; Galatians 6:9; Colossians 3:13; James 1:2–8

A teacher was helping a kindergarten student put on his cowboy boots. Even with her pulling and him pushing, the little boots didn't want to go on. By the time they got the second boot on, she had worked up a sweat. She almost cried when the little boy said, "Teacher, they're on the wrong feet." She looked, and sure enough, they were.

It wasn't any easier pulling the boots off than it was putting them on. She managed to keep her cool as together they worked to get the boots back on, this time on the right feet. He then announced, "These aren't my boots." She bit her tongue rather than get right in his face to scream, "Why didn't you say so?"

Once again, she struggled to help him pull off the boots. No sooner had they gotten the boots off when he said, "They're my brother's boots. My mom made me wear 'em." Now she didn't know if she should laugh or cry, but she mustered up what grace and courage she had left to wrestle the boots on his feet again.

Helping him into his coat, she asked, "Now, where are your mittens?" He said, "I stuffed 'em in the toes of my boots."

—John Beukema,
Chambersburg, Pennsylvania

ILLUSTRATION 392

A HANDFUL OF SUCKERS

Topics: Ambition; Dependence on God; Faith; Grace; Prayer; Self-centeredness; Striving; Trust; Waiting on God

References: Genesis 13:9; Psalm 16:5–6; 34:8–10; 84:11; 100:5; Matthew 7:7–11; Ephesians 3:20

A young boy went to the store with his mother. The shop owner, a kind man, passed him a large jar of suckers and invited him to help himself to a handful. Uncharacteristically, the boy held back. So the shop owner pulled out a handful for him.

When outside, the boy's mother asked why he wouldn't take a handful of suckers when offered.

"Because his hand is much bigger than mine!" said the boy.

—Brian Harris,
Mount Roskill, Auckland, New Zealand

PART 17: JUSTICE

ILLUSTRATION 393

RULING STRONG AND TENDER

Topics: Authority; Dependence on God; Discipline; Fear; Gentleness; Government; Grace; Help; Kingdom of God; Protection; Tenderness

References: Psalm 91:4; Isaiah 43:2; Matthew 11:28–30; Romans 13:1–7; 2 Corinthians 12:10; Titus 3:1; Hebrews 12:11

"People want to be lightly governed by strong governments." I read that a long time ago in a *Wall Street Journal* editorial, but it has stuck with me ever since.

You've wanted that since you were a small child. You wanted your dad to be big and strong and able to do anything you could think of — except that, when he dealt with you, it had to be with gentleness and tenderness. You wanted a policeman on the corner tough enough to handle any neighborhood bully but who would also hoist you to his shoulders and help you find your parents when you got lost in the crowd.

Lots of muscle with lots of restraint — there's an innate yearning in almost all of us for that rare combination. When evil people rise up, we want a government with the clout to back them down. Yet we never want that clout turned on us.

People want to be lightly governed by strong governments because that's how God governs. The omnipotent ruler of the universe is also the one who invites us tenderly: "Come to me, all you who are weary and burdened, and I will give you rest. Take my yoke upon you and learn from me, for I am gentle and humble in heart, and you will find rest for your souls. For my yoke is easy and my burden is light" (Matthew 11:28–30).

—Joel Belz, "Tender Toughness,"
World (July 22, 2006)

ILLUSTRATION 394

DOING THE RIGHT THING

Topics: Advice; Conscience; Consequences; Courage; Decisions; Friendship; Guilt; Heroes; Integrity; Outreach; Responsibility; Truth; Violence; Witnessing

References: Isaiah 59:1–4; Acts 24:16; James 4:17; 1 Peter 3:13–17

In September 2006, Matt Atkinson's three friends told him they were plotting a Columbine-style attack on their school. They would ignite bombs near bathrooms, set fire to exits, then shoot any of the fifteen hundred students and staff they didn't like.

Atkinson was torn. Though his friends' threats sounded serious, he wasn't certain they were genuine. Could he risk getting his friends into major trouble over what might turn out to be a joke? That night he talked to his mother.

The following morning—one day before his friends had scheduled their attack—Atkinson followed his mother's advice and talked to the school's assistant principal. Law enforcement officials immediately intervened. After taking the three would-be attackers into custody, police searched their homes. They found shocking confirmation of the intended assault: suicide notes, a large cache of weapons, ammunition, camouflage clothing, helmets, and gas masks.

When news of the foiled attack became public, Atkinson was lauded as a hero. "Do the right thing," he said, downplaying the incident. "That's all I can say: do the right thing. There's no harm in telling somebody about it. I didn't do it for fame. I had fear for the life of my fellow students and staff at East High School."

Atkinson did the right thing because he had a proper view of the consequences of his inaction—not just for his fellow students, but also for the attackers and himself. "If it wasn't true," he said, "at least they'd get the help they needed. If I didn't go, and they were serious, I couldn't live with that on my conscience."

—Hugh Poland, "Courageous Student Prevents School Shooting," PreachingToday.com; source: "Student Talks of Breaking Up Bomb Plot," MSNBC.com (September 21, 2006)

ILLUSTRATION 395

SUING FOR THE SABBATH

Topics: Career; Commitment; Convictions; Courage; Example; Freedom; Integrity; Overcoming; Persecution; Sabbath; Ten Commandments; Testing

References: Genesis 2:1–2; Exodus 20:8–11; 23:12; Joshua 24:15; Hebrews 4:9–11

A public library in Savannah, Missouri, decided to open on Sunday. As a result, Connie Rehm, a librarian for twelve years, found herself squeezed between honoring the Sabbath and keeping a job she considered to be "a gift from God." Rehm chose to worship on Sundays and was terminated by the library.

Rehm decided to file a lawsuit against the library, claiming religious discrimination. When it became clear that the ex-employee had a strong case, the library offered a financial settlement. According to Rehm's attorney, David Gibbs, the library wanted "to deal with it as a financial matter, attempting to simply pay to make Rehm and her claim go away." He added, "One of the unique elements of this case is that Connie wasn't interested in money; she wanted her job back. That's an uncommon situation."

Three years after her initial termination in 2003, a Missouri jury ordered the library to reinstate Connie Rehm to her job. It also awarded her $53,712 in damages as compensation for lost wages.

"A middle-American, mild-mannered, small-town library person—I attribute to the Lord a great sense of humor for having picked me for this test," Rehm said. "What price is my religious freedom? What is it worth? It's not a matter of displaying the Ten Commandments. It's being able to live the Ten Commandments, and that's what my employer was asking me not to do."

— Dana Fields, "Woman Wins
Religious Discrimination Case,"
Houston Chronicle (November 16, 2006)

ILLUSTRATION 396

SEX-CHANGE PROPOSAL DIES

Topics: Creation; Culture; Government; Human Condition; Human Nature; Sex Changes

References: Genesis 1:27; 2:22 – 25; Psalm 139:13; Proverbs 14:12; 1 Corinthians 6:19; 2 Timothy 4:3

The proposal to allow people to change the sex on their birth certificates without sex-change procedures got scrapped in January 2007 when the New York City Board of Health unexpectedly withdrew the motion.

Commissioner Thomas R. Frieden, who had enthusiastically supported the plan only a month before, told *The New York Times* that institutions such as hospitals and jails had raised concerns the board hadn't considered, such as, Would female patients end up in hospital beds next to men? Would male inmates wind up in women's cell blocks?

"This is something we hadn't thought through, frankly," Frieden said. "What the birth certificate shows does have implications beyond what the birth certificate shows."

— "The Buzz," *World* (December 23, 2006)

ILLUSTRATION 397

SUING HIMSELF

Topics: Blame; Consequences; Faults; Honesty; Human Nature; Self-deception; Sin

References: Psalm 19:12 – 13; Matthew 18:15 – 18; Romans 7:15 – 24

In March 2006, a city dump truck backed into Curtis Gokey's car. The car was damaged badly, so Gokey sued the city of Lodi, California, for $3,600.

The catch? Curtis Gokey was driving the city dump truck that crunched his personal car. He even admitted the accident was his fault. The city dropped the lawsuit, stating that Gokey could not sue himself.

Like Gokey, we are often our own worst enemies. Rather than shifting the blame for the damage we do, we would do well to acknowledge our fault and humbly accept the consequences.

— Lee Eclov, "Man Tries to Sue Himself,"
PreachingToday.com

ILLUSTRATION 398

CONFRONTING BENNY

Topics: Admonition; Confrontation; Gentleness; Guidance; Leadership; Love; Mentoring; Perspective; Reconciliation; Responsibility; Teaching

References: Matthew 18:15; Romans 1:11–12; Ephesians 4:15; Colossians 3:12–14; Philemon 1:7; James 5:19–20

Jim Slevcove was my supervisor for six summers at Forest Home, a Christian conference center in California. I held a responsible position over junior high and high school kids, but I couldn't pass up a chance to play a prank. Like the time I passed off laxative gum as chewing gum to some coworkers. Word of the rigorous purgative's effect got back to Jim.

He asked me to come to his office the next day for "a little chat." There was a long, awkward silence as he leaned back in his chair and looked up at the ceiling. Were those tears in his eyes? Then he whispered "Benny" with tender affection. "Benny" he repeated twice when he got control of his emotions.

My arguments disappeared like the vapor they were. I'd gone way over the line of propriety, not to mention compassion. I owed my victims an apology. We talked about my impulsiveness and vindictiveness, the meaning of Christian community, and the responsibilities that go with leadership. In saying the hard thing to me, Jim was always gracious. His goal was not to tear down but to build up.

— Ben Patterson,
He Has Made Me Glad (InterVarsity, 2005)

ILLUSTRATION 399

LOVING AWAY RAGE

Topics: Anger; Bitterness; Enemies; Family; Fathers; Forgiveness; Grudges; Hatred; Love; Malice; Murder; Resentment; Revenge; Self-control; Violence

References: Exodus 20:13; Romans 12:19; Ephesians 4:31; Colossians 3:13; Hebrews 10:30; 12:15; 1 John 2:9; 3:15

Rick Garmon's daughter, Katie, was date-raped in 2002 when she was age eighteen and a freshman in college. Too humiliated to speak about what had happened to anyone — even her family — Katie switched schools and attempted to move on with her life.

Over the next fourteen months, Katie withdrew from her family and friends. She developed an eating disorder and began losing weight. Finally confronted by her mother, Katie confessed the truth. A year of fervent prayer and therapy finally helped Katie to overcome the pain and return to a normal life.

Meantime, Katie's father was battling the desire to avenge his daughter's rape. He even developed a plan to kill the man who had so deeply wounded his daughter. He, too, pulled away from everyone as he plotted how he'd drive through the college campus, sit in the parking lot with his rifle until the rapist walked by, and then shoot him.

One weekend when Katie was home, he retreated from her pain by going to the basement to clean his gun. His son Thomas came downstairs and asked, "Whatcha doin', Dad? Can I help ya clean? You goin' huntin'?"

The father didn't respond. When he looked at Thomas, the boy's eyes brimmed with tears. *He knows. Dear God, I think my son knows my plan,* the father thought.

"Come here, boy. Give your daddy a hug," Rick Garmon said. When Thomas wrapped his arms around him, the father realized that the boy's love was somehow stronger than his hatred. "His hug began to crumble my rage like a sledgehammer breaking a wall," the father said. "Chip by chip."

Locking the gun in the cabinet, Rick Garmon made a choice to forgive the man who had harmed his daughter.

—Based on Rick Garmon, "My Secret Hate,"
Today's Christian (May–June 2006)

ILLUSTRATION 400

ON THE WRONG SIDE OF THE LAW

Topics: Accountability; Complacency; Consequences; Debt; God; Guilt; Judgment; Punishment; Sin

References: Matthew 12:36; Romans 3:10; 13:8; Hebrews 9:27; James 2:10; 1 Peter 4:5; Revelation 20:11–15

After moving to a new state, I went to the Department of Motor Vehicles to get a new driver's license. The guy behind the desk said he couldn't help me because my license was suspended.

"There must be some mistake," I said. "I've never done anything to deserve that."

The civil servant was very civil but said I had to clear up the problem with the State of Massachusetts before he could help me. I hadn't lived in Massachusetts for ten years, so I couldn't imagine what was wrong. Five long-distance phone calls later, I found out that when I moved from Massachusetts, I owed part of an excise tax of $2.

That tiny little bill began to accrue penalties and interest. I had to pay that bill plus the cost of a new Massachusetts driver's license and registration for a car that had long ago become scrap metal before I could become legal in my new home state. The price tag was nearly $300.

The whole thing was embarrassing. It wasn't so much the money that bothered me; it was knowing that I was on the wrong side of the law for all those years without even being aware of it.

How shocking it will be for those who stand before the God of the universe one day and realize, for the first time, that he holds them accountable for all the wrongs they do.

—John Beukema,
Chambersburg, Pennsylvania

ILLUSTRATION 401

CRUEL END FOR TEFLON DON

Topics: Despair; Justice; Retribution; Sowing and Reaping

References: Psalm 62:12; Galatians 6:7–8

Mafia boss John Gotti thought he was immune to the law. Nicknamed "the Teflon Don" for escaping punishment by bribing jurors, Gotti had eaten at the best restaurants, worn the most expensive suits, and had his hair trimmed daily by his personal barber.

But the FBI kept compiling evidence against Gotti and eventually convinced Gotti's under-boss, Salvatore Gravano, to testify against Gotti in court. In June 1992, Gotti was sentenced and taken to Marion, Illinois, the most secure federal prison. For eight years he spent nearly twenty-four hours a day in a concrete seven-by-eight-foot cell with a radio, a small television, a cot, a basin, and a toilet. He was allowed two showers a week, and he got his meals through a slot in the cell door.

Gotti conceded, "I'm cursed. I'm stuck in this joint here, and that's the end of it."

In 1998 Gotti was diagnosed with throat cancer. He died in June 2002.

—Rick Hampson, "Curtains Descend on Gotti, Family," *USA Today* (July 25, 2001)

ILLUSTRATION 402

HONORABLE TROOPER

Topics: Gentleness; Human Worth; Judging Others; Kindness; Self-control

References: Proverbs 15:1; 1 Corinthians 13:1–3; Galatians 5:22–23

I once questioned a state trooper presented with an "Outstanding Trooper" award about what the governor said when presenting the award. "He said you haven't once roughed up a drunk or used excessive force on anyone. How can you

be a state trooper for fifteen years, dealing with the kind of stuff you deal with, and have that happen?"

"Two things," the trooper said. "First, if I am called to break up a fight at a tavern, I never say to myself, 'There's a drunk'; I always say to myself, 'There's a man—someone's husband, someone's son, someone's neighbor—who got drunk.' I try to think of him as a man, not a crime.

"Secondly, the Bible says that a soft answer turns away wrath. So whenever I walk up to the window of an automobile, I always speak a little softer than the person I'm speaking to."

—Jay Kesler, in the sermon "Families That Succeed," Focus on the Family Ministries

ILLUSTRATION 403

HOLDING THE STICK

Topics: Beatitudes; Confidence; Divine Power; Gentleness; Human Power; Meekness; Strength

References: Psalm 37:11; Matthew 5:5; Philippians 1:27–30

President Theodore Roosevelt adopted as his pet proverb, "Speak softly and carry a big stick." He meant that if the United States had a strong military, it could work its will among the nations of the world.

In 1901, Roosevelt changed the saying to "If a man continually blusters, a big stick will not save him from trouble; and neither will speaking softly avail, if back of the softness there does not lie strength, power."

When Jesus said, "Blessed are the meek, for they will inherit the earth," he was not speaking of armies and foreign policy, but some principles are the same. The meek Christian does not need to bluster, as if self-confidence could win the day. Whether we're contesting a point, responding to criticism, or speaking of the hope within, we can do so in meekness, with quiet confidence. For in "back of the softness" within us lie the strength and power of God.

—Thomas Bailey and David Kennedy, eds.,
The American Pageant, 9th ed. (D. C. Heath, 1991)

ILLUSTRATION 404

JUMPING TO DEFY LAW

Topics: Defiance; Disobedience; Rebellion; Ten Commandments

References: Deuteronomy 4:1; 30:16

Jan Davis, sixty, a professional parachutist, was BASE jumping when she fell to her death. Her husband, who was filming the jump, and several reporters were stunned when Davis crashed onto the rocks. She was jumping off the thirty-two-hundred-foot granite cliff, El Capitan, in Yosemite National Park, California, when her chute failed to open.

She and the other jumpers knew that BASE jumping was illegal in Yosemite Park. The law was passed because six people and numerous others had been injured in Yosemite due to BASE jumping. The five jumpers, including Davis, were protesting the park's restrictions by proving the sport is safe. They knew the law, but they

deliberately chose to defy it. Davis paid for that disobedience with her life.

In a similar way, many people think they can deliberately violate God's law. Eventually they learn, sometimes the hard way, that God's laws exist to protect us.

—Jonathan Mutchler, "Parachutist Perishes,"
PreachingToday.com

ILLUSTRATION 405

GOVERNING WITH MORALITY

Topics: Ethics; Government; Law; Morality

Reference: Romans 2:28–29

In the ultimate analysis of what moral forces govern a society, it must generally be concluded that law alone is a feeble instrument. Laws will not be enacted or enforced unless there is a moral consensus to support them. Underlying every enforceable law there has to be a clear understanding of its moral objective and a willingness to accept it.

—Father Robert F. Drinan,
St. Mary's Law Journal, 1998

ILLUSTRATION 406

SUBMITTING TO A HIGHER LAW

Topics: Freedom; Law; Obedience

Reference: James 1:25

When I was in third grade, I was condemned to live under a law of nearsightedness. My eyes went bad, and today I am considered legally blind. I am not free; I am in bondage to this law. I hate it. But it doesn't matter. There is no escape.

One day I discovered there was a greater law that can overcome the law of nearsightedness. It is the law of glasses. When I submitted myself to the law of corrective lenses, the law of nearsightedness was overcome. The law of nearsightedness is still there, but it was overpowered by a greater law that enabled me to see.

Here's the irony: You would think if I want to be free, I should throw the glasses away. But that is not freedom. Only by submitting to the law of glasses do I become free.

—Jim Holm, "Free at Last,"
Mennonite Brethren Herald
(February 19, 1999)

ILLUSTRATION 407

AFTERMATH OF ANYTHING GOES

Topics: Family; Happiness; Morality; Self-control; Sexual Immorality; Suicide

References: Jeremiah 31:31–34; 1 Thessalonians 4:3–8

Let's face it; we are not a happier society as a result of the liberalization of the seventies. We have record rates of divorce, record rates of suicide, record rates of teenage pregnancy, record rates of youth crime, record rates of underage sex.

We should invite people to recognize that the Great Experiment has failed. You cannot have happiness without restraint.

—Anne Widdecombe,
Electronic Telegraph (April 3, 2000)

ILLUSTRATION 408

JUDGING THE JUDGMENT

Topics: Hell; Judgment; Justice; Punishment

References: Genesis 18:25; Psalm 9:7–8; Romans 11:33–36; 14:9–13

Imagine tuning into a TV courtroom trial. You can see only what the camera shows you. You don't hear all the testimony. You don't get to question the witnesses. You don't get to see all the evidence. You don't hear the instructions to the jury. You're not privy to the conversations between the lawyers and the judge.

When the jury comes in with its verdict and the sentence is passed by the judge, how adequately can you assess whether justice has been done?

How then can we sit in judgment on God's justice? We don't have all the information necessary to judge whether God has been just.

—John Walton, in the sermon "Auditing God"

ILLUSTRATION 409

TOPPING THE SENTENCE

Topics: Betrayal; Forgiveness; Redemption; Relationships; Restoration; Stealing; Trust

References: Matthew 6:12–15; 18:21–35; Colossians 3:12–14

Mark Gagnon worked as a clerk in a store owned by James Brazeau. Brazeau had promised to bring Gagnon a New England Patriots hat when he returned from the football game. Brazeau arrived as promised, hat in hand, only to discover Gagnon had stolen $4,382 worth of lottery tickets from the store.

Gagnon was prosecuted, and just before he was sentenced, his former boss, Brazeau, walked over to the defendant's table and presented Gagnon with a paper bag. He said, "I want this to be a learning experience for you." The judge made the hat part of the sentence, ordering Gagnon to wear the hat every time he appeared in public for the next two years.

—William H. Nix,
Character Works (Broadman & Holman, 1999)

ILLUSTRATION 410

MY ERRANT THUMB

Topics: Depravity; Faults; Final Judgment; Guilt; Redemption; Sin; Sinful Nature

References: Matthew 5:30; 10:28; 25:34; Mark 9:43; 2 Corinthians 5:10

After several months of pain in my right thumb, I went to a hand specialist. As the doctor examined my hand, a nurse stood by with a clipboard. The doctor looked closely at my hand, said, "Atrophy," and then, "No." The nurse wrote on her clipboard. He named something else—an acronym like CLJ—then again said, "No," and the nurse wrote on her clipboard.

I realized he was proceeding through a checklist of possible problems with my hand. As he named the next item on the checklist, I found myself hoping, wishing, that he would again say no.

I want my thumb to be free from pain. In the months prior to this appointment I had begun curtailing my use of the thumb to see if that would bring it back to normal. When typing on the keyboard, for example, I started using my left thumb to hit the space bar instead of my right, thinking that perhaps I had a repetitive motion injury. I was careful how I turned the key in the car ignition. I stopped shaking hands with my right hand. I was careful not to open bottles with my right hand. And so on.

Each time the doctor said no I felt relief. He named another item on the checklist, and again he said no. After seven nos, he sent me for X-rays. Minutes later the doctor showed me the film and said, "Here is the problem." The ligament on one side of my joint had stretched, and the thumb had gotten out of alignment. He described treatments but implied the situation might not get better. That was not what I wanted to hear.

As I thought later about this experience in the doctor's office, I couldn't get over the visceral yearning I had, as the doctor went through his checklist, to hear him find no fault in my hand. If that yearning is so strong regarding my hand, which I will be using for a limited number of years on earth, how much more should I yearn for a good report when I stand before the one who judges my soul?

—Craig Brian Larson,
Arlington Heights, Illinois

ILLUSTRATION 411

ABORTION SUPPORT DECREASES

Topics: Abortion; Babies; Culture; Family; Government; Justice; Morality; Parenting; Politics; Values

References: Exodus 20:13; Psalm 139; Proverbs 31:8; Isaiah 59:14; Jeremiah 1

Public support for the *Roe v. Wade* decision to legalize abortion continues to decline. According to a survey reported by a Harris poll in May 2006, only 49 percent of more than one thousand adults surveyed supported *Roe*, marking the first time that less than half of the United States population endorsed the ruling made by the U.S. Supreme Court in 1973. Forty-seven percent oppose *Roe*, while 4 percent are not certain or refuse to answer.

The lowest previous support for *Roe* in a Harris poll was in 1985 with 50 percent. The highest backing for *Roe* in a Harris survey was in 1991, when 65 percent of Americans said they endorsed the decision. In 1973, 52 percent supported *Roe*.

—Associated Press, "Support for Roe Dips to New Low," *Baptist Press* (May 8, 2006)

PART 18: LIFE AND DEATH

ILLUSTRATION 412

EPITAPH FOR RICK WARREN

Topics: Character; Compassion; Endurance; Leadership; Legacy

References: Deuteronomy 15:7–8; Proverbs 21:13; Micah 6:8; Matthew 25:31–46; Galatians 2:10; James 1:26–27; 1 John 3:16–18

In August 2006, Fox News featured a television special titled "Can Rick Warren Change the World?" Throughout the show, reporters interviewed Warren about his bestselling book *The Purpose Driven Life*, his ministry at Saddleback Church, and his leadership in the church growth movement.

They also spotlighted his attempts to move beyond the boundaries of this country with a global network of churches to revolutionize the way we tackle what he believes are the five biggest problems facing the world today: poverty, disease, illiteracy, spiritual emptiness, and egocentric leadership.

As the interview progressed, a nagging question seemed to taint the ambitious pastor's hopes and plans: Can it really work? Can one man — or one church, or one network, or one nation — really heal all of the hurts of the world?

Warren did not shy away from questions. At the end of the interview, he offered four words to be written on his tombstone: "At least he tried."

— "Can Rick Warren Change the World?" FoxNews.com (August 20, 2006)

ILLUSTRATION 413

DISARMING TO DEATH

Topics: Danger; Distractions; Indifference; Neglect; Responsibility; Warnings; Witnessing

References: Matthew 28:16–20; Luke 24:45–49; John 3:16–21; Acts 1:8; Romans 6:23; 10:14–15; 1 Corinthians 9:19–23; 1 Peter 3:15

In March 2007, in the Kuban region of southern Russia, at least sixty-two people were killed by a fire that quickly blazed through a home for the elderly. The greatest tragedy was that the deaths could have been prevented.

Authorities say a night watchman ignored two fire alarms. When the third alarm sounded and the watchman saw flames, he finally took the necessary action to evacuate residents. Even then, other staffers were notably absent from their posts, making the escape effort nearly impossible in some cases. By the time fire authorities and rescue workers arrived, many residents had already died from smoke inhalation.

—Associated Press, "Fire Kills 62 after Alarms Ignored," CNN.com (March 20, 2007)

ILLUSTRATION 414
WHAT REALLY MATTERS

Topics: Accomplishments; Courage; Love; Priorities; Success

Reference: Amos 5:18–24

The question to ask at the end of life's race is not so much "What have I accomplished?" but "Whom have I loved, and how courageously?"

—Geoff Gorsuch, "Journey to Adelphos," *Discipleship Journal*, issue 14 (March/April 1983)

ILLUSTRATION 415
THE BEST OF WORST TIMES

Topics: Healing; Perseverance; Preaching; Protection; Sorrow; Strength; Tears

References: 1 Corinthians 1:27; 2 Corinthians 12:9–10; Galatians 6:9

John Claypool, pastor of the Crescent Hill Baptist Church in Louisville, had a little daughter with leukemia. When she went into remission, everybody thought God had healed her. On an Easter Sunday morning she had a recurrence. In his book *Tracks of a Fellow Struggler*, Claypool

says his daughter asked, "Daddy, did you talk to God about my leukemia?"

He said, "Yes, we've been praying for you."

She asked, "Did you ask him how long the leukemia would last? What did God say?"

What do you say to your daughter when you can't help her and the heavens are silent? A few hours later, the little girl died. The following Sunday, John Claypool got up to preach. His text was Isaiah 40:31: "Those who hope in the LORD will renew their strength. They will soar on wings like eagles; they will run and not grow weary, they will walk and not be faint."

"There are three stages of life," Claypool said. "Sometimes we mount up with wings as an eagle and fly; we're on top of the world. Sometimes we run, and we don't grow weary; we just go through the routine. Sometimes the best we can do is to walk and not faint. That's where I am right now. I need your prayers."

At the moment that Claypool was at his lowest, he preached probably his most influential sermon. Like Paul, he could say, "For when I am weak, then I am strong" (2 Corinthians 12:10).

—R. L. Russell, "Triumphing over Trials," Preaching Today Audio, no. 119

ILLUSTRATION 416
SHOWING US HOW TO MOURN

Topics: Acceptance; Body of Christ; Christians; Community; Compassion; Example; Forgiveness; Grace; Grief; Kindness; Love; Mercy; Mourning

References: Matthew 5:7, 43–48; Luke 6:27–36; 17:4; Romans 12:17–19; Ephesians 4:32; Colossians 3:12–13

On the morning of October 2, 2006, Charles Carl Roberts barricaded himself inside West Nickel Mines Amish School. After murdering five young girls and wounding six others, Roberts committed suicide. It was a dark day for the Amish community of West Nickel Mines, but it was also a dark day for Marie Roberts, the wife of the gunman, and her two young children.

On the following Saturday, Marie went to her husband's funeral. She and her children watched in amazement as Amish families—about half of the seventy-five mourners present—came and stood alongside them in the midst of their blinding grief. Despite the horrific crimes the man had committed against them, the Amish came to mourn Charles Carl Roberts as a husband and daddy.

Bruce Porter, a fire department chaplain who attended the service, was profoundly moved: "It's the love, the heartfelt forgiveness they have toward the family. I broke down and cried seeing it displayed." He said Marie Roberts was also touched. "She was absolutely, deeply moved by the love shown."

—"Amish Mourn Gunman in School Rampage," *USA Today* (October 7, 2006)

ILLUSTRATION 417

TAKING ME HOME

Topics: Blessings; Death; Disease; Heaven; Home; Illness; Longing; Mortality; Needs; Perseverance; Suffering; Thankfulness; Valleys

References: 1 Kings 17:17–24; Job 29:18; Psalm 23:4; 56:5; Mark 5:35–43; Philippians 4:19

Fred Smith, an influential businessman who has mentored Christian leaders for several decades, was seriously ill in the summer of 2004. He was hospitalized, semiconscious, and not expected to live. Periodically he would mutter, "I want to go home, I want to go home." After an emotional family conference, the family concluded they should respect Fred's wishes and allow him to die. They agreed to remove him from dialysis, knowing that his death would come in a few days.

For the next thirty-six hours, Fred's family sang, read Scripture, prayed, and said their good-byes. Fred seemed to get worse; he went into pulmonary failure and choking aspiration. His daughter Brenda sat with him at midnight, begging God for answers. The coughing, however, broke through Fred's deep sleep, and he awoke. Brenda quietly told her dad of the family's decision to follow his desire to "go home." She explained that he would slip into unconsciousness and then step "from here to there."

Suddenly Fred's eyes were wide open: "Home? I didn't mean heaven; I meant Parkchester [his house on Parkchester Drive]." Laughing through tears, Brenda quickly called the doctors to reschedule his dialysis, and Fred returned to what he called "the washing machine." A year later, while still prepared to go to his heavenly home, Fred was happy to be at his current home in Dallas.

—Introduction to "Ask Fred," *Leadership* (Summer 2005)

ILLUSTRATION 418

CURING FEAR

Topics: Anxiety; Courage; Danger; Deliverance; Doubt; Fear; Growth; Healing; Overcoming; Sanctification; Self-discipline; Spiritual Formation; Testing; Trials; Worry

References: Romans 5:3–5; Philippians 4:6–7; 2 Timothy 1:7; Hebrews 2:14–15; James 1:2–4; 1 Peter 1:6–7; 1 John 4:18

I recently went to the doctor for allergy tests to determine what was triggering my asthma. The nurse practitioner pricked my forearm in eighteen places with different allergens and then said, "Don't scratch." I had to resist the urge to scratch the itch for fifteen of the longest minutes of my life!

Testing for allergies isn't a pointless exercise in cruel and unusual punishment, even though it might seem like it. It is a form of reverse engineering. My doctor wasn't satisfied with treating my allergy symptoms; she wanted to discover the root causes of my reactions. And the solution isn't just avoiding those allergens I reacted to. The cure is actually exposing myself to those allergens in small doses.

Here is my point: The cure for fear of failure is not success; it's failure. The cure for fear of rejection is not acceptance; it's rejection. You have to be exposed to small quantities of whatever you're afraid of. That's how you build up immunity to fear.

—Mark Batterson, *In a Pit with a Lion on a Snowy Day* (Multnomah, 2006)

ILLUSTRATION 419

AVALANCHE AHEAD

Topics: Alertness; Danger; Death; Perspective; Preparation; Second Coming; Threats; Training; Vulnerability; Warnings; Watchfulness

References: Psalm 73:2; Ecclesiastes 9:11–12; Isaiah 46:9–10; Jonah 3:3–6; Matthew 24:42; Colossians 4:2; 1 Peter 1:13; Revelation 16:15

When Dave Boon first saw the avalanche that swept his car over a guardrail on Interstate 40 in Denver, Colorado, it was only a puff of powder. After that brief warning, a snowy burst of wind knocked the car out of control. "Not even a second later, a freight train hit us," Boon said.

Boon had been traveling with his wife, June, and Gary Martinez, thirteen, on their way to a youth group ski trip. The three of them had been discussing the possibility of an avalanche. "We were talking about avalanches and how there was so much snow and stuff. Then we turned the corner and saw some white powder, and it slammed us into the guardrail," Boon said.

The wall of snow knocked the car over the rail and caused it to roll hundreds of feet down a steep mountain slope. In the middle of the descent, the car struck a tree and was knocked out of the avalanche's grasp. It came to a stop upside down and pointing back uphill.

Fortunately, Boon and his wife were well trained. After clearing an airway and freeing himself from the seat belt, Boon was able to exit the car along with Martinez and then cut his wife free from her restraints. Despite several bumps, bruises, and scrapes, none of the three required hospitalization.

For Boon, the experience was a reminder that warnings and hints of danger need to be respected. "The signs read, 'Avalanche Area, No Stopping,'" he said. "We've driven by that place hundreds of times. We've skied avalanche chutes, worn beepers, always carried an avalanche shovel. We've seen avalanches. But in our wildest dreams, we never imagined getting hit in a car by one."

— Patrick O'Driscoll,
"Avalanche Sends Travelers Tumbling,"
USA Today (January 8, 2007)

ILLUSTRATION 420

LAST WORDS

Topics: Afterlife; Death; Human Condition; Legacy; Limitations; Mortality; Salvation; Satisfaction

References: Psalm 49:10; Ecclesiastes 1:2; 12:6–7; John 11:25–26; Hebrews 9:27; James 4:14

What will be your last words? Here are some from other people:

"Nothing matters. Nothing matters" (Louis B. Mayer, film producer; died October 29, 1957).

"It is very beautiful over there" (Thomas Edison, inventor; died October 18, 1931; he may have been referring to the view outside of his window).

"I'm bored with it all" (Winston Churchill, statesman; died January 24, 1965; after saying this, he slipped into a coma and died nine days later).

"Am I dying, or is this my birthday?" (Lady Nancy Astor; died 1964; after waking briefly during her last illness and finding all her family around her).

"Why, yes, a bulletproof vest" (Domonic Willard, a foot soldier during the Prohibition, just before his death by firing squad, in response to being asked if he had any last requests).

"Don't let me die; I have got so much to do" (Huey Long, "The Kingfish," governor of and senator from Louisiana; died 1935).

"My work is done. Why wait?" (George Eastman, inventor; died 1932; from his suicide note).

"Jesus, I love you. Jesus, I love you" (Mother Teresa; died September 5, 1997).

— www.wikiquote.org

ILLUSTRATION 421

HOLDING HER TIGHT

Topics: Assurance; Attitudes; Discouragement; Faith; Love; Marriage; Overcoming; Peace; Security in God; Spouses; Testimony; Thankfulness; Tragedy; Victorious Living

References: Psalm 23:4; Matthew 5:4; John 16:20; Romans 8:35–39; Philippians 4:6–7; 1 Thessalonians 4:13–18

Kelly James, a landscape architect, and two of his friends were climbing Mount Hood in Welches, Oregon, when they encountered a blizzard. Kelly called his family on his cell phone, but the storm was too severe for rescue workers to come in. All three hikers perished.

On the *CBS Evening News*, Katie Couric asked Kelly's widow if she was angry with her husband for climbing the mountain. Karen James replied, "I'm really sad our journey is over for a while, and I miss him terribly. But he loved life so much, and he taught me how to love. He taught me how to live. And I don't know how you can be angry at someone who loved their family, who loved God … and gave back so much more than he took."

When asked how her husband would like to be remembered, Karen said, "Kelly had this little ornament, and he's had it since he was little. It's a manger. It's just this little plastic thing. And it's always the tradition that [our son] Jack and Kelly put it on the tree together. So I said this Christmas, 'We're going to put that ornament on the tree.' One of the things that we really understand about Christmas is how that little baby born in a barn is the reason our family has so much strength now. And that is really important to Kelly."

Couric asked if the family's confidence in God had been tested by her husband's death. "No, it was never tested," Karen answered. "I remember one time we were watching TV, and Kelly said to me, 'I can't wait to go to heaven.' I said, 'What?' We were watching some show that had nothing to do with heaven. And he said, 'Yeah, that's going to be really cool.' And I said, 'Can you hold off? Can we wait?' But he wasn't scared. Those conversations are what I hold on to."

When asked if there were any lessons to be learned from her husband's tragedy, Karen replied, "I've told a colleague of mine that men should hold their wives really, really tight, because you don't know when our journey's going to end. My journey ended with an 'I love you.' And … for others, if their journey ends with an 'I love you,' it's a lot to hold on to."

—Ted De Haas, "Widow Thankful for Her Husband's Life and Witness," PreachingToday.com; source; "Climber's Widow Tells Her Story," *CBS Evening News* (December 21, 2006)

ILLUSTRATION 422

CROC MAN KILLED BY PUSSYCAT

Topics: Complacency; Consequences; Creation; Danger; Death; Fear; Mortality; Nature; Respect; Risk; Tragedy; Vulnerability; Watchfulness

References: Psalm 39:5; Proverbs 6:27; 14:12; Galatians 6:7–8; James 1:14–15; 4:14; 1 Peter 1:24

Steve Irwin, the "Crocodile Hunter," was killed September 4, 2006, while filming wildlife along the Great Barrier Reef. Irwin was best known for the wildly popular, wildly dangerous antics on *Crocodile Hunter*, his long-running TV program. During the fourteen years the documentary was on, Irwin survived countless snakebites, was chased up a tree by a deadly komodo dragon, was spat on by a red spitting cobra, and was pulled into the water by a massive crocodile. At the time of his death, he was in the Great Barrier Reef to film a documentary on the ocean's deadliest creatures.

One of the ocean's least harmful creatures killed Irwin. Due to poor weather, his team had stopped filming for the "Ocean's Deadliest" series, so Irwin decided to do some work for a children's show that was to be hosted by his eight-year-old daughter, Bindi.

While swimming with his cameraman, Irwin came across a five-foot-wide stingray and began to follow it. Stingrays are often called the "pussycats of the sea" because of their docile nature. They can be hand-fed by tourists on excursions from cruise liners. Irwin reportedly got a little too close to the animal, which thrust its poisonous, barbed tail upward in a defensive reflex. The ten-inch, serrated barb went into Irwin's chest and pierced his heart.

Irwin was only the seventeenth person in the world known to have been killed by a stingray. If the barb had penetrated elsewhere on his body, he would have easily survived. He was rushed to the nearest island and picked up by a medical helicopter, but he died long before reaching the hospital.

—AnimalPlanet.com (September 7, 2006)

ILLUSTRATION 423
WHAT A WAY TO GO

Topics: Abundant Life; Fulfillment; Human Condition; Limitations; New Life; Perfection; Self-worth; Sports; Success; Weakness

References: Ecclesiastes 6:12; Jeremiah 29:11; Matthew 5:48; 1 Corinthians 15:58

Ed Lorenz bowled a perfect game, then had a heart attack and died. The sixty-nine-year-old retiree had started bowling in 1957 and had bowled two other perfect games in 2004. His per-game average for his last full season was 223, and in 2005 he was inducted into the Kalamazoo Metro Bowling Association Hall of Fame. He died after his third perfect game in January 2006.

"If he could have written a way to go out, this would have been it," said Johnny D. Masters, Lorenz's bowling partner.

—Andrew Hard, "Talk about Going Out on Top," FoxNews.com (January 3, 2006)

ILLUSTRATION 424
COURTING THE ROAD OF DEATH

Topics: Alertness; Consequences; Danger; Death; Disobedience; Eternal Life; Hell; Judgment; Mortality; Salvation; Sin; Temptation; Threats; Watchfulness; Worldliness

References: Psalm 23:4; Proverbs 2:11 – 15; 4:11; 14:12; Matthew 7:13 – 14; Hebrews 11:8

The dirt and rock road that stretches about forty miles and descends from La Paz (at twelve thousand feet) down to the beautiful rain forest town of Coroico at the edge of the basin of the Amazon River is a road of death.

In 1995, the Inter-American Development Bank called this stretch the "world's most dangerous road." An average of twenty-six vehicles fall off this road each year, and two hundred to three hundred people lose their lives. As if steep hillsides, cliffs, and drop-offs with no guardrails aren't bad enough, the road sometimes has room for only one vehicle. Rain and fog complicate the trip, along with muddy surfaces and loose rocks. On July 24, 1983, more than a hundred passengers were killed when a bus veered over the edge and crashed into a canyon.

Despite the danger, the road has become an increasingly popular tourist attraction since the early 1990s.

—Graham Gori, Associated Press, "Thrills on the Highway of Death" (November 24, 2002)

ILLUSTRATION 425
EMAILING AFTER DEATH

Topics: Communication; Computers; Death; Eternity; Grief; Inheritance; Legacy; Mortality; Perspective; Technology; Time

References: Deuteronomy 4:9; Psalm 78:4–7; Isaiah 38:18; Joel 1:3; 2 Corinthians 10:10–11; 2 Timothy 1:14; Hebrews 9:27–28

For a yearly fee of $19.95, you can send emails after you die. Credit Dr. David Eagleman, an assistant professor of neuroscience and psychiatry at Baylor College of Medicine, for that benefit. He created Deathswitch, an automated online service that allows a person to send an email after your death to preselected recipients, usually containing critical personal information of the deceased. "It can be anything from computer passwords or a love note to the last word in an argument," Eagleman says.

Eagleman sees his service as a way of bridging mortality. The idea for Deathswitch came from his love of the Internet and how it can extend the human experience. "It would be so interesting to receive an email from someone who passed away," Eagleman says. "I don't think there's any honor in being silent in death."

Brian Rosenthal, the CEO of the Silicon Valley-based e-commerce consulting firm Robocommerce, has signed up for Deathswitch. "It extends our reach," says Rosenthal. "You can store some part of yourself that lasts beyond your life."

Others have their doubts, including Rob Frankel, a Los Angeles-based branding consultant. "Nobody wants to think about their demise," he says. "It's hard enough to get someone to buy a cemetery plot."

—Associated Press, "One Enterprising Houston Scientist Is Using the Internet to Offer His Customers the Last Word," *Houston Chronicle* (January 9, 2007)

ILLUSTRATION 426
HOW LONG YOU'LL LIVE

Topics: Aging; Choices; Consequences; Death; Future

References: Deuteronomy 32:29;
Job 14:5; Psalm 39:4; 90:12;
Romans 3:23; 5:12–19; 6:23

How long will you live? Researchers with the San Francisco Veterans Affairs Medical Center say they have developed a test that predicts your chances of surviving with 81 percent accuracy.

They begin with zero, then factor in risk factors, such as diabetes, smoking, exhaustion, or good health habits such as moderate exercise. Men automatically lose 2 points just for being men. Dr. Sei Lee, a geriatrics researcher at the San Francisco Veterans Affairs Medical Center, said the quiz is designed "to try to help doctors and families get a firmer sense for what the future may hold" to plan health care accordingly.

—Lindsey Tanner, "Test Helps You Predict
Chances of Dying," news.yahoo.com
(February 14, 2006)

ILLUSTRATION 427

WHY GO ON LIVING?

Topics: Affliction; Life; Loss; Meaning; Perseverance; Purpose; Suffering

References: Matthew 10:39; Mark 12:30; Philippians 4:13

When Jewish psychiatrist Viktor Frankl was arrested by the Nazis in World War II and put in Auschwitz, the infamous death camp, he was stripped of everything: property, family, possessions—and a manuscript he had spent years researching and writing on finding meaning in life. The manuscript had been sewn into the lining of his coat.

"Now it seemed as if nothing and no one would survive me; neither a physical nor a spiritual child of my own," Frankl wrote. "I found myself confronted with the question of whether under such circumstances my life was ultimately void of any meaning."

A few days later, the Nazis forced the prisoners to give up what little clothing they still wore. "I had to surrender my clothes and in turn inherited the worn-out rags of an inmate who had been sent to the gas chamber," said Frankl. "Instead of the many pages of my manuscript, I found in the pocket of the newly acquired coat a single page torn out of a Hebrew prayer book, which contained the Jewish prayer 'Shema Yisrael' (Hear, O Israel! The Lord our God is one God. And you shall love the Lord your God with all your heart and with all your soul and with all your might.)

"How should I have interpreted such a 'coincidence' other than as a challenge to 'live' my thoughts instead of merely putting them on paper?"

Frankl later reflected on his ordeal in *Man's Search for Meaning*, saying, "There is nothing in the world that would so effectively help one to survive even the worst conditions, as the knowledge that there is meaning in one's life.... He who has a 'why' to live for can bear almost any 'how.'"

—Based on Viktor Frankl,
Man's Search for Meaning (Pocket, 1997)

ILLUSTRATION 428
LESSONS IN A HOSPITAL BED

Topics: Achievement; Death; Materialism; Meaning; Riches

References: Job 27:16–17; Psalm 39:6; Ecclesiastes 2:26; Matthew 6:19–21; James 5:3

Sudden loss often simplifies life. For example, a man who found himself in a hospital bed wrote:

> I came to realize I no longer really cared for what the world chases after, such as how much money you have in the bank and how many cars are parked in the garage. As it says in Ecclesiastes, chasing after these things is like chasing the wind, anyway. Suddenly, the rat race became vanity to me, utter vanity. I felt naked before God.
>
> If I died, I would take none of the stuff with me. All that really mattered ultimately was my relationship with the Lord, my relationship with family and friends. If it weren't for the loss of my health, I could have wasted the rest of my life chasing achievements and acquiring more transitory things.

I'd say his loss served him well, wouldn't you?

—Bill Hybels, "The Often-Overlooked Benefits of Losing," *Preaching Today Audio*, no. 80

ILLUSTRATION 429
WHAT'S REALLY IMPORTANT

Topics: Choices; Death; Decisions; Meaning; Mortality; Worth

References: Psalm 89:46–48; 90:12; Matthew 6:19–21; Luke 12:13–31; Hebrews 9:27; James 4:13–15

Remembering that I'll be dead soon is the most important tool I've ever encountered to help me make the big choices in life. Because almost everything—all external expectations, all pride, all fear of embarrassment or failure—these things just fall away in the face of death, leaving only what is truly important.

—Steve Jobs, cofounder of Apple and Pixar, Stanford University Commencement Address (June 2005)

ILLUSTRATION 430
HOPE FOR THE DYING

Topics: Aging; Assurance; Eternal Life; Evangelism; Future; Ministry; Mortality; Seekers; Witnessing

References: Ecclesiastes 8:8; Matthew 20:1–16; Ephesians 5:15–16; Hebrews 9:27; James 4:14; 1 Peter 1:24; 2 Peter 3:11–12

"Last Minute Ministry" began when a friend of Pastor Chuck Kent asked him to visit his dying ninety-two-year-old great-grandfather in the hospital. The elderly man, Elwyn, was an agnostic.

Pastor Chuck met with Elwyn and asked if he could share one of Jesus' stories. He told the story of the vineyard owner who hired people to work in the last hour. Elwyn, who was also in the "eleventh hour," prayed to accept Christ. A week later, Pastor Chuck conducted Elwyn's funeral. About a hundred people heard the gospel at the service.

When Kent's daughters said there were others in the hospital who needed to hear the gospel, the pastor got permission from the hospital to visit. He went room to room, asking each person if he could pray and then share the story of the eleventh hour. In one month he visited fifteen people, eight of whom accepted Christ.

During one of those visits, Chuck talked to a comatose man who had only a few hours to live. The man was unable to speak or open his eyes. So Chuck led him through the prayer of salvation by having him squeeze Chuck's hand one phrase at a time. Two hours later, the patient died.

"We started this ministry, not intending for it to be ongoing," Chuck says. "But the church got excited; it took off amazingly. It's an easy ministry to see progress, because these people are getting ready to die." He added, "People on the terminal floor are a lot more realistic about eternity."

—Elizabeth Diffin, "Eleventh-Hour Ministry," *Leadership* (Spring 2006)

ILLUSTRATION 431
UNREPENTANT TO THE END

Topics: Atheism; Death; Hard-heartedness; Repentance; Stubbornness

References: Acts 3:19; Hebrews 3:7–8

When my father was in intensive care, a priest was sent, presumably to administer last rites. After ascertaining the purpose of the visit, my father quickly dismissed the priest and sent him out. The doctor later said, "They say there are no atheists in the trenches, but … whew!"

Dad wouldn't let the priest do any sort of cursory prayer, Hail Mary, *anything*. But see, my father had as much patience for religion as he did for solicitors ringing the bell.

—Dave Eggers, *A Heartbreaking Work of Staggering Genius* (Simon & Schuster, 2000)

ILLUSTRATION 432
WHEN LIFE DISSOLVES

Topics: Afterlife; Death; Despair; Funerals; Hopelessness

References: 1 Corinthians 15:12–32; 1 Thessalonians 4:13–18

African Muslims have a unique funeral custom. Close family and friends circle the casket and quietly gaze at the corpse. There's no singing. No flowers. No tears.

A peppermint candy is passed to everyone. At a signal, each one puts the candy in his or her mouth. When the candy is gone, each participant is reminded that life for this person is over. For them, life simply dissolves.

—Philip Yancey, *Where Is God When It Hurts?* (Zondervan, 1997)

ILLUSTRATION 433

SINGING TO SAVE BABIES

Topics: Abortion; Desires; Dreams; Fulfillment; Goals; Hope; Ministry

References: 1 Samuel 1:1–11; Psalm 20:4; 37:4; 139:13–16

"Being single at forty-two, I'm realizing I may never have a child," says singer Kathy Troccoli. "But God has repeatedly brought me stories from women who have chosen life over an abortion as a result of hearing a song I wrote."

Troccoli had just finished singing at a concert in Dallas when a young woman's voice came over the loudspeaker. She said when she was pregnant with her second child, people told her to abort the baby. She went to one of Troccoli's concerts and heard the song "A Baby's Prayer," which says, "But if I should die before I wake, I pray her soul you'll keep. 'Forgive her, Lord; she doesn't know that you gave life to me.'"

The Holy Spirit used that song to help the young woman decide to keep her baby.

"God has shown me that more children have been born through that song than I could ever bear," Troccoli says.

— Kathy Troccoli and Dee Brestin, *Falling in Love with Jesus* (Word, 2001)

ILLUSTRATION 434

THAWING A FROZEN TODDLER

Topics: Children; Christ as Shepherd; Healing; Motherhood; Redemption; Repentance; Rescue; Salvation; Sin

References: Psalm 91:14; Luke 15:3–7, 11–32

On a cold February night in 2001, Erika, age one, somehow wandered out of her house and spent the entire night outside. When her mother, Leyla Nordby, found the little girl, Erika appeared to be totally frozen. Her legs were stiff and her body frozen, and all signs of life appeared to be gone.

Erika was treated at Edmonton's Stollery Children's Health Center. To the amazement of doctors, the toddler showed no sign of brain damage. They gave Erika a clear prognosis; she would soon hop and skip and play like other girls her age.

Some of us have wandered away from our Father's house, and it has brought us near the point of death. Our hearts have hardened, and our spiritual bodies look as lifeless as the little girl in the snow. But our Father knows we are missing and is searching for us. He can take our lifeless spirits and restore us to health.

Let the Father pick you up and take you back to his house.

— David Duncan, "Wandering from God's House," PreachingToday.com; source: Bob McKeown, "A Tiny Survivor," MSNBC *Dateline* (March 20, 2001)

ILLUSTRATION 435

DEATHBED CONVERSATION

Topics: Communication; Death; Family; Friendship; Honesty; Love; Relationships

Reference: 2 Corinthians 1:3–7

When my dad had died eight years earlier, Michael had stood by me. When the sympathy cards stopped coming and I began the terrifying freefall into grief, Michael had been my parachute. Now I stood vigil with him at his father's deathbed.

I tried to look into Al's eyes, which had always been playful. Under his silver eyebrows were dark circles; his lids were slightly open, but the eyes were rolled back and showed only white. Clear plastic tubing snaked from the wall to a mask covering his nose and mouth. The nurses said he might make it through the night, but they weren't sure. His kidneys were shutting down.

Out in the shiny hospital hallway, laundry carts stood silent. It was deep past midnight, and we were alone: a son, a wife, a dying dad, a friend.

Hearing is the last sense to fade, so Michael and his wife, Stephanie, spoke to Al—beautiful, tender words. "I love you, Dad," Michael said. "I'm here with you, and you won't be abandoned. You won't be left alone."

"Thank you for all you've given us," Stephanie added, holding his hand, which occasionally twitched. Al had always been generous, helping with school expenses or other needs. "Whenever you helped us and we said thank you, you just told us, 'That's what dads are for,'" Michael said.

He paused and repeated, "That's what dads are for."

Death changes conversation. It strips away cheap social conventions and calls us either to be silent or to speak from the heart. In that room, the only words that seemed appropriate were the kind that were deep and clear and true.

Death also changes the calculation. Whatever seemed so important during life—job or money or house or success—doesn't matter now. When you're *in extremis*, the most important thing, apart from being ready to meet God, is to be surrounded by people who love you.

—Kevin Miller, LeadershipJournal.net
(October 5, 2000)

ILLUSTRATION 436

WRITING BLIND

Topics: Death; Despair; Eternal Life; Fear; Hope

Reference: Psalm 23:4

When divers combed the wreckage of the *Kursk*, the Russian nuclear submarine on which 118 sailors perished, they found a letter written by Lieutenant Dmitri Kolesnikov, addressed to his wife, Olga. It was written after the explosion that felled the sub August 12, 2000, in the Barents Sea and confirmed speculation that all the crew had not died instantly.

Hours after the sub plunged to the bottom of the sea, Kolesnikov wrote, "All the crew from the sixth, seventh, and eighth compartments went over to the ninth. There are 23 people here.... None of us can get to the surface."

The last lines of the letter indicated that death was closing in as the auxiliary power failed. Kolesnikov wrote unevenly in the pitch-darkness: "I am writing blind."

The apostle Paul, blind and knowing that a martyr's death was near, also wrote good-bye letters. His writing, though, was filled with hope in Christ.

—Greg Asimakoupoulos, "Hope beyond Earthly Life," PreachingToday.com

ILLUSTRATION 437

SAILING INTO DEATH

Topics: Afterlife; Death; Eternity; Fear; Mortality; Peace; Trust

References: Hosea 13:14; Luke 23:43; 1 Thessalonians 4:13–18; Hebrews 2:14–15

"I have moments when fear makes me sit up in bed at night and weep like a three-year-old," says Cathy Hainer about her struggle with cancer. "I've become afraid of the long, lonely nights. Yet at other times I feel at peace, knowing I'm in the right place, secure in my beliefs about an afterlife."

Hainer takes solace in something a friend recently showed her: a parable found on the body of an American Jewish soldier, Colonel David Marcus, who helped establish the state of Israel. He wrote:

I am standing upon the seashore. A ship at my side spreads her white sails in the morning breeze and starts for the blue ocean. She is an object of beauty and strength, and I stand and watch her until at length she is only a ribbon of white cloud just where the sea and sky come to mingle with each other. Then someone at my side says, "There! She's gone!"

Gone where? Gone from my sight—that is all. She is just as large in mast and hull and spar as she was when she left my side, and just as able to bear her load of living freight to the place of destination. Her diminished size is in me, not in her, and just at the moment when someone at my side says, "There! She's gone!" there are other voices ready to take up the glad shout, "There! She comes!" And that is dying.

—Cathy Hainer, *USA Today* (December 6, 1999)

ILLUSTRATION 438

AM I GOING TO DIE?

Topics: Cross; Crucifixion; Death; God as Father; God's Love; Human Condition; Humanity of Christ; Limitations; Parenting; Sacrifice; Suffering

References: Matthew 26:39; John 3:16; Romans 8:32; Philippians 2:8

Last week my son, Bjorn, got sick. I took his temperature, and it was 102.5 degrees. The Children's Advil came out. He slugged down the appropriate dose for his size. Forty-five minutes later the fever was down to 100.

Just before bed I checked his temperature again. It was back up. More Advil. I checked again forty-five minutes later; now it was 103. Concerned, I asked Bjorn to drink more water. He obliged, but he was clearly languishing.

My wife, Mary, slept with our youngest son, Kristian, as I monitored Bjorn through the night. At 12:30 a.m., the thermometer went under the tongue of my lethargic son. His skin was hot; his affect dulled. 104.

I called the urgent care facility at the local medical center. They said, "Bring him in."

Mary took Bjorn in while I stayed home with Kristian. While she started the van, I got Bjorn ready. I jostled him. He awoke. I told him we were going to the doctor. He looked at me with weary, wondering eyes and asked, "Am I going to die, Daddy?"

I had three reactions. Common sense: "No, you are not going to die. We need to get this fever down." Emotional: "I'm scared." Visions of children with bizarre diseases flooded my heart. Spiritual: "Dear Jesus, cover him. Heal him. Love him."

I conveyed the commonsense reaction to Bjorn, not wanting to scare him and being fairly certain his fever was not life threatening. But my mind flashed to the many parents in this world who have had to look at their children, knowing that the ultimate answer to that question was yes. I can barely write as I contemplate that circumstance.

Bjorn recovered. Still, I wonder if there was once a conversation between the Father and the Son, when the Son asked the question, "Am I going to die, Daddy?" and in his heart the Father knew the answer was yes.

—Per Nilsen, Burnsville, Minnesota

ILLUSTRATION 439

COMPUTING YOUR DEATH

Topics: Death; Eternity; Life Span

Reference: Psalm 90:10–12

Want to make the most of your life? Consult a website to find out just how much time you have left.

If you enter your birth date and gender at The Death Clock (www.deathclock.com), you will get your projected date of death. If you were born, say, on March 16, 1969, and are male, you will die December 26, 2042, based on an average life span. That's less than 1.4 billion seconds away.

The Death Clock bills itself as "the Internet's friendly reminder that life is slipping away."

—Associated Press, "Magazine Lists Worst Sites on Internet," *Daily Herald*, Arlington Heights, Illinois (October 19, 1999)

ILLUSTRATION 440

UNBELIEVING TO THE END

Topics: Apologetics; Atheism; Belief; Death; Despair; Faith; Knowledge; Naturalism; Science; Skepticism

Reference: John 20:29

Carl Sagan was fascinated that educated adults, with the wonders of science manifest all around them, could cling to beliefs based on the unverifiable testimony of observers dead for two thousand years.

"You're so smart, why do you believe in God?" he once asked cleric Joan Brown Campbell. She found this a surprising question from someone who had no trouble accepting the existence of black holes, which no one has ever observed.

"You're so smart, why don't you believe in God?" she answered.

Sagan never wavered in his agnosticism, even when he was dying. "There was no death-bed conversion," his wife, Ann Druyan, says. "No appeals to God, no hope for an afterlife, no pretending that he and I, who had been insepa-rable for twenty years, were not saying good-bye forever."

"Didn't he want to believe?" someone asked.

"Carl never wanted to believe," she said fiercely. "He wanted to *know*."

—Jerry Adler, "Unbeliever's Quest," *Newsweek* (March 31, 1997)

ILLUSTRATION 441

BETTING ON DEATH

Topics: Ambition; Death; Greed; Money; Perspective; Time

References: Psalm 90:12; Luke 12:13 – 21

A man opens a newspaper and discovers it is dated six months in advance of the time he lives. Reading through the newspaper, he discovers stories about events that have not yet taken place. He turns to the sports page and sees scores of games not yet played. He turns to the financial page and discovers the rise or fall of different stocks and bonds.

He realizes this information can make him a wealthy man. A few large bets on an under-dog team can make him wealthy. Investments in stocks that are now low but will go high can fat-ten his portfolio. He is delighted.

He turns the page and comes to the obituary column and sees his picture and story. Everything changes. The knowledge of his death changes his view about his wealth.

—Haddon Robinson, "Life and Death Advice," Preaching Today Audio, no. 200

ILLUSTRATION 442

TOLSTOY'S REASON TO LIVE

Topics: Conversion; Meaning of Life; Pleasure; Purpose; Questions; Significance; Sin; Worldliness

References: Psalm 16:11; Matthew 6:19 – 21; 1 Timothy 1:12 – 17

Leo Tolstoy, known for his classic work *War and Peace*, also wrote *A Confession*, which tells the story of his search for meaning and purpose in life.

Tolstoy rejected Christianity as a child and went to a university seeking pleasure. In Moscow and St. Petersburg he drank heavily, lived pro-miscuously, and gambled frequently. His ambi-tion was to become wealthy and famous, but nothing satisfied him.

In 1862, he married a wonderful woman, and they had thirteen children. He had every-thing, yet he was so unhappy that he was on the verge of suicide. "Is there any meaning in my life which will not be annihilated by the inevitability of death, which awaits me?" he said.

Tolstoy searched for the answer in every field of science and philosophy. As he looked around, he saw that people were not facing up to the basic questions of life, such as: Where did I come from? Where am I going? Who am I? What is life all about? Eventually he found that the peasant people of Russia answered these questions through their Christian faith, and he, too, came to realize that only in Jesus Christ do we find the true meaning of life.

—Nicky Gumbel,
Questions of Life (Kingsway, 1993)

to live so freely. The mantra for my generation was 'Be your own man!' I always said, 'Hey, you can have whatever rules you want—I'm going to have mine. I'll accept the guilt. I'll pay the check. I'll do the time.' I chose my own way. That was my philosophical position well into my fifties. As I've gotten older, I've had to adjust."

But reality has a way of getting the attention of even Jack Nicholson. Later in the interview, he adds, "We all want to go on forever, don't we? We fear the unknown. Everybody goes to that wall, yet nobody knows what's on the other side. That's why we fear death."

—Dotson Rader, "I Want to Go On Forever,"
Parade magazine (December 9, 2007)

ILLUSTRATION 443

FEARING THE UNKNOWN

Topics: Consequences; Death; Eternal Life; Faith; Fear; Heaven; Hell; Hope; Jesus Christ; Lifestyle; Mortality; Peace; Resurrection; Salvation; Trust; Uncertainties

References: John 3:16; 11:25–26; 14:1–6; Romans 8:35–39; 2 Corinthians 5:1–10; Philippians 1:21; Hebrews 9:27; Revelation 21:1–5

In the 2007 film *The Bucket List*, two terminally ill men—played by Jack Nicholson and Morgan Freeman—take a road trip to do the things they always said they would do before they "kicked the bucket." Before the film's release, Nicholson was interviewed by *Parade* magazine. Reflecting on his personal life, Nicholson said, "I used

ILLUSTRATION 444

MARRYING THE RIGHT ONE

Topics: Commitment; Contentment; Divorce; Happiness; Intimacy; Love; Marriage; Relationships; Romance; Satisfaction; Spouses; Unfaithfulness; Vows

References: Genesis 2:24; Malachi 2:13–16; Matthew 7:24–27; 19:3–9; 1 Corinthians 7:10–11; Ephesians 5:22–33

If we are serious about pursuing spiritual growth through marriage, we must convince ourselves to refrain from asking the spiritually dangerous question, "Did I marry the right person?"

A far better alternative to questioning one's choice is to learn how to live with one's choice. A character in the Anne Tyler novel *A Patchwork Planet* realizes this too late. The book's thirty-two-year-old narrator has gone through a divorce and now works almost exclusively with elderly people. As he observes their long-standing marriages, he comes to a profound understanding:

> I was beginning to suspect that it made no difference whether they'd married the right person. Finally, you're just with who you're with. You've signed on with her, put in half a century with her, grown to know her as well as you know yourself or even better, and she's become the right person. Or the only person, might be more to the point.
>
> I wish someone had told me that earlier. I'd have hung on then; I swear I would. I never would have driven Natalie to leave me.

—Gary Thomas,
Sacred Marriage (Zondervan, 2000)

ILLUSTRATION 445

I'LL ALTER HIM

Topics: Anxiety; Brides; Fear; Love; Marriage; Spouses; Vows; Weddings

References: Genesis 2:24; Proverbs 18:22; 1 Corinthians 7:1–7; Ephesians 5:22–33; 1 Peter 3:1–7

A young bride was so nervous she said to her pastor, "I'm afraid I might not make it through the ceremony."

The pastor soothed her, saying, "When you enter the church tomorrow and the processional begins, you will be walking down the same aisle you've walked many times before. Concentrate on that aisle. When you get halfway down the aisle, you'll see the altar, where you and your family have worshiped for many years. Concentrate on that altar. Then, when you're almost to the altar, you will see your groom, the one you love. Concentrate on him."

The next day, the bride walked down the aisle with her chin up and eyes bright. But those along the center were a bit surprised to hear her muttering over and over, "Aisle, altar, him. Aisle, altar, him."

—J. R. Love, Rushton, Louisiana

ILLUSTRATION 446

TAKING A BREAK

Topics: Apathy; Commitment; Communication; Indifference; Intimacy; Love; Marriage; Spouses

References: Proverbs 18:22; Ephesians 5:25–33; Colossians 3:19; 1 Peter 3:7; Revelation 3:15–16

A businessman moved over slightly as a young man crowded into the airplane seat next to him. As they both fastened their seat belts, the businessman good-naturedly asked whether the young man was traveling on business or pleasure.

"Pleasure," the young man replied. "I'm on my honeymoon."

"Your honeymoon?" the businessman asked, mystified. "Where's your wife?"

"Oh, she's a few rows back. The plane was full, so we couldn't get seats together."

The plane hadn't started rolling yet, so the businessman said, "I'd be happy to change seats with her so that the two of you can be together."

"That's OK," the young man replied. "I've been talking to her all week."

—Gary Thomas,
Sacred Marriage (Zondervan, 2000)

ILLUSTRATION 447

DON'T COME HOME

Topics: Arguments; Attitudes; Confrontation; Emotions; Family; Fatherhood; Fighting; Guidance; Obedience; Parenting; Problems; Vows

References: Genesis 2:24; Proverbs 22:6; Mark 10:9; Ephesians 5:22–33; Titus 2:4; Hebrews 13:4

My husband, Mike, and I had been married only a few months when we had a major argument. In a fit of rage, I stormed onto our back porch and called my parents in Michigan, letting them know I'd be on the first flight out of Philadelphia. I expected them to say, "Of course! Come home!"

Instead, my father informed me that was not an option.

"You've never told me I couldn't come home! Why are you being so unfair?" I shouted.

"Jamie, your gut reaction has always been to bail when things get difficult," he said. "Your marriage vows were for better or worse, until death do you part. I know you didn't think the 'for worse' part was going to come so soon, but it did, and you need to learn how to deal with it. You're not welcome in our home under these circumstances. You need to work things out with Mike."

After I hung up, I reluctantly grabbed my Bible and opened it to Genesis 2:24: "For this reason a man will leave his father and mother and be united to his wife, and they will become one flesh." As I meditated on this Scripture, I realized my impulse to run home when Mike and I fought is disobedient to God. Sticking with my husband isn't something I do only when I feel like it—it's God's will for my marriage.

I broke down in tears—this time in joy for a father who knew what was best for me and pointed me to God. I went inside, truly broken at the way I'd treated Mike. After a brief, internal tug-of-war, I sat down humbly and explained the phone conversation I'd just had.

"I'm sorry I turned to my parents instead of you," I said. "From now on I promise I won't try to run home when things between us get tough."

I still miss my parents. Living with them made me feel safe, and some days it's difficult knowing I'll never have that security again. But I'm learning that's not necessarily bad. Because, in leaving my parents, I experience the joy that comes from cleaving only to my husband. And in doing that, I am pleasing God.

—Jamie Bartlett, "Why Can't I Come Home?"
Marriage Partnership (Summer 2006)

ILLUSTRATION 448

FIRST FIGHT

Topics: Arguments; Conflict; Division; Family; Fighting; Husbands; Marriage; Murder; Relationships; Spouses; Violence; Wives

References: Proverbs 12:4; 19:13; 27:15; Ephesians 4:26–27; 5:22–23; Colossians 3:19; 1 Peter 3:1–7

Three weeks after her wedding day, Joanna called her minister in hysterics. "Pastor," she cried, "John and I had our first fight. It was awful! What am I going to do?"

"Calm down, Joanna," her pastor answered, leaning back in his chair. "This isn't nearly as bad as you think. Every marriage has to have its first fight. It's natural."

"I know, I know," Joanna said impatiently. "But what am I going to do with the body?"

—Van Morris, Mount Washington, Kentucky

ILLUSTRATION 449

MARITAL ADVICE FROM ANIMALS

Topics: Acceptance; Change; Divorce; Husbands; Marriage; Spouses; Wives

References: Genesis 2:18–25; Proverbs 17:9; 18:22; 19:13; 27:15; Luke 17:4; Colossians 3:13; 1 Peter 3:1

After twelve years of marriage, journalist Amy Sutherland was still irked by some of her spouse's habits. It took some advice from animal trainers to help her. In a column in *The New York Times*, Sutherland wrote:

> These minor annoyances are not the stuff of separation and divorce, but they began to dull my love for Scott. I wanted—needed—to nudge him a little

closer to perfect, to make him into a mate who might annoy me a little less, who wouldn't keep me waiting at restaurants, a mate who would be easier to love.

So, like many wives before me, I ignored a library of advice books and set about improving him. My nagging only made his behavior worse: he'd drive faster instead of slower; shave less frequently, not more; and leave his reeking bike garb on the bedroom floor longer than ever.

A breakthrough came when Amy went to a school for exotic animal trainers in California to research a book. She wrote:

I listened, rapt, as professional trainers explained how they taught dolphins to flip and elephants to paint. Eventually it hit me that the same techniques might work on that stubborn but lovable species, the American husband.

The central lesson I learned is that I should reward behavior I like and ignore behavior I don't. After all, you don't get a sea lion to balance a ball on the end of its nose by nagging. The same goes for the American husband.

Back in Maine, I began thanking Scott if he threw one dirty shirt into the hamper. If he threw in two, I'd kiss him. Meanwhile, I would step over any soiled clothes on the floor without one sharp word, though I did sometimes kick them under the bed. But as he basked in my appreciation, the piles became smaller.

—Amy Sutherland, "What Shamu Taught Me about a Happy Marriage," *The New York Times* (June 25, 2006)

ILLUSTRATION 450

ARE YOU MAD AT ME?

Topics: Anger; Apathy; Arguments; Conflict; Emotions; Feelings; Insensitivity; Marriage; Needs; Passivity; Relationships; Spouses

References: 1 Corinthians 7:1–7; 13:4–7; Ephesians 5:22–33; Colossians 3:18–19; 1 Peter 3:7

Recently Jana and I weathered one of the most stressful weeks in our marriage. I had spent two weeks traveling for business, and now I had to prepare presentations to make to clients. It was also the week that Jana moved her mother into a retirement home. I couldn't help with the move because of my work commitments, plus I had to spend time watching the kids while she got her mom settled. By the end of that week, we were exhausted.

On Sunday evening I ran to my office (which is ten minutes away) to pick up some work. I left without telling Jana. She was busy checking her email, so I thought I'd just step out, go to the office, and come back; I wouldn't even be missed.

When I came home, Jana said: "Dave, you were gone for thirty minutes. You know I hate when you don't tell me you're leaving. Are you mad at me?"

I thought, *Am I?* I knew I wasn't. But by leaving without telling Jana, I was being passive-aggressive. I'd had a couple of weeks where I wasn't getting any attention, and I responded by becoming passive, thinking, *I'll just leave and see if she misses me.*

Passivity, or not taking initiative in your marriage, is a spiritual issue, because underneath is a deep current that says, "My needs aren't getting met, so I'm not going to meet your needs." That's a spiritually dangerous and crippling place to be.

—Dave Goetz, "Marital Drift,"
Marriage Partnership (Winter 2006)

ILLUSTRATION 451

OUT-OF-WEDLOCK BIRTHS

Topics: Abstinence; Babies; Chastity; Children; Cohabitation; Family; Home; Marriage; Monogamy; Parents; Premarital Sex; Sexual Immorality; Vows

References: Genesis 2:24; 1 Corinthians 6:18–20; 7:8–9; Ephesians 5:3; 1 Thessalonians 4:3–5; Hebrews 13:4; 1 Peter 2:11

Of the 4.1 million babies born in the United States in 2005, more than 1.5 were brought into the world by unmarried couples. That means, according to government reports, almost four of ten babies were born out of wedlock.

Several factors contributed to these statistics. While the rate of teen births dropped, unwed mothers in their twenties had a higher increase in birth rates than any other age group. In addition, the number of Americans choosing to live together without getting married continues to rise. In 1970, there were 200,000 unmarried- couple households with children. By 2005 that number had jumped to 1.7 million.

—Associated Press, "Almost 4 in 10 U.S. Children Born Out of Wedlock in 2005," *USA Today* (November 21, 2006)

ILLUSTRATION 452

MORE SINGLE WOMEN

Topics: Husbands; Lifestyle; Marriage; Singleness; Spouses

References: Genesis 2:18; Judges 21:14; Matthew 19:11; 1 Corinthians 7:32–35

Fifty-one percent of women lived without a spouse in 2006. According to a January 2007 article in *The New York Times*, this is the first time in American history that single women outnumbered married women.

That percentage was up from 35 percent in 1950 and 49 percent in 2000.

—Sam Roberts, "51 Percent of Women Are Now Living without a Spouse," *The New York Times* (January 16, 2007)

ILLUSTRATION 453

MEN AND MARRIAGE

Topics: Attitudes; Commitment; Contentment; Family; Husbands; Love; Marriage; Singleness; Wives

References: Genesis 2:24; Proverbs 12:4; 18:22; Malachi 2:16; Mark 10:9

It's better to marry than to stay single, men said. That was the finding of a study done in 2006 by the Centers for Disease Control and Prevention. About 66 percent of men agreed with the statement, "It is better to get married than go through life single," compared with only 51 percent of women.

In addition 76 percent of men and 72 percent of women agreed that "it is more important for a man to spend a lot of time with his family than be successful at his career."

The study involved more than 12,000 men and women, ages fifteen to forty-four, and comprised the government's first comprehensive glimpse into the male psyche. Relationship expert Neil Chethik said the data mirrors his own research, in which 90 percent of married men say they would marry the same woman if given a chance to do it again.

—Sharon Jayson, "Marriage Means More to Men," *USA Today* (June 1, 2006)

ILLUSTRATION 454

ADULTERERS BEWARE

Topics: Adultery; Betrayal; Community; Example; Faithfulness; Marriage; Purity; Relationships; Self-control; Tolerance; Unfaithfulness; Vows; Workplace

References: Exodus 20:14; Proverbs 6:20–35; Matthew 5:27–30; Romans 2:17–24

Sheriff's deputies in Pinellas County, Florida, will be suspended if they commit adultery. So says Country Sheriff Dennis Fowler. His reason is that adultery is not a victimless crime. Rather, it has created difficulties within his department that go beyond the offenders. "Adultery affects other people in the workplace, people's ability to do their job, and I think that is relevant," Fowler says.

—"County to Suspend 'Cheating' Sheriff's Deputies," local6.com (February 8, 2006)

ILLUSTRATION 455

MARITAL ASSETS

Topics: Divorce; Faithfulness; Finances; Lifestyle; Love; Loyalty; Marriage; Money; Possessions; Poverty; Prosperity; Relationships; Riches; Teamwork; Wealth

References: Malachi 2:16; Matthew 19:1–9; Mark 10:1–12; 1 Corinthians 7:10–11

People who marry and stay hitched accumulate nearly twice as much wealth as those who are single or divorced.

That's what a researcher at Ohio State University discovered. Economist Jay Zagorsky of Ohio State's Center for Human Resource Research tracked the financial and marital status of more than 9,000 people from 1985 to 2000. During that time, married people amassed 93 percent more wealth than single or divorced people.

Wealth was defined as a participant's total assets, such as bank accounts, stocks, bonds, and real estate, minus outstanding debt, such as a mortgage. The data came from the National Longitudinal Survey of Youth, a study funded by the U.S. Bureau of Labor Statistics, which has repeatedly surveyed the same individuals over time.

According to the report, published in the *Journal of Sociology*, people who married and stayed married showed a sharp wealth expansion after their wedding, growing to an average of about $43,000 by the tenth year of marriage. For single people, assets grew from less than $2,000 at the start of the survey to about $11,000 by the fifteenth year.

Those who divorced saw their wealth shrink by 77 percent—a larger decline than would occur by simply splitting a couple's assets in half. "You lose economies of scale in divorce—you need two places to live, two cars," Zagorsky says. "Divorce is quite expensive, paying for lawyers and court fees. Divorce is also time-consuming. It may take time away from work, which also reduces many people's incomes." In addition, divorce weakens the incentive to work harder in the future, particularly if a percentage of income is garnished to pay alimony.

On the other hand, wedded bliss has rich rewards: "Married people boosted their wealth by about 4 percent each year—just as a result of being married—with all other factors held constant."

—Laura Rouley, "Wedded, Wealthy, and Wise," finance.yahoo.com (January 27, 2006)

ILLUSTRATION 456

COSTLY ADULTERY

Topics: Adultery; Cost; Divorce; Faithfulness; Marriage; Vows

References: Genesis 2:24; Matthew 19:6; Mark 10:1–12

Adultery need not break up marriages. It's the civilized way of dealing with the fault line of marriage—desire.

So says social commentator Minette Marrin in London's *Sunday Times*. In America adultery is no longer a crime in half the states, and in the others adultery is seldom, if ever, prosecuted. But sexual straying from marriage remains a costly, if not criminal, practice. According to a recent estimate, the typical adulterous husband invests almost $26,000 over a four-month period in conducting an extramarital affair. Once his wife discovers his philandering, he can count on another $5,000 in legal bills, plus an $1,800 deposit on a place to live after she ejects him from their home.

Apart from its immorality, adultery is a terrible investment. Only 5 percent of men and women who leave their marriages for someone else actually end up marrying that person.

—David Yount, "The Cost of Adultery," knoxnews.com (November 29, 2004)

ILLUSTRATION 457

FIGHTING TO DEATH

Topics: Arguments; Conflict; Disunity; Family; Fighting; Marriage; Peace; Prayer; Presumption; Relationships; Strife

References: Proverbs 27:15; Ephesians 4:26–27; Philippians 2:14; Colossians 3:19; Hebrews 12:14; James 4:1

An elderly couple lived together in a nursing home. Though they had been married for sixty years, their relationship was strained with constant arguments, disagreements, and shouting contests. The fights didn't stop even in the nursing home; the couple argued and squabbled from the time they got up in the morning until they fell in bed at night.

The nursing home supervisor eventually threatened to throw them out if they didn't change their ways. Even then the couple couldn't agree on what to do.

Finally, the wife said to her husband, "I'll tell you what, Joe; let's pray that one of us dies. After the funeral is over, I'll go live with my sister."

—John Beukema,
Chambersburg, Pennsylvania

ILLUSTRATION 458

HOUSE WITH BRIDE FOR SALE

Topics: Brides; Dating; Internet; Loneliness; Marriage; Money; Romance; Wives

References: Proverbs 31:10; Hebrews 13:4

Deborah Hale wants to sell her home—with herself included. At age forty-eight, Hale, a jewelry maker, says she has a hard time meeting single men. Hale decided to advertise her home in the Washington Park section of Denver as an added incentive for prospective husbands. Since that time, she has had as many as fifteen thousand hits per hour on the website she established.

Hale acknowledges that she won't discount a prospective suitor who isn't interested in the home but makes it clear that for the right man, she "could become part of the deal."

—"House for Sale, Bride Included,"
msnbc.msn.com (November 11, 2005)

ILLUSTRATION 459

HEALING FOR A BROKEN MARRIAGE

Topics: Accepting Christ; Adultery; Awakenings; Beginnings; Change; Conversion; Desperation; Invitation; Reconciliation; Repentance; Restoration; Salvation; Worry

References: Isaiah 57:18; Joel 2:32; Romans 6:20–23; 2 Corinthians 7:9–10; Ephesians 5:8–10; Titus 3:3; 1 Peter 3:1–2

Shawna Pilat's husband still wasn't home from his Saturday night partying. "It was very common for Rick to be out all night. I always knew there was unfaithfulness," said Shawna, who was home with her three-year-old son. "That bothered me, naturally, but I was also worried that Rick was going to turn up some place dead. And that morning I was at the end of my rope."

As Shawna angrily washed dishes in the kitchen, she noticed a man speaking on television. He was funny and warm, and seemed to be speaking to her. "I felt something come over me that I can't explain," she remembers. "I couldn't quit crying. At the end of the program, it said, 'Join us,' and it gave the name of a church in Winnipeg. I couldn't get my son dressed fast enough."

On the way to the church, Shawna had one purpose in mind: getting emotionally strong enough to kick Rick out. But God had a surprise for her.

At the end of the message, the pastor invited people to give their lives to Christ. Shawna raised her hand. Three weeks later, Rick asked if he could join her at church.

After four or five weeks of attending church with his wife, Rick recognized his need for Christ. Still, the following months weren't easy. "I was going to church and wanting to do right, but I kept doing wrong," he said. It wasn't until a Promise Keepers seminar that he finally came to understand the importance of repentance and accepting the forgiveness God offers through Jesus Christ. That day Rick went home and told his wife, "I can be the husband you need me to be now."

Rick and Shawna's lives changed that day. They became active in their church and now serve as Promise Keepers volunteers who share the hope of God's restoration and forgiveness with struggling couples. "When I think of how Jesus can change people—no matter how deep in sin they are—that overwhelms me," Rick says. "If he did it for us, he can do it for anybody."

—Kristen Burke, "Winnipeg Couple Set Free," *Decision* (December 2006)

ILLUSTRATION 460

PROPOSING ON A BIKE

Topics: Determination; Love; Marriage; Passion; Purpose; Romance

References: Genesis 2:24; Proverbs 18:22; Mark 10:8; Ephesians 5:28

Brian Shipwash and his girlfriend, Shandra Miller, were riding a motorcycle up North Carolina's Pilot Mountain. At a curve in the road, Shipwash lost control and crashed into the side of an oncoming pickup truck. The couple went flying, and the motorcycle landed on top of Shipwash.

Ten other Harley-Davidson riders rushed to help and found the handlebars of the motorcycle stuck six inches into Shipwash's abdomen. When they pulled the handlebars from his stomach, Shipwash pulled a small box from his pocket. It was broken and bloody, but inside was a ring.

Later Shipwash told his girlfriend the reason they were going to Pilot Mountain was so he could propose. In front of reporters, he said, "I know this is not the best time in the world, but will you marry me?"

"I was crying at the time because of the wreck," Miller said. "But when I saw [the ring], I just started crying even more."

Though he suffered a broken hand and leg, Shipwash did not damage any major organs. No one else was injured in the accident. And Shandra Miller said yes.

—Associated Press, "Crashed Biker Proposes at Accident Scene," *Chicago Sun-Times* (December 31, 2003)

ILLUSTRATION 461

SHOCK THERAPY FOR MARRIAGE

Topics: Anxiety; Faith; Growth; Husbands; Marriage; New Life; Patience; Security in God; Stress; Trust; Vows; Wives

References: Matthew 10:34–39; 1 Corinthians 7:10–17; 1 Peter 3:1–2

When I met Christ, I was forty-nine years old and had been married to my husband for seventeen years. We had two children and a quiet suburban life. We had built a comfortable life. But I knew that if I fully followed Christ, everything in my life would change. I might lose it all — my marriage, my friends, and my family.

I weighed devotion for Christ against devotion to my kids and family. I asked whether a broken marriage with Christ was better than a marriage without Christ. But gradually, as Christ's words became my words, his love filled me and poured out of me, even to my husband, who now called me his enemy. I found that I could love my husband with a resolve I had never before experienced.

In the eighteen months that followed my full commitment to Christ, Christ has been shaping our marriage in a new way. My husband has changed dramatically from the man he was two years ago. From fighting my church attendance, he now encourages me to go. My children are going to youth group, and both are worshiping with me weekly. When I asked my husband if he would help my daughter and me to go on a mission trip to Mexico, he said, "We will make it happen."

I have learned many lessons in these past months, but none so much as loving and trusting my Lord.

—Anonymous

ILLUSTRATION 462

WEDDED TREES

Topics: Christmas; Church; Community; Friendship; Marriage; Spiritual Gifts; Teamwork; Unity

References: Proverbs 27:17; Ecclesiastes 4:9–11; Mark 10:6–9; Romans 12:3–8; 1 Corinthians 1:10; 12; Ephesians 4:11–16

Slats Grobnik, who sold Christmas trees, noticed one couple on the hunt for a Christmas tree. The guy was skinny with a big Adam's apple, and she was kind of pretty. Both wore clothes from the bottom of the bin of the Salvation Army store.

After bypassing trees that were too expensive, they found a Scotch pine that was OK on one side but pretty bare on the other. Then they picked up another tree that was not much better — full on one side, scraggly on the other. She whispered something, and he asked if $3 would be OK. Slats figured both trees wouldn't sell, so he agreed.

A few days later Slats was walking down the street and saw a beautiful tree in the couple's apartment. It was thick and well rounded. He knocked on their door, and they told him how they had pushed the two trees together where the branches were thin. Then they tied the trunks together. The branches overlapped and formed a tree so thick you couldn't see the wire. Slats described it as "a tiny forest of its own."

"So that's the secret," Slats asserts. "You take two trees that aren't perfect, that have flaws, that might even be homely, that maybe nobody else would want. If you put them together just right, you can come up with something really beautiful."

—Mike Royko, *One More Time*
(University of Chicago Press, 1999)

ILLUSTRATION 463

COMMON-LAW MARRIAGE

Topics: Cohabitation; Divorce; Marriage; Relationships; Romance; Sexual Immorality

References: Genesis 2:18–24; 1 Corinthians 7:1–7, 10–11

While marriage still accounts for the majority of relationships, its traditional dominance is giving way to the growing popularity of common-law unions. According to data from the 1995 General Social Survey in Canada, women whose first conjugal union was a common-law relationship were almost twice as likely to separate as women

who married first. Young people were more inclined to live in common-law union with their first partner. In 1995, only 1 percent of women ages sixty to sixty-nine lived common-law in their first union. By contrast, 38 percent of women ages thirty to thirty-nine chose common-law first, while 52 percent of those ages twenty to twenty-nine chose common-law.

The likelihood of the common-law relationship ending in divorce or separation has increased significantly. While 25 percent of women ages sixty to sixty-nine experienced a breakup at some point in their lives in 1995, more than 40 percent of those in their thirties and forties had already gone through one.

—Céline Le Bourdais and others,
"The Changing Face of Conjugal Relationships,"
Canadian Social Trends (Spring 2000)

ILLUSTRATION 464

FIRST WORDS

Topics: Hearing God; Listening; Love; New Life; Spiritual Perception

References: John 3:16; 10:1–16; Romans 6:4–7; 2 Corinthians 5:17

For fifty-seven years, Steve Henning of Huntley, Illinois, could not hear music, laughter, or human speech. Even though he lived a full life, he still longed to hear the voices of those he loved.

In the winter of 2001, he learned of a surgical procedure that would allow sound waves to bypass the nonfunctioning part of his ear and travel directly to the auditory nerve. On January 30, he was operated on. Because the implanted device could not be activated until the swelling in the ear decreased, doctors and Steve didn't know for six weeks if the operation was successful.

Finally, the six weeks was up. As Steve waited nervously, the audiologist programmed the cochlear implant. Then he invited Steve's wife to say something. Pat Henning leaned toward her husband and gently said, "I love you." Able to hear for the first time in six decades, Steve's face broke into a smile. The first words he heard were of love.

—Greg Asimakoupoulos, "Hearing God's Word of Love," PreachingToday.com

ILLUSTRATION 465

LESSONS FROM A VACUUM CLEANER

Topics: Help; Husbands; Love; Marriage; Servanthood; Wives

References: Acts 20:35; Ephesians 5:25; 1 Peter 3:7; 1 John 3:16

I learned some lessons about vacuuming one day. First, I learned that our cat is terrified of vacuum cleaners. That kept me entertained for about an hour.

As I vacuumed in one direction, a stripe would appear. Going the opposite direction would create a stripe of a different shade. Entranced, I striped the whole room. Then I went crossways, creating a checkerboard pattern. I got so carried away that I dusted the furniture and straightened the entire house.

I was embedded in the easy chair, working on a crossword puzzle, when my wife, Diane, came home from work. She struggled through the door with a bag of groceries under each arm, kicked the door shut with one foot, then took in the house with an expert glance. Her mouth dropped open. Slowly the bags slipped from her grasp and dropped to the floor. "Who did this?" she asked.

"I did," I said. Without warning, she attacked. Diving on me before I could get out of the chair, she smothered me with kisses and hugs. The kisses grew more passionate. We broke the chair. It was wonderful!

The vacuum cleaner taught me an important lesson that day: Love is expressed with more than just words.

—Ken Davis, *Lighten Up!* (Zondervan, 2000)

ILLUSTRATION 466

HIS SEVEN-YEAR FIT

Topics: Anger; Bitterness; Forgiveness; Gratitude; Husbands; Ingratitude; Marriage; Relationships; Resentment; Wives

Reference: Matthew 18:15–35

I collect old newspapers. I was humored by a story in the November 17, 1930, edition of the *Chicago Herald Examiner* about a husband and a wife. The article tells of a man named Harry Havens of Indiana, who went to bed—and stayed there—for seven years with a blindfold over his eyes because he was peeved at his wife.

Havens liked to help around the house — hang pictures, wipe the dishes, and such. But one day his wife scolded him for the way he was performing one of these tasks, and he resented it. He reportedly said, "All right. If that's the way you feel, I'm going to bed. I'm going to stay there the rest of my life. And I don't want to see you or anyone else again."

His last remark explains the blindfold. He said he finally got up when the bed started to feel uncomfortable.

— Van Morris, "Resentful Husband Retreats," PreachingToday.com

ILLUSTRATION 467

ANYTHING FOR SUGAR

Topics: Family; Generosity; Marriage; Materialism; Money; Responsibility

References: Proverbs 11:24 – 25; Ecclesiastes 5:8 – 15

Several men in the locker room of a private exercise club were talking when a cell phone rang. One man picked it up without hesitation and said, "Hello?"

"Honey, it's me," she said.

"Sugar!"

"I'm at the mall two blocks from the club. I saw a beautiful mink coat. It is absolutely gorgeous! Can I buy it? It's only $1,500."

"Well, OK, if you like it that much."

"Thanks! Oh, and I also stopped by the Mercedes dealership and saw the new models. I saw one I really liked. I spoke with the salesman, and he gave me a great price."

"How much?"

"Only $60,000!"

"OK, but for that price I want all the options."

"Great! Before we hang up, there's something else. It might seem like a lot, but, well, I stopped by to see the real estate agent this morning, and I saw the house we had looked at last year. It's on sale! Remember? The beachfront property with the pool and the English garden?"

"How much are they asking?"

"Only $450,000, a magnificent price, and we have that much in the bank to cover it."

"Well then, go ahead and buy it, but put in a bid for only $420,000, OK?"

"OK, sweetie. Thanks! I'll see you later! I love you!"

"I love you too."

The man hung up, closed the phone's flap, and raised it aloft, asking, "Does anyone know who this cell phone belongs to?"

— John Fehlen, Stanwood, Washington

ILLUSTRATION 468

NAMING THE CHILD

Topics: Conflict; Divorce; Marriage; Relationships

References: Malachi 2:16; Matthew 19:1 – 6; 1 Corinthians 7:10 – 11

A couple was in the midst of a hostile divorce. Six months into their case, their baby boy was born.

His mother named him a day later, only to find her husband had gone to court to bar her from naming the child. Shortly thereafter, they began legal mediation to see if they could agree on a name.

The overseeing judge urged the couple to work things out, saying, "I would hate to see this thing turn ugly."

—Abdon M. Pallasch,
"Wife Won't Have to Pump Milk,"
Chicago Sun-Times (December 14, 2000)

ILLUSTRATION 469

THE POWER OF A PAIR

Topics: Marriage; Ministry; Skills

References: Genesis 1:26–31; 2:4–25; Ecclesiastes 4:9–12; Luke 10:1; Ephesians 5:22–33

When the time came for a strategic decision during his ministry, Jesus made an interesting choice. He gathered seventy-two workers, like regional representatives, and sent them to various towns to prepare people for his visits (see Luke 10:1). He could have sent each disciple separately and reached more towns. Instead, he chose to send thirty-six teams of two.

When two people work together, one can protect the other. One can encourage another. Two can split the work, offset each other's weaknesses, and draw on each other's strengths. Companionship makes two more effective, not less, than one.

Today Jesus sends out Christian couples, just like he sent those pairs of disciples, because a pair has power. When we felt God was calling us to write this book, we knew neither of us could do it alone. I needed Kevin's skills in writing; he needed my background in marriage counseling. Together, with God's help, we could minister in a more powerful way.

Most Christians have been trained to think of serving Christ individually. How often might our ministries—and our marriages—be strengthened if we could find a way to draw on our spouse's strengths? It's not always possible, and it's not always easy. But God has called you to serve him. He also has called you to be married. Those two callings not only *can* go together; they *should* go together. When they do, you'll find a stronger Christian life and a stronger Christian marriage.

—Karen and Kevin Miller, *More Than You and Me* (Focus on the Family, 1994)

ILLUSTRATION 470

LETTING LOVE GO

Topics: Depravity; God's Love; Idolatry; Persistence; Sin

References: Ezekiel 16:15–63; Hosea 1:2; James 4:4

Have you ever had to turn a lover over to a mortal enemy to allow her to find out for herself what his intentions toward her really were? Have you ever had to lie in bed knowing she was believing his lies and [being intimate] with him every night? Have you ever sat helplessly by in a parking lot, while your enemy and his friends took turns [taking advantage of] your lover even as you sat nearby, unable to win her heart enough so she would trust you to rescue her?

Have you ever called this one you had loved for so long ... and asked her if she was ready to come back to you, only to have her say her heart was still captured by your enemy? Have you ever watched your lover's beauty slowly diminish and fade in a haze of alcohol, drugs, occult practices, and infant sacrifice until she is no longer recognizable in body or soul? Have you ever loved one so much that you even send your only son to talk with her about your love for her, knowing that she will kill him?

All this and more God has endured, yet he refuses to stop loving us.

— Brent Curtis and John Eldredge,
The Sacred Romance (Nelson, 1997)

ILLUSTRATION 471
STAYING MARRIED FOR THE KIDS

Topics: Child Rearing; Children; Divorce; Family; Marriage; Parenting

References: Matthew 19:3 – 12; Mark 10:10 – 12

Children don't need parents who like each other or are even civil to each other. But they do need them to stay together, for better or for worse. That's the conclusion of therapist Judith Wallerstein in *The Unexpected Legacy of Divorce.*

This imperative comes with asterisks, of course, but fewer than one might think. Physical abuse, substance addiction, and other severe pathologies cannot be tolerated in any home. Aside from these, Wallerstein stands firm: where

the children's welfare is concerned, a lousy marriage beats a great divorce.

— Walter Kirn, "Should You Stay Together for the Kids?" *Time* (September 15, 2000)

ILLUSTRATION 472
REMEMBERING THE ANNIVERSARY

Topics: Anniversaries; Family; Husbands; Marriage; Time

Reference: Ephesians 5:25 – 33

Margaret said her husband, George, couldn't remember their wedding anniversary on March 7. But one year, when they were en route to Australia, at five minutes before midnight on March 6, George proudly looked at Margaret and said, "This year I remembered. Just five more minutes till our anniversary."

Just then the pilot announced, "We have crossed the International Date Line. It's now March 8."

— Margaret Gunn, Mason, Michigan, "Lite Fare," *Christian Reader* (July – August 2000)

ILLUSTRATION 473
THE WORD HE LONGED TO HEAR

Topics: Accepting Christ; Invitation; Marriage; Romance; Salvation

References: John 1:12; Ephesians 5:31–32

Tedd was five years older than Janet, finished college before her, and was working in a city hundreds of miles from her. They always seemed to be at different places in their lives. But they had been dating for seven years.

Every Valentine's Day Tedd would propose marriage, and Janet would say, "No, not yet."

Finally, when they were both living in Dallas, Tedd reached the end of his patience. He bought a ring, took Janet to a romantic restaurant, and prepared to give her the diamond. Another no would mean he would get on with his life without her.

After salad, entree, and dessert, Tedd was ready. But realizing Janet had a gift for him, he asked, "What did you bring me?" She handed him a box the size of a book. He opened the package and slowly peeled away the tissue paper. It was a cross-stitch Janet had made that simply said, "Yes."

It was the word Tedd longed to hear. It's also the word that God, in his tireless pursuit of the sinner, longs to hear.

—Rubel Shelly, Nashville, Tennessee

ILLUSTRATION 474
SATISFIED WITH SEX

Topics: Cohabitation; Commitment; Family; Marriage; Pleasure; Sex

References: 1 Corinthians 6:15–20; 7:3–5

Married people have better sex lives than single people. And married people are about twice as likely as unmarried people to make love at least two or three times a week.

That's not all. Married sex is more fun, certainly, at least, for men. Forty-eight percent of husbands say sex with their partners is extremely satisfying, compared to just 37 percent of cohabiting men.

Marriage offers a promise of permanence, which may be why cohabiting men are four times more likely to cheat, and cohabiting women eight times more likely to be unfaithful, than husbands and wives.

—Linda J. Waite and Maggie Gallagher, *The Case for Marriage* (Doubleday, 2000)

ILLUSTRATION 475
SHOTGUN LOVE

Topics: Abuse; Anger; Conflict; Emotions; Family; Love; Marriage; Remorse; Revenge; Temper; Violence

References: Psalm 11:5; Matthew 5:21–22; Romans 13:10; Ephesians 4:26–27

I was a nurse in the operating room for several years. One day a couple arrived, both with gunshot wounds. He had awakened late for his first day on the job because his wife did not set the alarm. He expressed his displeasure by shooting her in the arm. Not to be outdone, she went to another room, got a shotgun, and shot him in the arm.

As I gathered their paperwork, I heard something one would only expect to hear in a country song. Separated by a deputy sheriff and handcuffed to their respective stretchers, the husband began, "I love you, baby, and I'm sorry I shot you."

The wife responded, "I love you too, baby. I'm sorry I shot you."

—David A. Slagle, Lawrenceville, Georgia

ILLUSTRATION 476
JOINED AT THE HIP

Topics: Commitment; Cooperation; Marriage; Relationships; Teamwork

Reference: Matthew 19:3–12

Side Show is a musical based on the true story of the Hilton twins. The Hiltons were Siamese twins who rose from poverty as a sideshow attraction to become a singing and dancing vaudeville act in the 1930s and, later, stars of some B-grade films.

One unusual element of this play is that the two lead actresses must play the parts of the Hiltons, who are "joined at the hip." It doesn't matter how good their individual talents are if they can't work together and if they can't do it convincingly. The success of the show depends on the success of their partnership. If one of them decides to go solo, the show is over.

That is a good metaphor of marriage. Once the commitment is made, husband and wife are, as it were, "joined at the hip." They succeed or fail together. Other people don't generally think of one without thinking of the other. Wherever life's drama takes them, their success depends on doing it together.

—Lee Eclov, Lake Forest, Illinois

ILLUSTRATION 477
MARRIAGE SUCCESS FACTORS

Topics: Commitment; Communication; Faithfulness; Gender Differences; Love; Marriage; Respect

Reference: Hebrews 13:4

Men and women vary about what factors are most important in a successful marriage. A research report by Taylor Nelson Sofres (TNS) points to these factors:

Mutual respect and trust: men, 90 percent; women, 95 percent
Open, regular communication: men, 82 percent; women, 92 percent
Marital fidelity: men, 74 percent; women, 85 percent

—Cindy Hall and Jerry Mosemak, *USA Today* "Snapshots" (October 11, 1999)

ILLUSTRATION 478
BEATLE LOVE

Topics: Adultery; Character; Children; Divorce; Family; Hypocrisy; Love; Parenting

Reference: Ephesians 6:4

"He was a hypocrite. Dad could talk about peace and love out loud to the world, but he could not show it to the people who supposedly meant the most to him: his wife and son," said Julian Lennon, who was abandoned at age five by his father, Beatle John Lennon.

"How can you talk about peace and love and have a family in bits and pieces—no communication, adultery, divorce? You can't do it, not if you're being true and honest with yourself."

—*Servant* (Summer 1998)

ILLUSTRATION 479

HIS CHEATING HEART

Topics: Adultery; Guilt; Marriage; Unfaithfulness

Reference: Hebrews 13:4

"Cheating was the worst mistake I ever made in my life," said a husband who admitted being unfaithful. "I don't know that we wouldn't have gotten a divorce, but I felt really bad that I cheated on my wife.

"I didn't really want a divorce. I didn't even really want to be with that other woman; it's just that she was telling me what I needed to hear. I wasn't getting any attention from my wife at home. We hadn't slept together in about three months.

"This other woman was giving me the attention I hadn't gotten in a long time. It all felt fine, until right after it happened. Then I just felt terrible."

—*Men's Health* (December 1998)

ILLUSTRATION 480

FINDING FREEDOM IN MARRIAGE

Topics: Dying to Self; Giving; Marriage; Sacrifice; Self-centeredness; Singleness

References: Acts 20:35; Romans 12:1; 2 Corinthians 8:9; Galatians 2:20

The biggest drawback to living alone is having nobody to forgive, says author D. J. Waldie. It's not that you don't get certain things, such as companionship, sex, and somebody to share the chores; it's that you can't give to them. You are deprived of a great opportunity: to learn to love your neighbor as yourself.

"This was a radical notion in Christ's time; it is radical now," Waldie says. "It will always be radical because it is the hardest way, the most illogical way, the 'unfairest' way—and the only way that can grant us the peace that passes all understanding.

"In a way I can see only dimly, marriage is causing me to be freer with my time, my money, my affections. It is changing my heart, one molecule at a time, from stone to flesh. Day by day, hour by hour, minute by minute, it is giving me the opportunity to die to myself."

And that, as Saint Francis said, is the only way to awaken to eternal life.

—Based on D. J. Waldie, *Holy Land: A Suburban Memoir* (Norton, 1996)

ILLUSTRATION 481

GETTING THE SCORE

Topics: Commitment; Family; Fatherhood; Parenting; Sports

References: Ephesians 6:4; Colossians 3:21

A wedding video on a recent TV show cracked me up. The video was shot from the back of the church looking up the aisle toward the bride and groom. Because of the camera angle, you could see several members of the congregation.

During the vows, a man jumped up from his pew and yelled, "Yes! Yes! Yes!" as he pumped his fist. Then he froze and slid down into his seat—sheepishly taking off his headphones. He had been listening to the Auburn-Alabama game, and his favorite team had just scored.

We've all had times when we were physically in one place but mentally in another. Most of the time, it's not a real problem—except when it comes to being a husband and father.

—John Trent, "A Father's Heart," *Christian Parenting Today* (November–December 1999)

ILLUSTRATION 482

GIVING A RAIN GAUGE

Topics: Anniversaries; Giving; God; Worship

References: Psalm 95:6; John 4:23–24; Hebrews 12:28–29

Early in our marriage, I gave my wife a terrific anniversary gift. At least I thought it was a great gift. Susan, after all, is a farmer's daughter and keeps close watch on the weather. I envisioned her delight and nostalgia while tracking our backyard precipitation on her new rain gauge.

Susan was not impressed. "A rain gauge for our anniversary?" she asked incredulously. The gauge is now a family joke, a classic example of a gift enjoyed by the giver but not the receiver.

One word I hear a lot these days is *authentic*, as in "We seek *authentic* worship." Usually this means we're trying to create an experience that helps worshipers feel something. There's nothing wrong with that, but if our focus is only on *our* experience, we may be giving God a rain gauge.

A real gift, real worship, means knowing what's important to the Receiver.

—Marshall Shelley, *Leadership* (Spring 1999)

ILLUSTRATION 483

ONE WOMAN FOR KEEPS

Topics: Commitment; Illicit Sex; Marriage; Relationships

Reference: Ephesians 4:19

The late Wilt Chamberlain had great numbers as a professional basketball star, but the number he will probably be remembered for most is twenty thousand. That is how many women Chamberlain, who never married, claimed to have slept with.

What few may remember though, says columnist Clarence Page, is Chamberlain went on to write that he would have traded all twenty thousand for the one woman he wanted to stay with for keeps.

—Clarence Page, "Remembering the Big Dipper's Other Statistics," *Chicago Tribune* (October 17, 1999)

ILLUSTRATION 484

HOUSE OF DIFFERENCES

Topics: Conflict; Cooperation; Diversity; Love; Marriage; Self-centeredness; Stubbornness; Submission

References: Ephesians 5:25 – 33; Philippians 2:3 – 4; Colossians 3:18 – 19

Castleward, a stately home, was built in the 1760s about thirty miles from Belfast, Ireland. The original owners of the house were Bernard Ward, the first Viscount of Bangor, and his wife, Lady Anne.

One of the most striking features of the house is its two styles of architecture. The rear of the house is built in Gothic style, while the front is neoclassical. It's built that way because Bernard and Lady Anne could not agree on one style. Not only did they differ in their architectural preferences; they apparently had other differences, because Lady Anne eventually walked out of the marriage.

Depending on your point of view, the house is either a celebration of diversity or a monument to stubbornness.

—Alan Wilson, Nyon, Switzerland

ILLUSTRATION 485

WORKING IT OUT

Topics: Character; Conflict; Decisions; Marriage; Relationships; Unity; Values

Reference: Colossians 3:15

A young, ambitious guy at Amoco got a promotion that required a transfer to Cairo. He went home to his new wife and young baby and said, "Great news, we're moving to Cairo."

Appalled, his wife said, "You're moving alone. I'm going home to my mother."

That was the first test of leadership in that family. There was no apparent compromise. If he gave up his promotion, he would resent his wife for ruining his career. But if she went along with the move, she would hate him for squashing her ideals for the baby and herself. What to do?

They had a long discussion, going back to the fundamentals, asking questions such as, Is this my career or ours? Is the baby yours or mine? Are we individuals, or do we operate as a team? What are our values?

The couple ended up going to Cairo, but not before their relationship had been transformed—she understanding that his career was important to her, and he recommitting to his values as a participant in the family.

What matters is not what they ended up choosing, but how. They took the courageous step to redefine from the inside out who they truly were. The *how* is what gives you character. The *what*, which at first appears paramount, is ultimately of no emotional significance.

—Peter Koestenbaum, "Fear and Trembling in the New Economy," *Fast Company* (March 2001)

ILLUSTRATION 486

GOLDFISH WIFE

Topics: Companionship; Marriage; Relationships; Self-centeredness

References: John 13:1–17; Ephesians 5:22–33; 1 John 3:16–18

A man had been dating a woman for several years, and she was wondering if they would ever marry. He told me he didn't know if he could marry her because she didn't make him happy.

I asked him why not, which was a mistake. He explained all the reasons why she didn't make him happy.

Finally, I interrupted and asked, "What kind of wife would make you happy?" The more he described what he was looking for in a wife, the more convinced I became that what he really needed was a goldfish, the pretty kind with the long tail that floats around. A goldfish just looks pretty and doesn't ask you to communicate. It doesn't ask you how your day was or expect you to listen to how its day was. The last thing he needed was a wife, because his whole understanding of why the world existed was to meet his needs.

A wife or husband will not meet your needs, but neither will friends, the church, or even a fish. You have needs that are important and ought to be met. But for that, you will have to pray to God, who alone can be your Savior when it comes to human need. Then you can be useful to the people around you.

—M. Craig Barnes, in the sermon "Learning to Speak Multiculturally," National Presbyterian Church, Washington, D.C. (October 3, 1999)

ILLUSTRATION 487

WAITING FOR LOVE

Topics: Courtship; Love; Marriage; Patience; Waiting

References: 2 Peter 3:8–9; Revelation 3:20

A man and woman spotted each other on the morning air shuttle. Sparks flew, but no words were exchanged as they stood together in the taxi line at Washington National. She got in a cab, looked back, and saw him running after her. She begged the cabbie to stop, but he kept going. In desperation she scrawled her phone number on a piece of paper and pressed it against the back window. But she knew the man was too far away to read it.

She went to her meeting, but she couldn't stop thinking about him. So she feigned illness and returned to the airport to wait for him to catch the shuttle back to New York. She waited all day, but he didn't show.

She took her flight. When she stepped into the gate area, he was there. "What took you so long?" he asked. "I've been waiting all day."

The couple eventually married.

How like God this story is. In his great love, he waits for us—as long as it takes—so he can make us his own.

—Dini von Mueffling, *The 50 Most Romantic Things Ever Done* (Doubleday, 1997)

ILLUSTRATION 488

BLESSING SEX

Topics: Blessings; Fidelity; Husbands; Intimacy; Love; Pleasure; Spirituality; Wives

References: Genesis 2:24; Song of Songs 4; 7; 1 Corinthians 7:1–7

A 2006 survey conducted by Beliefnet.com indicates a link between sex and spirituality. According to the survey results, a majority of religious people do not see sex as guilt inducing or sinful, but rather as a divine blessing. Some of the results of the survey:

- people who see sex as at least part of their spiritual lives: 55 percent
- women who see sex as a gift from God: 46 percent
- men who see sex as a gift from God: 51 percent
- people who have prayed before or after sex: 38 percent

— "Beliefwatch: God's Gift,"
Newsweek (October 22, 2006)

ILLUSTRATION 489

DEFINING MINISTRY

Topics: Jesus Christ; Leadership; Ministry; Pastors; Service

Reference: 2 Corinthians 5:18

The foundation of ministry is character.
The nature of ministry is service.
The motive for ministry is love.
The measure of ministry is sacrifice.
The authority of ministry is submission.
The purpose of ministry is the glory of God.
The tools of ministry are the Word of God
   and prayer.
The privilege of ministry is growth.
The power of ministry is the Holy Spirit,
The model for ministry is Jesus Christ.

—Warren W. Wiersbe and David W. Wiersbe,
Making Sense of the Ministry (Baker, 1989)

ILLUSTRATION 490

WINNING RECOGNITION

Topics: Christian Life; Ministry; Servanthood; Service

References: Matthew 6:1–4;
20:25–28; 1 Corinthians 15:58;
Colossians 3:23–24

There are no such things as prominent service and obscure service; it is all the same with God.

—Oswald Chambers,
So Send I You (Discovery House, 1993)

ILLUSTRATION 491

TEACHING MORE THAN MUSIC

Topics: Calling; Career; Dedication; Love; Ministry; Sacrifice; Vocation

Reference: Matthew 18:5–6

Jack Martens is a band teacher of teens in San Francisco. For thirty-three years he has braved the challenges of less-than-ideal teaching conditions at Ben Franklin Middle School to live out his faith. Over 50 percent of Martens's students are from broken homes, on welfare, and from families where English is not the first language. And funding for the arts has been all but cut off in Jack's school district.

Still the fifty-six-year-old, bearded band teacher shepherds his students through the less-than-green pastures of life. "I love these kids," he says. "And they love me. In me they can see my love for Jesus Christ."

Although Martens keeps a Bible and other Christian symbols on his desk, it is his interaction with the kids that is his primary witness. He eats lunch with his kids to help them talk through their problems. He stays after school to help them with difficult fingerings on their instruments. Through the mechanics of music he is able to show his students they are capable of something beautiful.

—Greg Asimakoupoulos,
Mercer Island, Washington

ILLUSTRATION 492

MOPPING UP THE MESS

Topics: Fatherhood; Leadership; Men; Parenting; Servanthood

References: Matthew 20:20–28; John 13:1–17; 1 Peter 5:3

Dad and I padded through the tall pines, our feet quiet on the carpet of brown pine needles. We had come to New Hampshire, just the two of us, something that had never happened before. I knew then that I, eleven years old, was becoming a man.

We placed our net, tackle boxes, and rods in the canoe, then slipped it quietly into the Ossipee River. As Dad paddled from the back, I cast my trustworthy Mepps lure near the lily pads. Father, son, canoe, water, fish, pines—this was heaven. I desperately wanted to show Dad I was worthy of the confidence he had placed in me by inviting me on this trip.

Two nights later, I awoke, sick to my stomach. I feared I might throw up. I needed to get to the bathroom. But the cabin was cold and dark, and I would have to climb out of my warm top bunk. Suddenly, I threw up over the side of the bunk.

My dad heard the awful splatter and came running in, flicked on the light, and surveyed the mess. "Couldn't you have gotten to the bathroom?" he asked.

"I'm sorry," I said, knowing I deserved every angry comment that would come. I had done something foolish, messy, embarrassing—and worst of all, childish.

My dad shook his head a little, then left. He came back with a bucket of sudsy hot water and a scrub brush. I watched, amazed, as he got on hands and knees and began scrubbing each pine board clean again.

When Dad died suddenly, he left me with that picture.

As Christian leaders, we face many awful and embarrassing messes. Our people may often let us down. But Jesus has already shown us what we must do in those situations: "Now that I, your Lord and Teacher, have washed your feet, you also should wash one another's feet" (John 13:14).

—Kevin Miller,
ChurchLeadersOnline.com (April 5, 2000)

ILLUSTRATION 493

CALLING BY THE THROAT

Topics: Calling; Experiencing God; Gospel; Ministry; Preaching; Scripture; Service; Spiritual Perception

References: Jeremiah 1:5–10; Acts 9:9–19; Romans 1:16; Philippians 3:7–8

Several denominational leaders were visiting the campus where I teach. In one meeting with faculty, we asked this diverse group about their call to the ministry. Some of them had extraordinary experiences. For others, their calling had been a fairly cerebral thing.

But as I listened to each response, I found one thing each had in common. Each person cited a text that had just leaped off the page, grabbed the person by the throat, and wouldn't let go. Underlying that was a profound, unswerving, immutable passionate belief that the gospel is so central in all of human life that nothing short of its proclamation is worth doing.

God calls some Christians to be chemists and others to be garbage collectors. But those who are called to proclaim God's message have a profound sense of the sheer nonnegotiable value of the gospel.

—Don Carson, "Preachers in the Hands of a Holy God," *Preaching Today* Audio no. 205

ILLUSTRATION 494
SHOEMAKER'S CALLING

Topics: Calling; Discipline; Evangelism; Goals; Missions; Passion; Self-discipline

References: Psalm 37:4; 1 Corinthians 1:26–31

He was just a shoemaker, after all, and an average one at that. But in the evenings, after work, he studied Greek, Hebrew, and a variety of modern languages. He devoured Captain Cook's *Voyages* to expand his horizons, which, because of his poverty, kept him bound to a small, forgotten English village. Some people said his time would have been better spent getting a second job to support his growing family.

But the young man's passion wasn't a curious, self-satisfying hobby. Early in life he had become concerned about the millions of unbelievers outside of Europe, and he was trying to figure out what could be done to bring them the gospel.

With God's help, he slowly figured it out. He ended up going to India to serve as the first Protestant missionary in the modern era. His passion inspired a generation of men and women, such as Adoniram Judson, Hudson Taylor, and David Livingstone, to take up the cause of missions.

Because one impoverished shoemaker named William Carey followed his God-given passion, large parts of the world that had little or no access to the gospel have large populations of people today who confess Christ as Lord.

—Ruth Tucker, *From Jerusalem to Irian Jaya* (Zondervan, 1983)

ILLUSTRATION 495
USING LAST DAYS

Topics: Consecration; Preparation; Prisons; Service; Stewardship; Study; Television; Wasting Time

References: Matthew 10:39; Philippians 3:7–14; 2 Timothy 2:15

References: Matthew 16:24–28; Luke 9:23–26; John 15:12–17; Philippians 2:5–11

Most of the death row inmates at Mississippi's Parchman Prison were in their bunks, wrapped in blankets and staring blankly at little black-and-white TV screens, killing time. But in one cell a man was sitting on his bunk reading. As I approached he looked up and showed me his book — an instruction manual on Episcopal liturgy.

John Irving, who had been on death row for more than fifteen years, was studying for the priesthood. Irving told me he was allowed out of his cell one hour each day. The rest of the time, he studied.

Seeing that Irving had nothing in his cell but a few books, I thought, *God has blessed me so much, the least I can do is provide something for this brother.* "Would you like a TV if I could arrange it?" I asked.

"Thanks," Irving said with a smile, "but no thanks. You can waste an awful lot of time with those things." Irving had determined not to waste the one commodity he had to give to the Lord — his time.

—Charles Colson,
A Dangerous Grace (Word, 1994)

ILLUSTRATION 496

LIFE WITH NO REGRETS

Topics: Calling; Commitment; Compassion; Evangelism; Example; Focus; Leadership; Ministry; Missions; Passion; Prayer; Purpose; Regret; Sacrifice

When William Borden graduated from a Chicago high school in 1904, he was heir to the Borden Dairy estate, which made him a millionaire. For his graduation present, his parents gave him a trip around the world. As the young man traveled through Asia, the Middle East, and Europe, he felt a growing burden for the world's hurting people. Finally, Borden wrote home to say, "I'm going to give my life to prepare for the mission field." At the same time, he wrote two words in the back of his Bible: "No reserves."

During his college years at Yale University, Borden became a pillar in the Christian community. One entry in his personal journal that defined the source of his spiritual strength simply said, "Say no to self and yes to Jesus every time."

During his first semester at Yale, Borden started a small prayer group that mushroomed into a movement that spread across the campus. By the end of his first year, 150 freshmen were meeting for weekly Bible study and prayer. By the time Bill Borden was a senior, one thousand of Yale's thirteen hundred students were meeting in such groups.

Borden met with fellow Christians to make sure every student on campus heard the gospel. Often he ministered to the poor in the streets of New Haven. But his real passion was missions. Once he narrowed his missionary call to the Kansu people in China, Borden never wavered.

Upon graduation from Yale, Borden wrote two more words in the back of his Bible: "No retreats." He turned down several high-paying job offers and enrolled in seminary. After graduating, he went to Egypt to learn Arabic so he could work with Muslims in China. While in Egypt, Borden came down with spinal meningitis. Within a month he was dead at age twenty-five.

Prior to his death, Borden wrote two more words in his Bible. Underneath the words "No reserves" and "No retreats," he wrote, "No regrets."

—Mrs. Howard Taylor,
Borden of Yale (Bethany, 1988)

ILLUSTRATION 497

ANT LEADERSHIP

Topics: Church; Community; Cooperation; Discipleship; Family; Growth; Leadership; Mentoring; Patience; Results; Sacrifice; Sanctification; Teaching; Training; Unselfishness

References: Romans 12:1 – 8; Ephesians 4:1 – 7; Colossians 3:12 – 17

Worker ants sacrifice time and efficiency to teach other ants how to find food, which benefits their society as a whole.

There's more. According to research published in January 2006, when a female ant of the species *Temnothorax albipennis* goes out to find food, she will often choose another ant to accompany her. If the second ant doesn't know the way to the food source, the leader will teach her through a process called "tandem running." As the teacher runs along the path to food, the student follows behind, often stopping to locate landmarks. That creates a gap between the leader and student. When ready, the student will run forward and tap the teacher on the back legs.

Ants participating in tandem running located a food source in an average of 201 seconds, while ants searching for food on their own took an average of 310 seconds (a 35 percent difference). However, the process is detrimental to the teachers. Research indicated that the lead ants traveled up to four times faster when not accompanied by a student.

So why do leaders sacrifice their time and efficiency to teach others? According to Nigel Franks, study leader, "They are very closely related nest mates, and their society as a whole will benefit." This occurs as the students gradually learn their way and are able to teach other ants, which increases the efficiency of the entire population.

—Bjorn Carey, "Ant School: The First Formal Classroom Found in Nature," FoxNews.com (January 13, 2006)

ILLUSTRATION 498

BUILDING COURAGE MUSCLE

Topics: Apathy; Church; Commitment; Complacency; Courage; Dedication; Leadership; Strength

References: Deuteronomy 3:6; 2 Chronicles 32:7; 1 Corinthians 16:13; Galatians 6:9; 2 Timothy 1:8

Courage is like a muscle. The more we exercise it, the stronger it gets. I sometimes worry that our collective courage is growing weaker from disuse. We don't demand it from our leaders, and our leaders don't demand it from us. The courage deficit is both our problem and our fault. As a result, too many leaders in the public and private sectors lack the courage necessary to honor their obligations to others and to uphold the essential values of leadership.

—U.S. Senator John McCain,
Fast Company magazine's "First Impression"
newsletter (August 2, 2006)

ILLUSTRATION 499

FROM GENERAL TO SERVANT

Topics: Leadership; Relationships; Servanthood; Team; Trust

References: Matthew 20:20–28; John 13:34–35

I've led from a place of servant leadership, and I've led from a place of top-down leadership—and there's no question which kind of leadership is more effective.

My classmates at Harvard Business School used to call me the Prussian general because for many years that was my approach to leadership. Then I was hit by a series of personal and professional setbacks. My wife died. A mail-order venture that I had started went bankrupt. Rather than launch another business, I accepted a friend's offer to head an aquarium project in Tampa.

I spent the next six years in a job that gave me no power, no money, and no knowledge. That situation forced me to draw on a deeper part of myself. We ended up with a team of people who

were so high-performing that they could almost walk through walls. Why, I wondered, was I suddenly able to lead a team that was so much more resilient and creative than any team that I had run before?

The answer: somewhere, amid all of my trials, I had begun to trust my colleagues as much as I trusted myself. And that is the essence of servant leadership.

—Jim Stuart, cofounder of the Leadership Circle, *Fast Company* (September 1999)

ILLUSTRATION 500

MARKING THE CALL

Topics: Calling; Failure; Ministry; Success

Reference: Exodus 5

Quite often the absence of immediate success is the mark of a genuine call.

—Bruce Larson, *My Creator, My Friend* (Word, 1986)

ILLUSTRATION 501

DEEPENING OURSELVES

Topics: Maturity; Meaning; Planning; Purpose; Understanding; Wisdom

References: Ecclesiastes 12:13–14; Philippians 2:12–13

Unless the distant goals of meaning, greatness, and destiny are addressed, we can't make an intelligent decision about what to do tomorrow morning—much less set strategy for a company or for a human life.

Nothing is more practical than for people to deepen themselves. The more you understand the human condition, the more effective you are as a businessperson. Human depth makes business sense.

—Peter Koestenbaum,
Fast Company (March 2000)

ILLUSTRATION 502

BILLY'S MESSAGE

Topics: Evangelism; Gospel; Greatness; Humility; Leadership; Meekness; Reputation; Respect; Witnessing

References: Proverbs 11:2; Matthew 18:4; John 3:16; Romans 10:14–15; 2 Corinthians 4:5; James 4:10; 1 Peter 3:15

Graeme Keith, treasurer of the Billy Graham Association and Billy's lifelong friend, was on an elevator with Billy Graham when another man recognized the evangelist. "You're Billy Graham, aren't you?" he asked.

"Yes," Graham said.

"Well," the man said, "you are truly a great man."

"No, I'm not a great man. I just have a great message," responded Graham.

—Harold Myra and Marshall Shelley,
The Leadership Secrets of Billy Graham
(Zondervan, 2005)

ILLUSTRATION 503

ANYTHING YOU WANT

Topics: Fruit of the Spirit; Fruitfulness

References: Romans 1:16; Galatians 5:22–23; 6:7–8

A woman dreamed that she wandered into a shop at the mall and found Jesus behind a counter.

"You can have anything your heart desires," Jesus said.

Astounded but pleased, the woman asked for peace, joy, happiness, wisdom, and freedom from fear. Then she added, "Not just for me, but for the whole earth."

Jesus smiled and said, "I think you misunderstood me. We don't sell fruits, only seeds."

—Bruce McNicol and Bill Thrall,
The Ascent of a Leader (Jossey-Bass, 1999)

ILLUSTRATION 504

REDEEMING THE NEIGHBORHOOD

Topics: Calling; Change; Commitment; Community; Evangelism; Example; Faith; Integrity; Leadership; Ministry; Neighbors; Service; Testimony

References: Leviticus 19:18; Matthew 22:37–40; Mark 12:28–33; Luke 10:25–37; John 13:34; Galatians 5:14; James 2:8

Kirsten and Lee Hildebrand had just settled into their first home in a suburban community where Kirsten practiced labor and employment law and Lee was working on a doctorate in counseling psychology. But when the couple attended East-brook Church, a nondenominational, inner-city Milwaukee church, they began to wonder, *Did we settle in the right place?* Gradually they became convinced that they needed to move out of sub-urbia into the city.

In three days they sold their home and bought one in Sherman Park on Grant Boule-vard, where old brick homes shoulder Mediterra-nean tile roofs and copper gutters, and neighbors take in the world from adjoining porches. As the couple unpacked boxes, a question hung over them. "We knew we were led here for a purpose, but we didn't know why," says Lee.

Six months later, after they had remodeled their own home, the Hildebrands noticed a fore-closure sign a few houses down. Along with two neighbors, Paul Handle and Dave Klevgard, they made an unsuccessful bid for the house, but in the process they identified a problem of absen-tee landlords. "The landlords didn't care about the properties, didn't put the work in, and then demanded rent," Kirsten says. "They're treating people this way, but everyone deserves a nice place to live."

After many late-night conversations, the four of them decided to systematically purchase rundown houses, restore them, rent them afford-ably to the residents of their city, and, hopefully, change the absentee landlord trend. They regis-tered as "City Ventures LLC" and brought their fifty-page business plan to Legacy Bank. "We didn't just go in jeans with stuff scribbled in a notebook," Lee says. "Kirsten is an attorney, Paul is a marketing manager, David is in insurance,

and I was doing my PhD at Marquette. We went as young professionals."

With investment capital from the bank and additional funds from individual home equity loans, City Ventures bought a single-family house and then a series of duplexes. The part-ners juggled full-time jobs with the new worlds of plumbing, electrical work, rent collecting, and the realities of the inner-city. At night drug dealers moved onto their construction sites. In the morning they'd see vandal scrawls on freshly painted walls. Once, a disgruntled tenant held a gun on Lee, forcing him to use his counseling skills to talk his way out of the room.

Still, the couple refuses to see crime as the neighborhood's defining characteristic. "That's not the sum of the neighborhood," they say. "Ninety percent of the people are people who just want to live their lives." Six years later Sher-man Park is a living illustration of that commit-ment. Seventy restored buildings boast colorful awnings and shutters, new bricks, or siding. "We worked hard, and God's grace was involved," Lee says. "We give him all the credit."

— "Building Up," *Trinity Magazine* (Fall 2006)

ILLUSTRATION 505

SELLING ONIONS

Topics: Attitudes; Meaning; Money; Motivation; Priorities; Traditions

References: Ecclesiastes 5:10–15; Matthew 4:4; 6:24; James 1:9–11

At the market in Mexico City, old Pota-lamo had twenty strings of onions for sale. An American tourist asked, "How much for a string of onions?"

"Ten cents," said Pota-lamo.

"How much for two strings?"

"Twenty cents."

"How much for all twenty strings?" asked the American.

"I would not sell you twenty strings," replied Pota-lamo.

"Why not? Aren't you here to sell your onions?"

"No," replied the old merchant. "I am here to live my life. I love this marketplace. I love the crowds and the red serapes. I love the sunlight and the wavering palmettos. I love to have friends come by and say *buenos dias* and talk about the babies and the crops.

"That is my life. For that I sit here all day and sell my twenty strings of onions. But if I sell all my onions to one customer, then my day is ended. I have lost the life I love—and that I will not do."

—Mark Moody, "In Search of Renewal," *Strategic Adult Ministry Journal* (no. 139)

ILLUSTRATION 506

MILLWRIGHT POET

Topics: Calling; Christian Life; Gifts; Purpose; Work

Reference: Acts 18:1–3

In the furniture industry of the 1920s, the machines of most factories were not run by electric motors but by pulleys from a central drive shaft. The millwright was the person on whom the entire activity of the operation depended. He was the key person, says Max DePree, former CEO of Herman Miller. He goes on:

One day the millwright at Herman Miller died. My father, being a young manager at the time, did not know what to do when a key person died but thought he ought to go visit the family. He went to the house and was invited to join the family in the living room.

The widow asked my father if it would be all right if she read aloud some poetry. Naturally, he agreed. She went into another room, came back with a bound book, and for many minutes read selected pieces of beautiful poetry. When she finished, my father commented on how beautiful the poetry was and asked who wrote it. She replied that her husband, the millwright, was the poet.

It is now nearly sixty years since the millwright died, and my father and many of us at Herman Miller continue to wonder: *Was he a poet who did millwright's work, or was he a millwright who wrote poetry?*

—Max DePree, in "Work and Spirituality," teambuildinginc.com

PART 21: PARENTING

ILLUSTRATION 507

I JUST DIDN'T KNOW

Topics: Appearances; Assumptions; Babies; Birth; Challenges; Confusion; Consequences; Ignorance; Knowledge; Motherhood; Neglect

References: Proverbs 2:1–5; 14:8; Isaiah 44:18; 50:10; John 16:21; Hebrews 5:12–14; 2 Peter 1:5–8

While an old proverb claims that ignorance is bliss, Amanda Brisendine, a twenty-six-year-old woman from Renton, Washington, would be the first to tell you that ignorance can have unexpected consequences.

Brisendine had gained thirty pounds in the past year and attributed her weight gain to eating rich foods and having quit smoking. But after several days of abdominal pain so intense that she had to stay home from work, she went to the hospital. She returned home later with a newborn son, Alexander.

Already a mother to a fourteen-month-old daughter, Brisendine was shocked when told she was nine months pregnant. She said she hadn't experienced the typical signs of a pregnancy. "Everything was normal as far as I knew," Brisendine said. "I don't know how I didn't know," she added. "I just didn't know."

Her ignorance could have had serious consequences. Ultrasounds showed low amniotic fluid in the placenta. Baby Alexander was not moving properly, and he was successfully delivered by an emergency C-section.

What we don't know can hurt us. The best antidote for spiritual ignorance is a faithful study of God's Word so that we never have to echo Brisendine's admission: "I don't know how I didn't know. I just didn't know."

—David Paulsen, "Woman Unaware of Pregnancy," PreachingToday.com

ILLUSTRATION 508

LETTING BABY GO

Topics: Babies; Control; Crisis; Dependence on God; Faith; Love; Rescue; Surrender; Trials; Trust

References: Exodus 2:3; Psalm 22:7–9; 91; Isaiah 43:1–3

Letting go of their children and watching them make their own way in the world is tough for any parent. For Tracinda Foxe, however, letting go came much too early in her baby's life.

In December 2005, Foxe's apartment building in the Bronx caught fire. With flames engulfing her third-floor bedroom, Foxe was forced to contemplate the unthinkable. As smoke billowed around her, Tracinda leaned out the window with her baby. Then she let go of her child. The infant tumbled three stories down into the waiting arms of Felix Vazquez, who performed mouth-to-mouth resuscitation on the baby until paramedics arrived.

Moments later, Tracinda was rescued from her apartment by firefighters and reunited with her child. Neither was seriously injured. Asked later about the painful decision to drop her baby from the window, Tracinda said, "I prayed that someone would catch him and save his life. I said, 'God, please save my son.' And he did."

—Catherine Donaldson-Evans,
"The Good News of 2005,"
FoxNews.com (December 30, 2005)

ILLUSTRATION 509

MAKING MOMS

Topics: Child Rearing; Children; Family; Home; Mothers

References: Proverbs 29:15; 31:10–31; Matthew 18:3; Mark 10:15

Here's how several elementary school students answered the following questions about moms:
Why did God make mothers?

- She's the only one who knows where the Scotch tape is.
- Mostly to clean the house.
- To help us out of there when we were getting born.

How did God make mothers?

- He used dirt, just like for the rest of us.
- Magic plus superpowers and a lot of stirring.
- God made my mom just the same like he made me. He just used bigger parts.

Of what ingredients are mothers made?

- God makes mothers out of clouds and angel hair and everything nice in the world, and one dab of mean.
- They had to get their start from men's bones. Then they mostly use string, I think.

Why did God give you your mother and not some other mom?

- We're related.
- God knew she likes me a lot more than other people's moms like me.

—Peg Beukema, Nyack, New York

ILLUSTRATION 510

DISRESPECTING MOMS

Topics: Career; Mothers; Resentment; Respect; Sacrifice; Work

References: Psalm 127; Proverbs 30:17; 31:10–31

Eighty-six percent of mothers think they don't get enough respect, and 80 percent agree that moms who stay home get even less. Even so, 77 percent of mothers who work full-time would rather stay home if they could. That's according to a poll by *Family Circle* magazine.

Moms in both camps are defensive: 73 percent of those at home think working moms look down on them, while 66 percent of those who work feel the same way about moms who are at home.

The upside of the research is that while 70 percent of mothers say that being a mom is more demanding than they expected, 92 percent say it is also more rewarding.

—Melissa August and others, "Mother's Day,"
Time (May 6, 2002)

ILLUSTRATION 511

WHY KIDS ARE RUDE

Topics: Child Rearing; Children; Civility; Conduct; Respect

References: Proverbs 22:6; 1 Corinthians 13:4–5; Ephesians 6:1–4

In 2002, only 9 percent of adults said the children they saw in public were respectful toward adults. In 2004, more than one of three teachers considered leaving their profession or knew another teacher who quit. The reason? Students' "intolerable behavior." So said Public Agenda, a nonprofit and nonpartisan research group.

In 2005, 70 percent of people surveyed said, "People are ruder than they were 20 or 30 years ago." Among the worst offenders were children, said an Associated Press–Ipsos poll. The reason, experts say, is because of what parents expect from kids. "The pressure to do well is up. The demand to do good is way down."

Dan Kindlon, a child psychologist at Harvard University, believes most parents want considerate, polite, well-behaved children. "But they're too tired, worn down by work, and personally needy to take up the task of teaching them proper behavior at home," Kindlon says. He says present-day parenting has more to do with training boys and girls to compete in school or on the soccer field, but competition doesn't teach civility.

"Parents are out of control," says Dr. Alvin Rosenfeld, a child psychiatrist. "We always want to blame the kids, but if there's something wrong with their incivility, it's the way their parents model for them."

—Judith Warner, "Kids Gone Wild,"
The New York Times (November 27, 2005)

ILLUSTRATION 512

MEAN, DANGEROUS, AND ANGRY

Topics: Blessings; Child Rearing; Children; Encouragement; Fatherhood; God

References: Psalm 68:5; Proverbs 22:6; Romans 8:15; Galatians 4:6–7; Ephesians 6:4; Colossians 3:21; 1 John 3:1

The seventeen kids who shot classmates in schools in various parts of the United States had one thing in common: a problem with their dads—a conclusion drawn by the FBI after studying the high school shooters in Paducah, Kentucky; Pearl, Mississippi; and Littleton, Colorado.

"When a man doesn't get along with his father, it makes him mean; it makes him dangerous; it makes him angry," writes former NFL pro Bill Glass, who has thirty-six years of prison ministry experience. Glass continues:

On the day before Father's Day, I was in North Carolina in a juvenile prison. I ate lunch with three boys. I asked the first boy, "Is your dad coming to see you tomorrow on Father's Day?" He said, "No; he's not coming."

"Why not?"

"He's in prison."

I asked the second boy the same question and got the same answer. I asked the third one why his dad wasn't coming, and he said, "He got out of prison about nine months ago, and he's doing good. I'm proud of my father. He's really going to be a good dad to me, and he's going to go straight."

He was protesting so much that I could tell something was wrong. So I asked, "How many times has your father been here to see you since he got out nine months ago?"

"He hasn't made it yet."

"Why not?"

"Well, he lives way, *way* away."

"Where does he live?"

"In Durham."

Durham was only two hours away. I had come fifteen hundred miles to visit the boy, but his dad couldn't come two hours? A lot of fathers are really deserters. When I'm in a prison, I always challenge inmates to bless their kids. If you want to keep your kids out of prison, bless them.

—Bill Glass, "The Power of a Father's Blessing," *Christianity Today* (January 2006)

ILLUSTRATION 513

DAD'S BEST GIFT

Topics: Accepting Christ; Assurance; Child Rearing; Children; Family; Fatherhood; Heaven; Testimony

References: Deuteronomy 6:4–9; Psalm 45:16; Proverbs 1:8; 4:1; Romans 6:23

At the funeral of Ronald Reagan, his son Michael described the greatest gift a child can receive:

I was so proud . . . to be Ronald Reagan's son. What a great honor. He gave me a lot of gifts as a child—a horse, a car, a lot of things. But there's a gift he gave me that I think is wonderful for every father to give every son. . . .

Last Saturday, . . . when he closed his eyes, that's when I realized the gift that he gave to me, the gift that he was going to be with his Lord and Savior, Jesus Christ. He had, back in 1988 on a flight from Washington, D.C., to Point Mugu, told me about his love of God, his love of Christ as his Savior. I didn't know then what it all meant. But I certainly, certainly know now.

I can't think of a better gift for a father to give a son. And I hope to honor my father by giving my son, Cameron, and my daughter, Ashley, that very same gift he gave to me. I know where my father is this very moment; that he is in heaven. I can only promise my father this: "Dad, when I die, I will go to heaven, too. And you and I and my sister, Maureen, who went before us, will dance with the heavenly host of angels before the presence of God. We will do it melanoma- and Alzheimer's-free."

—Associated Press, "Reagan's Children's Eulogy Remarks," *USA Today* (June 12, 2004)

ILLUSTRATION 514

MAKING THE GRADE AT FAMILY MEALS

Topics: Children; Community; Family; Fathers; Fellowship; Food; Lifestyle; Mothers; Prosperity; Relationships; Teens

References: Deuteronomy 6:7; Proverbs 22:6; Acts 2:42; Ephesians 6:4

"Kids who dine with the folks are healthier, happier, and better students, which is why a dying tradition is coming back." That's what an in-depth study by the National Center on Addiction and Substance Abuse at Columbia University concluded after nearly a decade of research.

Researchers identified several important patterns. For example, 55 percent of twelve-year-olds say they have dinner with a parent every night, compared with only 26 percent of seven-

teen-year-olds. Along ethnic lines, 54 percent of Hispanic teens say they eat with a parent most nights, compared with 40 percent of black teens and 39 percent of white teens.

Children who eat meals most often with their parents are 40 percent more likely to say they get mainly As and Bs in school than kids who have two or fewer family dinners a week. Children who participate in family meals fewer than three times a week are more than twice as likely to say there is a great deal of tension among family members and much less likely to think their parents are proud of them.

Finally, among those who eat together three or fewer times a week, 45 percent say the TV is on during meals (as opposed to 37 percent of all households), and nearly one-third say there isn't much conversation.

—Nancy Gibbs, "The Magic of the Family Meal," *Time* (June 12, 2006)

ILLUSTRATION 515

THE FATHER THEY WANT

Topics: Children; Desires; Family; Fathers; Girls; Love; Needs; Single Moms

References: Proverbs 17:6; Ephesians 6:4; Colossians 3:21

The enormous response to Bob Carlisle's 1996 ballad "Butterfly Kisses," which speaks of the tender love between a father and his daughter, makes Carlisle feel sad.

"I get a lot of mail from young girls who try to get me to marry their moms," he says. "That used to be a real chuckle because it's so cute, but then I realized they don't want a romance for mom; they want the father who is in that song. That just kills me."

— Mary A. Kassian, "Father of the Fatherless," *Journal for Biblical Manhood and Womanhood* (Spring 2000)

ILLUSTRATION 516

HUGGING YOUR KIDS

Topics: Affection; Assurance; Death; Fathers; Regret; Suicide

References: Genesis 31:28; Ecclesiastes 9:7 – 10; Luke 15:20; 1 Thessalonians 4:13 – 18

His eighteen-year-old son committed suicide near the end of the 2005 football season. At the funeral service, Tony Dungy, head coach of the Indianapolis Colts, offered a heartbreaking appeal to fathers.

"God can provide joy in the midst of a sad occasion," he said. "The challenge is to find that joy. I urge you not to take your relations for granted. Parents, hug your kids each chance you get. Tell them you love them each chance you get. You don't know when it's going to be the last time."

Tony Dungy last saw his son at Thanksgiving in Indianapolis. James Dungy was in a rush to get to the airport, and his father did not have a chance to hug him.

— Phil Richards, "Colts Convene in Tampa as Dungy Buries Son," *USA Today* (December 27, 2005)

ILLUSTRATION 517

TOO BUSY

Topics: Busyness; Children; Fathers; God as Father; Love; Priorities; Relationships; Schedules

References: Matthew 6:21; Luke 11:11 – 13; Colossians 3:21

Several months ago, I talked to a man who described one of the most painful experiences of his life. When he was seventeen years old, he was a star on his high school football team. But his father, a very successful man in the city, was always too busy to see him play.

The final game of the season came around, which was the state championship. The boy was desperate to have his dad there. The night of the big game, he was on the field, warming up, when he looked into the stadium just in time to see his father arrive with two other men, each wearing a business suit. They stood talking together for a moment or two and then left.

The man who told me this story is now fifty-eight years of age, yet tears still streamed down his cheeks as he recalled that long-ago moment. It's been forty years since that night, yet the rejection and pain are as vivid as ever. I was struck again by the awesome influence a father has in the lives of his children.

My friend's father died not long ago, and as he stood by his dad's body in the mortuary, he said, "Dad, I never really knew you. We could have shared so much love together — but you never had time for me."

— James Dobson, *Coming Home* (Tyndale, 2000)

ILLUSTRATION 518

AUCTIONING MOM'S TOUCH

Topics: Affirmation; Attitudes; Children; Feelings; Longing; Love; Mothers; Needs; Relationships; Self-esteem

References: Exodus 20:12; Isaiah 66:13; 1 Thessalonians 2:7

Dan Baber honored his mother by posting an auction on eBay titled "Best Mother in the World." The winning bidder would receive an email from his mom, Sue Hamilton, that would "make you feel like you are the most special person on the earth."

During the auction's seven-day run, 42,711 people—enough to fill most major league baseball stadiums—took a look. Ninety-two offered a bid, pushing the price from a $1 opening to a $610 closing.

Isn't it interesting how people will pay for something most mothers give for free?

—"A Mother's Touch," Focus on the Family *Citizen* (July 2002)

ILLUSTRATION 519

INDULGING KIDS

Topics: Children; Contentment; Discontent; Envy; Family; Greed; Materialism; Media; Money; Peer Pressure; Possessions; Prosperity; Riches; Television; Values; Worldliness

References: Matthew 6:19–21; Luke 12:15–33; 1 Timothy 6:17–19

Kids are significantly targeted and influenced by advertising. Following are some findings reported in *U.S. News & World Report* in 2004:

- Twenty-six percent of kids ages two and under have a TV in their room.
- Advertisers spend $15 billion a year telling kids what's hot.
- The average American child sees 40,000 commercials a year.
- Children recognize Lego bricks by eighteen months; by age two, many ask for products by brand name.

American parents do little to correct this trend; rather, they seem to be encouraging it. According to the magazine:

- American kids get an average of 70 new toys a year.
- In 1984, children ages four to twelve spent $4.2 billion of their own pocket money. In 2004, they were estimated to spend $35 billion.
- In 2004, children were predicted to influence $670 billion worth of parental purchases, both small (which snacks to buy) and large (which SUV).

—Katy Kelly and Linda Kulman, "Kid Power," usnews.com (September 13, 2004)

ILLUSTRATION 520

CELEBRATING MOTHER'S DAY

Topics: Caring; Compassion; Family; Gratitude; Honor; Influence; Love; Mothers; Nurture; Sacrifice

References: Exodus 20:12; Deuteronomy 5:16; Proverbs 31:28; Ephesians 6:1–2

Anna Maria Reeves-Jarvis of Grafton, West Virginia, organized a club of women to nurse wounded soldiers from the North and South during the Civil War. After the war, Reeves-Jarvis started "Mothers' Friendship Days" to reconcile families that had been divided by the conflict.

Throughout her life, Reeves-Jarvis modeled the ideals of Victorian motherhood. She gave up her dreams of college to care for an older husband and four children. She bore the loss of seven other children with grace. She taught Sunday school in the local Methodist church for twenty years and stayed active in benevolent work.

Her death in 1905 devastated her daughter Anna. She honored her mother's memory by initiating a holiday honoring all mothers. Mother's Day was first celebrated in 1908 in Grafton (where Anna grew up) and Philadelphia (where she lived as an adult). Later, in a resolution passed May 8, 1914, the U.S. Congress officially established the second Sunday in May as Mother's Day.

—Elesha Coffman, "Mom, We Salute You," *Christian History Newsletter* (May 10, 2002)

ILLUSTRATION 521

NAMING BLOOPER

Topics: Attitudes; Challenges; Courage; Destiny; Determination; Discouragement; Family; Overcoming; Perspective; Reputation; Respect; Strength; Trials

References: Job 23:10; Romans 5:3–5; James 1:2–4; 1 Peter 5:10

In 1958, a baby boy was born into the Lane family. Robert, the father, chose to name the boy Winner. How could the young man fail to succeed with a name like Winner Lane?

The Lanes had another son several years later. Robert named this baby Loser. Contrary to all expectations, Loser Lane *succeeded*. He graduated from college and later became a sergeant with the New York Police Department. No one feels comfortable calling him Loser. His police colleagues refer to him as Lou.

The most noteworthy achievement of Winner Lane, now in his midforties, is the sheer length of his criminal record—nearly three dozen arrests for burglary, domestic violence, trespassing, resisting arrest, and other mayhem.

Go figure.

—Steven Levitt and Stephen Dubner, *Freakonomics* (HarperCollins, 2005)

ILLUSTRATION 522

COSTLY LOVE

Topics: Affection; Caring; Compassion; Death; Disease; Love; Medical Care; Misery; Motherhood; Sickness

References: Matthew 3:17; Romans 8:35; Ephesians 2:4–5; 3:14–19; 1 John 3:1; 4:18

Princess Alice, daughter of Queen Victoria, had a little boy who became very sick with black diphtheria. Doctors quarantined the boy and told the mother to stay away.

She tried, until one day she overheard him whisper to the nurse, "Why doesn't my mother kiss me anymore?" Princess Alice ran to her son and smothered him with kisses. Within a few days, both died.

—Max Lucado, "Down Deep from Heaven,"
Today's Christian (March–April 2004)

ILLUSTRATION 523

GIVING ALL FOR BABY

Topics: Commitment; Cross; Love; Miracles; Mothers; Sacrifice; Self-denial

References: John 10:11; 15:13; 1 John 3:16

Years ago, a mother was walking across the hills of southern Wales carrying her baby when she was overtaken by a blizzard. When the storm subsided, her body was found beneath a mound of snow. Before she died, however, she had taken off all her outer clothing and wrapped it around her baby.

When unwrapped, the baby boy was found alive and well. Years later, that child, David Lloyd George, became the prime minister of Great Britain and one of England's greatest statesmen.

—J. John and Mark Stibbe,
A Box of Delights (Kregel, 2001)

ILLUSTRATION 524

HEROIC RESCUE

Topics: Cross; Fathers; Heroes; Jesus Christ; Love; Redeemer; Sacrifice; Salvation; Unselfishness

References: John 15:13; Romans 5:8; 2 Corinthians 5:15

David Saunders, forty-two, waited on the driveway of his home in Hanover, Michigan, for his daughter Danielle, four, to get off the school bus. A pickup truck was stopped behind the bus. Saunders crossed the street to meet Danielle at the bus, and then the two crossed the street together and stood in the Saunders's driveway.

Suddenly the father noticed that a car behind the bus was traveling too fast to stop before entering the crossing zone. The car swerved to avoid the pickup and headed into the Saunders's driveway. Saunders grabbed Danielle by the arm and flung her away from himself and into their front yard.

The car hit the father and killed him. Danielle was treated for minor injuries at a nearby hospital and soon released. The sixteen-year-old driver and a fifteen-year-old passenger were not injured.

"It was a heroic act by a father to save his child," said Tony Philipps, the sheriff's captain. "He did everything he could, and in the process, he lost his own life."

—"A Father's Love,"
Detroit Free Press (November 19, 2000)

ILLUSTRATION 525

LIVING WITH DECADENCE

Topics: Christian Life; Example; Faith; Family; Neglect; Parenting; Regret

References: Deuteronomy 6:6–9; 1 Samuel 2:12–25; Matthew 18:5–6; Ephesians 6:4

Former Hollywood bad boy Martin Sheen says watching his son, Charlie Sheen, lead a similarly decadent life fills him with remorse. He worries that he learned to be a father too late. He particularly regrets his failure to share his faith. "I never lost my faith," Sheen says. "But I felt for a time that I had outgrown the church. Now it is a bone of contention in my soul that I did not share my faith with my kids, as my parents did with me. It was a source of grace when I needed it. I have been greatly nurtured and inspired by my faith."

—*Electronic Telegraph*
interview with Martin Sheen

ILLUSTRATION 526

WINNING TIME WITH DAD

Topics: Busyness; Family; Fatherhood; Priorities; Schedules; Teens; Time

References: Malachi 4:6; Luke 10:38–42; John 12:1–8

Dr. Robert Schuller was on a whirlwind book promotion tour, visiting eight cities in four days. It was exhausting work in addition to his normal duties as pastor of a large church.

As Schuller reviewed his schedule with his secretary, she reminded him that he was scheduled to have lunch with the winner of a charity raffle. Schuller was suddenly sobered when he found out the winner of the raffle, for he happened to know that the $500 the person had bid to have lunch with him represented that person's entire life savings.

The winner was his own teenage daughter.

—Steve Farrar,
Standing Tall (Multnomah, 1994)

ILLUSTRATION 527

DASHING MOM'S HOPES

Topics: Dashed Hopes; Dependence on God; Despair; God as Father; Grace; Helplessness; Rebellion

References: Psalm 118:5; Luke 18:9–14; Hebrews 4:16

A teenage son rebelled against his parents and against God. For four years he protested his guilt and made innumerable promises to "straighten up." But each excuse was unjustified, and each promise was broken.

So much pain, embarrassment, and discouragement had been inflicted on these parents that the mother's heart hardened against her own child. What melted it again was a cry of desperation.

After another escapade, followed by more protests of innocence from the son, the mother walked away. As the young man sat alone on the sofa in the family room, he began to leaf through a family photo album. The pictures of better and happier days filled him with increasing emotion. He called his mother back into the room to look at one picture, which showed him as a young child, whom his mother smiled at in approval.

The teen said, "When I see this, I understand why you can't love me anymore. In the picture, hope fills your eyes as you look down at your little boy. But I dashed all your hopes, Mom. Please forgive me for dashing all your hopes."

The mother's hardness broke, and she embraced her son in love. What moved her were neither protests of innocence nor fresh promises to do better. Rather, she was moved by his absolute desperation.

The Bible tells us that is also what moves God.

— Bryan Chapell,
Holiness by Grace (Crossway, 2001)

ILLUSTRATION 528

EASING A CHILD'S PAIN

Topics: Comfort; Compassion; Empathy; Encouragement; Love; Pain; Pastors; Presence; Support

References: Psalm 46; Galatians 6:2; 1 Thessalonians 2:7–12; Hebrews 13:3

In June 2001, my son Jordan and I were working on our driveway, using a chisel and hammer to remove old asphalt and then patching it with new asphalt. We were both tired, so our accuracy declined. At one point Jordan pounded his finger with a hammer. He jumped up in agony, holding back tears as he ran for ice. I realized no one was in the house to help him, so I ran after him.

As soon as I got near the house, I heard him screaming in pain. I tried to calm him down and get some ice on the tender spot, but he was in too much pain to settle down. He hated icing down a wound as much as the pain of the wound itself. Finally, I put some ice in a bowl and filled it with water. He agreed to put his hand in the bowl as long as I would put my hand in the bowl also. So we sat there on the cold tile kitchen floor with both of our hands in the ice water.

Occasionally we would take our hands out to let the feeling return. After ten minutes Jordan started to feel better. "I'm glad you're here," he said.

I was reminded that as a pastor or even a father, I can seldom take the pain away, but my presence can somehow make it more tolerable.

— Jim Johnson, Longview, Texas

ILLUSTRATION 529

LETTING PARENTS BE PARENTS

Topics: Alcohol; Drugs; Education; Family; Substance Abuse; Teens

References: 1 Samuel 2:12–36; 1 Kings 1:6; Proverbs 22:6

Almost one in five American teens say they live with parents who fail to consistently set rules and monitor their behavior. These teens have a four-times-greater risk for smoking, drinking, and illegal drug use than their peers with "hands-on" parents. So said a survey conducted by Columbia University's Center on Addiction and Substance Abuse (CASA).

The survey of 1,000 children ages twelve to seventeen also found:

- Teens who believe their parents would "not be too upset" if they used marijuana are three times as likely to use drugs than those who believe their parents would be "extremely upset."
- Teens with parents who are "very unaware" of their academic performance are almost three times more likely to engage in substance use than their peers whose parents are "very aware" of their school performance.

"Mothers and fathers who are parents rather than pals can greatly reduce the risk of their children smoking, drinking, and using drugs," said Joseph A. Califano Jr. "The family is funda-mental to keeping children away from tobacco, alcohol, and drugs."

—"CASA 2000 Teen Survey,"
Columbia News (February 23, 2001)

ILLUSTRATION 530

SPENDING TIME WITH THE GIRLS

Topics: Children; Family; Fatherhood; Time

References: Ephesians 5:16; 6:4

During morning devotions with his two young daughters, our friend Bill Cage realized he hadn't been spending much time with his girls. After apologizing, he said, "You know, the quantity of time we spend together is not always as impor-tant as the quality of time we spend together."

Kristen, six, and Madison, four, didn't quite understand.

Bill further explained, "Quantity means how much time we spend together, and quality means how good the time is that we spend together. Which would you rather have?"

Not missing a beat, Kristen replied, "Quality time. And a lot of it!"

—Pat Ferguson, Virginia Beach, Virginia

ILLUSTRATION 531

IMPOSSIBLE DAD

Topics: Affirmation; Approval; Child Rearing; Criticism; Encouragement; Family; Fathers; Faultfinding

References: Proverbs 25:11; Ephesians 4:15; 6:4; Colossians 4:6; 1 Thessalonians 5:11

The town ball club was the Lake Wobegon Schroeders, so named because the starting nine were brothers, sons of E.J. Schroeder. E.J. was ticked off if a boy hit a bad pitch. He'd spit and curse and rail at him. If a son hit a home run, E.J. would say, "Blind man coulda hit that one. Your gramma coulda put the wood on that one. If a guy couldn't hit that one out, there'd be something wrong with him. Wind practically took that one out of here, didn't even need to hit it much," and lean over and spit.

So E.J.'s sons could never please him, and if they did, he forgot about it. Once, against Freeport, his oldest boy, Edwin Jim Jr., turned and ran to the center field fence for a long, long, long fly ball. He threw his glove forty feet in the air to snag the ball and caught the ball and glove. When he turned toward the dugout to see if his dad had seen it, E.J. was on his feet clapping, but when he saw the boy look to him, he immediately pretended he was swatting mosquitoes. The batter was called out, the third out. Jim ran back to the bench and stood by his dad.

E.J. sat chewing in silence and finally said, "I saw a man in Superior, Wisconsin, do that a long time ago. But he did it at night, and the ball was hit a lot harder."

—Garrison Keillor,
We Are Still Married (Penguin, 1990)

ILLUSTRATION 532

SAYING "I LOVE YOU"

Topics: Affirmation; Family; Fathers; Feelings; Relationships; Security; Unconditional Love; Words

References: Proverbs 27:5; 1 Corinthians 13:1–7; Ephesians 5:1–2

"I love you" wasn't spread around too much in our household. Not that it wasn't meant. I could tell every time my dad told me he loved me without saying it. It's just the way things were then.

The situation is different in my family. I want my kids to hear, "I love you no matter what," which means, "whether you're good or bad, happy or sad. It doesn't matter whatever you are. I love you. Unconditionally. Always."

It all goes back to security and telling them you'll always be there for them. Maybe you run the risk of telling them you love them so often that it loses meaning. I'll risk it.

—Mark Hyman,
Dad's Magazine (June–July 2000)

ILLUSTRATION 533

SUFFERING WITHOUT DAD

Topics: Child Rearing; Crime; Divorce; Family; Fatherlessness; Fathers

References: Proverbs 22:6; Mark 10:14; Ephesians 6:4

Are fathers necessary in the home? Consider these statistics:

- Children in single-parent families are five times more likely to be poor, and half the single mothers in the United States live below the poverty line.
- Children of divorce suffer intense grief, which often lasts many years. Even as young adults, they are nearly twice as likely to require psychological help.
- Children from disrupted families have more academic and behavioral problems at school and are nearly twice as likely to drop out of high school.
- Girls in single-parent homes are 2.5 times more likely to have a child out of wedlock.
- Crime and substance abuse are strongly linked to fatherless households. Sixty percent of rapists grew up in fatherless homes, as did 72 percent of adolescent murderers and 70 percent of all long-term prison inmates.

Bottom line? Most of the social pathologies disrupting American life today can be traced to fatherlessness.

—Charles Colson,
How Now Shall We Live? (Tyndale, 1999)

ILLUSTRATION 534

DEAR DADDY

Topics: Children; Divorce; Family; Fathers; God as Father; Intimacy; Love; Presence

References: Romans 8:15; Ephesians 6:4

Here's what some third graders had to say about their dads, bad spelling and all:

> *Dear Dad,*
> *I love it when you take me on dates! I like it when you play baseball with me, miniature golf with me, and watch movies with me. I really aprisheate it! I like it when you tell jokes to me. I like it when you hug me and kiss me.*
> *Daddy, I love you!*
>
> *Dear Daddy,*
> *I love you so much. When you are going to come see me agen? I miss you very much. I love it when you take me to the pool. When am I going to get to spend the night at your house? Have you ever seen my house before? I want to see what your house looks like. Do you? When am I going to get to see you agene?*
> *I love you, Daddy.*

One letter is from a child who knows her father's presence. The second is from a child whose father, for whatever reason, has chosen not to be present.

—John Trent, "Promise to Be There,"
Christian Parenting Today
(September–October 2000)

ILLUSTRATION 535

HARMING KIDS WITH PERMISSIVENESS

Topics: Child Rearing; Children; Discipline; Family; Guidance; Love; Support

References: Deuteronomy 6:6–7; Proverbs 22:6, 15; 23:13; 29:15; Ephesians 6:4

Parents are reluctant to set limits for their children. And this permissiveness is harming kids of all ages, psychologists and educators say.

Karen Stabiner writes in *The New York Times*, "It seems that the parents of today's parents, those strict disciplinarians of the 1950s and early 1960s, may have been right all along: Father and Mother did know best."

Nancy Samalin, a parent educator in New York City, explains one reason for the permissiveness: single- and two-parent families are simply overwhelmed. "Parents want their children to love them, and it's harder to say no than yes, especially if they've been working all day and are tired," she says.

Telling a child no is essential to raising healthy kids, says Linda Rubinowitz, psychologist at the Family Institute at Northwestern University in Chicago. "It gives the child a sense that you really understand what's going on. And it gives the child a way to deal with a problem in a social context. You can tell the child, 'Say your mom and dad won't let you do it, and grumble if you want.' That's face-saving for the child."

Revetta Bowers, head of the Center for Early Education in Los Angeles, says schools are replacing parents as disciplinarians. "Schools now make rules, which in many instances are the only rules that are not open to arbitration or negotiation," she explains. "What children really need is guidance and love and support. We expect them to act more and more like adults, while we act more and more like children. Then, when we're ready to act like parents, they bristle at the retaking of authority."

In other words, you can't leave it to Beaver.

—Karen Stabiner, "The Problem with Kids Today? Today's Parents, Some Say," *The New York Times* (June 25, 2000)

ILLUSTRATION 536

BREAKING TEEN REBELLION

Topics: Discipline; Obedience; Occult; Persistence; Teens

Reference: Ephesians 6:1–4

The young teen had become increasingly rebellious, wore dark clothing, and ran with bad kids. Then the mother found a folder in her daughter's room marked: "Leave this [blankety-blank] alone. This is my life." With trembling hands the mother opened the folder and found the most disturbing letters she'd ever seen. One note had blood smeared around the edges. The teen, who had grown up in the church, was involved with witchcraft and the occult.

The parents realized their daughter was beyond their ability to control. So they took drastic action. Within twenty-four hours they whisked her away to her aunt. The aunt, a dedicated Christian, insisted the girl go through a program called Bondage Breakers. She took her niece with her to Precept Bible Studies. She homeschooled her. One day this young girl devoted her life to Jesus Christ.

She was gone for three months, but she came back a new creature in Christ. Today she is active in youth group, and she recently gave her testimony. Her mother wrote me, "Bob, encourage people to be obedient to God even if it's embarrassing, even if it's drastic. We are thankful we did."

—Robert Russell, "When Teens Rebel," Preaching Today Audio, no. 207

ILLUSTRATION 537
POWERING UP WITH DAD

Topics: Dependence on God; God as Father; Prayer; Strength; Weakness

References: Psalm 46:1; Philippians 4:6, 13; James 4:2

A father watched through the kitchen window as his small son attempted to lift a large stone out of his sandbox. The boy couldn't get enough leverage to lift the rock over the side. Finally, he gave up and sat on the edge of the sandbox with his head in his hands.

"What's wrong, Son? Can't you lift that rock out?" the dad asked.

"No, sir," the boy said, "I can't do it."

"Have you used all the strength that's available to you?" the father asked.

"Yes, sir," the boy replied.

"No, you haven't," the father said. "You haven't asked me to help you."

—Bob Russell, Louisville, Kentucky

ILLUSTRATION 538
RAISING MORAL KIDS

Topics: Children; Empathy; Family; Morality; Values

References: Deuteronomy 6:6–7; Proverbs 22:6, 15; Ephesians 6:4

Eighty-one percent of mothers and 78 percent of fathers plan to send their young child to Sunday school or some other kind of religious training. That's according to *Newsweek*'s Karen Springen, who also found that, for many parents, raising a child who is empathetic, knows right from wrong, and attempts to follow the Golden Rule is more important than that child becoming wealthy or a president.

Parents have always made instilling moral values a priority. "But in today's fast-paced world, where reliable role models are few and acts of violence by children are increasingly common, the quest to raise a moral child has taken on a new urgency," says Springen.

—Karen Springen, "Raising a Moral Child," *Newsweek* special issue: "Your Child" (Fall–Winter 2000)

ILLUSTRATION 539

MORE PARENTS WORKING

Topics: Career; Children; Family; Marriage; Money; Work

Reference: Proverbs 29:15

The work status of parents with children has dramatically changed. According to the U.S. Census Bureau:

- Fifty-one percent of families had both spouses employed in 1998. That was up from 33 percent in 1976.
- Fifty-nine percent of married or single mothers with babies younger than a year old were employed at least part-time. That was up from 31 percent in 1976.
- Seventy-three percent of mothers ages fifteen to forty-four with children older than a year in 1998 were employed. Of them, 52 percent were working full-time. There was no data available for 1976.

—Tamar Lewin, "Two-Income Families Now the Norm, Census Bureau Says," *The New York Times* (October 23, 2000)

ILLUSTRATION 540

GRANDPARENT PARENTING

Topics: Children; Family; Grandparents; Orphans; Social Trends; Society

References: Psalm 68:5; 82:3; James 1:27

Abandonment, incarceration, drugs, death, and mental illness are some of the reasons 4 million kids in the United States no longer live with their parent(s). In more than 2.5 million families, grandparents are now parenting the children.

These "skipped generation households" have increased by more than 50 percent in the last ten years. In almost one-third of these families, parents are completely absent. In other cases, parents are occasionally present but are emotionally or financially incapable of taking care of their kids.

"Contrary to the stereotype of the inner-city welfare mom who is raising her teenage daughter's baby, the majority of grandparent caregivers are white, between the ages of 50 and 64, and live in non-metropolitan areas," reports *Newsweek*. There are more than seven hundred support groups nationwide that lobby government for legal rights and financial support for grandparent caregivers. Because their guardianship is often informal, grandparents also have problems getting medical care for the kids and enrolling them in school.

The first housing facility designed for grandparent-headed households opened in Boston in 1998. Carl Bowman, who shares an apartment with his wife and grandson, says, "I don't know where we'd be without this place. We're all in the same boat here. We all help one another."

—Lynette Clemetson, "Grandma Knows Best," *Newsweek* (June 12, 2000)

ILLUSTRATION 541

SUFFERING FROM COHABITATION

Topics: Children; Cohabitation; Commitment; Consequences; Faithfulness; Family; Love; Marriage; Parenting; Premarital Sex; Purity; Relationships; Sexual Immorality

References: Proverbs 14:12; 16:25; 1 Corinthians 7:2–6; Hebrews 13:4

Dr. A. Patrick Schneider II did a statistical analysis of cohabitation in America, based on the findings of a number of academic resources. Here are some conclusions he draws:

- Relationships are unstable in cohabitation. One-sixth of cohabiting couples stay together for only three years; one in ten survives five or more years.
- Cohabiting women often end up with the responsibilities of marriage—particularly when it comes to caring for children—without the legal protection. Research shows they also contribute more than 70 percent of the relationship's income.
- Cohabitation brings a greater risk of sexually transmitted diseases, because cohabiting men are four times more likely to be unfaithful than husbands.
- Poverty rates are higher among cohabitors. Those who share a home but never marry have 78 percent less wealth than the continuously married.

- Those who suffer most from cohabitation are the children. The poverty rate among children of cohabiting couples is fivefold greater than the rate among children in married-couple households. Children ages 12–17 with cohabiting parents are six times more likely to exhibit emotional and behavioral problems and 122 percent more likely to be expelled from school.

—Based on A. Patrick Schneider II, "Cohabitation: Ten Facts," *New Oxford Review* (September 2007)

ILLUSTRATION 542

MY HERO DAD

Topics: Example; Family; Fathers; Priorities

References: 2 Timothy 1:13; Titus 2:6–8

Here are two of the most important things Michael Tait of dc Talk learned from his dad:

- *Love people.* "That's what he taught," says Tait says, "and that's what he did. He cried with people, he laughed with people. Everybody was his friend. He couldn't care less about your race, your nationality, your socioeconomic status, whatever. All he cared about was you, your soul."
- *Live for God.* Tait sums up the lesson this way: "Don't get caught up in the things of this world, because they're just fleeting. The world will get the best of you if you let it, so live for God."

Tait was visiting his parents in Washington, D.C., during the Christmas holidays in 1997 when his dad complained of stomach pains. Michael took him to the hospital, where doctors found cancer. Michael was present a few weeks later when his dad breathed his last. "The man was my hero," Tait said.

—Mark Moring, "My Dad, My Hero," *Campus Life* (May–June 1999)

ILLUSTRATION 543

JABBA THE BUTT

Topics: Fear of God; God as Father; God's Holiness; God's Love

References: Luke 12:32; 2 Corinthians 5:11; Galatians 4:4–7

When my children got old enough to wrestle with me, we played a game we called "Jabba the Butt." The name came from a disgusting, evil character in the Star Wars trilogy called Jabba the Hutt.

I would play Jabba and roar around the room as the kids would shoot their laser guns at me and try to wrestle me to the floor. Sometimes I would get too much into the role. The kids would feel my great strength and hear my booming voice, and Daddy would become Jabba. Then I had to stop the game and hold them tenderly, reminding them I was Daddy.

The juxtaposition of overwhelming strength and tender love is as hard for a child to grasp as it is for an adult. But addressing God as Father can be electrifying if we can think of him as infinite love and tenderness combined with infinite holiness and power.

—Ben Patterson, *Deepening Your Conversation with God* (Bethany, 1999)

ILLUSTRATION 544

SAILING WITH DAD

Topics: Confidence; God as Father; Trust

References: Romans 8:15–17; 1 John 3:1

When I was learning how to sail, Dad would often say to me, "Go ahead and take the boat out, but take a friend with you."

A forty-two-foot sailboat on a body of water the size of Lake Michigan is a big responsibility. But I'd find a junior high friend, and we'd sail past the breakwater, hoist the sails, and head out to open water. If I saw any cloud formation coming our way or the wind seemed to be piping up, I'd head back toward shore, take the sails down, and regain my normal breathing pattern only when we were safely tied up in the slip. Most of the time it was fun having a friend along, but in a storm I knew the kid wouldn't be much help.

Other times my dad would come home from work and we'd take the boat out together. When I was sailing with my dad, I'd actually look for cloud formations and hope for heavy air. I loved the feel of the strong winds and huge waves when I was with him.

My dad had sailed across the Atlantic Ocean. He had endured five days of sailing through a hurricane. He was a veteran, and I was confident he would be able to handle anything Lake Michigan could throw at us. Everything changed when my dad was on board.

—Bill Hybels, *The God You're Looking For* (Nelson, 1997)

ILLUSTRATION 545

CARING FOR MOM

Topics: Child Rearing; Courage; Education; Mothers; Parenting

References: 2 Timothy 1:5; Titus 2:1–5

About the time he was in junior high, Dr. Benjamin Carson, now director of pediatric neurosurgery at Johns Hopkins Children's Center, Baltimore, Maryland, and author of several books, realized that his mother couldn't read. For years, Ben and his brother had read books and scratched out reports for their mother, assuming their mom was checking every word. But she didn't have a clue what they were writing.

Ben's illiterate mom didn't twist her hands over her lack of learning and give up hope of raising intelligent boys, however. Instead, she gave her boys what she had—interest, accountability, and the courage to demand extra work. And it paid off.

Years later, someone asked Ben why his mother still lived with him, even after he was married and had a family of his own. "You don't understand," Ben answered. "If it weren't for that

woman, I wouldn't be living here. She earned this."

—Kevin Leman, *What a Difference a Daddy Makes* (Nelson, 2000)

ILLUSTRATION 546

MOTHERING ME

Topics: Alcoholism; God's Strength; Ministry; Mothers; Service; Weakness

References: 2 Corinthians 3:4–6; 12:9

My parents divorced when I was five. My older sister, younger brother, and I were raised by my alcoholic mother.

While my mother meant well—truly she did—most of my memories are of my mothering her rather than her mothering me. Alcohol altered her love, turning it into something that wasn't love. I remember her weaving down the hall of our ranch home in Houston, Texas, glass of scotch in hand. She would wake me at 2:00 a.m. just to make sure I was asleep. I would wake her up at 7:00 a.m. to try to get her off to work.

Sure, there were good times, like Christmas and birthdays when she went all out and celebrated us as children. But even those days ended in the warped glow of alcohol. What she did right was lost in what she did wrong.

When I was asked to consider leading MOPS International, a vital ministry that nurtures mothers, I went straight to my knees, then to the therapist's office. How could God use me—who had never been mothered—to nurture other mothers?

The answer came as I looked into the eyes of other moms around me and saw their needs mirroring my own. God would take my deficits and make them my offering. He would answer his promise "My grace is sufficient for you, for my power is made perfect in weakness" (2 Corinthians 12:9).

—Elisa Morgan, "The Upside of an Upside-Down Life," *Christian Parenting Today* (May–June 1999)

ILLUSTRATION 547

LETTING KIDS GO

Topics: Child Rearing; Children; Family; Independence; Letting Go

References: Deuteronomy 11:19; Proverbs 22:6; Ephesians 6:4

The task of raising kids is rather like trying to fly a kite on a day when the wind doesn't blow, said humorist Erma Bombeck. Mom and Dad run down the road pulling the cute little device at the end of a string. It bounces along the ground and shows no inclination of getting off the ground.

Eventually and with much effort, they manage to lift it fifteen feet in the air, but great danger suddenly looms. The kite dives toward electrical lines and twirls near trees. It is a scary moment. Will they ever get it safely on its way? Then, unexpectedly, a gust of wind catches the kite, and it sails upward. Mom and Dad feed out line as rapidly as they can.

The kite begins pulling the string, making it difficult to hold on. Then they reach the end of their line. What should they do now? The kite is demanding more freedom. It wants to go higher. Dad stands on his tiptoes and raises his hand to accommodate the tug. The line is now grasped tenuously between his index finger and thumb, held upward toward the sky. Then the moment of release comes. The string slips through his fingers, and the kite soars majestically into God's beautiful sky.

Mom and Dad stand gazing at their precious "baby" who is now gleaming in the sun, a mere pinpoint of color on the horizon. They are proud of what they've done—but sad to realize their job is finished. Raising this child was a labor of love. But where did the years go?

—James Dobson, *Complete Marriage and Family Home Reference Guide* (Tyndale, 2000)

ILLUSTRATION 548

APOLOGIZING TO YOUR KIDS

Topics: Apology; Children; Family; Integrity; Mistakes; Respect

Reference: Ephesians 6:4

One day I found my son, four, trying to give his sister, two, a drink of water from his cup. Pam's clothes were soaked, and I scolded my son for his carelessness. Later I realized the boy had been trying to share his water with his little sister. But because I spoke on impulse, his generosity earned him criticism.

"I'm sorry, Harry," I told him. "I shouldn't have scolded you when you were being so nice to share." His look of relief told me I'd done the right thing.

No matter how much we love our children, we still make mistakes. Apologizing shows integrity and encourages our children to do the same when they make mistakes.

—Elsie Brunk, "R-E-S-P-E-C-T," *Christian Parenting Today* (March–April 2000)

ILLUSTRATION 549

SAVING CECILIA

Topics: Atonement; Children; Cross; Devotion; Jesus Christ; Love; Mothers; Protection; Sacrifice; Salvation

References: John 3:16; 12:20–33; Romans 8:38–39; Philippians 2:5–11

Northwest Airlines flight 225 crashed just after takeoff from Detroit on August 16, 1987, killing 155 people. Only one person survived: Cecilia, four, of Tempe, Arizona.

When rescuers found Cecilia, they did not believe she had been on the plane. They thought she had been a passenger in one of the cars on the highway onto which the airliner crashed. But when the passenger list was checked, there was Cecilia's name.

Cecilia survived because, as the plane was falling, Cecilia's mother, Paula Chican, unbuckled her own seat belt, got down on her knees in front of her daughter, wrapped her arms and body around Cecilia, and would not let her go. Nothing could separate that child from her mother's love—neither tragedy nor fall nor the flames that followed.

Such is the love of our Savior for us. He left heaven, lowered himself to us, and covered us with the sacrifice of his own body to save us.

—Bryan Chapell, *In the Grip of Grace* (Baker, 1992)

ILLUSTRATION 550

BELTING OUR LOVE

Topics: Commands; Law; Love; Obedience; Safety; Ten Commandments

References: Exodus 20:1–17; John 14:23–24; 1 John 5:3

Until a few years ago, there were no laws about child safety seats and automobile restraint systems. Many young children who were not safely belted in their seats died in car accidents.

Today laws prohibit children from riding in a car without special seating facing the right direction and properly installed. New mothers must have the seat in place before taking a child home from the hospital.

A parent's love for a child is beautiful. Yet when a child's safety is at stake, it seems a parent's love is not always enough. Many parents needed a seat belt law to ensure the safety of their children.

The same is true of our love and devotion for God and other people. Feelings are not enough. We needed laws and boundaries in the form of commands to help us love God and others.

—Troy Dean, Fullerton, California

PART 22: PRAYER

ILLUSTRATION 551

CLICKING PRAYERS TO GOD

Topics: God; Heaven; Technology

References: Matthew 6:5–18;
1 John 5:14–15

You can now send your prayers to God via a website.

Newprayer.com says, "Simply click on the Pray button and transmit your prayer to the only known location of God." The site claims it can send prayers via a radio transmitter to God's last known location: the star cluster M13, believed to be one of the oldest in the universe.

Crandall Stone, fifty, a Cambridge, Massachusetts, engineer and freelance consultant, set up the site after a winter's night of sipping brandy and philosophizing with friends in Vermont. The conversation turned to Big Bang theories of creation. Someone suggested that if everything was in one place at the time of the explosion, God must have been there too.

"It's the one place where we could be sure he was," Stone said. "We thought that if we could find that location and had a radio transmitter, we could send a message to God."

After consulting with NASA scientists, the friends settled on M13 as the likely location.

They chipped in about $20,000 to build a radio wave–transmitting website.

Newprayer.com transmits about 50,000 prayers a week from seekers around the globe.

Note: Newprayer.com is no longer operational.

—Judith Gaines, "Tapping into God,"
Denver Rocky Mountain News (March 13, 2000)

ILLUSTRATION 552

WAKING UP TO PRAYER

Topics: Children; Edification;
Encouragement; Example; Fathers;
Guidance; Mentoring; Parenting;
Spiritual Disciplines

References: Deuteronomy 6;
Matthew 13:44–46; 2 Corinthians
4:18; Ephesians 6:4, 18

Many kids wake up to the smell of coffee brewing or the sound of a rooster crowing. My wake-up call was my father's passionate praying. Sometimes I'd ease downstairs and join him. One knee was usually raised, so I'd slip in underneath, shielded by his body as he pleaded for my soul.

I never caught Dad praying for our happiness. He realized that the pursuit of happiness for its own sake is a frustrating, disillusioning, often futile effort. Happiness usually hides from those addicted to its sugar, while it chases after those caught up in something more lasting than momentary excitement.

I never heard him pray for a bigger house, car, or bank account. Instead, he prayed that our hearts would be ignited and inspired to do things of eternal consequence. "Turn our eyes from the temporal, the physical, and the menial," he prayed, "and toward the eternal, the spiritual, and the noble."

My father never pressured us toward achievement. He knew that the push had to come from inner reserves, not outward designs. He simply dangled before us the possibilities. Thanks to his example, we sometimes took the bait.

—John Ashcroft, *Lessons from a Father to His Son* (Nelson, 1998)

ILLUSTRATION 553

OPENING A BAG OF PRAYERS

Topics: Faith; Grace; Help from God; Waiting on God

References: Job 30:20; Matthew 10:29–31; Luke 12:6–7; 18:1–8; 2 Corinthians 12:8–10; Ephesians 6:18; 1 John 5:14–15

Bill Lacovara was fishing near Atlantic City, New Jersey, when he spotted a plastic bag floating in the water. Inside he found about 300 requests for prayer that had been mailed to a local pastor. Most of the letters were unopened. The pastor had died two years earlier, and authorities specu-

lated that the letters had been dumped as garbage after his house was cleaned out.

Some of the prayers were frivolous. "I'm still praying to hit the lottery—twice," wrote one man. "First $50,000—then, after some changes have taken place—let me hit the millionaire."

Many of the letters were heartbreaking. They came from anguished spouses, children, and widows, all crying out to God. Some prayed for relatives who were using drugs, gambling, or cheating on them. One man wrote from prison, saying that he was innocent and wanted to be back home with his family. A teenager poured out her heart on yellow, lined paper, begging God to forgive her and asking for a second chance. "Lord, I know that I have had an abortion, and I killed one of your angels," she wrote. "There is not a day that goes by that I don't think about the mistake I made."

Lacovara felt sad that so many prayers had been tossed away unheeded. "How many letters like this all over the world aren't being opened or answered?" he wondered. "There are hundreds of lives here, a lot of struggle, washed up on the beach."

—Wayne Perry, Associated Press, "Letters to God End Up in Ocean, Unread" (November 3, 2006)

ILLUSTRATION 554

PRAYING OUT OF EGO

Topics: Attitudes; Bondage; Ego; Self-centeredness

References: Romans 1:18–32; 6:16

Those people who pray know what most around them either don't know or choose to ignore: centering life in the insatiable demands of the ego is the sure path to doom. They know that life confined to the self is a prison, a joy-killing, neurosis-producing, disease-fomenting prison.

— Eugene Peterson,
Where Your Treasure Is (Eerdmans, 1993)

ILLUSTRATION 555

DISTURB US, LORD

Topics: Apathy; Boldness; Change; Complacency; Desires; Presence of God; Revival; Self-reliance; Spiritual Direction; Testing; Trials

References: Nehemiah 1:1 – 10; Psalm 85:6; Isaiah 6; Jeremiah 1:13 – 19; Revelation 3:15 – 16

Disturb us, Lord, when we are too well pleased with ourselves, when our dreams have come true because we have dreamed too little, when we arrive safely because we have sailed too close to the shore.

Disturb us, Lord, when with the abundance of things we possess, we have lost our thirst for the waters of life; having fallen in love with life, we have ceased to dream of eternity; and in our efforts to build a new earth, we have allowed our vision of the new heaven to dim.

Disturb us, Lord, to dare more boldly, to venture on wider seas where storms will show your mastery; where losing sight of land, we shall find the stars. We ask you to push back the hori-

zons of our hopes and to push us into the future in strength, courage, hope, and love.

— Sir Francis Drake, 1577, explorer and naval pioneer during the Elizabethan era

ILLUSTRATION 556

WHEN A COMMUNITY PRAYS

Topics: Body of Christ; Church; Comfort; Community; Encouragement; Grief; Guidance; Help; Ministry; Pain

References: Romans 12:15; 2 Corinthians 1:3 – 7; Galatians 6:2; 1 Thessalonians 5:11; Hebrews 10:25; James 5:16

On Christmas morning 1998, Russ Robinson and his family climbed into their motor home and headed from Chicago to Phoenix, Arizona. Russ and his wife took turns driving all day and into the night. While cruising along in the darkness, the headlights suddenly revealed a woman dressed in black, walking in the middle of the road. Russ swerved, but it was too late. The motor home crashed into the woman. Her head hit the windshield, and her body smashed into the right side of the vehicle, tossing her into the ditch.

The woman, who was trying to commit suicide, survived. But Russ was devastated. He phoned a friend in his small group. His wife called someone in her group. The two groups gathered to pray for Russ. He writes:

Their prayer support helped me begin the road to emotional recovery. My community listened during long conversations while I tried to process confusing emotions. When I wrestled with God—seeking to make sense of the experience—people offered reassurance and other help. I needed people to pray with and for me, and I came to know what it was to have someone "weep with those who weep" (Romans 12:15). I experienced how the body of Christ can extend real, personal hands to someone in pain.

You need to invest in community today so you can reap the benefits during tomorrow's seasons of deprivation and loss.

—Based on Bill Donahue and Russ Robinson, *Building a Church of Small Groups* (Zondervan, 2001)

ILLUSTRATION 557

SAVING HOBBY LOBBY

Topics: Business; Despair; Discouragement; Growth; Help from God; Overcoming; Security in God

References: Psalm 91:15; Isaiah 65:24; Matthew 7:7; Luke 18:1–8; John 14:13–14; 15:7; Philippians 4:6

In the offices of his multimillion-dollar hobby and craft business, Hobby Lobby, David Green read the bad news: the bank was ready to foreclose on the product of years of his life and labor.

In 1986, Hobby Lobby wasn't the only business in trouble. The oil business in Oklahoma had gone bust, and the overextended banks were failing. Many business owners in Oklahoma City had already closed their doors in defeat and declared bankruptcy.

Although the foreclosure of the business was the worst thing he could imagine, Green came to see it as a defining moment in his spiritual life. "I know I prayed prior to that time, but that's when I got really serious about it," he said.

The space beneath his desk became his prayer closet. He would crawl under his desk in his corporate office and seek God's help. It was God's response to those prayers for their business that the family believes pulled the company out from under looming bankruptcy and set it on its feet again.

Hobby Lobby was projected to produce more than $1.5 billion in sales throughout 2006.

—Suzanne Jordan Brown, "Prayer-Driven Enterprise," *Pray!* (July–August 2006)

ILLUSTRATION 558

HELPING UNCLE JOE

Topics: Attitudes; Children; Compassion; Example; Faith; Forgiveness; Grace; Love for Enemies; Patience

References: Matthew 18:3, 21–35; Mark 11:25; Luke 10:21; Romans 12:19–21; Ephesians 4:32; Colossians 3:13

When I went to pick up Shanna for Sunday school one week, she was crying and had blood on her dress. "It's my uncle Joe!" she said. I knew that her family was "going through changes" because of Uncle Joe and his drug addiction.

Shanna had particular reason to feel bitter toward her uncle. For years she had dreamed of owning a bicycle, and that Christmas a donation from a church made her dream come true. Shanna rode her shiny, new blue bike everywhere, bragged on it, polished it, and treasured it. Within a month, her uncle had sold the bike to buy drugs — an ample reason to embitter a nine-year-old.

Now, on this morning, there was one more reason. Uncle Joe had come home wearing a T-shirt that read, "Say No to Drugs." Shanna commented, "Why don't you read your own shirt?" He hit her, causing a nosebleed. The white collar and yellow lace of her Sunday dress were a mess. Nothing else was clean, and everyone else was still asleep. We went to church to wash out the bloodstain.

When it came time in the service for individual prayer petitions, Shanna's voice sounded bright and clear as a trumpet: "I pray for my uncle Joe. He needs your help, Lord. Please, Jesus, help my uncle."

What a privilege to drink from the same chalice as Shanna.

—Heidi Neumark,
Breathing Space (Beacon, 2003)

ILLUSTRATION 559
PUTTING FEET ON PRAYER

Topics: Abortion; Calling; Commitment; Dedication; Evangelism; Example; Guidance; Hearing God; Justice; Mission; Purpose; Responsibility

References: Matthew 7:7–8; Luke 18:1–8; Philippians 4:6; Colossians 4:2; 1 John 5:14–15

In a small apartment in Washington, D.C., a group of Christians are devoted to radical intercessory prayer. Each person in the group prays in shifts six days a week for eight hours each day. Then, in two-hour shifts, groups of six to ten gather on the steps of the Supreme Court to pray silently with red duct tape covering their mouths. The word "LIFE" is scrawled across the tape in black marker.

Matt Lockett, one member of the group, used to think of prayer like most of us do. "I knew it was something I was supposed to do," he says. But in September 2004, Matt had a vivid dream in which he saw God end abortion in America in response to prayer.

"My whole life changed after that," Lockett said. Lockett and his family sold their home in Denver, Colorado, and moved to the nation's capital to join a budding prayer movement called The Cause. On the opening day of the Supreme Court session in October 2004, The Cause gathered on the court steps to pray.

From that point on, the members of The Cause have centered on prayer as a dynamic action rather than a passive event. "God has called us to put feet to our prayers," Lockett says. "My understanding of prayer is this: Stop living the American dream and live God's dream."

—"A Cause Worth Fighting For,"
Relevant (November–December 2006)

ILLUSTRATION 560

TOO BUSY TO PRAY

Topics: Busyness; Help; Lifestyle; Pressure; Problems; Rescue; Stress; Trials

References: Proverbs 3:5–6; Matthew 11:28–30; Luke 18:1–8; John 14:27; Ephesians 6:18; Philippians 4:6–7

The top ten reasons you are too busy to pray today:

1. You wake up feeling rested, then realize your alarm should have gone off an hour ago.
2. Your spouse is away on a two-day business trip that has lasted all week.
3. None of the clean clothes you were able to find match.
4. Your teenager shaved ... the left half of his head.
5. Your bills are due and your toddler hid the checkbook.
6. A strange fluid is dripping from your car.
7. You accidentally delete your quarterly report ten minutes before meeting with your boss.
8. You're in charge of games for the church youth night tonight.
9. Your dog is throwing up.
10. Your toilet's overflowing, but at least you found the checkbook.

Ten reasons you really should pray today: (See list above.)

— "The Top Ten Reasons You Are Too Busy to Pray Today," *Marriage Partnership* (1996)

ILLUSTRATION 561

SURGICALLY ASSISTING PRAYER

Topics: Calling; Community; Evangelism; Great Commission; Guidance; Outreach; Passion; Testimony; Vocation

References: Matthew 9:10–13; 28:18–20; Mark 2:17; Luke 19:10; Ephesians 6:6–8, 18; Philippians 4:6; Colossians 4:2; 1 Timothy 2:8; 1 John 5:14–15

I am a surgical assistant—the surgeon's right-hand man. At one point in my career, I lost my passion. I wanted a job with spiritual significance, and I prayed for that. Imagine my shock when God led me to a position in plastic surgery. *Why would God want me in a hotbed of vanity?* I wondered.

During my quiet times, the Lord assured me that this was part of his plan and that I should wait for his direction. So I obeyed, continuing to pray that the Lord would use me in this job.

The first directive when I started my new position was "Gather and pray in my name." There were only a few Christians who worked in the plastic surgery department, but I started with them. "I'm going to start praying for our workplace each Monday, fifteen minutes before we clock in," I told them. "I'll be in Operating Room 2, and I hope you will join me."

We met each week, praying for our work, our colleagues, and our patients. Soon we were praying boldly for opportunities to witness. By the end of that year, God had answered many prayers, which included ten friends who accepted Christ as their Savior!

God has given me a purpose far beyond patient care. He expanded my circle of influence by transferring me to the main surgery department, where I now rotate through all four departments in the hospital campus. I have started several prayer groups throughout the hospital. Each group focuses on inviting the Holy Spirit to move in their department. We encourage each other in Christ, pray for opportunities to witness, seek God's will, and ask that Christ be glorified in our work.

Since I realized that I could advance the kingdom of God through praying at work, I have found renewed passion for my job, as well as for the opportunities for ministry it provides.

—Brandon A. Bradley, "Prayer at Work: Surgical Assistant," *Pray!* (July–August 2006)

ILLUSTRATION 562

PRAYING OUT OF FEAR

Topics: Anxiety; Confrontation; Fear; Help from God; Security in God; Sexual Immorality; Surrender; Temptation; Trust

References: Ephesians 4:15; 6:18; Philippians 4:6; Colossians 3:16; 4:2; James 5:19–20; 1 Peter 5:7

Carrie was an outgoing person with a quick smile and ready words of encouragement. But something told me all was not as it seemed. I learned this single Christian was in a compromising sexual situation. I quietly interceded for her for some time until the Holy Spirit prompted me to talk to her about it.

I met Carrie for coffee on a Saturday morning. After chatting for a few minutes, I said, "Carrie, I've been praying for you. I think the Lord is saying that you are trapped by fear. Am I hearing correctly?"

Carrie did not take long to react. She was indeed very afraid, she admitted. Finances were tight, almost desperate, for her. She was afraid of being alone. These fears were nearly consuming her. She had been trying to cope with everything on her own, which was carrying her further and further from God and from peace of mind.

While fear is a normal human reaction to danger, the sin of fear is a fleshly response to circumstances that seem beyond our control. I gently pointed this out to Carrie. When I suggested that she tell this to God, she wholeheartedly agreed. First, she confessed her sin of fear—her lack of trust in the Lord's provision and presence and her quickness to turn to earthly substitutes. Then, without my saying a word, she tearfully confessed to God her temptation to enter into an immoral relationship because of the security it would provide.

I then took the opportunity ask God to pour out his comfort, love, provision, and presence on her. There was still practical follow-up to be done, to be sure. But it would be easier because the hard work of restoring Carrie's heart had already started.

—Arlyn Lawrence, "The Other Great Commission?" *Pray!* (May–June 2006)

ILLUSTRATION 563

BLESSINGS IN PERSECUTION

Topics: Blessings; Enemies; Overcoming; Persecution; Perspective

References: Numbers 23:11; Proverbs 25:21–22; Matthew 5:44; Romans 12:20–21

Serbian bishop Nikolai Velimirovic spoke out against Nazism in the early 1940s. For that he was arrested and taken to the Dachau concentration camp. There he prayed:

> Bless my enemies, O Lord. Even I bless them and do not curse them. Enemies have driven me into your embrace more than friends have. Friends have bound me to earth; enemies have loosed me from earth and have demolished all my aspirations in the world.
>
> Just as a hunted animal finds safer shelter than an unhunted animal does, so have I, persecuted by enemies, found the safest sanctuary, having ensconced myself beneath your tabernacle, where neither friends nor enemies can slay my soul.
>
> Bless my enemies, O Lord. Even I bless and do not curse them.

—Bishop Nikolai Velimirovic, *Prayers by the Lake* (Serbian Orthodox Metropolitanate of New Gracanica, 1999)

ILLUSTRATION 564

A TEACHER'S PRAYERS

Topics: Evangelism; Harvest; Intercession; Results; Teachers

References: Romans 10:1; 1 Corinthians 3:6–9; Philippians 4:6

My wife, Angie, went to a rough high school. There were few Christians there apart from one teacher, David Bunton, who taught manual arts. Years after leaving Bunton's classroom, dozens of his former students became believers. Many have entered the ministry and become pastors and missionaries. I tracked down Bunton, who is now seventy years old and retired. He was stunned with emotion when I told him of the many conversions of his former students.

I asked how his influence had brought such a harvest. He told me that many times he had prayed softly over his classes as he sat at his desk and watched them work. Apart from that, he had done nothing to influence these students toward Christ. The only common point of spiritual connection the students shared was that they were prayed over by their teacher.

—Brian Roennfeldt, Perth, West Australia

ILLUSTRATION 565

MIRACLE MANDY

Topics: Doubt; Faith; Infertility; Miracles

References: Genesis 25:21; 1 Samuel 1:10 – 20; Psalm 13; Matthew 19:26

The doctor told Marsha Mark and her husband they would never have biological children. In their disappointment, Marsha clung to a friend's words: "Somehow, God is going to use your struggle with infertility for his glory." Marsha began to pray for a glimpse of that glory.

"I asked everyone I knew to pray," she said. "One five-year-old prayed, 'Dear God, please send Marsha a baby. Maybe someone could give her one, or she could just find one on the street.'"

Marsha's husband, Tom, a scientist, stopped praying when Marsha showed signs of menopause. Tom had seen lots of data. And in his lifetime, he'd never seen prayer change scientific facts.

Six months later, Marsha made an appointment for another pregnancy test. The doctor said no because Marsha hadn't had a period for seven months. "Asking for another pregnancy test indicates you are not accepting things as they are," he said. Marsha begged for the extra test anyway. And it came back positive.

"Over the next fourteen days, I had four more pregnancy tests and three more sonograms at the hospital's request. I think this time the doctor was having trouble dealing with the facts," Marsha said.

Her full-term pregnancy was uneventful. On October 22, 1996, Amanda Joy was born. "We call her Miracle Mandy," Marsha said.

—Marsha Marks, "Special Delivery," *Christian Reader* (September – October 2000)

ILLUSTRATION 566
BAMBOO PRAYER

Topics: Faith; Perseverance; Power; Supplication

References: Matthew 7:7; 17:20; 21:21 – 22; James 1:5 – 8

The largest and finest bell in the East was in the great Buddhist Temple, Shwee-da-gone, in Rangoon. During a war the bell sank in a river. Over the years, various engineers tried but failed to raise it. At last a clever priest asked permission to try, but only if the bell was given to his temple.

The priest had his assistants gather an immense number of bamboo rods. One by one the rods were fastened to the bell at the bottom of the river. After thousands of them had been fastened, the bell began to move. When the last bamboo rod was attached, the buoyancy of the accumulated rods lifted the bronze bell from the mire of the river bottom to the stream's surface.

"Every whisper of believing prayer is like one of the little bamboo rods," writes author A. B. Simpson. "For a time they seem to be in vain, but there comes a last breath of believing supplication, and lo, the walls of Jericho fall, the mountain becomes a plain, and the host of Amalek is defeated."

—Cregg Puckett, "One More Prayer," PreachingToday.com

ILLUSTRATION 567

ASKING FOR MORE

Topics: Daily Bread; Dependence on God; Experiencing God; Faith; Help from God; Money; Needs; Provision

References: Luke 11:9 – 13; 2 Corinthians 9:6 – 11; Ephesians 3:20

In the mid-1980s my family moved to northern Saskatchewan to start a church. As a church planter, part of my support was funded by the local mission. Most months were financially difficult.

One week in April, when the ground was still frozen and snow covered, we were down to a few dollars in the bank. Our usual reaction was to look for our own solution. This time, however, in a stroke of faith, I went before God and told him that we needed eggs, bread, and milk. I would wait on him.

That afternoon a man came to my little fix-it shop with a leaky teakettle. He said, "I know I could get another, but it's my favorite kettle. Please fix it." In minutes the job was done, and I didn't even charge him for it. But he pulled out a $10 bill and insisted that I take it. It was enough to buy a gallon of milk, a dozen eggs, and a loaf of bread.

As he left, with a bit of pride in my faith decision, I thanked God, to which he replied, "Don't you wish you had asked for half a beef?"

—Len Sullivan, Tupelo, Mississippi

ILLUSTRATION 568

TRUSTING THE SUBAUDIBLE

Topics: Agnosticism; Dependence on God; Faith; Fear; Help from God; Trust

References: Psalm 23:1 – 4; Matthew 6:9; 28:20; 1 Peter 5:7

Trisha McFarland stopped on a family hike across the Appalachians to go to the bathroom. In trying to catch up with her family, she found herself on the wrong trail, lost and alone. She sat down, closed her eyes, and tried to pray for rescue. But praying was hard. She said, "Our Father," and it came out of her mouth flat and uncomforting.

She couldn't remember discussing spiritual matters with her mother, but she had asked her father not a month before if he believed in God.

"I'll tell you what I believe in," said Larry McFarland. "I believe in the Subaudible. Do you remember when we lived on Fore Street? Do you remember how the electric baseboard units would hum, even when they weren't heating?"

Trisha shook her head.

"That's because you got used to it," the father said. "But take my word, Trisha, that sound was always there. Even in a house where there aren't baseboard heaters, there are noises. The fridge goes on and off. The traffic goes by outside. We hear those things all the time, so most of the time we don't hear them at all. They become ..."

"Subaudible," Trisha said.

"Pree-cisely. I don't believe in a God who marks the fall of every bird, who records all of our sins in a big golden book and then judges us when we die. But I believe there has to be something. Some sort of insensate force for the good."

"The Subaudible," she said.

"You got it."

So, here's this girl in the woods, lost and sensing that there must be something more. Then she remembers her baseball hero, the great closer of the Boston Red Sox, Tom "Flash" Gordon. He pulls out miraculous saves for the Sox, and when he wins, he points his finger to the sky, giving credit to a personal God who has revealed himself to the world in Jesus Christ.

After nine days of being bug-bitten, scared, cut, sick from drinking bad water and eating poisonous berries, Trisha finally pleads to a personal God to bring her out of the woods.

"Please God, help me find the path," she says to the God of Tom Gordon, not her father's Subaudible. She needs a God who is really there, one you can point to when and if you get the save. "Please, God, please, help me."

> —Based on Stephen King, *The Girl Who Loved Tom Gordon* (Scribner, 1999)

ILLUSTRATION 569

HEARING GOD IN A CHILD

Topics: Blessings; Children; Encouragement; Experiencing God; Hearing God; Identity in Christ

References: Psalm 8:2; Matthew 7:7–11

Two days ago, I was kneeling in prayer in the front room of our house at 6:30 a.m. I'd just confessed sins and was asking God for a blessing that day, needing to feel loved by him.

Our little boy, Timothy, twenty-two months old, had just gotten up, and I noticed out of the corner of my eye that he had sneaked quietly into the front room. He is always quiet in the morning when I'm praying because his mom tells him to be, but this time he ambled straight over to me, put a hand on my clasped hands, and said, "Hi, special one. Hi, special one. Hi, special one."

Never once has he called me that before. Six times he called me "special one." He said it enough for me actually to get it—that God was speaking to me and giving me a blessing.

> —Bill White, Paramount, California

ILLUSTRATION 570

PRAYING FOR RAIN

Topics: Belief; Circumstances; Faith; Prayer

References: Matthew 21:22; Mark 11:24; John 20:29

Three farmers gather daily during a horrible drought. The men are down on their knees, praying the skies will open and pour forth rain. The heavens are silent, however, and the petitioners become discouraged. Nonetheless, they continue to pray every morning.

One morning, a stranger asks the men what they are doing. They say, "We're praying for rain."

The stranger looks at each of them and shakes his head. "I don't think so."

The first farmer says, "We are down on our knees, pleading for rain. Look around; see the drought. We haven't had rain in more than a year!"

The stranger says their efforts won't work.

The second farmer says, "We need the rain; we aren't asking only for ourselves, but for our families and livestock."

The stranger still isn't impressed. "You're wasting your time," he says.

The third farmer in anger says, "What would you do if you were in our shoes?"

"You really want to know?" the stranger asks.

"We really want to know!" the farmers say. "The future of our farmlands is at stake."

The stranger says, "I would have brought an umbrella!"

—Larry King, *Powerful Prayers*
(Renaissance, 1998)

ILLUSTRATION 571

THE MIRACLE WELL

Topics: Dependence on God; Faith; Miracles; Supernatural Occurrences; Trust

References: Matthew 17:20–21; 19:26; Luke 1:37; James 5:13–16

During Desert Storm the United States Marine Corps was ordered to push up the Saudi Arabian coast through the minefields in southern Kuwait and capture Kuwait City. To move 80,000 marines up that coast, we had to build a logistics support base. We built that base at Kabrit, 30 kilometers south of Kuwait and 30 kilometers in from the Persian Gulf. We picked Kabrit because it was an old airfield that had water wells that provided 100,000 gallons of water a day. The marines needed that much water daily to carry troops into Kuwait.

Fourteen days before the war began, General Norman Schwarzkopf, commander in chief of the central command, made a daring move called the "great left hook." This sweep of forces flanked the Iraqi army. It was a great move, but it forced the Marine Corps to move 140 kilometers to the northwest and locate a new logistic space at the Gravel Plains.

There was no water. For fourteen days we had engineers digging desperately to find water. We went to the Saudi government and asked if they knew of any water in this area, and their answer was no. We brought the exiled Kuwaiti government down to our command post and asked, "Do you know if there's any water in this area?" They said no. We went to the Bedouin tribes and the nomads, the people who lived in that area, and said, "Do you know where there's water on the Gravel Plain?"

They said, "There's no water there." We kept digging wells hundreds of feet deep — to no avail.

Every morning at 7:15 a.m., during my devotional time, I asked the Lord to help us find water. On the Sunday before we were to enter Kuwait, I was in a chapel service, where we were praying for water, when a colonel came to the tent and said, "General, I need to show you something."

We drove down a road we had built through the desert from the Gravel Plains to the border of Kuwait. About a mile down that road, the officer said, "Look over there." About twenty yards off the road was a tower that reached fifteen feet into the air. It was a white tower, and at the top of the tower was a cross. Off the ends of the cross were canvas sleeves used in old train stations to put water into train engines. At the base of that cross was an eight-foot-high pump, newly painted red. Beside that pump was a diesel engine, and beside that, four batteries still in their plastic. On the engine were an On button and an Off button.

I pushed the On button, and the engine kicked over immediately. I called one of my engineers and asked him to test the flow coming out of the pipes. An hour later he said, "Sir, it is putting out 100,000 gallons a day."

—General Charles Krulak, in a message given at the Leadership Prayer Breakfast, Wheaton, Illinois, October 2000

ILLUSTRATION 572
NO-ANSWER PRAYER

Topics: Christian Life; Truth

References: Matthew 21:22; Romans 8:26–27

However much he may want to, I do not believe God will answer the prayer of the student who turned in his test and prayed, "O God, please let Paris be the capital of England!"

—Nicky Gumbel, "How and Why Should I Pray?" *Alpha Evangelism Series* (HTB Publications, 1994)

ILLUSTRATION 573
SHIFTING THE WINDS

Topics: Dependence on God; Divine Power; Help from God; Miracles

References: Joshua 10:1–14; Matthew 17:20

The prevailing winds in the Persian Gulf area blow from northeast to southwest. So if you attack from the southwest, your enemy can release biological weapons into the air, and the chemicals will blow right into your face. That was a tremendous concern for the military during operation Desert Storm and the subject of many prayers in the Gulf and back home in the United States.

On February 21, 1991, American forces attacked from the southwest at 4:00 a.m. Only three hours before, the prevailing winds had shifted from southwest to northeast, exactly 180 degrees from the direction the prevailing winds normally blow. The winds blew in that direction for four days, the duration of the war. Within thirty minutes of the surrender, the winds shifted back. That is the unbelievable power of prayer.

—General Charles Krulak, in a message given at the Leadership Prayer Breakfast, Wheaton, Illinois, October 2000

ILLUSTRATION 574
KEEPING ONE EYE OPEN

Topics: Spiritual Disciplines; Watchfulness

References: Matthew 26:41;
Colossians 4:2

Hannah, three, came home from Bible school and announced that her new teacher "makes everyone bow their heads and close their eyes when we pray, but then keeps his eyes open."

I asked Hannah how she would know that if her eyes were closed.

"I only close one eye at a time," she replied.

—Malinda F., Roanoke Rapids,
North Carolina, "Life in Our House,"
Christian Parenting Today (May–June 2000)

ILLUSTRATION 575

PERSISTENCE PAYS

Topic: Persistence

References: Matthew 7:7–8;
Luke 11:5–10; 18:1–8

A huge magazine fulfillment firm in Chicago sends out renewal and expiration notices for hundreds of magazines. But one day the company's computer malfunctioned. A rancher in Powder Bluff, Colorado, got 9,734 separate mailings informing him that his subscription to *National Geographic* had expired.

The rancher dropped what he was doing and traveled ten miles to the nearest U.S. post office, where he sent money for a renewal along with a note that said, "I give up—send me your magazine!"

Multiplied requests often break down resistance. For reasons known only to God, that is true also of prayer.

—*Stand Firm* (September 1999)

ILLUSTRATION 576

SHE'D BE PRAYING

Topics: Example; Mothers

References: Psalm 78:1–7; Ephesians 6:18; Philippians 4:6–7; 1 Thessalonians 5:17

A black woman remembered how her mother, a slave whose work schedule left little free room for anything else, nonetheless found time and strength to talk to God.

"My mother, all the time she'd be praying to the Lord," the woman said. "She'd take us children to the woods to pick up firewood, and we'd turn around to see her down on her knees behind a stump, praying. We'd see her wiping her eyes with the corner of her apron—first one eye, then the other—as we came along back. Then, back in the house, down on her knees, she'd be praying."

—"Did You Know?" *Christian History*,
no. 62 (Spring 1999)

ILLUSTRATION 577

HE HAD A HAT

Topics: Contentment; Mothers;
Thanksgiving

Reference: Philippians 4:6

A mother and son lived in a forest. One day a tornado roared through. The mother clung to a tree and tried to hold her son, but the swirling winds carried him into the sky.

The woman began to weep and pray: "Please, O Lord, bring back my boy! He's all I have. I'd do anything not to lose him. If you'll bring him back, I'll serve you all my days."

Suddenly the boy toppled from the sky, right at her feet. He was a bit mussed up but safe and sound.

His mother joyfully brushed him off. Then she stopped for a moment, looked to the sky, and said, "He had a hat, Lord."

—*Stand Firm* (September 1999)

ILLUSTRATION 578
TOGETHERNESS IN PRAYER

Topics: Church; Community; Lord's Prayer

References: Matthew 6:9 – 13; Luke 11:2 – 4; Acts 2:42 – 47

I like to fly-fish, and when I do, I spend a lot of time alone. Even when I go on a trip with my son, we usually split up and take different parts of the river to fish. Later we come back and swap stories.

Even when I'm casting by myself, though, in front of a gentle riffle, I never feel alone. I know my son is fishing with me even though he's not fishing with me.

That's how it is with the Lord's Prayer. Even though we say it alone, it reminds us that we're not alone. That's the point of the words *our* and *us* that run through it. Even when you pray alone, you are reminded that you're part of a community—in particular, a group that honors Christ,

that prays to him regularly, and also, from time to time, says the prayer he taught.

—Mark Galli, *The Complete Idiot's Guide to Prayer* (Macmillan, 1999)

ILLUSTRATION 579
PRAYING FOR MISTER ROGERS

Topics: Children; Community; Disabilities; Humility; Intercession; Self-image; Self-worth

Reference: Colossians 4:2 – 4

The late Mister Rogers once visited a teenager with cerebral palsy. At first the boy was so nervous about the visit that he began hitting himself. His mother had to take him to another room.

Mister Rogers waited patiently, and when the boy came back, the star of children's television asked the boy, "Would you do something for me?" The boy answered yes on his computer. "I would like you to pray for me," Mister Rogers said. "Will you pray for me?"

The boy was shocked because nobody had ever asked him for something like that. The boy had always been the object of prayer, and now he was being asked to pray for Mister Rogers. At first he didn't know if he could do it, but then he said he'd try.

From then on, the boy kept Mister Rogers in his prayers. He didn't talk about wanting to die anymore, because he figured Mister Rogers was close to God, and if Mister Rogers liked him, that must mean God liked him too.

When Mister Rogers was asked how he knew what to say to make the boy feel better, he said, "I didn't ask prayers for him; I asked them for me. I asked because I think that anyone who has gone through challenges like that must be very close to God. I asked him because I wanted his intercession."

—Wendy Murray Zoba, "Won't You Be My Neighbor?" *Christianity Today* (March 6, 2000)

ILLUSTRATION 580

JESUS' UNANSWERED PRAYER

Topics: Cross; Easter; Jesus Christ; Salvation

References: Matthew 26:36–46; Mark 14:32–42; Luke 22:39–46

When Jesus prayed to the one who could save him from death, he did not get that salvation; he got instead the salvation of the world.

—Philip Yancey, "Jesus' Unanswered Prayers," *Christianity Today* (February 9, 1998)

ILLUSTRATION 581

PRAYING IN FRONT OF A GROUP

Topics: Affirmation; Communion; Discipleship; Encouragement; Failure; Kindness; Mentoring

References: Romans 12:6–8; Ephesians 4:29; 1 Thessalonians 5:11; Hebrews 3:13

Young men in his church were expected to pray aloud in Communion services. So the young Larry Crabb felt pressured to pray, even though he had a problem with stuttering. He remembers offering a terribly confused prayer in which he thanked the Father for hanging on the cross and praised Christ for triumphantly bringing the Spirit from the grave. When he was finished, he vowed he would never again pray out loud in front of a group.

At the end of the service, Crabb made for the door. Before he could get out, an older man caught him. "Larry, there's one thing I want you to know," the man said. "Whatever you do for the Lord, I'm behind you 1,000 percent."

"Even as I write these words, my eyes fill with tears," says Crabb, who has since become a best-selling book author, psychologist, and speaker. "Those words were life words. They had power. They reached deep into my being."

—Based on Larry Crabb, *Encouragement* (Zondervan, 1984)

ILLUSTRATION 582

JUST ASK

Topics: Boldness; Friendship; God; Receiving

References: Matthew 7:7–11; James 4:2

In 1962, Robert White, fourteen, wrote to President John F. Kennedy's personal secretary requesting the president's autograph. Within a few weeks Evelyn Lincoln sent the boy a signature.

That began a thirty-three-year relationship of correspondence. Impressed with White's passion for presidential history, the president's secretary gave the boy thousands of documents and mementos. She saved whatever could be saved, including the doodles JFK drew during meetings. Today White has the largest private collection of Kennedy memorabilia, over fifty thousand items.

Receiving begins with the courage to ask.

—Greg Asimakoupoulos, "Ask,"
PreachingToday.com

PART 23: RELATIONSHIPS

ILLUSTRATION 583

POTATO CHIP LOYALTY

Topics: Commitment; Friends; Loyalty

References: Psalm 16:8;
Proverbs 3:5–6; John 16:13;
2 Corinthians 3:17–18

Recently I was shopping at our local grocery store. After picking up some staples, I headed to the all-important potato chip aisle. Unlike my usual routine, I had already decided what kind of chips to buy. With my eyes set like flint, I walked down the center of the aisle, ignoring the siren calls of various brands until I reached the Mike Sells chip display.

After I had picked up two bags of Mike Sells chips, I heard a familiar voice behind me saying, "Thanks a lot, buddy." It was my friend Chuck, a member of the congregation I pastor and a deliveryman for Mike Sells.

Now, imagine how I would have felt if Chuck had seen me hugging a bag of Ruffles. Thirty minutes earlier I had run into Chuck at the local bakery. He and I had spent a few minutes talking together, and then we each went our way. When I arrived at the grocery store and began considering what chips to buy, I remembered that Chuck worked for Mike Sells and would probably be pleased if I purchased the brand he

sold. So, spending some time together influenced my choice.

The whole experience reminded me of something important. Spending time with my heavenly Father and being reminded of what pleases him will likely result in making decisions pleasing to him. Perhaps I'll even get a "Way to go, Van!"

—Van Morris, Mount Washington, Kentucky

ILLUSTRATION 584

MORE THAN A TRUCK

Topics: Bitterness; Conflict; Enemies; Perspective; Priorities; Reconciliation; Relationships; Revenge; Values

References: Matthew 5:39;
Luke 6:28–29; Romans 15:1;
1 Corinthians 6:7; Colossians 3:13;
1 Thessalonians 5:14–15

While Tom Wiles was university chaplain at Grand Canyon University in Phoenix, Arizona, he picked up Leonard Sweet at the airport in his new Ford pickup to take him to a leadership conference. Since Sweet was still mourning the trade-in of his Dodge truck, the two men immediately bonded, sharing truck stories and laughing at the bumper-sticker truism "Nothing is more beautiful than a man and his truck." Sweet tells what happened next:

As I climbed into Tom's 2002 Ranger for the ride back to the airport a day later, I noticed two big scrapes by the passenger door. "What *happened*?" I asked.

"My neighbor's basketball post fell on the truck," Tom replied sadly.

"You're kidding! How awful," I said. "This truck is so new I can smell it."

"What's even worse is my neighbor doesn't feel responsible for the damage."

I immediately rose to my friend's defense. "Did you contact your insurance company? How are you going to get him to pay for it?" I asked.

"This has been a real spiritual journey for me," Tom replied. "After a lot of soul-searching and discussions with my wife about hiring an attorney, it came down to this: I can either be in the right, or I can be in a relationship with my neighbor. Since my neighbor will probably be with me longer than this truck, I decided that I'd rather be in a relationship than be right. Besides, trucks are meant to be banged up, so I got mine initiated into the real world a bit earlier than I expected."

— Based on Leonard Sweet, *Out of the Question ... into the Mystery* (WaterBrook, 2004)

ILLUSTRATION 585

RUBBER, METAL, AND GLASS

Topics: Choices; Direction; Discernment; Family; Guidance; Perspective; Priorities; Relationships; Self-discipline; Spiritual Disciplines; Testing; Time

References: Psalm 90:12; Matthew 6:19–21; 16:26; Luke 16:13; Ephesians 5:15

Tim Sanders, former chief solutions officer at Yahoo! and author of *Love Is the Killer App*, says the following about establishing priorities:

Take your life and all the things that you think are important, and put them in one of three categories, represented by three items: glass, metal, and rubber.

Things of rubber, when you drop them, will bounce back. No harm is done when these things get dropped. So, for instance, if I miss a Seahawks' game, my life will bounce along fine. Missing a game or a season of football will not alter my marriage or my spiritual life. I can take 'em or leave 'em.

Things of metal, when dropped, create a lot of noise. But you can recover from the drop. If you miss a meeting at work, you can get the CliffsNotes. If you don't balance your checkbook and lose track of how much you have in your account, and the bank notifies you of an overdraft — that will create some noise in your life, but you can recover from it.

Things of glass, when dropped, shatter into pieces and will never be the same again. They can be glued back together, but they are altered forever. They may be missing some pieces, and they probably can't hold water again without leaking. The consequences of this brokenness will forever affect how the glass is used.

You're the only person who knows what those things are that you can't afford to drop. More than likely, they have a lot to do with your relationships with spouse, children, family, and friends.

—Tim Sanders, www.sanderssays.typepad.com
(August 25, 2006)

ILLUSTRATION 586

NO SHORTCUTS TO LOVE

Topics: Commitment; Community; Companionship; Friends; Love; Neighbors; Patience; Priorities; Time

References: Matthew 22:39; John 13:34–35; 15:12; Acts 2:42–47; Romans 12:10; 1 Corinthians 10:24; Galatians 6:9; 1 Peter 1:22

While a college student, Heidi Neumark took a year off to serve in a volunteer program sponsored by Rural Mission. She went to Johns Island off the Carolina coast, where she listened to the stories of the sons and daughters of plantation slaves. This is what she learned:

The most important lesson I learned on Johns Island was from Miss Ellie, who lived miles down a small dirt road in a one-room, wooden home. We'd sit in old rocking chairs on the front porch, drinking tall glasses of sweet tea, while she'd tell me stories. I never could find out Miss Ellie's precise age, but it was somewhere between ninety and one hundred. Maybe she didn't know herself. She still chopped her own firewood, stacked in neat little piles behind the house.

Miss Ellie had a friend named Netta, whom she'd known since they were small girls. To get to Netta's house, Miss Ellie had to walk for miles through fields of tall grass. This was the sweet grass that Sea Island women make famous baskets out of, but it was also home to numerous poisonous snakes.

Actually, Netta's home was not that far from Miss Ellie's place, but there was a stream that cut across the fields. You had to walk quite a distance to get to the place where it narrowed enough to pass. Poor Miss Ellie, I thought, old and arthritic, having to walk all that way, pushing through the thick summer heat, not to mention avoiding the snakes.

I hit upon the perfect plan. I arranged with some men to help build a simple plank bridge across the stream near Miss Ellie's house. I scouted out the ideal place—not too wide, but too deep to cross. Our bridge was built in a day. I was so excited that I could hardly wait to see Miss Ellie's reaction. I went to her house and practically dragged her off with me. "Look!" I shouted, "a shortcut for you to visit Netta!"

Miss Ellie did not look grateful. Instead, she shook her head and looked at me with pity. "Child, I don't need a shortcut," she said. Then she told about all the friends she kept up with on her way to visit Netta: Mr. Jenkins, with whom she always swapped gossip; Miss Hunter, who so looked forward to the quilt scraps she'd bring by; the raisin wine she'd taste at one place in exchange for her biscuits; and the chance to look in on the "old folks" who were sick.

"Child, you can't take shortcuts if you want friends in this world," she told me. "Shortcuts don't mix with love."

— Heidi Neumark,
Breathing Space (Beacon, 2003)

ILLUSTRATION 587

HOLD THE APOLOGY

Topics: Accountability; Apology; Conflict; Cursing; Forgiveness; Hypocrisy; Insensitivity; Reconciliation; Remorse; Sincerity; Speech; Tongue; Words

References: Psalm 32:5; Matthew 6:14 – 15; Ephesians 4:32; James 3:1 – 12; 5:12

Insincere apologies may be worse than none. Take note:

"It has come to the editor's attention that the *Herald-Leader* neglected

to cover the civil rights movement. We regret the omission" (July 4, 2004). [*The Herald-Leader* of Lexington, Kentucky, apologizing for the forty-year-old policies of the paper to relegate the coverage of sit-ins, marches, and the like to brief mentions in a column called "Colored Notes."]

"The comment was not meant to be a regional slur. To the extent that it was misinterpreted to be one, I apologize" (October 17, 2003). [Assistant U.S. Attorney Kenneth Taylor, apologizing for referring to potential jurors in the Eastern Kentucky Mountains as "illiterate cave-dwellers."]

"I really, from the very bottom of my heart, want to apologize for statements I made about Christianity. I did it mainly out of frustration. At one time or another, I've offended almost every group. I'm sure I'll be apologizing again" (June 13, 1990). [CNN founder Ted Turner, apologizing for repeatedly calling Christianity "a religion for losers."]

— Paul Slansky and Arleen Sorkin,
My Bad (Bloomsbury USA, 2006);
"Unconvincing Apologies,"
The Week (June 9, 2006)

ILLUSTRATION 588

COSTLY RECONCILIATION

Topics: Acceptance; Attitudes; Communication; Double-mindedness;

Fear; Friendship; Hospitality; Prejudice; Racism; Reconciliation; Unity

References: 1 Samuel 20:42; Luke 10:5–8; Acts 10:24–28; Galatians 3:28; 1 John 2:9–11

It was my third year with the ministry. I got a call from a prominent white Christian leader asking me to go to lunch with him. As we're sitting down to eat, all of a sudden this guy started crying. He explained that God had blessed him—his children were healthy, he was known throughout the country. But, he said, "I've had a hard time sleeping throughout the night." And I was thinking to myself, "Why is he telling me this? I'm not a therapist."

"I just came back from an annual conference on the other side of the country," the man told me. "A bunch of us got together to discuss reconciliation and cross-cultural ministry. Usually, when black leaders come into the meeting, we make them feel right at home and let them be part of the decision-making process. But to be honest with you, the decisions are made before your leaders ever get there. I'm used to hearing the jokes and the use of the *N*-word. But this time, when the jokes were going on and people were saying things, it didn't sound right to me."

"How can I get over this?" the leader asked me, sobbing. "How can we be friends?"

I was silent for a moment then asked him, "Do you like football?" He seemed a little puzzled, but he said yes.

"I do, too," I told him. "I used to coach high school and college ball, and I have a lot of friends who play pro. I love a good game, and I love to cook out. So here's what we do: I need to get to know you, and you need to get to know me. Why don't you come over to my house?" I was the only black in my suburban neighborhood at the time. I said, "Bring your wife and meet my wife, and we'll just sit and talk and get to know each other. I'll barbecue some steaks, and let's start there."

He said, "You want me to come to your house?"

"Yes," I said. "If you want me to sit here and clear your conscience for all the crap you did, I can't do that. Friendship is not cheap. It takes time and commitment." I gave him my home phone number and told him to give me a call.

I never heard from him again.

—Ed Gilbreath, *Reconciliation Blues* (InterVarsity, 2006)

ILLUSTRATION 589

CLOSED FOR DINNER

Topics: Busyness; Community; Evangelism; Fellowship; Food; Friendship; Hospitality; Kindness; Loneliness; Time

References: John 13:35; Acts 2:42–47; Romans 12:13; 16:2–3; Ephesians 2:19–22; 1 Thessalonians 5:11; 1 Timothy 5:10; 1 Peter 4:9; 3 John 1:8

How hospitable are we? The following responses to the question "How often do you entertain guests for dinner?" in a May 2005 survey are telling:

once a week: 6 percent
once a month: 21 percent

more than once a month: 12 percent
a few times a year: 37 percent
rarely or never: 24 percent

—*USA Today* "Snapshots" (June 6, 2006)

social incentives against crime, the main one being shame.

—Steven Levitt and Stephen Dubner, *Freakonomics* (HarperCollins, 2005)

ILLUSTRATION 590

PAYING FOR BAGELS

Topics: Behavior; Cheating; Community; Crime; Dishonesty; Honesty; Morality; Neighbors; Self-control; Shame; Stealing; Values; Vigilance

References: Psalm 44:13; 133:1; Proverbs 26:18–19; Romans 12:17; 14:12; Hebrews 12:14–15

Paul Feldman has a bagel business. He delivers bagels to companies and allows individuals to pay on the honor system. Over the years, Feldman has kept meticulous records, which show that smaller offices are more honest than big ones. An office with a few dozen employees generally outpays (for bagels) by 3 to 5 percent an office with a few hundred employees.

This may seem counterintuitive. In a bigger office a bigger crowd is bound to convene around the bagel table, providing more witnesses to make sure you drop your money in the box. But in the big office/small office comparison, bagel crime seems to mirror street crime. There is far less street crime per capita in rural areas than in cities, in large part because a rural criminal is more likely to be known (and therefore caught). Also, a small community tends to exert greater

ILLUSTRATION 591

THE BEST ARGUERS

Topics: Arguments; Attitudes; Church; Community; Conflict; Cooperation; Fellowship; Marriage; Reconciliation; Spouses; Teamwork

References: Romans 12:9–21; Ephesians 4:1–6; 1 John 3:11–18

The best arguers don't point their fingers. That's according to a study reported in *Psychological Science*. The study also said the person who says "we" the most during an argument suggests the best solutions.

Researchers from the University of Pennsylvania and the University of North Carolina at Chapel Hill studied fifty-nine couples. Spouses who used second-person pronouns (*you*) tended to be negative in interactions. Those using first-person plural pronouns (*we*) provided positive solutions to problems.

The study concluded, "'We' users may have a sense of shared interest that sparks compromise and other ideas pleasing to both partners. 'You'-sayers tend to criticize, disagree, justify, and otherwise teem with negativity."

—Rachel A. Simmons and others, "Pronouns in Marital Interaction: What Do 'You' and 'I' Say about Marital Health?" *Psychological Science*, vol. 16, no. 12 (December 2005)

ILLUSTRATION 592

CHUNNEL CONFLICT

Topics: Church; Conflict; Cooperation; Division; Unity

References: John 17:11; Ephesians 4:4–6; James 1:5–8

The English Channel tunnel connecting England with France, later called the Chunnel, was a two-headed beast from the start. Two mammoth firms were heading the project—one charged with finance and operation, the other responsible for building the chunnel. Each of these companies was also two-headed—equally French and British.

No one was allowed to take charge. Leadership, more times than not, was reduced to the management of conflict. Said a high-ranking executive, "The project ... created a lot of tension because it [was] not geared to solving problems; it [was] geared to placing blame." The English yelled at the French, and the French yelled at the English. Said another executive, "There were nervous breakdowns galore."

The problems were primarily due to a lack of shared standards. The two countries had a different word for everything. The French had their accounting system; so did the English. The French ran on 380 volts; the British on 420. Instruction manuals were bilingual. There were even two different standards used to measure sea level.

"When you have people coming from two different nations," said one of the engineers, "each believes that only their regulations are right."

—Robert Lewis with Rob Wilkins, *The Church of Irresistible Influence* (Zondervan, 2001)

ILLUSTRATION 593

BONO BONDING

Topics: Acceptance; Compassion; Consideration; Cooperation; Friendship; Kindness; Love; Mercy; Politics; Respect

References: Romans 15:7; Colossians 3:13; Titus 3:2; James 3:17–18

As lunch ended in the ornate United States Senate Foreign Relations Committee conference room, Senator Jesse Helms stood to bid farewell to the guest of honor: U2 singer Bono.

Bono stayed at the conservative patriarch's right hand, doing what he could to help. For the photographers, it would have been hard to imagine a stranger image than this delicate dance between the aging senator and the rock superstar.

"You know, I love you," Helms said softly.

The singer gave Helms a hug. This private session with a circle of senators during U2's recent Washington stop wasn't the first time Bono and Helms have discussed poverty, plagues, charity, and faith. Nor will it be the last. Blest be the ties that bind.

"What can I say? It's good to be loved—especially by Jesse Helms," Bono said two days later, as his campaign for Third World debt relief continued on Capitol Hill.

Bono can quote the book of Leviticus as well as the works of John Lennon. While his star power opens doors, it is his sincere, if often unconventional, Christian faith that creates bonds with cultural conservatives in the Vatican and inside the Beltway. Bono has shared prayers and his sunglasses with Pope John Paul II.

—Terry Mattingly, "The Scripture according to Bono," Scripps-Howard News Service (June 20, 2001)

ILLUSTRATION 594

INSPIRED BY TEDDY

Topics: Inspiration; Jesus Christ; Leadership; Presence of God; Vision

References: Matthew 4:19; Mark 1:17; John 6:68–69; 7:46; Acts 9:1–22

"I had never known such a man as he and never shall again," said journalist William Allen White after meeting President Theodore Roosevelt in 1897 for the first time. "He overcame me. And in the hour or two we spent that day at lunch, he poured into my heart such vision, such ideals, such hopes, such a new attitude toward life and patriotism and the meaning of things, as I had never dreamed men had.

"After that, I was his man."

If a mere mortal can have such an effect on another, how much more our Lord? If we will spend time with him in prayer and in Scripture, we too will find our hearts filled with vision, with hopes, with a new attitude toward life and the meaning of things, and afterward we too will say with thankfulness, "I am his."

—Thomas Bailey and David Kennedy, eds., *The American Pageant*, 9th ed. (D. C. Heath, 1991)

ILLUSTRATION 595

APOLOGY FOR A FEE

Topics: Apology; Forgiveness; Reconciliation; Relationships

References: Matthew 5:23–24; 18:15–18; 1 John 1:9–10

"As a society, China lacks the spirit of apologizing," says Zhou Xiaozheng, a sociology professor at People's University in China. That difficulty has given rise to the Tianjin Apology and Gift Center, a company that delivers apologies and attempts to facilitate reconciliation. The company's motto is "We Say Sorry for You."

An apology in China involves a formal procedure and is a very stressful process for all concerned. Hence Zhou isn't sure how long the Tianjin Apology and Gift Center will last. "In our increasingly commercialized society, people have the idea that you can pay money to others to do your work for you, and that includes apologizing," he says. "But if you are sincere, you should go and apologize by yourself."

—Elisabeth Rosenthal, "For a Fee, Chinese Firm Will Beg Pardon for Anyone," *The New York Times* (January 3, 2001)

ILLUSTRATION 596

SENSING LIKE A CHILD

Topics: Attitudes; Childlikeness; Children; Maturity

References: Matthew 18:1–6; Luke 18:16–17

When I look at a patch of dandelions, I see a bunch of weeds that are going to take over my yard. Kids see flowers for Mom and white fluff you can wish on.

When I look at a drunk and he smiles at me, I see a smelly, dirty person who probably wants money. Kids see someone smiling at them, and they smile back.

When I hear music I love, I know I can't carry a tune and don't have much rhythm, so I sit self-consciously and listen. Kids feel the beat and move to it. They sing the words, and if they don't know them, they make up their own.

When I feel wind on my face, I brace myself against it. I feel it messing up my hair and pulling me back when I walk. Kids close their eyes, spread their arms, and fly with the wind until they fall to the ground laughing.

When I pray, I say "thee" and "thou" and "grant me this" and "give me that." Kids say "Hi, God! Thanks for my toys and my friends. Please keep the bad dreams away tonight. Sorry, I don't want to go to heaven yet; I would miss Mommy and Daddy."

When I see a mud puddle, I step around it. I see muddy shoes and clothes and dirty carpets. Kids sit in the puddle. They see dams to build, rivers to cross, and worms to play with.

I wonder if we are given kids to teach or to learn from? No wonder God loves the little children!

—Anonymous

ILLUSTRATION 597

LONE RANGER CREED

Topics: Community; Friendship; Redemption

Reference: Psalm 133:1

The Lone Ranger Creed was once as familiar to boys in America as The Boy Scout Oath. Written by Fran Striker, it was the kind of creed that felt good. The creed said, "I believe that to have a friend, a man must be one."

—Lee Eclov, Lake Forest, Illinois

ILLUSTRATION 598

I KNEW YOU WOULD COME

Topics: Compassion; Devotion; Faithfulness; Friendship; Love; Loyalty

References: Proverbs 17:17; 18:24; 27:10; Romans 12:10

Jim and Phillip did everything together when they were kids. They even went to high school and college together. After college they joined the marines together. They were both sent to Germany, where they fought side by side in one of history's ugliest wars.

During a fierce battle, they were given the command to retreat. As the men were running back, Jim noticed that Phillip hadn't returned with the others. Jim begged his commanding officer to let him go after his friend, but the officer forbade the request, saying it would be suicide.

Jim disobeyed and went after Phillip. His heart pounding, he ran into the gunfire, calling out for Phillip. A short time later, his platoon saw him hobbling across the field carrying a limp body in his arms. The commanding officer shouted at Jim for his outrageous risk. "Your friend is dead," he said. "There was nothing you could do."

"No sir," Jim replied. "I got there just in time. Before Phillip died, he said, 'I knew you would come.'"

—John C. Maxwell and Dan Reiland,
The Treasure of a Friend (J. Countryman, 1999)

ILLUSTRATION 599
SIX DEGREES OF SEPARATION

Topics: Acceptance; Grace; Knowing God; Presence of God

Reference: Isaiah 43:18 – 25

Everyone on the planet can be connected to everyone else on the planet by no more than six steps. So says Pulitzer prize–winning playwright John Guare in his play *Six Degrees of Separation*.

Recently a leading news magazine in Germany, *Die Zeit*, tested this theory. It asked Salah Ben Ghaly, an Iraqi immigrant who owns a local *falafel* stand, to whom he would most like be linked. Ghaly chose Marlon Brando. It took some months, but *Die Zeit* managed to find the connection. A friend of Ghaly who lives in California works in the same company as Ken Carson, boyfriend of Michelle Bevin, sorority sister

to Christina Kutzer, daughter of Patrick Palmer, producer of *Don Juan de Marco*, in which Brando starred.

The idea of six degrees of separation suggests two encouraging things for Christians. First, we can be thankful that knowing God is a personal experience, so there are no degrees of separation between us and God when we are willing to repent and receive his grace. Second, if there is any truth to six degrees of separation, no person on the planet is beyond the range of hearing the gospel.

—Rich Tatum, "Six Degrees of Separation,"
PreachingToday.com

ILLUSTRATION 600
HOOKING UP

Topics: Commitment; Courtship; Dating; Immorality; Relationships; Sex

References: Colossians 3:5 – 9;
2 Timothy 2:22

Dating a male in hopes of finding a lifelong mate has been replaced by "hooking up." Hooking up usually is fueled by alcohol and involves sexual activity. According to a survey done by the Institute for American Values titled "Hooking Up, Hanging Out, and Looking for Mr. Right," 40 percent of the one thousand college women surveyed admitted hooking up with men, and one in ten said she had done so at least six times.

"[The women] wish they could really get to know a guy without necessarily having a sexual relationship," said Elizabeth Marquardt, coauthor of the report. The survey was conducted after the National Marriage Project at Rutgers University released a report in 1999 that concluded that fewer Americans are marrying, and those who do marry are less happy.

—Michael Fletcher, "Campus Romance, Unrequited," *Washington Post* (July 26, 2001)

ILLUSTRATION 601

WHAT HE WANTS OF HER

Topics: Communication; Gender Differences; Love; Marriage; Men; Romance; Women

References: Genesis 2:18–25; Ephesians 5:25–33

Here are ten rules men wish women would follow:

1. If you ask a question you don't really want an answer to, expect an answer you didn't want to hear.
2. Sometimes we're not thinking about you. Live with it.
3. Don't ask us what we're thinking about unless you are prepared to discuss topics such as navel lint, the shotgun formation, and monster trucks.
4. When we have to go somewhere, absolutely anything you wear is fine. Really.
5. Crying is blackmail.
6. Ask for what you want. Let's be clear on this one: Subtle hints don't work. Strong hints don't work. Really obvious hints don't work. Just say it!
7. No, we don't know what day it is. We never will. Mark anniversaries on a calendar you know we check.
8. We're not mind readers, and we never will be. Our lack of mind-reading ability is not proof of how little we care about you.
9. Yes and no are perfectly acceptable answers to almost every question.
10. Come to us with a problem only if you want help solving it. That's what we do. Sympathy is what your girlfriends are for.

—Cheryl Lavin, "Rules Guys Wish Girls Played By," *Chicago Tribune* (April 23, 2000)

PART 24: SALVATION

ILLUSTRATION 602

INTERPRETING SIGNS ON AN SUV

Topics: Change; Choices; Commitment; Conversion; Double-mindedness; Loyalty

References: Matthew 16:24–26; Mark 8:34–38; Luke 9:23–26; Romans 12:1–2; 2 Corinthians 6:14–18; Colossians 3:1–4; James 4:4; 1 John 2:15–17

On the way to work, I noticed some interesting signs on the SUV in front of me. The spare tire mounted on the back had the words "Texas Longhorns" and an orange, steer-head icon on it. The trailer hitch displayed another steer-head icon and the word "Texas." The license plate frame was bordered with the words "Longhorns" on top and "University of Texas" at the bottom.

But something didn't add up. The license plate frame was screwed into a "Land of Lincoln" license plate with a picture of old Abe on it. I live in Illinois, and the SUV's license plate showed that this driver now did too. I assumed the owner of this SUV had moved but had not yet identified with his new home and had no plans of changing loyalties.

When we move, we often go through a slow transition of loyalties to our new home. And so it is as a Christian. When we come to Christ, the kingdom of God becomes our home, but the kingdom of this world does not easily leave our hearts. The great challenge of the Christian is to overcome divided loyalties and fully identify with God's kingdom.

—Craig Brian Larson,
Arlington Heights, Illinois

ILLUSTRATION 603

POLLUTING AIR PURIFIERS

Topics: Conversion; Cross; Grace; Justification; Redemption

References: Matthew 23:1–33; Luke 11:39; Romans 3:21–26; 6:23; 10:1–4; Galatians 2:15–16; 2:21; Ephesians 2:8–9; Philippians 3:8–9

In May 2006, *Journal of the Air and Waste Management Association* published a study conducted by the National Science Foundation revealing that certain ionic air purifiers (those using a process called ozonolysis) actually pollute their environment. Here's how it works. Ionic air purifiers function by charging airborne particles through a process called ionization. Once charged, these particles then stick to metal electrodes. Theoretically, the air is cleaner after passing through the purifier because it has fewer particles. However, the study found that the ionization process itself produces ozone. This gas is helpful when located way up in the atmosphere because it blocks harmful UV rays. However, at the surface of the earth, ozone is better known as smog. Human exposure to high levels of ozone can cause damaged lungs, shortness of breath, throat irritation, and a worsening of asthma.

Study leader Sergey Nizkorodov, a chemistry professor at the University of California, Irvine, said, "People operating air purifiers indoors are more prone to being exposed to ozone levels in excess of public health standards." Indeed, the study revealed that some homes and cars using indoor air purifiers registered ozone levels exceeding 350 parts per billion, which would trigger a Stage 2 Smog Alert if measured outside.

In 2005, the acting chairperson of the California Air Resources Board (ARB) delivered this warning about ionic air purifiers that use ozonolysis: "These machines are insidious. Marketed as a strong defense against indoor air pollution, they emit ozone, the same chemical that the ARB and U.S. Environmental Protection Agency have been trying to eliminate from our air for decades. More chilling is that some people susceptible to the ill effects of ozone will eagerly bring these Trojan horses home."

In the same way, in our efforts to be pure in God's sight, we can make our problems even worse. If we try to make ourselves clean before God by relying on our own goodness rather than on the cross of Jesus Christ, we make ourselves even more unclean in the sight of God.

— Robert Roy Britt, "Isn't It Ionic? Air Purifiers Make Smog," LiveScience.com (May 9, 2006)

ILLUSTRATION 604

MAGDALENE'S TRUE LOVE

Topics: Community; Deliverance; Experiencing God; Freedom; Help from God; New Life; Overcoming; Prostitution; Trials; Unconditional Love; Worth

References: Matthew 21:32; Hebrews 11:31; James 2:25

Her story of addiction is all too typical. Cynthia, of Nashville, Tennessee, was introduced to moonshine at age five and to marijuana at age six. She was raped by a cousin at age eight. Her father died when she was nine. Angry and afraid, Cynthia left home and began living on the streets.

She had a baby when she was thirteen, thinking a baby would give her the love she yearned for. "I didn't have anybody to show me the way," Cynthia says. Things continued to decline as she got into drugs. She had two more children while bouncing in and out of drug treatment programs. At one point she weighed only sixty-four pounds. When she finally hit rock bottom, she asked God to either take her life or send her to jail.

She went to jail. In prison she prayed fervently for a month before she finally found a sense of God. After prison, Cynthia went to Magdalene, a two-year residential community for women with a criminal history of prostitution and drug abuse, which was founded in 1997 by Rev. Becca Stevens. For the first time in her life, Cynthia knew the love of Christ in a caring community. "From that day forward, I was blessed," she says. "These people didn't know me, and yet the love was so unconditional."

In April 2006, Cynthia celebrated her nineteenth month of being clean from drug addiction. She is the store manager for Thistle Farms, Magdalene's cottage business that sells bath and beauty products.

According to Rev. Stevens, women like Cynthia often get into trouble because of a combination of family failures, community breakdowns, and poor choices. Drugs become a way to escape the pain, and prostitution the means to acquire the drugs. Even so, Stevens is quick to emphasize that nobody's situation is hopeless. "There's a myth that once you are a prostitute, you're never going to get better," she says. "It's not true."

— Jane Lampman, "Where Women Build New Lives," *Christian Science Monitor* (April 13, 2006)

ILLUSTRATION 605

PROSTITUTES AND THE PROUD

Topics: Complacency; Emptiness; Human Condition; Pride; Prosperity; Self-centeredness

References: Joshua 6:17 – 23; Matthew 19:24; 21:32

"I tell you the truth, the tax collectors and the prostitutes are entering the kingdom of God ahead of you," Jesus announced to the religious authorities of his day.

After puzzling over that statement, C. S. Lewis concluded, "Prostitutes are in no danger of

finding their present life so satisfactory that they cannot turn to God. The proud, the avaricious, the self-righteous, are in that danger."

— Philip Yancey, "Back from the Brothel," *Christianity Today* (January 2005)

ILLUSTRATION 606

SHRINKING IN GOD'S LIGHT

Topics: Acceptance; Arrogance; Body of Christ; Cooperation; Envy; Neighbors; Pride; Relationships; Self-righteousness; Unity

References: Romans 12:5; 1 Corinthians 8:9 – 13; James 2:1 – 4

When we see ourselves as "pretty good," we misunderstand the gravity of sin and our desperate need for grace. We place ourselves above others, become their judges, and give them the power to disappoint us.

A physicist friend uses this analogy: Each of us is like a lightbulb. One shines with fifty watts of holiness, another has only twenty-five watts. Maybe the most stellar Christians are two hundred watts. But these comparisons become trite in the presence of the sun.

In the face of God, our different levels of piety are puny and meaningless. It makes no sense to compare ourselves with one another, because we are all much more alike than we are different.

— Mark McMinn, *Why Sin Matters* (Tyndale, 2004)

ILLUSTRATION 607

WANTING TO BE WANTED

Topics: Fathers; Identity; Lying; Providence; Restoration; Satan; Worth

References: Proverbs 19:5; Luke 15:20–24; John 10:10–15

In 1996, a thirty-eight-year-old security guard at a Pennsylvania middle school convinced Tanya Kach, fourteen, to leave her father and live with him. For the next ten years, the security guard kept Tanya captive in the home he shared with his elderly parents.

To keep Tanya from running away, her captor convinced the girl that no one cared that she was gone and that her parents weren't even looking for her. He told her, "You're stupid. You're immature. Nobody cares about you but me."

Eventually the security guard became so confident in Tanya's loyalty to him that he allowed her to leave the house for short periods of time while he was at work. Through these daily excursions, Tanya became friends with Joseph Sparico, the owner of a local Deli Mart.

In March 2006, Tanya finally confessed her true identity to Sparico, who shared the information with his son, a retired police officer. Before long, Tanya was rescued and reunited with her father. Commenting on the girl's situation, Sparico said, "She wanted to be wanted, that's all."

Tanya's father, Jerry, who had desperately tried to find his daughter through the years, posting her picture several thousand times on flyers and milk cartons, was overjoyed to see her. "There wasn't a day that went by that I didn't think of her," he said. "I just say thank you, there is a God—and he brought my little girl back home."

Tanya, too, was delighted to learn that her father had never given up looking for her. "He's crying; I'm crying. All he kept saying was, 'I got my baby,'" she said, describing their reunion. "I'm touching blood, and I get to say, 'I love you, Dad.'"

—Daniel Lovering, "Woman Missing Since She Was 14 Is Found," news.yahoo.com (March 23, 2006)

ILLUSTRATION 608

TAKING CARE OF DINNER

Topics: Atonement; Cross; Depravity; Grace; Jesus Christ; Justification; Redemption

References: John 3:16; 19:30; Romans 3:21–26; Ephesians 2:13

Author James Herriot tells of an unforgettable wedding anniversary he and his wife celebrated early in their marriage. His boss had encouraged Herriot to take his wife to a fancy restaurant, but Herriot balked. He was a young veterinarian and couldn't really afford it. "Oh, do it!" the boss insisted. "It's a special day!" Herriot reluctantly agreed and surprised his wife with the news.

En route to the restaurant, Herriot and his wife stopped at a farm to examine a farmer's horse. Having finished the routine exam, the young vet returned to his car and drove to the restaurant, unaware that his checkbook had fallen in the mud. After a wonderful meal, Herriot reached for his checkbook and discovered it was gone. Quite embarrassed, he tried to offer a way of making it up.

"Not to worry," the waiter replied. "Your dinner has been taken care of!" Herriot's employer had paid for the dinner in advance.

God has done the same for us. Jesus' word on the cross, "It is finished," is a Greek term meaning "paid in full."

— Greg Asimakoupoulos,
Mercer Island, Washington

ILLUSTRATION 609

LEAVING GIFTS UNCLAIMED

Topics: Accepting Christ; Apathy; Assurance; Complacency; Eternal Life; Grace; Neglect; Righteousness

References: John 3:16; 14:6; Romans 6:23; Ephesians 2:8 – 9; Hebrews 2:3; 12:25; Revelation 22:17

One of five gift-card recipients never used their cards in 2005, representing about $972 million in unredeemed cards. According to Consumer Reports National Research Center, the top reasons for not using gift cards:

- didn't have time: 50 percent
- didn't find anything they wanted: 37 percent
- lost the card: 14 percent
- card expired: 12 percent

— Jae Yang and Adrienne Lewis,
"Americans Neglect a Billion in Gift Cards,"
USA Today (November 20, 2006)

ILLUSTRATION 610

GOING PUBLIC WITH SIN

Topics: Bondage; Confession; Culture; Depravity; Guilt; Human Condition; Regret; Shame; Sin; Vices

References: 2 Chronicles 7:14; Ezra 10:1 – 16; Proverbs 28:13; Matthew 7:6; James 5:16; 1 John 1:9

In 2006, two performing artists named Laura Barnett and Sandra Spannan created an exhibit in a storefront in Manhattan that allowed passersby to alleviate their guilt.

The two women dressed as nineteenth-century washerwomen and sat in the storefront. One underlined the words on the glass — "Air your dirty laundry. 100 percent confidential. Anonymous. Free." Onlookers were encouraged to write their deepest secrets on pieces of paper. The washerwomen then collected the confessions and displayed them in the window for all to see.

The sins and secrets ranged from slightly humorous to sordid:

- "The hermit crab was still alive when I threw it down the trash shoot [sic]."
- "I want to see SUVs explode. Those people are so selfish."
- "My girlfriend and I both think Osama Bin Laden has a sweet-looking face."
- "I make fun of this one friend behind her back all the time. She just enrages me! But I get freaked out when I think of what she might say about me. I worry this means we're not really friends. Human relationships are infinitely confusing!"

- "I haven't slept with my husband in a year, and I am about to start an affair with — —."
- "I haven't yet visited my dead parents' grave."
- "I am dating a married man and getting financial compensation in exchange for the guilt. I'm twenty-five, and he's a millionaire. It pays to be young."
- "New York makes me feel lonely."

Barnett said the onlookers are often overwhelmed by the weight of others' sins: "We go there, and the window is empty, and we're wearing all white. At the end, the window is full. It's exhausting. Some of those things are really, really sad. And afterward I need to take a bath."

—Kathryn Shattuck, "Artists Display
Confessions of Passersby on a 44th Street
Storefront," *The New York Times* (May 6, 2006)

ILLUSTRATION 611

SPIRITUALLY DIRECTING THE PRESIDENT

Topics: Commitment; Conversion; Discipleship; Encouragement; Evangelism; Friendship; Influence; Mentoring; Ministry; Purpose; Spiritual Direction; Spiritual Growth

References: John 15:15; Proverbs 17:17; 18:24

Gerald R. Ford found Christ with the help of a Hollywood director. When Ford was a young congressman in Michigan, Billy Zeoli, a gospel film executive, stopped by Ford's office and gave him a Bible. Over the next few years, the two men became so close that Ford called Zeoli "an alter ego, a second self."

They both loved sports. Ford had been an All-American football player, and Zeoli created a ministry for professional athletes. Zeoli was holding a service for the Dallas Cowboys at a Washington-area Marriott hotel. Ford went to hear his friend preach on "God's game plan." Ford was especially moved by the sermon and hung around to talk with Zeoli about Christ and forgiveness and what it meant. The inquiry felt real and raw; but was that the moment Ford committed himself to Christ? "It's hard to say when a man does that," Zeoli says plainly. "That's a God thing. But I think that day is the day he looked back to as an extremely important day of knowing Christ."

When Ford became vice president in the fall of 1973, Zeoli began sending him a weekly devotional memo titled *God's Got a Better Idea*. Ford referred to those memos as "profound in their meaning and judicious in their selection." Beyond the memos, Ford and Zeoli would meet privately every four or five weeks for prayer and Bible study.

—Nancy Gibbs and Michael Duffy,
"The Other Born-Again President,"
Time (January 15, 2007)

ILLUSTRATION 612

REFUSING BULLET-POINT FAITH

Topics: Beliefs; Choices; Curiosity; Decisions; Faith; Longing; Questions; Seekers; Witnessing

References: Matthew 16:24–28; Luke 9:23–26; Hebrews 4:12

A man once appeared at my office door asking for some quick points on Christianity to help make sense of the dinner conversations he was having with his wife, a recent convert. He made it clear that he was very busy and very successful and didn't really have time to study her beliefs—just bullet points, if you please.

It would have been easy to hand him a book or pamphlet. But instead, I said, "I can see you are a very busy and very successful person, so I don't think this is a good idea."

"Why?" he asked, frustrated.

"Because if I were to give you the bullet points and you were to really understand them, they might work in you so significantly that your life could really get messed-up. You would have to rethink the meaning of success, of time, of family—of everything, really. I don't think you really want to do that, do you?"

It was an effort to raise his thirst, not to give him answers. In his case, it worked.

—Mark Labberton, "Pastor of Desperation," *Leadership* (Winter 2006)

ILLUSTRATION 613

DANCING WITH DANGER

Topics: Assurance; Danger; Fear; Hell; Protection; Safety; Security in God; Seen and Unseen; Trust

References: Ezra 9:8–9; Psalm 91; 118; Luke 4:9–11

The construction of the Golden Gate Bridge was so risky that newspaper reporters dubbed it "Dance of Danger." Workers on top of swaying catwalks and high towers, sometimes hundreds of feet in the air, would be blown by powerful winds. Predictions were that for every $1 million spent, one life would be lost.

Engineers on the Golden Gate Bridge, however, believed the risks could be lowered. When construction began in 1932, numerous safety measures were put into place and strictly enforced: mandatory use of hard hats and prescription filtered eyeglasses, implementation of a no showboating policy (cause for automatic firing), use of tie-off lines, and establishment of an on-site hospital greatly reduced the casualty rate. After nearly four years of construction and $20 million spent, only one worker had died.

The most effective safety device, without question, was the use of a trapeze net. This large net, costing $130,000, was draped sixty feet below the roadbed under construction, extending ten feet to either side. This net caught so many falling workers that the newspapers began running box scores on the total number of lives saved. Workers saved by the net were said to have joined the "Halfway to Hell Club."

Beyond that, the net freed many of the workers from an often-paralyzing sense of fear, which helped them work more productively.

—Robert Lewis with Rob Wilkins,
The Church of Irresistible Influence
(Zondervan, 2001)

ILLUSTRATION 614

REDEEMING FORGIVENESS

Topics: Forgiveness; Opportunity; Salvation

References: 1 Corinthians 6:2; Hebrews 3:7 – 8

Gift cards often come with expiration dates. Sometimes I will stuff one in my wallet and forget about it. A gift card can be worth $100 one day, and then the next day you might as well throw it in the garbage because it has expired. You have missed the opportunity to spend it!

God's gift of forgiveness is like a gift card that is more valuable than anything we can imagine. He paid for it with his Son's life. God is holding that priceless gift card out to us, waiting for us to take it. If we don't accept it and use it, however, it's of no value to us.

A gift card is only plastic unless it is redeemed. Don't wait to claim God's gift before it's too late.

—Mike Silva, *Would You Like Fries With That?* (Word, 2005)

ILLUSTRATION 615

SANKEY AND THE SNIPER

Topics: Deliverance; Enemies; Hymns; Jesus Christ; Mercy; Protection

References: Psalm 20:1; Proverbs 18:10

Ira Sankey was traveling on a steamer in the Delaware River when he was recognized by some passengers who had seen his picture in the newspaper and knew he was associated with evangelist D. L. Moody. When they asked him to sing one of his own compositions, Sankey said he preferred the hymn by William Bradbury, "Savior, Like a Shepherd Lead Us."

He suggested that everyone join in the singing. One of the stanzas begins, "We are thine, do thou befriend us; be the guardian of our way."

When he finished, a man stepped out of the shadows and asked, "Were you in the army, Mr. Sankey?"

"Yes, I joined up in 1860."

"Did you do guard duty at night in Maryland, about 1862?"

"Yes, I did."

"I was in the Confederate Army," said the stranger. "I saw you one night at Sharpsburg. I had you in my gun sight as you stood in the light of the full moon. Then just as I was about to pull the trigger, you began to sing. It was the same hymn you sang tonight. I couldn't shoot you."

—Kenneth R. Hendren, "In the Gun Sights,
Men of Integrity (April 17, 2001)

ILLUSTRATION 616

SHOCKED INTO BELIEF

Topics: Conversion; Evil; God's Holiness; Hatred; Humanism; Racism; Sin

References: Proverbs 14:12; Romans 3:9–26

Many Germans who had immigrated to the United States were sitting in a theater when the movie *Psyche* was shown. The propaganda movie, produced by Hitler's Third Reich in 1940, followed the invasion and Blitzkrieg through Poland. Whenever a Polish person appeared on the screen, people in the audience would scream, "Kill him! Kill him!" in a frenzied commitment to the destruction of Germany's enemies.

W. H. Auden, the Pulitzer prize–winning poet, playwright, and literary critic, was so shocked that he walked out of the theater. He later said one question ran through his mind: "What response can my enlightened, humanistic tradition give to this evil, to those who cry out for the blood of innocent victims?" He began to sense that the only answer to evil was not in humanism, but in God and the revelation of God in the Bible.

He was convicted of God's holiness and his own sinfulness. In 1940 he became a Christian.

—John Yenchko, "Hell," *Journal of Biblical Counseling* (Fall 2000)

ILLUSTRATION 617

HEALING HARD FEELINGS

Topics: Forgiveness; God's Love; Reconciliation; Sacrifice

References: Romans 5:9–11; 2 Corinthians 5:14–21

In January 2001, Seiko Sakamoto, a Japanese plasterer in a Tokyo subway station, fell into the path of an oncoming train. Lee Su Hyun, a Korean student in Japan, leaped down on the tracks to save Sakamoto. Both Hyun and Sakamoto were killed.

This selfless act by the Korean student on behalf of the Japanese laborer has caused many people in Japan to reconsider their long-held prejudices against Koreans. Strong feelings of distrust between the two countries go back to World War II atrocities that the Japanese inflicted on Koreans. Many Japanese people, including the prime minister of Japan, have openly expressed sorrow over their stereotypes of Koreans and have begun to talk about reconciliation.

Nobuaki Fujioka, sixty-two, of Japan, says, "I felt a kind of shame. A young foreigner sacrificed his life for a Japanese. This is not an easy thing to do."

By giving his one and only Son, God took the initiative in healing our broken relationship with him. He made the supreme sacrifice for us that we might be reconciled to him.

—Shigehiko Togo and Doug Struck, "Japan Searches Its Soul to Fathom Fatal Gesture," *Washington Post*, January 30, 2001

ILLUSTRATION 618

A PILOT'S SACRIFICE

Topics: Cross; Jesus Christ; Sacrifice; Salvation

References: John 15:13; Philippians 2:5–8

I was leading a beach mission with children on the sands of Scarborough, North Yorkshire, when a Royal Air Force Lightning jet flew by, skimming the surface of the sea before it turned and flew inland. A minute or two later it returned and went into a steep incline over Scarborough Castle. I thought the pilot was doing a stunt. Then, to our horror, the plane flipped and dropped to the sea. It crashed less than two hundred yards away from the beach. The pilot was killed.

The next day the newspaper headline on the crash was "Pilot Gives Life to Save Crowds." The story reported how, when his plane began to fail, the pilot chose not to eject himself and risk having the plane crash onto the crowded beach but instead steered it away from the crowds.

When the pilot climbed into the plane that day, he had no idea that he would sacrifice his life to save us. By contrast, the Lord Jesus deliberately left heaven and came to earth with the express intention of going to a death to "save the crowds."

—Roger Carswell,
How Small a Whisper (Kregel, 2000)

ILLUSTRATION 619

GUILTY BUT FREE

Topics: Confession; Forgiveness; Freedom; Grace; Guilt

References: Romans 10:9–10; 1 John 1:9

"Guilty Plea Sets Inmate Free" was the headline of a story in the *Chicago Tribune* about a man who was imprisoned eight years before cutting a deal with the state's attorney so that the time he served satisfied his sentence.

What struck me was that headline. My first reaction was, "Another criminal gets off with a plea bargain." Then I realized that I, too, was guilty and set free.

Freedom is not in a plea of innocence but in the admission of guilt. My story is different, but the headline "Guilty Plea Sets Inmate Free" fits perfectly.

—Lee Eclov, Lake Forest, Illinois

ILLUSTRATION 620

IT'S WHO YOU KNOW

Topics: Dependence; Help from God; Intercession; Jesus Christ; Prayer; Relationships; Trials

References: Ephesians 3:20; Philippians 4:6; 2 Timothy 4:17; 1 Peter 5:7

A motorcade carrying the security service chief of Gaza came under bullet fire from Israeli troops in the midst of the Israeli-Arab conflict in April 2001. The frightened security official called Yasser Arafat from his car for help.

Arafat, in turn, called the U.S. ambassador, who then called the U.S. secretary of state, Colin Powell. Colin Powell phoned Ariel Sharon, the Israeli prime minister, who ordered the shooting to stop. And it did. The security chief's connections eventually saved his life.

In a similar way, Christians have a divine connection to the ultimate power of the universe that can make a world of difference in any situation.

—Kevin Short, "Connections in High Places,"
PreachingToday.com

ILLUSTRATION 621

LOVING CANNIBALS TO CHRIST

Topics: Enemies; Forgiveness; Love; Mercy

References: Matthew 5:38–48; Luke 23:34

Missionaries brought the gospel to cannibals in Africa in the nineteenth century. Some missionaries, such as Bishop Hamilton, were eaten.

His two sons went to Uganda to replace him. Eventually they baptized and gave Communion to men who had digested their own father's flesh. The new Christians told the sons that the bishop,

while being led to his death, repeated unceasingly Jesus' words "Love your enemies."

—Richard Wurmbrand, *In the Face of Surrender* (Bridge-Logos, 1998)

ILLUSTRATION 622

LANDING TOO LATE

Topics: Last Things; Peace with God; Watchfulness

Reference: Matthew 25:1–13

On July 25, 2000, Air France Concorde flight 4590 crashed on takeoff in Paris. A hundred passengers were killed along with nine crew and four people on the ground as the Concorde banked, stalled, and then plunged to the ground, exploding on impact.

The cause of the crash was a sixteen-inch strip of metal on the runway. The metal burst the aircraft's tire, and debris from the blowout ruptured a fuel tank in the aircraft's wing. With the plane on fire, the pilot could not halt the takeoff, though he planned to make an emergency landing at a nearby airport. His last words as he fought to save his stricken craft were "too late."

We only have one life to live. If we fail to make our peace with God before life ends, it will also be too late for us.

—Owen Bourgaize,
Guernsey, United Kingdom

ILLUSTRATION 623

THE GOOD NEWS OF SIN

Topics: Human Condition;
Reconciliation; Repentance; Sin

Reference: James 5:16

Sin is the best news there is, because with sin, there's a way out. You can't repent of confusion or psychological flaws inflicted by your parents—you're stuck with them. But you can repent of sin. Sin and repentance are the only grounds for hope and joy, the grounds for reconciled, joyful relationships.

—John Alexander, *The Other Side*,
quoted in *Leadership* (Summer 2000)

ILLUSTRATION 624

LOVING TRACY TO CHRIST

Topics: Conversion; Example;
Kindness; Love; Mercy; Patience;
Self-control

References: Matthew 5:14–16;
1 John 4:7–11

Gavin and I were helping my pastor guide thirty lively teens through an all-night "lock-in" at church. Early in the evening, Gavin challenged me to a game of table tennis in the fellowship hall. Our game quickly heated up.

With the score tied and only three points to go before the end of the game, Tracy, an eighth-grader, grabbed the ball and kept it from us. My first impulse was irritation. But then a Scripture passage that our group had read that afternoon came to mind: "Love is patient, love is kind. It does not envy, it does not boast, it is not proud. It is not rude, it is not self-seeking, it is not easily angered, it keeps no record of wrongs."

Gavin and I joked with Tracy until she finally tossed the ball back onto the table. We thanked her and finished the game.

Hours later, after an evangelistic film, Tracy walked down the aisle with six others to receive Christ as Savior. Later that night, when we gathered for testimonies, Tracy said, "I grew up in a family where nobody goes to church. I've learned to get attention by making people mad at me. But earlier this evening I saw something different."

Gavin and I looked at each other and raised our eyebrows. "When I stole the ball from those guys," she said, pointing at us, "they didn't get mad at me. They didn't fight back. I decided right then that I wanted whatever it was they have."

—Clark Cothern, "I Saw Something Different
in Those Guys," *Decision* (May 2000)

ILLUSTRATION 625

TERMINATOR HITS HOME

Topics: Conversion; God as Father;
Salvation; Unconditional Love

Reference: John 3:16

David Mains, director of Chapel Ministries, was sitting in a dental chair when his orthodontist asked David if he would go with him to see a movie. "I've seen this film five times already," said the orthodontist, "and each time I break down and weep at the same part of the story. I'm hoping you can help me understand why that scene in the movie makes me cry."

"Sure," David said. "What movie is it?"

His orthodontist replied, *Terminator 2,* with Arnold."

When David sat with his friend through the movie, the orthodontist broke down as before during the scene where the Terminator gives his life to save a child.

Over coffee after the film, the two men talked. The orthodontist hinted at an inner longing for a father's love. David identified the symbol of sacrificial love, so poignantly displayed in the movie, as a picture of God's love. "I believe that's what you are looking for," David said.

The orthodontist agreed. Together they bowed in prayer, and the orthodontist received the forgiveness and love of his heavenly Father.

—Greg Asimakoupoulos,
Mercer Island, Washington

ILLUSTRATION 626
SURVIVING THE SAHARA

Topics: Desires; Discontent; Longing; Satisfaction; Thirst

References: Psalm 42:1; John 4:6–29

Lag Lag and a companion were crossing the desert when their truck broke down. As their bodies dehydrated, they became willing to drink anything to quench their terrible thirst. The sun forced them into the shade under the truck, where they dug a shallow trench. Day after day

they lay there. They had food but did not eat, fearing it would magnify their thirst.

Dehydration, not starvation, kills wanderers in the desert, and thirst is the most terrible of all human sufferings. Lag Lag progressed from *eudipsia,* "ordinary thirst," through bouts of *hyperdipsia,* meaning "temporary intense thirst," to *polydipsia,* "sustained excessive thirst," which is the kind of thirst that drives one to drink anything, including urine and blood.

Radiator water is what Lag Lag and his assistant started drinking during the polydipsia phase. To survive, they were willing to drink poison.

Many people do something similar in the spiritual realm. They depend on things like money, sex, and power to quench spiritual thirst. But such thirst quenchers are in reality spiritual poison, a dangerous substitute for the "living water" Jesus promised.

—William Langewiesche,
Sahara Unveiled (Vintage, 1997)

ILLUSTRATION 627
SERENDIPITY GRACE

Topics: Body of Christ; Community; Ministry; Salvation; Service; Stewardship

References: Matthew 7:12; 22:39; Luke 6:38; 10:27; 1 Corinthians 12:12–26; 2 Corinthians 8:14; 9:12–15; Galatians 6:7–8

In 1999, Kevin Stephan of Lancaster, New York, was a batboy for his younger brother's Little League baseball team. During one game, a player who was warming up accidentally hit Kevin in the chest with a bat. Kevin fell to the ground, unconscious. His heart stopped beating.

"All I remember is that, all of a sudden, I got hit in the chest with something, and I turned around and passed out," Kevin says. Penny Brown, a nurse whose son played on the team, was able to revive Kevin.

Seven years later, Penny Brown was eating at the Hillview Restaurant in Depew, New York, when she began to choke on her food. "The food wasn't going anywhere, and I totally couldn't breathe," said Penny. "It was very frightening."

Patrons screamed for help. One of the restaurant employees — a volunteer firefighter — ran out from the back. He wrapped his arms around the victim, applied the Heimlich maneuver, and saved the woman's life. The firefighter was Kevin Stephan, the boy whom Penny had saved seven years earlier.

—Aaron Saykin, "Teen Saves Life of Woman Who Once Saved His," wusatv9.com (February 4, 2006)

ILLUSTRATION 628

PASSING THE LIFELINE

Topics: Cross; Jesus Christ; Love; Purpose; Sacrifice; Unselfishness

Reference: Philippians 2:5–11

On January 13, 1982, Air Florida Flight 90 crashed into the Potomac. Ice on the wings prevented the plane from having a successful take-off. Almost all of the passengers perished. The few that survived struggled in the icy river as rescuers tried to reach them.

Five times a helicopter dropped a rope to save Arland D. Williams Jr. Five times Williams passed the rope to other passengers in worse shape than he was. When the rope was extended to Williams the sixth time, he was too weak to take hold and succumbed to the frigid waters.

His heroism was not rash. Aware that his own strength was fading, he deliberately handed hope to someone else over the space of several minutes. The bridge near where he died has now been named the Arland D. Williams Jr. Memorial Bridge.

Jesus did not rashly give his life for us either. Being a sacrifice for us was his destiny from eternity past. We need only take the lifeline handed to us to be saved by his sacrificial death on the cross.

—David A. Slagle, "Giving Hope and Life Away," PreachingToday.com

ILLUSTRATION 629

REWRITING THE BOOK

Topics: Challenges; Despair; Goals; Hope; Loss; Perseverance; Persistence; Perspective

Reference: Matthew 6:11

Thomas Carlyle had just spent two years writing a book on the French Revolution. He gave his only copy to a colleague, John Stuart Mill, to read and critique. Then the unthinkable occurred: Mill's servant used Carlyle's manuscript as kindling to start a fire.

As Mill reported the devastating news, Carlyle's face paled. Two years of his life were lost. Thousands of long, lonely hours spent in writing had been wasted. He could not imagine writing the book again. He lapsed into a deep depression.

Then one day while walking the city streets, Carlyle noticed a stone wall under construction. He was transfixed. That tall sweeping wall was being raised one brick at a time. He realized that if he wrote one page at a time, one day at a time, he could write his book again. That is exactly what he did.

When faced with seemingly impossible situations, we often see the wall and not the individual bricks, but taken day by day, task by task, the load is more manageable. Jesus prayed for daily bread. He didn't worry about tomorrow, next week, or next year. God's help comes day by day.

— Rick Christian, *Alive* (Zondervan, 1995)

PART 25: SIGNS AND WONDERS

ILLUSTRATION 630

I BELIEVE

Topics: Healing; Holy Spirit; Miracles; Prayer; Supernatural Occurrences

References: Matthew 19:26; Acts 2:22

We believe in miracles. That's what a recent poll by *Newsweek* revealed. Here are the percentages:

- Americans who believe in divine miracles: 84 percent
- those who believe in the reality of miracles described in the Bible: 79 percent
- those who have personal experiences with miracles: 48 percent
- those who know of people who have experienced miracles: 63 percent
- those who have prayed for a miracle: 67 percent
- those who believe God or the saints heal sick people who have been given no chance of survival by medical doctors: 77 percent

— "Newsweek Poll: Most Americans Believe in Miracles," *Newsweek* (May 1, 2000)

ILLUSTRATION 631

THE EARS HAVE IT

Topics: Hearing God; Listening; Signs; Spiritual Perception

Reference: 1 Kings 19:9–13; Matthew 20:1–16

When the telegraph was the fastest means of long-distance communication, a young man applied for a job as a Morse code operator. Answering an ad in the newspaper, he went to the address that was listed. When he arrived, he entered a large, noisy office. In the background a telegraph clacked away. A sign on the receptionist's counter instructed job applicants to fill out a form and wait until they were summoned to enter the inner office.

The young man completed his form and sat down with seven other applicants. After a few minutes, the young man stood up, crossed the room to the door of the inner office, and walked right in. The other applicants perked up, wondering what was going on. Why had this man been so bold? They muttered among themselves that they hadn't heard any summons yet. They took more than a little satisfaction in assuming the young man who went into the office would be reprimanded for his presumption and summarily disqualified for the job.

Within a few minutes the young man emerged from the inner office escorted by the interviewer, who announced to the other applicants, "Gentlemen, thank you very much for coming, but the job has been filled by this young man."

The other applicants began grumbling. Then one spoke up saying, "Wait a minute—I don't understand something. He was the last one to come in, and we never even got a chance to be interviewed. Yet he got the job. That's not fair."

The employer said, "I'm sorry, but all the time you've been sitting here, the telegraph has been ticking out the following message in Morse code: 'If you understand this message, then come right in. The job is yours.' None of you heard it or understood it. This young man did. So the job is his."

God uses many means to demonstrate his care—not only through his Word, his Spirit, and the ministry of Christian friends, but also through more unconventional methods—like burning bushes, talking donkeys, hungry creatures of the sea, visiting angels, or a bright star in the darkened sky. We need only to be alert to these signs.

—Gary Preston, *Character Forged from Conflict* (Bethany, 1999)

ILLUSTRATION 632

SHIELDED FROM HARM

Topics: Appearances; Faith; Light; Perception and Reality; Spiritual Perception; Trust; Watchfulness

References: Numbers 12:8; Isaiah 48:6; Matthew 5:14; Mark 4:22; Luke 9:45

A copper object can be protected from microwave radiation by using a special "cloaking device." That's what researchers discovered in the fall of 2006. The cloaking device used special materials to divert the microwaves around the copper can, like water flowing around a smooth stone. As a result, what could previously be "seen" by microwave detectors became "unseen." Designer David Schurig compared the breakthrough to a mirage in the desert, where heat causes the bending of light rays and cloaks the road ahead behind an image of the sky. "We have built an artificial mirage that can hide something from would-be observers in any direction," Schurig said.

So far Schurig's device does not work with visible light, meaning that it does not affect the way human eyes perceive what is here or not here. But the first step has been taken on a scientific quest that may one day change the way we see the world around us.

—Randolph E. Schmid, "Scientists Create Cloak of Invisibility," ABCNews.com (October 19, 2006)

ILLUSTRATION 633

SAVED FROM SUICIDE

Topics: Addiction; Conversion; Gambling; Grace; Holy Spirit; Mercy; New Life; Outreach; Salvation; Suicide

References: Psalm 30; 2 Corinthians 5:17–20

I sat in my car in front of the Delaware Memorial Bridge. I had just driven back from a three-day gambling binge in Atlantic City, where I had lost more than $5,000. I had maxed out my credit cards trying to recoup my losses that now surpassed $300,000.

My past flashed before me as I tried to get up enough nerve to jump five hundred feet into the Delaware River. *I was a decent sort until my marriage broke up and I began womanizing, drinking, and betting on anything anywhere,* I thought.

I am a retired chief master sergeant of the Air Force. I had previously won numerous awards, including Citizen of the Year in Delaware and Sergeant of the Year in the Air Force, and I had shared the National Freedom Foundation's highest award. My works of patriotism were entered into the *Congressional Record* of the U.S. Senate. Back then I had a purpose in life. Now I was an addicted sleaze.

I took a swig of the drink I had carried out of the Resorts Hotel and Casino, opened the door, and walked toward the bridge. A state trooper came by and yelled, "Car trouble?"

"No, sir, just getting some air," I said.

I climbed back in my blue Sprint and drove home, where I spent a lot of lonely hours contemplating my failures. It was 4:00 a.m. on a Sunday. I drank more booze to help me sleep.

About 3:00 p.m., the phone woke me up. It was Jim, an old friend who always wanted me to go to church with him. He said, "I prayed for you this morning, Joe," and invited me to go with him that night to hear a guest speaker. I said OK, figuring he would buy me a hamburger after church.

At the Pentecostal church, the visiting speaker gave an eloquent sermon and then invited individuals who were hurting to come forward.

A long line of people came to the platform. The pastor stood in front of each. Several fell backward. "Those people are being slain in the power of the Holy Spirit," my friend explained. "Let's go up." I waited until there were only a few people left. When I got close to the pastor, he asked, "What can God do for you, my son?"

I blurted out something about my asthma. He raised his hand, closed his eyes, and began to pray. I felt peace come over me. The next instant I was lying in Jim's arms. *Did he push me down?* I wondered as I glanced around and saw I was the only one left on the platform.

"How long have I been lying here?" I asked.

"About eight minutes," Jim said as he helped me to my feet.

From that day on, I began to walk in Christ. Today I think of how wonderfully God works. If my friend hadn't called, if I hadn't been hungry for a hamburger, if the visiting pastor had not grabbed my interest, I might have ended my life jumping off a bridge.

—Joseph J. Pfister, "The Comeback," *Pentecostal Evangel* (October 15, 2000)

ILLUSTRATION 634

OLAF'S CONVERSION

Topics: Conversion; Great Commission; Ministry; Power; Prophecy

Reference: Matthew 28:18–20

Olaf Trygvesson of Norway was the Viking's Viking. He was unmatched in climbing and swimming and leaping and could juggle five daggers in the air, always catching them by the handle. Early in life he conducted successful raids on Holland and France.

Then he turned to England, the greatest prize. After burning villages, laying waste the land, putting numbers of people to death by fire and sword without regard to gender, and sweeping off an immense booty, Olaf was offered 22,000 pounds of silver to cease.

While the deal was being made, Olaf heard of a hermit who had the gift of prophecy. So he went to the hermit's retreat and asked about his future.

"Thou wilt become a renowned king and do celebrated deeds," the hermit said. He predicted that Olaf's men would mutiny, and in the ensuing fight, Olaf would be wounded. After seven days, he would recover and would allow himself to be baptized as a Christian. "Many men wilt thou bring to faith and baptism," the prophet said, "both to thine own and others' good."

The mutiny and Olaf's wounding took place precisely as the hermit had predicted. After his recovery, the Viking went back to the seer and asked him how he had gained such wisdom. "The God of the Christians has blessed me so that I can know all that I desire," the hermit said. At that, Olaf submitted to baptism.

Olaf vowed never again to visit war upon England, and he returned to Norway to begin converting his people. We can't exactly say everyone lived happily ever after, but over the next two centuries, Norway became not only an increasingly unified country but a Christian nation as well. It remained such for nearly a thousand years.

—James Reston, *The Last Apocalypse*
(Doubleday, 1998)

ILLUSTRATION 635

MIRACLE IN THE STORM

Topics: Assumptions; Attitudes; Awe; Education; Faith; Fear of God; Glorifying God; Miracles; Power; Reverence; Wonder; Worship

References: Job 25:2; Habakkuk 3:2; Matthew 8:23–27; 9:8; 11:25; Mark 4:35–41; Luke 5:26; 7:16; 8:22–25; 10:21; Hebrews 12:28

A group of Laotian refugees who had been attending the church I pastored in Sacramento, California, approached me after the service one Sunday and asked to become members. Our church had sponsored the newcomers, and they had been attending the church only a few months.

They had only a rudimentary understanding of the Christian faith, so I suggested we study the gospel of Mark together for a few weeks to make sure they knew what a commitment to Christ and his church involved. They happily agreed.

Despite the Laotians' lack of Christian knowledge — or maybe because of it — the Bible studies were some of the most interesting I've ever led. After reading the passage in which Jesus calms the storm, I asked about the storms in their lives. There was a puzzled look among my Laotian friends, so I explained that we all have storms — problems, worries, troubles, crises — and this story teaches that Jesus can give us peace in the midst of those storms. "So what are your storms?" I asked.

Again, more puzzled silence. Finally, one of the men asked, "Do you mean that Jesus actually calmed the wind and sea in the middle of a storm?"

I didn't want to get distracted with the problem of miracles, so I replied, "We should not get hung up on the details of the miracle. We should remember that Jesus can calm the storms in our lives."

Another stretch of awkward silence ensued until someone said, "Well, if Jesus calmed the wind and the waves, he must be a powerful man!" At this, they all nodded vigorously and chattered excitedly to one another in Lao. Except for me, the room was full of wonder. I suddenly realized that they grasped the story better than I did.

—Mark Galli,
Jesus Mean and Wild (Baker, 2006)

ILLUSTRATION 636
ALIVE TO THE UNSEEN

Topics: Blindness; Experiencing God; Spiritual Perception; Spiritual Vitality

References: John 3:1–16; 1 Corinthians 2:9–16

Humans can perceive only 30 percent of the range of the sun's light and 1/70 of the spectrum of electromagnetic energy. Many animals exceed those abilities. Bats detect insects by sonar; pigeons navigate by magnetic fields; bloodhounds perceive a world of smell unavailable to us.

Perhaps the spiritual or "unseen" world requires senses activated only through some sort of spiritual quickening. As Jesus said, "No one can see the kingdom of God without being born from above." And the apostle Paul said,

"The man without the Spirit does not accept the things that come from the Spirit of God, for they are foolishness to him, and he cannot understand them, because they are spiritually discerned."

Both expressions tell us that some truths are available only to a person who is spiritually alive.

—Philip Yancey, "Seeing the Invisible God,"
Books and Culture (May–June 2000)

ILLUSTRATION 637
PARALYZED ATHLETE WALKS

Topics: Example; Glorifying God; Hope; Purpose; Sports; Tragedy

References: Psalm 46; Isaiah 40:29–31; 43:7

Dennis Byrd was an up-and-coming defensive superstar for the New York Jets, who was expected to help turn the Jets around. But on November 29, 1992, when the Jets were playing the Chiefs, Byrd was about to sack the quarterback when he collided with a teammate. His spinal cord snapped.

He awoke in the middle of the night at Lenox Hospital in a halo brace, not knowing where he was, why he couldn't move, and what was happening. Suddenly, he went from dreaming of making it to the Pro Bowl to hoping that someday he could once more hold his daughter in his arms.

From a worldly perspective, Byrd was no longer able to reach his potential. But in God's eyes, Byrd was capable of more than sacking quarterbacks. As the world watched and listened, Byrd told the media that Christ was his source of comfort in his time of tragedy. The doctors said Byrd would likely never walk again, but Byrd said that with God's help, he would.

On opening day of the 1993 football season, less than a year after his spinal-cord injury, Byrd walked to the middle of the Meadowlands Stadium while 75,000 fans cheered. The miracle in Byrd's life is not that he broke his neck and walked again. The miracle is that the injury that destroyed his career didn't destroy his life.

—Steve May, Sermonnotes.com

PART 26: SORROW AND STRESS

ILLUSTRATION 638

TEEN STRESS

Topics: Achievement; Choices; Drinking; Drugs; Parenting; Peer Pressure; Sex; Teens

References: Romans 12:2; 1 Peter 2:11–12

Teens are stressed. Here's what they say stresses them, according to a 1999 survey by Peter D. Hart Research Associates:

- pressure to get good grades: 44 percent
- pressure to get into college: 32 percent
- pressure to fit in socially: 29 percent
- pressure to use drugs or alcohol: 19 percent
- pressure to be sexually active: 13 percent

— *USA Today* "Snapshots" (November 8, 1999)

ILLUSTRATION 639

IDOLIZING EXHAUSTION

Topics: Balance; Family; Rest; Sabbath; Work

References: Exodus 23:12; 31:12–17

I do not mean to make an idol of health, but it seems to me that at least some of us have made an idol of exhaustion. The only time we know we have done enough is when we are running on empty and when the ones we love most are the ones we see the least.

When we lie down to sleep at night, we offer our full appointment calendars to God in lieu of prayer, believing that God—who is as busy as we are—will surely understand.

— Barbara Brown Taylor,
"Divine Subtraction,"
Christian Century (November 3, 1999)

ILLUSTRATION 640

FATIGUE DISASTERS

Topics: Busyness; Rest; Sabbath; Work

References: Exodus 20:8–11; Mark 6:31–32

Our most notorious industrial accidents in recent years—*Exxon Valdez*, Three Mile Island, Chernobyl, and the fatal navigational error of Korean Air Lines Flight 007—all occurred in the middle of the night. This may indicate that fatigue, more than anything, was a contributing factor.

When the USS *Vincennes* shot down an Iranian A300 airbus, killing all 290 people aboard, fatigue-stressed operators in the high-tech Combat Information Center on the carrier misinterpreted radar data and repeatedly told their captain the jet was descending as if to attack, when the airliner actually was remaining on a normal flight path.

In the *Challenger* space shuttle disaster, key NASA officials made the ill-fated decision to go ahead with the launch after working twenty hours straight and getting only two to three hours of sleep the night before. Their error in judgment cost the lives of seven astronauts and nearly killed the U.S. space program.

We ignore our need for rest at the peril of others and ourselves.

—Martin Moore-Ede, *The Twenty-Four-Hour Society* (Addison-Wesley, 1994)

ILLUSTRATION 641

SHAKING THE DIRT

Topics: Adversity; Attitudes; Faith; Hope; Overcoming; Perseverance; Praise

References: Romans 5:3–5; James 1:2–4

A dog fell into a farmer's well. After assessing the situation, the farmer decided that neither the dog nor the well was worth the bother of saving. He'd bury the old dog in the well and put him out of his misery.

When the farmer began shoveling dirt down the well, initially the old dog was hysterical. But as the dirt hit his back, the dog realized every time dirt landed on his back, he could shake it

off and step up. "Shake it off and step up; shake it off and step up!" he repeated to himself.

No matter how painful the blows were, the old dog kept shaking the dirt off and stepping up. It wasn't long before the dog, battered and exhausted, stepped triumphantly over the wall of that well. What seemed as though it would bury him actually benefited him—all because of the way he handled his adversity.

The adversities that come along to bury us usually have within them the potential to bless us. Forgiveness, faith, prayer, praise, and hope are some of the biblical ways to shake it off and step up out of the wells in which we find ourselves.

—Bruce Shelley, Denver, Colorado

ILLUSTRATION 642

TURNIP AND MUD

Topics: Creation; Goodness of God; Praise; Thanksgiving

References: Isaiah 25:1–9; Ephesians 5:20

One winter I sat in army fatigues somewhere near Anniston, Alabama, eating my supper out of a mess kit. The infantry training battalion that I had been assigned to was on bivouac. There was a cold drizzle of rain, and everything was mud. The sun had gone down.

I was still hungry when I finished and noticed that a man nearby had left something that he was not going to eat. It was a turnip. When I asked him if I could have it, he tossed it over to me. I missed the catch, and the turnip fell to the ground, but I wanted it so badly that I picked it up and started eating it, mud and all.

Time deepened and slowed down. With a lurch of the heart, I saw suddenly that not only was the turnip good, but the mud was good too, even the drizzle and cold were good, even the Army that I had dreaded for months was good.

Sitting there in the Alabama winter with my mouth full of cold turnip and mud, I could see at least for a moment how if you ever took truly to heart the ultimate goodness and joy of things, even at their bleakest, the need to praise someone or something for it would be so great that you might even have to go out and speak of it to the birds of the air.

—Frederick Buechner,
The Sacred Journey (HarperOne, 1991)

ILLUSTRATION 643
FREEING THE SQUIRREL

Topics: Advent; Christmas; Freedom; Incarnation; Patience; Redemption; Salvation; Waiting on God

References: Psalm 27:14; Acts 9:1–19

One Christmas we had an unexpected houseguest. A squirrel had fallen down the chimney into the wood burner stove in the basement of our home in Michigan.

I thought if it knew we were there to help, I could just reach in and gently lift it out. Nothing doing. As I reached in, it began scratching like it had overdosed on espresso.

We finally managed to construct a cardboard box "cage" complete with a large hole in one side, into which the squirrel waltzed when we placed the box against the wood burner's door. We let it out into the safety of our backyard.

Later, I thought, *Isn't it funny how, before its redemption, our little visitor had frantically tried to bash its way out of its dark prison? It seemed that the harder it struggled to get free, the more pain it caused itself.* In the end, it had to wait until one who was much bigger—one who could peer into its world—could carry it to that larger world where it really belonged.

That is what the Lord will do for us.

—Clark Cothern, *Detours* (Multnomah, 1999)

ILLUSTRATION 644
DEATH COMES CALLING

Topics: Afterlife; Death; Doubt; Hopelessness; Meaning of Life; Priorities; Skepticism; Values

Reference: John 11:25

Samuel Johnson once said the prospect of being hanged concentrates a man's mind wonderfully. I can testify that the prospect, extended over an hour or two, of dying in a gasoline fireball after an automobile crash does much the same. It dissolves your more commonplace troubles.

—Robert Hughes, "In Death's Throat,"
Time (October 11, 1999)

ILLUSTRATION 645

MONEY WORRIES

Topics: Anxiety; Fear; Future; Money; Provision

References: Matthew 6:25–34; Philippians 4:19

People are fearful about money. According to a 2000 survey, here are some of the things they are worried about:

- not being able to pay medical bills: 36 percent
- Social Security going bust: 35 percent
- caring for elderly parents: 31 percent
- no inheritance to pass on: 22 percent
- stock market crash: 20 percent

— *USA Today* "Snapshots" (February 10, 2000)

ILLUSTRATION 646

THE ZEIGARNIK EFFECT

Topics: Emotions; Failure; Human Condition; Limitations; Psychology; Regret

References: 1 Kings 19:1–9; John 21:15–19

Failures take on a life of their own because the brain remembers incomplete tasks or failures longer than success or completed activity. That is called the "Zeigarnik effect." When a project or a thought is completed, the brain places it in a special memory. The brain no longer gives the project priority or active working status, and bits and pieces of the achieved situation begin to decay.

But failures have no closure. The brain continues to spin the memory, trying to come up with ways to fix the mess and move it from active to inactive status.

— Perry Buffington, "Forgive or Forget," Universal Press Syndicate (August 29, 1999)

ILLUSTRATION 647

STRESS MAKES YOU SICK

Topics: Anxiety; Illness; Peace; Security in God; Stress; Trust; Worry

References: Psalm 55:22; Matthew 11:30; 1 Peter 5:7

In times of emotional stress, a hormone, neuropeptide Y (NPY), is released into the body. This hormone undermines the body's immune system and literally makes you sick.

That's what a team of Australian researchers at Sydney's Garvan Institute scientifically confirmed in 2005. According to Fabienne Mackay of the institute, "During periods of stress, nerves release a lot of NPY, and it gets into the bloodstream where it inhibits the cells in the immune system that look out for and destroy pathogens in the body.

"That stress makes you sick is no longer a myth; it is a reality, and we need to take it seriously."

— "Australian Scientists Find Proof That Stress Makes You Sick," Breitbart.com (December 4, 2005)

ILLUSTRATION 648

WOMEN AND STRESS

Topics: Anxiety; Stress; Women

References: Matthew 6:25–34;
Philippians 4:6

Women are stressed; that's for sure. Here's what they say about how often they are stressed:

- all the time: 8 percent
- almost every day: 21 percent
- once/twice a week: 29 percent
- a few times a month: 31 percent
- a few days a year: 11 percent

— *USA Today* "Snapshots" (March 20, 2000)

ILLUSTRATION 649

THE FOG OF WORRY

Topics: Confusion; Faith; Fear;
Happiness; Worry

References: Matthew 6:25–34;
2 Corinthians 4:16–18; Philippians
4:6–7

A dense fog covering seven city blocks to a depth of a hundred feet condensed into water wouldn't quite fill a drinking glass. That's according to the U.S. Bureau of Standards.

Like fog, our worries can thoroughly block our vision of the light of God's promises, but in the final analysis, they have little substance to them.

— Brian Heckber, Burlington, Kentucky

ILLUSTRATION 650

LEAKING GRIEF

Topics: Coping; Forgetting; Grief;
Memories; Pain; Sorrow

References: Job 16:12; John 16:20;
2 Corinthians 4:16;
1 Thessalonians 4:13

Fifty years ago, industrialists thought they could just bury toxic waste and it would go away. We have since learned it doesn't just go away. Toxic waste leaks into the water table, contaminates crops, and kills animals.

Buried grief does the same thing. Raw time doesn't heal a thing. Buried pain leaks into our emotional system and wreaks havoc there. It distorts our perceptions of life, and it taints our relationships. That contamination happens subconsciously.

— Bill Hybels, "A Better Kind of Grieving,"
Preaching Today Audio, no. 108

ILLUSTRATION 651

RUNNING FROM PAIN

Topics: Mourning; Pain; Sorrow

References: Matthew 5:4; John 16:20;
1 Thessalonians 4:13

What should people do when dealing with loss? I recently asked a seasoned Christian counselor about that. "I tell them to feel their feelings," she said. "But I also urge people to reduce radically the pace of their lives. I urge them to review their loss, talk about it openly, think about it thoroughly, write about it reflectively, and pray through it."

She continued, "It's my experience that people want to run from their pain. They want to replace pain with another feeling as soon as they can. To recover from pain, you have to face it. You must stand in it and process it before it will dissipate. That's God's way."

I didn't grieve well when my father died; I replaced pain real fast. I think I missed only four days of work. And I just replaced the feeling of loss and disappointment with a frenzied ministry schedule. In short, I ran from grief. That was a bad move for me and for people around me.

I wonder how many of us do that. Is anybody running from pain today? Are you trading in your pain prematurely for some other feeling? That's not God's way.

—Bill Hybels, "A Better Kind of Grieving," Preaching Today Audio, no. 108

ILLUSTRATION 652

HOW ADVERSITY STRENGTHENS US

Topics: Adversity; Hardship; Science; Suffering

References: Job 23:10; Isaiah 48:10; 2 Corinthians 4:17

For two years, scientists sequestered themselves in an artificial environment called Biosphere 2. Inside their self-sustaining community, the Bio-

spherians created a number of mini-environments, including a desert, rain forest, and ocean. Nearly every weather condition could be simulated except one: wind.

Over time, the effects of their windless environment became apparent. A number of acacia trees bent over and snapped. Without the stress of wind to strengthen the wood, the trunks grew weak and could not hold up their own weight.

Though our culture shuns hardship, we would do well to remember that God uses hardship "for our good, that we may share in his holiness" (Hebrews 12:10).

—Jay Akkerman, in *Fresh Illustrations for Preaching and Teaching* (Baker, 1997)

ILLUSTRATION 653

WHEN A BEAR LURKS

Topics: Danger; Family; Fear; Habits; Sin; Temptation; Thoughts

References: Matthew 5:29–30; 26:41; 1 Timothy 6:9; 1 Peter 5:8

One Sunday afternoon in December of 2005, Pedro Sainvil's children, who had been outside playing in the snow, came rushing into the house screaming, "Dad, there's a bear under the house!"

Sainvil discovered that day that a seven-hundred-pound black bear was hibernating under his porch. The discovery was not a total shock, since neighborhood trash cans had been tampered with for several weeks. However, it was obviously a concern for Sainvil and his family.

Local authorities determined to remove the bear, especially since there was a school bus stop across the street from the house. State Game Commission spokesman Jerry Feaser said that situations like this are fairly common in the Northeast but can be prevented by blocking access to crawl spaces and other areas that would be tempting to large animals during denning season. The space under Sainvil's porch was uncovered.

"It's very scary," said Sainvil's mother, who lives with the family. "I'm just praying that he'll take off. It's like a bomb under the house."

—Dan Berrett, "An Unbearable Guest," poconorecord.com (December 6, 2005)

ILLUSTRATION 654

HONEY, I MISS YOU

Topics: Death; Devotion; Emotions; Eternal Life; Faith; Grief; Heaven; Hope; Loss; Love; Marriage; Mortality; Perspective; Promises; Spouses

References: 2 Samuel 14:14; Psalm 116:15; John 11:25–26; 14:1–6; Romans 6:23; 14:8; 1 Thessalonians 4:13–18; 1 Peter 1:3

As he reflected on the death of his beloved wife, Margaret, Lyman Coleman wrote the following:

The most painful decision of my life was asking God to take her home. She had been suffering from repeated brain seizures and her body was wasted. I whis-

pered in her ear: "Honey, I love you. I love you. Jesus wants you to come home. We are going to be all right. We give you permission to let go." She closed her eyes and fell asleep....

As I write this letter, I realize I am without my editor. My greatest critic. My teammate. Soul mate. Prayer mate. Partner in everything. We traveled the roads less traveled together in hard times and good times.

Honey, I miss you. I miss you. I miss you. I will keep the light on for the kids. I will be there for friends. And one day we are going to join you. All of us. Because Jesus promised it.

"Precious in the sight of the Lord is the death of his saints" (Psalm 116:15).

—Bill Donahue and Russ Robinson, *Building a Church of Small Groups* (Zondervan, 2001)

ILLUSTRATION 655

BAD GRIEVING INSTRUCTIONS

Topics: Death; Grief; Mourning; Sorrow; Worldliness

References: Matthew 5:4; 1 Corinthians 7:29–30; 1 Thessalonians 4:13

When his dog dies, Johnny, five, bursts out crying. His dog has been his constant companion; it slept at the foot of his bed. Now the dog is gone, and little Johnny is a basket case.

Johnny's dad stammers a bit and says, "Uh, don't feel bad, Johnny, we'll get you a new dog."

It is lesson one in society's grief management program: Bury your feelings; replace your losses. Once you have the new dog, you won't think about the old one anymore.

Years later, Johnny falls in love with a high school freshman girl. The world has never looked brighter until she dumps him. Suddenly a curtain covers the sun. Johnny's heart is broken with big-time hurt. He is a wreck. But Mom comes to the rescue, saying, "Don't feel bad, John, there are other fish in the sea."

Lesson two: Bury the pain, replace the loss.

Much later, John's grandfather dies — the one he fished with every summer and felt close to. A note is slipped to him in math class. He reads the note and breaks into sobs. The teacher sends him to the school office.

John's father picks him up from school. His mother is weeping in the living room, and John wants to hug her. But his dad says, "Don't disturb her, John; she needs to be alone. She'll be all right in a little while. Then the two of you can talk."

Lesson three: Grieve alone.

Let's review. Bury your feelings; replace your losses; grieve alone; let time heal; live with regret; never trust again. That has been society's approach for years.

—Bill Hybels, "A Better Kind of Grieving," Preaching Today Audio, no. 108

ILLUSTRATION 656

TROUBLE IN THE FAMILY

Topics: Abuse; Anxiety; Children; Conflict; Family; Fatherhood; Health; Motherhood; Stress

References: Ephesians 6:4; Colossians 3:21

Childhood can be a very stressful time, but there is a difference between stresses caused inside and outside the home. Family stressors cause the most devastation.

Researchers measured levels of cortisol, a hormone that is produced in a child's saliva when under stress. They also collected health records and interviews to get a complete picture of the effects of stress. What they found was that stress that continues over days, weeks, or years will put a child's developing systems on hold, sometimes permanently. Unusually high cortisol levels from constant stress will slow physical growth, delay sexual maturity, and stunt the growth of brain cells.

Poverty, schoolwork, or conflicts with peers raises cortisol levels very little. Rather, family issues cause the most harm, such as when a family experiences some sort of trauma, Father and Mother fight, Dad leaves, or Grandma hits a child.

The continual absence of a mother or father in the home also has a major effect. The study showed that "girls between the ages of nine and sixteen are much more affected by the absence of their mother than are boys of this age. And infant boys respond to the absence of their father with abnormally low cortisol levels and slow growth."

Other findings: Children react the same way each time parents fight or leave home. While adults learn to adapt to relentless stressful circumstances, children always react as if they are encountering it for the first time. Many diseases suffered by middle-age adults, such as heart disease or high blood pressure, can be traced back to unresolved patterns of stress initiated during childhood.

—Meredith F. Small, "Trouble in Paradise,"
New Scientist (December 16, 2000)

ILLUSTRATION 657

SAINT-SINNER CONFLICT

Topics: Apathy; Busyness; Choices; Compromise; Desires; Distractions; Human Nature; Hypocrisy; Self-indulgence; Temptation; Time Management; Values; Vices; Weakness; Weariness

References: Matthew 6:24; Luke 16:13; 1 Corinthians 6:13 – 18; 10:21; Galatians 6:7 – 8; 1 Thessalonians 4:1 – 8; James 4:8

We want to be a saint, but we also want to feel every sensation experienced by sinners; we want to be innocent and pure, but we also want to be experienced and taste all of life; we want to serve the poor and have a simple lifestyle, but we also want all the comforts of the rich; we want to have the depth afforded by solitude, but we also do not want to miss anything; we want to pray,

but we also want to watch television, read, talk to friends, and go out.

It's a small wonder that life is often a trying enterprise, and that we are often tired and pathologically overextended.

—Ronald Rolheiser,
The Holy Longing (Doubleday, 1999)

ILLUSTRATION 658

WHEN BOSSES MAKE YOU SICK

Topics: Criticism; Employees; Employers; Health; Stress

References: Mark 10:42 – 45; Ephesians 6:5 – 9; Colossians 4:1; James 5:1 – 6; 1 Peter 3:8 – 17

Research in England revealed that employers who unfairly treat their employees can actually make them sick. That's according to a study in which 6,400 civil servants in London were asked questions such as, "Do you ever get criticized unfairly?" and "Do you ever get praised for your work?"

A follow-up study ten years later showed that men who reported low scores on their bosses' fairness were 30 percent more likely to have coronary heart disease, which is the number-one killer in Western societies. Ongoing stress is a major contributor to this affliction.

Labor experts say the effect on employees' health might be even greater in the United States than in Britain, since workers in the United

States spend more time at their jobs than their overseas counterparts.

> — "When the Boss Is a Jerk,"
> *The Week* (November 11, 2005)

ILLUSTRATION 659

DE-STRESSING AT KIDDIES' CAMP

Topics: Busyness; Career; Childlikeness; Escape; Faith; Fun; Jobs; Joy; Leisure; Play; Pressure; Responsibility; Sabbath; Stress; Work

References: Matthew 18:1–4; 19:14; Mark 10:13–16; Luke 18:16

When stress at work gets to be too much, many executives are finding new ways to escape. Instead of retreating to the beach, to the mountains, or to a golf outing, many adults are, well, acting like kids.

At California's Camp GetAway, an adult can participate in sing-alongs, water balloon fights, kickball, s'mores around the campfire, and sneaking out of the cabin to toilet paper the cars and cabins of other campers.

Some adults opt for the increasingly popular Rock 'n' Roll Fantasy Camps, where even unskilled participants can jam with real rock musicians.

Helen Oseen founded The Ultimate Pajama Party, a camp where older women can don their pajamas, pillow fight, and sit on the bed and share confidences late into the night. Oseen

began the camp when she realized she worked a lot and didn't save time for play.

Christopher Noxon calls the trend "rejuveniling" in his book *Rejuvenile: Kickball, Cartoons, Cupcakes, and the Reinvention of the American Grown-Up.* A father of three in Los Angeles, Noxon said, "In a world where pressure and problems pile on nonstop, more grown-ups are seeking a vacation from their adult side."

> — Kitty Bean Yancey, "Get Away from It All,"
> *USA Today* (July 28, 2006)

ILLUSTRATION 660

RESTING IN JAIL

Topics: Emotions; Family; Husbands; Marriage; Neglect; Relationships; Resentment; Responsibility; Rest; Sabbath; Wives

References: Ecclesiastes 2:17–23; Isaiah 40:28–31; Matthew 11:28; Hebrews 4:9–11; Revelation 14:13

Maria Brunner, of Poing, Germany, was willing to go to jail to get a break.

Brunner's husband is unemployed, so she supports their three young children by cleaning other people's houses. Even without a job, her husband managed to run up $5,000 worth of unpaid parking tickets. The husband kept the tickets a secret, but as the owner of the vehicle, Maria was responsible. She couldn't pay the fine, and unless her husband could come up with the money, she would spend three months in jail.

She welcomed the thought. "I've had enough of scraping a living for the family," she says. "As long as I get food and a hot shower every day, I don't mind being sent to jail. I can finally get some rest and relaxation."

Police reported that Maria repeatedly thanked them for arresting her.

— "Family of the Week,"
timesonline.co.uk (May 15, 2005)

ILLUSTRATION 661

NAPPING FOR SHOPPERS

Topics: Leisure; Limitations; Rest; Sabbath; Stress; Vacation; Weariness; Work

References: Psalm 62; Jeremiah 6:16; Matthew 11:28–30; Hebrews 4:1–11

MinneNAPolis opened in Minnesota's Mall of America in 2005. It rents comfy spots where weary shoppers can take naps for seventy cents a minute. Founded by PowerNap Sleep Centers of Boca Raton, Florida, the new store includes themed rooms such as Asian Mist, Tropical Isle, and Deep Space. The walls are thick enough to drown out the sounds of squealing children outside.

The company's website reads, "Escape the pressures of the real world into the pleasures of an ideal one." "It's not just napping," according to the press release. "Some guests will want to listen to music, put their feet up, watch the water trickling in the beautiful stone waterfall, breathe in the positive-ionization-filtered air, enjoy the full-body massager, and just take an enjoyable escape from the fast-paced lifestyle."

— www.powernapsleepcenters.com
(October 28, 2005)

ILLUSTRATION 662

MESSAGING STRESS

Topics: Ambition; Business; Busyness; Career; Communication; Competition; Emptiness; Jobs; Lifestyle; Pressure; Sabbath; Stress; Weariness; Work

References: Exodus 20:8–11; 23:12; Psalm 127:2; Matthew 11:28–30; 13:22; Luke 21:34; Philippians 4:6–7

The average office gets 220 messages a day in emails, memos, phone calls, interruptions, and ads.

No wonder a survey of 1,313 managers on four continents found that "one-third of managers suffer from ill health as a direct consequence of stress associated with information overload. This figure increases to 43 percent among senior managers."

— Kevin Miller, "Managing Chaos,"
Christian Management Report (June 2006)

ILLUSTRATION 663

TWO-PHONE JOE

Topics: Busyness; Holiness; Lifestyle; Outreach; Peace; Prayer; Pressure; Seekers; Stress; Weariness

References: Psalm 46:10; Matthew 11:28–30; 13:22; Luke 10:38–42; Ephesians 6:18

I called him Two-Phone Joe. The first time I met him, I was sitting at an outdoor table at my favorite coffee spot. He came out, cell phone pressed between shoulder and ear, talking a blue streak. He had a cup of coffee in one hand, a Coke in the other, and another phone on his belt. When he put his cup down to hang up, I said, "Man, you've got to relax a little!" And that's how my friendship got started with one of the most hyper guys I've ever known.

Joe and I talked often. Actually, Joe ranted and raved, and I mostly listened. Once I was sitting at an inside table and he came in, assaulting his phone as usual. He talked, loud and angry, the whole time he ordered, and then, after he sat down, he kept arguing for the whole coffee shop to hear. When he finally got off the phone, I said, "Joe, come here."

"What?" he barked guardedly.

"Sit down here," I repeated.

"Why?" he asked, but he sat down.

"Joe, I don't know if anyone has ever done this for you before, but I am going to pray for you right now." Joe's eyes got big, and he looked at me like I was crazy. Before he could run, I just put my hand on his arm and quietly prayed for a few seconds, asking God to quiet Joe and to give him peace.

"Thank you," Joe said softly, and I wondered if that might have been the first holy moment in Joe's entire tumultuous life.

—Lee Eclov, "Christ in a Coffee Shop," *Trinity Magazine* (Spring 2006)

ILLUSTRATION 664

NEEDING A BREAK

Topics: Busyness; Leisure; Rest; Sabbath; Stress; Success; Time; Work

References: Exodus 23:12; Matthew 11:28–30; Hebrews 4:1–11

We're working too hard in the United States. At least we think we are. Here's what 1,220 workers said about themselves in a Hilton Generational Time survey in January 2001:

- need more fun: 68 percent
- need a long vacation: 67 percent
- often feel stressed: 66 percent
- feel time is crunched: 60 percent
- want less work, more play: 51 percent
- feel pressured to succeed: 49 percent
- feel overwhelmed: 48 percent

—Lori Joseph and Bob Laird, "Americans Working Too Hard," *USA Today* "Snapshots"

ILLUSTRATION 665

TOO MUCH TO DO

Topics: Burnout; Focus; Priorities; Work

References: Matthew 22:35–40; Luke 10:41–42; Philippians 3:7–8

When animal trainers go into a cage of lions, they carry whips and pistols. But invariably they also carry a stool. According to William H. Hinson, the stool is the most important tool.

The trainer holds the stool by the back and thrusts the legs toward the face of the wild animal. The animal tries to focus on all four legs at once. In the attempt to focus on all four, a kind of paralysis overwhelms the animal. It becomes tame, weak, and disabled because its attention is fragmented.

Likewise, the stress of having too much to do can paralyze us.

—John Maxwell, *Developing the Leader within You* (Nelson, 1993)

ILLUSTRATION 666

FORGETTING BIRTHDAY BOY

Topics: Birthdays; Celebration; Children

References: Matthew 15:7–9; Luke 11:42; John 4:23–24

The party on June 3, 2006, was for Michael Emmanuel's sixth birthday, and friends and family were celebrating at the local Chuck E. Cheese in Boca Raton, Florida.

The party went just fine. The problem came when it was over. All the children and adults climbed into three different vehicles and headed home. Everyone, that is, except Michael.

Apparently, the birthday boy returned to the play area, and when the partygoers departed, the boy was left behind. Employees found Michael wandering around the restaurant at 10:00 p.m. and called the police.

Michael's mother, who assumed that her son was staying with his grandmother, didn't realize the boy was missing until the next morning. Unfortunately for Michael (and his mother), it is possible to have a joyful celebration and still forget the guest of honor.

— "Mother Forgets Child at 6th Birthday Party," CBS4.com (June 5, 2006)

ILLUSTRATION 667

REVEALING SECRET SANTA

Topics: Christmas; Generosity; Giving; Hope; Money; Stewardship; Testimony

References: Leviticus 25:35; Deuteronomy 15:7; Proverbs 11:25; 22:9; Matthew 6:3; 19:16–26; Luke 6:38; 11:39–41; Acts 20:35; 2 Corinthians 9:7

Just prior to the 2006 Christmas season, Larry Stewart, fifty-eight, a successful businessman from Lee's Summit, Missouri, revealed that he was the Secret Santa who has been doling out hundred-dollar bills to the needy every Christmas for the past twenty-six years. Stewart said he decided to go public after it became apparent that a tabloid newspaper was going to reveal his name. Now he hopes to inspire others to become Secret Santas.

In the winter of 1971, Stewart was working as a door-to-door salesman, when the company he was working for went out of business. Stewart quickly ran out of money. He hadn't eaten in two days when he went to Dixie Diner and ordered a breakfast he eventually admitted he couldn't pay for. Ted Horn, the restaurant owner, acted like he found a twenty-dollar bill on the floor underneath Stewart's chair. "Son, you must have dropped this," Horn said.

"It was like a fortune to me," Stewart said. His response was to vow, "Lord, if you ever put me in a position to help other people, I will do it."

Over the years, Stewart estimates that he has given away about $1.3 million, for which he has been amply rewarded. "I see looks of hopelessness turn to looks of hope in an instant," he says. "After all, isn't that what we're put here on earth for—to help one another?"

—Nanci Hellmich, "Santa Shares His Secret," *USA Today* (December 22, 2006)

ILLUSTRATION 668

TURNING CHRISTMAS UPSIDE DOWN

Topics: Advent; Christmas; Greed; Holidays; Materialism; Secularism

References: Isaiah 9:6–7; Matthew 1:22–24; Luke 1:1–20; 3 John 1

The Upside-Down Christmas Tree. That's what Hammacher Schlemmer, a retail company based in New York, is currently offering for sale.

Standing at seven feet tall and prelit with over eight hundred commercial grade lights, this technological marvel can be yours for $599.95. But why would anyone want an upside-down Christmas tree? According to Hammacher Schlemmer's website, "The inverted shape makes it easier to see ornaments, which hang away from the dense needles," while "allowing more room for the accumulation of presents underneath."

Other retail outlets are following suit, including ChristmasTreeForMe.com, which offers five- to seven-and-a-half-foot bizarro trees from $280 to $504. Even Target is getting in on the action, with upside-down trees ranging from $299 to $499 on its website. Target also claims that the trees "leave more room on the floor for gifts."

—Andrew Hard, "Christmas on the Flip Side," FoxNews.com (November 9, 2005)

ILLUSTRATION 669

WHO'S TO BLAME FOR CHRISTMAS?

Topics: Advent; Attitudes; Christmas; Cynicism; Holidays; Jesus Christ; Stress

References: Isaiah 7:14; 53; Matthew 1:18–25; 2:1–12; 11:28–30; Luke 2:1–20

A woman was doing her last-minute Christmas shopping at a crowded mall. She was tired of fighting the crowds. She was tired of standing in lines. She was tired of fighting her way down long aisles looking for a gift that had sold out days before.

Her arms were full of bulky packages when an elevator door opened. It was full. The occupants of the elevator grudgingly tightened ranks to allow a small space for her and her load.

As the doors closed, she blurted out, "Whoever is responsible for this whole Christmas thing ought to be arrested, strung up, and shot!"

A few others nodded their heads or grunted in agreement.

Then, from somewhere in the back of the elevator, came a single voice that said: "Don't worry. They already crucified him."

—*Homiletics*, vol. 18
(November–December 2006)

ILLUSTRATION 670

OUR DUMPSTER-DIVING GOD

Topics: Advent; Christmas; God's Love; Grace; Help; Human Worth; Incarnation; Jesus Christ

References: Luke 2:6–7; 15:11–24; 2 Corinthians 5:21; Hebrews 2:17

I love ribs, so when I heard about a restaurant that had amazing ribs, a bunch of my friends and I drove fifty minutes to get there. The place was packed, and the food was great. It was "all-you-can-eat rib night," and rib bones were piling up as fast as the line to get in.

Eating ribs is messy business. Barbecue sauce gets on your face, fingers, and clothes. Dirty napkins pile up next to half-eaten bowls of baked beans and coleslaw. When our crew had eaten all we could, we paid our tab and waddled out to the car.

I reached into my pocket for my keys and came up with nothing but lint. Panicking, I looked through the window at the ignition. I hoped that I had locked my keys in the car, because in the back of my mind a more disgust-ing possibility was taking shape. When I saw that the ignition was empty, I knew exactly where my keys were—to my car, my house, and my office. Only seconds earlier, those precious keys had slid off my tray and followed a half-eaten corncob and many bones to the bottom of a trash can. I had thrown away my keys on all-you-can-eat rib night.

My friends weren't going to do the dirty work for me. So I dove into the dumpster, fish-ing through bones, beans, barbecue, corn, cake, coleslaw, and a host of saliva-soaked napkins. A shiny layer of trash can slime coated my arms before I finally grabbed those precious keys.

As I meditate on the incarnation this Christ-mas season, I think about our dumpster-diving God. I mean no disrespect by calling him that. On the contrary, I have a soaring adoration for the infinite God who left a pristine, sinless heaven to search through the filth and rubbish of this fallen world for something precious to him—me.

—David Slagle, Decatur, Georgia

ILLUSTRATION 671

POSTAL BLESSING

Topics: Advent; Atonement; Christmas; Cross; Gift of Righteousness; Jesus Christ; Justification; Pardon; Reconciliation; Redemption; Salvation

References: Isaiah 53:3–5; John 3:16; Acts 20:28; 1 Corinthians 6:20; 7:23; Ephesians 1:7; 1 Peter 1:18–19; 1 John 2:2; 4:9–10; Revelation 5:9

Just prior to Christmas, I went to the post office. After helping me, the pleasant postal clerk uttered what is surely her standard line: "Is there anything else I can do for you?"

I quipped, "Can you help me pay for Christmas?"

Without missing a beat, she replied, "He has already paid for it."

I was stunned. Pleased, surprised, a tad embarrassed, but most of all, stunned. I murmured something profound in response—like, "He certainly did"—and left.

A simple phrase had put everything in perspective.

—Pete Winn, "Citizen Link Update"
(December 24, 2003)

ILLUSTRATION 672

JESUS AT CHURCH

Topics: Easter; Jesus Christ; Resurrection

References: John 2:19; Acts 2:22–24; Romans 1:3–4

While driving to church on Easter Sunday a few years ago, I told my children the Easter story. "This is the day we celebrate Jesus' coming back to life," I explained.

Right away, my son, Kevin, three, piped up from the backseat, "Will he be in church today?"

—Peggy Key, Portage, Michigan

ILLUSTRATION 673

COMING ALIVE ON EASTER

Topics: Easter; Hope; Jesus Christ; New Life; Priorities; Resurrection; Work

References: John 6:35; 11:25; 2 Corinthians 1:6; Titus 3:4–5; 1 Peter 1:3

It was Good Friday. My house looked more like a set for *Rescue 911* than a place of solemn preparation for the pinnacle of the church year. Barbara, my wife of fifteen years, had gotten home at 3:00 a.m. after a long shift as a hospital nurse. Her heart started to pound more than a hundred beats a minute. Her pulse raced so fast we couldn't measure it. We tried massage and relaxation exercises, but nothing helped. Desperate, I called 911.

In the darkness, the emergency medical services unit arrived and rushed my normally healthy, forty-three-year-old wife to the hospital. In the early morning hours, when many churches would sing "Go to Dark Gethsemane" and reflect on Christ's agony on the cross, I was deep in my own darkness. I wept as I thought the unthinkable.

Doctors finally controlled Barbara's racing heart and admitted her to the intensive care cardiac unit. She had another episode on Saturday, which the doctor again brought under control.

I returned to our empty parsonage, facing an Easter I couldn't cancel and didn't have much heart for. I prayed, wept, and pleaded for God to give me the strength to be both a good husband and a good pastor. The question pulled at me. How can I celebrate Easter when I'm living Good Friday?

I prayed, cried, and paced the room. A seminary classmate called me at 11:30 p.m. He asked me what I planned to preach on Easter Sunday. I responded by pouring out my heart to him. My friend gave me a couple of thoughts to hang on to. "First, Christ is Savior and rose from the grave," he said. "Dave, you are not Christ, but you will find the energy to do Easter. Second, Barb knows you love her. She wants you to be the best pastor you can be on Easter morning."

Though I barely got three hours of sleep the night before Easter, somehow Christ strengthened me the next day. I was able to proclaim the eternal message "He is risen!"

When the Communion server gave me the bread and wine and said, "Take and eat; this is the body and blood of Christ, broken and shed for you," it struck me that Christ was present with us in all his majesty, just as he was with Barbara in the ICCU.

After church I found Barbara in great shape at the hospital. We concluded that Barb's working two jobs to pay off our bills wasn't worth her life. Our priorities changed dramatically, thanks to the Easter weekend when we truly lived — not just observed — the journey to new life.

—David Coffin, "Celebrating Easter
When You're Living Good Friday,"
Leadership (Winter 1999)

ILLUSTRATION 674

LAYING WREATHS FOR SOLDIERS

Topics: Holidays; Honor; Mourning; Respect; Thanksgiving; Victory

References: Matthew 26:26–29; Mark 14:22–25; Luke 22:19–20; 1 Corinthians 10:16; 11:23–24

Every December since 1992, Morrill Worcester and volunteers have been laying wreaths on the graves of soldiers in Arlington National Cemetery.

Worcester, owner of one of the world's largest holiday wreath companies, started Wreaths Across America, the volunteer wreath-laying program, after one of his warehouses called to report an overproduction of several thousand wreaths. "Well, I'm not just gonna throw them away," Worcester said. He called Washington and asked for permission to lay his wreaths on graves in Arlington. He got it.

"When people hear about what we're doing, they want to know if I'm a veteran," Morrill said. "I'm not. But I make it my business never to forget."

Wreaths Across America is helping reclaim the true meaning of a wreath, Worcester says. "We wanted to get back to the simple idea of what a wreath represents — respect, honor, and victory."

—Rick Hampson, "Gift of Wreaths Touches
Nation," *USA Today* (December 15, 2007)

ILLUSTRATION 675

IS HE ALIVE?

Topics: Easter; Faith; Jesus Christ; Passion; Purpose; Resurrection; Witnessing

References: Job 32:17–19; Hosea 6:3; Mark 16:19; Acts 13:32–33; 2 Corinthians 2:14; Colossians 1:3–6; 2 Timothy 1:8; 1 Peter 3:22

Following an Easter service in 2003, a woman approached a pastor and asked, "So what happened with Jesus after the resurrection?"

"Well, he ascended into heaven and he's still alive," the pastor said.

"I know he was resurrected, but is he really alive?" she asked.

"Yes, he's alive."

"Alive? *Alive?* Why didn't you tell me?"

For the next two weeks, she telephoned everyone she knew and exclaimed, "Jesus is alive! Did you know he's alive?"

—Eric Reed, *Leadership Weekly*
(April 13, 2004)

ILLUSTRATION 676

GIVING THAT COSTS SOMETHING

Topics: Christmas; Dishonesty; Generosity; Giving; Lying; Money; Sacrifice; Stewardship

References: 1 Chronicles 21:24; Matthew 6:1–4; 2 Corinthians 9:12–15

A. A. Milne, author of the Winnie the Pooh books, wrote a seasonal piece titled "A Hint for Next Christmas." He tells of William who went to a big Christmas party and was stunned to discover that everyone had brought gifts for everyone else, a courtesy he had completely missed. He gave some thought to this problem and then went alone into the dining room while all the other people were in the parlor. There in the dining room the gifts were piled at each person's place at the table. Milne writes:

> The top parcel said, "To John and Mary from Charles." William took out his fountain pen and added a couple of words to the inscription. It then read, "To John and Mary from Charles and William."
>
> He moved on to the next place. "To Angela from Father," said the top parcel. "And William," wrote William. At his hostess's place he hesitated a moment. The first present there was for "Darling Mother, from her loving children." It did not seem that "and William" was quite suitable. But his hostess was not to be deprived of William's kindly thought, so twenty seconds later the handkerchiefs "from John and Mary and William" expressed all the nice things he was feeling for her.

Nice try, but how pitiful. We only truly give when it costs us something.

—Based on A. A. Milne, "A Hint for Next Christmas," *A Christmas Treasury* (Viking, 1982)

ILLUSTRATION 677

EXCLUDING JESUS

Topics: Burdens; Christmas; Dependence on God; Jesus Christ; Problems; Self-reliance; Unbelief

References: Jeremiah 17:5–8; Matthew 11:28–30; Hebrews 4:15–16; 1 John 5:5

It was nearing Christmas, and I received a phone call from a man who needed to talk to a counselor. I met him at my church office, where he told me his tale of woe. A decade earlier he had killed his wife in a fit of anger, was convicted of manslaughter, and spent several years in prison. He and his wife had a daughter who was in the custody of his in-laws. He had not seen her since the crime.

Now, as Christmas neared, his heart ached. Tears streaming down his face, he lamented, "I could pass her on the streets of this city and not even know who she was."

What I remember most about our counseling session, however, was what he said when he first walked into my office. Dramatically raising his arms, he said, "Now, preacher, let's just leave Jesus out of this, OK?"

As he sadly went his way that day, I thought to myself, *That's the whole problem. You've left Jesus out of everything.*

—Phil LeMaster, Grayson, Kentucky

ILLUSTRATION 678

PLAYING THE VIRGIN

Topics: Celibacy; Chastity; Christmas; Jesus Christ; Purity

References: Psalm 51:10; Luke 1:26–45; 2 Corinthians 11:2; Ephesians 5:3–4; 2 Timothy 2:22; Hebrews 13:4

Olivia, five, and her best friend, Claire, were in a nativity play at school. Claire was playing Mary, and Olivia was an angel. Before the show, a young boy went around the dressing room saying, "I'm a sheep; what are you?" Each child responded politely, including Olivia, who proudly declared that she was an angel.

The boy then turned to Claire and repeated the question to her: "I'm a sheep; what are you?"

Claire simply said, "I'm Mary."

Realizing Claire was a lead character, the boy tried to justify his own role. "It's hard being a sheep, you know," he said.

"Yes," said Claire innocently, "but it's also hard being a virgin."

—Jeremy M. Basset, Oklahoma City, Oklahoma

ILLUSTRATION 679

HOME FOR THE HOLIDAYS

Topics: Children; Christmas; Deceit; Family; Holidays; Lying; Parenting

Reference: Ephesians 6:1–4

An elderly man in Phoenix calls his son in New York and says, "I hate to ruin your day, but I have to tell you that your mother and I are divorcing—forty-five years of misery is enough."

"Pop, what are you talking about?" the son asks.

"We can't stand the sight of each other any longer," the old man says. "We're sick of each other, and I'm sick of talking about this, so you call your sister in Chicago and tell her."

Frantic, the son calls his sister, who explodes on the phone. "Like heck they're getting divorced," she shouts. "I'll take care of this."

She calls Phoenix and screams at her father, "You are *not* getting divorced. Don't do a single thing until I get there. I'm calling my brother back, and we'll both be there tomorrow. Until then, don't do a thing."

The old man hangs up the phone and turns to his wife. "OK," he says. "They're coming for Thanksgiving and paying their own fare. Now what do we do for Christmas?"

—Anonymous

ILLUSTRATION 680

DRUNK WITH YEARNING

Topics: Bible; Christmas; Conversion; Drunkenness; Fathers; Heaven; Longing; Praise; Redemption; Surrender; Worship

References: Isaiah 45:21; Luke 2:28–32; Romans 6:17

One of my fondest memories of Christmas Eve is singing "Angels We Have Heard on High" alongside my father when I was about nine years old. Dad was a shy man, so he normally would sing hymns very softly. On this night, though, he sang it full bore, off-key, and with the deepest yearning that I had ever heard in him. Dad was drunk that night.

He was a melancholic, battered man, a World War II army veteran who saw many of his friends blown to bits. He sought refuge in alcohol, which made life pretty frightening for Mom, my older brother, Randy, and me. But in church I saw the gentle Cajun who grew up Catholic and who still feared God.

Only a few years after this Christmas Eve service, my brother became a Jesus freak. Dad began reading the Bible to help my brother realize how far he had stepped off the deep end into religious extremism. Within a year Dad realized that my brother had found a relationship with Jesus that Dad had not discovered. So Dad surrendered to Jesus.

Then his drinking simply stopped. He still struggled with anger. We still argued about the length of my hair, my failure to practice the piano, and my halfhearted efforts at homework. Still, I began associating Dad more with love than with fear.

I spent nearly every Christmas with Dad until his death in 1992. We sang "Angels We Have Heard on High" together many times, but somehow my keenest memory is of Dad singing it with such yearning. Now, when I sing this carol, I know a small measure of the yearning Dad felt when I was a boy. I close my eyes and imagine Dad in heaven, singing along at the top of his redeemed lungs, feeling drunk on his adoration for God.

—Douglas LeBlanc, Chesterfield, Virginia

ILLUSTRATION 681

UNHAPPY NEW YEAR

Topics: Crime; Death; Depravity; Fall of Humanity; Greed; Human Condition; Injustice; Robbery; Sin

References: Luke 10:27–37; John 10:10; Romans 1:28–32; 6:12–14, 19–23; 2 Timothy 3:1–4

The drivers of the first two vehicles that struck Lynette Spiller, forty-two, in Las Vegas on New Year's Day 2002, hit her and drove off. While Spiller's body was pinned under the third car, passersby combed through her purse, wallet, and backpack, taking what they wanted. Detective Doug Nutton said one person later gave police Spiller's identification card, saying it had been found elsewhere.

Spiller was jaywalking, but the drivers of the first two cars could be charged with felony hit-and-run. The driver of the third car stopped.

—Associated Press, "Passersby Rob Dead Woman," (January 3, 2002)

ILLUSTRATION 682

LAUGHING ON EASTER

Topics: Easter; Experiencing God; Jesus Christ; Laughter; Resurrection

References: Acts 2:24–32; Romans 5:9–11

Let's celebrate Easter with the rite of laughter.
Christ died and rose and lives.
Laugh like a woman who holds her first baby.
Our enemy death will soon be destroyed.
Laugh like a man who finds he doesn't have cancer, or he does, but now there's a cure.
Christ opened wide the door of heaven.
Laugh like children at Disneyland's gates.
This world is owned by God, and he'll return to rule.
Laugh like a man who walks away uninjured from a wreck in which his car was totaled.
Laugh as if all the people in the whole world were invited to a picnic and then invite them.

—Joseph Bayly, *Psalms of My Life* (David C. Cook, 2000)

ILLUSTRATION 683

SAYING YES ON CHRISTMAS

Topics: Christmas; God's Sovereignty; Hope; Incarnation; Providence; Salvation

Reference: 2 Corinthians 1:18–20

Songs, good feelings, beautiful liturgies, nice presents, big dinners, and sweet words do not make Christmas. Christmas is saying yes to something beyond all emotions and feelings. Christmas is saying yes to a hope based on God's initiative, which has nothing to do with what I think or feel. Christmas is believing that the salvation of the world is God's work and not mine.

—Henri Nouwen, *New Oxford Review* (November 1986)

ILLUSTRATION 684

OPENING THE DOOR OF ADVENT

Topics: Advent; Christmas; Freedom; Grace; Hope; Waiting

Reference: Luke 1:76–79

A prison cell, in which one waits, hopes, does various unessential things, and is completely dependent on the fact that the door of freedom has to be opened from the outside is not a bad picture of Advent.

—Dietrich Bonhoeffer, *Letters and Papers from Prison* (SCM Press, 1953)

ILLUSTRATION 685

EXPECTING THE UNEXPECTED

Topics: Christmas; Divine Power; Holiness; Humility; Incarnation

Reference: Philippians 2:5–11

Those who believe in God can never in a way be sure of him again. Once they have seen him in a stable, they can never be sure where he will appear or to what lengths he will go or to what ludicrous depths of self-humiliation he will descend in his wild pursuit of man. If the holiness and the awful power and majesty of God were present in this least auspicious of all events, this birth of a peasant's child, then there is no place or time so lowly and earthbound but that holiness can be present there too.

And this means that we are never safe, that there is no place where we can hide from God, no place where we are safe from his power to break in two and recreate the human heart, because it is just where he seems most helpless that he is most strong, and just where we least expect him that he comes most fully.

—Frederick Buechner, *The Hungering Dark* (HarperSanFrancisco, 1985)

ILLUSTRATION 686

FINDING HIS SWEET GIFTS

Topics: Birth of Christ; Christmas; Favor; Grace; Love; Salvation; Savior

References: John 3:16–17; Ephesians 2:1–10

There are many reasons God saves you: to bring glory to himself, to appease his justice, to demonstrate his sovereignty. But one of the sweetest reasons God saved you is because he is fond of you. He likes having you around. He thinks you are the best thing to come down the pike in quite a while.

If God had a refrigerator, your picture would be on it. If he had a wallet, your photo would be in it. He sends you flowers every spring and a sunrise every morning. Whenever you want to talk, he'll listen. He can live anywhere in the universe, and he chose your heart. And the Christmas gift he sent you in Bethlehem? Face it, friend. He's crazy about you!

—Max Lucado, *A Gentle Thunder* (Word, 1995)

ILLUSTRATION 687

LOSING THE BABY

Topics: Advent; Christmas; Distractions; Priorities; Worship

Reference: Matthew 6:1

Evangelist Luis Palau tells of a wealthy European family that decided to have their newborn baby baptized. Dozens of guests were invited to the elaborate affair, and they all arrived at the mansion dressed to the nines. After depositing their elegant wraps on a bed in an upstairs room, the guests were entertained royally.

Soon the time came for the main event—the infant's baptism. But where was the baby? No one seemed to know. The child's governess ran upstairs and returned with a desperate look on her face. Everyone searched around frantically. Finally, someone recalled having seen him asleep on one of the beds.

The baby was buried beneath a pile of coats, jackets, and furs. The object of that day's celebration had been forgotten, neglected, and nearly smothered.

The baby whose birthday we celebrate at Christmas may also be hidden beneath the piles of stuff we load up during the season. We need to enter every Advent asking, "Where's the baby?"

—Greg Asimakoupoulos,
Mercer Island, Washington

ILLUSTRATION 688

CELEBRATING CHRISTMAS ANYTIME

Topics: Advent; Attitudes; Celebration; Christmas; Happiness; Holidays; Joy

References: Matthew 8:17; Hebrews 2:4

I was waiting to see my doctor in June when an older couple arrived. "Merry Christmas! Merry Christmas!" the gentleman said to everyone in the waiting room. His enthusiasm was infectious.

Most of the patients ignored the outburst, but I decided to respond, "Merry Christmas to you too!"

Sensing a sympathetic ear, the wife quietly said, "It started this past year. For no reason, my husband would get the Christmas spirit. At first we dismissed it, but then we realized how much joy it brought him. So we started decorating the house, singing carols, having a spur-of-the-moment celebration.

"You know, after doing this a number of times, we look forward to it. Christmas can come anytime, anyplace. It's always a pleasant surprise."

—Donald Castle, Lombard, Illinois

ILLUSTRATION 689

WAKING UP ON CHRISTMAS

Topics: Christmas; Healing; Miracles; Supernatural Occurrences

References: Matthew 8:17; Hebrews 2:4

Patti White Bull, of Albuquerque, New Mexico, was in a coma for sixteen years. But on Christmas Day, she awoke and resumed normal activities: she dressed herself, walked without support, and talked in complete sentences. Unlike most coma patients, who awaken gradually, White Bull became fully conscious and showed no signs of any mental or physical disability.

Neurologist Randy Chestnut of Oregon Health Sciences University says White Bull's awakening is "extraordinary but not out of the realm of possibility." He speculates that decreased brain stimulation may have been caused by a kind of brain-stem blockage that finally shifted. White Bull may have been interacting with people in subtle ways that went unnoticed, he suggested, adding, "Maybe on Christmas Day, people noticed more than they ever had before, and that made it seem like a dramatic recovery."

Her family and friends prefer to think the spontaneous healing was a Christmas miracle.

—Shawna Vogel, "A Christmas Miracle? Woman Out of 'Vegetative State' after 16 Years," ABCNews.com (December 29, 1999)

ILLUSTRATION 690

REVISING THE WISH LIST

Topics: Children; Christmas; Desires; Gifts; Grace; Humanity; Manipulation; Prayer; Will

References: Isaiah 55:6–9; Hebrews 5:7; 1 John 5:14–15

A small boy was writing a letter to God about the Christmas presents he wanted. "I've been good for six months now," he wrote. After a moment's reflection, he crossed out "six months" and wrote "three." After a pause he changed that to "two weeks." There was another pause and another erasure.

Finally, the boy got up from the table and went over to the little nativity scene that had the figures of Mary and Joseph. He picked up the figure of Mary and went back to his writing and started again: "Dear God, if ever you want to see your mother again ..."

—Stephen Arterburn and Bill Farrel, *The One Year Book of Devotions for Men on the Go* (Tyndale House, 2004)

ILLUSTRATION 691

BREAKING THE MOLD

Topics: Humanity; Significance; Worth

References: Job 7:17; John 3:16; Romans 8:31–32

Many years ago, I purchased a Christmas plate for my wife, Judy. The price was $21.95. It was the first Christmas plate produced by Hummel in Germany, and the store clerk assured me it would increase in value.

Recently Judy and I attended an auction and were surprised to see a Hummel Christmas plate just like ours being sold for more than $1,000. What was it about the plate that caused this remarkable growth in value? Its substance had not changed; it was not more beautiful, nor had it changed in size. But it was in greater demand. The original mold had been broken. Now only a limited number of plates were available, with no opportunity for replacement. All of these factors had contributed to an increased value.

So it is with us: there is only one mold per person and no opportunity for replacement.

—C. William Pollard,
The Soul of the Firm (Zondervan, 2000)

ILLUSTRATION 692
MAKING A DEAL WITH GOD

Topics: Anger; Changed Heart; Children; Christmas; Love; Mercy; Receiving Christ

Reference: John 1:12

I once taught a Bible class at the home of Barbara Holmyard, the Champion Spark Plug heiress. Princess Alexandra of Greece was invited to come, and she did. Rose Kennedy came with her.

When I saw that Rose was present, I immediately changed my subject for the day to a little homily on death, making three points:

1. You can fight it.
2. You can take flight from it.
3. You can make a deal with God.

After the class, Rose whispered in my ear, "I made that deal a long time ago.

"I was a spoiled young bride of a strong-willed man, a socialite who attended every function possible," she began. "We were expecting a child and elated at the prospect. The day came

when our child was born. She was a beautiful child.

"But it wasn't long until we realized that there was something terribly wrong with her. We took her to the doctor, who confirmed our fears. She was retarded, and nothing could be done."

"Anger grew within my heart," Rose said. "How could God do such a thing to this child—to me? I turned my back on God, my husband, my closest friends—and became a recluse.

"One evening a major event was happening in the city. I wanted to go, but I was so filled with wrath that I thought I might create a scene. My husband feared it, too, so we decided to stay home. A lovely woman, who was one of our maids, gently said to me, 'Please excuse me, Mrs. Kennedy, but I've been watching you the last few weeks. I love you very much, and I hate to see this destroy your life. Mrs. Kennedy, you'll never be happy until you make your heart a manger where the Christ-child may be born.'

"I fired her on the spot! Yet later that night my mind ruminated relentlessly, keeping me awake. I could not forget that lovely face, the sweetness of the maid, the joy in her spirit, and especially her words.

"I have loved Christ all my life, and tried to be a good Catholic, but now I knelt beside my bed and prayed, 'Dear God, make my heart a manger where the Christ-child may be born.' I felt a fresh new divine entry into my life, and there was born in me a love for retarded children.

"Oh, by the way, I rehired the lovely maid. She was with us until her death."

—Jess Moody, *Club Sandwich*
(Broadman & Holman, 1999)

ILLUSTRATION 693

RETRIEVING THE JOY

Topics: Advent; Christmas; Death; Grief; Light; Loneliness; Loss; Mourning; Peace; Redemption

References: Matthew 4:16; John 8:12

It looked like Stella Thornhope would be alone at Christmas. Her husband had died of cancer a few months before. Now she was snowed in. She decided not to bother with decorating the house.

Late that afternoon, the doorbell rang. It was a delivery boy with a box. He asked her to sign for the package. After she did, she asked, "What's in the box?" The young man opened the box. Inside was a little puppy, a golden Labrador retriever. The delivery boy picked up the squirming pup and said, "This is for you, ma'am. He's six weeks old, completely housebroken."

"Who sent this?" Thornhope asked.

The young man set the animal down and handed her an envelope and said, "It's all explained here, ma'am. The dog was bought last July while its mother was still pregnant. It was meant to be a Christmas gift to you." The young man then handed her a book, *How to Care for Your Labrador Retriever.*

She again asked, "Who sent this puppy?"

As the young man turned to leave, he said, "Your husband, ma'am. Merry Christmas."

She opened the letter from her husband. He had written it three weeks before he died and left it with the kennel owners to be delivered with the puppy at Christmas. Her husband admonished her to be strong and said he was waiting for the day when she would join him. He had sent her this young animal to keep her company until then.

She picked up the golden furry ball and held it to her neck. Then she looked out the window at the lights that outlined the neighbor's house. Suddenly she felt the most amazing sensation of peace. Her heart felt a wonder greater than the grief and loneliness.

"Little fella," she said to the dog, "It's just you and me. But you know what? There's a box down in the basement that's got a little Christmas tree in it and some decorations and some lights that are going to impress you. And there's a manger scene down there. Let's go get it."

God has a way of sending signals to remind us that life is stronger than death, and light more powerful than darkness. Open the Book and reach for the joy.

—Robert Russell, "Jesus Came to Be the Light," *Preaching Today Audio*, no. 195

ILLUSTRATION 694

KEEPING THE LIGHTS ON

Topics: Anticipation; Christmas; Hope; Light

References: Matthew 4:16; Luke 2:32

A house near the entrance of our subdivision kept its Christmas lights burning long after the season was past. They burned through January and then into February. Finally, I became a bit caustic. "If I were too lazy to take my Christmas lights down, I think I'd at least turn them off at night," I said.

But about the middle of March a sign outside the house explained why the lights were still on. It simply said, "Welcome home, Jimmy." We learned the family had a son in Vietnam, and they had left their Christmas lights on in anticipation of his return.

Lights are a symbol of hope.

—Robert Russell, "Jesus Came to Be the Light," Preaching Today Audio, no. 195

ILLUSTRATION 695

PRICING A ROYAL VISIT

Topics: Advent; Christmas; Humility; Incarnation

References: Isaiah 40:1–11; Philippians 2:5–11

In London, looking toward the auditorium's royal box where the queen and her family sat, I caught glimpses of the way rulers stride through the world: with bodyguards, a trumpet fanfare, and a flourish of bright clothes and flashing jewelry.

Queen Elizabeth II had recently visited the United States, and reporters delighted in spelling out the logistics involved: her four thousand pounds of luggage included two outfits for every occasion, a mourning outfit in case someone died, forty pints of plasma, and white kid-leather toilet seat covers. She brought along her own hairdresser, two valets, and a host of other attendants. A brief visit of royalty to a foreign country can easily cost $20 million.

By contrast, God's visit to earth took place in an animal shelter with no attendants present and nowhere to lay the newborn King but a feed trough. Indeed, the event that divided history, and even our calendars, into two parts may have had more animal than human witnesses. A mule could have stepped on him.

—Philip Yancey, *The Jesus I Never Knew* (Zondervan, 1995)

ILLUSTRATION 696

LIVING IN THE SATURDAY

Topics: Easter; Holy Week; Hope; Jesus Christ; Kingdom of God; Patience; Resurrection; Second Coming; Waiting on God

References: John 20:1–18; Romans 8:18–25; 1 Corinthians 15:1–11

Good Friday and Easter Sunday have earned names on the calendar. Yet in a real sense we live on Saturday, the day with no name. What the disciples experienced in small scale—three days in grief over one man who had died on a cross—we now live through on a cosmic scale.

Human history grinds on between the time of promise and fulfillment. Can we trust that God can make something holy and beautiful and good out of a world that includes Bosnia and Rwanda and inner-city ghettos and jammed prisons in the richest nation on earth? It's Saturday on planet Earth. Will Sunday ever come?

—Philip Yancey, *The Jesus I Never Knew* (Zondervan, 1995)

ILLUSTRATION 697

FINDING RESURRECTION COMFORT

Topics: Comfort; Death; Easter; Hope; New Life; Resurrection

Reference: 1 Thessalonians 4:13–18

My wife, Debbie, had the flu. When she didn't get better, we went to the hospital for tests. The first thing the doctor said to Debbie was, "You've got some serious problems."

Debbie learned she had stomach cancer. Four months later, she passed away at age forty-three.

During Debbie's suffering, I took refuge in the truth of Jesus' resurrection. It had been my major research area for twenty-five years, and I appreciated a student who asked, "What would you do now if Jesus hadn't been raised from the dead?" I told him that Jesus' bodily resurrection is the center of the Christian faith. After he died on the cross to pay for our sins, Jesus was raised from the dead. He appeared to many people in his physical body that was now immortal.

Knowing that helped me while Debbie was dying. I imagined what God might say to me in response to my questions about Debbie. He would ask, "Gary, did I raise my Son from the dead?"

"Of course you did, Lord," I would say. "But why is Debbie dying?"

"Gary, did I raise my Son from the dead?" the question would come again.

I imagined God repeating the same question until I got the point. If Jesus has been raised, I can trust that Debbie will be raised someday too.

It was sufficient to know that because of Jesus' resurrection, and because Debbie and I belong to Jesus, we will be together again—for all eternity!

—Gary Habermas, *Decision* (April 2000)

PART 28: SPIRITUAL DIRECTION

ILLUSTRATION 698

LOOKING THE WRONG WAY

Topics: Expectations; Kingdom of God; Repentance

Reference: Mark 1:14–18

I once visited a village in the Madras diocese. There was no road into the village; you reached it by crossing a river, and you could do this either on the south side of the village or on the north. The congregation assumed I would come by the southern route, and they had prepared a welcome that only an Indian village can prepare. There was music and fireworks and garlands and fruit and *silumbum* (South Indian martial art done on ceremonial occasions) — everything you can imagine.

Unfortunately, I entered the village at the north end and found only a few goats and chickens. Crisis! I had to disappear while word was sent to the assembled congregation, and the entire village did a sort of U-turn to face the other way. Then I duly reappeared.

That is what *metanoia* means in Mark 1:14–18. The reign of God has drawn near, but you can't see it because you are looking the wrong way. You are expecting the wrong thing. What you think is God isn't God at all. You have to go through a mental revolution; otherwise the reign of God will be totally hidden from you.

—Lesslie Newbigin,
Mission in Christ's Way (AbeBooks, 2005)

ILLUSTRATION 699

FINDING THE EXITS

Topics: Fear; Focus; Spirituality; Vision; Worry

Reference: Matthew 6:22–34

Tree-skiing may sound like a death wish, but some skiers love the risk of skiing virgin powder through a stand of aspen or spruce. The key, of course, is not hitting the trees. And that can be tricky.

Even more so than in deep snow or moguls, what you focus your eyes on becomes critical in the woods. Look at the spaces between the trees — the exits where you hope to be traveling.

Or, in the words of extreme skiing world champion Kim Reichelm: "Don't stare at what you don't want to hit."

—Tim Etchells, "The Trees: Lovely, Dark, and Deep," *Outside* (November 1999)

ILLUSTRATION 700

SEEING EAGLES WITH EDWARD

Topics: Empathy; Intimacy; Knowing God; Presence of God; Relationships

References: Psalm 139:7; 1 John 3:18–20

My husband, Edward, is devoted to hawks, especially to the golden eagles that are returning to Georgia. Driving down the highway with him can be a test of nerves as he peers over the steering wheel at a particularly large bird. Is it an eagle or just a turkey vulture? He has to know, even if it means weaving down the road or running off it from time to time.

My view is a bit different: "Keep your eyes on the road!" I yell at him. "Who cares what it is? I'll buy you a bird book; I'll even buy you a bird—just watch where you're going."

A couple of summers ago, we spent two months apart, and I thought I'd get a break from hawks. Instead, I began to see them everywhere—looping through the air, spiraling in rising thermals, hunkered down in the tops of trees. Seeing them, really seeing them for the first time in my life, I understood that I was not seeing them with my own eyes but with Edward's eyes. He was not there, so I was seeing them for him. He was present in me.

—Barbara Brown Taylor,
The Best Spiritual Writing (Harper, 1999)

ILLUSTRATION 701

MARKING THE CROSSING

Topics: Acceptance; Death; Grace; Grief; Love; Mercy; Parents

References: Romans 5:20; 2 Peter 3:18

Fifty-five years ago, sitting up with you after midnight while the nurse rested, I watched you take your last breath. A few minutes before you died, you raised your head and said, "Which ... way?" I understood that you were at a dark, unmarked crossing. Then a minute later you said, "You're a good ... boy ... Wallace," and died.

My name was the last word you spoke; your faith in me and love for me were your last thoughts. I could bear them no better than I could bear your death, and I went blindly out into the November darkness and walked for hours with my mind clenched like a fist.

—Wallace Stegner, *Where the Bluebird Sings
to the Lemonade Springs* (Penguin, 1993)

ILLUSTRATION 702

DON'T WASTE THE PAIN

Topics: Growth; Ministry; Overcoming; Pain; Perspective; Suffering; Thankfulness; Weakness

References: Romans 8:28; 2 Corinthians 12:7–10; Philippians 2:12–13; James 1:2–4

Judy agreed to accompany me to Australia where I was to speak at a conference. I was thankful to enjoy a few weeks of my daughter's company, and we excitedly planned our trip together.

However, two days before we were to leave, my back went out. I became more thankful than ever for Judy. As we climbed aboard the plane, Judy asked, "Are you OK?"

"The long rest will help," I said hopefully. But by the time we arrived in Sydney, I couldn't move. Airline personnel carried me off the plane and laid me gently on the airport floor. I looked up at a circle of worried faces. The welcoming committee, clutching huge bunches of flowers, did not look thankful to see their guest speaker from this angle.

That night, awake from jet lag, Judy and I began to plan. "You'll have to help me, Judy," I told her. "I'll try to take two meetings a day, but you'll have to do the rest."

"Mother, I've only given two talks to the youth group," she protested.

"What were they about?" I asked.

"Stress and anxiety," she answered, grinning.

"Perfect," I said. "I'll help you with them." That night we worked on her talks.

At the first meeting I noticed Judy praying for me as I spoke. And when she spoke, the women loved her. Somehow we struggled through together. We thanked God for each other, for the privilege of ministering together, and for the funny things that gave us relief along the way. We thanked God for showing Judy her own unique gifts.

We had nearly given up, but God gave us the strength to finish the course. By the time we boarded the plane to fly back home, we had a new vision of a ministry together that has now come to fruition in new and deeper ways.

—Jill Briscoe, *Decision* (November 1999)

ILLUSTRATION 703

FLIPPING TO THE END

Topics: Assurance; Faith; Heaven; Hope; Resurrection; Trust

References: 1 Thessalonians 4:13–18; Hebrews 6:19; Revelation 21:3–5

I am a tremendous sports fan. Since many sporting events take place when I am not at home, I record them. When it's time to sit in my easy chair and view the game, unlike most people, I don't start at the beginning. Instead, I fast-forward to the end to see who won and who lost. If my team lost, I'll stop watching, but if my team won, I'll start the game at the beginning, get out some snacks, and watch the whole game.

Some say this method can't be much fun. But I love it. No matter how bad things look for my team, I don't have to worry because I know the end of the story.

That's how we might think about what Jesus did for us on the cross: no matter how bad things look, we don't have to worry because we know the end of the story.

—Charles Ellis, Indianapolis, Indiana

ILLUSTRATION 704

GRIEVING THE WRONG

Topics: Love; Rejection; Relationships; Success

References: John 15:9–17; Romans 12:18

I was talking to my spiritual director about a deep spiritual grief. I kept telling him how woefully I must have failed someone I loved for that person to have wronged me so destructively.

He said to me calmly, "Who are you to think you are better than our Lord? After all, he was singularly unsuccessful with a great many people."

That remark has stood me in great stead time and again. I have to try, but I do not have to succeed. Following Christ has nothing to do with success as the world sees success. It has to do with love.

—Madeleine L'Engle,
Walking on Water (Shaw, 2001)

ILLUSTRATION 705

AVOIDING ICEBERGS

Topics: Security; Spiritual Warfare; Temptation; Threats; Watchfulness

References: Matthew 26:41; 1 Corinthians 10:1–13; Ephesians 6:10–18

The Hibernia oil platform in the North Atlantic is 189 miles southeast of St. John's, Newfoundland, Canada. The total structure is 246 yards high from ocean floor to the top of the derricks.

Unlike the fated Ocean Ranger, a platform that sank in 1982, killing the eighty-four men aboard, Hibernia's design incorporates a gravity-based structure (GBS), which anchors it to the seabed. The structure does not move. It is an artificial island. It was built that way because it is in the middle of "iceberg alley," where an iceberg can be as large as an ocean liner.

Hibernia is built to withstand a one-million-ton iceberg (expected every five hundred years), and to withstand a six-million-ton iceberg (expected once in ten thousand years) with repairable damage. Even so, Hibernia's designers take no chances. Radio operators plot and monitor all icebergs within twenty-seven miles. Any that come close are "lassoed" and towed away from the platform by powerful supply ships. Smaller ones are diverted by the ship's high-pressure water cannons or with propeller wash. As rugged and as strong as this platform is, Hibernia will not allow an iceberg even to come close.

One thing seems obvious: the engineers of this oil platform are not guilty of the kind of false security that may have contributed to the sinking of the *Titanic*. Christians need to take spiritual threats just as seriously.

—J. Richard Love, "Oil Platform Designed to Survive the Worst," PreachingToday.com

ILLUSTRATION 706

STEP-BY-STEP FREEDOM

Topics: Leadership; Preparation; Racism; Seasons

Reference: Romans 5:3

Rosa Parks's decision not to ride in the "blacks only" section of the bus in 1955 was anything but impulsive. Rather, the woman whose action ignited the bus boycott in Montgomery, Alabama, becoming a key victory in the civil rights movement, had been working for the emancipation of blacks for many years.

Parks had spent the previous twelve years helping lead the local NAACP chapter. The summer before, she had attended a ten-day training session in Tennessee at a labor and civil rights organizing school. For some time she had been studying other bus boycotts, and she had already been arrested in Baton Rouge, Louisiana, two years earlier for participating in one.

So when she boarded that bus in Montgomery and sat where blacks weren't allowed, she was armed, chapter and verse, for what would follow.

— "Change Happens Slowly,"
Utne Reader (July–August 1999)

ILLUSTRATION 707

PILOT MAKES FATAL CHOICE

Topics: Choices; Goals; Morality; Priorities; Values

Reference: Proverbs 14:12

American Airlines Flight 965 left Miami for Cali, Columbia, in December 1995. Before landing, the pilot of the 757 needed to select the next radio navigation fix, named Rozo. He entered an R into his navigation computer. The computer returned a list of nearby navigation fixes starting with R, and the pilot selected the first of these, whose latitude and longitude appeared to be correct.

Unfortunately, the pilot selected Romeo, 132 miles to the northeast. Following indications on the flight computer, the pilots began an easterly turn and slammed into a granite peak at ten thousand feet. Only 4 of the 156 passengers survived; 152 plus all the crew perished.

The National Transportation Safety Board declared that the crash was due to human error. The navigational aid the pilots were following was valid but not for the landing procedure at Cali. In the literal definition of the phrase, this was indeed human error, because the pilot selected the wrong radio beacon.

The computer told the pilot he was tracking precisely to the beacon he had selected. Unfortunately, it neglected to tell him the beacon he selected was a fatal choice.

—Alan Cooper, *The Inmates Are Running the Asylum* (SAMS, a division of Macmillan Computer Publishing, 2004)

ILLUSTRATION 708

THE WEIRD ORBIT OF MERCURY

Topics: Doubt; Mysteries; Promises; Purpose; Questions; Suffering; Trust; Understanding

References: Proverbs 3:5; Romans 11:33–36

Physicists had scratched their heads for some fifty years over the unexplainable orbit of the planet Mercury. Newton's theories of gravity had served well for centuries to understand the orbits of all the other planets, but in Mercury's elliptical orbit, the point nearest the sun drifted by a small amount. Astronomers conjectured that another small hidden planet, which they named Vulcan, might be orbiting the sun and exerting gravitational force on Mercury. But Vulcan was never discovered.

Then Albert Einstein formulated his general theory of relativity. When he applied this gravitational formula to the eccentric orbit of Mercury, the numbers fit. Mercury was a mystery no more.

On occasion my life has an orbit, which, like Mercury, defies my best efforts to explain it. Nonetheless, as surely as there is order in the universe, there is a heavenly reason for my circumstances that is utterly consistent with God's Word and character. I just cannot understand it yet.

—Craig Brian Larson,
Pastoral Grit (Bethany, 1998)

ILLUSTRATION 709

WALKING STRAIGHT AND TRUE

Topics: Beauty; Creativity; Curiosity; Goals; Lifestyle; Planning; Success

References: Psalm 19:1 – 6; Romans 1:20

When Frank Lloyd Wright was nine, he went walking across a snow-covered field with his uncle. As the two of them reached the end of the field, his uncle stopped him. He pointed out his own tracks in the snow, straight and true as an arrow's flight, then young Frank's tracks meandering all over the field. "Notice how your tracks wander aimlessly from the fence to the cattle to the woods and back again," his uncle said. "See how my tracks aim directly to my goal? There is an important lesson in that."

Years later, the world-famous architect told how this experience had greatly contributed to his philosophy in life. "I determined right then not to miss most things in life, as my uncle had," he said.

—Jeff Arthurs, "Life Goals,"
PreachingToday.com

ILLUSTRATION 710

KNOWING THE TERRAIN

Topics: Guidance; Jesus Christ; Leading of the Holy Spirit

References: Exodus 13:21 – 22; Psalm 23:1 – 3; John 10:11 – 18

Bob, my father-in-law, hunts deer every fall in the mountains of California. A number of farmers and ranchers in the area are willing to let individuals or small groups hunt on their property—if the hunters ask permission and show respect for the land.

Last year my father-in-law asked if he might drive through a certain gate and do some hunting in the evening. The rancher gave Bob a thoughtful look and said, "Yeah, you can come on the land. But you'd better let me ride with you in the truck for a while. I want to show you some things."

Bob could have argued, but he didn't. So the pair drove through the gate onto the ranch. They had been skimming across a wide, seemingly featureless field when the rancher suddenly said, "You'd better slow down."

Bob pulled his foot off the accelerator. There was no deer. As far as he could see, there were no creeks, gullies, or fences. Just a wide pasture stretching out to the dusky foothills.

"Park right here," the rancher said. "Want to show you something."

They got out of the truck in the cool, mountain air and began walking. Then the rancher put his hand on Bob's shoulder and said, "Look up ahead."

My father-in-law stopped dead in his tracks. Cleaving at right angles across their path—and across the pasture as far as he could see in both directions—was a yawning, black tear in the surface of the earth. The crack was probably thirty feet across. Peering over the edge, the hair on Bob's neck bristled. The sheer, rock-ribbed sides of the great volcanic fissure plunged to unknown depths. Cold, still air seemed to exhale from the blackness below.

Walking back to the truck, Bob marveled at how difficult it was to see the fissure from just yards away. He smiled. Having a guide wasn't such a bad thing. He had a new appreciation for a man who knew the terrain—and where to park the truck.

—Larry Libby, *No Matter What, No Matter Where* (WaterBrook, 2000)

ILLUSTRATION 711

FOLLOWING THE JUDAS GOAT

Topics: Compromise; Influence; Satan; Sheep; Teens; Temptation

References: Psalm 119:176; Isaiah 53:6; Matthew 9:36; 1 Peter 2:25

Shepherds and ranchers tell us that sheep are virtually defenseless against predators, not very resourceful, inclined to follow one another into danger, and absolutely dependent on their human masters for safety. Thus, when Isaiah wrote, "We all, like sheep, have gone astray," he was referring to our tendency to move as an unthinking herd away from the watchful care of the Shepherd.

A documentary on television was filmed in a packinghouse where sheep were being slaughtered for the meat market. Huddled in pens outside were hundreds of nervous animals that seemed to sense danger. A gate opened that led up a ramp and though a door to the right.

To get the sheep to walk up that ramp, the handlers used a "Judas goat." The goat did his job very efficiently. He walked to the bottom of the ramp and looked back. Then he took a few more steps and stopped again. The sheep looked at each other skittishly and then began moving toward the ramp. Eventually, they followed the goat to the top, where he went through a little gate to the left, while they were forced to turn to the right and to their deaths. It was a dramatic illustration of unthinking herd behavior and the deadly consequences it often brings.

—James Dobson, *Life on the Edge* (Word, 1995)

ILLUSTRATION 712

RESETTING THE COMPASS

Topics: Church; Direction; Perspective; Preaching; Truth; Worship

References: Colossians 3:15 – 17; 1 Timothy 3:15; Hebrews 10:24 – 25

My sister bought a new car loaded with high-tech options. The first time she drove the car in the rain, she turned a knob she thought would start the windshield wipers. Instead a message flashed across the dash: "Drive car in 360 degrees." She had no idea what that meant, so when she got home, she read the car manual.

She learned that while trying to turn on the windshield wipers she had inadvertently turned off the internal compass, and the car had lost its sense of direction. To correct the problem, the car had to be driven in a full circle, pointed north, and then the compass had to be reset.

Each time we gather to worship, we are resetting our internal compass. We establish "true north" in our soul, remembering who God is and what his truth proclaims.

—Nancy Cheatham, Olathe, Kansas

ILLUSTRATION 713

NO-PURPOSE CLIMBING

Topics: Dedication; Emptiness; Priorities; Purpose; Values

References: Ecclesiastes 1:2; 12:13 – 14; Philippians 3:7 – 11

"One of the things that really attracts me about mountaineering is its total pointlessness. So I've dedicated my life to it."

—Tom Whittaker, mountaineer, Prescott, Arizona, *Time* (April 20, 1998)

ILLUSTRATION 714

FLYING LESSONS

Topics: Confusion; Devotional Life; Focus; Guidance; Holy Spirit; Prayer; Trials

Reference: Psalm 119:105

In the aftermath of the death of John Kennedy Jr. in 1999, amateur pilot Stephen Hedges wrote about the difficulty of flying a plane by instruments alone — a necessary skill if you want to fly at night or in fog. Without this skill, it is easy for a pilot to fall into an uncontrolled bank and crash.

During one instrument lesson, Hedges noted, "I flew the headings and turns as instructed, but even with ten hours of instrument flying in my logbook, I was amazed at how quickly the plane slid into a banking turn if I diverted my attention for just a few moments. The first time it happened, a pang of panic shot through me, a momentary fear that made it even more difficult to comprehend what the plane was doing."

But when he heard his instructor next to him calmly say, "Watch your bank," Hedges quickly leveled the plane.

There are a lot of times in the Christian life when we're forced to fly in fog or at night, when it's hard to get our bearings, when we can't see the horizon and get the perspective necessary to stay level. At such times it's doubly important to keep our eyes fixed on God's guiding Word and to stay attentive to his calming guidance.

—Mark Galli, "Guidance: Lesson from JFK Jr. Crash," PreachingToday.com

ILLUSTRATION 715

LOST IN THE SNOW

Topics: Choices; Confusion; Consequences; Decisions; Direction; Discernment; Help; Loneliness; Redemption; Rescue; Salvation

References: Psalm 143:10; Proverbs 3:5–6; Matthew 7:13–14; 15:14; Luke 19:10; Romans 12:2; Colossians 2:8

After spending Thanksgiving with family in Seattle, Washington, the Kims began their long journey back to San Francisco on November 24, 2006. James and Kati, along with their daughters Penelope (four) and Sabine (seven months), traveled south on Interstate 5 until late in the evening, intending to spend the night in an upscale lodge. But they missed their turn.

Instead of backtracking, the Kims decided to follow an alternate route. Using an official Oregon Department of Transportation road map, they traveled sixty-two miles south and drove onto Bear Camp Road, which seemed to be a more direct path to the Oregon coast. Both James and Kati failed to notice a small box on the map indicating that the road might be closed during winter. The Kims eventually encountered warning signs announcing that snowdrifts had blocked the pass and decided to turn off onto a spur road.

After struggling for fifteen miles along the unpaved road, their station wagon got stuck in the snow. The family decided to remain with the car and hope for rescue. They were there a week, running the car intermittently for heat and rationing their small amount of food. Once the gas ran out, they burned magazines, wet wood, and eventually car tires to keep warm.

Finally, James Kim set off on foot to find help. From the map, he determined that the town of Galice was about four miles away. According to state police officer Gregg Hastings, the distance was actually fifteen miles. A few days later, James died of exposure and hypothermia.

Katie waited two days for her husband to return, then gathered up her children and began her own trek to find help. She was spotted by rescue helicopters and rescued.

In March 2005, Peter Stivers survived a seventeen-day ordeal on a similar road with his wife, two children, and mother. Stivers's family had a motor home and more abundant supplies, but he still understands the terror that the Kims must have felt. "You're all alone," he said, "and you don't know if anybody's coming for you."

—Martin Kasindorf and Andrea Stone,
"Rescuers Laud Dad as Hero,"
USA Today (December 8, 2006)

ILLUSTRATION 716

RUNNING RED LIGHTS

Topics: Blindness; Conscience; Danger; Disobedience; Lawlessness; Sin; Will

References: Romans 1:28–32; 1 Timothy 1:19; 4:1–2

During my college years, I decided it made no sense to stop at red traffic lights when there was no traffic around. So I began to stop briefly, just long enough to check for cars, and then proceed.

My stops became shorter and shorter, and eventually I no longer stopped at all. I simply checked out the landscape, and if no cars were coming, I proceeded full speed through the red light.

One day I approached a light. I had already checked out the landscape and was near the empty intersection when a car topped the hill to my left. It was too far to pose any threat, but it was a police car. That is not what changed my ways, though, because I got the car stopped and received no more punishment than a dirty glance.

What scared me enough to quit running red lights was what occurred in the split second between spotting the patrol car and stopping the car. In that instant, my foot moved from the gas pedal to the brake pedal, then back to the gas pedal. I didn't will it; my foot just did it because that's how I had trained my mind to respond. I had continually ignored what was once a clear signal to stop—a red light—and as a result my mind was confused about what to do.

The same occurs with sin. Our God-given conscience gives us warning signals. We can heed those signals or ignore them. If we ignore them often enough, we may eventually fail to recognize them as signals at all and rush headlong into danger.

—J. Douglas Burford, Mission, Kansas

PART 29: SPIRITUAL GROWTH

ILLUSTRATION 717

HURRY NOT

Topics: Busyness; Mentoring; Rest; Spiritual Disciplines; Spirituality; Time; Work

References: 2 Corinthians 7:1; Galatians 5:22–23; 1 Timothy 4:7; Hebrews 4:1–11

Not long after moving to the Chicago area to serve as teaching pastor of Willow Creek Community Church, John Ortberg called a friend to ask for spiritual direction.

"I described the pace of life in my current ministry," Ortberg writes. "The church where I serve tends to move at a fast clip. I also told him about our rhythms of family life: we are in the van-driving, soccer-league, piano-lesson, school-orientation-night years. I told him about the present condition of my heart, as best I could discern it. What did I need to do, I asked him, to be spiritually healthy?"

After a long pause, the friend said, "You must ruthlessly eliminate hurry from your life."

"OK, I've written that one down," I told him, a little impatiently. "That's a good one. Now, what else is there?" Ortberg had many things to do, and this was a long-distance call, so he was anxious to cram as many units of spiritual wisdom into the least amount of time possible.

There was another long pause.

"There is nothing else," the friend said. "You must ruthlessly eliminate hurry from your life."

Ortberg eventually got it. "I have concluded that my life and the well-being of the people I serve depends on following his prescription, for hurry is the great enemy of spiritual life in our day," he said. "Hurry destroys souls."

—John Ortberg, "Ruthlessly Eliminate Hurry," LeadershipJournal.net (July 4, 2002)

ILLUSTRATION 718

A LESSON IN SHEEP CALLING

Topics: Christ as Shepherd; Hearing God; Influence; Leadership; Listening; Preaching; Responsibility; Spiritual Growth; Teaching

References: Ezekiel 3:16–21; John 10:2–4, 27; Acts 20:28; Hebrews 13:17; James 3:1; 5:19–20

Bill Donahue tells of a lesson he learned while visiting a farm where two of his students lived. When their father, Tom, asked if Bill would help call in the sheep, Bill enthusiastically agreed.

Sheep calling was like preaching, he thought, as he watched twenty-five sheep graze.

"Go ahead," Tom dared Bill. "Call them in."

"What do you say?" Bill asked.

"I just say, 'Hey, sheep! C'mon in!'"

No sweat, Bill thought. A city kid with a bad back and hay fever could do this. He began speaking, but Tom interrupted. "You are seventy-five yards away, downwind, and they have their backs to you. Yell! Use your diaphragm, like they teach you in preaching class."

Bill took a deep breath and put every inch of stomach muscle into a yell that revival preachers around the world would envy: "Hey, sheep! C'mon in!" The blessed creatures didn't move. Not one even turned an ear.

Tom smiled sarcastically. "Do they teach you the Bible in that seminary? Have you ever read, 'My sheep hear my voice, and I know them, and they follow me'?" Raising his voice only slightly, he said, "Hey, sheep! C'mon in!" All twenty-five sheep turned and ambled toward Tom.

"Now, don't you ever forget," Tom said to Bill. "You are the shepherd to my kids."

—Based on Bill Donahue and Russ Robinson,
Building a Church of Small Groups
(Zondervan, 2001)

References: Isaiah 65:5; Matthew 7:3, 13–14; 23:1–3; Romans 2:1; 8:33; 1 Corinthians 11:28–32; 2 Corinthians 7:1; 1 Peter 1:16

When our children were young, my husband and I decided we wouldn't watch R-rated movies. We made this decision in good conscience and never regretted it. I found, however, that it made me feel judgmental toward other parents who watched R-rated movies. I began to feel they weren't fully committed to Christ because they watched things I'd decided not to watch.

I realize how ridiculous it is to judge someone's relationship with God by what movies he or she watches, but my evaluation was so subtle at the time. As I made this judgment, I never thought about my own sin or all the things the person I was judging was doing right. Instead, I focused on this one thing I thought they were doing wrong.

Being a Pharisee is so easy. It's great to make rules to guide our own behavior, but when we extend those rules to everyone around us, we're in danger of becoming like the Pharisees, whom Jesus denounced as hypocrites.

—JoHannah Reardon, in newsletter
introduction at ChristianBibleStudies.com

ILLUSTRATION 719
WHEN I WAS A PHARISEE

Topics: Attitudes; Convictions; Entertainment; Faultfinding; Holiness; Humility; Hypocrisy; Judging Others; Legalism; Lifestyle; Presumption; Respect; Self-righteousness; Tolerance

ILLUSTRATION 720
STRETCHING TOO HIGH

Topics: Child Rearing; Children; Discouragement; Encouragement; Fathers; Growth; Parenting

References: Ephesians 6:4; 1 Thessalonians 5:11; Hebrews 3:13; 10:24

My ten-year-old son was "helping" me paint the laundry room. I brushed; he rolled. When he disappeared to get a Coke, I rerolled where he'd painted.

I didn't mind this. But I did mind his repeated efforts to reach higher than he should; standing on tiptoe, his arm straight up, wobbly, trying to control the roller heavy with paint. "Let Daddy get the high stuff," I said. "I'm afraid you'll drop the roller or lose your balance and fall in the paint."

I had to leave the room briefly and returned to find Justin once again stretched — ambitiously but precariously — with a shaky roller in his fingertips. "Justin," I barked, "I told you to stop stretching! I'll get that."

"OK, Daddy. I won't do it again."

In the silence that followed, I wondered how many times over the years I have given my children that message: "Stop stretching." How often have I said, "You can't do this; it's too hard. Let me do it. Don't be unrealistic. Don't reach so high"? Too often, I'm afraid. Now that I think about it, I kind of hope they weren't listening.

— Ken Langley, Zion, Illinois

On October 31, 1999, a full airplane took off from JFK International Airport in New York on a routine flight to Cairo, Egypt. Shortly after takeoff, the relief first officer waited for the pilot to leave the cockpit; then he disengaged the autopilot. He moved the throttle levers from cruise power to idle, cutting the engines. The airplane began to pitch nose-downward and then descended into a freefall.

In the final moments before impact, the horrified pilot dashed back to his seat and battled the copilot for control of the plane. The pilot pulled back on his controls, desperate to bring the nose of the Boeing 767 up, while the suicidal first officer pushed his own controls forward to keep the jet diving. EgyptAir Flight 990 crashed into the Atlantic Ocean south of Nantucket, Massachusetts. All 217 people aboard were killed.

The battle in that airliner's cockpit is like the inner life of a Christian. Each day, we choose either to hijack control of our lives — plunging ourselves into sin — or to remain locked in the direction of God's will.

— Jim Bennett, "A Fatal Loss of Control," PreachingToday.com

ILLUSTRATION 721
COCKPIT BATTLE FOR CONTROL

Topics: Bondage; Choices; Depravity; God's Will; Human Condition; Self-control; Self-discipline; Sin; Sinful Nature

References: Romans 7:14–25; 12:1–2; 2 Corinthians 5:17; Ephesians 4:22–24

ILLUSTRATION 722
INTERRUPTING LIFE TO HEAR GOD

Topics: Contentment; Desires; Freedom; Money; Needs; Perspective; Possessions; Poverty; Prosperity; Riches; Sacrifice; Simplicity; Stewardship

References: Proverbs 15:16; Matthew 16:26; Philippians 4:11–12; 1 Timothy 6:6; Hebrews 13:5

"I've become more convinced than ever that God finds ways to communicate with those who truly seek him, especially when we lower the volume of the surrounding static," says writer Philip Yancey.

Yancey talks about reading the account of a spiritual seeker who interrupted a busy life to spend a few days in a monastery. "I hope your stay is a blessed one," said the monk who showed the visitor to his cell. "If you need anything, let us know, and we'll teach you how to live without it."

— Based on Philip Yancey,
"What 147 Elk Taught Me about Prayer,"
Christianity Today (March 2006)

ILLUSTRATION 723

FEARING HEIGHTS

Topics: Awe; Divine Power; Experiencing God; Fear; God's Glory; God's Wrath; Wonder; Worship

References: Deuteronomy 6:13; Psalm 11:4–6; 19:1–6; 24; 33:6–19; Isaiah 8:13; Matthew 10:28; Revelation 1:8; 4:1–11

A few summers ago we took a family vacation to Toronto. We'd never been there, but all the guidebooks said, "You have to go up the CN Tower, the world's tallest building and freestanding structure."

Just the thought of being 1,815 feet above the ground made me queasy. But the kids said, "Aw, Dad, we gotta go," so against my better judgment, we went.

I was the last one into the elevator. We started up, which was when I realized that the door of this elevator was actually made of glass, and that this elevator was affixed to the outside of the tower. As we rushed up the side of the CN Tower, I could see the city of Toronto falling away at my feet. My palms started sweating, my throat got tight, and I started breathing really fast. I told myself, "Just hang on. Soon you'll be on the observation floor."

I stumbled out of the elevator onto the observation floor, where I thought it would be safe. But I found that some sadist had installed a glass floor there so that people could walk on it and look straight down to the ground.

The kids were laughing as they walked onto the glass floor, jumped up and down, and even laid down.

"C'mon, Dad!" they yelled.

That same year, we went to the Grand Canyon, where you can stand at the South Rim and peer 6,000 feet straight down. At the Grand Canyon, you are not separated from your doom by blocks of glass 2.5 inches thick. So every year, an average of four or five people die while visiting because of (in one website's words) "overly zealous photographic endeavors."

Still, the Grand Canyon is so beautiful that I was drawn to it. I had to see it, to get near it. I wouldn't do anything too foolish near the edge, but the same awesome beauty that caused me fear also drew me toward it.

When the Bible talks about "fearing God," what is it talking about? Is it talking about the kind of fear I felt at the CN Tower? Or is it more like the fear I felt at the Grand Canyon?

For years, preachers and writers have told me that it's like the fear I felt at the CN Tower. "When the Bible says to fear God," they explained, "it doesn't really mean fear. It means awe or reverence. You should respect God, of course, but you don't need to actually fear him. It's like you're standing on the glass floor 1,100 feet up in the CN Tower. Being there may give you a thrill or a quick feeling of awe, but you're completely safe. So if you do feel any terror with God, that's unnecessary or even irrational."

But the Bible disagrees. Isaiah prophesies, "The LORD Almighty is the one ... you are to fear, he is the one you are to dread" (Isaiah 8:13). And Jesus says, "Fear God, who has the power to kill you and then throw you into hell" (Luke 12:5 NLT).

So when the Bible talks about fearing God, it means not just awe and not just reverence. It also means fear. It's the kind of fear I felt at the Grand Canyon, where I was drawn to amazing beauty, but I also felt a realistic fear at the danger, because people who acted foolishly near it have died.

—Kevin Miller, Wheaton, Illinois

ILLUSTRATION 724

WHEN KNOWLEDGE IS TOO HEAVY

Topics: Answers; Childlikeness; Faith; Fathers; God as Father; God's Sovereignty; Mysteries; Questions; Trust

References: Job 38–40; Isaiah 55:8–9; Matthew 18:5; Mark 9:42

Corrie ten Boom, at about age ten, was reading a poem as she and her father traveled by train from Amsterdam to Haarlem. "What does 'sex sin' mean?" she asked. She describes what happened next:

He turned to look at me, as he always did when answering a question, but, to my surprise, he said nothing. At last he stood up, lifted his traveling case from the rack over our heads, and set it on the floor. "Will you carry it off the train, Corrie?" he asked.

I stood up and tugged at it. It was crammed with watches and spare parts he had purchased that morning. "It's too heavy," I said.

"Yes," he said. "And it would be a pretty poor father who would ask his little girl to carry such a load. It's the same way, Corrie, with knowledge. Some knowledge is too heavy for children. When you are older and stronger, you can bear it. For now you must trust me to carry it for you."

And I was satisfied. More than satisfied—wonderfully at peace. There were answers to this and all my hard questions; for now, I was content to leave them in my father's keeping.

God is mysterious not simply because he is God, but because we are children. And in his love our childhood is protected. We should view both childhood and God's mysteries as a source of wonder and even comfort; there is a Creator, and we are among the created. There are answers to all things safely in our Father's keeping.

—Based on Corrie ten Boom, *The Hiding Place* (Guideposts Associates, 1971)

ILLUSTRATION 725

SPIRITUALLY MALNOURISHED

Topics: Bible; Devotional Life; Maturity; Spiritual Growth; Teaching

References: 1 Corinthians 13:11; Ephesians 4:14; Hebrews 5:14

One spring, our family was driving from Fort Lauderdale to Tampa, Florida. As far as the eye could see, orange trees were loaded with fruit. When we stopped for breakfast, I ordered orange juice with my eggs. "I'm sorry," the waitress said. "I can't bring you orange juice. Our machine is broken."

I was dumbfounded. We were surrounded by millions of oranges, and orange slices garnished our plates. We were surrounded by thousands of gallons of juice, but we couldn't have it because the restaurant was dependent on a machine to get it.

Christians are sometimes like that. They are surrounded by Bibles, but if they couldn't get to a Sunday morning preaching service, they would have no nourishment for their souls. The problem is not a lack of spiritual food; it's that many Christians haven't grown enough to know how to get it for themselves.

—Leroy Eims, *The Lost Art of Disciple Making* (Zondervan, 1978)

ILLUSTRATION 726

HEARING LESSONS

Topics: Healing; Last Things; Potential; Regeneration; Restoration; Sanctification; Waiting on God

References: Romans 8:18–39; 2 Corinthians 5:17; Philippians 1:6

A little girl in England, Josie Caven, was born profoundly deaf. She often felt isolated as a child because of her inability to hear, but that changed after she received a cochlear implant during the Christmas season. At the age of twelve, she heard clearly for the first time. The first sound she heard was the song "Jingle Bells" coming from the radio.

Was Josie's hearing restored? Yes—completely. Was she hearing well immediately? Not exactly. Her mother said, "She is having to learn what each new sound is and what it means. She will ask, 'Was that a door closing?' and has realized for the first time that the light in her room hums when it is switched on. She even knows what her name sounds like now, because before she could not hear the soft *s* sound in the middle of the word. Seeing her face light up as she hears everything around her is all I could have wished for this Christmas."

Josie's hearing was restored, but that restoration introduced her to the daily adventure of learning to distinguish each new sound in the hearing world. It's the already and the not yet—a phrase that aptly describes the perspective of believers in Christ who have not yet experienced the fullness of redemption that will one day be realized in heaven.

— "Christmas Carols Music to the Ears of Deaf Girl," Yorkshireposttoday.com

ILLUSTRATION 727
ACCIDENTS WITH GOD

Topics: Bible Reading; Devotional Life; Experiencing God; Fasting; Knowing God; Listening; Meditation; Quiet Time; Reflection; Seeking God; Self-discipline; Solitude; Spiritual Disciplines; Worship

References: Matthew 6:1–18; John 17:3; 1 Corinthians 9:24–27; Colossians 4:2; 1 Thessalonians 5:17; Hebrews 4:16

Experiences of God cannot be planned or achieved. "They are spontaneous moments of grace, almost accidental," a rabbi said.

His student asked, "If God-realization is just accidental, why do we work so hard doing all these spiritual practices?"

"To be as accident-prone as possible," said the teacher.

— Philip Yancey, *Prayer* (Zondervan, 2006)

ILLUSTRATION 728
DOING THE UNNATURAL

Topics: Behavior; Conduct; Depravity; Desires; Ethics; Habits; Human Nature; Lust; Morality; Pleasure; Sexual Immorality; Sinful Nature

References: Romans 1:26–27; 12:1; 1 Corinthians 6:9–20; Galatians 5:17–23; Colossians 3:5; Titus 2:11–12

Many people justify a variety of behaviors by calling them "natural." Here's what M. Scott Peck says about that: "Calling it natural does not mean it is essential or beneficial or unchangeable behavior. It is also natural to defecate in our pants and never brush our teeth. Yet we teach ourselves to do the unnatural until the unnatural itself becomes second nature. Indeed, all self-discipline might be defined as teaching ourselves to do the unnatural."

— M. Scott Peck,
The Road Less Traveled (Touchstone, 1998)

ILLUSTRATION 729
CLEANING MAKEOVER

Topics: Christian Life; Cleansing; Purity; Renewal; Repentance; Sanctification; Spiritual Formation

References: 2 Chronicles 29; Psalm 139:23–24; 2 Timothy 2:20–21

On the Style Channel's *Clean House*, experts sweep into a cluttered home with the purpose of leaving it more comfortable, attractive, and livable. The experts face the challenges of clothes strewn across the floor, bulging cabinets, closets filled from top to bottom, cluttered countertops, and overflowing kitchens, bedrooms, bathrooms, and living rooms — not a clean room in the house!

The experts' first step is to take an inventory of all the stuff. Then, decisions are made about what to sell at a yard sale and what to keep. The homeowners try to hold on to favorite clothes from years gone by, childhood keepsakes, and space-taking trivia, but then they yield. They have a yard sale, and the money they earn helps with the makeover. Then the family leaves, and the work begins.

Rooms are cleaned out, redone for more efficiency and attractiveness, and repainted. Curtains are hung, cabinets set in, and walls decorated. When the family returns, nervous anticipation quickly gives way to excitement and laughter. "Thank you, thank you," the family says amid smiles and tears.

In the spiritual realm, there comes a time for each of us to take inventory of what's in our hearts, get rid of some things, and do some repairing and remodeling. Like the families on *Clean House*, we have an expert in remodeling and renovation — Jesus Christ — who can make our makeover an astounding success.

— Ted De Haas, Bedford, Iowa

ILLUSTRATION 730

HEART FIX

Topics: Abundant Life; Behavior; Conduct; Freedom; Fulfillment; Fullness; Gratitude; Healing; Heart; Hope; Lifestyle; Sanctification

References: Ezekiel 11:19; Romans 6:6–11; 2 Corinthians 5:17; Ephesians 4:22–24; Colossians 3:5–10; Hebrews 9:13–15; 1 Peter 1:23

From his hospital bed on the eve of open-heart surgery, Pastor Bruce McIver asked his cardiologist, Dr. Dudley Johnson, "Can you fix my heart?"

The physician said, "Sure." Then he walked away.

Following the twelve-hour surgery, McIver asked Johnson, "In light of the blocked arteries that I had when I checked into the hospital, how much blood supply do I now have?"

"All you'll ever need," replied the terse surgeon.

Upon his discharge from the hospital, McIver's wife, Lawanna, asked the doctor, "What about my husband's future quality of life?"

Dr. Johnson paused and then said, "I fixed his heart; the quality of his life is up to him."

— Bruce McIver, *Stories I Couldn't Tell While I Was a Pastor* (Wolgemuth and Hyatt, 1991

ILLUSTRATION 731

RESOLUTION FOLLOW-UP

Topics: Determination; Discipline; Faithfulness; Humility; Imitation of Christ; Obedience; Self-discipline; Self-examination

References: Mark 8:34–35; Philippians 1:9–10; James 4:10

Jonathan Edwards, the eighteenth-century revivalist, sat down at age seventeen and penned twenty-one resolutions by which he would live his life. He added to this list until, by his death, he had seventy resolutions.

He put this at the top of his list: "Being sensible that I am unable to do anything without God's help, I do humbly entreat him by his grace to enable me to keep these resolutions."

To follow up, each week Edwards did a self-check. He regularly summed up how he was doing and sought God's help in the process.

— Jan Brown, Christianity Online Connection (January 8, 1999)

ILLUSTRATION 732

WHAT IS REQUIRED OF US

Topics: Humility; Justice; Love; Mercy; Righteousness

References: Micah 6:8; Matthew 16:24

"The only thing that God requires from us is to enjoy life — and love," said singer Paul Simon in a February 2001 interview with *Rolling Stone*. "It doesn't matter if you accomplish anything. You don't have to do anything but appreciate that you're alive. And love, that's the whole point."

By contrast, the Old Testament prophet Micah wrote, "And what does the LORD require of you? To act justly and to love mercy and to walk humbly with your God" (6:8).

— David Slagle, "Paul Simon: What God Requires," PreachingToday.com

ILLUSTRATION 733

FACING FEAR

Topics: Attitudes; Challenges; Confidence; Fear; Panic; Preparation; Spiritual Warfare

References: Luke 22:31–34; 1 Corinthians 10:11–13; Ephesians 6:10–18; 2 Timothy 1:7

On July 21, 1861, raw Yankee recruits marched toward the Confederate Army camping at Bull Run, thirty miles southwest of Washington. The Union soldiers were overconfident and acted as if they were headed toward a sporting event. Congressmen, ladies, and all sorts of spectators trailed along with lunch baskets to observe the fun.

But the courage of the Confederates, who stood their ground like a stone wall — giving their leader, Thomas J. Jackson, the nickname of "Stonewall" — and the arrival of Confederate reinforcements threw the Union forces into a panic, even though the Union had superior forces.

One observer wrote, "We called to them, tried to tell them there was no danger, called them to stop, implored them to stand. We called them cowards, denounced them in the most offensive terms ... but all in vain; a cruel, crazy, mad, hopeless panic possessed them."

Likewise, fear and panic can overwhelm us emotionally, even though we have the spiritual resources to deal with the situation. We are better able to face fearful situations—and stop a "mad, hopeless panic" from possessing us—if we prepare ourselves soberly for the challenges life will hand us.

—Thomas Bailey and David Kennedy, eds.,
The American Pageant, 9th ed. (D. C. Heath, 1991)

ILLUSTRATION 734

PRAYING FOR CLARITY

Topics: Dependence; Direction; Guidance; Prayer; Spiritual Perception; Trust

References: Psalm 37:3–6; Proverbs 3:5–6

When John Kavanaugh, a renowned ethicist, went to work at "the house of the dying" in Calcutta, he was seeking a clear answer about how to spend the rest of his life. On the first morning there he met Mother Teresa. She asked, "And what can I do for you?"

Kavanaugh asked her to pray for him. "What do you want me to pray for?" she asked.

He said, "Pray that I have clarity."

She said firmly, "I will not do that."

When he asked her why, she said, "Clarity is the last thing you are clinging to and must let go of."

When Kavanaugh commented that she seemed to have the clarity he longed for, she laughed and said, "I have never had clarity; what I have always had is trust. So I will pray that you trust God."

—Brennan Manning,
Ruthless Trust (HarperCollins, 2000)

ILLUSTRATION 735

THE BOMB UNDER THE BED

Topics: Anger; Bitterness; Confession; Hindrances; Repentance; Shame

References: Psalm 90:8; Matthew 5:21–22; Ephesians 4:26

During World War II, Zinaida Bragantsova of Ukraine was sitting by the window sewing. Suddenly she heard a whistling noise. Then she was struck by a blast of wind. When she came to, her sewing machine was gone, and there was a hole in the floor.

She told people there was a bomb in the floor, but she couldn't get any officials to check out the situation. So she moved her bed over the hole and lived with it for the next forty-three years.

Then, one day, phone cable was being laid in the area and demolition experts were called in to probe for buried explosives. "Where's your bomb, Grandma?" asked the smiling army lieutenant of Bragantsova. "No doubt, under your bed?"

"Under my bed," Bragantsova responded dryly.

Sure enough, they found a five-hundred-pound bomb. After evacuating two thousand people from surrounding buildings, the bomb squad detonated the bomb. Bragantsova moved to a new apartment.

Many people live as if they have a bomb under their bed. They cover up a terrible secret, a great hurt, a seething anger while everyone goes on about their business. But no one is truly safe until the bomb is uncovered and removed.

—Lee Eclov, "Danger of Bitterness,"
PreachingToday.com

ILLUSTRATION 736
FUELING HAPPINESS

Topics: Desires; Fulfillment; Happiness; Joy; Peace; Purpose; Satisfaction

References: Psalm 42:1; Isaiah 26:3; John 14:6, 27; 15:11

A car is made to run on petrol [gas], and it would not run properly on anything else. Now God designed the human machine to run on himself. He himself is the fuel our spirits were designed to burn, or the food our spirits were designed to feed on. There is no other. That is why it is just no good asking God to make us happy in our own way without bothering about religion. God cannot give us a happiness and peace apart from himself, because it is not there. There is no such thing.

—C. S. Lewis,
Mere Christianity (Macmillan, 1952)

ILLUSTRATION 737
THANKS FOR THE TREES

Topics: Criticism; Gratitude; Ingratitude; Thankfulness

Reference: Luke 17:12–19

I was helping a friend plant a tree at the local park. She had planted twenty-three trees already, most of them without any help. The trees were donated by family members in remembrance of loved ones. While we were working, a woman approached us. I recognized her and assumed she was there to say thank you.

"Remember the tree you planted for me the other day?" she asked.

My friend nodded.

"You planted it too close to the road. It needs to be moved." Then she turned and left.

I don't think this woman was intentionally rude. She was probably distracted, or maybe she'd had a bad day, but, still—of the twenty-three trees my friend planted, only two people remembered to say, "Thank you."

—Teresa Bell Kindred,
Kentucky Living (October 2000)

ILLUSTRATION 738
WAYS OF SHOWING THANKS

Topics: Prayer; Thankfulness

References: Philippians 4:6–7; 1 Thessalonians 5:16–18

We give thanks to God, who is the source of all good things. According to Yankelovich Partners for Lutheran Brotherhood, here's how we do that:

- praying: 45 percent
- being a good role model: 39 percent
- volunteering: 36 percent
- participating in a place of worship: 35 percent
- giving money to charity: 30 percent

—*USA Today* "Snapshots"
(November 23, 1999)

ILLUSTRATION 739

RUNNING WITH INNER SPRINGS

Topics: Holy Spirit; Power

References: Romans 15:13; Galatians 2:20; Philippians 4:13

You can put a spring back into your step, thanks to Nike. After sixteen years of research, the giant shoe company produced sneakers called Shox, which have four strong springs in the heel. When you press down, the brightly colored springs, made of high-density foam, push back up. Shox help you run faster and jump higher than you could on your own.

Bruce Kilgore, director of advanced research and development at Nike, describes what happened when runners tested out a prototype: "Smiles ... would break out on people's faces as they were running," he said.

Christians also have inner springs. With the power of the Spirit, we can do things we never could do on our own.

—Ron Lieber, "Boing!"
Fast Company (November 2000)

ILLUSTRATION 740

MOVING ACCORDING TO PLAN

Topics: Faith; God's Will; Guidance; Providence; Trust

Reference: Psalm 13:1–2

In December 1958, I came to America from Germany on the USS *Butner*, a transport ship. After we left Bremerhafen, we passed through the North Sea into the North Atlantic. Huge waves buffeted the ship, and every day seemed the same—water, water everywhere, to the north, the south, the east, and the west. All we could hear was the monotonous grinding of the ship's engine.

Finally, the scene changed. There was water to the east and the south, but to the west stood the Statue of Liberty gleaming in the morning sun. We had come home.

Walking by faith can be like that. Waves of opposition battle us with no change in sight. In all directions there seems to be nothing, with the Lord seemingly asleep. Then, finally, a special day arrives, revealing that we have been moving all along according to his plan.

—Helmar Heckel, Excelsior, Minnesota

ILLUSTRATION 741

UNPLUGGED

Topics: Holy Spirit; Power; Prayer

References: 1 Corinthians 1:24; 4:20;
2 Timothy 3:5

While visiting Grand Coulee Dam, my family and I were surprised to see that the visitor's center was dark. It was a sunny day, so we thought the center might have tinted windows, but as we got closer, we realized no lights were on. We went in and saw that none of the displays were working.

It soon became clear that there was no power to the center. Due to a technical difficulty, the visitor's center that sat only hundreds of feet from a hydroelectric dam had no power.

How could something be so close to the power source yet not be "plugged in"?

—Paul Dawson, Pendleton, Oregon

ILLUSTRATION 742

LIFE GOALS

Topics: Ambition; Character; Contentment; Goals; Greed; Lifestyle; Money; Possessions; Prosperity; Purpose; Riches; Spiritual Growth; Spiritual Poverty; Stewardship; Teens; Worldliness

References: Deuteronomy 15:7; Proverbs 19:17; Matthew 6:1–4; 19:21; Acts 5:1–11

What is "essential" in the mind of the typical college freshman? An extensive survey conducted by the Higher Education Research Institute found that 85.8 percent say it is getting rich. That's a 43 percent increase over what the typical college freshman thought in 1967. As for developing a meaningful philosophy of life? Only 45 percent found it to be of any real worth. That's a 29 percent drop.

According to research collected by Pew Research for the MacNeil/Lehrer Productions' Generation Next project, 18- to 25-year-olds listed the following as their top life goal:

- be rich: 81 percent
- be famous: 51 percent
- help people who need help: 30 percent
- be leaders in their community: 22 percent
- become more spiritual: 10 percent

—Van Morris, "Goals of 'Generation Next,'"
PreachingToday.com

ILLUSTRATION 743

PERSONALIZING GOD'S WILL

Topics: Character; Example; God's Will; Grace; Integrity; Men; Obedience

References: Romans 1:16–17; 2 Timothy 1:13

God has no more precious gift to a church or an age than a man who lives as an embodiment of his will, and inspires those around him with the faith of what grace can do.

—Andrew Murray, *Leadership* (Fall 1986)

ILLUSTRATION 744

A RUNNING PLAN

Topics: Christlikeness; Maturity; Perseverance; Planning; Spiritual Growth

References: Luke 14:27 – 31; Romans 8:29; Philippians 3:7 – 16

When I first ran track in prep school, my coach invited me to his home for dinner. After the meal, he pulled out a notebook with my name on the front cover. He turned to the back page, which bore the heading "June 1957" — three and a half years away.

"Gordon, these are the races I'm going to schedule you to run about four years from now. Here are the times you will achieve."

I looked at those times. They were light-years away from where I was as a runner. Then Coach began turning back the pages of that book, page by page, showing the forty-two months he had scheduled for workouts. These were the graduated, accelerated plans for my increasing skill on the track in the coming months.

Coaches and other leaders know the necessity of strategic, long-range planning. Similarly, a wise and all-knowing God has a plan for our lives, as down through the years we gradually become more like Jesus.

> — Gordon MacDonald, from a message delivered at the Promise Keepers "Go the Distance" conference (August 11, 2000)

ILLUSTRATION 745

WAITING LESSONS

Topics: Hope; Patience; Perseverance; Seasons; Waiting on God

References: Psalm 27:14; Romans 8:22 – 25; Hebrews 10:36

I'm an impatient, restless person. Slowing down and waiting seem like a waste of time. Yet waiting seems to be an inevitable part of the human condition.

Henri Nouwen said, "Waiting is a period of learning. The longer we wait, the more we hear about him for whom we are waiting."

Eugene Peterson's paraphrase of Romans 8:24 resonates with Nouwen: "Waiting does not diminish us any more than waiting diminishes a pregnant mother. We are enlarged in the waiting" (*The Message*).

During times of waiting, God is vibrantly at work within us.

> — Luci Shaw, "Nourishment for the Journey," in *Nouwen Then*, Christopher deVinck, ed. (Zondervan, 1999)

ILLUSTRATION 746

TAMING EAGLES

Topics: Brokenness; Dependence; Ministry; Spiritual Formation; Weakness

References: Psalm 51:17; 102:23; Acts 9:1 – 19

The capture, taming, training, and keeping of hunting eagles in Asia is highly ritualized. Most of the birds, which have a life span of about forty years, are caught when very young — either snatched from a nest or trapped in a baited net. Once captured, the eagle is hooded and placed in a cage with a perch that sways constantly so it cannot rest or sleep.

For two or three days the eaglet is also deprived of food. During this time, the *berkutchi*, or eagle hunter, talks, sings, and chants to the bird for hours on end. Finally, the man begins to feed and stroke the bird. Slowly the weakened creature comes to rely on its master. When the berkutchi decides that their relationship has become strong enough, the training begins.

Not all eagles will become hunters, but those who take to life with a master display intense loyalty.

The training and breaking of the eagle may seem harsh, but it is a picture of how over time God breaks our independent spirit to draw us close to him.

> — Stephen Kinzer, "A Hunter
> Whose Weapon Is Also His Friend,"
> *The New York Times* (November 4, 1999).

ILLUSTRATION 747
HEARING THE FLUTES

Topics: Hearing God; Holy Spirit; Quietness; Spiritual Disciplines; Spiritual Perception

References: 1 Samuel 3:1 – 14; Psalm 16:7

A child was told by his father during a concert, "Listen for the flutes in this song. Don't they sound beautiful?" The child looked up at his father with a puzzled look, "What are flutes, Father?"

A child first needs to learn what flutes sound like on their own, separate from the whole orchestra, before he can hear them in a symphony. So it is with us as children of God. Unless we take the time to hear his voice in the quiet moments of life, we will not be able to hear him in the symphony sounds of life.

> — Stephen Macchia,
> *Becoming a Healthy Church* (Baker, 1999)

ILLUSTRATION 748
THE BIGNESS OF LITTLE CHOICES

Topics: Character; Choices; Crisis; Decisions; Honesty; Integrity; Mistakes; Temptation; Truth

Reference: Ephesians 4:25

My wife, Jana, was working as a nurse in a clinic when a young mother came in with her eighteen-month-old son. He needed his final shot for a routine immunization, and she needed a physical. Both patients — and Jana — were new to the clinic.

Jana gave the boy his shot, and his mother took him back to the waiting room to his sister and grandmother. The mother went back for her physical. When Jana went to record the vaccination on the boy's chart, she noticed that the seal on the vial inside her lab coat was unbroken. Quickly Jana realized that she had given the boy the wrong vaccine.

She gasped when she realized her mistake. Here is the sequence of the thoughts that followed:

"No one will ever know. No harm done."

"I can't tell the doctor."

"This is my first day on the job."

"The doctor will think I'm incompetent."

"It can't hurt the boy, can it?"

"It doesn't hurt to be immunized twice for the same thing."

"But he needs the right vaccine."

"What will the mother say?"

"But I will always know, and so will God."

Following Jesus is often cast as a series of big things — the big decision to be more committed, the big decision to forsake all and become a missionary, the big decision to become a pastor, the big decision to do big things for God. Yet the real battles are often fought internally, in quickly passing moments.

When the doctor walked out of the room, Jana told him her mistake. After a few moments, he walked back in the room, told the mother what happened, and asked her to schedule another time for her child's immunization. Jana's anxiety released; she was now free.

— Dave Goetz, Wheaton, Illinois

ILLUSTRATION 749

HELPING STUDENTS WITH MORAL STRUGGLES

Topics: Conscience; Maturity; Punishment; Purity; Temptation

References: Proverbs 28:13; Hebrews 3:13; James 5:16; 1 John 1:9

As associate dean of students at Trinity International University, Matthew Perrault helps students grow closer to Jesus. He also disciplines students who fall short of the university's moral guidelines. Amazingly, Perrault has come up with a system that allows him to accomplish both at the same time.

"No one is expected to come to Trinity perfect," Perrault says, "but in the past, there has been a misconception that you cannot be open about your struggles or you'll get into trouble. For example, a student who entered Trinity and tried to quit smoking at the same time might try really hard but fail and be in violation of our community expectations. This left many students feeling scared, guilty, and alienated from the very community they needed to help them."

A few years ago, Perrault and the Student Development staff officially included the "Restoration Program" in the student handbook. If a student has broken community expectations or has a behavioral pattern that is in violation of Scripture, the student can approach any staff or faculty member and ask to enter the program. The new policy states that, rather than facing normal disciplinary procedures, the student will work with Student Development to determine the relationships and accountability measures needed to face the problem. The student will then enter into a mentoring relationship for a set period of time.

Perrault has noticed a shift in students' attitudes about discipline in response to the program. Increasingly over recent years, instead of trying to hide their struggles, students trust the dean's office as a safe place. "What a humbling privilege it is to be entrusted with these fragile lives and these students' desire to grow in Christ," he says. "Through this process, they're committing to us, but we're also committing to them."

— "Invested Time,"
Trinity Magazine (Spring 2006)

The command "Be ye perfect" is not idealistic gas. Nor is it a command to do the impossible. [God] is going to make us into creatures that can obey that command.

—C. S. Lewis,
Mere Christianity (Macmillan, 1952)

ILLUSTRATION 750

JUMPING HURDLES

Topics: Goals; Inspiration; Leadership; Motivation; Passion; Spiritual Desires; Vision

Reference: Titus 2:7–8

An Olympic equestrian champion was asked, "How does your horse know when it has to leap the hedges and hurdles, and why do some horses turn away or stumble?"

The woman answered, "That's simple. You tear your heart out of your body and throw it over the hedge. The horse knows how desperate you are to catch up to your heart. So it leaps."

—Martin Marty, foreword in Quentin Schultze,
Communicating for Life (Baker, 2000)

ILLUSTRATION 751

BECOMING PERFECT

Topics: Christian Life; Holiness; Maturity; Perfection; Sanctification

References: Matthew 5:48; Philippians 1:6

ILLUSTRATION 752

RUNNING ACROSS THE SAHARA

Topics: Ambition; Attitudes; Challenges; Courage; Dedication; Determination; Faith; Faithfulness; Goals; Motivation; Passion; Patience; Perseverance; Persistence; Self-discipline; Strength; Trials; Victory

References: Acts 20:24; 1 Corinthians 4:9–13; 9:24–27; 2 Corinthians 1:8–11; 2 Timothy 2:1–13; 4:6–8; Hebrews 11:1–12:13; Revelation 3:10

For 111 days. Charlie Engle, Ray Zahab, and Kevin Lin ran across the Sahara Desert. They touched the waters at Senegal and then made their way through Mauritania, Mali, Niger, Libya, and Egypt to touch the waters of the Red Sea.

Along the way, the trio faced blazing afternoons of 100-plus degrees; jarring, freezing nights; sandstorms; tendonitis; violent sickness; aches, pains, and blisters. But the biggest challenge they faced was finding water. Finding it in its purest, cleanest form gets to be a bit of a chore while in the middle of nowhere.

Running 4,000 miles across the Sahara Desert is an amazing accomplishment. But just as commendable are these marathon finishers:

- Christians who finish their lives still growing, still serving
- husbands and wives who stay faithful to each other "until death do us part"
- young people who preserve their virginity until marriage despite crushing peer pressure
- pastors who stay passionate about ministry until their last breath
- church members who weather conflict and remain joyful, loving, and faithful

—Anna Johnson, "3 Ultra-athletes Run across Sahara," *USA Today* (February 20, 2007)

PART 30: SPORTS

ILLUSTRATION 753

LOSING THE BIG GAME

Topics: Grief; Healing; Loss; Optimism; Pain; Pessimism; Sorrow

References: 2 Corinthians 4:16; 1 Thessalonians 4:13; Revelation 2:3

Relief pitcher Donny Moore couldn't resolve his anguish over losing an American League championship series game a few years ago. In a moment of torment, he shot his wife and then himself.

Compare that with the reaction of Dave Dravecky, who lost not only a game but a career, a livelihood, his pitching arm, and his shoulder. He is energetically rebuilding his life and looking forward to whatever tomorrow might bring. You tell me how important it is to grieve appropriately.

—Bill Hybels, "A Better Kind of Grieving," Preaching Today Audio, no. 108

ILLUSTRATION 754

MORE THAN A SUPER BOWL

Topics: Emptiness; Human Condition; Meaning; Purpose; Seeking God; Significance; Success

References: Ecclesiastes 2:22–26; Mark 8:35–36; Philippians 3:4–14

At age twenty-eight Tom Brady has already won three Super Bowls and is ranked as one of the best quarterbacks ever. But it isn't enough.

"Why do I have three Super Bowl rings and still think there's something greater out there for me?" he asked in a 2005 interview. "I mean, maybe a lot of people would say, 'Hey man, this is what is. I reached my goal, my dream, my life.' Me, I think, God, it's got to be more than this. I mean this isn't, this can't be, what it's all cracked up to be."

—*60 Minutes* (November 6, 2005), CBSNews.com

ILLUSTRATION 755

GRIDIRON REGRETS

Topics: Ambition; Consequences; Drugs; Glory; Meaning; Purpose; Sin; Success

References: 1 Corinthians 9:24–27; Galatians 6:7–8; Philippians 3:14–21

For sixteen years, linebacker Bill Romanowski ruled the NFL gridiron with vicious tackles and cheap hits. Known as "Romo," he played with intense hatred and violence on the field, breaking bones and injuring opposing players. Driven by a fear of failure, he pushed his body to the limit, not only through weight training, but with dietary supplements and illegal steroids.

"I compromised my morality to get ahead, to play another year, to play two more years, to win another Super Bowl," he said in a 2005 interview. Worse than the pain from all the vicious hits was the embarrassment he caused to his family, friends, teammates, team owners, the league, and ultimately a little boy who asked, "Dad, do you do drugs?"

"That one hurt me more than anything," Romanowski said.

Romo suffered dozens of concussions while playing football. Toward the end of his career, he couldn't see straight. He had headaches and nausea. Two years after retirement, doctors say he shows profound slowing in cognitive function.

Greater than the physical pain is Romanowski's pain of living without purpose and meaning after he was done with football. "You know, I think you have these illusions, dreams, nightmares, that maybe you can still do it," he said. He admitted that he hadn't cleaned out his locker in Oakland after he retired in 2003.

— *60 Minutes* (October 16, 2005),
CBSNews.com

ILLUSTRATION 756

SKIPPING THE SUPER BOWL

Topics: Commitment; Good Deeds; Medical Care; Ministry; Missions; Passion; Priorities; Sacrifice; Service

References: Matthew 6:19–20; Luke 9:23–26; 12:33

Kathy Holmgren, wife of Seattle Seahawks head coach Mike Holmgren, decided to skip Super Bowl XL in 2006 for something she considered more important—a faith-based humanitarian trip to Africa.

Holmgren, a nurse, and her daughter, Calla, who is an obstetrician, left three days before the big game on a seventeen-day medical training mission with Northwest Medical Teams—a relief group based in Portland, Oregon—to the northwest region of the Democratic Republic of Congo. The two joined six other physicians with experience as missionaries.

During the three days it took to reach the region, the medical team traveled over marginal roads that narrowed to near nonexistence, waded through streams, and crossed rough-hewn and often improvised bridges. The team then worked with the staff of a hospital operated by the Evangelical Covenant Church.

The hospital is the only medical facility for 300,000 people in the region, and the staff is often forced to use rudimentary equipment when treating 2,500 patients a month. More than 3.9 million Congolese have died since 1998, most from preventable disease, according to the British medical journal *The Lancet*.

Kathy Holmgren spent ten months in the region in 1970 but gave up her dream of being a Covenant medical missionary to marry. Last October, Mike Holmgren's birthday present to his wife was the trip back to the country she loves.

—Stan Friedman, "Seahawks Coach's Family Choose Mission to Africa over Super Bowl," belief net.com (Religion News Service, January 30, 2006)

ILLUSTRATION 757

A BULL RIDER WITH FAITH

Topics: Courage; Danger; Death; Evangelism; Faith; Fear; Peace; Prayer

References: Joshua 1:9; Isaiah 26:3; Matthew 28:19; Philippians 4:6–7; 1 Peter 5:7

Adriano Moraes is one of the best bull riders in the world. His flawless technique and natural riding ability have won him two world championships. Moraes is also deeply committed to Jesus Christ. "Work, faith, and humbleness" is the motto by which he and his family live. "When I'm close to my God, I'm doing well," he says.

During one rodeo, his faith was severely tested after he saw a fellow Brazilian rider get thrown from his bull and go down hard. The rider didn't move as a crowd of cowboys and officials gathered around him, loaded him on a gurney, and took him to the nearest hospital.

Suddenly Moraes was gripped with fear. He didn't want the same thing to happen to him. Later, in his hotel room, he knelt by the side of his bed and prayed, "Lord Jesus, strengthen me through your Holy Spirit, who lives in me." The Lord blessed him with peace and courage. "I can die now," Moraes said.

While still a champion rider, Moraes heads up "Rodeo with Christ," a multifaceted ministry in Brazil. The ministry includes TV shows and an annual evangelistic "Rodeo with Christ." The primary goal is to spread the truth of Jesus Christ to those who need to hear it.

— *Beyond the Bull* television series, "Out of the Gate" (The Learning Channel, January 10, 2005)

ILLUSTRATION 758

BROKEN BEFORE GOD

Topics: Anxiety; Assurance; Brokenness; Consequences; Danger; Despair; Doubt; Eternal Life; Faith; Fame; Heaven; Mortality; Pain; Seeking God; Suffering; Trials

References: Job 6:10; John 11:25–26; 14:1–4; Acts 16:31; Romans 3:10–26; 10:8–12; Revelation 21:4

The motorcyclist Evel Knievel became "the most famous daredevil on earth" during the 1960s and 1970s. Jumping over buses, cars, and anything else put before him earned him $30 million. But the price he paid was forty bone fractures and a broken back (seven times). He was in a coma for weeks following a crash at Caesars Palace in Las Vegas.

In 2007, he was also a broken man. Pins and fasteners held him together. He was hooked up to oxygen, and synthetic heroin was shot into his spine to control pain. His lungs were scarred with pulmonary fibrosis due to smoking. His liver was destroyed by alcohol.

On April 1, 2007, Knievel announced to a worldwide audience that he "believed in Jesus Christ" for the first time. He professed his personal faith in Christ to more than four thousand people who gathered inside the Crystal Cathedral for Palm Sunday services in Garden Grove, California, and to presumably millions via an *Hour of Power* telecast of the service to more than one hundred countries.

At his request he was baptized before the congregation and TV cameras by Dr. Robert

H. Schuller, founder of the Crystal Cathedral. *Christianity Today* reported that "Daredevil Knievel's testimony triggered mass baptisms at Crystal Cathedral."

—Jim Saraceno, "Long-Retired Knievel Frail, Feisty, Still Cheating Death," USAToday.com (January 3, 2007)

ILLUSTRATION 759

SCORING FOR THE TEAM

Topics: Attitudes; Church; Cooperation; Faithfulness; Humility; Loyalty; Meekness; Reputation; Teamwork; Thankfulness; Togetherness; Unselfishness

References: Matthew 18:4; Luke 22:26; John 13:1–17; Romans 12:3–8; 1 Corinthians 12:7–27; Ephesians 4:11–16; Philippians 2:3–4; James 4:10

In a game between the San Diego Chargers and the Denver Broncos in December 2006, LaDainian Tomlinson, running back for the Chargers, took his position the same way he had done hundreds of times before. But this time he took the ball and sprinted around two defenders for a seven-yard gain into the end zone for his NFL record-breaking twenty-ninth touchdown of the season.

Impressive as that accomplishment was, Tomlinson's selfless behavior after the run really stole the show. Instead of raising his hands in victory or dancing across the turf, Tomlinson beckoned for his offensive line—those inconspicuous behemoths who cleared the path for his success—to join him. With more than 67,000 fans wildly cheering, he helped his entire team bask in the glory.

He also refused to acknowledge individual accomplishment when talking with reporters after the game. Instead, he consistently used plural pronouns to include his teammates: "When we're old and can't play this game anymore, those are the moments that we're going to remember, being able to tell our kids and tell our grandchildren. We made history today, and there's no better feeling than to share it with the group of guys in that locker room."

—Mark Bergin, "Head of the Class," *World* (December 23, 2006)

ILLUSTRATION 760

MAKING IT TO THE FINISH LINE

Topics: Anxiety; Commitment; Courage; Dedication; Despair; Discouragement; Doubt; Endurance; Fear; Limitations; Motivation; Overcoming; Perseverance; Quitting; Steadfastness; Testing; Trials; Weariness

References: Luke 21:12–19; Acts 20:24; 1 Corinthians 9:24; Galatians 5:7; 6:9; 2 Timothy 4:7; Hebrews 10:36; 12:1; James 1:2–4

The first half of the New York City Marathon is a party. You're swept along by 28,000 runners and the crowds lining the streets. You're touring the ethnic neighborhoods of Brooklyn and Queens. You feel like you could run forever. At mile 13, you cross over into Manhattan and start heading north, away from the finish line. The crowds are thinner now. The party's over.

At about mile 16 or 18, you hit the wall. You're absolutely miserable. Physically and psychologically, you're busted. I remember passing one of the first-aid stations, where runners were lying on cots—pale and gaunt, with IVs dripping into their arms. I thought, *Those lucky dogs.* At that point I began to despair. I imagined myself having to go home and tell everybody I didn't finish. Why did I ever sign up for this race? What made me think I could do this?

That's when it hit me: one way or another, I had to get to Central Park. I had no car, no money. I would have to get there on my own two feet. So I might as well keep running. Just keep putting one foot in front of the other. Don't think about the next six miles; just think about the next step. Gradually the miles will pass. And when you cross that finish line, it feels like glory—even when you're in 10,044th place.

Some of you may be hitting the wall right now—feeling like you can't go on, like you'll never make it. Following Christ is harder than you ever imagined it would be, and you're thinking about giving up—about doing something foolish. Don't do it!

There's no magic to endurance racing. It's all about making it to the finish line.

—Bryan Wilkerson, "Endurance,"
PreachingToday.com

ILLUSTRATION 761

JUICED ON JESUS

Topics: Anointing; Christian Life; Divine Power; Experiencing God; Holy Spirit; Jesus Christ; New Life; Sports

References: Isaiah 40:31; Joel 2:28–29; John 7:37–39; Ephesians 5:18

At age forty-seven, Julio Franco became the oldest player in major league baseball history to hit a home run. A week later, on April 27, 2006, he became the oldest player in ninety-seven years to steal a base.

With a cloud of skepticism surrounding the sport, Franco's longevity has met suspicion from players and outsiders who doubt that he has stayed in top shape through natural training alone. In 2004, retired outfielder Andy Van Slyke accused Franco of using steroids. Franco's response demonstrated the true source of his remarkable life: "Tell Andy Van Slyke he's right—I'm on the best juice there is. I'm juiced up every day, and the name of my juice is Jesus. I'm on his power, his wisdom, his understanding. Andy Van Slyke is right, but the thing he didn't mention was what kind of steroids I'm on. Next time you talk to him, tell him the steroid I'm on is Jesus of Nazareth."

—"It Wasn't All Bad,"
The Week (May 5, 2006)

ILLUSTRATION 762

IRONMAN ATTITUDES

Topics: Advice; Bitterness; Complaining; Counsel; Cynicism; Discouragement; Encouragement; Guidance; Motivation; Optimism; Perseverance

References: Nehemiah 4:1–15; Isaiah 41:13; Galatians 6:2; Ephesians 4:15, 29; 5:15–16; Philippians 2:14; 1 Thessalonians 5:11; 2 Timothy 4:2; Hebrews 3:13

I discovered the importance of healthy counsel in a half Ironman triathlon. After the 1.2-mile swim and the 56-mile bike ride, I didn't have much energy left for the 13.1-mile run. Neither did the fellow jogging next to me. I asked him how he was doing and soon regretted posing the question.

"This stinks. This race is the dumbest decision I've ever made." He had more complaints than a taxpayer at the IRS. My response to him? "Good-bye." I knew if I listened too long, I'd start agreeing with him.

I caught up with a sixty-six-year-old grandmother. Her tone was just the opposite. "You'll finish this," she said. "It's hot, but at least it's not raining. One step at a time … don't forget to hydrate … stay in there." I ran next to her until my heart lifted and my legs were aching. I finally had to slow down. She waved and passed me.

Which of these two describes the counsel you seek?

—Max Lucado, *Facing Your Giants*
(W Publishing Group, 2006)

ILLUSTRATION 763

JASON'S AMAZING GAME

Topics: Blessings; Dedication; Disabilities; Faith; Fulfillment; Joy; Overcoming; Sports; Talents; Team; Unselfishness; Victory

References: Romans 12:3–8, 15–16; 1 Corinthians 12:14–26

Jason McElwain, a high school senior with autism, was the basketball team manager for three seasons, diligently fetching water, chasing rebounds in warm-ups, and mopping up sweat. However, in February 2006, for the last game of the season, Jason's coach decided to reward the young man by allowing him to suit up. Then, with the team ahead by twenty points and only four minutes to go, the coach put Jason in the game.

Jason missed his first two shots, but his third was a three-point swish. As the ball went through the net, the gymnasium erupted with applause. Jason went on to make six three-pointers—a Greece Athena High School record—to finish with twenty points in a little more than four minutes.

With each basket, the crowd became more enthusiastic. By the time Jason hit his last shot, everyone was jumping up and down. When the game ended, the bleachers emptied onto the court as the crowd gathered around Jason, and his teammates hoisted him onto their shoulders.

After the game, Jason's mother said, "This is the first moment Jason has ever succeeded and could be proud of himself. I look at autism as a Berlin Wall, and he cracked it." But Jason's success touched many more lives than his own, as those who celebrated with him experienced the selfless joy of delighting in others.

—Jim Aroune, "Beyond Rudy: Athena Senior Inspires" rnews.com (February 17, 2006)

ILLUSTRATION 764

NO STEROIDS, SON

Topics: Admonition; Confrontation; Deliverance; Direction; Drugs; Fatherhood; Guidance; Love; Parenting; Wisdom

References: Proverbs 12:15; Romans 8:15; Ephesians 6:4; 2 Timothy 4:2; Hebrews 12:11; 1 John 3:1

Before Bill Curry was an ESPN analyst, he was a college football coach, and before that he was a lineman in the National Football League. Today he wears two Super Bowl rings. But in the spring of 1965, it was unclear whether he would ever wear an NFL uniform.

He had been drafted in the twentieth round by the Green Bay Packers of the Vince Lombardi era but was convinced he would never make the team unless he gave himself an edge. So, a few months before the tryouts, Curry began lifting weights and taking steroids. He went from 220 to 240 pounds in just a few weeks.

When his father, a weightlifter, came to visit, Curry talked about his remarkable improvement. "It's just incredible what these pills can do, Dad!"

His father asked for the pills, walked to the bathroom, and poured them down the toilet.

The younger Curry panicked. "What are you doing?"

His father warned his son about steroids and how they would eventually destroy his body. Curry was shaken but convinced, and he never took steroids again. Today he simply says, "I'm so glad I had a father who loved me like that."

—Mark Galli, *Jesus Mean and Wild* (Baker, 2006)

ILLUSTRATION 765

FREE TO CRASH

Topics: Choices; Consequences; Free Will; Growth; Maturity; Perspective; Pride; Pruning; Recreation; Spiritual Growth; Trials; Understanding

References: Romans 8:2; 1 Corinthians 8:9; Galatians 5:13; 6:7–8; 1 Peter 2:16

Pittsburgh Steelers quarterback Ben Roethlisberger is the youngest signal-caller ever to win a Super Bowl. In July 2005, a reporter asked Roethlisberger why he didn't wear a helmet when riding his motorcycle.

"It's not the law," Roethlisberger said. "If it were the law, I'd definitely have one on every time I rode. But it's not the law and I know I don't have to. You're just freer when you're out there with no helmet on."

Less than a year later, Roethlisberger was involved in a serious motorcycle accident.

Surgeons spent over seven hours repairing his broken jaw, fractured skull, and several facial injuries.

Roethlisberger later apologized to the fans, his family, and his team for risking his health. "In the past few days, I've gained a new perspective on life," he said. "By the grace of God, I'm fortunate to be alive." He said if he ever rides a motorcycle again, he'll wear a helmet.

—David Slagle, "Quarterback Experiences Consequences of Freedom," PreachingToday.com

ILLUSTRATION 766

LOYALTY WINS GOLD

Topics: Assurance; Faith; Guidance; Loyalty; Providence; Trials

References: Proverbs 3:5–6; Jeremiah 29:11; Philippians 4:6–7

Vonetta Flowers was the first person of African descent to win a gold medal for the United States in the Olympic Winter Games. She did that in 2002 after she and teammate Jill Bakken jumped into a speeding bobsled and hurled themselves downhill in record time.

In the whirlwind of press coverage that followed, Flowers was named one of *People* magazine's "50 Most Beautiful People." She appeared on the *Today* show with Katie Couric and Matt Lauer. In the intense media spotlight, Flowers said time and time again, "I thank God for this win, because without him I wouldn't be here."

When she was age nine, Flowers was singled out as an athlete with Olympic potential. Her first track coach, Dewitt Thomas, told her she could be the next Jackie Joyner-Kersee. "I believed him," Flowers says.

Flowers went to the University of Alabama, Birmingham, on a full-ride athletic scholarship. She became one of the school's most decorated student athletes and the first person from her family to graduate from college. She tried out for the U.S. Olympic track and field team in 1996 as a college senior, but ankle injuries contributed to a disappointing thirteenth-place finish. Flowers began questioning her future. "I had achieved a lot of success in track and field based on my individual efforts, and I believed if I trained hard enough and stayed healthy, that would be enough for me to make the Olympic team. I didn't yet realize I needed God in my life to understand that what he wanted for my life was far greater than anything I ever could have imagined."

Flowers started attending church with a friend. Soon she made the decision to accept Christ as her Savior. In 1999, Flowers married Johnny, a fellow athlete and pastor's kid. With Johnny coaching her, Flowers started training again for the 2000 Olympics. Another ankle injury kept her off the team.

Then Johnny saw a flyer inviting athletes to try out for the U.S. bobsled team. Two weeks later, Bonny Warner, a world-class bobsled driver, invited Flowers to come to Germany to learn how to push a bobsled. After several weeks of training, Flowers asked to be brakeman on Warner's two-person sled. By the end of 2001, the duo was ranked third in the world. It looked like an easy slide to the 2002 Winter Olympics.

Then Warner dumped Flowers for another brakeman.

"I was devastated," Flowers says. For almost two weeks she didn't do anything. But then Johnny stepped in. "God put you in this sport for a reason, so we're going to start training again," he said to his wife.

A dubious Flowers agreed to start training again. Within a week of returning to the track, she received a phone call from Jill Bakken, the number-two driver in the world, asking Flowers to join her team. Together Flowers and Bakken made it to the 2002 Winter Olympics in Salt Lake City. But the night before what would be their history-making competition, Flowers got another phone call. Jean Racine, the number-one driver in the world, asked Flowers to leave Jill and join her sled. Was she tempted?

Not a bit. Flowers stayed with Bakken, and they took the gold.

—Lisa Ann Cockrel, "Golden Girl,"
Today's Christian Woman
(November–December 2005)

ILLUSTRATION 767

PASS THE BATON!

Topics: Discipleship; Generations; Growth; Guidance; Leadership; Maturity; Parenting; Practice; Teachers; Training

References: Deuteronomy 6:1–9, 20–25; Proverbs 22:6; Ephesians 6:4; 2 Timothy 1:5

The American women's relay race team was favored to win the gold medal in the 4-by-100 relay race in the 2004 Summer Olympic Games in Athens, Greece. The team featured Marion Jones, a sprinter who had won four gold medals at the previous games in Sydney. Indeed, the American team was off to a strong start when Jones took the baton for the second leg of the race. She gained ground as she ran her 100 meters and approached Lauryn Williams, who would run the third leg.

Williams began running as Jones got close, but when she reached back to receive the baton, the women couldn't complete the handoff. Jones thrust the baton forward three times, but each time Williams failed to grab it. Finally, on the fourth try, the runners made the connection. But by that time, they had crossed out of the twenty-yard exchange zone and were disqualified. Everyone knew they were the fastest team on the track, but because they couldn't complete the handoff, they lost the race.

It is important for one generation to set the pace for others by living authentically, but at a certain point a handoff must be made to the next generation. That handoff isn't as easy as it looks. It's the result of thousands of practice runs.

—Bryan Wilkerson, "From Generation to Generation," PreachingToday.com

ILLUSTRATION 768

MISTAKEN IDENTITY

Topics: Assumptions; Behavior; Character; Dignity; Dishonor; Gossip; Identity; Injustice; Integrity; Name; Reputation; Respect; Responsibility; Virtue

References: Proverbs 10:18–19; 11:13; 16:28; 22:1; 2 Corinthians 12:20; Ephesians 4:29–32; 1 Timothy 5:13; Titus 3:1–2; James 3:1–12; 1 Peter 3:10

It may take former NBA star and current Phoenix TV commentator Edward Arnett Johnson a long time to get over the worst day of his life. After his NBA career ended, the six-foot-eight-inch basketball champ, who is forty-seven, spent many years working with children, giving motivational speeches, and serving his community.

But in 2006, another former NBA star — six-foot-two-inch, fifty-one-year-old "Fast Eddie" Johnson — was arrested for sexual battery and burglary. Some reporters around the country picked up the story and mistakenly assumed that Edward Johnson of Phoenix was the criminal. His phone started ringing off the hook. Neighbors, even friends, were quick to tell him how disappointed they were with him.

"The thing that disappointed me the most is some people were overzealous enough to think it was me and attack me with a ferocity I can't comprehend," Johnson said in a telephone interview from his home in Phoenix. "That's the part that didn't allow me to sleep last night. That's the part that forced me to reach out to as many people as I could and say, 'Shame on you; that's not me.'"

Eddie Johnson of Phoenix said his goal for the next several days was to get the word out about who he really is — *and isn't.*

"I don't fault the other Eddie Johnson for having that name," said Johnson. "I think it's a great name. He just doesn't happen to be a great guy."

—Eddie Pells, "It Ain't Me,"
Houston Chronicle (August 11, 2006)

ILLUSTRATION 769

TALKING OUT TEAMWORK

Topics: Communication; Community; Listening; Problems; Relationships; Teamwork; Unity

References: Psalm 133:1; Romans 15:5; Philippians 2:1–4

In 1997, the Washington Capitals were hot, skating their way into the Stanley Cup finals. By the fall of 1999, they had slipped to one of the worst records in the NHL. Coach Ron Wilson decided drastic measures were necessary and quickly changed their strategy. Yet injuries abounded, and the losses mounted. The team was skating on thin ice and couldn't figure out what was wrong.

Just before Christmas, the team embarked on a late-night, seven-hour flight from Vancouver and did what they typically do on a flight of that duration: they popped in a video to pass the time. Then the VCR froze.

As the plane winged its way through the evening sky, one by one the players started talking with each other. They talked strategy. Obstacles. Key plays. Out of necessity, they rediscovered the ancient art of conversation. By the time the plane touched down, the Capitals had picked apart their game and knew what needed to be done.

In the weeks that followed, they became virtually unstoppable, going on an eleven-game winning streak. Team goaltender Olaf Kolzig reflected, "Maybe it was fate the VCR didn't work. It gave us a chance to just roam about the plane and talk with guys. It was a good way to clear the air." Indeed. They went 12–2–3 after the busted VCR incident.

—Bob De Moss, *Plugged In* radio broadcast (April 4, 2001)

ILLUSTRATION 770

PITCHER ON HOLD

Topics: Commitment; Humility; Regret; Sacrifice; Service

References: Philippians 2:5–8; 3:7–8

Bob Feller, a pitcher for the Cleveland Indians, had already thrown a no-hitter and won 107 games in the major leagues when the Japanese bombed Pearl Harbor. Feller volunteered to fight for his country at the age of twenty-three. After the war Bob returned to pitching and had three no-hitters, twelve one-hitters, and won 266 games.

But his years of military service cost Bob much of the fame he deserved. When baseball fans elected the All-Century Team in 1999, Bob and his 266 victories were ignored in favor of two other pitchers. Some suggest Feller may be the most underrated baseball player of all time.

Feller was once asked if he regretted his wartime service. "No," he said, "I've made many mistakes in my life. That wasn't one of them."

—Based on John B. Holway, "Underrated: Bob Feller," *American Heritage* (September 2001); bobfellermuseum.org

ILLUSTRATION 771

WINNING AS A TEAM

Topics: Church; Community; Ego; Pride; Self-centeredness; Sports; Teamwork; Unity; Unselfishness

References: Ephesians 4:11–16; Philippians 2:3–4

Men often talk about their glory years in high school, says A. C. Green, an NBA player. "At Benson High School, in Portland, Oregon, I was a sports-minded, egotistical maniac. I was the tallest guy on the team and could have broken scoring records, but Coach Gray wouldn't let me. Even with the brakes on, twice that year I scored thirty-nine points, and in the season finale against Wilson I scored forty.

"I averaged twenty-seven points per game. As a team we scored more than one hundred points in seven games and averaged over ninety. I was voted the *Oregonian*'s 1981 All-Metro area player of the year."

The coach wouldn't allow Green to be a hot-shot scorer, however, because he was more interested in the final stat—becoming number one in basketball in the state. He knew the only way the players could reach that championship level was for them to become team players.

"In basketball and in life, everyone starts out with a what's-in-it-for-me attitude," Green says. "That natural selfishness has to be broken to be a winner. You have to realize you can't do it all by yourself. You need the team. Coach Gray made me pass the ball and play unselfishly. Regardless of individual stats, we, the team, reached the top. We went all the way."

—A. C. Green, *Victory* (Creation, 1994)

ILLUSTRATION 772

MY NAME'S NOT FOR SALE

Topics: Character; Christians; Compromise; Convictions; Glorifying God; Identity in Christ; Integrity; Money; Name

Reference: 1 Peter 4:14–16

Mark Cuban, owner of the NBA's Dallas Mavericks, recently offered WGN Chicago Radio sports-talk host David Kaplan $50,000 to change his name legally to "Dallas Maverick." When Kaplan declined, Cuban sweetened the offer. Cuban would pay Kaplan $100,000 and donate $100,000 to Kaplan's favorite charity if he took the name for one year.

Despite some soul-searching and email bombardment from listeners, who said he was crazy to turn down the money, Kaplan held firm. "I'd be saying I'd do anything for money, and that bothers me," Kaplan said. "My name is my birthright. I'd like to preserve my integrity and credibility."

"Christian" is the birthright of every follower of Jesus Christ. We have a responsibility to live every day in a way that brings honor to that name.

—Skip Bayless, "Radio Host Prefers Class over Crass," *Chicago Tribune* (January 10, 2001)

ILLUSTRATION 773

WOODEN'S WINNING WAYS

Topics: Example; Integrity; Leadership; Priorities; Success; Teaching; Values; Winning and Losing

Reference: Hebrews 13:7

John Wooden's UCLA teams won ten NCAA championships in twelve years. Still, the 1960s were a turbulent time when Bill Walton played for UCLA under Wooden, and young people were asking hard questions of anyone in authority.

Wooden's answers to such questions never varied. "We thought he was nuts, but in all his preachings and teachings, everything he told us turned out to be true," Walton said. "His interest and goal was to make you the best basketball player but first to make you the best person. He would never talk wins and losses but what we needed to succeed in life. Once you were a good human being, you had a chance to be a good player. He never deviated from that.

"He never tried to be your friend. He was your teacher, your coach. He handled us with extreme patience."

Today Walton and Wooden, ninety, talk frequently. "He has thousands of maxims," Walton says. "He is more John Wooden today than ever. He is a man who truly has principles and ideas."

"When you're touched by someone that special, it changes your life," Walton adds. "You spend your life chasing it down, trying to recreate it."

—Hal Bock, Associated Press, "A Coach for All Seasons," *Spokane Review* (December 4, 2000)

ILLUSTRATION 774

CHAMPIONSHIP RING

Topics: Cross; Grace; New Life; Rebirth; Redemption; Salvation

References: Job 19:25; Romans 3:24; 8:3–4; 1 Corinthians 1:30; 2 Corinthians 5:16–21; Ephesians 1:7; Colossians 1:14

Lou Johnson, a 1965 World Series hero for the Los Angeles Dodgers, tried for thirty years to recover the championship ring he had lost to drug dealers in 1971. Drug and alcohol abuse cost him everything from that magical season, including his uniform, glove, and the bat he used to hit the winning home run in the deciding game.

When Dodger president Bob Graziano learned that Johnson's World Series ring was about to be auctioned on the Internet, he immediately bought the ring for $3,457 and gave it to Johnson, sixty-six, who has been drug-free for years and a Dodger community relations employee. He did for Johnson what Johnson could not do for himself.

The ball player wept when given the gold ring. "It felt like a piece of me had been reborn," he said.

Likewise, Christians can testify to a spiritual rebirth as a result of the price that Jesus paid on the cross in their place. He did for them what they could not do for themselves.

—Rick Kauffman, "Team President Redeems Athlete," PreachingToday.com

ILLUSTRATION 775

REJECTING THE HELMET

Topics: Accepting Christ; Choices; Decisions; Judgment; Neglect; Salvation

Reference: John 1:12

On Sunday, February 18, 2001, NASCAR driver Dale Earnhardt, known as "The Intimidator," was in third place on the last lap of the Daytona 500 when his car was hit from behind and sent into the wall at 180 miles per hour. An autopsy revealed Earnhardt died of blunt trauma to the head.

Some have suggested that if Earnhardt had been wearing the HANS (Head and Neck Safety Device) he would have survived the crash. Although this device was available, Earnhardt, like many other drivers that day, chose not to use it. That neglect may have cost him his life.

The Bible tells us that every individual is on a collision course with God's judgment. God has provided a safety device designed to keep people from suffering eternal death and separation from him. But like Dale Earnhardt and the other drivers in the race that day, each of us must decide whether to accept or neglect this offer.

—Michael Owenby, Carrollton, Georgia

ILLUSTRATION 776

STOLEN TROPHIES

Topics: Disappointment; Glory; Hope; Promises; Rewards; Success

References: Matthew 6:18; Philippians 3:7–14; Hebrews 6:10; 11:24–26; James 1:12

When I was a senior in high school, I was presented with two trophies at the annual sports assembly, one for being cocaptain of the basketball team and one for being the most improved player on the team. I have kept those two tiny trophies for more than thirty years.

Last year I drove back to my hometown for a thirty-year reunion of our school's first football team. I arrived early, so I walked through the old high school to see what it looked like after three decades. I found the lobby where the sports awards are displayed and looked for the two plaques where my name would be inscribed in honor of my awards.

I found both plaques, but the name of a teammate had been substituted where my name belonged. My glory had been stolen from me.

In this sinful world we are often promised rewards that are not delivered to us. We are foolish to place our ultimate hope on any of those worldly promises. Only our Father in heaven can be trusted to deliver on his promises.

—David Gibson, Idaho Falls, Idaho

ILLUSTRATION 777

HITTING A FLAWED RIM

Topics: Dedication; Discernment; Experience; Spiritual Disciplines; Spiritual Perception; Sports

References: Proverbs 14:33; Philippians 1:10; 1 Timothy 4:8; Hebrews 5:13–14; 1 John 4:1

The floor of the Princeton gym was being resurfaced, so Princeton basketball player (and later United States senator) Bill Bradley had to practice at Lawrenceville School. His first afternoon at Lawrenceville, he began by shooting fourteen-foot jump shots from the right side. He got off to a bad start, and he kept missing them. Six in a row hit the back rim of the basket and bounced out.

He stopped and seemed to make an adjustment in his mind. Then he went up for another jump shot from the same spot and hit it cleanly. Four more shots went in without a miss. Then he paused and said, "You want to know something? That basket is about an inch and a half low."

Some weeks later, I went back to Lawrenceville with a steel tape measure. I borrowed a stepladder and measured the height of the basket. It was nine feet, ten and seven-eighths inches above the floor, or one and one-eighth inches too low.

—John McPhee, *A Sense of Where You Are*
(Farrar, Straus & Giroux, 1965)

ILLUSTRATION 778

RUNNING BLIND

Topics: Achievement; Hope; Perseverance; Persistence; Success; Winning and Losing

References: Acts 20:24; 2 Corinthians 4:18; Colossians 3:1–4; 2 Timothy 4:7; Hebrews 12:1–3

U.S. runner Marla Runyon, legally blind for twenty-two years, competed in the 2000 Summer Olympic Games in Sydney, Australia. She qualified for the finals in the 1,500-meter race, then finished eighth, just seconds behind the medal winners.

Runyon can't see in color; all she sees is a fuzzy blob. So when she races, she just follows the blob of figures in front of her. The real difficulty is rounding the final turn and racing toward a finish line she can't see. "I just know where it is," she said.

—Today Show, September 22, 2000

ILLUSTRATION 779

LETTING GOD WATCH

Topics: Dependence on God; Experiencing God; Prayer

References: Psalm 127:1–2; Zechariah 4:6; Philippians 4:13; 1 Thessalonians 5:17

The baseball game was tied with two outs in the bottom of the ninth inning. The batter stepped into the batting box and made the sign of the cross on home plate with his bat. Yogi Berra, Hall of Fame catcher for the New York Yankees, was behind the plate. A Catholic as well, Berra wiped off the plate with his glove and said to the pious batter, "Why don't we let God just watch this game?"

Letting God watch. That may be OK for a baseball game, but it's terrible theology when applied to the way we live our lives and carry out the work of the church.

—Ben Patterson in "Why We Don't Pray," *Prayer Book* (March 23, 1997)

ILLUSTRATION 780

HORMONES AND SPORTS

Topics: Ambition; Anger; Competition; Ego; Gender Differences; Winning and Losing

References: Romans 8:37; 2 Corinthians 2:14

Consider these stats on what happens to a man's hormones when his team plays:

- average percentage points by which a male sports fan's testosterone level rises when his team wins: 20
- average points by which the level falls when his team loses: 20

—Paul Bernhardt and others, "Testosterone Changes during Vicarious Experiences of Winning and Losing among Fans at Sporting Events, *Physiology and Behavior*, vol. 65, no. 1 (August 1998)

ILLUSTRATION 781

UPSTAGING THE UMPIRE

Topics: Authority; Judgment; Law; Morality; Power

References: 1 Corinthians 3:10–15; 2 Corinthians 5:10

In Cuba baseball rules, except when Fidel Castro, Cuba's former dictator, would go up to bat.

During an exhibition game against Venezuela, the Cuban dictator grabbed an aluminum bat and walked to the plate. Not to be outdone, the president of Venezuela, Hugo Chavez, went to the pitcher's mound.

The first pitch didn't even reach the plate. Castro kept his bat on his shoulder. The next pitch was over the plate, and Castro swung and missed. A couple more balls and an attempted bunt later, the two heads of state were locked in a full count. Castro watched the 3–2 pitch sail through the middle of the strike zone and listened as the umpire called him out.

"No," Castro said. "That was a ball." He took first base. No one argued. Chavez said nothing. The opposing team said nothing, and the umpire said nothing. Later Castro joked, "Today just wasn't Chavez's day."

It's hard to get a batter out when he has the power to overrule the umpire's calls. In God's economy, dictators can't do that. Everyone will face God's ultimate judgment, whose word will be final.

—Jim Wilson, "Fidel Castro Plays Baseball," PreachingToday.com

ILLUSTRATION 782

LESSONS FOR SPARKY

Topics: Adversity; Character; Winning and Losing

References: Romans 5:1–5; James 1:2–4; 1 Peter 4:12

Hall of Famer Sparky Anderson is the only manager in history to win World Series titles in both the National and American Leagues. He led the Cincinnati Reds to the top in 1975 and '76, and the Detroit Tigers to the top in 1984.

But even Sparky can't win 'em all. In 1989, the Tigers finished a miserable 59–103. Sparky suffered such mental and physical exhaustion early in the season that he had to leave the team for seventeen days. Looking back on that time, he says, "If you think you're destined never to fail, you'd better keep one eye open when you fall asleep at night.

"For my first nineteen years as a manager, I was blessed by so much good fortune I thought maybe the devil had forgotten where I lived. In 1989, I found out that Sparky Anderson has to pay his dues too. I never got over the point of bleeding a little bit after every loss, but I finally learned to let go. I can't say I'm happy with the pain I went through in 1989. But I'm grateful for what it taught me."

—Sparky Anderson and Dan Ewald, *They Call Me Sparky* (Sleeping Bear, 1998)

ILLUSTRATION 783

WALKER'S REWARD

Topics: Communication; Eternal Life; Glory; Honor; Rewards

References: Hebrews 12:25–29; 2 Peter 1:11

Kenny Walker, born deaf, felt like an outsider. As Walker matured, however, he compensated for his deafness with physical strength. His large frame, extensive knowledge of football, and intense focus attracted the attention first of his

1001 ILLUSTRATIONS THAT CONNECT

high school football coaches and then of college coaches.

When Walker's high school coach asked him where he wanted to play college football, he signed *N* for Nebraska. Nebraska's coaches immediately recruited him and made arrangements to have an interpreter present at every game.

At Nebraska, Walker made All-American and was named Big Eight Conference "Defensive Player of the Year." But the crowning moment of his college football career came during his final home game. Traditionally, senior players were introduced alphabetically and ran onto the field, welcomed by a cheering crowd. But because Walker was deaf, the university found a unique way to honor the player. The *Omaha World Herald* explained to fans how to sign an ovation by standing, holding their hands above their heads, spreading their fingers, then waving their hands from side to side.

When Walker stood in the stadium tunnel, he felt the vibration of the cheering crowd as each senior ran out on the field. But when he ran onto the field, he felt no vibrations. Puzzled, he looked around the stadium to see over seventy-five thousand fans standing for him, waving their hands in a way that only a deaf person would recognize as applause.

Likewise, we who know Christ as Savior will be welcomed into glory. As 2 Peter 1:11 reads, "You will receive a rich welcome into the eternal kingdom of our Lord and Savior Jesus Christ."

—John G. Hubbell, "Kenny Walker Listens with His Heart," *Reader's Digest* (October 1993)

ILLUSTRATION 784

CHEERING THE SWIMMER IN

Topics: Acceptance; Church; Community; Encouragement; Perseverance; Weakness; Witnessing

References: Philippians 3:13–14; 2 Timothy 4:7–8; Hebrews 10:24; 12:1–3

Eric Moussambani of Equatorial Guinea was an unlikely hero of the 2000 Olympic Games in Sydney, Australia. The twenty-two-year-old African had learned to swim only nine months before the games, had only practiced in a twenty-meter pool without lane markers, and had never raced more than fifty meters. Through a special program that permits poorer countries to participate, even though their athletes don't meet customary standards, Moussambani had been entered in the 100-meter men's freestyle.

When the other two swimmers in his heat were disqualified because of false starts, Moussambani was forced to swim alone. He was reportedly "charmingly inept." He never put his head under the water's surface and flailed wildly to stay afloat. With ten meters left to the wall, he virtually came to a stop. Some spectators thought he might drown. Even though his time was more than a minute slower than what qualified for the next level of competition, the capacity crowd at the Olympic Aquatic Center stood up and cheered him on.

After what seemed like an eternity, the African reached the wall and hung on for dear life. When he had caught his breath and regained his composure, he said through an interpreter, "I want to send hugs and kisses to the crowd. It was their cheering that kept me going."

—Greg Asimakoupoulos and Rubel Shelly, "Help for Long Race," PreachingToday.com

the record for the 100-meter dash if the race is 400 meters long."

—Gordon MacDonald, Promise Keepers "Go the Distance" conference (August 11, 2000)

ILLUSTRATION 785

WAITING AT THE FINISH LINE

Topics: Arrogance; Endurance; Perseverance; Pride

References: Hebrews 10:36; 12:1–2; James 1:3–4

I was at the Pennsylvania Relays, a famous Eastern track meet, and our relay team was running in the championship race. I was the leadoff man and in the second lane. The man in the first lane held the 100-meter dash record for prep school runners at that time. He also held a record for arrogance, because when I got to the line and put my starting blocks down, he said, "May the best man win. I'll be waiting for you at the finish line."

We went into the blocks. The gun sounded. He took off, and seven of us settled in behind him. We went around the first turn and down the back stretch. About 180 meters into the race, I suddenly saw the record holder in front of me, holding his side, bent over and groaning as he jogged along. We passed him like he was standing still, and because I'm such a gentleman, I waited for him at the finish line.

At the end of the race, my coach took me aside and said, "I hope you've learned a lesson today. It makes little difference whether you hold

ILLUSTRATION 786

INSPIRATIONAL QUITTING

Topics: Caring; Empathy; Sacrifice; Unselfishness

References: Matthew 20:26–28; Philippians 2:1–11

Cleveland Browns linebacker Chris Spielman had to retire from football early in the 1999 season after suffering an injury that resulted in the narrowing of his spinal canal. Spielman had skipped the entire '98 season to care for his wife, Stefanie, who was battling breast cancer.

After spending ten NFL seasons with other teams, Spielman, who grew up in Ohio, was finally getting a chance to play for his beloved Browns—only to have it taken away almost as soon as the season started.

Was he bitter? His wife Stefanie said, "He had a couple of emotions. He said that he felt like he was letting down our children because they'd never get to see him play. And he said he felt sorry for all those people who had bought his #54 SPIELMAN jersey.

"That shows what kind of man I married. He feels so much for other people."

When Spielman told Browns coach Chris Palmer he had to quit, Spielman said, "I'm sorry I let you down."

"Let me down?" Palmer said later. "He had to be kidding. This guy's one of the most inspirational players the league has seen."

—Peter King, "Knowing When, and Why, to Go," *Sports Illustrated* (September 6, 1999)

ILLUSTRATION 787
JUMPING OFF CHRIST

Topics: Apostasy; Invitation; Rest; Safety

References: Matthew 11:28–30; 1 Corinthians 15:2; Hebrews 12:25

An extreme sports fanatic scaled the 120-foot *Christ the Redeemer* statue on Brazil's Corcovado mountain and jumped from its outstretched arms.

For the first ever such leap, Felix Baumgartner, thirty, an Austrian, smuggled his parachute on board the little train that takes dozens of tourists up the two-thousand-foot mountain to visit the statue. He scaled the gray stone figure, climbed onto one of its fingers, and jumped. Baumgartner's parachute worked, and he was not injured.

How many people approach life like this daredevil? Rather than turning to the one who invites all who are weary to come to him and find rest, many prefer to jump from the safety of his hands. Unlike this thrill seeker, theirs will be a far different end, for there are no spiritual parachutes for those who spurn Christ.

—Alan Wilson, "Spurning Christ," PreachingToday.com

ILLUSTRATION 788
LINEBACKER GOALS FOR LIFE

Topics: Compassion; Family; Ministry; Service; Significance

References: Matthew 22:37–40; John 13:34–35

"The first thing in my life by far, and the reason I do everything, is my love for Jesus Christ," says Mike Singletary, former linebacker for the Chicago Bears who was inducted into the Pro Football Hall of Fame in 1998. "The second is my family—being there for them and making sure I'm not missing time that I can't get back. Third is my work, speaking to corporations about teamwork, leadership, and cultural diversity and trying to help people come together.

"I don't care where I'm at or what I'm doing. The thing I want to do now in my life is make a difference and serve with a capital *S*. Serve in my home. Serve in my relationship with my wife. And serve my fellow man.

"For me, it's a matter of 'What am I doing to make a difference? What am I doing except making money?' There are a lot of people out there who are hurting."

—Rick Morrissey, "For Singletary, Religion Goes Far beyond Words," *Chicago Tribune* (November 14, 1999)

ILLUSTRATION 789
PAYTON'S SWEETNESS

Topics: Compassion; Empathy; Ministry

References: 1 Corinthians 12:26; Ephesians 4:32; 1 Peter 3:8

After ten seasons as place kicker with the Chicago Bears, Bob Thomas was notified by the management that he was being cut.

Thomas, a born-again Christian, waited until he knew the locker room would be cleared of players to clear out his things. He didn't have the emotional strength to face the players he'd grown to love. His celebrated teammate, Walter Payton, another believer, learned about Thomas's termination and waited alone at the kicker's locker. When Bob saw Walter, he buried his face in the running back's chest and allowed his friend and fellow Christian to comfort him.

After Walter Payton's death in 1999, Thomas recalled that emotional moment in the locker room. "To share your grief with a Hall of Fame running back with that kind of compassion, empathy, and ability is really my fondest memory of the guy we called Sweetness," he said.

— Christy Gutowski, "Payton's Was a
Shoulder to Cry On," *Daily Herald*,
Suburban Chicago, Illinois (November 2, 1999)

ILLUSTRATION 790

KEEPING THE DREAM ALIVE

Topics: Hardship; Humility; Perseverance; Persistence; Testimony; Trials

References: Romans 5:3–5; 11:36

While at the University of Northern Iowa, Kurt Warner was a second-string player on the football team. During college he met a single mom who had two kids, one of whom was blind. Warner married the woman and adopted both kids.

He wasn't drafted by the NFL after college, so he went to work stocking groceries. But he kept his dream alive by playing in the Arena Football League and eventually for the Amsterdam Admirals in the European NFL. In 1998, he was signed by the St. Louis Rams but barely played. In 1999, his opportunities didn't look much better. The Rams had signed quarterback Trent Green to a multimillion-dollar contract. Kurt got the league minimum for a second-year player, $250,000.

In a preseason game, Green got hurt, which allowed Warner to prove himself as a starting quarterback. And he did. Kurt Warner was named the NFL's most valuable player for 1999 and the MVP of the Super Bowl.

Warner keeps success in perspective. During the Billy Graham crusade on October 15, 1999, at the TWA Dome in St. Louis, where the Rams play their home games, Warner announced to more than 40,000 cheering fans, "People often ask the secret to my success as a football player. It has nothing to do with how I work out in the off-season or my diet. The secret to my success is Jesus Christ."

Warner says his faith, as well as the hardships and tragedies his family has faced, has helped him understand what truly is important in life. In turn, this helps him on the football field, particularly in pressure situations.

— Greg Asimakoupoulos,
Mercer Island, Washington

PART 31: SUFFERING

ILLUSTRATION 791

EMPATHIZING WITH SUFFERING

Topics: Compassion; Empathy; Incarnation; Mercy; Ministry; Suffering

References: John 11:35; Hebrews 4:14–16; 5:1–10

When sportswriter Mitch Albom heard that his favorite college professor, whom he hadn't seen in twenty years, was dying of Lou Gehrig's disease, he began visiting him weekly. In his bestselling book *Tuesdays with Morrie*, Albom describes their visits, focusing on his old professor's wit and insights.

One time, Mitch asked Morrie why he bothered following the news since he wouldn't be around to see how things turned out. Morrie responded, "It's hard to explain, Mitch. Now that I'm suffering, I feel closer to people who suffer than I ever did before. The other night on TV, I saw people in Bosnia running across the street, getting fired on. I just started to cry. I feel their anguish as if it were my own. I don't know any of these people. But—how can I put this? I'm almost drawn to them."

Jesus understands our sufferings, too, but it's more than empathy; he has suffered and is with us when we suffer.

—Greg Asimakoupoulos, Mercer Island, Washington

ILLUSTRATION 792

MATURING IN HARDSHIP

Topics: Commitment; Devotion; Maturity; Ministry; Obedience; Sacrifice

References: Romans 8:17–18; Philippians 3:7–11

Gladys Aylward, a missionary to China during and after World War II, brought a hundred orphans, ages four to fifteen, safely over the mountains of China to Sian in Shensi.

But it was not without cost.

When Aylward arrived in Sian with the children, she was gravely ill. She had suffered internal injuries from a beating by the Japanese invaders in the mission compound at Tsechow. In addition, she was wracked with fever, typhus, pneumonia, malnutrition, shock, and fatigue.

Through her ordeal Aylward learned to choose Christ over anything else life had to offer. When the man she loved, Colonel Linnan, came to visit her in Sian and asked her to marry him, she declined because she knew marriage would interfere with the work God had given her among the children of China. She said good-bye to Linnan at the train station, and they never met again. Gladys continued serving God in China and England until her death in 1970.

Through our suffering in ministry, God wants us to learn obedience to increase our maturity in Christ.

—Gary D. Preston, *Character Forged*
from Conflict (Bethany, 1999)

ILLUSTRATION 793

BREAKING THE ICE

Topics: Attitudes; Caring; Compassion; Empathy; Mercy

Reference: Matthew 25:31–40

Each day I worked in the emergency room, I became more insensitive to people and their real needs. Five years of emergency room exposure took its toll. Then God intervened.

I was registering a young woman who had overdosed on drugs and attempted suicide. Her mother sat before me, unkempt and bleary eyed. She had been awakened in the night by the police to come to the hospital. She could only speak to me in a whisper.

"Hurry up!" I said to myself as she slowly gave me information. My impatience was raw as I finished the report and jumped to the machine

to copy the medical cards. Then God stopped me, saying, "You didn't even look at her."

I felt his grief for the woman and her daughter then, and I bowed my head, saying, "I'm sorry, Lord. I am so sorry."

I sat by the distraught woman and covered her hands with mine. I looked into her eyes with all the love that God could flood through me and said, "I care. Don't give up." She wept as she poured out her story. For years she had dealt with a rebellious daughter who was a single mom. Finally, after the weeping stopped, she thanked me for listening. Me—the coldhearted one with no feelings.

My attitude changed that night. My God, who so loved the world, broke that self-imposed barrier around my heart. Now he could reach out, not only to me, but to a lost and hurting woman.

—Adapted from Patricia Miller,
"The Emergency Room," *Pentecostal Evangel*
(October 15, 2000)

ILLUSTRATION 794

LEARNING TO ACCEPT

Topics: Acceptance; Desires

References: Psalm 20:4; Romans 8:18;
2 Corinthians 6:4–10

Suffering is getting what you don't want, and not getting what you do want.

—J. I. Packer

ILLUSTRATION 795

STANDING ON HOLY GROUND

Topics: Compassion; Empathy; Grandmothers; Love; Ministry; Presence; Understanding

References: Matthew 25:40; John 15:13

Today I visited a little girl dying of cancer. Her body was disfigured by her disease and its treatment. She was in constant pain. As I entered her room, I was overcome by her suffering, which seemed unjust, unfair, unreasonable. Even more overpowering was the presence of her grandmother lying in bed beside her with her huge body embracing this precious eight-year-old.

I stood in awe, knowing I was on holy ground. I will never forget the great, gentle arms of this grandmother. She never spoke but simply held her granddaughter, participating in suffering that she could not relieve. No words could express the magnitude of her love.

—Leonard Sweet, *Postmodern Pilgrims* (Broadman & Holman, 2000)

ILLUSTRATION 796

PREYING ON THE VULNERABLE

Topics: Death; Ethics; Euthanasia; Evil; Murder; Suicide

Reference: Exodus 20:13

Jack Kevorkian preyed on the vulnerable, says a study of the sixty-nine suicides Kevorkian assisted in Oakland County, Michigan. Seventy-five percent of those people would have lived for at least another six months. The vast majority—67 percent—were divorced, widowed, or never married, suggesting they had no social or family support. Only 35 percent were in pain, and 7 percent—five patients—had no evidence of disease at all.

The findings of Oakland County medical examiner and longtime Kevorkian critic L. J. Dragovic were published in the letters section of *The New England Journal of Medicine*. Kevorkian was convicted of murder and sentenced to ten to fifteen years in jail. He was recently released and vows he will no longer help people end their lives.

—Christianity Today Online Weblog (December 8, 2000)

ILLUSTRATION 797

CAREY'S EXTREME LOSS

Topics: Faith; God's Sovereignty; Loss; Missions; Trials; Trust

Reference: Psalm 46:10

William Carey, called the father of modern missions, went to India in 1793 and worked there for forty years, never once returning to his native England. He translated portions of Scripture into more than a dozen Indian languages.

One afternoon, after twenty years of plodding translation work in India, a fire raged through Carey's printing plant and warehouse. All of his printing equipment was destroyed, but most tragically, many of his precious manuscripts were completely consumed. Twenty years of nonstop labor were gone within a few hours.

"The ground must be laboured over again, but we are not discouraged," Carey wrote to his pastor-friend Andrew Murray in England. "We have all been supported under the affliction, and preserved from discouragement. To me the consideration of the divine sovereignty and wisdom has been very supporting. I preached on this affliction last Lord's Day, from Psalm 46:10, 'Be still and know that I am God.' I principally dwelt upon two ideas: (1) God has a sovereign right to dispose of us as he pleases. (2) We ought to acquiesce in all that God does with us and to us."

—Bill Mills and Craig Parro,
Finishing Well in Life and Ministry
(Leadership Resources International, 1999)

ILLUSTRATION 798

ACCEPTING GOD'S CRUSHING

Topics: God's Sovereignty; Imitation of Christ; Motivation; Obedience; Sacrifice; Surrender

References: Matthew 11:29–30; John 20:21; Philippians 2:5–11, 17; Hebrews 10:5–7

God can never make me wine if I object to the fingers he uses to crush me. If God would only crush me with his own fingers and say, "Now, my son, I am going to make you broken bread and poured-out wine in a particular way, and everyone will know what I am doing." But when he uses someone who is not a Christian, or someone I particularly dislike, or some set of circumstances that I said I would never submit to, and begins to make these the crushers, I object.

I must never choose the scene of my own martyrdom; nor must I choose the things God will use to make me broken bread and poured-out wine. His own Son did not choose. God chose for his Son that he should have a devil in his company for three years. We say, "I want angels; I want people better than myself; I want everything to be significantly from God; otherwise I cannot live the life or do the thing properly; I always want to be gilt-edged."

Let God do as he likes. If you are ever going to be wine to drink, you must be crushed. Grapes cannot be drunk; grapes are only wine when they have been crushed. I wonder what kind of coarse finger and thumb God has been using to squeeze you, and you have been like a marble and escaped? You are not ripe yet, and if God had squeezed you, the wine that came out would have been remarkably bitter. Let God go on with his crushing, because it will work his purpose in the end.

—Oswald Chambers,
So Send I You (Discovery House, 1993)

ILLUSTRATION 799

BEING ONE WITH GOD IN SUFFERING

Topics: Adversity; Affliction; Courage

References: Matthew 5:11; 10:39; Acts 5:41; Romans 8:17; 2 Corinthians 4:11

It is good to learn early enough that suffering and God are not a contradiction but rather a unity, for the idea that God himself is suffering is one that has always been one of the most convincing teachings of Christianity.

I think God is nearer to suffering than to happiness, and to find God in this way gives peace and rest and a strong and courageous heart.

—Dietrich Bonhoeffer, in a letter to his twin sister, Sabine; *Christian History*, no. 32

and the outline of the path. Then, to his utter astonishment, he saw the figure of a man standing just a few feet away, armed with a bow and arrow. It was the boy's father, who had been there all night long.

Likewise, God is always present with us in our trials. His presence is unseen, but it is more real than life itself.

—Leonard Sweet, *SoulSalsa* (Zondervan, 2000)

ILLUSTRATION 800

SENSING GOD IN THE FOREST

Topics: Fear; God as Father; God's Faithfulness; Loneliness; Presence of God; Protection; Trials

References: Deuteronomy 31:6; Matthew 28:20; Hebrews 13:5

A tribe of Native Americans had a unique practice for training young braves. On the night of a boy's thirteenth birthday, he was blindfolded and taken miles away. When he took off the blindfold, he was in the midst of thick woods. He had to stay there all night by himself.

Every time a twig snapped, he probably visualized a wild animal ready to pounce. Every time an animal howled, he imagined a wolf leaping out of the darkness. Every time the wind blew, he wondered what more sinister sound it masked.

After what seemed like an eternity, the first rays of sunlight lightened the interior of the forest. Looking around, the boy saw flowers, trees,

ILLUSTRATION 801

FRAGRANCE OF THE BROKEN

Topics: Brokenness; Cross; Grace; Prayer

References: Romans 5:12–21; Ephesians 2:1–10

I had stacked some rocks out at this little place in the woods, a place I had gone to pray, desperate for God to do something, to show up, or to have some sort of breakthrough. As I was praying, I remember smelling cedar so strong it distracted me from my prayer.

I looked around to see this little cedar tree that had been snapped in half from my stepping in there. That was where the smell was coming from. It was a tangible sign of grace. I wrote down on a little notepad "the fragrance of the broken."

—Steven Curtis Chapman in *CCM* (July 1999)

ILLUSTRATION 802

ASKING GOD WHY

Topics: Cross; Loneliness; Mysteries; Pain; Questions; Resentment

References: Job 7:20 – 21; Psalm 10:1; Habakkuk 1:1 – 4; Mark 15:34

It is always best to go first for our answers to Jesus himself. He cried out on the cross, "My God, my God, why have you forsaken me?" It was a human cry, a cry of desperation, springing from his heart's agony at the prospect of being put into the hands of wicked men and actually becoming sin for you and me.

We can never suffer anything like that, yet we do at times feel forsaken and cry, "Why, Lord?"

The psalmist asked why. Job, a blameless man who suffered horrible torments on an ash heap, asked why. It does not seem sinful to ask the question. What *is* sinful is resentment against God and his dealings with us.

—Elisabeth Elliot, *Keep a Quiet Heart* (Vine, 1995)

ILLUSTRATION 803

GROWING TOGETHER IN PAIN

Topics: Church; Comfort; Community; Death; Mourning; Suffering

References: 2 Corinthians 1:3 – 11; 1 Peter 4:13; 5:9

Recently I experienced, for the first time, a profound sense of biblical community. For the past seven years, my wife and I have participated in a small group, which included five couples. This past year our group celebrated a couple's first child. We also cheered when two other women in the group announced their pregnancies, and then we prayed fervently for safe deliveries and healthy babies.

In October, the woman who was due first became concerned when her due date came and went. She said the baby seemed to be moving less. That was Saturday. On Tuesday there was no heartbeat. On Wednesday morning she gave birth to Ian Patrick Lincoln, whom we never got to know. The umbilical cord was wrapped twice around his neck.

My wife and I—and several others from our small group—were at the hospital when Ian was born. We huddled together, sobbing, staring down at our shoes. We attempted to pray. Then we all went to the delivery room to see Ian and his mom.

The week dragged by. After the funeral we collapsed from exhaustion. In grieving with the parents and the other members of my small group, I learned an old truth: much of our spiritual development happens only through suffering. But in this life suffering is not evenly meted out. I had gone twelve years without deep mourning. Now community forced me into relationship with a small circle of people who had become closer than family. I was forced to suffer loss—vicariously but still real.

Community is not just a place for the suffering to find comfort but for the comfortable to find suffering. Together we join Christ in his suffering, and as a result, as 2 Corinthians 1:4 says, "We can comfort those in any trouble with the comfort we ourselves have received from God."

—Dave Goetz, "Community for the Comfortable," ChurchLeadersOnline.com (November 17, 1999)

ILLUSTRATION 804

TIME-TESTED CONVICTIONS

Topics: Convictions; Faith; Temptation; Testing

Reference: James 2:14–26

You don't have convictions unless you have been tested.

—Crawford W. Loritts Jr., in a message at the Institute for Biblical Preaching (March 10, 1999)

ILLUSTRATION 805

SHARING THE GLORY

Topics: Glory; Inheritance; Persecution; Rewards

References: Romans 8:17; Revelation 3:21

The documents of surrender officially ending World War II were signed by the Japanese and designated representatives of allied nations on September 2, 1945. General Douglas MacArthur, officiating the ceremony aboard the USS *Missouri*, was the last to sign on behalf of the United States.

MacArthur took his Parker fountain pen and simply signed his first name, "Douglas." He then passed the pen to General Wainwright, who signed "Mac." MacArthur then handed the pen to General Percival, who signed "Arthur."

This unusual procedure was MacArthur's way of honoring the two U.S. generals who had suffered severe persecution as prisoners of war. They had persevered, and now they were allowed to share in the glory of victory.

Likewise, Paul describes those who persevere in the spiritual battles fought this side of heaven. In Romans 8:17 he calls them "co-heirs." Those who share in the sufferings of Christ will also share in his glory.

—Greg Asimakoupoulos, Mercer Island, Washington

ILLUSTRATION 806

A PRAYER IN SUFFERING

Topics: Commitment; Devotion; Discipleship; Ministry; Sacrifice; Surrender

Reference: Philippians 2:5–11

I am no longer my own, but thine.
Put me to what thou wilt, rank me with whom thou wilt.
Put me to doing, put me to suffering.
Let me be employed by thee or laid aside for thee,
Exalted for thee or brought low by thee.
Let me be full, let me be empty.

Let me have all things, let me have nothing.
I freely and heartily yield all things to thy
pleasure and disposal.
And now, O glorious and blessed God,
Father, Son, and Holy Spirit,
Thou art mine, and I am thine. So be it.
And the covenant which I have made
on earth,
Let it be ratified in heaven. Amen.

—John Wesley, "A Covenant Prayer
in the Wesleyan Tradition,"
The United Methodist Hymnal

ILLUSTRATION 807

PRODUCING FRUIT

Topics: Discouragement; Fruitfulness;
Growth; Spiritual Formation; Trials

References: Psalm 119:71; Romans
5:3–5; James 1:2–4; 1 Peter 1:6–7

Mountaintops are for views and inspiration, but
fruit is grown in the valleys.

—Billy Graham, Montreat, North Carolina

ILLUSTRATION 808

PROFITING FROM SUFFERING

Topics: Disabilities; Inclusion; Justice

Reference: Amos 5:24

Lost causes are big business in the United States.
There is more effort put into curing spinal cord
injuries or discussing the legal issues involved in
suicide for the severely disabled than in integrat-
ing disabled folks into society at large.

Pray to be normal, no matter how impossible
it seems, is the sentimental message. The alternative is too horrible to contemplate.

—John Hockenberry, wheelchair-using
MSNBC news anchor,
Moving Violations (Hyperion, 1995)

ILLUSTRATION 809

SELF-DENIAL GOD'S WAY

Topics: Acceptance; Patience; Sacrifice;
Self-denial; Spiritual Disciplines

References: Matthew 16:24–25;
2 Corinthians 1:5–7; 1 Peter 1:6–7

Self-denial has its place in a Christian's life, but
God doesn't ask you to choose what is most painful to you. If you followed this path, you would
soon ruin your health, reputation, business, and
friendship.

Self-denial consists of bearing patiently all
those things that God allows to pass into your
life. If you don't refuse anything that comes in
God's order, you are tasting of the cross of Jesus
Christ.

—François Fénelon, *The Seeking Heart*
(Library of Spiritual Classics, vol. 4)

ILLUSTRATION 810

OUT OF HARM'S WAY

Topics: Discipline; Pain; Problems; Rescue

References: Psalm 119:6, 71; Hebrews 12:4–13; James 1:2–4

A train was rolling down the rails of Lafayette, Indiana, at twenty-four miles per hour. Suddenly the conductor, Robert Mohr, spotted an object on the tracks roughly a city block away. Initially the engineer, Rod Lindley, thought it was a dog on the tracks. Then Mohr screamed, "That's a baby!"

The baby was Emily Marshall, a nineteen-month-old toddler who had wandered away from home while her mother planted flowers in her yard.

Lindley hit the brakes. Mohr bolted out the door and raced along a ledge to the front of the engine. Realizing there was no time to jump ahead of the train and grab the baby, he ran down some steps, squatted at the bottom of the grill, and hung on.

As the train drew close to Emily, Mohr stretched out his leg and pushed her out of harm's way. Mohr then jumped off the train, picked up the little girl, and cradled her in his arms. Little Emily ended up with just a cut on her head and a swollen lip.

Sometimes, like this train conductor, God must hurt us in order to save us.

—Charles Kimball,
Winston-Salem, North Carolina

ILLUSTRATION 811

SHOWING CONCERN

Topics: Caring; Compassion; God as Father; God's Love

References: John 3:16; Romans 8:31–32; 1 Peter 5:7

While Patrick, the two-day-old son of President John F. Kennedy, was fighting for his life because of a lung condition, Kennedy went to see him on the hospital's fifth floor, which had been cleared of all visitors.

On his way to the room, President Kennedy passed by an open door and saw two girls, three or four years old, playing in bed. They were both terribly burned and bandaged.

Kennedy learned one of the children would probably lose one of her hands. The president wrote a note to each girl. After several minutes he went to his own son's room. Patrick died the next day.

If a mere man—even a president—can show love and concern to two unknown children while his own son is suffering and dying, how much more will our infinite Father in heaven take concern in us?

—Seymour M. Hersh, *The Dark Side of Camelot* (Little, Brown, 1997)

ILLUSTRATION 812

UNAFFECTED BY HORROR

Topics: Atonement; Awe; Blood of Christ; Cross; Crucifixion; Holy Week

Reference: Philippians 2:5–11

It is curious that people who are filled with horrified indignation when a cat kills a sparrow can hear the story of the killing of God told Sunday after Sunday and not experience any shock at all.

—Barbara Brown Taylor,
God in Pain (Abingdon, 1998)

ILLUSTRATION 813

SCALDED FOR CHRIST

Topics: Baptism; Commitment; Courage; Evangelism; New Life; Opposition; Oppression; Persecution; Testimony; Threats; Victorious Living; Wholehearted Devotion

References: Matthew 24:7–14; 28:19; Mark 1:9–13; Philippians 1:29; 2 Timothy 3:12; 1 Peter 1:6–7

Through Athens, Greece, runs one of the world's refugee highways, on which millions of desperate people travel after being forced from their homelands by violence, terror, and persecution. These refugees seek a safe place to end their journey and begin new lives in freedom and silence. In May 2006, a missionary in Athens, Kallie Skaife, reported what happened to an Iranian man identified as "M":

In 2003, everything M knew was destroyed by an earthquake measuring 7.45 on the Richter scale. He was tortured by the question of why something like this would happen. He went to live with relatives in Afghanistan, was married, and had a daughter. But he was still filled with despair.

Leaving his family behind, M headed west and ended up in Athens, staying with other relatives. Though he and all his family were Muslims, M became interested in Christianity, finding himself strangely drawn to the crosses he saw decorating the Orthodox churches in the city. M was given a Bible and started reading. Since his relatives forbade such a thing, M used a tiny flashlight to read during the night after his uncles were asleep.

He studied the Bible this way for two years. Finally, M realized God was calling him to be born again. He contacted the refugee ministry center, declared his faith in Christ, and asked for more information.

On Sunday, May 7, 2006, M set his alarm for 6:00 a.m. He wanted to spend time reading his Bible and praying because on that day he was to be baptized at a fellowship with other Iranian believers. But M's cousin had discovered the plan. Before M's alarm went off, the cousin boiled water in a saucepan and poured it on M while he slept, scalding both thighs and one arm.

M came to the baptism anyway. Standing before those gathered, the burn on his arm clearly visible, M declared, "No matter what they do to me, I will love Jesus."

—Kallie Skaife,
International Teams, personal email

ILLUSTRATION 814

STRENGTHENED IN ATTACK

Topics: Courage; Dedication; Devotion; Love for Christ; Martyrdom;

Overcoming; Persecution; Trials; Victorious Living; Wholehearted Devotion

References: Psalm 27:1–6; Matthew 5:10; 10:22; 16:24–26; Acts 5:41; 14:19; 2 Corinthians 11:24–26; Philippians 1:29

On a Sunday morning in January 2006, five young men attacked and threatened to kill a Protestant church leader in Turkey. Kamil Kiroglu, twenty-nine, had just left his church in Adana when he was ambushed and beaten so severely that he fell unconscious twice.

"They were trying to force me to deny Jesus," Kiroglu said. "But each time they asked me to deny Jesus and become a Muslim, I said, 'Jesus is Lord.' The more I said, 'Jesus is Lord,' the more they beat me." One of the attackers pulled out a long knife and threatened to kill Kiroglu if he did not deny his Christian faith and return to Islam. Kiroglu refused.

After the incident, he said, "I am praising God—not because he saved me from death, but because he helped me not to deny him in the shadow of death."

—"Convert Christian Beaten Unconscious," *Compass Direct* (January 20, 2006)

ILLUSTRATION 815

ACCEPTING TRAGEDY

Topics: Acceptance; Attitudes; God's Will; Loss; Tragedy

References: Job 1:21; 2:10; Matthew 26:42

When United States district judge Joan Lefkow came home to suburban Chicago on February 28, 2005, she found her mother and husband murdered. The killer was a man whom she had ruled against in court.

She later told the *Chicago Tribune*, "As a sojourner on this earth, I don't feel terribly entitled. I believe the Lord giveth and the Lord taketh away. It's your responsibility to accept the adversity as well as the abundance."

—Mary Schmich, "The Journey of Judge Joan Lefkow," *Chicago Tribune* (November 20, 2005)

ILLUSTRATION 816

CHILD'S MURDER INSPIRES MOM

Topics: Conversion; Crime; Forgiveness; Freedom; Murder; New Life

References: Genesis 50:15–21; Matthew 18:15–35; Ephesians 2:10; 1 Peter 4:12–19

Yvonne Pointer was one of ten children born to a wonderful mother and father, though she admits, "I was the worst. I did everything my parents did not want me to do."

For three years a friend of her father tried to reach her. "He would come to where I was getting high and say, 'You need to change your ways.' He was a thorn in my flesh," Pointer says. But in time the high turned on her. Then she remembered the words of her father's friend, went to church, and cried out to God. And on May 4, 1975, she turned her life over to Christ.

Less than ten years later, Pointer experienced what some say is the greatest pain on earth — the loss of a child. On December 6, 1984, her daughter Gloria was raped and murdered while on her way to school in Cleveland, Ohio. "After she died, I would spend hours in the church when no one was there, because Gloria's death didn't make sense to me," Pointer says. "I had come through drugs, through street life — and now this? I could not fathom why this would happen. But because I'd had that personal experience with God, I went to God."

People from the church rallied around her, washing clothes, cooking, and cleaning when the mother didn't have the strength. Slowly, a new sense of direction emerged. "In the beginning it was all about the injustice done to my child. Period," Pointer says. But soon she became aware of others with similar losses. She wrote letters and talked to police, to reporters, and to anyone who would listen.

Meantime, Pointer cofounded Parents Against Child Killing, which later became Positive Plus, a women-helping-women organization. "We started out with mothers who had lost children," Pointer says, "but I found out pain is pain. If your husband walked out and left you with five babies, that's pain. We felt we could find solutions by helping each other."

Pointer has received numerous honors for her work as an advocate for child safety. She even speaks in prisons, sharing the love of God with inmates. "I found hatred too heavy a load to carry. Would I want the person who murdered Gloria over for Sunday dinner? No. But if I didn't forgive him, unforgiveness would kill

me too," she says quietly. "Forgiveness releases you to live."

—Audrey T. Hingley, "Gloria's Legacy,"
Today's Christian (May–June 2006)

ILLUSTRATION 817

GOING PUBLIC WITH PAIN

Topics: Circumstances and Faith; Comfort; Compassion; Death; Despair; Emotions; Faith; Funerals; Grace; Grief; Ministry; Mortality; Mourning; Murder; Overcoming

References: Psalm 23:4; 46:1–3; 121; Isaiah 41:10–13; 43:1–2; John 14:27; 2 Corinthians 1:3–4; 1 Thessalonians 5:11; 1 Peter 5:7

The day Martin Luther King Jr. was assassinated (April 4, 1968), Robert F. Kennedy was in Indianapolis, speaking to a crowd of African-Americans. He had to break the terrible news to the large crowd that had gathered.

He sought to comfort his hearers by sharing his grief over the assassination of his brother, John F. Kennedy — something he had never before done publicly. In the midst of that sharing, he quoted Aeschylus, his favorite Greek poet: "Even in our sleep, pain which cannot forget falls drop by drop upon the heart until, in our own despair, against our will, comes wisdom through the awful grace of God."

—Joe Klein, "Psst, Who's Behind the Decline of Politics?" *Time* (April 17, 2006)

ILLUSTRATION 818

SUFFERING IS PERSONAL

Topics: Adversity; Burdens; Despair; Help from God; Jesus Christ; Misery; Overcoming; Pain; Problems; Providence; Questions; Security in God; Struggles; Trials; Trust

References: Matthew 11:28–30; Romans 5:3–5; 8:17; 2 Corinthians 4:11; Hebrews 4:15; James 1:2–4; 1 Peter 1:6–7; 2:24; 5:10

The answer to suffering cannot just be an abstract idea, because this isn't an abstract issue; it's a personal issue. It requires a personal response. It's not a bunch of words, it's *the* Word. It's not a tightly woven philosophical argument; it's a person. *The* person. The answer must be someone, not just something, because the issue involves someone—*"God, where are you?"*

—Lee Strobel,
The Case for Faith (Zondervan, 2000)

ILLUSTRATION 819

WHY IS THIS HAPPENING TO ME?

Topics: Affliction; Fear of God; Mercy; Vindictiveness

References: Job 16:12; Psalm 90:7; 102:9–10

Is not the question "Why is God letting this happen to me?" really a question that seeks to find out how God feels toward me? When I have pursued the "why" question by asking, "Could you tell me what you think might be the answer?" I have usually gotten a response that reveals the person's perception of their present relationship with God. Often it is concern that the suffering indicates a vindictive God who is angry with them.

—Arthur H. Becker, *Ministry with Older Persons* (Augsburg Fortress, 1986)

ILLUSTRATION 820

HOPING BACK TO HEALTH

Topics: Attitudes; Despair; Discouragement; Faith; Hope; Overcoming; Pain; Strength; Trials; Victory; Waiting on God

References: Isaiah 40:28–31; Romans 12:12; Hebrews 11:1

Ernest Gordon, dean of the chapel of Princeton University for twenty-six years, was called to the ministry in a Japanese concentration camp during World War II. Gordon and his fellow prisoners were used as slave labor to build the Thailand-Burma Railroad. Hundreds of them perished from mistreatment. As an officer, Gordon struggled to help his men make sense of the suffering they had to endure. He became deathly ill, however, and was spared only by the care of Chaplain Dusty Miller, who shared his precious rations with Gordon.

At one point, as Chaplain Miller nursed Gordon's broken body back to health, he spoke the words that nursed Gordon's broken soul back to health and called him to ministry. Miller told him, "A man can experience an incredible amount of pain and suffering if he has hope. When he loses his hope, that's when he dies."

—Bill White, Paramount, California

ILLUSTRATION 821

A SMILE FROM HEAVEN

Topics: Dependence on God; Experiencing God; Grace; Happiness; Joy; Prayer; Strength; Weakness

References: 2 Corinthians 12:8–10; Philippians 4:13

Honesty is always the best policy, especially when you are surrounded by women in a restroom during a break at a Christian women's conference. One woman, putting on lipstick, said, "Oh, Joni, you always look so together, so happy in your wheelchair. I wish that I had your joy!" Several women around her nodded. "How do you do it?" she asked as she capped her lipstick.

"I don't do it," I said. "May I tell you honestly how I woke up this morning?"

"This is an average day. After my husband, Ken, leaves for work at 6:00 a.m., I'm alone until I hear the front door open at 7:00 a.m. That's when a friend arrives to get me up. While she makes coffee, I pray, 'Lord, my friend will soon give me a bath, get me dressed, sit me up in my chair, brush my hair and teeth, and send me out the door. I don't have the strength to face this routine one more time. I have no resources. I don't have a smile to take into the day. But you do. May I have yours? God, I need you desperately.'"

"So what happens when your friend comes into the bedroom?" one of them asked.

"I turn my head toward her and give her a smile sent straight from heaven. It's not mine; it's God's." I point to my paralyzed legs. "Whatever joy you see today was hard won this morning."

I have learned that the weaker we are, the more we need to lean on God; and the more we lean on God, the stronger we find him to be.

—Joni Eareckson Tada, "Joy Hard Won," *Decision* (March 2000)

ILLUSTRATION 822

USEFUL TO GOD

Topics: Character; Ministry; Service; Trials

References: 2 Corinthians 1:3–7; 1 Thessalonians 2:9–13

If you are going to be used by God, he will take you through a multitude of experiences that are not meant for you at all; they are meant to make you useful in his hands.

—Oswald Chambers

ILLUSTRATION 823

BREAKING WISHBONE FAITH

Topics: Belief; Christianity; Faith; Loyalty; Support; Trust; Unbelief

References: 2 Timothy 1:12; Hebrews 10:23, 35–39; 11

Alumni and fans made UCLA football coach Pepper Rodgers's life miserable the year his Bruins got off to a horrible start. Nobody in Southern California would hang out with him. "My dog was my only true friend," Rodgers said.

"I told my wife that every man needs at least two good friends. She bought me another dog."

Rodgers is tough in the face of adversity, however. When his players at UCLA were having difficulty adapting to the wishbone offense he'd installed and the school's alumni demanded that he adopt another system, Rodgers didn't budge. "The wishbone is like Christianity," he said. "If you believe in it only until something goes wrong, you didn't believe in it in the first place."

—"A Look at Our Legacy," coachwyatt.com (August 29, 2003)

ILLUSTRATION 824

KEEP GETTING UP

Topics: Courage; Endurance; Failure; Perseverance; Persistence; Strength; Success; Winning and Losing

References: Proverbs 24:16; Romans 5:3–5; 1 Corinthians 9:24–27; Galatians 6:9–10; Hebrews 10:36; James 1:2–4

Walter Payton, who was five feet ten inches and 202 pounds, was not a particularly large running back for the National Football League. But he set one of sport's greatest records: the all-time rushing record of 16,726 yards. During his twelve-year career, Payton carried the football over nine miles.

What is truly impressive, though, is that, on average, he was knocked to the ground every 4.4 yards of those nine miles by someone bigger than himself. He kept getting up, and he kept getting up, and he kept getting up.

Great victories await those with great endurance.

—Bill White, Paramount, California

ILLUSTRATION 825

THANKS IN HARD TIMES

Topics: Blessings; Gratitude; Old Age; Thanksgiving

References: Deuteronomy 8:10; Psalm 100:4

During the Depression, William Stidger was in a restaurant with friends who were all talking about how terrible things were: suffering people, rich people committing suicide, joblessness. The conversation got more miserable as it went on.

A minister in the group interrupted. "In two or three weeks I have to preach a sermon on Thanksgiving Day," he said. "What can I say that's affirmative in a period of world depression like this?"

Stidger felt the Spirit of God saying to him, "Why don't you give thanks to those people who have been a blessing in your life and affirm them during this terrible time?"

He began to think about that. He remembered a schoolteacher who was very dear to him, a wonderful teacher of poetry and English literature who had gone out of her way to put a great love of literature and verse in him, which has affected all his writings and his preaching. So he sat down and wrote a letter to this woman, now up in years. It was only a matter of days until he got a reply in the feeble scrawl of the aged:

> *My dear Willy,*
>
> *I can't tell you how much your note meant to me. I am in my 80s, living alone in a small room, cooking my own meals, lonely, and like the last leaf of autumn lingering behind. You'll be interested to know that I taught in school for more than fifty years, and yours is the first note of appreciation I ever received. It came on a blue, cold morning, and it cheered me as nothing has done in many years.*

"I'm not sentimental, but I found myself weeping over that note," Stidger said. Then he thought of a kind bishop, now retired, who had recently faced the death of his wife and was all alone. This bishop had taken a lot of time giving Stidger advice and counsel and love when he first began his ministry. So he sat down and wrote the old bishop. In two days a reply came back.

> *My dear Will,*
>
> *Your letter was so beautiful, so real, that as I sat reading it in my study, tears of gratitude fell from my eyes. Before I realized what I was doing, I rose from my chair and I called my wife's name to share it with her, forgetting she was gone. You'll never know how much your letter has warmed my spirit. I have been walking around in the glow of your letter all day long.*

—David A. Seamands, "Instruction for Thanksgiving," Preaching Today Audio, no. 62

PART 32: TEMPTATION

ILLUSTRATION 826

CORPSE FLOWER

Topics: Deception; Emptiness; Pleasure; Promises; Sin; Temptation

References: Genesis 3:6–24; Proverbs 9:17–18; 14:12; 1 Peter 1:18

The corpse flower (*titan arum*), native to the equatorial forests of Sumatra, can grow up to ten feet tall. Once open, the spiky, bright red bloom looks like rotten meat, a veritable welcome mat for the insects that pollinate it—flies and carrion beetles.

According to Matthew Opel, University of Connecticut research assistant, the corpse flower "looks like something has died. It smells like something has died. It has the same chemicals that dead bodies produce."

The flower, which begins to disintegrate after two days, is nothing but a big practical joke to the flies and other carrion insects, says Opel. "Unlike other plants that offer nectar, there's no real reward here. They think they're going to get a meal because it smells like something dead."

How like the corpse flower is the story of sin. It is attractive. It holds out promises yet has no true rewards. And it ends in death.

—"Smelly Corpse Flower to Bloom," rednova.com (June 23, 2004)

ILLUSTRATION 827

STOPPING THE LIP PRINTS

Topics: Consequences; Sin; **Temptat**ion; Warnings

Reference: Galatians 6:7–8

At a middle school in Oregon, some girls were putting on lipstick and then pressing their lips to the mirrors, leaving dozens of lip prints.

The principal called the girls to the bathroom and told them how the lip prints were causing a major problem for the custodian, who had to clean the mirrors every day. To demonstrate how difficult it was, she asked the custodian to clean one of the mirrors. He took out a long-handled brush, dipped it into the toilet, and scrubbed the mirror.

Since then there have been no lip prints on the mirrors.

When tempted to sin, if we could only see the real filth we'd be kissing, we wouldn't be attracted to it.

—Brett Kays, Brownstown, Michigan

ILLUSTRATION 828

APPRECIATING SEX

Topics: Morality; Sex; Temptation

References: 1 Corinthians 6:12–20;
1 Thessalonians 4:3–8

There is a tendency to think of sex as something degrading. It is not. It is magnificent, an enormous privilege. But because of that the rules are tremendously strict and severe.

— Francis Charles Devas,
British army chaplain

ILLUSTRATION 829

HITTING THE INTERSECTION

Topics: Choices; Consequences;
Temptation; Wisdom

Reference: Matthew 7:13–14

The most dangerous intersection for accidents in the United States during 1999 and 2000 was the corner of Flamingo Road and Pines Boulevard in Pembroke Pines, Florida, just north of Miami.

So reported State Farm Insurance in 2001. During the two-year period, there were 357 reported crashes at this intersection, which is surrounded by three malls and the C.B. Smith Park. According to State Farm statistics, nearly 90,000 cars pass through the intersection daily. The intersection averages nearly one auto accident every two days, costing over $1 million dollars in property damage each year.

Life is full of dangerous intersections.

— "Ten Most Dangerous Intersections,"
InjuryBoard.com (July 2, 2001)

ILLUSTRATION 830

EXPANDING THE NET OF PORN

Topics: Addiction; Holiness;
Internet; Lust; Pornography; Purity;
Self-control; Sex; Sexual Immorality;
Temptation

References: Isaiah 33:15;
Matthew 5:27–30; Romans 1:24–32;
1 Thessalonians 4:3–8

What makes online sex far more compelling than any shrink-wrapped smut is instant gratification in endless variety—you never get to the end of the magazine and have to start looking at the same pictures again.

With old porn, once you view it, you've consumed it. You've chewed the flavor out of the gum. This can't be done on the Net, where the gum never runs out of flavor because a new piece of flesh waits behind every old one, and expectation bids you to go further. Much further.

Because as long as there's more to come, you'll keep coming. This is all so new. No stimulus like this ever existed before.

— Greg Gutfield, "The Sex Drive,"
Men's Health (October 1999)

ILLUSTRATION 831

TALK LOUDER, GOD

Topics: Devil; Hearing God; Holy Spirit; Listening; Obedience; Sin; Temptation

References: 2 Corinthians 4:3–6; Galatians 5:16–25; James 1:13–15; 4:7; 1 Peter 5:8–9

Barbara, five, had disobeyed me and was sent to her room. After a few minutes, I went in to talk with her about what she had done. Teary-eyed, she asked, "Why do we do wrong things, Mommy?"

"Sometimes the Devil tells us to do something wrong, and we listen to him," I said. "We need to listen to God instead."

"But God doesn't talk loud enough!" she wailed.

—Jo M. Guerrero, *Christian Reader*
(September–October 1996)

ILLUSTRATION 832

ESCALATING CONFLICT

Topics: Apology; Conflict; Gossip; Integrity; Relationships; Slander; Speech; Temptation; Truthfulness

References: Proverbs 21:23; Ephesians 4:29–32; Philippians 4:2–3; Colossians 3:12–14; James 3:1–12

A family in our church recently had their basement finished by a contractor. The process ended up being a construction nightmare. I somehow got caught in the middle of the dispute.

As the conflict escalated, I got calls from both sides, each trying to use me to reinforce his case. Such conversations quickly turned negative. The home owner once told me, "Not only does the contractor do shoddy work, but I've heard stories about how unethical he has been in paying former employees."

The contractor was guilty of the same kind of talk. Eventually I, too, found myself succumbing to the temptation of letting my knowledge of the other party leak out in conversations with each side. Soon I caught myself and moved back to a neutral position. But by then I had already said too much. One party confronted me about my loose tongue. I had to admit my error to both parties. In the end, my error turned out to be a lesson for all three of us.

Conflict has a way of growing a small snow-slide into a full-scale avalanche. On its way downhill, it can sweep victims into its wake. A conflict has the potential to mar the integrity of combatants on both sides. That happens as each side seeks to garner support for its position—making exaggerated statements, shading the truth, and impugning the motives of others.

—Gary Preston, Boulder, Colorado

ILLUSTRATION 833

A MATCH AGAINST TEMPTATION

Topics: Desires; Hell; Sin; Temptation

References: Proverbs 1:10–17; Titus 2:11–12; 1 John 3:7–10

Muhammad Ali once said that he had come up with a way to resist temptation. Wherever he went, he always carried a small box of matches. "Whenever I go to a party and I'm tempted by a beautiful woman, I simply pull out one of the matches and strike it," Ali said. "Then I put it out with my fingers and remind myself, 'Hell is a lot hotter than this.'"

—Keith Todd, "Muhammad Ali Faces Temptation," PreachingToday.com

ILLUSTRATION 834

SINKING WITH THE TUNA

Topics: Addiction; Pride; Sin; Temptation

References: James 1:13–15; 2 Peter 3:8–15

For the first time in forty-seven years, the tuna were running only thirty miles off Cape Cod. And they were biting. All you needed to catch one was a sharp hook and some bait. And the rumor was that Japanese buyers would pay $50,000 for a nice bluefin.

Many inexperienced fishermen ignored coast guard warnings and headed out to sea in small boats. What they didn't realize was that the problem wasn't catching the fish; it was reeling in the giant tuna and pulling it aboard.

The *Christi Anne*, a nineteen-foot boat, capsized while doing battle with a tuna. That same day the twenty-seven-foot boat *Basic Instinct* suffered the same fate, while *Official Business*, a twenty-eight-footer, was swamped after it hooked a six-hundred-pound tuna. Fishermen on these boats underestimated the power of the fish they were trying to catch.

That is what temptation does to us. It looks great on the surface. Only after we hook into it do we discover its strength.

—Kent Edwards,
South Hamilton, Massachusetts

ILLUSTRATION 835

EXPOSING KIDS TO PORNOGRAPHY

Topics: Children; Lust; Pornography; Purity; Teens; Temptation

References: Matthew 18:6; Mark 9:42; Luke 17:2; 1 Corinthians 6:18

Nine of ten kids between ages eight and sixteen have been exposed to pornography online according to the U.S. Justice Department.

Furthermore, 47 percent of school-age children receive pornographic spam on a daily basis, reports software company Symantec. And representatives from the pornography industry told Congress's COPA (Child Online Protection Act) Commission that as many as 20 to 30 percent of the visitors to some pornographic websites are children.

—Daniel Weiss, "Pornography: Harmless Fun or Public Health Hazard?" citizenlink.org (May 19, 2005)

ILLUSTRATION 836

DYING WITH PORNOGRAPHY

Topics: Addiction; Death; Foolishness; Lust; Perversion; Pleasure; Pornography; Self-indulgence; Sexual Immorality; Temptation; Unrighteousness; Vices

References: Matthew 5:27–30; Romans 13:13; 1 Corinthians 6:18; Galatians 5:19–21; Colossians 3:5; Jude 1:7

In 2006, Vladimir Villisov of Russia designed his own coffin to accommodate his vast collection of pornography.

"The girls in those magazines have been my companions for years," said Villisov, sixty-six, "and I want them to accompany me to the next life."

—Brian Mavis, "Going to the Grave with His Porn," SermonNews.com (June 22, 2006)

ILLUSTRATION 837

PEPSI REFUSES COKE SECRETS

Topics: Business; Competition; Ethics; Fairness; Golden Rule; Honesty; Integrity; Morality; Temptation; Values; Virtue

References: Exodus 23:8; Deuteronomy 16:19; Proverbs 10:9; 11:3; 15:27; Ephesians 4:25; 1 Timothy 1:19; 6:10

In 2006, an administrative assistant at Coca-Cola's Atlanta headquarters left work with classified materials in her purse, which included recipes for upcoming products, future promotions, and a beverage sample for an upcoming product.

With the help of two other employees, the secretary sent a letter to Pepsi—Coke's oldest and biggest competitor—offering to sell the secrets. Pepsi could have seriously damaged its competitor for a relatively low price.

Pepsi officials immediately responded, however, by contacting Coca-Cola officials, who then called the FBI. The Feds conducted a sting operation that netted the three conspirators when they agreed to part with the secrets for $1.5 million.

"We were just doing what any responsible company would do," said Pepsi spokesperson Dave DeCecco. "Despite the fierce competition in this industry, it should also be fair."

—Kathleen Kingsbury, "You Can't Beat the Real Thing," *Time* (July 17, 2006)

ILLUSTRATION 838

WATCHING SEX

Topics: Entertainment; Example; Lust; Media; Movies; Music; Pornography; Premarital Sex; Sexual Immorality; Teens; Television; Temptation

References: Job 31:1; Matthew 5:28; 6:22–23; Luke 11:34; 1 Corinthians 15:33

Kids who watch violence on television and in movies tend to become more violent, research has shown. Now research shows that kids who watch sexual activity on TV and in movies tend to become more sexually active.

In a study published in 2006 by the American Academy of Pediatrics, researchers studied 1,017 adolescents, ages twelve to fourteen, over a period of two years. During that time, the teens were exposed to 264 episodes on movies, TV shows, music and magazines, which were then analyzed for their sexual content. In general, the survey found that teens exposed to higher levels of sexual media participated in a higher level of sexual activity. For example, teens exposed to a high amount of sexual media were 2.2 times more likely to have had intercourse between the ages of fourteen and sixteen than teens with less exposure.

One explanation for the increase in sexual activity is the entertainment industry's role as a peer, researchers say. In an age when parents rarely talk to their children about sex, the media becomes an educator, teaching that sex is fun and there are no risks. Researchers suggest that teenagers exposed to a large amount of sexual media "may begin to adopt the media's social norms as their own. Some, especially those who have fewer alternative sources of sexual norms—such as parents or friends—may use the media as a kind of sexual super-peer that encourages them to be sexually active."

— Michael Conlon, "Sexy Media a Siren Call to Promiscuity?" Reuters News Service (April 3, 2006)

ILLUSTRATION 839

EXCELLING WITH PATIENCE

Topics: Addiction; Appetites; Contentment; Desires; Fruit of the Spirit; Greed; Limitations; Lust; Patience; Self-control; Self-indulgence; Temptation

References: Genesis 25:27–34; Psalm 37:7; 40:1; Proverbs 25:28; Acts 1:4; Galatians 5:22–23; 2 Timothy 3:2–4; James 5:7–11

Kids who can wait for something do better in school.

That's what Walter Mischel proved in an experiment in 1970 with four-year-olds. He would leave one child in a room with a bell and a marshmallow. If the child rang the bell, Mischel would come back and the child could eat the marshmallow. If the child waited for Mischel to come back on his own, the child could have two marshmallows.

In videos of the experiment, you can see children squirming, kicking, hiding their eyes—desperately trying to exercise self-control so they could wait and get two marshmallows. Their performance varied widely. Some broke down and rang the bell within a minute. Others lasted fifteen minutes.

The children who waited longer went on to get higher SAT scores. They got into better colleges and, on average, achieved more as adults. The children who rang the bell quickest were more likely to become bullies. They received worse teacher and parental evaluations ten years later and were more likely to have drug problems at age thirty-two.

Mischel concluded that children may be taught "that it pays to work toward the future instead of living for instant gratification."

—David Brooks, "Marshmallows and Public Policy," *The New York Times* (May 7, 2006)

ILLUSTRATION 840

SAVED FROM THE LIONS

Topics: Jesus Christ; God's Love; Salvation; Savior; Temptation

References: John 3:16; 1 John 4:9

Several years ago, my wife, Kathy, and a friend took their kids to the St. Louis Zoo. "Big Cat Country" had just opened, which took the lions and tigers out of their cages and allowed them to roam in large enclosures. Visitors could observe the cats by walking on elevated skyways above the habitats.

As my wife and her friend took the children up one of the skyway ramps, a blanket got tangled in a stroller wheel. Kathy knelt to help untangle the wheel while our preschool boys went ahead. When Kathy looked up, she discovered that the boys had walked through a small gap in the fencing and had climbed up on the rocks some twenty or twenty-five feet from the lion pen.

Pointing to the lions below, they called back to their mother, "Hey, Mom, we can see them!" They had no concept of how much danger they were in. But what could Kathy do? If she screamed, she might startle the boys perched precariously above the lions. The gap in the fence was too small for her to get through.

So she knelt down, spread out her arms, and said, "Boys, come get a hug." They came running for the love that saved them from danger greater than they could perceive.

With similar love, our Savior beckons us from temptation that would devour us.

—Bryan Chapell, *Holiness by Grace* (Crossway, 2001)

ILLUSTRATION 841

PLEDGING ABSTINENCE

Topics: Abstinence; Commitment; Sex; Teens; Temptation

References: 1 Corinthians 6:12–20; Galatians 5:16–25; 1 Thessalonians 4:1–8

Teens who take public pledges to remain virgins wait about eighteen months longer to have sex than those who don't, says a new study published in the *American Journal of Sociology*.

"Adolescents who pledge are much less likely to have intercourse than adolescents who do not pledge," says Peter S. Bearman of Columbia University and Hannah Bruckner of Yale University, authors of the study. "The delay effect is substantial and robust. Pledging delays intercourse for a long time. In this sense, the pledge works."

The pledge works because taking a public stand for virginity helps to give teens a sense of identity and community, Bearman and Bruckner say. Unfortunately, if a school's students accept the pledge as a fashionable stance (with more than 30 percent pledging), the effect diminishes. Those results come from the National Longitudinal Study of Adolescent Health, which surveyed about 90,000 American teens and found that by 1995, about 10 percent of teen boys and 16 percent of teen girls had taken virginity pledges—that's about 2.5 million teens.

The University of North Carolina's J. Richard Udry, who helped design the survey, told Canada's *National Post*, "We were cynical about the likelihood that the pledge would produce [significant results]. But we were wrong."

—Ted Olsen, "True Love Actually Does Wait, Study Finds," ChristianityToday.com (January 1, 2001)

ILLUSTRATION 842

LOVING TO SAY YES

Topics: Brokenness; Christian Life; Evil Desires; God's Love; Obedience; Sin; Temptation

References: Galatians 2:20; 5:16–25

I cannot continuously say no to this or no to that unless there is something ten times more attractive to choose. Saying no to my lust, my greed, my needs, and the world's powers takes an enormous amount of energy. The only hope is to find something so obviously real and attractive that I can devote all my energies to saying yes.

One such thing I can say yes to is when I come in touch with the fact that I am loved. Once I have found that in my total brokenness I am still loved, I become free from the compulsion of doing successful things.

—Henri Nouwen, "Hearing God's Voice and Obeying His Word," *Leadership* (Winter 1982)

ILLUSTRATION 843

NO DRUG FOR GAMBLING

Topics: Addiction; Appetites; Gambling; Greed; Love of Money; Money; Self-control; Temptation; Vices

References: Psalm 103:2–5; John 8:34; Romans 6:16; Titus 2:11–12; 2 Peter 2:19; 1 John 1:9

In 1999, between 0.6 and 0.9 percent of Americans were compulsive gamblers who had a pathological addiction to gambling, reported the National Gambling Impact Study Commission. Seven years later, that figure rose to 1.1 percent, said the National Center for Responsible Gambling.

Other studies reveal higher percentages in areas where there are many casinos. For example, a white paper for the National Coalition Against Legalized Gambling estimated addiction rates as high as 6.4 percent in Nevada and 4.9 percent in Mississippi. What's more, the study says, these areas provide a reasonable reference for what all of America could become if the trend toward increased gambling continues.

For some people such statistics are a clear warning about the dangers of gambling in our culture. For others like executives at Somaxon Pharmaceuticals, they represent a potential gold mine. For years the San Diego–based drug maker has tried to produce a drug that could treat gambling addiction. If the lowest projections are correct, millions of people in the United States have a gambling problem. A pharmaceutical treatment for such an addiction would be worth billions of dollars.

Sadly, such a treatment will not be available anytime soon. In December 2006, Somaxon said the results of drug trials were not encouraging. Gamblers taking a prototype drug called nalmefene hydrochloride experienced meager improvements over those given placebos. They also suffered serious side effects, such insomnia, nausea, and dizziness.

"It's a disappointment," said Somaxon founder Jeff Raser.

—Timothy Lamer, "No Easy Cure,"
World (December 23, 2006)

ILLUSTRATION 844
TEACHING KIDS TO KILL

Topics: Killing; Murder; Teens;
Temptation; Video Games; Violence

References: Exodus 20:13;
Proverbs 3:31; 22:6; Matthew
6:22–23; 1 Corinthians 15:33;
Philippians 4:8

David Grossman, a retired U.S. Army psychologist, believes that violent video games are teaching our kids to kill. Grossman first became aware of this issue while conducting research for his Pulitzer prize–nominated book *On Killing*, which tells about the army's solution to the problem that as many as 85 percent of soldiers did not fire their weapons during World Wars I and II.

Grossman said, "Hardwired into the brains of most healthy members of most species is a response against killing their own kind." To deal with the problem, the army desensitized soldiers by having them shoot at human-shaped targets made of wood. As technology improved, the military began using video games to simulate the killing of other human beings.

Grossman believes that modern video games like Doom and Grand Theft Auto have the same desensitizing effect on teens. David Walsh, director of the National Institute on Media and the Family, agrees: "What happens when a teen spends a lot of time playing violent video games is [that] the aggression center of the brain activates, but the emotional center of the brain deactivates—exactly the combination that we would not want to see."

As an example, Grossman writes about Michael Carneal, of Paducah, Kentucky, who in 1997 opened fire in the lobby of his high school, seriously injuring five of his classmates and killing three others. A subsequent police investigation found that Michael's parents had converted their two-car garage into a playroom lined with point-and-shoot arcade games. Years of playing violent video games had provided Michael with the emotional training needed to kill human beings.

Those video games also provided Michael with the physical training needed to use a deadly weapon. Prior to the night before his killing spree, he had never shot an actual pistol. However, when he opened fire on his fellow students, he did so with a surprising degree of accuracy. "I have trained the FBI. I have trained Navy SEALS, Green Berets, and Texas Rangers," Grossman writes. "And when I tell them about this case, they're simply stumped. Nowhere in the annals of law enforcement, military, or criminal history can we find an equivalent achievement."

— Tom Neven, "Teaching Kids to Kill,"
Plugged In (July 2006)

ILLUSTRATION 845

ROUSING SEX WITH MUSIC

Topics: Influence; Media; Music; Sex; Sexual Immorality; Teens

References: Proverbs 22:6; Matthew 6:22–23; Romans 12:2; 1 Corinthians 15:33; Philippians 4:8; 1 Thessalonians 4:1–5; 2 Timothy 2:22; 1 John 2:15–17

Teens who listen to raunchy, sex-filled lyrics are more likely to indulge in early sexual activity than teens who don't. So said a survey done in 2001 of 1,461 teenagers between the ages of twelve and seventeen.

Most of the participants were virgins at the beginning of the study. Between 2002 and 2004, the researchers did follow-up interviews to track the sexual activity of the teens. About 51 percent of teens who collected sexually degrading music began having sex within two years of the three-year study, compared to 29 percent of those who did not listen to such music. The research was first published in *Pediatrics* journal.

"A lot of teens think that's the way they're supposed to be," says seventeen-year-old Natasha Ramsey. She is editor of sexetc.com, a Rutgers University website on teen sexual health. "They

think that's the cool thing to do." She agrees that music is a major decision driver. "Teens will try to deny it; they'll say, 'No, it's not the music.' But it *is* the music! It is one of the biggest impacts on our lives."

— Sunil Vyas, "Raunchy Lyrics Trigger Earlier Onset of Sexual Activity among Teens," earthtimes.org (August 7, 2006)

ILLUSTRATION 846

MURDERING BY VIDEO

Topics: Addiction; Confession; Death; Entertainment; Guilt; Hypocrisy; Media; Murder; Parenting; Play; Stumbling Blocks; Violence

References: Exodus 20:13; Ezekiel 8:17; 1 Timothy 3:2–3; 2 Timothy 3:1–5; 2 Peter 2:19

I have used swords and shotguns, handguns and grenades. I have shot, stabbed, and bludgeoned. I have crushed skulls with golf clubs and hammers and baseball bats. I have slaughtered men and women, drug dealers and crime bosses, soldiers and secret agents, mad scientists and aliens, zombies and the pizza guy. I have killed hundreds, even thousands—so many that I lost count long ago. I have taken up machine guns, plasma rifles, and chain saws. I have learned to aim for the head.

I have killed with Xbox and GameCube, PlayStation, and PC. I have killed with joystick, mouse, and keyboard. I have killed for hours at a time on screens big and small, on laptops and high-resolution monitors. I have killed in my basement, in my living room, at the local arcade, at a neighbor's house, with a coworker's teenage son. I have killed late into the night, until 3:00 a.m., because my adrenaline was surging, because my kids were safely in bed, because I was simply on a roll. Because I was winning and they were dying....

Every weeknight I play, most nights later than the one before. And every night I slink up the stairs and ease my weary frame into bed, trying not to disturb my wife, who went to sleep hours ago. My body is spent, yet I cannot sleep. The bedroom is silent, yet I can still hear those ominous refrains. I close my eyes, yet I can still picture the endless corridors, each one leading to another door or outcropping, another blind corner, another enemy, another target....

Come Saturday morning I'm at the computer again. That's when I hear it: the muted thud of feet on the stairs. And there, standing to my right, eyes fixed on the screen, is my little boy. I tell him to go back upstairs, but he doesn't budge. In his mind there is a cartoon on the computer, the likes of which he's never seen before. He somehow knows this is forbidden fruit that he must possess or at least observe. I call for my wife, asking her to please come get her son.

Later on, this boy who has never operated a joystick in his life asks me a question I never saw coming: "Daddy, can I watch you play the bad game?"

Forgive me, Father, for I have killed.

—Jeff Hooten, "Point. Click. Kill.," *Citizen* (February 2006)

ILLUSTRATION 847
WORKING IN CHOCOLATE

Topics: Appetites; Bondage; Eating; Gluttony; Moderation; Sinful Nature; Temptation

References: Psalm 9:16; Proverbs 29:6; Matthew 26:41; Mark 14:38; 1 Corinthians 10:13

A twenty-one-year-old man was taken to the hospital for treatment of minor injuries after being trapped waist-deep in a vat of chocolate.

The employee of Debelis Corporation, a company that supplies chocolate ingredients, told police he stepped into the tank of molten chocolate to unplug it. He became stuck and soon sank up to his waist in the viscous confection.

The man's coworkers and local police and firefighters tried to pull him loose, but they couldn't free him for two hours until the chocolate had thinned out.

—Associated Press, "Man Trapped Waist-Deep in Chocolate," news.yahoo.com (August 18, 2006)

ILLUSTRATION 848
MUSIC'S EFFECT ON KILLER

Topics: Entertainment; Influence; Mind; Music; Thoughts

References: Romans 12:2; 1 Corinthians 15:33; Philippians 4:8

"I used to think this ain't affecting me; you'd have to be weak-minded to let this stuff affect you—and the whole time it affected me." So said Jamie Rouse on how music affected his behavior. On November 15, 1995, Rouse walked into his Lynnville, Tennessee, high school carrying a .22 caliber rifle. He then killed a teacher and student.

—Bob Waliszewski, "Confessions of a School Shooter," *Plugged In* (March 2001)

ILLUSTRATION 849

PLAYING WITH BOMBS

Topics: Children; Choices; Consequences; Danger; Discernment; Foolishness; Maturity; Sin; Temptation; Wisdom

References: Matthew 7:13–14; Ephesians 5:15–18; 2 Timothy 2:22; Hebrews 5:14

Children will play with virtually anything they get their hands on. It's no surprise, then, that when Dutch children in the town of Barneveld uncovered an unexploded World War II artillery shell, they played with it. In fact, they had games with it for several months.

That shell was still live and contained high explosives. Thankfully, the deadly plaything did not explode in the Barneveld playground as the children tossed it about. Eventually the authorities learned about the shell, confiscated it, and exploded it in a safe place.

Those who are not yet mature often fail to recognize the danger in what they are doing. For children, the world is a playground, and bombs make great toys.

—Craig Brian Larson, "Children Play with a Bomb," PreachingToday.com

PART 33: TRUST

ILLUSTRATION 850

HOLDING COMFORT FOOD

Topics: Needs; Provision; Shepherd; Trust

References: Psalm 23:1; Matthew 6:25–34; Philippians 4:19

The Allied soldiers gathered many hungry, homeless children after World War II and placed them in large camps. The children were abundantly fed and cared for. However, at night they did not sleep well; they seemed restless and afraid.

Finally, a psychologist offered a solution. After the children were put to bed, they each received a slice of bread. If they wanted more to eat, they could have it, but this particular slice was not to be eaten—it was just to hold.

The slice of bread produced marvelous results. The child would go to sleep, subconsciously feeling there was something to eat tomorrow. That calmed the child.

In Psalm 23 David says, "The Lord is my shepherd; I shall not want." Instinctively, the sheep knows the shepherd has made plans for its grazing. He knows the shepherd has made ample provision, so he will lie down in peace, with the piece of bread in his hand.

—Charles L. Allen,
God's Psychiatry (Revell, 1988)

ILLUSTRATION 851

FEARING NOT THE RHINO

Topics: Fear; Provision; Trust; Vulnerability

References: Psalm 91:2; Proverbs 3:5–6; Daniel 6:23

A young girl stands in a picturesque meadow. In another part of the field is a gigantic African rhinoceros, which begins charging toward the girl. Her serene and happy face remains unmoved.

As the rhinoceros gets closer, the words appear on the screen, "Trust is not being afraid." A split second before the rhino tramples the helpless child, it stops, and the girl, her smile never wavering, reaches up and pets the animal on its massive horn. The final words then appear, "even when you are vulnerable."

The commercial was designed to tout the abilities of an insurance company to protect its clients from the uncertainties of life. How much more does it describe the believer, who can say with the psalmist, "I will say of the Lord, 'He is my refuge and my fortress, my God, in whom I trust'" (Psalm 91:2)!

—Stephen Nordbye, Charlton, Massachusetts

ILLUSTRATION 852

TRUSTING LIKE A CAT

Topics: Assurance; Confidence; Provision; Trust

References: Psalm 9:10; Proverbs 3:5

When our cat, Clement of Alexandria, goes outside, he looks around as though it's a jungle, and he is terrified. But when he comes in the house, he lies on the floor between the kitchen and the dining room—where we walk most frequently—and falls asleep in total trust. My wife, Kathy, or I could squash Clement's head, but he trusts us.

Our cat lives in complete, total confidence in his human companions. Every time I see Clement just lying there, I say to myself, "That's what Jesus wants me to do—to trust him." The kind of trust the cat shows in us is the kind of trust the Lord Jesus Christ invites from us.

—Dale Bruner, "Is Jesus Inclusive or Exclusive?" *Theology, News & Notes* (October 1999)

ILLUSTRATION 853

TAKING CARE OF THE CHECK

Topics: Assurance; Atonement; Choices; Dependence on God; Doubt; Faith; Gift of Righteousness; Grace; Help from God; Promises; Salvation; Trust

References: Exodus 32:30; John 3:16; Romans 3:21–26; 5:11; Ephesians 1:7;

2:8–9; Titus 3:3–7; 1 Peter 1:17–19; 1 John 1:9

I was having breakfast with my dad and my younger son at the Real Food Café in Grand Rapids, Michigan. As we were finishing our meal, I noticed that the waitress brought our check, then took it away, then brought it back again. She placed it on the table, smiled, and said, "Somebody in the restaurant paid for your meal. You're all set." Then she walked away.

I had the strangest feeling of helplessness. There was nothing I could do. To insist on paying would have been pointless. All I could do was trust that what she said was actually true and then live in that—which meant getting up and leaving the restaurant. My acceptance of what she said gave me a choice to live like it was true or to create my own reality in which the bill was not paid.

That is our invitation—to trust that we don't owe anything. To trust that something is already true about us, something has already been done, something has been there all along.

To trust that grace pays the bill.

—Rob Bell, *Velvet Elvis* (Zondervan, 2005)

ILLUSTRATION 854

WAITING IN TRUST

Topics: Faith; Hope; Patience; Prayer; Trust; Waiting on God

References: Psalm 25:1–10; 27:14; 31:15; Micah 7:7

The Flying Roudellas, who were trapeze artists, said there is a special relationship between flyer and catcher on the trapeze. The flyer is the one who lets go, and the catcher is the one who catches.

As the flyer swings high above the crowd on the trapeze, the moment comes when he must let go. He arcs out into the air. His job is to remain as still as possible and wait for the strong hands of the catcher to pluck him from the air.

The flyer must never try to catch the catcher but must wait in absolute trust. The catcher will catch him, but he must wait.

—John Ortberg, "Waiting on God,"
Preaching Today Audio, no. 199

ILLUSTRATION 855

CUDDLING IN THE STORM

Topics: Children; Courage; Fear; Loneliness; Marriage; Mothers; Parenting; Relationships; Togetherness; Trust

References: Genesis 15:1; Deuteronomy 1:21; Joshua 1:9; Luke 8:22–25

During a violent thunderstorm a mother was tucking her small boy into bed. She was about to turn off the light when he asked with a tremor in his voice, "Mommy, will you sleep with me tonight?"

The mother gave him a smile and a reassuring hug. "I can't, dear," she said. "I have to sleep with your daddy."

A long silence was broken at last by his shaky little voice: "The big sissy."

—Anonymous

ILLUSTRATION 856

DRINKING MUD

Topics: Faith; Healing; Medicine; Miracles; Prayer; Trust

Reference: John 9:1–7

My daughter, suffering from anorexia and bulimia, was undergoing treatment at Baptist Medical Center in Kansas City. On a particularly difficult day she was told to drink a glass of milk, but she just couldn't.

Her doctor was called in. He sat down beside her on the bed and said, "You are a Christian, correct?"

When she answered yes, he said, "Do you remember the man Jesus healed near the pool of Siloam? Jesus put mud on his eyes to bring about his healing. But what really healed him?"

She thought for a moment and then answered, "His faith."

"Good!" he said. "Now drink your mud."

—Steve T., Florence, Kansas

ILLUSTRATION 857

TRUSTING THE GREAT WALL

Topics: Betrayal; Morality; Security; Trust; Values

References: Proverbs 14:34;
Ephesians 6:14

In ancient China, people wanted protection from barbarian hordes from the North. So the Great Wall of China was built: thirty feet high, eighteen feet thick, and more than fifteen hundred miles long.

The Chinese goal was to build an absolutely impenetrable defense — too high to climb over, too thick to break down, and too long to go around. The people trusted this wall to keep them safe. But during the first hundred years of the wall's existence, China was successfully invaded three times.

It wasn't the wall's fault. During all three invasions, the barbaric hordes never climbed over the wall, broke it down, or went around it; they simply bribed a gatekeeper and then marched in through an open door. The purpose of the wall failed because of a breakdown in values.

—James Emery White, *You Can Experience a Purposeful Life* (Word, 2000)

ILLUSTRATION 858

POISONING BEETHOVEN

Topics: Authority; Beliefs; Consequences; False Beliefs; Heresy; New Age; Postmodernism; Seeking God; Sowing and Reaping; Spirituality; Thirst

References: Leviticus 19:31; Deuteronomy 18:10 – 14; Proverbs 14:12; Isaiah 2:6; Zechariah 10:2; Romans 6:12; Galatians 6:7 – 8; Colossians 2:8; 1 Timothy 4:1

Beethoven may have poisoned himself. That's what William Walsh, a scientist from Illinois, suggested after studying strands of hair from the body of famous classical composer Ludwig van Beethoven. Walsh discovered that Beethoven's body had one hundred times the normal amount of lead. He concluded that Beethoven's untimely death at the age of fifty-seven was due to lead poisoning.

Beethoven's lead poisoning may have been due to the mineral spa he went to for relaxation. The very thing he thought was bringing him relief was slowly poisoning him to death.

Spiritual poison is like that. As people engage in practices and embrace ideas that are spiritually poisonous, they think they're becoming more spiritual. But in reality, they're gradually being poisoned to eternal death.

—Tim Peck, "Deepening Your Life with God," PreachingToday.com

ILLUSTRATION 859

SATAN AND SANTA

Topics: Belief; Demons; Devil; Doctrine; Doubt; Evil; False Beliefs; Perception and Reality; Satan; Skepticism; Unbelief

References: Genesis 3:1 – 7; John 8:44; 2 Corinthians 4:4; 11:14; Ephesians 6:12; 1 Peter 5:8; 1 John 4:1 – 3

Two boys were walking home from Sunday school after hearing a strong sermon on the Devil. One said to the other, "What do you think about all this Satan stuff?"

The other boy replied, "Well, you know how Santa Claus turned out. It's probably just your dad."

—Dale W. Decker,
Mount Washington, Kentucky

ILLUSTRATION 860

CHECKING TRUTH

Topics: Culture; Denial; Humanity; Writing

References: Proverbs 2:1–11; John 1:1–3; Romans 1:21

Cultures are always dancing with denial. Writers tap us on the shoulder and say, "May I cut in?"

—Susan Shaughnessy, *Walking on Alligators* (HarperSanFrancisco, 1993)

ILLUSTRATION 861

GENERIC BAPTISM

Topics: Apathy; Baptism; Church; Compromise; Culture; False Beliefs; Halfheartedness; Heresy; Pluralism; Postmodernism; Sacraments; Tolerance; Traditions

References: 1 Timothy 6:3–5; 2 Timothy 4:3–4; 1 Peter 3:21; 2 Peter 2:1; Revelation 3:15–16

There are now baptism-style ceremonies in which God is never mentioned. They are offered to parents seeking to initiate their children into a world of all faiths, says Ema Drouillard of San Francisco, who runs the website Ceremonyway.com.

Drouillard conducted such an event for a couple in Marin County, California, in 1998, for their baby. "We just wanted a larger spirit to guide our daughter, but we didn't want to get

specific. I wanted all her bases covered," the mom said.

The couple grew up Presbyterian, but now, Mom says, "We do Christianity L-I-T-E for our baby, who believes in angels and fairies, leprechauns and Santa Claus."

—Cathy Lynn Grossman, "Rite of Baptism Trickles Away," *USA Today* (April 13, 2006)

ILLUSTRATION 862

PASTOR OPRAH

Topics: Authenticity; Entertainment; Idolatry; Integrity; Longing; Spirituality; Teachers; Television

References: Deuteronomy 11:16; Mark 13:22; Acts 17:29; 2 Timothy 4:3–4; 2 Peter 2:1; 1 John 5:21

She has hosted *The Oprah Winfrey Show* for more than twenty years, amassing billions of dollars in assets and attracting more than 49 million viewers each week in the United States. People look to Oprah Winfrey for advice on everything from genocide in Rwanda to the best-tasting oatmeal cookies.

Many people also regard her as a spiritual leader. According to *USA Today*, "By the late 1990s, Winfrey's focus was Change Your Life TV, and a New Age message was more prevalent. She preached, making the message of her life—take responsibility, and greatness will follow—the substance of the show. Keep a personal journal, purchase self-indulgent gifts, take time for you because you deserve it. The notes rang true to millions of viewers."

Cathleen Falsani, religion writer for the *Chicago Sun-Times*, asks straight out: "Has Oprah become America's pastor?"

There is evidence to support this conclusion. According to a November 2006 poll conducted by Beliefnet.com, which looks at how religion and spirituality intersect with popular culture, 33 percent of its sixty-six hundred respondents said Winfrey has had "a more profound impact" than their pastors on their spiritual lives.

Chris Altrock, pastor of Highland Street Church of Christ in Memphis, Tennessee, says, "Our culture is changing as churches are in decline and the bulk of a new generation is growing up outside of religion. People are now turning up at The Church of Oprah instead."

Jim Twitchell, a professor at the University of Florida, believes that Oprah reverence makes sense. "Religion essentially is based on high anxiety of what's going to happen to you," he says. "Winfrey pushes the idea that you have a life out there, and it's better than the one you have now, and go get it. It has to do with this deep American faith and yearning to be reborn. To start again."

In *The Gospel according to Oprah*, Marcia Nelson says Oprah's integrity has enhanced her spiritual stature. "One of the things that's key is she walks her talk," Nelson says. "That's really, really important in today's culture. People who don't walk their talk fall from a great pedestal—think of scandals in the Catholic Church and in televangelism. If you're not doing what you say you do, woe be unto you."

—Ann Oldenburg, "The Divine Miss Winfrey?" *USA Today* (May 11, 2006)

ILLUSTRATION 863
REALITY CHECK

Topics: Belief; Depravity; Human Nature; Repentance; Truth; Vision; Worldview

References: John 3:19–21; 8:31–47; Ephesians 4:15

Face reality as it is, not as you wish it to be.

—Peter Koestenbaum,
Fast Company (March 2000)

ILLUSTRATION 864
SHAM VETERAN CONFESSES

Topics: Boasting; Bondage; Conscience; Deception; Falsehood; Guilt; Hypocrisy; Lying; Regret; Repentance; Sin; Truthfulness

References: 2 Samuel 12; 24:10; Proverbs 28:13

Werner "Jack" Genot wanted to be a hero. So, he concocted a story about serving as a marine and being taken as a prisoner of war during a bloody Korean War battle.

Genot, now seventy-one, is from the small Illinois town of Marengo, where he serves as an alderman. His story grew until the uniform he wore on special occasions became laden with fake medals he had ordered from a catalog—a Bronze Star, a Silver Star, and two Purple Hearts. He would march in parades and talk to schoolchildren. He even got a special license plate reserved for wounded veterans by forging discharge papers.

However, a veteran's league eventually noticed a lack of records on file and numerous factual holes in Genot's military record and began an investigation. For two years, Genot denied the accusations and danced around the questions. But he finally confessed his deception in an interview with a local newspaper, claiming he could no longer stand the facade.

"You can't imagine what I'm going through," he said. "I really didn't know how to shake this demon. But I went to bed with it every night, and I looked at it in the mirror every morning. I don't want to meet my Maker with this on my heart."

—Jeff Long, "He Lied So He Could Be a Hero," *Chicago Tribune* (November 22, 2005)

ILLUSTRATION 865

LEGALLY NAMED CHRIST

Topics: Arrogance; Control; Jesus Christ; Lordship; Pride; Reality; Rebellion; Submission; Surrender; Will

References: Exodus 3:14–15; 34:14; Acts 4:12; 19:13–20; Philippians 2:9–11; James 4:6; 1 Peter 3:15

In 2006, a judge in New York allowed Jose Luis Espinal to legally change his name to Jesus Christ. Following the decision, Espinal said he was happy and grateful that the judge approved the change. He also said that he was moved to seek the name change about a year prior to the decision when he realized, "I am the person that is that name."

We're all a little like Jose—we're just more subtle. We grab at the title of "Lord" every time we reclaim the management of our life.

—Samuel Maull, "Judge Lets Man Change Name to Jesus Christ," Breitbart.com (December 23, 2005)

ILLUSTRATION 866

INTERNET RELIGION

Topics: Absolutes; Authority; Beliefs; Bible; Doctrine; False Beliefs; Humanism; Inspiration of Scripture; Postmodernism; Relativism; Religion; Scripture; Secularism; Truth

References: 2 Samuel 23:1–2; Nehemiah 9:13–14; Matthew 24:35; 1 Corinthians 14:36–37; Galatians 1:11–12; 1 Thessalonians 2:13; 2 Timothy 3:16; 2 Peter 1:20–21; 1 John 5:9

Wikipedia, the online encyclopedia, has inspired a new religion. Yoism, invented by a Massachusetts psychologist, is based on the "open source" principle that the general public creates a combined, creative authority and source of truth.

Yoism operates and evolves over the Internet and has numerous contributors. It shuns traditional religious authorities and divine inspiration in favor of the wisdom of humans. Bob Dylan, Albert Einstein, and Sigmund Freud are among its revered saints.

Dan Kriegman founded Yoism in 1994 to make religion open to change and responsive to the wisdom of people everywhere. "I don't think anyone has ever complained about something that didn't lead to some revision or clarification in the Book of Yo," Kriegman says. "Every aware, conscious, sentient spirit is divine and has direct access to truth.... Open source embodies that. There is no authority."

—Charles Piller, "Divine Inspiration from the Masses," *LA Times* (July 23, 2006)

ILLUSTRATION 867

JESUS UNTOUCHED BY HYENAS

Topics: Creeds; Crucifixion; Easter; Faith; Family of God; Gospel; Jesus Christ; Love; Missions; Perspective; Protection; Resurrection; Victory

References: Proverbs 25:11; Isaiah 55:5; Acts 4:13; 1 Corinthians 9:19–23; 15:3–5; Philippians 3:20–21; Hebrews 1:1–3

Judaism has its *shema* and Islam its *shahadah*, but Christians, responding to Jesus' question "Who do you say that I am?" have produced literally thousands of statements of faith across the centuries.

As a capstone to his lifelong interest in the central texts of the Christian faith, Jaroslav Pelikan edited (with Valerie Hotchkiss) *Creeds and Confessions of Faith in the Christian Tradition*, a four-volume critical edition with a one-volume historical and theological guide called simply *Credo*.

Pelikan's collection includes several hundred creeds, including the Masai Creed from Nigeria, which Africanizes Christianity by declaring that Jesus "was always on safari doing good." It also declares that after Jesus had been "tortured and nailed hands and feet to a cross, and died, he lay buried in the grave, but the hyenas did not touch him, and on the third day, he rose from the grave. He ascended unto the skies. He is the Lord."

This creed was brought to Pelikan's attention by one of his students, a woman who had been a member of a religious order working in a hospital in East Nigeria. Pelikan wrote, "She brought it to me, and I just got shivers. Just the thought, you know, the hyenas did not touch him, and the act of defiance—God lives even in spite of the hyenas."

—Timothy George, "Delighted by Doctrine," *Christian History and Biography* (Summer 2006)

ILLUSTRATION 868

TRUMPING GOD WITH SCIENCE

Topics: Afterlife; Atheism; Belief; Creation; Creator; Experiencing God; Fellowship with God; Hope; Knowing God; Meaning of Life; Nature; Religion; Science; Worldview

References: Genesis 1:1–2; Psalm 14:1; 104; Isaiah 40:26; John 1:1–3; Romans 1:18–23; Colossians 1:15–17

According to a 2006 *Newsweek* poll, people in the United States said they believed in God by a margin of 92 to 6. Only 2 percent answered, "Don't know." Still, many people are atheists.

Astronomer Carolyn Porco believes science is a better system than God. "Science itself should attempt to supplant God in Western culture by providing the benefits and comforts people find in religion: community, ceremony, and a sense of awe," Porco says. "Imagine congregations raising their voices in tribute to gravity — the force that binds us all to the earth, and the earth to the sun, and the sun to the Milky Way."

Porco admits there are limits to finding spiritual fulfillment by exploring the universe — namely, our innate desire to understand what is beyond the universe. She writes, "The people who want to know that they're going to live forever and meet Mom and Dad in heaven? We can't offer that."

—Jerry Adler, "The New Naysayers," *Newsweek* (September 11, 2006)

ILLUSTRATION 869

SNAKE KILLS EVANGELIST

Topics: Belief; Discernment; Doctrine; Faith; False Beliefs; Hermeneutics; Interpretation; Presumption; Testing God; Theology; Traditions; Trust

References: Mark 16:17 – 18; Luke 10:19; Acts 28:1 – 6

John Wayne Brown Jr., a snake-handling evangelist, was bitten by one of his own timber rattlesnakes in the middle of his sermon. Though

Brown continued to speak to the people of Rock House Holiness Church that October night in 1998, he soon collapsed. The congregation gathered around him, praying and trying to cool him with an electric fan, but Brown was dead within minutes.

Brown, thirty-four, had handled snakes since he was seventeen and had survived twenty-two previous bites. He left behind five orphaned children. His wife, Melinda, died from a snakebite during a revival service in 1995.

One pastor who was onstage with Brown the night of his death said he didn't think the tragedy would make the church change its practices: "I think they will be more careful about handling serpents," he said. "I think they will wait until the Lord moves on them."

"A lot of people don't understand us," he offered. "We are just normal people, but we believe God's Word."

—Kent Faulk, "Snake Kills Evangelist, but Pastor Says Congregation Will Hold Firm to Its Traditions," *Birmingham News* (October 6, 1998)

ILLUSTRATION 870

FLAT DAVE TRUMPS REAL ONE

Topics: Appearances; Authenticity; Community; Companionship; Family; Humanity; Idolatry; Relationships

References: Exodus 20:4 – 6; Isaiah 44:9 – 23; Matthew 5:16; Acts 17:29; Romans 12:11; Revelation 3:15 – 16

1001 ILLUSTRATIONS THAT CONNECT

Dave Davila, twenty-four, took a job in Chicago and had to leave his close-knit family in East Moline, Illinois. But family gatherings just weren't the same without Dave. So his mother took a digital photo of Dave, had it blown up to his actual height—five feet eight inches—and mounted the photo on heavy cardboard.

At first Flat Dave just showed up and stood quietly by at family gatherings. Then word spread throughout the community, and he became something of a celebrity in East Moline. "Complete strangers want to pose with him," said his brother Dan. He also said, "I think Flat Dave's actually better looking than Dave."

Sometimes things get somewhat awkward for the real Dave—the one the family now calls Thick Dave. "I'm in Chicago talking to my mom on the phone, and she says, 'Hold on, I've got to load you into the van.' It's a little weird."

—Rex W. Huppke, "Meet Flat Dave.
He's a Real Stand-Up Guy,"
Chicago Tribune (July 2, 2006)

ILLUSTRATION 871

COLLECTING RELIGION

Topics: Belief; Doctrine; Experiencing God; Faith; False Beliefs; Idolatry; Legalism; Religion; Self-righteousness

References: Ezekiel 33:32; Matthew 23; Mark 7:9; John 14:6; Galatians 5:6; 1 Timothy 5:4; Titus 1:16; James 1:26–27

One can love religion like anything else in life: sports, science, stamp collecting. One can love it for its own sake without relation to God or the world or life.

Religion fascinates; it is entertaining. It has everything that is sought after by a certain type of person: aesthetics, mystery, the sacred, a feeling of one's importance and exclusive depth, etc. That kind of religion is not necessarily faith.

—Alexander Schmemann,
The Journals of Alexander Schmemann, 1973–1983
(St. Vladimir's Seminary Press, 2000)

ILLUSTRATION 872

FEELING THE BUBBLES

Topics: Confusion; Darkness; Discernment; Doubt; Emotions; Feelings; Questions; Scripture; Truth

References: Psalm 43:3; 119:105; Matthew 15:14; Luke 6:39; 2 Timothy 3:16

A scuba diver told me that he had been in water so deep and dark that it was almost impossible to keep from becoming disoriented. What a terrifying feeling—being underwater, unable to see your hands in front of your face, not knowing which way is up, panic engulfing you. I asked my friend, "So what do you do?"

"Feel the bubbles," he said.

"Feel the bubbles?" I asked.

"That's right. When it's pitch-black and you have no idea which way to go, you reach up with your hand and feel the bubbles. The bubbles always drift to the surface. When you can't trust your feelings or judgment, you can always trust the bubbles to get you back to the top."

Sometimes in life we get disoriented and desperate. At other times, we find ourselves drifting aimlessly. God knew we would need advice and instructions about how to live. In the sixty-six books of the Bible, we have a reality library—stories, letters, guidelines, and examples from God that tell us what is true and real.

—Terry Carter, Scott Duvall, and Daniel Hays, *Preaching God's Word* (Zondervan, 2005)

ILLUSTRATION 873

OPRAH ON TRUTH

Topics: Apology; Dishonesty; Honesty; Humility; Regret; Repentance; Truthfulness; Values; Words

References: Acts 5:1–11; 1 Corinthians 13:6; 2 Corinthians 13:5–10

After being included in Oprah Winfrey's famous book club, James Frey's memoir, *A Million Little Pieces*, quickly sold more than 3.5 million copies. Controversy erupted, however, when members of the press began to question whether the stories contained in Frey's book were actually true.

On January 11, 2005, Oprah Winfrey went on CNN's *Larry King Live* to defend the book and its author, stating that the controversy over his truthfulness was "much ado about nothing." She said Frey's writing was the "essential truth" of his life.

She reversed herself weeks later after new information came out confirming Frey's dishonesty. Oprah apologized on her own show, saying, "I left the impression that the truth does not matter. And I am deeply sorry about that, because that is not what I believe. To everyone who has challenged me on this issue of truth, you are absolutely right."

—Edward Wyatt, "Live on 'Oprah,' a Memoirist Is Kicked Out of the Book Club," nytimes.com (January 27, 2006)

ILLUSTRATION 874

CHEATING ON EXEMPTIONS

Topics: Character; Deceit; Dishonesty; Ethics; Government; Honesty; Integrity; Lying; Motives; Taxes; Temptation; Truthfulness; Values

References: 2 Kings 17:4; Micah 6:10–11; Mark 12:17; Luke 20:25; Romans 13:6–7

Cheating is a prominent feature in just about every human endeavor. So says economist Steven Levitt in *Freakonomics*. Although he doesn't declare cheating part of human nature, Levitt notes the prevalence of it among ordinary schoolteachers, wait staff, and payroll managers.

While evidence for cheating is often hard to uncover, at times it is overwhelming. Consider what happened one spring evening at midnight in 1987, when 7 million American children suddenly disappeared. It was April 15, and the Internal Revenue Service had just changed a rule. Instead of merely listing the name of each dependent child, tax filers were now required also to provide a Social Security number for each child. Suddenly 7 million children who had existed only as phantom exemptions on the previous year's 1040 forms vanished, representing about one in ten of all dependent children in the United States.

—John Beukema, "Phantom Exemptions Show the Prevalence of Cheating," PreachingToday.com

ILLUSTRATION 875

NONREBEL TEENS

Topics: Apathy; Conformity; Culture; Internet; Leadership; Outreach; Rebellion; Technology; Teens; Thoughts; Witnessing; Worldview

References: 1 Samuel 17; 1 Corinthians 9:23; Philippians 2:14–16; 1 Timothy 4:12; James 5:20

Two teens are combating the myth that teens are rebellious and apathetic. They're doing that by blogging.

Twin brothers Alex and Brett Harris, seventeen, created therebelution.com to debunk the myth that being a teenager means freedom from responsibility. Alex Harris reasons that if teens think adolescence is the time to have fun, they won't become responsible as adults. He says, "Low expectations affect you, even if you're not into drugs, sex, etc., and they continue to affect you until someone intentionally remedies that irresponsibility."

The twins are volunteering to lead a "rebelution" (a cross between rebellion and revolution) to rise up against social norms. "We are refusing to be defined by an ungodly, rebellious culture," they say.

Jonathan McCarthy, eighteen, also has a heart for teens, though he specifically targets Christian kids. "The biggest threat that I see facing Christian teens today is a deadness to spiritual things and a conforming to the world in the areas of music, movies, and books," McCarthy says.

McCarthy's blog, christianthink.blogspot.com, emphasizes a worldview based on Scripture and the necessity of a changed heart. As he continues to mature, McCarthy hopes to encourage teens to become spiritual leaders through technology. "We need to produce better, deeper media products and preach a gospel of judgment and mercy," he says.

—Jessica McCaleb, "Blogging Teens," *World* (September 16, 2006)

ILLUSTRATION 876

FROM POLYGAMY TO CHRIST

Topics: Baptism; Beliefs; Bible; Conversion; Cults; Faith; Faith and Works; False Beliefs; Gospel; Mormonism; Shame; Teachers; Theology

References: Mark 13:22; John 14:6; Galatians 1:9; Ephesians 2:8–9; 2 Timothy 4:3–4; Titus 3:3–7; 2 Peter 2:1

Kathy was one of thirteen children raised by one father and three mothers in a polygamist community in Utah. The community was a part of the Fundamentalist Church of Jesus Christ of Latter-Day Saints, a sect that split from the Church of Jesus Christ of Latter-Day Saints in the 1890s. Growing up, she was burdened by the unrealistic expectations of the cult: "We were constantly told to 'keep sweet,' and that 'perfect obedience produces perfect faith.' Behind these sugary slogans lay the impossible duty of living in complete obedience to the prophet."

This prophet was Leroy Johnson. "We called him Uncle Roy," says Kathy. "He was a feeble old man who prophesied that he would never die — that he'd become young again and be lifted up to heaven. If I kept sweet, I'd be taken with him. I looked forward to that glorious day with hope and fear."

Johnson passed away at the age of ninety-three and was succeeded by a new prophet. These events shattered Kathy's faith in Mormonism. In an act of rebellion, she ran away with a young man named Matt. The two were married and moved to California, but Kathy found that physical distance was not enough to separate her from her former life.

Kathy and Matt divorced. Years later, she met Brian, who was a Christian. Kathy describes what happened next:

We began attending church, and Brian and I spent more time together. He had a purpose to his life, a steadiness I wanted. When I told him about my past, he talked about how Mormonism differed from the truth of the Bible. We began praying together. God seemed more real and different than I'd ever expected.

One day, Brian's mother talked about a baptism. I asked many questions: What did a person need to do to be baptized? Did he say a vow or go through a ceremony? How much did it cost? She assured me baptism was free, that it was an outward statement of an inward commitment to Christ. I admitted I wasn't sure I'd made that commitment. How did I get this faith? Did you have to keep sweet and be perfectly obedient? She said good deeds don't save us. The Bible teaches that trusting in Christ's finished work on the cross saves us.

I was amazed at the simplicity of the gospel message. I cried as I realized I could come to Christ just as I was; he didn't require perfection. I prayed to receive Jesus as my Savior. After counseling sessions with the pastor to make sure I fully understood, I was baptized.

By God's grace, I am now a woman of faith.

—Story told to Jan Brown, "I Grew Up in a Polygamist Family," *Today's Christian Woman* (November–December 2006)

ILLUSTRATION 877

DARK MISSION

Topics: Christianity; Darkness; Evil; Seekers; Self-examination; Youth

References: 2 Corinthians 13:5; 1 John 1:5

Alternative rocker Tori Amos's mission is to expose the dark side of Christianity.

"The problem with Christianity is they think everything is about outside forces, good and evil," she says. "With Christianity there's not a lot of inner work encouraged. Kids get into weird cults [because] they're desperately searching for the dark side of themselves. I think a lot of kids are starving in high school because they want tools to do the inner work."

—Steven Daly, "Her Secret Garden," *Rolling Stone* (July 25, 1998)

ILLUSTRATION 878

NO REASON FOR ATHEISM

Topics: Atheism; Faith; Mind; Reason; Thoughts; Unbelief

References: Job 12:7–25; Isaiah 42:1–9; Romans 1:19–20

If there is no intelligence behind the universe, then nobody designed my brain for the purpose of thinking. Thought is merely the by-product of some atoms within my skull.

If so, how can I trust my own thinking to be true? And if I can't trust my own thinking, I can't trust arguments leading to atheism and therefore have no reason to be an atheist, or anything else. Unless I believe in God, I can't believe in thought; so I can never use thought to disbelieve God.

—C. S. Lewis, *Broadcast Talks* (London, 1946)

ILLUSTRATION 879

THE BEAR AND THE ATHEIST

Topics: Atheism; Creation; Crisis; Evolution; Gratitude; Ideologies and Belief Systems; Judgment; Prayer; Thanksgiving; Unbelief

Reference: Romans 1:18–22

An atheist was walking through the woods, admiring all the "accidents" that evolution had created. "What majestic trees! What powerful rivers! What beautiful animals!" he said.

Suddenly he heard a rustling in the bushes behind him. Turning to look, he saw a seven-foot grizzly bear charging toward him. He ran as fast as he could up the path.

He looked over his shoulder and saw the grizzly was closing in on him. He was so scared that tears came to his eyes. His heart was pounding. He tried to run faster but then tripped and fell to the ground. He rolled over to pick himself up, but the bear was over him, raising its right paw to strike him.

"O my God!" cried the atheist.

Time stopped. The bear froze. The forest was silent. Even the river stopped moving.

As a bright light shone on the man, a voice came out of the sky, "You deny my existence for all these years, teach others that I don't exist, and even credit creation to a cosmic accident. Do you expect me to help you out of this predicament? Am I to count you as a believer?"

The atheist looked directly into the light and said, "I would feel like a hypocrite to become a Christian after all these years, but perhaps you could make the bear a Christian?"

"Very well," said the voice.

The light went out. The river ran. The sounds of the forest resumed. Then the bear dropped its right paw, brought both paws together, bowed its head, and spoke: "Lord, for this food which I am about to receive, I am truly thankful."

—Anonymous

ILLUSTRATION 880

SECONDHAND DOUBT

Topics: Atheism; Doubt; Hypocrisy; Skepticism

Reference: 2 Peter 3:3–4

We hear so much criticism from skeptics about what they often brand as "secondhand faith." It is implied that many people believe in God only because of the context of their birth or family or determined conditions.

If the criticism is justified, and undoubtedly it sometimes is, why do we not show the same distrust of secondhand doubt? If it is possible for a person's belief to be merely an echo of someone else's faith, are there not hypocrites in doubt also?

—Ravi Zacharias, *Jesus among Other Gods* (Word, 2000)

ILLUSTRATION 881

LINCOLN'S CRITICS RECANT

Topics: Character; Compromise; Convictions; Criticism; Integrity; Leadership; Persecution; Rewards

References: Matthew 10:17–20; Acts 5:27–39

After Abraham Lincoln announced the Emancipation Proclamation, freeing the slaves during the Civil War, he was condemned by the *London Times* as "a sort of moral American pope" destined to be "Lincoln the Last."

After Lincoln's assassination, the paper realized his greatness, saying, "Abraham Lincoln was as little a tyrant as any man who ever lived. He could have been a tyrant if he pleased, but he never uttered so much as an ill-natured speech."

In the Christian life, there will be times when we must take an unpopular stand—at work, at school, even at church—and stubbornly stick to principle. We will be called all manner of names, but if we're in God's will, we will be vindicated, certainly in the next life, but sometimes in this one.

—Thomas Bailey and David Kennedy, eds., *The American Pageant*, 9th ed. (D. C. Heath, 1991)

ILLUSTRATION 882

CHEATING ON TAXES

Topics: Behavior; Deceit; Honesty; Integrity; Lying; Money; Responsibility; Taxes

Reference: Romans 13:6–7

The percentage of Americans who approve of cheating on their income taxes: 19 percent.

—IRS Oversight Board Fiscal Year 2005 Special Report (March 2004)

ILLUSTRATION 883

KEEPING PROMISES

Topics: Church; Community; Integrity; Promises

References: Exodus 20:16; James 3:1–12

Toward the end of his three volumes on the history of the French Revolution, Thomas Carlyle concluded that the revolution failed, not because of corruption in high places, but because ordinary people in their ordinary places neglected to keep their promises.

If we do not keep our promises, what once was a human community turns into a combat zone of competitive self-maximizers. We are at sea, loose-jointed, uncertain, leery of each other, untrusting. Nobody can trust his or her neighbors. And without trust, no law, no police force, and no legal contracts can keep a community human. We are a people who can join together in a permanently free society only if we are a people who can keep promises together.

—Lewis B. Smedes, *A Chorus of Witnesses*
(Eerdmans, 1994)

ILLUSTRATION 884

INCOMPLETE CLEANSING

Topics: Atonement; Divine Power; False Beliefs; Healing

References: Matthew 24:4–5; 2 Corinthians 11:14–15

It is midnight in Israel, and three hundred worshipers gather in a floodlit enclosure as they thump tambourines and clap hands in the warm night. They sing *ya'ase shalom*, which means "he will make peace." Though the words refer to God, the crowd thinks of another.

"I will clean the people," says Rabbi Yaakov Ifargan, thirty-four, slinging candles into a brazier until the flame rises six meters and wax sizzles onto the dusty ground. Ifargan is the most prominent new leader in a wave of cabalistic mysticism sweeping Israel, particularly among the 60 percent of the population known as Mizrahis, those who have emigrated from North Africa and the Middle East. Ifargan is a *tzaddik*, a holy man.

Almost four hours into this ceremony, the rabbi turns to a row of followers confined to their wheelchairs sweating near the fire. "Are you a believer?" he asks. Gabriel Rafael, twenty-two, has multiple sclerosis. People in the crowd raise him by his arms. He takes a few steps, scuffing his feet through the dirt, then collapses into his wheelchair. Those around him wait to hear that a miracle has taken place. What they hear instead is Gabriel say, "I *do* feel stronger."

It's hardly enough—and far short of what the true Messiah offers: complete healing through the cleansing power of his blood.

—Matt Rees, "Miracle Makers,"
Time (September 25, 2000)

ILLUSTRATION 885

BELIEVING IN GHOSTS

Topics: Supernatural Occurrences

References: Matthew 14:26;
Luke 24:37

Do you believe in ghosts? When asked, Americans said:

No: 57 percent
Yes: 40 percent
Unsure: 3 percent

—2000 Zogby America poll of 1,021 adults

ILLUSTRATION 886

NO TRIVIA FOR EINSTEIN

Topics: Concentration; Discipline;
Focus; Priorities; Values

Reference: 1 Corinthians 10:31

A student once asked Albert Einstein how many feet were in a mile. He was astonished when Einstein replied, "I don't know."

The student was sure the great professor was joking. Surely Einstein would know a simple fact that every schoolchild is required to memorize. When the student pressed for an explanation, the professor declared, "I make it a rule not to clutter my mind with simple information that I can find in a book in five minutes."

Albert Einstein was not interested in trivial data. His passion was to explore the deep things of the universe. And his passion for mathematical and physical truth made him a pivotal fixture in world history.

—R. C. Sproul Jr., *In the Presence of God*
(Word, 1999)

ILLUSTRATION 887

TEENS AND RELIGION

Topics: Religions; Spirituality; Teens

References: John 4:23–24;
Romans 10:1–3

When George Gallup asked teens how much interest they had in learning more about other religions, there was "a great deal of interest" or "some interest" in these faiths:

- Roman Catholic Christianity: 54 percent
- Protestant Christianity: 52 percent
- Native American spiritual worship: 44 percent
- Islam: 29 percent
- Buddhism: 27 percent
- Judaism: 27 percent
- Hinduism: 22 percent
- Pagan religion: 16 percent
- Mormonism: 15 percent

—Princeton Religion Research Center,
Emerging Trends (September 1999)

ILLUSTRATION 888

BEING YOURSELF WITH GOD

Topics: Grace; Prayer; Surrender

References: Romans 8:15–17; Colossians 1:22

I took Bekah, six, to audition for the part of a munchkin in *The Wizard of Oz*. The thought that she might not get the part seemed never to occur to her. I encouraged her but didn't say anything about her chances.

I had no idea that 250 children would show up for 50 parts. In a huge gym, the two directors had the children line the four edges of the cavernous building, the tallest on one end trailing down to the shortest on the other end. The directors went through the line, having each child say his or her name and age. They did it again, this time urging, "Say your name loud. Say it with animation." The boisterous, enthusiastic kids were told to sit down, marking them in a kind of first cut. I watched as they finally got to Bekah. I was at the opposite end, but my heart sank when I could not hear her. She was too quiet, too restrained.

The directors gave the kids other chances, other quick assignments. But I could never hear Bekah. I knew she was not standing out. The expressive, outgoing kids were getting the parts.

Finally, the long two hours came to a close with the kids all gathered in a knot around the directors. The names of the chosen 50 were read off a list. I knew already that Bekah hadn't made it.

Bekah threaded her way to me afterward, cheeks flushed. She hugged me hard as we pre-pared to walk out. "I'm proud of you," I said. "I am so impressed that you auditioned." Then I said, quietly, "I'm sorry you didn't get a part."

That broke Bekah's tear floodgates. She grabbed at me and sobbed. I picked her up, and she buried her face in my shoulder.

The next morning, I overheard Bekah talking with her mother. "The kids who got parts didn't behave right," she said. "I was good. I was quiet like I was supposed to be. And I didn't get a part!" She had equated goodness with restraint. She was trying hard but in the wrong way. She thought the directors wanted reserve, stiff attention, frozen alertness. That was "good." But Bekah didn't understand: The directors wanted energy, emotion, loudness. They wanted kids who could be themselves with abandon.

Many people, I suspect, feel that way around God — restrained, rigid, tight. They can't relax and simply receive God's wondrous grace. And they miss the opportunity to awaken to the grace-filled kindness of God.

—Timothy Jones, *Awake My Soul* (Doubleday, 1999)

ILLUSTRATION 889

MEDIA-DRIVEN RELIGION

Topics: Authority; Leadership; Media; Publishing

Reference: 1 Timothy 3:15

"For the first time in American history, whatever is happening in religion is being driven by the media instead of ecclesiastical institutions." So said Phyllis Tickle, religion editor of *Publishers*

Weekly, about the explosive growth in sales of books on religion and spirituality.

— *Life@Work* (November–December 1998)

ILLUSTRATION 890

DECOY LOVE

Topics: First Commandment; Idolatry; Love; Reality

References: 1 Thessalonians 1; 1 John 5:21

One hundred decoys were placed on the Izu islands of Japan to encourage endangered albatrosses to breed. For more than two years, a five-year-old albatross named Deko tried to woo a wooden decoy by building fancy nests and fighting off rival suitors. He spent his days standing faithfully by her side. Japanese researcher Fumio Sato, talking about the albatross's infatuation with the wooden decoy, said, "He seems to have no desire to date real birds."

— *World* (February 20, 1999)

ILLUSTRATION 891

MARKET BEATERS

Topics: Arrogance; Humility; Pride

References: Mark 9:33–37; Luke 18:10–14; Philippians 2:3

When researchers at Duke, Harvard, and Northwestern asked investors how their mutual funds performed last year compared with Standard & Poor's 500 stock index, a third claimed their funds outperformed the market by at least 5 percent. One in six said their funds fared better by more than 10 percent.

However, a check of the portfolios of those claiming to have beaten the market showed that 88 percent had overestimated their earnings. The study discovered that some "market beaters" lagged between 5 and 15 percent behind the S&P. Said Don Moore of Northwestern, "Everybody wants to believe they're better than average."

Unfortunately, the same thing is true in the spiritual realm. It is human nature for us to look at our neighbors and conclude that we are more righteous.

— Rick Kauffman, "I'm Better," PreachingToday.com

ILLUSTRATION 892

SHOUTING MATCH FOR TRUTH

Topics: Philosophy; Postmodernism; Relativism; Religions; Truth

References: John 18:38; Acts 17:16–34; 1 Timothy 3:15

The notion that there are many truths might seem well suited to a diverse society. But when everyone is free to define truth as he or she prefers, as at present, the result is an intellectual and moral shouting match in which the people with the loudest voices are most likely to be heard.

—Mary Lefkowitz, *The New York Times Book Review* (January 23, 2000)

ILLUSTRATION 893

LIMITS OF UNDERSTANDING

Topics: Church; Doctrine; Gospel; Humility; Mysteries; Paradoxes

Reference: Romans 11:33–36

Respect for differing views provides some defense against the natural desire to probe incessantly the mystery of the gospel. (There are those who would consider it the ultimate intellectual achievement to unravel the hidden counsel of God.) But the pursuit of doctrine for the sake of doctrine can be idolatrous. The gospel will not be demystified. God will not be mocked by the pretensions of those who believe they might fully and certainly know his mind.

Was that, after all, not the sin of the Garden?

—Chuck Colson, *The Body* (Word, 1992)

ILLUSTRATION 894

WHEN WE FAKE IT

Topics: Authenticity; Confession; Honesty; Hypocrisy; Sin; Truth; Worship

References: Psalm 51:1–12; Luke 18:9–14; James 5:16; 1 John 5:5–10

Research psychologists have found there are at least three situations when we are not ourselves.

1. The average person puts on airs when visiting the lobby of a fancy hotel.
2. The average person stifles emotion to bamboozle the salesman when entering the new-car showroom.
3. The average person in church tries to fake out the Almighty about being good all week.

—Dr. Perry Buffington, "Playing Charades," Universal Press Syndicate (September 26, 1999)

ILLUSTRATION 895

UMP REWARDS HONEST PLAYER

Topics: Character; Children; Honesty; Integrity; Name; Reputation; Trust; Truth; Virtue

References: Exodus 20:16; Proverbs 11:3; 12:19; Zechariah 8:16; Ephesians 4:25; Colossians 3:9; James 4:17

It pays to be honest. That's what Tanner Munsey, seven, discovered. While playing T-ball as a first baseman in Wellington, Florida, Tanner fielded a ground ball and tried to tag a runner going from first to second base.

The umpire, Laura Benson, called the runner out, but young Tanner immediately ran to her side and said, "Ma'am, I didn't tag the runner." Umpire Benson reversed her call and sent the runner to second base.

Two weeks later, Laura Benson was again the umpire as Tanner was playing shortstop. This time Benson ruled that Tanner had missed the tag on a runner going to third base, and she called the runner safe. Tanner, obviously disappointed, tossed the ball to the pitcher and returned to his position. Benson asked Tanner what was wrong, and Tanner quietly said he had tagged the boy.

The ump's response was to declare the runner out. When the opposing coach rushed on the field to protest, Benson explained what had happened two weeks before, saying, "If a kid is that honest, I have to give it to him."

—Bill White, "Child Ballplayer Rewarded for Integrity," PreachingToday.com

ILLUSTRATION 896

CHEATING TEENS

Topics: Deceit; Dishonesty; Lying; Morality; Success; Teens; Truth

References: Exodus 20:16; Proverbs 11:1; 12:19–22; John 8:44; Ephesians 4:25; Colossians 3:9

A study shows that 70 percent of nearly 70,000 U.S. college and high school students admit to cheating. This distressing statistic highlights a 14 percent increase since 1993, and a 44 percent hike since 1963. The Duke University report also indicated that Internet plagiarism has quadrupled in the past six years.

A separate poll of 25,000 high schoolers found that nearly half agreed with the statement "A person has to lie or cheat sometimes in order to succeed."

—"Culture Clips," *Plugged In* (June 2006)

ILLUSTRATION 897

THIEVING CODE OF CONDUCT

Topics: Ethics; Judgment; Justice; Law; Morality; Righteousness; Standards; Ten Commandments; Truth

References: Psalm 7:11; Isaiah 64:6; Romans 3:10–23; 14:9–13; 2 Corinthians 5:10; Revelation 20:11–15

Dennis Lee Curtis was arrested for stealing in 1992 in Rapid City, South Dakota. In his wallet the police found a sheet of paper on which was written the following code of conduct:

1. I will not kill anyone unless I have to.
2. I will take cash and food stamps—no checks.
3. I will rob only at night.
4. I will not wear a mask.
5. I will not rob mini-marts or 7-Eleven stores.
6. If I get chased by cops on foot, I will get away. If chased by vehicle, I will not put the lives of innocent civilians on the line.
7. I will rob only seven months out of the year.

1001 ILLUSTRATIONS that CONNECT

8. I will enjoy robbing from the rich to give to the poor.

Curtis had a sense of morality, but it was flawed. When the thief stood before the court, he was not judged by the standards he had set for himself but by the higher laws of the state.

Likewise, when we stand before God, we will not be judged by the code of morality we have written for ourselves but by God's perfect law.

—Brian Burrell,
Words We Live By (S&S Trade, 1997)

ILLUSTRATION 898

ADDICTED TO HARMFUL WORDS

Topics: Bitterness; Boasting; Complaining; Criticism; Cursing; Discouragement; Faultfinding; Gossip; Insensitivity; Lying; Self-control; Speech; Tongue; Weakness

References: Proverbs 4:24; 12:18; 13:3; 18:21; Matthew 12:36; 15:11; 2 Corinthians 12:20; Ephesians 4:29; James 1:26; 3:1–12; 1 Peter 3:10

Rabbi Joseph Telushkin, author of *Words That Hurt, Words That Heal*, often lectures on the impact of words. He asks audiences if they can go twenty-four hours without saying any unkind words about another person or to another person. Invariably, a small number of listeners raise their hands, signifying yes. Others laugh, and quite a large number call out, "No!"

Telushkin says, "Those of you who can't answer yes must recognize that you have a serious problem. If you cannot go twenty-four hours without drinking liquor, you are addicted to alcohol. If you cannot go twenty-four hours without smoking, you are addicted to nicotine. Similarly, if you cannot go twenty-four hours without say-

ing unkind words about others, then you have lost control over your tongue."

—Rick Ezell, *One-Minute Uplift* (July 21, 2006)

ILLUSTRATION 899

GIFT OF BOLOGNA

Topics: Assumptions; Generosity; Giving; Help; Judging Others; Kindness; Sacrifice; Self-centeredness; Service

References: Deuteronomy 15:7; Proverbs 19:17; Matthew 25:31–46; Luke 6:38; Romans 12:13; 2 Corinthians 8:12; 9:7

Long before Sebastian Junger wrote *The Perfect Storm*, he decided to hitchhike across the country. He writes of what took place while making his way through the aftermath of a blizzard in Gillette, Wyoming:

> After two or three hours I saw a man working his way toward me along the on-ramp from town. He wore filthy canvas coveralls and carried a black lunchbox, and as he got closer I could see that his hair was matted in a way that occurs only after months on the skids. I put my

hand on the pepper spray in my pocket and turned to face him.

"You been out here long?" he asked. I nodded.

"Where you headed?"

"California."

"Warm out there."

"Yup."

"You got enough food?"

I thought about this. Clearly he didn't have any, and if I admitted that I did, he'd ask for some. That would mean opening my backpack and revealing all my expensive camping gear. I felt alone and ripe for pillage, and I just didn't want that. "I got some cheese," I said.

"You won't make it to California with just a little cheese," he said. "You'll starve."

At first I didn't understand. What was he saying, exactly? I kept my hand on the pepper spray.

"Believe me," he said, "I know. Listen, I'm living in a car back in town, and every day I walk out to the mine to see if they need me. Today they don't, so I won't be needing this lunch of mine."

I began to sag with understanding. In his world, whatever you have in your bag is all you've got, and he knew "a little cheese" would never get me to California. "I'm fine, really," I said. "I don't need your lunch."

He shook his head and opened his box. It was a typical church meal—a bologna sandwich, an apple, and a bag of chips—and I kept protesting, but he wouldn't hear of it. I finally took his lunch and watched him walk toward town.

I learned a lot of things in college. I learned things in Europe and in Mexico and in my hometown of Belmont, Massachusetts. But I had to stand out there on that frozen piece of interstate to learn generosity from a homeless man.

—Sebastian Junger, "Welcome Stranger," *National Geographic Adventure* (June 2006)

ILLUSTRATION 900

DRUGS, SEX, AND DEPRESSED TEENS

Topics: Addiction; Consequences; Depression; Drinking; Drugs; Emotions; Morality; Premarital Sex; Teens; Temptation

References: Job 4:8; Proverbs 5:22–23; Romans 2:8–9; Galatians 6:7–8; Ephesians 4:17–19

Doctors and social scientists have long assumed that many teens get into drugs and sex to deal with depression. However, a study published in the October 2005 edition of the *American Journal of Preventive Medicine* reverses that assumption. According to health policy researcher Denise Dion Hallfors, a recent study shows teens get depressed *after* substance abuse and sexual activity, not the other way around.

The national survey of 13,491 adolescents showed that about 25 percent, called "abstainers," had never had sex, smoked, drunk alcohol, or taken drugs. Only 4 percent of those teens experienced depression. The girls in the 75 percent who had taken drugs and experimented with sex were two to three times more likely to experience depression than abstaining girls. Boys who engaged in binge drinking were 4.5 times more likely to experience depression than boys in the abstaining group. Boys smoking marijuana were more than three times more likely to be depressed than those who abstained.

Dr. Hallfors warns, "Parents, educators, and health practitioners now have even more reason to be concerned about teen risk behaviors and to take action about alcohol, drugs, and sex."

—Taunya English, "Teen Sex and Drug Use May Be Cause of Depression, Not the Effect," Health Behavior News Service (September 2005)

ILLUSTRATION 901

PROFANITY RISING

Topics: Blasphemy; Cursing; Profanity; Speech; Tongue; Ungodliness; Vices

References: Exodus 20:7; Psalm 19:14; Ephesians 5:4–5; Colossians 3:8; James 3:7–12

The use of profanity in America is increasing. According to an AP-Ipsos poll conducted in March 2006, nearly 75 percent of people questioned said they encountered profanity in public frequently or occasionally. Two-thirds said they think people swear more often than they did twenty years ago.

Not surprisingly, the respondents were more than "hearers of the words." Sixty-four percent

said they use the *F* word—ranging from several times a day (8 percent) to a few times a year (15 percent). In addition, younger people admitted using bad language more often than older people. They also encounter it more frequently and are less offended by it. The poll showed that 62 percent of people ages eighteen to thirty-four acknowledged swearing in conversation at least a few times a week, compared to 39 percent of those thirty-five and older. Swearing is also more pronounced among men; 54 percent of men swear at least a few times a week, compared to 39 percent of women.

One bit of good news: the poll showed that many people who regularly swear believe it's wrong for them to do so.

—Associated Press, "Poll: Americans See, Hear More Profanity," news.yahoo.com (March 29, 2006)

ILLUSTRATION 902

A WAY TO SAY THANKS

Topics: Generosity; Giving; Good Deeds; Gratitude; Respect; Sacrifice; Unselfishness

References: Matthew 19:30; 20:16; Mark 10:31; Luke 13:30; Romans 12:1–10; 1 Corinthians 10:24; Philippians 2:3–4

Twelve United States soldiers were flying home from Iraq on a two-week leave in July 2004. Before one of the soldiers boarded the plane, a passenger traded his first-class ticket for the soldier's coach ticket. As the plane was boarding, other passengers asked to trade their first-class seats for the coach seats occupied by the remaining soldiers.

Devilla Evans, a flight attendant on the American Airlines flight from Atlanta to Chicago, said, "I was so privileged to be flying with these two groups of unselfish people. Here you have these kids who are putting their lives on the line, protecting our freedom, and here are these people who gave up these seats that are usually fought over. You really have to have a large heart to do something like that."

—Rummana Hussain, "Passengers Give Up Seats So Soldiers Can Go First-Class," newsbull.com (July 16, 2004)

ILLUSTRATION 903

SEX SITE SELLS FOR $12M

Topics: Internet; Lust; Morality; Pornography; Sex; Technology

References: Romans 13:12–14; 1 Corinthians 6:12–20; 1 Thessalonians 4:3–8

Sex.com was one of the most sought-after domain names in cyberspace for years before it sold in January 2006 for $12 million.

According to an article on the USAToday .com tech page, the transaction ranks as one of the most expensive website domain name transfers ever, topping the $7.5 million paid for business.com in 1999, at the peak of the dotcom boom.

—"Sex.com Appeals, Sells for $12M," USAToday.com (January 24, 2006)

ILLUSTRATION 904

INVESTING IN VICE

Topics: Depravity; Drinking; Foolishness; Gambling; Greed; Human Nature; Immorality; Money; Morality; Pleasure; Sin; Smoking; Spiritual Poverty; Temptation; Vices; Wickedness; Worldliness

References: Jeremiah 17:11; Matthew 18:6–7; Mark 8:36; Luke 17:1–2; John 3:19–20; Romans 6:19–23; 1 Timothy 6:10; 1 Peter 2:16; 4:3; 2 Peter 2:19

Though the stock market boasted in 2006 that it had 150 "socially responsible" mutual funds that invested in companies meeting the ethical standards of fund managers, a new investment fund quietly surfaced in 2002. It's the Vice Fund.

According to its prospectus, the Vice Fund favors "products or services often considered socially irresponsible." These include companies linked to alcohol, tobacco, gambling, and military contracts. The Vice Fund and another fund, the Gaming and Casino Fund, exploit the dark side of human nature, which is a great investment during times of economic downturns. Dan Ahrens, former manager of the Vice Fund and founder of the Gaming and Casino Fund, believes that bad habits don't change, even in bad economic times. People still indulge in vices, regardless of what happens in the stock market; they continue to smoke, drink, and gamble.

Investors in vice have profited; the Vice Fund has returned positive monetary gains, some reaching beyond 20 percent over five years.

—"Would You Invest in Human Vices?" *Omaha Sunday World-Herald* (July 16, 2006)

ILLUSTRATION 905

APOLOGIZING AT A COST

Topics: Apology; Confession; Foolishness; Greed; Human Nature; Hypocrisy; Reconciliation; Repentance; Self-centeredness; Sports

References: Psalm 32:5; 62:10; Proverbs 22:1; Joel 2:12–13; Acts 3:19; Hebrews 10:22; 1 John 1:8–10

Pete Rose has finally admitted that he bet on baseball games while employed as manager of the Cincinnati Reds, an infraction that produced a lifetime ban from the sport in 1989. Rose's admission of guilt in his autobiography in 2004 came after almost fifteen years of denying wrongdoing.

He has not stopped confessing. In September 2006, Rose began using his website to personally apologize to each fan he had failed or offended. For only $299 (plus $4.95 for shipping and handling), Pete Rose will send you an autographed baseball that reads, "I'm sorry I bet on baseball."

The marketing copy on the website says: "Now you can get the baseball collectible everyone's talking about— Pete Rose's personal apology for betting on baseball, newly inscribed on an actual baseball— at a fantastic price."

—Associated Press, "Rose Says 'Sorry,' but It'll Cost You," *Houston Chronicle* (September 20, 2006)

ILLUSTRATION 906

PRESCRIPTION DRUG ABUSE RISES

Topics: Addiction; Desires; Drugs; Lawlessness; Pleasure; Teens; Temptation; Vices

References: Romans 6:16; 12:2; 13:13–14; Ephesians 5:18; 1 Peter 5:8; 2 Peter 2:19

In 2003, 6.3 million people were misusing prescription drugs, such as stimulants, painkillers, sedatives, and tranquilizers. That's more than twice the number of people who use cocaine, according to the U.S. National Survey of Drug Use and Health.

A 2006 study reported in *Drug and Alcohol Dependence* found that large numbers of people are using the Internet to search for and trade advice on how to tamper with prescription drugs. Edward Cone, author of the study and a toxicologist at ConeChem Research in Maryland, explains: "Drug misusers are tampering with the drugs to get high, and you get high by getting the drug in faster or giving a bigger dose. All of these drugs are toxic or lethal at certain levels, so this is a very real health issue. In the U.S., the abuse of pharmaceutical drugs is reaching epidemic proportions."

Abuse of prescription drugs by teens and young adults in particular is on the rise. Drug counselors are getting numerous reports of pill-popping get-togethers called "pharm parties" at which teens trade prescription drugs like baseball cards. According to a 2005 survey by the Partnership for a Drug-Free America, 19 percent of

U.S. teenagers—roughly 4.5 million—reported having taken prescription painkillers such as Vicodin or OxyContin, or stimulants such as Ritalin or Adderall, to get high.

In May 2006, the U.S. Substance Abuse and Mental Health Services Administration reported that overdoses of prescription and over-the-counter drugs accounted for about one-fourth of the 1.3 million drug-related emergency room admissions in 2004.

—Hazel Muir, "Abuse of Prescription Drugs Fueled by Online Recipes," NewScientist.com (June 2006); Donna Leinwand, "Prescription Drugs Find Place in Teen Culture," *USA Today* (June 12, 2006)

ILLUSTRATION 907

IQ AND GOOD JUDGMENT

Topics: Choices; Decisions; Depravity; Discernment; Insight; Intelligence; Limitations; Mistakes; Understanding; Wisdom

References: Proverbs 1:7; 3:13; 4:7; 9:10; 14:12; 16:25; 23:23; 1 Corinthians 1:18–31; 3:19

The world-famous geneticist William French Anderson was convicted of child molestation in July 2006. In a press conference, Anderson's attorney said, "Nothing about having a 176 IQ means you have good judgment."

—"The Buzz," *World* (July 29, 2006)

ILLUSTRATION 908

VIRTUES LEADING TO PRIDE

Topics: Arrogance; Good Deeds; Human Power; Hypocrisy; Legalism; Limitations; Pride; Sanctification; Self-reliance; Vices; Virtue

References: Proverbs 16:18; Isaiah 64:6; Romans 4:2; 9:30–33; 1 Corinthians 5:6; Ephesians 2:8–9

Humanist Benjamin Franklin rejected the graces of religion and wrote his own. For example:

Silence: "Speak not but what may benefit others or yourself; avoid trifling conversation."
Frugality: "Make no expense but to do good to others or yourself, that is, waste nothing."
Industry: "Lose no time, be always employed in something useful, cut off all unnecessary actions."
Tranquility: "Be not disturbed at trifles or accidents common or unavoidable."

Franklin set up a book with a page for each virtue, with a column in which to record "defects." Choosing a different virtue to work on each week, he daily noted every mistake, starting over every thirteen weeks to cycle through the list four times a year. For many decades Franklin carried his little book with him, striving for a clean thirteen-week cycle.

As he made progress, he found himself struggling with yet another defect: pride. Franklin wrote, "There is perhaps no one of the natural passions so hard to subdue as *pride*. Disguise it. Struggle with it. Stifle it. Mortify it as much as one pleases. It is still alive, and will every now and then peep out and show itself.... Even if I could conceive that I had completely overcome it, I should probably be proud of my humility."

—Philip Yancey, *What's So Amazing about Grace?* (Zondervan, 1997)

ILLUSTRATION 909

EATEN BY ANGER

Topics: Anger; Bitterness; Forgiveness; Rage; Vindictiveness

References: Psalm 37:8; Ecclesiastes 7:9; Luke 6:28; Colossians 3:8; James 1:19–20

Of the seven deadly sins, anger is possibly the most fun. To lick your wounds, to smack your lips over grievances long past, to roll over your tongue the prospect of bitter confrontations still to come, to savor to the last toothsome morsel both the pain you are given and the pain you are giving back—in many ways it is a feast fit for a king.

The chief drawback is that what you are wolfing down is yourself. The skeleton at the feast is you.

—Frederick Buechner, *Wishful Thinking* (Harper, 1993)

ILLUSTRATION 910

TOP COUCH POTATO

Topics: Achievement; Emptiness; Entertainment; Laziness; Sloth; Television; Time

References: 1 Thessalonians 5:14; 2 Thessalonians 3:6–15

Suresh Joachim is the world's most incredible couch potato. In September 2005, Joachim broke the *Guinness Book of World's Records'* previous mark of spending the longest time watching TV.

Joachim spent sixty-nine hours and forty-eight minutes in front of the tube, with only a five-minute break every hour and a fifteen-minute break each eight hours. The rest of that time he had his eyes on the screen.

—Associated Press, "Toronto Man Breaks 'Couch Potato' World Record" (September 17, 2005)

ILLUSTRATION 911

UNORTHODOX GRILL STARTER

Topics: Alcohol; Consequences; Drunkenness; Foolishness; Judgment; Sowing and Reaping

References: Proverbs 20:1; Romans 6:23; 13:13; Galatians 6:7–8; Ephesians 5:18

While preparing for a cookout July 3, 2006, a Delaware man decided to use gunpowder rather than charcoal or lighter fluid to get the coals glowing in his grill. The unorthodox fire preparation method blew up on him. He was severely burned.

Police said the man had been drinking.

— "Quick Takes," *World* (July 22, 2006)

ILLUSTRATION 912

WATER INTOXICATION

Topics: Appetites; Consequences; Desires; Greed; Idolatry; Thirst

References: 2 Samuel 14:14; Proverbs 25:16 – 17; John 4:1 – 26; Ephesians 5:18

Jennifer Strange, twenty-eight, died trying to win a Nintendo.

In January 2007, a radio station in Sacramento, California, staged a water-drinking contest, promising a Nintendo Wii video game system to the person whose bladder held out the longest.

Strange did her best, but she didn't win the contest. Furthermore, several hours after the contest, Jennifer left work with a terrible headache. Later that day she was found dead in her house. An autopsy revealed that too much water had disrupted the electrolyte balance in her blood. Jennifer Strange literally died of water intoxication.

— Associated Press, "Woman Dies after Water-Drinking Contest," MSNBC.com (January 13, 2007)

ILLUSTRATION 913

MORE BULLIES

Topics: Conflict; Enemies; Fear; Fighting; Oppression; Persecution; Safety; Threats; Violence; Vulnerability; Youth

References: Matthew 5:10 – 12; John 15:20; 16:33; Colossians 3:13

Bullies abound. According to the U.S. Department of Education, here are the stats on the number of students ages twelve to eighteen who were bullied at school during 2006:

- inside school: 79 percent
- outside on school grounds: 28 percent
- on the school bus: 8 percent
- somewhere else: 5 percent

— David Stuckey and Alejandro Gonzalez, "Scared at School," *USA Today* (December 20, 2006)

ILLUSTRATION 914

DON'T LOOK AT ME

Topics: Behavior; Darkness; Disobedience; Hiding; Lifestyle; Light; Sin; Temptation; Worldliness

References: Genesis 3:8 – 10; John 3:19 – 21; Romans 3:23; 1 Corinthians 4:5; Galatians 5:1, 13; Ephesians 2:3; 5:11; James 1:14 – 15, 22 – 25; 1 John 1:5 – 9

A little girl discovered the secret to making mud one day, which she called "warm chocolate." After her grandmother cleaned up the mess, she told little Larissa not to make any more chocolate.

The little girl soon resumed making her chocolate, saying sweetly, "Don't look at me, Nana. OK?" Nana, being a little codependent, agreed.

Larissa continued to work the mud, but three times she said, "Don't look at me, Nana. OK?"

"Thus the tender soul of a little child shows us how necessary it is to us that we be unobserved in our wrong," writes Dallas Willard, a professor in the School of Philosophy at the University of Southern California in Los Angeles and author of numerous resources on spiritual formation.

Anytime we choose to do wrong or to withhold doing right, we choose hiding as well. It may be that out of all the prayers that are ever spoken, the most common one—the quietest one, the one that we least acknowledge making—is simply this: Don't look at me, God.

It was the very first prayer spoken after the fall. God came to walk in the garden to be with the man and the woman and called, "Where are you?"

"I heard you in the garden, and I was afraid," Adam answered, "so I hid."

Don't look at me, God.

—John Ortberg, *God Is Closer Than You Think* (Zondervan, 2005)

ILLUSTRATION 915

ANGER FINISH

Topics: Anger; Human Nature; Integrity; Regret; Reputation; Revenge; Self-control; Shame; Temper; Temptation; Victory

References: Psalm 37:8; Proverbs 16:32; 25:28; Acts 20:24; Romans 12:19; 1 Corinthians 9:24; 2 Timothy 4:7; James 1:19–20

Zinedine Zidane led the French national team to a World Cup championship in 1998. Eight years later, Zidane reported that he would retire after the 2006 World Cup. The French team was not expected to go far, partly because Zidane was rumored to have lost a step. He proved them wrong.

In France's second-round match against Spain, Zidane led the team to victory when he beat goalkeeper Iker Casillas for a goal. He was also instrumental in the team's victory over highly ranked Brazil in the quarterfinals, using precision passes and his trademark spin move to split the Brazilian defense. In a semifinal match against Portugal, Zidane scored the game-winning goal on a penalty kick. When the smoke cleared, Zidane had led his team to a second World Cup championship game, this time against Italy.

Things started out brilliantly for the superstar in what would be the final game of his exceptional career. However, his temper intervened. During the first half of overtime play, Zidane had a verbal confrontation with Italian defender Marco Materazzi. Zidane then wheeled around to face Materazzi, lowered his head, and slammed into the Italian's chest, knocking him to the ground. The referee flashed a red card, ejecting the French captain from the game.

As large screens around the stadium replayed Zidane's inability to control his temper, the once-proud legend walked off with his head lowered in shame.

— "Zidane Sent Off in Extra Time for Head Butt," *ESPNsoccernet* (July 9, 2006)

ILLUSTRATION 916

THE WOMAN WHO CAN'T FORGET

Topics: Circumstances; Consequences; Extremes; Forgetfulness; Forgiveness; Limitations; Memories; Mind; Past; Perception and Reality; Science; Thoughts

References: Genesis 41:51; Psalm 103:1–5, 11–13; Proverbs 3:1; Isaiah 43:18–19, 25; 49:14–16; Philippians 3:12–14; Hebrews 8:12

A.J. has the most astonishing memory scientists have ever tested. She can replay decades of her life like a movie. Give her any date, and she can recall the day of the week, usually what the weather was like, personal details of her life at that time, and major news events that occurred.

After testing A.J. over the last six years, Dr. James McGaugh of the University of California at Irvine has decided that A.J. is not using mnemonic devices to memorize data; nor is she a savant with exceptional memory in one area. This foremost authority on memory can't explain A.J.'s recall.

"The woman who can't forget" simply says that she intensely feels each day and remembers trivial details as clearly as major events. Asked what happened on August 16, 1977, she knew that Elvis Presley had died. But she also remembered that a California tax initiative passed on June 6 of the following year, and a plane crashed in Chicago on May 25 of the next year.

A great memory is not all it's cracked up to be. A.J. had to study for exams in school, struggled to memorize dates for history class, and still has to make a weekly grocery list. When asked if she considered her memory a gift, A.J. said, "Well, if I'm able to cure a disease, it's a gift. But to remember, like, the end of every relationship — it's hard."

Perhaps the ability to forget should be considered a gift as well.

— Michelle Trudeau, "Unique Memory Lets Woman Replay Life Like a Movie," NPR's *Morning Edition* (April 19, 2006)

ILLUSTRATION 917

PASSING ALONG BAD HABITS

Topics: Adolescence; Character; Children; Choices; Community; Decisions; Drinking; Drugs; Example; Family; Home; Integrity; Teens

References: Proverbs 22:1, 6; Romans 14:1–15:13; 1 Corinthians 5:6; 8; 11:1; 1 Timothy 4:12; Titus 2:7; 1 Peter 2:21

Many siblings pass along bad habits. A girl with an older, pregnant teenage sister is four to six times as likely to become a teen mom herself, says Patricia East, a developmental psychologist at the University of California, San Diego.

The same pattern holds for substance abuse. According to a paper published in the *Journal of Drug Issues* in 2006, younger siblings whose older siblings drink are twice as likely to pick up the habit. When it comes to smoking, the risk increases fourfold.

—Jeffrey Kluger, "The New Science of Siblings," *Time* (July 10, 2006)

ILLUSTRATION 918

WHAT THEY SEE IN YOUR HOUSE

Topics: Behavior; Character; Conduct; Example; Godliness; Integrity; Leadership; Lifestyle; Righteousness; Sanctification; Testimony; Witnessing

References: Matthew 5:13–16; Acts 1:8; 1 Corinthians 11:1; Galatians 5:22–23; 1 Timothy 4:12; 2 Timothy 1:5; Titus 2:7; 1 Peter 3:8–11

The five things most guests notice when they enter our homes:

1. *Piles of mail.* Keep an empty drawer in the kitchen for your correspondence.
2. *Dust bunnies and cobwebs.* Use a broom and a hand vacuum weekly.
3. *A messy bathroom.* Use glass cleaner for the mirror and other handy cleanup aids for the floors and appliances.
4. *Dirty dishes in the sink.* Throw them in the dishwasher. Or rinse and place them in the oven.
5. *Bulging wastebaskets.* Empty the trash into a larger receptacle that can be kept out of sight.

—"Five Things People Really Notice," *Good Housekeeping* (November 2006)

ILLUSTRATION 919

COMPASSION CHILLS ON MOUNT EVEREST

Topics: Ambition; Apathy; Brotherly Love; Caring; Compassion; Distractions; Evangelism; Goals; Golden Rule; Hard-heartedness; Indifference; Negligence; Self-centeredness; Servanthood

References: Genesis 4:9; Leviticus 19:18; Proverbs 3:27; Matthew 7:12; 22:37–40; Luke 6:31; 10:25–37; Acts 3:1–10; James 2:8; 4:17

In 1953, Sir Edmund Hillary and Tenzing Norgay climbed the 29,035-foot peak of Mount Everest. Thousands followed, thanks to Nepal's lifting its tight restrictions on climbing the legendary mountain. By 2006, more than 2,700 people had reached the summit of the world's tallest mountain, many paying more than $60,000 for the experience.

One result of this commercial influx has been the erosion of the traditional moral code of mountaineering. In the rush to the top, amateurs who have paid a fortune will do anything it takes to get to the summit, including abandoning other climbers.

David Sharp became a casualty in March of 2006. The thirty-four-year-old engineer from Cleveland managed to reach the summit on his own. However, he ran out of oxygen on the way back down. As he lay dying, forty climbers passed him by, too eager to achieve their own goals to take a chance on offering their oxygen to someone else. David Sharp froze to death.

Ed Viestrus, who has scaled fourteen of the world's eight-thousand-meter peaks, says passing people who are dying is not uncommon. "Unfortunately, there are those who say, 'It's not my problem. I've spent all this money, and I'm going to the summit.'"

This attitude has produced disgust in many climbers, including Sir Edmund Hillary. "On my expedition, there was no way you'd have left a man under a rock to die," he said.

> — "The Crowd on Mount Everest,"
> *The Week* (June 30, 2006)

ILLUSTRATION 920

LOSING OUR PATIENCE

Topics: Patience; Self-control; Self-discipline; Temper; Waiting

References: Galatians 5:22; Ephesians 4:2; Colossians 1:11; 3:12; James 5:7

We are not a patient people. A survey of 1,003 adults done in 2006 by the Associated Press and Ipsos discovered the following:

• While waiting in line at an office or store, most people take an average of seventeen minutes to lose their patience.

• On hold on the phone most people lose their patience in nine minutes.

• Women lost their patience after waiting in line for about eighteen minutes. Men lost it after fifteen minutes.

• People with lower income and less education are more patient than those with a college education and a high income.

• People who live in the suburbs are more patient than people who live in the city.

> — Trevor Tompson, "Impatience-Poll Glance,"
> www.hosted.ap.org (May 28, 2006)

ILLUSTRATION 921

POLICEMAN TICKETS HIMSELF

Topics: Accountability; Character; Conscience; Conviction of Sin; Honesty; Integrity; Truth

References: Psalm 32:5; Proverbs 28:13; Romans 14:12; Ephesians 4:25; James 4:17; 1 Peter 5:6

Police chief Richard Knoebel of Kewaskum, Wisconsin, accidentally drove past a stopped school bus with its emergency lights flashing. So Knoebel wrote himself a $235 ticket, docked himself four points on his driving record, and paid the fine.

Most people wouldn't have known about the officer's deed, but months after the ticket, a newspaper reporter discovered the record of Knoebel's ticket and fine.

While on patrol, Knoebel said he had become distracted by a stopped dump truck. Worried that a car quickly approaching the truck might collide with it, he moved to the next lane to pass the truck and give the oncoming car more room to stop. That's when he realized he was passing a stopped school bus in the far lane.

That didn't excuse breaking the law, however. The honest officer held himself accountable, even when most people weren't looking.

—Associated Press, "Wisconsin Police Chief Tickets Himself $235," MSNBC.com (February 3, 2007)

ILLUSTRATION 922

YOUR WORTH IN PROMISES

Topics: Accomplishments; Commitment; Identity; Promises; Self-centeredness; Self-image; Self-worth

References: Leviticus 19:11 – 12; Matthew 5:33; 7:16; 12:33

Some people ask, "Who am I?" and expect the answer to come from their accomplishments. Other people ask, "Who am I?" and expect the answer to come from what other people think about them.

A person who dares to make and keep promises discovers who she is by the promises she has made and kept to other people.

—Thomas G. Long and Cornelius Plantinga, eds., *A Chorus of Witnesses* (Eerdmans, 1994)

ILLUSTRATION 923

WATERING DOWN THE CHEMO

Topics: Evangelism; Gospel; Greed; Ministry; Preaching; Scripture; Truth

References: Leviticus 19:17; Matthew 18:15 – 17; Luke 17:3; 2 Timothy 2:15

In 2001, a Kansas City pharmacist was charged with diluting the cancer treatment drugs Taxol and Gemzar to make a profit. After pleading guilty, the pharmacist, Robert Courtney, was sentenced to thirty years in prison. Judge Ortrie D. Smith told the man, "Your crimes are a shock to the civilized conscience." Judge Smith also ordered Courtney to pay $10.4 million in restitution and a $25,000 fine. In his plea agreement, Courtney admitted diluting drugs for profit since 1992, affecting as many as 4,200 patients.

This man held life-saving power in his hands and for the sake of greed and personal gain diluted it to the point where it could not help people. We can do the same with God's life-saving truth.

—"30-Year Sentence for Druggist," *The New York Times* (December 6, 2002)

ILLUSTRATION 924

READING CORRECTIONS

Topics: Confession; Honesty; Humility; Hypocrisy; Truth

References: Proverbs 28:13; Matthew 5:25 – 26; James 5:16

The Guardian, a major newspaper in England, has a daily column of "Corrections and Clarifications." Edited by Ian Mayes, the column breaks the stodgy English tradition of rarely admitting error.

Sometimes done with humor at the paper's own expense, the column averages about five corrections a day, ranging from typos and simple misspellings to substituting "ex-patriots" for "expatriates," and "having insight" for "having incited." Thinking that more people read the corrections than the original story, Maye began working the columns into a book of his favorite mishaps, *Only Correct: The Best of Corrections and Clarifications.*

If a newspaper has learned that confession expands readership rather than turns people away, perhaps individuals will catch on too. Neither newspapers nor human beings can avoid making mistakes. It is candor in admitting them and taking responsibility for them that is unique.

—Rubel Shelly,
Nashville, Tennessee, from CNN.com

ILLUSTRATION 925

CODE OF HONESTY

Topics: Character; Cheating; Honesty; Integrity; Legacy

References: Psalm 41:12; Proverbs 6:16 – 19; Ephesians 4:25

My alma mater has an honor code that is respected throughout the university. Freshmen pledge to do their own academic work with integrity and to report those who do not to the student-run honor council.

Student signatures remain on display in the lobby of the Sarratt Student Center throughout their four years at the university. Alongside the signatures is a statement of the honor code as well as the words of the man for whom the building is named. Madison Sarratt, longtime dean of men at Vanderbilt University and a teacher in the mathematics department, died in 1978. He wrote, "Today I am going to give you two examinations, one in trigonometry and one in honesty. I hope you will pass them both, but if you must fail one, let it be trigonometry, for there are many good [people] in this world today who cannot pass an examination in trigonometry, but there are no good [people] in the world who cannot pass an examination in honesty."

Sarratt's former students still speak of the effect those words have had on their adult lives.

—Gaynelle Doll, "The Nature of Virtue,"
Vanderbilt Today (Summer – Fall 1999)

ILLUSTRATION 926

SOPRANO REGRETS

Topics: Fall of Humanity; Guilt; Human Condition; Regret; Sinful Nature

References: Isaiah 53:6; Romans 3:23

The Sopranos, a TV series about today's gangsters, attracted millions of viewers each week. According to James Gandolfini, who played New Jersey mob boss Tony Soprano, "We show people sometimes being at their worst and regretting it. And people identify with that because we've all had times when we were at our worst."

—Greg Asimakoupoulos,
Mercer Island, Washington

ILLUSTRATION 927
FOLLOWING ORDERS

Topics: Obedience; Questions; Trust

Reference: 1 John 5:1–3

It was probably a clerical error, but when Specialist Jeff Lewis, twenty-three, got the order to parachute out of an airplane, he followed the order, even though he'd had no formal training in jumping.

Lewis landed unhurt. "The Army said I was airborne-qualified," he said. "I wasn't going to question it. I had a job to do, and I had to believe in what I was doing."

—Associated Press, "Army Clerk Leaps
at Opportunity to Parachute,"
Milwaukee Journal Sentinel (May 20, 2000)

ILLUSTRATION 928
ADMITTING ANGER

Topics: Anger; Honesty; Rage; Self-control

References: Matthew 5:21–22; Ephesians 4:26

Many hotheads suffer from Intermittent Explosive Disorder (IED). The good news is that there is a drug that can control it.

So says Dr. Emil Coccaro, a researcher and professor of psychiatry at the University of Chicago Hospitals, who has studied anger for several decades and is championing a new drug called Depakote introduced by Abbott Laboratories in 1995.

The problem is that an effort to find volunteers with volatile tempers for the clinical studies has been unproductive. Apparently few people see their anger as a problem.

The doctor cites an example: "The other day I got into a friend's car and I noticed the visor on the passenger's side was gone. I asked what happened, and the driver told me, 'Don't get me started on that. My wife ripped it off.' I told him these things are hard to rip off, and he told me, 'Well, she was really angry.'"

—Mike Conklin,
Chicago Tribune (July 28, 2000)

ILLUSTRATION 929
HOLD THE CRITICISM

Topics: Acceptance; Criticism; Family; Sabbath; Spiritual Formation; Teens; Tongue; Words

References: Proverbs 12:18; James 1:26; 3:1–12

A family with teens decided that as part of their Sabbath commitments they would not criticize each other on Sundays.

As the months went on, they realized more and more of their children's friends were coming over on Sundays just to hang around. No one in the family had talked about their commitment to withhold criticism, but somehow other teens knew this home was a good place to be.

—Tilden Edwards,
Sabbath Time (Upper Room Books, 1992)

ILLUSTRATION 930
LIFE WITHOUT ANGER

Topics: Addiction; Anger; Change; Choices; Repentance; Sin

Reference: James 1:19–20

A Christian counselor told me about a man who came to counseling because he was having trouble controlling his anger. His outbursts were affecting his work and his family life. So he finally decided to get some help.

The counselor asked, "What would your life look like if you got rid of your anger?"

He was quiet a long time. Then he said, "But if I get rid of my anger, what will I have left?"

—Kevin Miller, Wheaton, Illinois

ILLUSTRATION 931
HAPPY IN GOD

Topics: Happiness; Meditation; Seeking God; Spiritual Disciplines

Reference: Matthew 6:33

Seek God, not happiness—that is the fundamental rule of all meditation. If you seek God alone, you will gain happiness—that is the promise of all meditation.

—Dietrich Bonhoeffer,
Life Together (HarperSanFrancisco, 1954)

ILLUSTRATION 932
TRUE HUMILITY

Topics: Attitudes; Human Condition; Humility; Purpose; Rewards; Self-denial; Self-image; Weakness

References: Philippians 2:5–8; Hebrews 2:9

What is humility? It is that habitual quality whereby we live in the truth of things: the truth that we are creatures and not the Creator; the truth that our life is a composite of good and evil, light and darkness; the truth that in our littleness we have been given extravagant dignity.

Humility is saying a radical *yes* to the human condition.

—Bishop Robert F. Morneau,
Green Bay, Wisconsin

ILLUSTRATION 933
MEETING GOD IN SILENCE

Topics: Contemplation; Listening; Meditation; Pleasure; Reflection; Silence

References: 1 Kings 19:9 – 13;
Psalm 46:10

I read *A Hole Is to Dig* to my children when they were young. Each charmingly illustrated page declares the purpose of something: "A pile of leaves is to jump in; a mud puddle is to slide in and go 'Oodlee-oddlee-oo!'" And so on.

The reasoning is sound if you're a child. The world is made for our entertainment; it gives us things to do and pleasures to revel in. Reading the book as an adult, however, offers a more pragmatic perspective: like holes are something to fill in before someone trips and sues you, or piles of leaves are to be put into plastic bags before the Thursday pickup, or mud is to be scraped off boots before stepping on the carpet.

The same pragmatism that turns a tired and jaundiced eye toward holes and mud seems to inform the liturgy of many churches with regard to the purpose of silence. Silence, it seems, is something that must be filled.

Perhaps it would help us to hear more regularly the story of Elijah on Mount Horeb, waiting for the Lord to pass by. The Lord was not in the great wind, or the earthquake, or the fire, but, as the NRSV translates it, in the "sound of sheer silence."

The church's long history of contemplative practice seems to suggest that there is some knowledge of God that can come only in stillness—a silence large and long and intentional enough to open a sacred space for the Holy One to enter.

—Marilyn Chandler McEntyre,
"Silence Is to Dwell In,"
Christianity Today (August 7, 2000)

ILLUSTRATION 934
RETURNING LOST MONEY

Topics: Character; Honesty;
Integrity; Loss

References: Exodus 20:15;
Ephesians 4:28

A newlywed couple left a black-zippered case on the roof of their car as they sped away from the reception. The case had all their wedding gift money in it—$12,000. By the time they reached their honeymoon destination, they realized what they had lost. "I feel numb," the bride said. "Overwhelmed."

David Yi, who was unemployed and struggling to pay bills, found the black bag. He tracked the couple down and returned their satchel, with every dollar intact. When asked why he turned in all the money, Yi said, "I guess it doesn't matter whether it's $50 or $1,000 or $1 million. It doesn't belong to me."

—"Fairy Tale Princess Story Turns Sour after
Newlyweds Lose Money," *Daily Herald*,
Suburban Chicago, Illinois (February 20, 1996)

ILLUSTRATION 935
LOVE-IN AT THE DRIVE-IN

Topics: Compassion; Giving;
Kindness; Love

References: John 13:34 – 35;
1 John 4:19

The owner of a drive-through coffee business in Portland, Oregon, was surprised one morning when a customer not only paid for her mocha but also for the mocha of the person in the car behind her. The owner smiled as she told the next customer her drink had already been paid for.

The second customer was so pleased that she bought coffee for the next customer. This string of kindnesses — one stranger paying for the mocha of the next customer — continued for two hours and twenty-seven customers.

That's how it is with God's love. It starts with his unexpected love for us, which is passed on to others, who in turn pass it on.

—Glen Zander, Portland, Oregon

ILLUSTRATION 936

TASTING BITTERNESS

Topics: Anger; Bitterness; Conflict; Forgiveness; Relationships

References: Ephesians 4:31; Hebrews 12:15; James 3:14

Bitterness is like drinking poison and waiting for the other person to die.

—Ron McManus, Springfield, Missouri

ILLUSTRATION 937

SEGMENTED STOMACH

Topics: Desires; Hunger; Prayer; Seeking God; Spiritual Disciplines

References: Psalm 42:1; Jeremiah 29:13; John 6:26 – 27

One night as his family was finishing dinner, Mike Benson noticed six green beans left on his daughter's plate. Ordinarily this wouldn't bother Mike, but this night he was irked and said to his eight-year-old, "Eat your green beans."

"I'm full to the top," she said.

"You won't pop," he responded.

"Yes, I will pop!" she said.

"Risk it!" he said. "It will be OK."

"Dad, I can't eat another bite."

Mike knew the dessert, pumpkin pie squares, was his daughter's favorite. So he asked, "How would you like a double helping of pumpkin pie squares with two dollops of whipped cream on top?"

"That sounds great!" she said as she pushed back her plate.

"How can you have room for a double helping of pumpkin pie squares with two dollops of whipped cream and not have room for six measly green beans?"

She stood up and pointed to her belly, saying, "This is my vegetable stomach. This is my meat stomach. They are both full. Here is my dessert stomach. It is empty. I am ready for dessert!"

What we eat reveals what we hunger for.

—Phillip Gunter, "Hungry for God,"
PreachingToday.com

1001 ILLUSTRATIONS THAT CONNECT

ILLUSTRATION 938

HOMELESS MAN FINDS TREASURE

Topics: Gratitude; Integrity; Poverty; Rewards; Riches; Self-centeredness; Stinginess

References: Proverbs 10:9; Matthew 6:19–21; 7:12; 16:26; 19:23; Luke 6:31; 12:15–34; 1 Timothy 6:10; Hebrews 13:5; James 2:8

In 2006, Charles Moore lost his job as a roofer in Toledo, Ohio, and decided to return to his hometown of Detroit to look for work. He couldn't find a job, however, and soon found himself homeless. In July, while looking through a trash bin for bottles, Moore found thirty-one U.S. Savings Bonds. With the help of the Neighborhood Service Organization, a local nonprofit group, Moore tracked down the owner of the bonds, Ernest Lehto, who had bought the bonds during the 1980s at a face value of $8,900. By the time Moore found them, the bonds were worth $20,738. Ernest Lehto died in 2004, but Moore returned the bonds to his son, Neil Lehto. For his honesty and effort, Moore was given $100. He was thankful for the money.

When local media picked up the story, however, Neil Lehto began receiving phone calls and emails from angry people calling him cheap and ungrateful. Lehto, a lawyer, blamed his eighty-two-year-old mother, saying that she was the sole beneficiary and had determined the reward amount. "That generation of people would consider $100 to be an adequate reward," he said.

Now aware of Moore's need, the community began to support the homeless man. One man sent him eight trash bags filled with bottle returns and a bowl of coins. Jesse Nyikon, a local billiards owner, offered Moore a night on the town, complete with food, drinks, and unlimited pool. As the story began to grow, so did the number of people expressing gratitude for Moore's integrity. Dick Wolski and Ken Zorn—two businessmen from Troy, Michigan—pulled together a gift of $1,200. They also paid for $250 worth of clothing at Men's Wearhouse. Best of all, they lined him up with a job interview at a local cleaning company.

"Here's a man who by all rights should be worried and thinking about himself but who takes the time to think about others," Wolski said. "What a lesson! Isn't that what we're all supposed to be doing?"

—Kim Kozlowski, "Virtue, $100 Not His Only Reward," *Chicago Tribune* (July 26, 2006)

ILLUSTRATION 939

A JERK WITH MONEY

Topics: Character; Money

References: Proverbs 22:1;
Matthew 19:23–24

If you were a jerk before, you'll be a bigger jerk with a billion dollars.

—Warren Buffet, billionaire businessman

ILLUSTRATION 940

WHEN A DIAMOND ISN'T FOREVER

Topics: Advice; Choices;
Consequences; Finances;
Foolishness; Guidance; Investments;
Money; Stewardship

References: Matthew 25:14–30;
Luke 19:11–27; 1 Corinthians 4:2;
1 Timothy 6:10

It was our first financial mistake, and it was a big one. After my wife and I said "I do" in June of 2003, we found ourselves with a sizable chunk of money (sizable to us, anyway). We viewed this money as part of an eventual down payment on our future house. In the meantime we needed to invest it.

At the time, the stock market was languishing in the wake of 9/11. Through some rather interesting circumstances, we came in contact with a diamond wholesaler. This man was very charming, very knowledgeable, and very optimistic about the investment potential of small, sparkling rocks.

And so, in spite of the advice of our parents and other financially sound naysayers, my wife and I purchased a lovely 1.07 carat, museum-quality diamond. We marveled at it for several days, delighting in its brilliance and largesse. Then we hid it under our bathroom sink in the middle of a roll of toilet paper (what thief would ever check there?).

Two long, stressful years later, we sold the diamond online to an estate liquidator for about half of what we had paid for it. As I say, it was our first financial mistake. It was also our first big lesson on the consequences of poor stewardship.

—Sam O'Neal, Saint Charles, Illinois

ILLUSTRATION 941

MONEY DRAIN

Topics: Finances; Frugality; Habits;
Lifestyle; Money; Possessions;
Prosperity; Riches; Self-control;
Spending; Stewardship; Women

References: Proverbs 21:20; 31:10–31;
Matthew 6:19; 1 Timothy 6:10;
Hebrews 13:5

What spending habits are the most difficult to break? A Harris Interactive poll of 1,202 women discovered these habits are toughest to control:

- eating out or getting takeout: 49 percent
- shopping for clothes: 28 percent

- daily coffee fix: 17 percent
- personal beauty products: 14 percent

> —Mary Cadden and Julie Snider, "Money
> Matters," *USA Today* "Snapshots"
> (February 6, 2006)

ILLUSTRATION 942

SHOPPING SABBATICAL

Topics: Community; Finances;
Godliness; Growth; Holiness;
Materialism; Renewal; Responsibility;
Sacrifice; Sanctification; Self-control;
Thankfulness

References: Proverbs 23:5; Ecclesiastes
5:10; Matthew 6:19 – 21, 24; 16:26;
19:23; Mark 4:19; Luke 12:15;
1 Timothy 6:10; Hebrews 13:5

What would it be like to go through an entire year without purchasing anything new? That's the question a small West Coast group of environmental activists asked themselves a year ago.

In January 2006, ten friends declared a sabbatical from American consumerism. The Compact, as they titled their agreement — bound them in a mutual pledge to abstain from shopping sprees. Other than food, essential toiletries, underwear, and items for health and safety, the friends purchased virtually nothing new.

They learned much about themselves in the process. After going through a time of "retail withdrawal," they were amazed at how the items they needed just "showed up" as they shared and interacted with others. Rachel Kesel, twenty-six, says, "I found a lot of times there were things I thought I needed that I didn't need that much." Rediscovering the library and paying down credit cards were two unexpected dividends. John Perry, forty-two, says one of the by-products of the Compact is having a different relationship with things. "I appreciate the stuff I have more," he says. He has developed a knack for fixing things rather than replacing them with new.

The group enjoyed the freedom of their Compact so much that they chose to renew their pledges for 2007.

> —Associated Press, "Group Went on Shopping
> Sabbatical in '06," *Houston Chronicle*
> (January 3, 2007)

ILLUSTRATION 943

HOW BRANDS BUY US

Topics: Appetites; Belonging; Choices;
Culture; Entertainment; Idolatry; Lifestyle; Possessions; Satisfaction;
Self-centeredness; Self-worth

References: Psalm 86:11; 115:4 – 8;
Proverbs 8:10 – 11

When you buy something, you can join any number of tribes on any number of days and feel part of something bigger than yourself. You can belong to the Callaway tribe when you play golf, the VW tribe when you drive to work, and the Williams-Sonoma tribe when you cook a meal. You're part of a select clan (or so you feel) when you buy products from these clearly differentiated companies. So says Marty Neumeier, author of *The Brand Gap*.

Brands are the little gods of modern life, each ruling a different need, activity, mood, or situation. Yet you're in control, Neumeier says. If your latest god falls from Olympus, you can switch to another one.

—Based on Marty Neumeier, *The Brand Gap* (AIGA, 2006)

ILLUSTRATION 944
COSTLY MOVE

Topics: Ambition; Judgment; Loss; Luxury; Money; Mortality; Possessions; Prosperity; Riches; Stewardship; Value; Vulnerability; Worth

References: Psalm 39:6; 144:4; Proverbs 21:6; 23:5; Ecclesiastes 5:10; Matthew 6:19–21; 16:26; Luke 12:13–21; James 5:1–6

The man who would have sold his Picasso painting for $139 million put an elbow through it minutes before completing the sale.

Throughout his life, Pablo Picasso produced an estimated 13,500 paintings and designs, 100,000 prints and engravings, 34,000 book illustrations, and 300 sculptures and ceramics. The painting titled *The Dream* was completed in 1932.

In 1997, at an art auction at Christie's in New York City, casino magnate Steve Wynn purchased *The Dream* for $47 million. Less than a decade later, Wynn completed a deal to sell the painting for $139 million. The transaction would have set a record for the sale of a piece of art.

It would have—if Wynn, who was standing close to the painting, hadn't turned and inadvertently clobbered the Picasso with his elbow, punching a six-inch hole in the middle of the masterpiece. While no one is certain what that does to the value of the painting itself, the effect on the sale price was immediate. Even more quickly than it had come, the record-breaking $139 million sale evaporated.

—Associated Press, "Vegas Tycoon Pokes Hole in a Picasso," CBSNews.com (October 18, 2006)

ILLUSTRATION 945
MORE SPACE FOR STUFF

Topics: Appetites; Contentment; Foolishness; Greed; Lifestyle; Luxury; Materialism; Money; Possessions; Prosperity; Riches; Satisfaction; Stewardship; Stinginess

References: Exodus 16:11–31; Amos 6:1–7; Matthew 6:19–21, 24; 25:14–30; Luke 12:15–21; 1 Timothy 6:10; James 5:1–6; 1 John 3:17

People in the United States possess about 1.9 billion square feet of personal storage space outside of the home. This self-storage space is in nearly 40,000 facilities owned and operated by more than 2,000 entrepreneurs, including a handful of publicly traded giants such as Public Storage, Storage USA, and Shurgard. So reports the Self Storage Association, a trade group charged with monitoring such things.

According to a recent survey, the owners of one of every eleven homes rent a self-storage space. This represents an increase of 75 percent since 1995. Operators of self-storage facilities report 90 percent occupancy, with average rental of fifteen months. In 2004 alone, there was a 24 percent spike in the number of self-storage units on the market.

As the amount of storage space required by homeowners has grown, so has the average size of the American house. The National Association of Homebuilders reports that the average American house increased from 1,660 square feet in 1973 to 2,400 square feet in 2004.

So let's get this straight—houses get bigger, average family sizes get smaller, yet we still need to tack on almost two billion square feet of extra space to store our stuff?

—Tom Vanderbilt, "Americans Are Storing
More Stuff Than Ever," Slate.com (July 18, 2005)

ILLUSTRATION 946

HOARDING IS NO FUN

Topics: Contentment; Generosity; Greed; Happiness; Possessions; Self-centeredness; Self-indulgence; Sinful Nature; Stinginess; Unselfishness

References: Proverbs 15:27; 28:25; Ecclesiastes 5:10; Habakkuk 2:5; Luke 12:15; Ephesians 5:5; Hebrews 13:5

A little boy sat on the floor of the church nursery with a red rubber ball in each arm and three Nerf balls clenched on the floor between his pudgy little knees. He was trying to protect all five from the other children in the nursery. The problem was, he could not hold all five at once, and the ball nearest to his feet was particularly vulnerable to being stolen. So whenever another child showed an interest in playing with one of the balls, the little boy snarled to make it clear these toys were not for sharing.

I suppose I should have stepped in and made the little guy give up one or two of the balls, but I was too wrapped up in the drama. For about five minutes, this little guy growled, postured, and kept the other children away from the balls. Like a hyena hunched over the last scraps of a carcass, this snarling little canine was not in the mood for sharing. The other kids circled like vultures around the kill, looking for a way to jump in and snatch a ball without being attacked and bitten. I honestly did not know whether to laugh or cry as I watched.

Then it struck me: this little boy was not having any fun. There was no cheer within ten yards of this kid. Not only was he unhappy, but all the other kids seemed sad as well. His selfishness created a black hole that sucked all of the joy out of that nursery.... When church was over and his parents came to pick him up, he left the balls behind. I guess the old saying is true: you can't take it with you.

—Kevin G. Harney,
Seismic Shifts (Zondervan, 2005)

ILLUSTRATION 947

WHO GETS WHAT

Topics: Ambition; Comparisons; Competition; Contentment; Coveting; Desires; Envy; Greed; Human Nature;

Jealousy; Money; Pride; Prosperity;
Riches; Service

References: Proverbs 14:30; 27:4;
Luke 9:25; 12:15; 17:18; 2 Corinthians
10:12–18; Galatians 5:26;
1 Timothy 6:6

I am talking with the head of a mighty American corporation. We're in his window-lined office, high in midtown Manhattan. The view—silver skyscrapers stacked one against another, dense, fine-lined, sparkling in the sun—is so perfect, so theatrical. It's like a scrim, like a fake backdrop for a 1930s movie about people in tuxes and tails. Edward Everett Horton could shake his cocktail shaker here; Fred and Ginger could banter on the phone.

The CEO tells me it is "annual report time," and he is looking forward to reading the reports of his competitors.

Why? I ask. I wonder what he looks for when he reads the reports of the competition.

He says he always flips to the back to see what the other CEOs got as part of their deal—corporate jets, private helicopters, whatever. "We all do that," he says. "We all want to see who has what."

The CEO is a talented and exceptional man, and I think afterward that he might, in an odd way, be telling me this about himself so I won't be unduly impressed by him. But what I think, instead, is that it must be hard for him to keep some simple things in mind each day as he works, such as a job creates a livelihood, a livelihood creates a family, a family creates a civilization. Ultimately this CEO is in the civilization-producing business. Does he know it? Does that give him

joy? Does he understand that is probably why he is there?

This man creates the jobs that create the world in which we live. And yet he can't help it; his mind is on the jet.

—Peggy Noonan, *John Paul the Great*
(Viking, 2005)

ILLUSTRATION 948

BRAND BURNING

Topics: Abundant Life; Addiction;
Appetites; Belonging; Conformity;
Contentment; Emptiness; Identity;
Lifestyle; Meaning; Possessions;
Prosperity; Temptation

References: Proverbs 15:16;
Ecclesiastes 5:10; Isaiah 55:1–2;
Matthew 6:24; Mark 4:19; Luke 12:15;
1 Timothy 6:10; Hebrews 13:5

Neil Boorman decided to burn every branded thing in his possession after he realized he was addicted to brands. He explained:

From an early age, I have been taught that to be accepted, to be lovable, to be cool, one must have the right stuff. At junior school, I tried to make friends with the popular kids, only to be ridiculed for the lack of stripes on my trainers. Once I had nagged my parents to the point of buying me the shoes, I was duly accepted at school, and I became much happier. As long as my parents continued to buy me the brands, life was more fun. Now, at the age of thirty-one, I still behave according to playground law.

The manner in which we spend our money defines who we are. In this secular society of ours, where family and church once gave us a sense of belonging, identity, and meaning, there is now Apple, Mercedes, and Coke.

So, this is why I am burning all my stuff. To find real happiness, to find the real me.

— Neil Boorman, "Bonfire of the Brands,"
BBC Magazine (August 29, 2006)

ILLUSTRATION 949

PACIFIC ISLAND SELLS SOUL

Topics: Choices; Consequences; Cost; Foolishness; Mistakes; Past; Regret; Responsibility; Shame; Stewardship

References: Ecclesiastes 6:2; Luke 12:15; 1 Timothy 6:10; Hebrews 13:5

Around the year 1900, two scientists from the Pacific Islands Company studied a piece of rock picked up on Nauru, a tiny Pacific Island east of New Guinea and twelve hundred miles from any sizable landmass. Instead of a fossilized rock, it was rich phosphate so valuable that it plunged Nauru violently into the industrial era.

During the years that followed, the country was colonized by a succession of European and Asian nations, who turned the island into a strip mine. Nauru achieved independence in 1968, but the Nauruan government continued the mining practices that had, by then, brutalized the island.

By the early 1980s, Nauru boasted the world's highest per capita income, but it didn't last. Midway through the 1990s, Nauru's wealth had been embezzled by corrupt financial managers, gambled away on risky investments, and squandered on extravagant luxuries. More than 70 percent of the island is a mined-out ruin, unable to offer the infrastructure or natural resources needed to support anyone. Nauru must now look for a new piece of land on which to relocate its population.

"When you're on Nauru, there's a palpable sense of shame at what was done," said reporter Jack Hitt. "The Nauruans literally sold off their homeland for a pot of wealth that is now lost."

— *This American Life*, "The Middle of Nowhere," Public Radio International, episode 253 (December 5, 2003)

ILLUSTRATION 950

NO POWER FOR FIFTEEN YEARS

Topics: Daily Bread; Grace; Gratitude; Holy Spirit; Light; Needs; Neglect; Neighbors; Poverty; Power; Powerlessness; Provision; Suffering; Weakness

References: Psalm 37:18–19; Isaiah 58:11; John 4:14; Acts 1:8; Ephesians 3:20; 6:10

When a hurricane hit South Florida, Norena's home was severely damaged. The elderly woman received an insurance settlement, and the repair work began. However, when the money ran out, so did the contractor, leaving an unfinished home with no electricity.

Norena had been living without power ever since Hurricane Andrew. For more than fifteen years, Norena had been living in a dark house with no heat, no air-conditioning, and not a single hot bath or shower. She got by with extension cords running into her house, plugged into a tiny refrigerator and a cook top, and a small lamp or two in the front of the house.

Acting on a tip, the mayor of Miami-Dade finally got involved. A few hours of work by electrical contractor Kent Crook restored power to the house. Norena planned to let the water get really hot and then take her first bubble bath in a decade and a half. "It's hard to describe having [the electricity] come on, to switch on," she said. "It's overwhelming."

—CBS Broadcasting, "Woman Has Power for the First Time in 15 Years," cbs4.com (February 19, 2007)

ILLUSTRATION 951

SETTLING FOR SOCKS

Topics: Accepting Christ; Behavior; Change; Conduct; Contentment; Desires; Eternal Life; Experiencing God; Foolishness; Knowing God; New Life; Prosperity

References: Ezekiel 11:19; Romans 6:6–7; 1 Corinthians 5:7; 2 Corinthians 5:17; Ephesians 4:22–24; 1 Peter 1:22–23

Thelma and Victor Hayes won more than $7 million in 2005 in Canada. When asked what the couple, who were then age eighty-nine, would do with the money, they said that at this stage of life they were unlikely to become "giddy high spenders." They planned to stay put in their retirement home.

Victor Hayes planned to buy a Lincoln Town Car, but his wife simply wanted a new pair of nylons. Her response was widely reported as comical, if not foolish. How could someone win a fortune and change nothing but her nylons?

In the same way, how can those who have won the spiritual grand prize of eternal life not live in a way that is consistent with being a new creation in Christ?

—John Beukema, "Lottery Winner Only Wants New Nylons," PreachingToday.com

ILLUSTRATION 952

OOPS INVITATION

Topics: Freedom; Grace; Prisons; Redemption

References: Matthew 9:10–13; 22:1–14; Luke 4:14–19; Romans 5:6–8; Ephesians 4:7–8

The Republican Party mistakenly invited an Ohio prisoner to a $2,500-a-plate fund-raising dinner in Washington with President George W. Bush. The invitation and a letter from Vice President Cheney were sent to Robert Kirkpatrick at the Belmont Correctional Institution in eastern Ohio. Kirkpatrick, thirty-five, was sentenced last year to nearly three years for drug possession and escape.

"I'm going to tell him that I'd be happy to attend," said Kirkpatrick, "but he's going to have to pull some strings to get me there."

—John Bacon (from staff and wire reports),
"Guess Who's Not Coming to a Bush Dinner,"
USA Today (June 5, 2002)

ILLUSTRATION 953

CHECK OUT THIS PHONE BILL

Topics: Atonement; Debt; Dependence on God; Grace; Guilt; Human Condition; Limitations; Powerlessness; Salvation; Spiritual Poverty

References: Isaiah 64:6; Matthew 18:21–35; John 14:6; Romans 3:23; 6:23; Ephesians 2:8–9

When Yahaya Wahab's father passed away in January 2006, Yahaya had his father's phone disconnected and paid the final bill of 84 ringgit (approximately $23) to Telekom Malaysia. He was then surprised to receive another bill from the phone company in April. He was utterly shocked, however, after looking at what was inside.

It was a bill for 806,400,000,000,000.01 ringgit (approximately $218 trillion), along with a threatening letter informing Yahaya that he must pay the bill within ten days or face pros-

ecution. It wasn't initially clear whether the monstrous charge was a mistake or if Yahaya's father's phone line had been used illegally after his death. What was immediately clear, however, was that the bill represented a debt that Yahaya would never be able to pay.

—Associated Press, "Man Gets $218 Trillion Phone Bill," *Chicago Tribune* (April 10, 2006)

ILLUSTRATION 954

PARKING THE ROLLS-ROYCE

Topics: Money; Resourcefulness; Stewardship; Wisdom

References: Matthew 10:16; 25:14–30

Before going to Europe on business, a man drove his Rolls-Royce to a downtown New York City bank, then went in to ask for a loan of $5,000. The loan officer requested collateral. The man said, "Here are the keys to my Rolls-Royce."

The loan officer had the car driven into the bank's underground parking for safekeeping and gave the owner $5,000.

Two weeks later, the man walked into the bank and asked to settle up his loan and get his car back. "That will be $5,000 in principal and $15.40 in interest," the loan officer said. The man wrote out a check, got up, and started to walk away.

"Wait sir," the loan officer said. "While you were gone, I found out you're a millionaire. Why in the world would you need to borrow $5,000?"

The man smiled. "Where else could I safely park my Rolls-Royce in Manhattan for two weeks and only pay $15.40?"

—Adapted from a commercial

ILLUSTRATION 955

ALL ABOUT MONEY

Topics: Ambition; Goals; Greed; Money; Possessions; Priorities; Purpose; Self-centeredness; Wealth

References: Matthew 6:19–21; Mark 10:17–22

Paul Dinin, a twenty-year-old employee of Interland, a web-hosting company in Atlanta, Georgia, was asked what his prized possessions were. Dinin, a high school dropout, listed four cars, including a Jaguar and a 1981 DeLorean.

When asked for his philosophy on life, Dinin said, "It's all about money. All those guys who say they just want to make a difference in the world, that's bull."

—Rochelle Sharp, "Teen Internet Moguls," *Business Week* (May 29, 2000)

ILLUSTRATION 956

QUICK RETURN ON INVESTMENT

Topics: Attitudes; Giving; Impatience; Money; Patience; Perseverance; Waiting

References: Luke 6:38; Romans 8:25; Galatians 6:9

When our eldest daughter was old enough to understand what saving money was all about, my wife and I sat down with her and explained the value of money. We explained how you save, and when the piggybank is full, you take the money out and deposit it in a bank so that it can draw interest. She seemed to understand and couldn't wait to open a savings account in our local bank.

I called the banker in our little town and told him our daughter was on the way to open her savings account. We would stop in later and sign the necessary papers.

What a thrill! The president of the bank waited on her. She handed over her savings, and he gave her a receipt and thanked her for her business. But she wouldn't leave. She just stood there like she was waiting for something.

"Is there anything else I can help you with?" he asked.

"Yes," she said, "I want my interest."

—Don Young Sr., Bern, Kansas

ILLUSTRATION 957

SMALL CHANGES FOR BIG RESULTS

Topics: Christian Life; Investments; Small Things; Spiritual Disciplines; Spiritual Formation; Stewardship

References: Matthew 10:42; 12:36–37; 25:21; 2 Corinthians 7:1

Making a few small changes can make a big difference in your savings and retirement. For example:

- Giving up potato chips with lunch could save you $176.80 a year and generate retirement savings of $10,483.62 in twenty years, assuming a 10 percent return.
- Giving up two doughnuts a week could boost your nest egg by $6,552.26 in two decades. Switch from double lattes with whipped cream to regular coffee, and you could save $429 per year—a whopping $27,028.07 at 10 percent over twenty years.
- Dropping the potato chips would also eliminate close to 10,000 calories per year. Skipping the cream cheese on a bagel would toss 54,000 calories a year from your diet and save $117—or $7,371.29 over a twenty-year investment period.

That's according to Bryan Olson of the Schwab Center for Investment Research, who gathered the data to stress the proven investment strategy that regular investments, even in small amounts, will make a big difference in savings and retirement.

All the positive steps you take, even the smallest ones, make a significant difference over time.

—Rubel Shelly, "Small Changes Net Big Rewards," PreachingToday.com

ILLUSTRATION 958

RICHES BEYOND WEALTH

Topics: Contentment; Joy; Materialism; Meaning; Money; Riches

References: Ecclesiastes 5:10–12; 2 Corinthians 6:10; Philippians 4:11–13

Happiness is not determined by wealth or fame but by character, says Billy Graham in his autobiography *Just as I Am*. He goes on to say:

Ruth and I had a vivid illustration of this on an island in the Caribbean. One of the wealthiest men in the world asked us to come to his lavish home for lunch. He was 75 years old, and throughout the entire meal he seemed close to tears. "I am the most miserable man in the world," he said. "Out there is my yacht. I can go anywhere I want to. I have my private plane, my helicopters. I have everything I want to make my life happy, yet I am as miserable as hell." We prayed with him, trying to point him to Christ, who alone gives lasting meaning to life.

Later that afternoon we met with the pastor of the local Baptist church. He was an Englishman, and he too was 75, a widower who spent most of his time taking care of his two invalid sisters. He was full of enthusiasm and love for Christ and others. "I don't have two pounds to my name," he said with a smile, "but I am the happiest man on this island."

Billy asked Ruth after they left, "Who do you think is the richer man?" She didn't have to reply, because they both already knew the answer.

—Billy Graham, *Just as I Am* (HarperCollins, 1999)

ILLUSTRATION 959

WELFARE RECIPIENTS DWINDLE

Topics: Government; Money; Poor People; Poverty; Welfare; Work

References: Deuteronomy 24:21; Malachi 3:6 – 15; 1 Timothy 5:9 – 16

The number of welfare recipients in the United States is going down. Here are some U.S. Health and Human Services Department statistics:

- 1965: 4.3 million
- 1971: approximately 10 million
- 1981: approximately 11.5 million
- 1989: approximately 11 million
- 1994: 14.2 million
- 2000: 5.8 million

—Adrienne Lewis, "*USA Today* "Snapshots" (May 15, 2001)

ILLUSTRATION 960

FOOD STAMP PURCHASES

Topics: Criticism; Empathy; Faultfinding; Judging Others; Self-righteousness; Welfare

References: Proverbs 30:12 – 13; Matthew 7:1 – 5; Luke 16:15; 18:9 – 14; Romans 2:1

A grocery store cashier wrote to advice columnist Ann Landers to complain that she had seen people buy birthday cakes and bags of shrimp with their food stamps. People on welfare who treated themselves to such nonnecessities were "lazy and wasteful," the writer said.

A few weeks later, Landers' column was devoted entirely to responses to that letter.

One woman wrote, "I didn't buy a cake, but I did buy a big bag of shrimp with food stamps. So what? My husband had been working at a plant for fifteen years when it shut down. The shrimp casserole I made was for our wedding anniversary dinner and lasted three days. Perhaps the grocery clerk who criticized that woman would have a different view of life after walking a mile in my shoes."

Another woman wrote, "I'm the woman who bought the $17 cake and paid for it with food stamps. I thought the checkout woman in the store would burn a hole through me with her eyes. What she didn't know is the cake was for my little girl's birthday. It will be her last. She has bone cancer and will probably be gone within six to eight months."

You never know what other people are dealing with.

—Terrie Williams,
The Personal Touch (Warner, 1994)

ILLUSTRATION 961

THE GOD OF MONEY

Topics: Catechism; Greed; Idolatry;
Money; Worldliness

References: Exodus 20:1–3;
Matthew 6:24

What is the chief end of man?

A. To get rich.

In what way?

A. Dishonestly if we can; honestly if we must.

Who is God, the one only and true?

A. Money is God. Gold and Greenbacks and Stock—father, son, and ghosts of same, three persons in one; these are the true and only God, mighty and supreme.

—Mark Twain, "Revised Catechism,"
New York *Tribune* (September 27, 1871)

ILLUSTRATION 962

OVERLOOKED ASSET

Topics: Coveting; Greed; Help;
Money; Needs; Provision

References: 1 Kings 17:1–16;
Matthew 6:25–34; 1 Timothy 6:6–11

Danny Simpson, twenty-four, robbed a bank in Ottawa, Canada, of $6,000 in 1990. He was caught and sentenced to six years in prison. He used a .45 caliber Colt semiautomatic in the robbery, which turned out to be an antique made by the Ross Rifle Company, Quebec City, in 1918.

It was worth up to $100,000—much more than Simpson stole. If he had just known what he carried in his hand, he wouldn't have robbed the bank.

In other words, Danny already had what he needed.

—*The Province*, Vancouver, British Columbia
(September 19, 1990)

ILLUSTRATION 963

CREDITING WEALTH

Topics: Dependence; Money; Pride;
Provision; Self-reliance; Work

References: Daniel 4:30; Romans
1:21; 11:36

Senior corporate executives with a net worth of $1 million or more, not including primary residence, credit their financial status to various factors. Here's the percent on each (from the 2000 Phoenix Wealth Management Survey):

hard work: 99 percent
intelligence and good sense: 97 percent
higher-than-average IQ: 83 percent

being the best in every situation: 62 percent
luck: 32 percent

— *USA Today* "Snapshots"
(November 13, 2000)

ILLUSTRATION 964

OVERWHELMED WITH MONEY

Topics: Generosity; Giving; Greed;
Money; Stewardship

References: Matthew 6:24;
1 Timothy 6:10, 17–19

Warren Bailey, eighty-eight, died in July 2000.
He had no family. And to the best of anybody's
recollection in St. Mary's, Georgia, Bailey
hadn't been to church in at least twenty years.
He did, however, make annual donations of
about $100,000 to St. Mary's United Method-
ist Church, a 350-member congregation with an
annual budget of less than $300,000.

Members of St. Mary's probably weren't
surprised when Bailey bequeathed money to the
church. But there was stunned silence among the
assembled parishioners when Rev. Derek McAleer
broke the news that the man who owned 49 percent of the region's Camden Telephone Company
had left the church $60 million.

"This is a number that doesn't have any
reality," the pastor said. Bailey's will included no
instructions on how the money was to be used,
so the church has set up an advisory board to
decide how to handle the money.

McAleer has been besieged by calls from
people asking for money. And he admits worrying that greed could consume his congregation.
"How do we remain a Christian church with all
this money?" he laments.

—Associated Press (October 30, 2000)

ILLUSTRATION 965

THE 90 PERCENT CLUB

Topics: Failure; Greed; Humility;
Money; Risk; Stewardship; Success

References: Matthew 6:24;
1 Timothy 6:10, 17–19

Michael Donahue, founder of InterWorld Corporation in New York City, was elated when his
company's share price skyrocketed in a public
stock offering in August 1999, earning him $448
million. So he splurged big-time.

He bought a $9.6 million second home in
Palm Beach, spent $100,000 to help sponsor his
polo team in Florida, and dropped a bundle rent-
ing a private jet so he could whisk off to Palm
Beach on weekend jaunts with his wife. "It was a
lifestyle thing," he says.

Today Donahue is a member of another
club—call it the 90 percent club—of executives whose companies' stock prices have fallen
that much or more from their peak. The value
of Donahue's InterWorld stake has plunged to
$12.6 million; the share price falling 96.8 per-
cent to $2.94 from a peak of $93.50 on December 31, 1999. Donahue was asked to repay part
of a $14 million loan he took out with his Inter-
World stock as collateral. And he had to put his

Palm Beach house on the market for more than $13 million.

"Going up was easy," Donahue says. "But when it starts going down, no one wants to talk to you. It's been the most challenging personal experience of my career."

— Susan Pulliam and Scott Thurm, "Echelon of Ex-centimillionaires Sees Stakes Plunge as Net Craze Fades," *Wall Street Journal* (October 20, 2000)

ILLUSTRATION 966

PRIORITIZING SPENDING

Topics: Knowledge; Money; Priorities; Study; Understanding

References: Proverbs 2:1–11; 23:12

When I get a little money, I buy books; and if any is left, I buy food and clothes.

— Desiderius Erasmus, "Letter to Jacob Batt" (April 12, 1500)

ILLUSTRATION 967

MONEY MY LOVE

Topics: Example; Fathers; Greed; Money; Priorities; Values

References: Matthew 6:19–21; 1 Timothy 6:8–9

When I was thirteen my dad owned his own business — a tiny shack where he sold chicken, ribs, hamburgers, hot dogs, and fries. One day the frying oil caught fire, and the whole place exploded in flames. My dad bolted from the store before the flames could engulf him.

Mom, Dad, and I stood outside, watching the fire burn. Suddenly my dad realized he had left his money in the metal cash register inside the building and ran back into the inferno.

He tried to open the metal register, but the drawer was sealed shut. So Dad picked up the scalding metal box and carried it outside. When he threw the register on the ground, the skin on his arms and chest came with it. He had escaped the fire safely once, untouched. Now he was severely injured.

That taught me money was more important than life. From that point on, earning money — lots of money — not only became what drove me professionally, but also became my emotional priority.

— Suze Orman, *9 Steps to Financial Freedom* (Random House, 2000)

ILLUSTRATION 968

MISSING THE VISION

Topics: Change; Complacency; Leadership; Opportunity; Success; Vision

References: Galatians 6:9–10; Hebrews 13:20–21

After my first year at Stanford Business School, I went to see Jim Levy, who was president of Activision, Inc., one of the fastest-growing companies in the world. Activision made games for the Atari 2600 game system and was rolling in dough.

I wanted to work for Levy that summer, so I made a bold proposal: "Hey, you've got all this cash and all these smart marketers and programmers. Why not go into the computer game business? You can dominate the PC the way you dominate the Atari 2600."

Looking back twenty-five years ago, that wasn't such a bad idea. After all, the PC market was only an inch or two away from the market that Activision was already in. But Levy disagreed with my proposition and told me, "We're in the cartridge business — and those machines use floppy disks. Forget it."

Sometimes success robs us of the eyes to see opportunity.

— Seth Godin, "Gear Shops Are No Longer the Engine of Our Economy," *Fast Company* (October 2000)

ILLUSTRATION 969

FINDING HAPPINESS

Topics: Happiness; Money; Poverty; Wealth

References: Proverbs 13:7; Ecclesiastes 5:8 – 15

It's pretty hard to tell what does bring happiness. Poverty and wealth have both failed.

— Ken Hubbard, Plymouth, Michigan

ILLUSTRATION 970

LEAVING THE TOYS BEHIND

Topics: Contentment; Goals; Greed; Heaven; Love of Money; Possessions; Rewards; Seeking God; Simplicity

References: Luke 12:13 – 34; Philippians 4:11 – 19; Hebrews 10:34; 1 John 3:17

There we were, in love and on the rim of the Grand Canyon on New Year's Eve. As we watched the sun go down, we remembered the hotel was full and we needed a place to stay.

My husband had a brainstorm. "I'll bet the ranger at the bottom of the canyon is lonely, especially tonight. Let's call him and see how he would feel about having guests."

The ranger's telephone number was in the book. We dialed, explained our situation, and offered to bring groceries down. Ranger Gary said he and his wife, Gina, would love company.

After an uneventful passage down the curving canyon, we arrived at the bottom. We were invited into the ranger's large cabin and served a nice dinner. Then Gary and Gina showed us their "sports room." It was full of abandoned sports equipment — high-class hiking boots, expensive backpacks, fancy hats, and even fancier walking sticks that people had left behind.

"People can walk in easily enough with all of this stuff," Gary said. "They just can't walk out."

— Donna Schaper, *All Is Calm* (St. Mary's Press, 1999)

ILLUSTRATION 971

UPPING THE PRICE OF A COKE

Topics: Cost; Grace; Value; Worth

References: Isaiah 55:1–2; Ephesians 2:8–9; Hebrews 13:8

Coca-Cola Company was working on a vending machine that would automatically increase the price of the soft drink when the temperature rises. Coke chairman Doug Ivester told the Brazilian magazine *Veja* that the machine was designed to reconcile supply and demand by raising the price when demand increased.

After a storm of protest, Coca-Cola backtracked, saying: "Contrary to some erroneous press reports, the Coca-Cola Company is not introducing vending machines that raise the price of soft drinks in hot weather." Instead, the company said it is exploring "innovative technology and communication systems that can actually improve product availability, promotional activity, and even offer consumers an interactive experience when they purchase a soft drink from a vending machine."

Some people still weren't buying it. "Who the heck wants to have an interactive experience buying a Coke?" responded a further disillusioned customer. "All I want to do is plunk in my money and out comes the cold can. I don't want machines saying, 'Hello, hope you enjoy your cold drink' or even 'Thank you.' I like to interact with people, not with machines."

Isn't it refreshing to know God doesn't change with the weather? His offer of salvation is sure, his promises never-changing. He is the same yesterday and today and forever.

—Yahoo! News (October 28, 1999)

ILLUSTRATION 972

CHOOSING MONEY OR TIME

Topics: Contentment; Family; Greed; Money; Pressure; Priorities; Schedules; Time

References: Ecclesiastes 5:10; Philippians 4:10–13

If you could have one more hour per day at home or a $10,000-a-year raise, which would you choose? Here's how the readers of *Fast Company* responded:

- money: 83 percent
- time at home: 17 percent

—*Fast Company* (July–August 1999)

ILLUSTRATION 973

COUNTING THE CHANGE

Topics: Children; Generosity; Giving; Kindness; Money; Relationships; Respect; Unselfishness

References: Galatians 5:22; 1 Timothy 6:18

Many years ago, a boy walked up to the counter of a soda shop and climbed onto a stool. He asked the waitress, "How much is an ice cream sundae?"

"Fifty cents," the waitress replied.

The boy reached into his pockets, pulled out a handful of change, and began counting. The waitress frowned impatiently.

The boy squinted up at the waitress. "How much is a dish of plain ice cream?"

The waitress rolled her eyes. "Thirty-five cents," she said.

Again, the boy counted his coins. "I'll have the plain ice cream, please." He put a quarter and two nickels on the counter. The waitress took the coins, brought the ice cream, and walked away. About ten minutes later, she returned. The ice cream dish was empty. The boy was gone. She picked up the empty dish then swallowed hard.

There, next to the wet spot where the dish had been, were two nickels and five pennies. The boy had had enough for a sundae, but he ordered plain ice cream so he could leave a tip.

—Pat Williams with James D. Denney,
Mr. Littlejon's Secrets to a Lifetime of Success
(Revell, 2000)

ILLUSTRATION 974

FREEZING THE ASSETS

Topics: Afterlife; Ambition; Death; Eternal Life; Human Condition; Immortality; Life; Limitations; Money; Mortality; Power; Resurrection

References: Amos 4:12;
Matthew 6:19–21; Luke 12:13–31;
1 Timothy 6:6–10; Hebrews 9:27

At least twelve American multimillionaires are looking forward to life beyond death. Confident in the continued progress of modern medicine, they have arranged for their bodies to be frozen after they have died. They also have set up "personal revival trusts," which are designed to ensure their present wealth will be waiting for them when they have been resuscitated one hundred or two hundred years in the future.

David Pizer, sixty-four years old, figured that the "roughly $10 million" he left to himself—after all the compound interest has been added in—will make him "the richest man in the world" when he wakes up.

—"Only in America,"
The Week (February 3, 2006)

PART 37: WORK AND LEISURE

ILLUSTRATION 975

HIDING WEB ACTIVITY

Topics: Accountability; Dishonesty; Employees; Honesty; Hypocrisy; Integrity; Internet; Lying; Secrets

References: Psalm 32:5; Proverbs 28:13; Matthew 12:36; Luke 2:2–3; Hebrews 4:13; 1 Peter 4:5

A Spherion Workplace poll asked 1,601 employed adults, "If you knew your employer could see content from your social network website—such as MySpace, Friendster, or Facebook—would you remove any content from it?" The results:

Yes: 33 percent
No: 37 percent
Neutral: 30 percent

—Jae Yang and Robert Ahrens,
USA Today "Snapshots" (November 14, 2006)

ILLUSTRATION 976

REVERSING OUR ROLES

Topics: Compromise; Control; Goals; Greed; Insensitivity; Marriage; Motives; Sacrifice; Self-centeredness; Unselfishness

References: Acts 20:35; 1 Corinthians 10:24; Ephesians 5:21–33; Philippians 2:3–4; Colossians 3:18–19; 1 Peter 3:7

I've asked my wife through the years to support me in various ventures. When we were first married, I was a youth pastor and was taking classes at the University of Colorado at Denver. I then decided to be a writer. So Jana and I moved to the Chicago suburbs so I could take a job as a writer and editor. About four years later, I became restless, so I began working on a master's degree in business. I expected her again to sacrifice.

By that time, we had one child, and I got a book contract. So I was working full-time, going to graduate school two nights a week, and writing a book. Then I decided to start my business. By this time, we had two children. The week I told Jana I was leaving my secure job to start a business, she told me she was pregnant. Again, who sacrificed?

Recently Jana told me she wanted to go back to school. How did I respond? I became unsupportive and critical. *We don't have the money,* I thought. Or, *You actually need to work more, because . . .* It didn't matter that we didn't have the money when I wanted my MBA or wanted to start my business. This was different. Or was it?

I had a great opportunity to give up power, to sacrifice some of the things I wanted so I could help my wife with her dreams. But I told Jana the other day, "I know in my head that I need to do this, and it's killing me because it's so difficult." Why? Because I think about what I have to give up. I want to meet *my* goals.

—Interview with Dave Goetz,
Marriage Partnership (Winter 2006)

ILLUSTRATION 977

STRESSING JAPANESE WORKERS

Topics: Ambition; Busyness; Career; Competition; Consequences; Depression; Greed; Materialism; Money; Prosperity; Riches; Stress; Suicide; Values

References: Matthew 11:28–30; 16:26; Luke 12:22–34; Philippians 4:11–12; 1 Timothy 6:10; Hebrews 13:5; 1 Peter 5:2

In 2006, Japanese workers had higher rates of anxiety, mental illness, depression, and suicide than ever before, partly due to Western culture.

In previous decades Western business practices upset traditional Japanese values to the detriment of Japanese workers. In an attempt to globalize, corporate Japan adopted the working practices of the United States and England. These efforts included merit-based pay and promotions, which deviated from the traditional Japanese emphases on seniority and teamwork. More temporary staff and greater salary disparities were other ill effects of the switch.

The intense competition and individualism generated by these practices negatively affected the mental health of the Japanese workforce. According to government officials, "Sixty percent of workers suffer from high anxiety, and 65 percent of companies report soaring levels of mental illness."

Directors of the Japanese Mental Health Institute blamed the infiltration of Western values for rising levels of depression among workers and the country's suicide rate, which remained the highest among rich nations. The male suicide rate alone had doubled since 1976.

—Leo Lewis, "Western Values Are Causing Mental Illness," timesonline.co.uk (August 10, 2006)

ILLUSTRATION 978

TAKING THE TALE OUT OF "VEGGIETALES"

Topics: Absolutes; Bible; Culture; Entertainment; Media; Morality; Opposition; Religion; Scripture; Secularism; Television; Tolerance; Truth

References: Matthew 5:10–12, 18; John 14:6; 15:20; 16:33; Acts 4:12; Romans 1:16; 1 Corinthians 1:23; 2 Corinthians 6:14–16; 2 Timothy 2:15; 3:16

NBC added VeggieTales—a popular and thoroughly Christian cartoon—to its Saturday morning lineup in 2006. But before showing any episodes, the network first eliminated Bob the Tomato, Larry the Cucumber, and many of the references to God and Scripture.

Initially NBC said the cuts were necessary to fit each episode into a tight, twenty-three-minute slot. But upon further investigation, it became clear there was more to the story. After pressure from several Christian organizations, NBC released the following statement: "NBC is committed to the positive messages and universal values of VeggieTales. Our goal is to reach as broad an audience as possible with these positive messages, while being careful not to advocate any one religious point of view."

Phil Vischer, cocreator of VeggieTales, expressed deep disappointment in the edits. "It's a mistake to pitch VeggieTales as just values," he said, "because fundamentally it's about God." Bob Bozell, president of Parents Television Council and the Media Research Center, was also disappointed. He said, "Today no one in network TV fears what the children are watching—unless it makes them think about God."

—David Slagle, "NBC Removes Biblical Content from 'VeggieTales,'" PreachingToday.com

ILLUSTRATION 979

FINDING SUCCESS AT WORK

Topics: Achievement; Career; Family; Fulfillment; Goals; Happiness; Joy; Meaning; Money; Motivation; Prosperity; Purpose; Relationships; Satisfaction; Self-worth; Success

References: Jeremiah 29:11; Matthew 6:19–21; 16:26; Mark 8:36; Luke 9:25; Romans 12:2; 1 Timothy 6:10; Hebrews 13:5

Our views of what success in business means vary. According to a study by *Success* magazine in 2006, 60 percent of respondents said business was a success if it added value to the lives of others. Only 18.8 percent said success meant "making a lot of money."

Other findings: In answer to the question, "What is the single, most important element for success?" respondents said:

faith: 41.0 percent
family: 25.5 percent
a balanced life: 11.7 percent
happiness: 7.3 percent

What are the most important factors for success?

good relationship with family— 89.9 percent
good relationship with spouse— 89.6 percent
good relationship with God— 86.0 percent
freedom to do what you want— 61.7 percent
financial security—57.5 percent
good career—47.1 percent
leaving a legacy—43.4 percent
money/wealth—32.3 percent

—"The New American Dream," *Success* (Summer 2006)

ILLUSTRATION 980

STARTING OVER

Topics: Career; Change; Contentment; Dissatisfaction; Jobs; Opportunity; Satisfaction

References: Genesis 4:12; Psalm 62:5; Ecclesiastes 3:22; 4:4–8

"If you could start your career over in a completely different field, would you?" That was the question asked in a 2006 study of 1,733 executives conducted by Korn/Ferry International. The results:

Yes: 51 percent
Maybe: 24 percent
No: 25 percent

—*USA Today* "Snapshots" (February 27, 2006)

ILLUSTRATION 981

RETIRING TO DEATH

Topics: Abundant Life; Apathy; Diligence; Husbands; Leisure; Lifestyle; Meaning; Purpose; Retirement; Self-discipline; Self-indulgence; Television; Wives

References: Ecclesiastes 2:24; Jeremiah 29:11; Philippians 3:13–14; 2 Thessalonians 3:11–12

At a community prayer breakfast, I sat with a group of men who began talking about retirement. The man next to me, who appeared to be in his early fifties, said how much he was looking forward to the end of his career. He talked about a conversation he'd had with his wife that morning.

"When she asked, 'What are you going to do when you retire?' I told her, 'I'm going to sit on the couch and watch TV all day,'" he said.

The table was silent, but I couldn't keep quiet for long. "If you do that, you'll be dead in a year," I said.

He looked at me wide-eyed and asked why.

I told him, "If the lack of purpose in your life doesn't kill you first, your wife will."

—John Beukema,
Chambersburg, Pennsylvania

ILLUSTRATION 982

WARNING FOOLS

Topics: Discernment; Foolishness; Human Condition; Ignorance; Warnings

References: 1 Samuel 25:25; Psalm 14:1; 53:1; Proverbs 6:27; 10:23; 18:2; Ecclesiastes 10:2; Matthew 7:24–27

The following warnings were found on consumer products:

- on a Duraflame fireplace log: "Caution: Risk of Fire."
- on a Batman costume: "Warning: Cape does not enable user to fly."
- on a bottle of hair coloring: "Do not use as an ice cream topping."

- on a cardboard sun shield for a car: "Do not drive with sun shield in place."
- on a portable stroller: "Caution: Remove infant before folding for storage."

—Amy Simpson, Winfield, Illinois

ILLUSTRATION 983
CONFRONTING BIG JOHN

Topics: Assumptions; Authority; Conflict; Confrontation; Expectations; Fear; Power; Relationships; Rights; Strength; Vindictiveness; Weakness

References: Psalm 37:7; Romans 8:31–39; 1 John 4:18

One day a bus driver was driving along his usual route when a big hulk of a man got on. He was six feet eight inches tall, built like a wrestler, and his arms hung to the ground. He glared at the driver and told him, "Big John doesn't pay!" Then he sat at the back of the bus.

The driver was five feet three inches tall, thin, and very meek, so he didn't argue with Big John. But he wasn't happy.

The next day the same thing happened, and the next. The bus driver began to lose sleep over the way Big John was taking advantage of him.

Finally, he could stand it no longer. He signed up for bodybuilding, karate, judo, and self-esteem classes. By the end of the summer, the bus driver had become stronger and more confident. So when Big John entered the bus and again declared, "Big John doesn't pay!" the driver finally took him on. He stood up, glared at Big John, and bellowed, "And why not?"

With a surprised look on his face, Big John replied, "Big John has a bus pass."

—Ed Rowell, Monument, Colorado

ILLUSTRATION 984
DOING THE PRESIDENCY

Topics: Ambition; Behavior; Desires; Fruitfulness; Hypocrisy; Integrity; Leadership; Motivation; Name; Reputation

References: Matthew 3:10; 7:15–20; 20:20–28; Luke 3:9; 6:43–44; John 15:5–8; Romans 12:1–8; Philippians 2:4–11; Colossians 1:10

In the spring of 1970, when I was twenty-nine, I learned I had won a fellowship from the American Council on Education, which would allow me to serve an administrative internship with Purdue University President Fred Hovde for the 1970–71 academic year. I was elated by the opportunity. Despite having only recently been awarded tenure and promoted to associate professor of electrical engineering at Purdue, I was already leaning toward a career in administration. . . .

Soon after the award was announced, I happened to bump into a colleague, Vern Newhouse, who was a highly respected senior member of the electrical engineering faculty. "So, Sample," Newhouse said to me, "I see you've won some sort of administrative fellowship in the president's office."

"Yes, that's true," I said.

"And you'll be learning how to become an administrator?"

"I suppose so."

"And then you'll probably want to be president of a university somewhere down the road?"

"Well, I don't know. I guess I've thought about it now and then," I said, somewhat disingenuously.

He smiled and said, "Personally, I've never had any ambition whatsoever to be an administrator. I am totally inept at managing things.... But I've been a careful observer of ambitious men all my life. And here, for what it's worth, is what I've learned: many men want to *be* president, but very few want to *do* president." And with that he wished me well and walked away.

—Steve Sample, *The Contrarian's Guide to Leadership* (Jossey-Bass, 2002)

ILLUSTRATION 985

INSTILLING MISSION IN WORKERS

Topics: Career; Dependence on God; Devotional Life; Example; Godliness; Integrity; Prayer; Righteousness; Service; Spiritual Disciplines; Temptation; Weakness; Work

References: Psalm 25:21; Matthew 6:9–13; Luke 11:1–4; Ephesians 6:18–19; Colossians 4:2

Here's some advice from Israel Gaither, national commander for the Salvation Army, on how to instill employees with a sense of mission:

- Begin the day with prayer.

- Organizations involve humans, and humans sometimes falter. Leaders should pick up those who have fallen but also have the option to fire them.
- Serving leadership is active leadership, not a mantra.
- Guard against mission creep. Be courageous to say no.

When asked about the first tip, "Can it be that simple? Can everyone stay out of trouble with a morning prayer?" Gaither responded, "I serve in a world weakened by sin. That's the context in which I serve, and I have to ask God to protect me—my mind, my thinking, and my behavior. Is that the path to help an organization do what is right? Yeah, I think that's the way to do it."

—Del Jones, "Salvation Army's Chief on a Mission," *USA Today* (November 20, 2006)

ILLUSTRATION 986

WORKING BEYOND WINNING

Topics: Dedication; Diligence; Integrity; Meekness; Responsibility; Sacrifice; Self-discipline; Values

References: Colossians 3:23; 1 Thessalonians 5:12–15; Hebrews 12:1

In February 2006, eight workers at a Nebraska meatpacking plant contributed $5 apiece to buy a block of 40 Powerball lottery tickets. The men usually worked sixty to seventy hours a week and earned $9.00 to $10.00 an hour. This group, however, ended up winning the largest jackpot in U.S. history; each person in the pool got $15.5 million after taxes.

Some of the winners did not quit their jobs. David Gehle, for example, arrived at the morning news conference four hours after finishing his overnight shift as a supervisor. He said that if he had not worked, the plant would have been short of help. "We couldn't just leave 'em in a bind," he said.

Gehle then shocked reporters by stating that he would report to his 10:00 p.m. shift later that evening and politely asked them not to seek interviews at his home, saying, "I need to get some sleep."

—Jeff Zeleny, "Powerball Winners Go from Meatpacking Plant to Life as Millionaires," *Chicago Tribune* (February 23, 2006)

ILLUSTRATION 987

TRAINING HOUSEHOLD SERVANTS

Topics: Christmas; Example; Humility; Jesus Christ; Self-denial; Service

References: John 13:13–17; Galatians 5:13–14; Philippians 2:5–11; 1 Timothy 6:1–2

We need more servants today. But a good servant is hard to find.

In the past decade, the number of American households worth $10 million or more has quadrupled, and the newly rich want help managing their large homes and busy lifestyles. Mary Starkey's International Institute for Household Management of Denver, Colorado, is trying to meet the need. With household managers earning $60,000 to $120,000 a year, applications are at an all-time high, but servanthood is not easy to learn.

Those enrolled in the rigorous eight-week, $7,200 course devote themselves to mastering the mundane aspects of running a large household: dealing with trades and outside vendors, managing household staff, learning table manners, and taking cooking classes. They learn how to set a formal dinner table and iron table linens so they are crisp and wrinkle-free.

Perhaps the most difficult aspect of servanthood, however, is self-denial. A consulting beautician at the school recently told an attractive young female student to trim her long blond hair, lose the showy earrings, and lay off the red lip liner. It seemed her makeup was drawing attention away from her employers to herself.

That violated the primary goal of a servant: to meet the needs of others rather than self.

—Chris Easton, in a sermon "Real Life: Making It Personal," Newark Church of the Nazarene, Newark, Ohio (October 15, 2006)

ILLUSTRATION 988

BUYING BOOKS

Topics: Books; Gender Differences; Men; Reading; Women

References: 1 Chronicles 28:9; Psalm 1:2; Matthew 22:37; Romans 12:2; Colossians 3:1–2

A study of book purchases from 1998 to 2000 shows that the leading genre of books purchased by men was nonfiction/religion. Espionage/thriller books were the second most popular, followed by science fiction, computer, and mystery/detective books.

Women spent the most money on romance books, followed by general fiction, mystery/detective, nonfiction religion, and religious fiction.

— "The Story Behind What We Read," *Chicago Tribune* (November 21, 2001)

ILLUSTRATION 989

FINDING SATISFACTION IN WORK

Topics: Career; Jobs; Money; Prestige; Satisfaction

References: Ecclesiastes 2:10 – 11; Colossians 3:23

The three things people in the United States value most in a job, according to a 2001 Gallup poll:

- job satisfaction: 65 percent
- being paid well: 34 percent
- having an important title: 1 percent

— "Workers Take Happiness over Money," *USA Today* "Snapshots" (September 20, 2001)

ILLUSTRATION 990

PERSEVERANCE PAYS OFF

Topics: Failure; Perseverance; Persistence; Success

References: Romans 5:3 – 5; James 1:2 – 4; 5:11

John Grisham's first novel, *A Time to Kill*, was rejected by twenty-eight agents and publishers. When an agent finally took him as a client, the book's first press run was only 5,000 copies. Grisham himself purchased 1,000 copies and hawked his work to bookstores from the trunk of his car.

Only after his second novel, *The Firm*, hit the bestseller list did Grisham get his big break. Six of his books have now been made into movies, and the press run of his most recent volume, *A Painted House*, was 2.8 million copies. Grisham now has more than 100 million books in print in thirty-one languages.

— Rubel Shelly, "John Grisham: Rewards of Perseverance," PreachingToday.com

ILLUSTRATION 991

RIDING WAVES OF CHANGE

Topics: Change; Decisions; Leadership; Planning; Risk; Vision

Reference: Matthew 25:15

Sewell Avery, former chairman of Montgomery Ward & Co., was responsible for Ward's failure

to open a single new store from 1941 to 1957. Instead, the big retailer piled up cash and sat on it. Montgomery Ward amassed $607 million, earning it the Wall Street nickname "the bank with the department storefront."

Avery did not follow Americans to the suburbs because he was convinced that depression had followed every major war since the time of Napoleon. "Who am I to argue with history?" Avery said. "Why build $14-a-foot buildings when we soon can do it for $3 a foot?"

Meantime, Ward's rival, Sears, Roebuck & Co., had a different idea. In 1946, Sears began a costly expansion into suburbia. Had another depression occurred, Sears would have been financially devastated. Instead, Sears doubled its revenues while Ward stood still. Sears never looked back, and Ward never caught up. Ward eventually went bankrupt.

How could corporate planning go so wrong? Sewell Avery banked on wisdom from an earlier era, misread the cultural cues of his day, and eventually wiped out his business.

—John McCormick, "You Snooze You Lose," *Newsweek* (July 21, 1997)

ILLUSTRATION 992

REPORTING WORK VIOLATIONS

Topics: Character; Circumstances and Faith; Convictions; Dishonesty; Dying to Self; Guidance; Honesty; Integrity; Persecution; Work

References: Psalm 41:12; Proverbs 11:3; Matthew 5:10; 16:24–26; Galatians 2:20; Philippians 3:7–17

George Galatis, an engineer at Millstone Nuclear Power Station in Waterford, Connecticut, found several unsafe practices at his plant. Federal guidelines required the Millstone plant to store only one-third of spent fuel rods in holding pools, but Galatis found all of the hot fuel had been dumped into them. Also, fuel was unloaded just 65 hours after a shutdown, far sooner than the mandated period of 250 hours.

Supervisors winked at the routine violations, knowing they were saving millions through shortcuts.

Fearing the violations could threaten thousands of lives, Galatis told a colleague they should contact the Nuclear Regulatory Commission (NRC). The friend warned him, "You do that and you're dogmeat."

Galatis urged plant managers to stop the hazardous practices, but they refused. Since many of his supervisors were churchgoers, he was baffled. "This was not splitting hairs," Galatis says. "These were moral issues." Galatis warned his supervisors what could happen: eventual shutdown, decommissioning of the plants, and criminal investigations. But after two years nothing had changed except other workers' attitudes toward Galatis. When he sat down in the cafeteria, coworkers left. When he entered a meeting, the room fell silent. Rumors spread that he was an alcoholic. His performance evaluation took a hit.

Galatis searched for God's guidance, rising every morning at 4:00 a.m. to pray and read Scripture. During lunch breaks, he drove to a secluded place to pray and search the Bible.

During one of these prayer times Galatis believed God whispered to him, "Will you die for me?"

Though he feared for his safety, Galatis realized there were many ways of dying; his livelihood, his reputation, and his family could also be destroyed. Previous whistleblowers' families had broken under intense emotional strain. Northeast Utilities, owner of the nuclear plants, would likely hire one of the nation's top law firms to fight him.

Still, he pressed on. He contacted the NRC, asking the government agency to suspend Millstone's license. As the petition became public, pressure at work increased. Coworkers confronted him, calling him a fool and troublemaker. He was harassed for months.

After four years of battling Millstone, Galatis finally got a severance agreement and left. The NRC never suspended Millstone's license, but three reactors were shut down for repairs at a cost of over $1 billion. A criminal investigation was launched.

Galatis went on to graduate from seminary and is now a pastor.

—Adam Bowles, "A Cry in the Nuclear Wilderness," *Christianity Today* (October 2, 2000)

ILLUSTRATION 993

BATTLING BUSINESS SIGNS

Topics: Attitudes; Business; Creativity; Hope

Reference: Proverbs 3:13–14

Three men owned shops in the same building. Times were tough, so the owner of the shop at one end of the building put a sign above his front entrance that said YEAR-END CLEARANCE!

The owner of the shop at the other end of the building responded with: ANNUAL CLOSEOUT!

The owner of the middle store, after careful consideration, hung a sign over his front door. It said, MAIN ENTRANCE.

—Ivan R. Misner, *The World's Best-Known Marketing Secret* (Bard, 1997)

ILLUSTRATION 994

TURNING DOWN A DREAM JOB

Topics: Commitment; Devotion; Ministry; Priorities; Sacrifice

Reference: Luke 14:25–33

Years ago, I worked part-time on the loading docks of various trucking companies. At one company I met a fine Christian man named Rufus Kidd. He had just completed his associate's degree in transportation and wanted to make it a full-time career. Since the company was beginning to open up to minorities at that time, Rufus, an African-American, interviewed for a position.

Later I asked him how the interview went, and he said they offered him a job in sales, which would pay well and offer unlimited opportunity. I was excited for him, but he said he wasn't going to take it. Although it was everything he wanted, he would have to give up his ministry with singles at his church. He said he would wait for a job to come along that would allow him to continue to teach his class.

Rufus sacrificed his chance to leave the sweltering docks and gave up a brand-new career to continue teaching.

—Kenneth Mitchell, Jacksonville, Florida

ILLUSTRATION 995

REFUELING IN REST

Topics: Energy; Preparation; Rest; Sabbath; Success; Work

Reference: Psalm 127:1–2

Two men had to clear a field of trees. The contract called for them to be paid per tree.

Bill wanted the day to be profitable, so he grunted and sweated, swinging his ax relentlessly. Ed, on the other hand, seemed to be working about half as fast. He even took a rest and sat off to the side for a few minutes. Bill kept chopping away until every muscle and tendon in his body was screaming.

At the end of the day, Bill was terribly sore, but Ed was smiling and telling jokes. What's more, Ed had cut down more trees. Bill said, "I noticed you sitting while I worked without a break. How did you outwork me?"

"Did you notice I was sharpening my ax while I was sitting?" Ed said, smiling.

—Robert M. Dubrul, *Stand Firm* (Morris, 2000)

ILLUSTRATION 996

UNHAPPY AT HOME AND WORK

Topics: Depression; Despair; Expectations; Family; Happiness; Meaning; Suicide; Weariness

References: Matthew 11:28–30; John 10:10

Ten percent of the British people believe they would be better off dead, according to a survey. One in four was unhappy in his or her job, while one in three felt exhausted, unappreciated, or underpaid.

Christine Webber, the psychotherapist who did the survey, said, "Sadly, it comes as no surprise to me that so many people are unhappy at home and work. It seems that people's lives do not live up to their extremely high expectations. It is particularly worrying to see so many people dwelling on morbid thoughts, with a large proportion just plainly exhausted by life."

—Sally Pook, "One in Ten Believe Their Lives Are Not Worth Living," *London Daily Telegraph* (June 19, 2001)

ILLUSTRATION 997

HONORING GOD WITH CHICK-FIL-A

Topics: Business; Character; Giving; Integrity; Ministry; Obedience; Sabbath; Work

References: Matthew 25:34–40; James 1:22

Truett Cathy, the founder of Chick-fil-A restaurants, is a successful businessman, but many know and respect him more for how faith guides his work.

For example, Cathy's restaurants have been closed on Sundays since 1948. The seventy-nine-year-old CEO of the nearly one thousand Chick-fil-A restaurants doesn't mind losing millions of dollars of business to honor the Lord's Day.

Also, at his first restaurant in 1948, Cathy hired Eddie J. White, twelve, an African-American. This was an unpopular choice during a time of segregation. Cathy also mentored an orphan, Woody Faulk, from the time Woody was thirteen. Woody eventually became vice president of product development at Chick-fil-A.

Cathy also developed a successful foster home system called WinShape Homes. There are now eleven homes in the United States and one in Brazil. His daughter Trudy and son-in-law John were Southern Baptist missionaries at the Brazil home for ten years. His Camp WinShape and the WinShape Foundation provide scholarships for kids and college students.

One of Cathy's favorite sayings is "It's easier to build boys and girls than to mend men and women." So Chick-fil-A Kids Meals don't come with promotional toys from the latest popular movie; instead, they offer VeggieTales books, audiocassettes of Focus on the Family's "Adventures in Odyssey," and other character-building materials.

Woody Faulk gives a good summary of Cathy's character: "A lot of people look on Truett as Santa Claus, but he's not. He'll meet you halfway so that you can learn a lesson from the process. He's the personification of James 1:22: 'Do not merely listen to the word, and so deceive yourselves. Do what it says.' I sincerely owe my life to that man."

—Tom Neven, "A Doer of the Word," *Focus on the Family Magazine* (September 2000)

ILLUSTRATION 998

RACING TO DEATH

Topics: Balance; Control; Human Effort; Rest; Sabbath; Stress; Work

Reference: Mark 6:31

John Henry once raced a steam drill tunneling through a mountain. He beat the machine, only to fall dead from the superhuman effort.

Sherman James, an epidemiologist at the University of Michigan, named a syndrome after John Henry, saying people with it believe that anything can be conquered as long as you work hard enough. They are the ones who, when completing questionnaires, answer yes to statements such as, "When things don't go the way I want, it just makes me work even harder," or "Once I make up my mind to do something, I stay with it until the job is completely done."

They believe that with enough effort and determination they can regulate all outcomes.

—Robert M. Sapolsky, *Why Zebras Don't Get Ulcers* (W. H. Freeman, 1998)

ILLUSTRATION 999

CHANGING JOBS

Topics: Change; Determination; Motives; Sanctification

References: Matthew 22:1 – 14; Galatians 5:16 – 25

My wife, Carol, a career counselor, was meeting with a client, George, who said to her in their first session, "I've got to get out of the rubber industry."

She gave him some homework to do before their next session. He came back the next week without having done a lick of homework. My wife asked, "What will happen if you don't get out of the rubber industry?"

"My wife will divorce me," George said.

"Do you want that to happen?" Carol asked.

He couldn't keep the smile off his face. She knew then that he would never change his job till it gave him what he wanted: a divorce, with his wife taking the initiative and the guilt.

Carol named this behavior "the doctrine of the prior agenda." "You can't help people change or find their mission when they have a conflicting prior agenda," she said. People will not change until they want to.

—Daniel H. Pink, "What Happened to Your Parachute?" *Fast Company* (September 1999)

ILLUSTRATION 1000

WORKING WITH JESUS

Topics: Fulfillment; Ministry; Pastors

References: Matthew 6:33; 1 Timothy 4:9 – 10

If you don't love Jesus, you will soon discover that being a pastor or a church leader is not really a very good job. You will be overworked, underpaid, overstressed, and underappreciated. But if you do love Jesus, you will discover, as so many others have, that it can be the most wonderful and exciting job in the world.

—Mark Allan Powell, Columbus, Ohio

ILLUSTRATION 1001

PERFECTING A LITTLE SWITCH

Topics: Church; Community; Influence; Ministry; Service; Small Things; Teamwork

References: Mark 12:41 – 44; Ephesians 4:16; Colossians 3:23 – 25

I was asked to speak at the funeral of a man who had helped develop the Boeing 747 aircraft. After the service I spoke with the widow and commented on what a remarkable thing her late husband had done.

"The truth is, he worked on a little switchbox smaller than a loaf of bread," she said. "That's all he worked on for fifteen years. But when that 747 lifted off the ground for the first time, it was the happiest day of his life."

He worked on a tiny switchbox for more than a decade, yet the Boeing 747 couldn't have lifted off without this man's contribution. Often we think our seemingly small efforts aren't very important. But when the great kingdom of God "lifts off," we'll be thrilled to find out that our efforts were essential.

—M. Craig Barnes, in a sermon delivered
at Christianity Today International
(September 19, 2000)

SCRIPTURE INDEX

1001 ILLUSTRATIONS that CONNECT

1001 ILLUSTRATIONS that CONNECT

6:9	156, 220, 234, 277, 325, 418, 514	4:26	406, 501	6:6–8, 18	310
		4:26–27	253, 258, 266	6:7	172, 173
6:9–10	68, 172, 449, 519	4:28	125, 503	6:10	511

Ephesians

1:7	373, 427, 464	4:29	57, 78, 320, 487	6:10–18	17, 22, 126, 134, 159, 390, 405
1:18–23	144	4:29–32	423, 453	6:12	467
1:22–23	40	4:31	18, 226, 504	6:14	465
2:1–10	120, 174, 380, 439	4:32	92, 215, 234, 308, 326, 433	6:18	306, 310, 311, 318, 368
2:3	494	5:1–2	295	6:18–19	528
2:4–5	291	5:1–17	81		
2:8–9	37, 98, 120, 158, 210, 335, 339, 464, 475, 492, 513, 521	5:2	108, 181	**Philippians**	
		5:3	255	1:6	34, 54, 199, 402, 413
		5:3–4	377		
2:10	172, 445	5:4–5	489	1:9–10	405
2:13	143, 176, 338	5:5	97, 509	1:10	428
2:19–22	327	5:8–10	258	1:21	249
3	49	5:11	494	1:21–24	168
3:6–7	63	5:15	324	1:27–30	228
3:14–19	291	5:15–16	63, 123, 242, 420	1:29	69, 444, 444
3:20	221, 314, 344, 511	5:15–18	462	2:1–4	174, 424
3:20–21	43	5:16	294	2:1–11	114, 432
3:21	40	5:18	419, 491, 493, 494	2:2–3	75
4:1–6	328	5:20	44, 98, 200, 358	2:3	155, 482
4:1–7	277	5:21–33	523	2:3, 5–11	52
4:1–13	45	5:22–23	253	2:3–4	270, 418, 425, 489, 523
4:1–16	46	5:22–33	217, 218, 251, 251, 252, 254, 264, 271	2:4–11	84, 527
4:2	498			2:5–8	76, 344, 425, 502
4:4–6	329			2:5–11	108, 276, 304, 348, 380, 385, 441, 443, 529
4:7–8	512	5:25	262		
4:11–16	32, 260, 418, 425	5:25–33	252, 265, 270, 333	2:5–11, 17	438
4:14	402	5:28	259	2:8	246
4:14–15	132	5:31	138	2:9–11	470
4:15	152, 226, 295, 311, 469	5:31–32	265	2:12–13	278, 388
		6:1–2	290	2:14	258, 420
4:15, 29	420	6:1–3	157	2:14–16	475
4:16	535	6:1–4	285, 297, 377	2:17	110
4:17–19	488	6:4	57, 140, 267, 269, 285, 287, 287, 292, 294, 295, 296, 297, 298, 303, 303, 364, 398, 421, 423	3:4–14	415
4:19	269			3:7–8	274, 369, 425
4:20–32	81			3:7–9	192
4:22–24	110, 399, 404, 512			3:7–11	394, 435
4:25	411, 455, 483, 484, 498, 500	6:4, 18	305	3:7–14	275, 427
		6:5–9	365		

TOPICAL INDEX

doctrine, 18, 26, 467, 470, 472, 473, 483

double-mindedness, 82, 326, 335

doubt, 20, 24, 26, 35, 64, 190, 198, 205, 213, 236, 312, 359, 391, 417, 418, 464, 467, 473, 478

dreams, 203, 244

drinking, 357, 488, 490, 496

drugs, 115, 125, 202, 294, 357, 415, 421, 488, 491, 496

drunkenness, 115, 378, 493

dying to self, 108, 268, 531

E

Easter, 27, 189, 320, 374, 373, 376, 379, 385, 386, 471

eating, 461

edification, 305

education, 106, 294, 302, 354

ego, 20, 52, 306, 425, 429

emotions, 41, 199, 252, 254, 266, 360, 363, 366, 446, 473, 488

empathy, 46, 174, 183, 293, 298, 388, 432, 433, 435, 436, 437, 516

employees, 365, 523

employers, 365

emptiness, 9, 28, 64, 90, 135, 152, 191, 192, 195, 337, 367, 394, 415, 451, 493, 510

encouragement, 41, 44, 57, 124, 140, 160, 193, 210, 201, 285, 293, 295, 305, 307, 315, 320, 340, 398, 420, 431

endurance, 68, 156, 197, 233, 418, 432, 449

enemies, 61, 91, 136, 159, 173, 226, 312, 323, 342, 345, 494

energy, 533

entertainment, 130, 398, 455, 460, 461, 468, 493, 507, 524

enthusiasm, 17, 41

environmentalism, 48, 53

envy, 215, 289, 337, 509

escape, 366

eternal death, 164, 194

eternal life, 10, 11, 98, 163, 164, 164, 164, 165, 166, 168, 239, 242, 245, 249, 339, 363, 417, 430, 512, 522

eternal versus temporary, 9

eternity, 168, 216, 240, 246, 247

ethics, 229, 403, 437, 455, 474, 484

euthanasia, 437

evangelism, 11, 21, 24, 29, 35, 44, 59, 59, 60, 61, 61, 62, 63, 65, 66, 66, 67, 68, 69, 70, 70, 70, 71, 72, 72, 75, 76, 77, 78, 87, 110, 160, 175, 177, 180, 242, 275, 276, 279, 279, 309, 310, 312, 327, 340, 417, 444, 497, 499

evidence for God, 50, 56

evil, 123, 126, 126, 129, 133, 134, 134, 135, 138, 147, 343, 437, 467, 476

evil desires, 458

evolution, 50, 105, 477

example, 10, 11, 53, 72, 76, 77, 78, 78, 84, 94, 101, 155, 171, 189, 224, 234, 256, 276, 279, 292, 300, 305, 308, 309, 318, 346, 355, 409, 426, 455, 496, 497, 519, 528, 529

excuses, 38, 87, 207

exercise, 156

expectations, 140, 164, 387, 527, 533

experience, 211, 428

experiencing God, 25, 67, 83, 109, 140, 190, 192, 193, 198, 199, 274, 314, 315, 336, 355, 379, 400, 403, 419, 429, 448, 471, 473, 512

extremes, 496

F

factions, 37

failure, 52, 203, 211, 278, 320, 360, 449, 518, 530

fairness, 455

faith, 11, 20, 26, 36, 39, 52, 64, 79, 105, 106, 107, 139, 144, 145, 189, 189, 190, 193, 194, 197, 198, 198, 200, 213, 221, 237, 247, 249, 260, 279, 283, 292, 306, 308, 312, 313, 314, 314, 315, 316, 341, 352, 354, 358, 361, 363, 366, 376, 389, 401, 408, 413, 417, 417, 420, 422, 422, 437, 441, 446, 447, 449, 464, 464, 465, 471, 473, 475, 477

faith and works, 32, 73, 82, 167, 210, 475

faithfulness, 14, 31, 79, 96, 178, 192, 256, 256, 257, 267, 300, 331, 405, 413, 418

fall of humanity, 52, 123, 189, 196, 379, 500

false beliefs, 20, 467, 467, 468, 470, 472, 473, 475, 479

falsehood, 469

fame, 417

family, 14, 40, 46, 79, 102, 107, 115, 116, 163, 208, 209, 215, 217, 226, 230, 232, 245, 252, 253, 255, 255, 258, 263, 265, 265, 266, 266, 267, 269, 277, 284, 286, 287, 287, 289, 290, 290, 292, 292, 294, 294, 295, 295, 296, 296, 297, 298, 299, 299, 300, 300, 303, 303, 324, 357, 362, 364, 366, 377, 433, 472, 496, 501, 521, 525, 533

humanity of Christ, 246

humility, 25, 39, 44, 52, 60, 76, 84, 112, 173, 183, 212, 220, 279, 319, 380, 385, 398, 405, 405, 418, 425, 434, 474, 482, 483, 499, 502, 518, 529

humor, 213, 220

hunger, 112, 168, 504

husbands, 14, 218, 253, 253, 255, 255, 260, 262, 262, 265, 272, 366, 526

hymns, 342

hypocrisy, 82, 155, 196, 216, 267, 326, 365, 398, 460, 469, 478, 483, 491, 492, 499, 523, 527

I

idealism, 150

identity, 52, 176, 338, 423, 499, 510

identity in Christ, 315, 426

ideologies and belief systems, 477

idolatry, 13, 264, 468, 472, 473, 482, 494, 507, 517

ignorance, 283, 526

illicit sex, 269

illness, 14, 141, 144, 149, 152, 174, 194, 235, 360

illumination, 49, 82

imitation of Christ, 90, 143, 155, 177, 405, 438

immorality, 332, 490

immortality, 10, 10, 164, 522

impatience, 514

Incarnation, 70, 76, 112, 114, 118, 119, 120, 359, 373, 379, 380, 385, 435

inclusion, 442

independence, 303

indifference, 17, 32, 196, 217, 233, 252, 497

individualism, 40, 45

inerrancy, 18, 20, 26

inexplicability of evil, 129

infertility, 312

infidelity, 256

influence, 57, 77, 130, 290, 340, 393, 397, 460, 461, 535

ingratitude, 80, 262, 407

inheritance, 240, 441

injustice, 379, 423

insecurity, 203

insensitivity, 151, 254, 326, 487, 523

insight, 26, 492

insignificance, 203

inspiration, 117, 330, 413

inspiration of Scripture, 18, 20, 20, 22, 26, 470

integrity, 53, 90, 125, 178, 198, 216, 223, 224, 279, 303, 409, 411, 423, 426, 426, 453, 455, 468, 474, 478, 478, 479, 483, 495, 496, 497, 498, 500, 503, 505, 523, 527, 528, 528, 531, 533

intelligence, 492

intercession, 312, 319, 344

Internet, 258, 452, 475, 490, 523

interpretation, 18, 20, 472

intimacy, 11, 14, 35, 107, 137, 151, 251, 252, 272, 296, 388

investments, 506, 514

invitation, 127, 258, 265, 433

involvement, 42, 178

irreverence, 108

Islam, 21, 72, 120, 121, 173

Israel, 59

J

jealousy, 136, 509

Jesus Christ, 24, 27, 44, 59, 64, 72, 76, 109, 112, 113, 113, 114, 115, 116, 117, 117, 120, 120, 121, 166, 189, 190, 191, 193, 202, 249, 273, 291, 304, 320, 330, 338, 342, 344, 344, 348, 372, 373, 373, 374, 374, 376, 377, 377, 379, 385, 392, 419, 447, 457, 470, 471, 529

Jesus, one with the Father, 118, 120

jobs, 48, 366, 367, 526, 530

joy, 31, 41, 42, 70, 74, 192, 200, 214, 219, 366, 381, 407, 420, 448, 515, 525

Judaism, 59, 120, 121

judging others, 59, 60, 151, 173, 196, 228, 398, 487, 516

judgment, 29, 108, 166, 227, 230, 239, 427, 429, 477, 484, 493, 508

justice, 115, 227, 230, 232, 309, 405, 442, 484

justification, 98, 166, 176, 335, 338, 373

K

killing, 459

kindness, 77, 84, 94, 97, 173, 174, 175, 179, 184, 184, 228, 234, 320, 327, 329, 346, 487, 503, 521

kingdom of God, 22, 73, 223, 385, 387

knowing God, 70, 105, 119, 332, 388, 403, 471, 512

knowledge, 14, 26, 79, 82, 247, 283, 519

L

last things, 202, 345, 402

laughter, 214, 379

law, 151, 229, 229, 304, 429, 484

lawlessness, 138, 395, 491

laziness, 156, 211, 493

344, 394, 413, 417, 418, 421, 422, 434, 437, 439, 442, 444, 447, 447, 448

Trinity, 42

trust, 20, 35, 36, 93, 107, 113, 132, 144, 148, 189, 190, 191, 194, 200, 201, 221, 231, 246, 249, 260, 278, 283, 301, 311, 314, 316, 341, 352, 360, 389, 391, 401, 406, 408, 437, 447, 449, 463, 463, 464, 464, 464, 465, 465, 465, 472, 483, 501

truth, 18, 21, 23, 24, 26, 27, 78, 109, 117, 119, 126, 152, 153, 167, 199, 223, 317, 393, 411, 469, 470, 473, 482, 483, 483, 484, 484, 498, 499, 499, 524

truthfulness, 132, 453, 469, 474, 474

U

unbelief, 20, 24, 26, 52, 64, 164, 213, 377, 449, 467, 477, 477

uncertainties, 26, 136, 249

uncleanness, 138

unconditional love, 120, 295, 336, 346

understanding, 14, 105, 117, 278, 391, 421, 437, 492, 519

unfaithfulness, 251, 256, 268

ungodliness, 489

unity, 37, 40, 48, 85, 128, 260, 270, 326, 329, 337, 424, 425

unrighteousness, 455

unselfishness, 174, 178, 277, 291, 348, 418, 420, 425, 432, 489, 509, 521, 523

untamed Christ, 119

urgency, 166

V

vacation, 367

valleys, 235

value, 508, 521

values, 79, 88, 88, 158, 172, 209, 232, 270, 289, 298, 323, 328, 359, 365, 391, 394, 426, 455, 465, 474, 474, 480, 519, 524, 528

vanity, 151, 155

vices, 53, 82, 153, 216, 339, 365, 455, 458, 489, 490, 491, 492

victorious living, 53, 192, 237, 444, 444

victory, 198, 201, 375, 413, 420, 447, 471, 495

video games, 459

vigilance, 328

vindictiveness, 447, 493, 527

violence, 36, 85, 123, 129, 135, 136, 223, 226, 253, 266, 459, 460, 494

virtue, 84, 423, 455, 483, 492

vision, 24, 34, 39, 48, 56, 57, 60, 100, 110, 203, 330, 387, 413, 469, 519, 530

visions, 193

visions and dreams, 136

vocation, 273, 310

vows, 251, 251, 252, 255, 256, 257, 260

vulnerability, 17, 236, 238, 463, 494, 508

W

waiting, 271, 380, 497, 514

waiting on God, 10, 189, 191, 221, 306, 359, 385, 402, 410, 447, 464

war, 20

warnings, 29, 82, 233, 236, 451, 526

wasting time, 275

watchfulness, 236, 238, 239, 317, 345, 352, 390

weakness, 9, 17, 37, 43, 53, 150, 239, 298, 302, 365, 388, 410, 431, 448, 487, 502, 511, 527, 528

wealth, 166, 256, 514, 520

weariness, 11, 33, 365, 367, 367, 368, 418, 533

weddings, 251

welfare, 516, 516

wholehearted devotion, 444, 444

wickedness, 490

widows, 180

will, 135, 382, 395, 470

winning and losing, 426, 428, 429, 430, 449

wisdom, 82, 139, 211, 278, 421, 452, 462, 492, 513

wishful thinking, 19

witchcraft, 130

witnessing, 27, 59, 59, 60, 61, 61, 62, 63, 64, 65, 66, 67, 72, 73, 74, 75, 76, 87, 160, 172, 173, 175, 176, 177, 180, 223, 233, 242, 279, 341, 376, 431, 475, 497

wives, 14, 218, 253, 253, 255, 258, 260, 262, 262, 272, 366, 526

women, 10, 53, 333, 361, 506, 529

wonder, 48, 56, 354, 400

Word of God, 17, 20, 21, 24, 28, 29, 52, 113

words, 81, 128, 218, 295, 326, 474, 501

work, 11, 13, 13, 14, 33, 48, 99, 211, 281, 284, 299, 357, 357, 366, 367, 367, 368, 369, 374, 397, 516, 517, 528, 531, 533, 533, 534

workplace, 256

Bonus CD-ROM with this book:

We have included in this book a bonus CD-ROM to facilitate your use of the 1001 illustrations that are included in the text. The disk contains electronic files for the complete book. The disk can be used in Windows or Mac OsX systems. You will be able to use it with your word-processing software to do the following:

- Cut and paste illustrations and insert them into your documents.
- Search to find a word, topic, or text.

1001 Quotations That Connect

Timeless Wisdom for Preaching, Teaching, and Writing

Craig Brian Larson and Brian Lowery, General Editors

Many times people wrack their brains for succinct, "preachable" quotations to drop into sermons or teaching materials. Now they can relax! *1001 Quotations That Connect* features inspiring observations from a wide spectrum of influential people of the past two millennia, culled from the collection of Christianity Today International. This volume—which contains the reflections of church fathers, missionaries, poets, and celebrities—is a gold mine for preachers, teachers, and writers.

The sayings are arranged under eight descriptive categories, including Ancient Words from Fathers and Founders, Rattling Words from Prophets and Activists, and Keen Words from Writers and Preachers. They are helpfully listed by source, then according to key topics and Scripture references, making retrieval of just the right quote a snap. What's more, a CD-ROM from which text files of all the quotations can easily be pasted into word processing documents comes with the book.

Whether you are driving home the point of a sermon or simply want a quote book for reflective reading, this unparalleled collection is a must-have resource!

Softcover: 978-0-310-28036-1

Pick up a copy today at your favorite bookstore!

Preach with Power

With a membership to **PreachingToday.com** you will have access to countless materials to increase your skills and improve your preaching. Discover how this online resource can help you reach your congregation.

PreachingToday.com will help you:

- **Find the right illustrations quickly** with over 10,000 top-quality illustrations and 10 NEW added each week—all in a powerful, searchable database.

- **Prepare your sermons** with the help of series builders, sermon outlines, transcripts, and thousands of title suggestions.

- **Enhance your knowledge and teaching** with audio sermons, videos, images for your presentations, and PowerPoints—all indexed by topic, Bible reference, and speaker.

- **Preach confidently** with new understanding gained from preaching articles designed to sharpen your skills.

As a benefit of purchasing this book, we would like to offer you a **FREE 90-DAY TRIAL** *and* **$10 OFF a Yearly Membership** to PreachingToday.com

Go to:
PreachingToday.com/offer/IllustrationBook
to sign up today!

PreachingToday.com
Advancing the Art of Biblical Preaching

Share Your Thoughts

With the Author: Your comments will be forwarded to
the author when you send them to *zauthor@zondervan.com*.

With Zondervan: Submit your review of this book
by writing to *zreview@zondervan.com*.

Free Online Resources at
www.zondervan.com/hello

 Zondervan AuthorTracker: Be notified whenever your favorite authors publish new books, go on tour, or post an update about what's happening in their lives.

 Daily Bible Verses and Devotions: Enrich your life with daily Bible verses or devotions that help you start every morning focused on God.

 Free Email Publications: Sign up for newsletters on fiction, Christian living, church ministry, parenting, and more.

 Zondervan Bible Search: Find and compare Bible passages in a variety of translations at www.zondervanbiblesearch.com.

 Other Benefits: Register yourself to receive online benefits like coupons and special offers, or to participate in research.

ZONDERVAN®
.com